THE PRENTICE HALL READER

ELEVENTH EDITION

THE PRENTICE
HALL READER

GEORGE MILLER
University of Delaware

PEARSON

Boston   Columbus   Indianapolis   New York   San Francisco   Upper Saddle River
Amsterdam   CapeTown   Dubai   London   Madrid   Milan   Munich   Paris   Montréal   Toronto
Delhi   Mexico City   São Paulo   Sydney   Hong Kong   Seoul   Singapore   Taipei   Tokyo

For Evan, Adam, and Nathan: Their Book

Senior Editor: Brad Potthoff
Editorial Assistant: Amanda Norelli
Development Editor: Karen Mauk
Senior Supplements Editor: Donna Campion
Executive Marketing Manager: Roxanne McCarley
Executive Digital Producer: Stefanie Snajder
Digital Editor: Sara Gordus
Content Specialist: Erin Jenkins
Project Manager: Denise Phillip Grant

Project Coordination, Text Design, and Electronic Page Makeup: S4Carlisle Publishing Services
Text Permissions: Aptara
Photo Research: Integra
Cover Designer/Manager: Wendy Ann Fredericks
Cover Art: © Kate Graham/Getty Images
Printer and Binder: Courier Companies, Inc.
Cover Printer: Courier Companies, Inc.

For permission to use copyrighted material, grateful acknowledgment is made to the copyright holders on page 555–559, which are hereby made part of this copyright page.

Library of Congress Cataloging-in-Publication Data

The Prentice Hall reader / [compiled by] George Miller.—Eleventh edition.
     pages cm
     Includes index.
     ISBN-13: 978-0-321-89971-2
     ISBN-10: 0-321-89971-7
1. College readers.   2. English language—Rhetoric—Problems, exercises, etc.
I. Miller, George, 1943-
     PE1417.P74 2014
     808'.0427—dc23

                                                                    2013022438

3 4 5 6 7 8 9 10 CRW 16 15 14

Student Edition: ISBN-13: 978-0-321-89971-2
Student Edition: ISBN-10:   0-321-89971-7
A la Carte ISBN-13: 978-0-321-95923-2
A la Carte ISBN-10:   0-321-95923-X

Contents

CHAPTER 2

NARRATION 103

CHAPTER **3**

DESCRIPTION **149**

CHAPTER 4

DIVISION AND CLASSIFICATION   197

CHAPTER **5**

COMPARISON AND CONTRAST 247

MARTIN ESPADA, "Coca-Cola and Coco Frio"   263

WILLIAM ZINSSER, "The Transaction: Two Writing Processes"   265
"A school in Connecticut once held 'a day devoted to the arts,' and I was asked if I would come and talk about writing as a vocation. When I arrived I found that a second speaker had been invited—Dr. Brock . . . a surgeon who had recently begun to write."

SUZANNE BRITT, "Neat People vs. Sloppy People"   268
"I've finally figured out the difference between neat people and sloppy people. The distinction is, as always, moral. Neat people are lazier and meaner than sloppy people."

LIBBY SANDER, "Colleges Confront a Gender Gap in Student Engagement"   272
"Men and women, it turns out, tend to view college differently—and those differences often shape their willingness to get invested in academic pursuits and other activities."

JUSTIN POPE, "MOOCs Gaining Popularity"   278
"Credit's the coin of the realm in higher education, the difference between knowing something and the world recognizing that you do."

MICHAEL POLLAN, "The Consumer—A Republic of Fat"   282
"Because of diabetes and all the other health problems that accompany obesity, today's children may turn out to be the first generation of Americans whose life expectancy will actually be shorter than that of their parents."

MEGHAN DAUM, "Virtual Love"   288
"It was the courtship ritual that had seduced us. E-mail had become an electronic epistle, a yearned-for rule book. It allowed us to do what was necessary to experience love."

CHAPTER 6

PROCESS   299

CHAPTER **7**

CAUSE AND EFFECT   347

CHAPTER 8

DEFINITION   397

CHAPTER **9**

ARGUMENT AND PERSUASION   **441**

CHAPTER 10

THE RESEARCH PAPER   507

Thematic Contents

Children and Family

Violence and Punishment

Media and Computers

Stereotypes, Prejudice, and the Struggle for Equality

WOMEN'S ROLES, WOMEN'S RIGHTS

GROWING OLDER

READING, WRITING, AND LANGUAGE

SCHOOL AND COLLEGE

Preface

The Prentice Hall Reader is predicated on two premises: that reading plays a vital role in learning how to write and that writing and reading can best be organized around the traditional division of discourse into a number of structural patterns. Such a division is not the only way that the forms of writing can be classified, but it does have several advantages.

First, practice in these structural patterns encourages students to organize knowledge and to see the ways in which information can be conveyed. How else does the mind know except by classifying, comparing, defining, or seeking cause-and-effect relationships? Second, the most common use of these patterns occurs in writing done in academic courses. There, students are asked to narrate a chain of events, to describe an artistic style, to classify plant forms, to compare two political systems, to tell how a laboratory experiment was performed, to analyze why famine occurs in Africa, to define a philosophical concept, or to argue for or against off-shore drilling. Learning how to structure papers using these patterns is an exercise that has immediate application in students' other academic work. Finally, because the readings use these patterns as structural devices, they offer an excellent way in which to integrate reading into a writing course. Students can see the patterns at work and learn how to use them to become more effective writers and better, more efficient readers.

WHAT IS NEW IN THE ELEVENTH EDITION?

The eleventh edition of *The Prentice Hall Reader* features 55 essays, 20 of which are new, 11 papers written by students, and nine poems or short, short stories that show the organizational strategies at work. As in the previous editions, the readings are chosen on the basis of several criteria: how well they demonstrate a particular pattern of organization, appeal to an audience of first-year students, and promote interesting and appropriate discussion and writing activities.

The eleventh edition of *The Prentice Hall Reader* includes a number of new features:

- **New readings.** Nearly 40 percent of the readings are new in this edition. Readings come from a variety of emerging genres including graphic novels, blogs, self-help books, and Web pages and include many new voices.

- **Expanded treatment of how to read an essay,** with sections on how to write a summary and a critical analysis. A new essay dealing with the "soft skills" that employers are looking for in new hires is annotated, summarized, and analyzed.

- **New apparatus for each essay.** The "Writing Suggestions" and the section "For Further Study" for each essay have been recast and rewritten.
  1. "Finding Reading Connections" links each essay to another in the *Reader* and provides an essay topic through which that link can be explored.
  2. "Exploring Links Online" extends the conversation by suggesting how a reading might be paired with online sources and then offering a writing suggestion that links the two.
  3. "Writing the Research Paper" suggests topics that can be explored through the Web and print sources for writing an academic essay with formal documentation.

- **Revised chapter on argument and persuasion** now includes material on the role of rhetoric in creating a writer's voice. The readings range from opinion writing to clusters of opposing arguments with formal documentation. A new casebook presents a pair of readings debating the question "Is a Vegan Diet Healthier Than a Balanced Diet?"

- **Revised chapter on the research paper** now moves from providing simple documentation in a traditional essay to preparing and documenting an academic research paper. Special attention is given to using and documenting online sources.

- **New student examples in Chapters 7 and 9,** with first drafts, revision suggestions, and final drafts.

- **Learning Objectives have been added to each chapter,** clearly establishing chapter goals at the start.

- **Timely readings appealing to college students.** The new essays add topics such as job skills, discrimination based on physical appearance, campus suicide, campus engagement by gender, MOOCs, how to avoid being "hacked," children's exposure to junk food, and vegan versus balanced diets.

WHAT IS DISTINCTIVE ABOUT *THE PRENTICE HALL READER*?

The eleventh edition retains and improves on some of the popular student features from earlier editions:

- **Selections arranged by difficulty.** *The Prentice Hall Reader* offers flexibility in choosing readings. No chapter has fewer than five selections; most have six or more. The readings are scaled in terms of length and sophistication—moving from a student example in the chapter's introduction to examples written by professional writers arranged in increasing length, difficulty, and sophistication.

- **Clear introductions to each chapter.** Each chapter's introductory material is organized around key questions about writing.

- **Links between chapter introductions and readings.** Sections labeled "Links Between Writing and Reading" connect introductory material with the chapter's readings.

- **Detailed and extensive writing suggestions.** Each reading is followed by seven writing suggestions: the first asks for a critical analysis of the essay; the second suggests a journal or blog entry; the third, a paragraph-length response; the fourth, an essay; the fifth, an essay linking two readings in the text; the sixth, an essay linking to an online reading; and the seventh, an essay involving research. Each suggestion is related to the content of the reading, and each calls for a response in the particular pattern being studied. In addition, each chapter contains an extensive new list of writing suggestions related to the chapter's organizational strategy. In all, the *Reader* has nearly five hundred writing suggestions.

- **Links between grammar and writing and between reading and writing.** In addition to the three opening units on reading, writing, and revising, each reading has a "Focusing on Grammar and Writing" activity.

- **Glossary and Ready Reference.** This tool at the end of the book explains and illustrates common problems with grammar and writing.

- **Literary examples of each organizational strategy.** A poem or short story is included in most of the chapters. These creative examples show how the strategies can be used to structure not just essays but poetry and fiction as well. Each selection has discussion questions and writing suggestions.

- **Emphasis on critical reading skills.** In addition to the unit "How to Read and Then Analyze an Essay," which appears at the beginning of the text, each chapter has an example of how critical-reading skills can be applied to reading each strategy. Each essay is preceded by two questions that invite students to connect the reading to their own experience and to focus their attention on a close reading of the essay. Each reading has a "Critical-Reading Activity" (in the *Instructor's Manual*).

- **Extensive Web activities.** Throughout the text, students are directed to the Web. To enhance student use of the Web, advice is given on Web searching and evaluating Web resources.

- **Writing about images.** Chapters include a section with a visual image and suggestions on writing about such images.

- **Extensive chapter on writing the research paper.** The research paper is traced from idea to finished draft. Detailed advice indicates how to locate and evaluate print and online sources.

WHAT ADDITIONAL RESOURCES ARE AVAILABLE TO THE INSTRUCTOR?

A separately published *Instructor's Manual With Quizzes* (ISBN 0-321-94600-6), available in downloadable form at www.pearsonhighered.com, includes the following:

- **Teaching writing resources.** These resources for planning the writing and reading in a composition course include sections on teaching the writing process, including how to use prewriting activities, to conference, to design and implement collaborative learning activities, and to grade. In addition, they offer advice on how to plan a class discussion, how to avoid pointless discussions, and how to conduct a writing assessment. They also include a variety of sample course materials including reproducible worksheets.

- **Annotations for each essay.** A teaching strategy suggests ways in which to teach the essay and to keep the students' attention focused on how the essay works as a piece of writing. The strategy includes

  - **Explanations of allusions and contexts.** Appropriate background information that explains allusions and historical contexts

  - **Essay activities.** Specific critical reading activities for each essay

  - **Discussion question responses.** Possible responses to all of the discussion questions included in the text

  - **Writing ideas for essays.** An additional writing suggestion to accompany each essay

  - **Quizzes.** Two quizzes are provided for each essay in the *Reader*, one on content and the other on vocabulary. Each quiz has five multiple-choice questions and is printed in a reproducible form. The quizzes are intended to be administered and graded quickly. They provide the instructor with a brief and efficient means of testing the students' ability to extract significant ideas from the readings and to demonstrate their understanding of certain vocabulary words from the readings. Keys to both quizzes are included.

MyWritingLab MyWritingLab is an online homework, tutorial, and assessment program that provides engaging experiences to today's instructors and students. By incorporating rubrics into the writing assignments, faculty can create meaningful assignments, grade them based on their desired criteria, and analyze class performance through advanced reporting. For students who enter the course under-prepared, MyWritingLab offers a diagnostic test and personalized remediation so that students see improve results and instructors spend less time in class reviewing the basics. Rich multimedia resources, including a text-specific ebook, are built in to engage students and support faculty throughout the course. Visit www.mywritinglab.com for more information.

Acknowledgments

Although writing is a solitary activity, no one can publish without the assistance of others. This text, as always, owes much to many people. To the staff at Pearson who over the years have continued to play a role in shaping and developing this text: Brad Potthoff, Senior Editor; Karen Mauk, Development Editor; Joseph Opiela, Vice President; Roxanne McCarley, Executive Marketing Manager; and Amanda Norelli, Editorial Assistant.

To my reviewers who wrote extensive critiques of the previous edition and made many helpful suggestions: April M. Dolata, Northwestern Connecticut Community College; William M. Folden, York Technical College; Roger Walton Jones, Ranger College; Miriam Moore, Lord Fairfax Community College; Jean Sorensen, Grayson College; Verne Underwood, Rogue Community College; Joette Waddle, Roane State Community College; and Sam Worley, Arkansas Technical University.

To the writing program staff at the University of Delaware. To my former students, both graduate and undergraduate, who tested materials, offered suggestions, and contributed essays to the introductions. To Kristen LaPorte, whose comments on her writing process and research papers are reproduced (exactly as they were written) in Chapter 10. To Susan Brynteson, the May Morris Director of Libraries at the University of Delaware, and her staff, who are always accommodating and helpful.

To my wife Vicki, who is always there to encourage. And to my children. Lisa, Jon, Craig, Valerie, Eric, Evan, Adam, and Nathan, and my stepchildren Alicia and Eric, who have learned over the years to live with a father who writes.

George Miller

How to Read and Then Analyze an Essay

LEARNING OBJECTIVES

In this section, you will learn how to

1. Apply the techniques of active reading to any essay you read
2. Summarize any essay
3. Analyze critically how any essay is constructed
4. Recognize how and why any visual image works

Key Questions

EXPLORING THE LINKS BETWEEN READING AND WRITING

Why do you read essays in a writing course?

How does reading an essay help you write an essay?

How does writing help you become a better reader?

What is the difference between being an active reader and a passive reader?

What steps do you follow to become an active reader?

    Prereading

    Reading

    Rereading

PRACTICING ACTIVE READING: A MODEL

    Nick Schulz, "Hard Unemployment Truths About 'Soft' Skills"

ANALYZING AN ESSAY

How do you write a summary of an essay?

How do you write a critical analysis of an essay?

READING A VISUAL IMAGE

How do you recognize the purpose or thesis of an image?

How do you analyze the composition and structure of an image?

How do you know who the intended audience might be?

PRACTICING READING A VISUAL: A MODEL

    "Don't Let Texting Blind You"

Exploring the Links between Reading and Writing

Why Do You Read Essays in a Writing Course?

Why should you "read" in a writing course? After all, your grade in most writing courses is determined by the papers you write rather than by exams based on the essays you have read. How do the activities of reading and writing fit together?

You read in a writing course for three purposes:

1. Essays *provide information* that can be used in your writing, and they suggest ways in which to research topics more fully.
2. Essays *offer a perspective* on a particular subject, one with which you might agree or disagree. In this sense they serve as catalysts to spark your writing.
3. Essays *offer models for writing.* They show how another writer dealt with a particular subject or writing problem.

How Does Reading an Essay Help You Write an Essay?

The first two purposes of readings—as a source of information and as a stimulus to writing—seem fairly obvious, but the third purpose might be confusing. Exactly how do you, as a student writer, use an essay written by a professional writer as a model?

To *model*, in the sense that the word is used here, does not mean to produce an imitation. You are not expected to use another writer's organizational structure or to imitate someone else's style, tone, or approach. Rather, from these writers you can learn how to select information; how to address a particular audience; how to structure the body of an essay; how to begin, make transitions, and end; and how to construct effective paragraphs and achieve sentence variety. In short, readings represent an album of performances, examples that you can use to study writing techniques.

Models, or examples, are important to you as a writer because you learn to write effectively in the same way that you learn any other activity. You study the rules or advice on how the activity is done; you practice, especially under the watchful eye of an instructor or coach; and you study how others have mastered similar problems and techniques.

To improve your writing, remember these steps:

- Follow the advice of your instructor and textbooks.
- Practice by writing frequently.
- Share your work with peers and listen to their comments.
- Study carefully what other writers do.

How Does Writing Help You Become a Better Reader?

Reading and writing work together: being a good reader will help you become a more effective writer, and being a good writer will help you become a more effective reader. As a writer, you learn how to plan an argument and how to make an effective transition from one point to another. You learn how to write beginnings, middles, and ends, and most important, you learn how to organize an essay. As a reader, you learn that comparison and contrast essays can be organized in either the subject-by-subject or the point-by-point pattern, that narratives are structured chronologically, and that cause-and-effect analyses are linear and sequential. So devices such as structure and pattern are not only creative tools used in writing, but also analytical tools that can be used in reading. By revealing an underlying organization, such devices help you understand what the essay says. To become an efficient reader, however, you need to exercise the same care and attention that you do when you write. In other words, become an active reader rather than a passive reader.

What Is the Difference between Being an Active Reader and a Passive Reader?

As a reader your first concern is usually plot or subject matter: What happens? What is the subject? Is the subject new and interesting? Generally, that first reading is done quickly, even superficially. You are a spectator waiting passively to be entertained or informed; you might even skim or hurry through the text. Then, if it is important for you to use that piece of writing in some way or to understand it in detail or in depth, active reading begins. You ask questions, seek answers, look for organizational strategies, and concentrate on themes and images or on the thesis and the quality of the evidence presented. Careful reading requires active participation. Writing and reading are social acts of communication; as such, they involve an implied contract between writer and audience. A writer's job is to communicate clearly and effectively; a reader's job is to read attentively and critically.

As a reader you are an active participant in the process of communication. Therefore, always read any piece of writing that you are using in a course or on your job more than once. Rereading an essay or a textbook involves the same types of critical activities involved in rereading a poem, a novel, or a set of directions. You must examine how the writer embodies meaning, purpose, or direction in the prose. You must seek answers to a variety of questions: How does the author structure the text? How does the author select, organize, and present information? To whom is the author writing? How does that audience influence the essay?

You can increase your effectiveness as an active and critical reader by following a three-step model.

What Steps Do You Follow to Become an Active Reader?

As you read here about the three steps of prereading, reading, and rereading, look briefly at the format of the first essay in this book, "Hard Unemployment Truths About 'Soft' Skills."

When you prepare to write a paper, you engage in preliminary activities such as finding a topic, narrowing that into a thesis, and gathering information. Similarly, you start the active reading process with preliminaries: Get an overview of the text you are about to read. Size it up; get a sense of what it is about and how it seems to work. Active reading involves a process that starts before you actually begin to read the essay itself.

PREREADING -----> READING -----> REREADING

Prereading Selected Essays

1. Look closely at the title of the essay. What expectations does it set up?
2. Read the biographical note about the author.
3. Check where the text was first published. What does that tell you?
4. Think about the two Before Reading questions.
5. Check for obvious subdivisions (e.g., subheadings, extra white space between paragraphs). What do they suggest about structure?
6. Read the first sentence of each paragraph.
7. Look at the questions that follow the essay. What do they want you to watch for when reading the essay?
8. Get a marker, pencil, or pen to annotate the text and ask questions.
9. Have a dictionary to look up unfamiliar words.

After you have finished prereading, you are ready to read the essay. When you begin to read a selection in this book, you already have an important piece of information about its structure. Each essay was chosen to demonstrate a particular type of writing (narration, description, exposition, or argumentation) and a particular pattern of organization (chronological, spatial, division, classification, comparison, contrast, process, cause and effect, definition, induction or deduction). As you read, think about why the essay was placed into that category.

PREREADING -----> **READING** -----> REREADING

Reading Selected Essays

1. What is the essay's subject?
2. What particular point is the author trying to make about this subject?
3. How is the essay organized?
4. Why might the author have begun the essay with that introduction?

5. How does the author bring the essay to a conclusion?

6. What examples or evidence does the author use? Where did they come from? Are they appropriate and convincing?

7. How readable is the essay? What makes it either easy or difficult to read?

8. To whom does the author seem to be writing? How do you sense that?

9. What purpose does the author seem to have for writing this essay?

Remember that an essay typically expresses a particular idea or assertion (*thesis*) about a *subject* to an *audience* for a particular reason (*purpose*). One reading of an essay will probably be enough to answer questions about its subject, but you may have to reread the essay several times to identify the author's thesis and purpose. Keep these elements separate and clear in your mind; it will help to answer the following questions as you read and reread:

Subject: What is this essay about?

Thesis: What particular point is the author trying to make about this subject?

Audience: To whom does the author seem to be writing? How does this intended audience help shape the essay and influence its language and style?

Purpose: Why might the author have written this essay? Is the intention to entertain? To inform? To persuade?

Rereading, like rewriting, is not always a discrete stage in a linear process. When writing, you might pause after several sentences and go back and make immediate changes. As a reader, you might stop at the end of a paragraph, then go back and reread what you have just read. Depending on the difficulty of the essay, it might take several rereadings for you to be able to answer the questions posed about the writer's thesis and purpose. Even if you feel certain about your understanding of the essay, a final rereading is important. A rereading is also the time to focus on the essay as an example of the writer's craft. Strive not only for a detailed understanding of what is happening in the essay, but also for what you (a practicing writer) can learn about the craft of writing.

PREREADING -----> READING -----> REREADING

Rereading Selected Essays

1. Use the questions at the end of each selection as a way to gauge your understanding of the essay.

2. Outline the essay to reveal its structure—a simple one will do.

3. Look carefully at how the essay is paragraphed. Paragraphs can represent shifts in thought or content, or they might be required because of the format in which an essay was originally published.

4. Pay attention to the author's sentence structures. How do these sentences differ from those you typically write?

5. Is there anything unusual about word choice? Do you use a similar range of vocabulary when you write?

6. How has the author kept the intended audience in mind?

7. How effective are the details and examples? Could any have been better?

8. Is the introduction effective? Do you want to keep reading? Does the conclusion seem like the right place at which to stop?

9. Jot down a few things that you have learned about writing from reading and studying this essay.

Practicing Active Reading: A Model

Before you begin reading in *The Prentice Hall Reader*, you can see how one student used the techniques of prereading, reading, and rereading on the following essay. The student's annotations required several rereadings of the essay. Following the essay are the student's prereading, reading, and rereading notes. Remember, one reading of any essay is never enough.

Hard Unemployment Truths About 'Soft' Skills

NICK SCHULZ

> *Nick Schulz is DeWitt Wallace Fellow at the American Enterprise Institute and editor-in-chief of American.com, the Institute's online magazine which focuses on business, economics, and public affairs. Schulz writes the "Economics 2.0" column for* Forbes.com, *and has published essays in many newspapers and magazines including the* Washington Post, *the* Los Angeles Times, *and* USA Today. *This essay originally appeared in the "Opinion" section of* The Wall Street Journal *on September 20, 2012.*

Before Reading

Connecting: What does the phrase "soft skills" mean to you? They are "soft" as opposed to what other type of skill?

Anticipating: What skills do you think you will need to get a job once you graduate?

1   **A**t a recent dinner in Washington, D.C., with representatives from major manufacturing companies, I listened as the talk turned to how hard it is to find qualified applicants for jobs.

2   His assumption   "What exactly are the skills you can't find?" I asked, <u>imagining that openings for high-tech positions went begging</u> because, as we hear so often, the training of the U.S. workforce doesn't match up well with current corporate needs.

3   Surprising answer   One of the representatives looked sheepishly around the room and responded: "To be perfectly honest . . . <u>we have a hard time finding people who can pass the drug test</u>." Several other reps gave a knowing nod. Applicants were often so underqualified, they said, that simply finding someone who could properly answer the telephone was sometimes a challenge.

4   Statistic to document job shortages   More than 600,000 jobs in manufacturing went unfilled in 2011 due to a skills shortage, according to a survey conducted by the consultancy Deloitte.

5   Expectation of policy makers   The <u>problem seems soluble</u>: Equip workers with the skills they need to match them with employers who are hiring. That explains the emphasis that policy makers of both parties place on science, technology, engineering and math degrees—it is such a (mantra) that they're known by shorthand as STEM degrees.

Mantra:

6   American manufacturing has become more advanced, we're told, and requires computer aptitude, intricate problem solving, and greater dexterity with complex tasks. Surely if Americans were getting STEM education, they would have the skills they need to get jobs in our modern, high-tech economy.

7   First source to document lack of "soft" skills   But considerable evidence suggests that many employers would be happy just to find job applicants who have the sort of "soft" skills that used to be almost taken for granted. In the Manpower Group's 2012 Talent Shortage Survey, nearly 20% of employers cited a lack of soft skills as a key reason they couldn't hire needed employees. "<u>Interpersonal skills and enthusiasm/ motivation" were among the most commonly</u> identified soft skills that employers found lacking.

Examples of missing "soft" skills

8   AARP: American Association of Retired Persons   Employers also mention a lack of elementary command of the English language. A survey in April of human-resources professionals conducted by the Society for Human Resource Management and the AARP

Second source to document need for "soft" skills

compared the skills gap between older workers who were nearing retirement and younger workers coming into the labor pool. More than half of the organizations surveyed reported simple grammar and spelling were the top "basic" skills among older workers that are not readily present in younger workers.

9

Third source

The SHRM/AARP survey also found that "professionalism" or "work ethic" is the top "applied" skill that younger workers lack. This finding is bolstered by the Empire Manufacturing Survey for April, published by the Federal Reserve Bank of New York. It said that manufacturers were finding it harder to find punctual, reliable workers today than in 2007, "an interesting result given that New York State's unemployment rate was more than 4 percentage points lower in early 2007 than in early 2012."

10   Although there is a shortage of people with STEM skills, that is not why unemployment numbers are high.

The skills shortage is not just an absence of workers who can write computer code, operate complex graphics software or manipulate cultures in a biotech lab—as real as that scarcity is. Many people lack what the writer R.R. Reno has called "forms of social discipline" that are indispensable components of a person's human capital and that are needed for economic success.

11

Suggest some causes but does not analyze

This is not an exercise in blaming the victim. There's plenty of fault to go around, from America's inadequate K–12 education system to the collapse of intact families and the resultant erosion of human and social capital in many communities. But we shouldn't delude ourselves about the nature of the problem facing many of the millions who can't find work. ∎

Prereading Notes

The essay appeared on the "opinion" page of a newspaper devoted to business and finance. Essay uses evidence—statistics and quotations—gathered from sources but does not provide any formal documentation since it appeared in a newspaper. Title seems to play with the opposition between "hard" and "soft" and hints that the reasons for a high unemployment rate might be more complicated than people think.

Reading Notes

Outline:
pars. 1–3 Begins with a reported dinner conversation with manufacturing employers. Direct quotations—his question, one person's surprising reply.

pars. 4–5 Documenting number of unfilled jobs in 2011 and the skills that policy makers assume are needed. Train more people in STEM fields and unemployment will drop.

pars. 7–9 Lack of "soft" skills in many seeking jobs. Soft skills include interpersonal skills, enthusiasm, motivation, simple grammar and spelling proficiency, professionalism, and a good work ethic. Three sources of documentation are used, one in each paragraph.

pars. 10–11 Suggested reasons for lack of soft skills—inadequate educational background, collapse of the family, erosion of human value.

Rereading Notes

Schulz is documenting a problem: business and industry needs not only workers with "hard" or technical skills and training, it also needs people who possess "soft" skills as well. He suggests that the high unemployment rate is more complicated than policy officials might think, that increasing STEM training will not solve everything. Schulz is not arguing for a specific agenda; he is not suggesting how this problem might be addressed; he does not provide a real cause and effect analysis of why soft skills are declining.

Analyzing an Essay

The model for prereading, reading, and rereading is one based on asking questions and taking notes. If you have carefully read the essay and annotated it, you might be asked to go a step further and write about the essay in much the same way that you might write about an imaginative work of literature. You can analyze an essay as an example of writing in two different ways. You can write a **summary,** a paragraph that objectively summarizes what the writer is saying, or you can write a **critical analysis** of how the writer says what she or he is saying.

How Do You Write a Summary of an Essay?

A summary, sometimes called an "abstract," tells the reader what the essay is about. It summarizes in a short paragraph the main points and the conclusions of the essay, objectively recording the **content** of the essay. It does not evaluate the essay or its conclusions; it is not a place where you react to the essay. If you have carefully read and reread an essay, writing a summary is a fairly simple task.

Begin by asking some basic questions:

1. What is the subject of the essay?
2. What is the main thesis or point that the essay is making about that subject?
3. What are the details or examples that support that thesis or point?

Remember that your goal is to summarize accurately the content of the essay. You are not to critique or to state your own opinion about the essay. Remember also that a summary is not a group of sentences quoted from the essay, but rather a paraphrase of its contents written in your own words. Write in the present tense—Schulz *cites*, not *cited*. Often summaries begin by identifying the essay's title and its author. A possible summary of Schulz's article might look something like this:

> In "Hard Unemployment Truths About 'Soft' Skills," Nick Schulz cites evidence showing that the high unemployment rates in the U.S. are not just the result of workers lacking the appropriate technical skills needed in modern industries. Many employers have difficulty finding workers who have the necessary "soft" skills such as interpersonal communication, motivation, and enthusiasm.

How Do You Write a Critical Analysis of an Essay?

If a summary accurately condenses the content of an essay into a paragraph or two, a critical analysis offers a close examination of how the author presents and organizes the essay. A critical analysis can focus on many different aspects of the essay. Each essay in this text has a critical analysis essay topic listed in the "writing suggestions." You might be asked, for example:

- to analyze how a writer uses language to create a humorous tone;
- how and why a particular organizational strategy is used;
- how dialogue contributes to the portrayal of a character;
- how the use of sources and quotations contribute to the argument.

A critical analysis looks at how and why a piece of writing works. When you are asked to write a critical analysis, go first to the questions provided after each essay—the questions on purpose, strategy and audience, and vocabulary and style. They will prompt you to look closely at how the essay is put together.

A critical analysis of Nick Schulz's "Hard Unemployment Truths About 'Soft' Skills" could explore a variety of approaches. What do the author's biography and the place of publication suggest about the essay? How are those things reflected in the essay, its word choice, its argument, its imagined audience? The essay is an editorial opinion, but what type of evidence and documentation does Schulz use so that it is not simply a personal opinion? How convincing do you find that evidence to be? How does Schulz structure his essay? What purpose do you think he might have in the essay? Is he suggesting any solutions to the problems he sees? Why or why not? Do you agree or disagree with Schulz's argument and why?

Each of the essays in *The Prentice Hall Reader* will repay you for the time and effort you put into reading it carefully and critically. Each essay shows an artful craftsperson at work, solving the problems inherent in communicating experiences, feelings, ideas, and opinions to an audience. Each writer is someone from whom you, as a reader and as a thinker, can learn.

So when your instructor assigns a selection from the text, remember that as a reader you must assume an active role. Don't assume that reading an essay once—to see what it is "about"—will mean that you are prepared to write about it or that you have learned all that you can learn from the essay. Ask questions, seek answers to those questions, analyze, and reread.

Reading a Visual Image

Reading a text is not just limited to paying attention to the words. Increasingly, we live in a world filled with images—some static (a photograph or a cartoon), some moving (like a video). Your textbooks for other courses are full of images; articles in magazines are heavily illustrated. Even the papers you write in school might include visuals—photographs, diagrams, charts—as well as words. Moreover, not every image is part of a written text. You study paintings and photographs in art and art history classes; you pass billboards on a highway. You post and watch videos on YouTube; your Facebook page is full of images; you take photographs and even videos with your cell phone.

The context in which a visual appears varies. Visuals or images can stand alone, such as a photograph, a painting, a cartoon in a magazine, with no accompanying text. Visuals can include some text which is clearly subordinated to the image itself—advertisements or graphic novels, for example. Finally, visuals can be a relatively small part of a larger written text—like the illustrations that accompany an article in a newspaper or a chapter in a textbook.

Visuals can be "read"—that is, analyzed and interpreted just like a text composed only of words. In order to do so, you need to ask and answer a series of questions similar to those you ask about a text containing only words.

- **Context:** In what context is this image used? Does it stand alone? Is it part of a written text and if so, how does it contribute to your understanding of or interest in the reading?
- **Purpose:** What purpose or thesis does this image seem to have?
- **Structure:** How is the image composed or structured? What elements in the image seem to be most important? What does the composition of the image reveal?
- **Audience:** Who seems to be the image's intended audience? What effect does the visual seem to have on you, its viewer? How is the image appropriate for its audience? Visuals communicate just as words do and both imply an audience.

How Do You Recognize the Purpose or Thesis of an Image?

Visual images, like writing, can have a wide range of purposes. Sometimes they are included or chosen simply to make a text more eye-catching. Unbroken pages of words can seem oppressive—images add another dimension to the reading experience. Sometimes images are simply intended to make us laugh. Sometimes images allow us to see something that could not be effectively described in words—think about photographs that accompany articles about natural disasters or exotic locations. Sometimes images help us to understand how to do something: "How to Assemble" instructions are often composed only of a sequence of images or drawings with few to no words. Sometimes images are manipulative—seeking to persuade us to act in a certain way, believe in a particular point of view, or buy a certain product. All of these purposes may be seen in the visuals that are included in the chapters that follow.

How Do You Analyze the Composition and Structure of an Image?

If you have ever taken a photograph or studied a work of art, you know that visual images are carefully composed and arranged. When you take a photograph, for example, you decide what you want to capture and why; who or what will be in it; the angle at which it is taken. Your task as a reader of visual images is to analyze how the image is presented to an audience. In each of the chapters that follow, you are given an image to analyze along with some specific questions to answer. You are then invited to write an analysis of the image. The images included here exhibit the rhetorical patterns that you are studying in writing and reading. An image can, for example, portray a process or suggest a cause and effect relationship. Images can have narrative or descriptive functions.

How Do You Know Who the Intended Audience Might Be?

The context and purpose of an image are keys to its intended audience. Identifying an audience depends on the nature of the visual image. An article about travel or science might use visuals to interest a reader in taking a trip or to explain a complex concept. The clearest relationship between purpose and audience can always be found in print advertisements that appear in magazines. The goal of an advertisement is to persuade you to purchase the product or service. Most goods and services are targeted to particular audiences—determined by gender, or age, or socio-economic background, or interest—and not to everyone; it is pretty easy to define who is being targeted.

Practicing Reading a Visual: A Model

Let's look at a sample analysis to see how you can apply what you know about writing and critical reading to an image.

SAMPLE ANALYSIS:

Context and Purpose: The image is a poster, created by the National Highway Traffic Safety Administration (NHTSA) in partnership with the Ad Council and the Outdoor Advertising Association of America (OAAA). It appeared in May 2013 as one of the images used on more than 1,000 billboards and posters. The text in the center of the image simply reads, "Don't Let Texting Blind You." The advertising campaign appeared in May because, as the OAAA noted in its press release, summer driving is "twice as deadly" for teenager drivers. The NHSTA reports that drivers using hand-held devises are four times more likely to have car accidents in which they are injured. Its purpose is, therefore, persuasive.

Composition: The image, photographed through the windshield of a car, depicts a male driver behind the wheel of a car holding a cell phone, presumably reading a text. The driver is alone—probably people are more likely to read or send texts if they are alone. The message, in large white capital letters, is spaced over three lines. The image, a wide rectangle, is large enough that the words could have been spaced over two lines or even one. Arranged in this way, the words, however, obscure the driver's face in the same way that texting blinds us by drawing our eyes away from the road. Studies have shown that on average a driver's eyes are off the road for five seconds while texting. At 55 mph, in that time the car will have traveled the length of a football field. The dimensions of the rectangle were chosen surely to fit billboards and poster spaces in bus stops, the targeted placement of the advertisements. The composition of the image is simple and could easily be grasped if quickly viewed on a billboard.

Audience: The message is aimed at all drivers; the campaign particularly targeted teenagers. The driver is male. The minimal text presents no statistics, examples, or facts. It simply makes its point by obscuring the viewer's face. If you cannot see the driver, the driver cannot see you.   ■

Checklist: Some Things to Remember When Reading and Analyzing an Essay

- ❑ Read the headnote to the selection. How does this information help you understand the author and the context in which the selection was written?
- ❑ Look at the questions that precede and follow each reading. They will help focus your attention on the important aspects of the selection. After you read, write out answers to each question.
- ❑ Read through the selection first to see what happens and to satisfy your curiosity.
- ❑ Reread the selection several times, taking notes or underlining as you go.
- ❑ Write or locate in the essay a thesis statement. Remember that the thesis is the particular point that the writer is trying to make about the subject.
- ❑ Define a purpose for the essay. Why is the author writing? Does the author make that purpose explicit?
- ❑ Imagine the audience for such an essay. Who is the likely reader? What does that reader already know about the subject? Is the reader likely to have any preconceptions or prejudices about the subject?
- ❑ Isolate a structure in the selection. How is it put together? Into how many parts can it be divided? How do those parts work together? Outline the essay.
- ❑ Be sure that you understand every sentence. How does the writer vary sentence structures?
- ❑ Look up every word that you cannot define with some degree of certainty. Remember, you might misinterpret what the author is saying if you simply skip over unfamiliar words.
- ❑ Reread the essay one final time, reassembling its parts into the artful whole it was intended to be.

How to Write an Essay

LEARNING OBJECTIVES

In this section, you will learn how to

1. Recognize what a writing topic is asking you to do
2. Design your own topic for an essay
3. Select appropriate information for your essay using personal experience or research
4. Write a thesis statement for an essay
5. Devise an effective structure for an essay

Key Questions

GETTING READY TO WRITE

Where do you start when you have an assigned topic?

Where do you start when you choose your own topic?

How do you gather information?

How do you write a thesis statement?

WRITING A DRAFT

How do you structure your paper?

How do you check the structure of your paper?

Getting Ready to Write

Where Do You Start When You Have an Assigned Topic?

In most college courses, you will be writing papers in response to a specific assignment. That assignment will contain a set of clues or instructions about what you are to do in the paper. Before you begin to write, before you even begin to gather information, spend time analyzing the assignment and the directions you have been given. Look at five areas in the assigned topic to see what clues they give you about the paper you are going to write.

Using Length as a Clue   How long is the paper to be? If your instructor specifies length (a certain number of pages or an approximate number of words), you have an idea of how detailed your paper must be. If the subject seems fairly large and the length modest, then clearly you must focus your paper on the key or significant issues. If your instructor wants a longer paper or a research paper, then you must respond to the assignment with extensive detail or evidence.

Using Purpose as a Clue   Do not confuse the reason why your instructor assigned a paper (e.g., to have something to grade!) with the purpose of the paper as it is stated in the assignment. To establish that, look for verbs or descriptive phrases in the assignment. For example, does it ask you to *narrate, argue for, evaluate, analyze, summarize, recommend, explain*? As you begin work on the paper, keep that purpose verb in mind.

Using Structure as a Clue   Purpose and structure are often closely related. Look at the accompanying table which connects assignment verbs with both purposes and structures. If you are told to *analyze*, you are dividing something into its component parts or assessing strengths and weaknesses. If you are to *argue for*, you will use an inductive or a deductive order.

Using Audience as a Clue   Audience can be more complicated than it sounds. The answer to "who?" is not simply "I'm writing to my instructor." You need to think about how much your audience (typically peers as well as instructor) knows about the subject. Are you going to be using words or concepts that might not be familiar to those readers? Will you have to find analogies that will help your audience understand? Will you have to define technical words and phrases? Is your audience likely to know everything that you are writing about? If so, then why would the audience be interested in reading your paper? If you are arguing for something, how deeply does your audience feel about the topic? Does the topic, for example, challenge your audience's deeply held beliefs?

Using Possible Sources as a Clue   What does the assignment suggest about where to find the information you need? Are you expected to draw from the readings that might be part of the assignment? From class lectures or discussions? Are you to use your own personal experiences? Are you to do some research? Interview people? Search the Internet? Locate books and articles on the topic?

Looking for Key Words	Usually Means	Likely Organizational Pattern
Narrate or Tell	to tell a story; to describe how something works	chronological; flashbacks can be used; first step to last
Summarize	to rehearse the key points	structure according to what is being summarized
Describe	to tell how something was perceived by the senses	spatial patterns: top to bottom, side to side, front to back, prominent to background
Classify	to place similar items into categories or groups	largest to smallest; most important to least
Divide	to separate a whole into its parts	largest to smallest; most important to least
Analyze	to show component parts; to assess correctness	how something works; component parts; strengths and weaknesses
Compare	to show similarities between two or more items	subject-by-subject (A, B), point-by-point (A1/B1, A2/B2)
Contrast	to show differences between two or more items	subject-by-subject (A, B), point-by-point (A1/B1, A2/B2)
Explain	to clarify an idea, a process; to make clear	step-by-step
Identify Causes and Effects	to identify causes of a certain event; to identify effects that arise from a certain event	forward or backward; causes to event; event and its effects
Define	to provide an explanation for a word, concept, or event	placement in a class and addition of distinguishing features; definition followed by examples
Argue or Persuade	to get a reader to agree with your position	inductive; deductive; logical (argument); emotional (persuasion)

PRACTICING WITH CLUES

Let's look at two sample writing assignments from this text. The first follows "The Inheritance of Tools" by Scott Russell Sanders (Chapter 3). In the essay, Sanders is building an interior wall in his house when he learns that his father has died. He has inherited from his father both the physical tools he is using and the knowledge of how to use them. In the essay, he reflects on that "inheritance" and what it means to him. Here is one of the writing assignments that follows that essay:

> **For an essay:** Think about a skill, talent, attitude, or habit that you have learned from or share with a family member. What does that inheritance mean to you? How does it affect our life? In an essay, describe the inheritance and identify its effects on you.
>
> **Using clues as a way of preparing to write:**
> **Length:** An essay, typically defined as three to four pages
> **Purpose:** "Describe the inheritance and identify its effect on you." You are asked to do two things. First, you are to select a "skill, talent, attitude, or habit" that you have inherited from or share with a family member and describe it. Second, you are to identify the effects that inheritance has had on you.
> **Structure:** The key phrases "describe" and "identify the effects" suggest that the essay will have two main parts. The first part of the essay will involve description, focusing on something and explaining or describing what it is. The second part of the essay will trace the effects that inheritance has had on you. The complete essay will be a description followed by an analysis of effects.
> **Audience:** Not specified, but typically imagined as an audience of peers
> **Sources of information:** Personal experience and reflection

The second example follows Peter Singer's "The Singer Solution to World Poverty" (Chapter 9).

> **For an essay:** Singer notes (citing the research of someone else) that a donation of two hundred dollars would "help a sickly two-year-old transform into a healthy six-year-old." That works out to about fifty-five cents per day yearly. Could you and your friends, even as college students, find a way to trim fifty-five cents a day (or less than four dollars a week) out of what you already spend? In an essay aimed at undergraduates at your school, argue for a schoolwide campaign to get everyone to contribute to such a cause.
>
> **Using clues as a way of preparing to write:**
> **Length:** An essay, typically defined as three to four pages
> **Purpose:** "Argue for a schoolwide campaign"
> **Structure:** Establish the problem and define a solution, which would involve showing how such a small sum of money could be saved no matter how tight the students' budgets
> **Audience:** "Undergraduates at your school" (who would have relatively little extra money)
> **Sources of information:** Some research on the problem (probably drawn from Singer's essay) and some research on the cost of the items consumed daily (e.g., cup of coffee, can of soda, candy)

Where Do You Start When You Choose Your Own Topic?

Writing from an assigned topic can seem frustrating and confining. At some point, probably every writer has resented being told what to write and has felt confined to a topic about which she or he has little or no interest. Devising your own topic may be more rewarding but also more difficult. You might be excited or terrified about a completely open-ended assignment that simply says, "Write a paper on a topic of your choice." Your response might be a series of questions that we have referred to as clues: "How long should this paper be?" "What is it supposed to do?"

Whether the topic is given to you or you choose it, the key is to define the set of parameters within which you will write. Before you start to write, answer each of the following questions:

> **Length:** How long will my paper be? Is it a one-page response paper, a three-to-four page essay, a research paper with documentation? What level of detail will I need?
>
> **Purpose:** What do I want my paper to do? Am I narrating or describing what happened? Am I conveying information? Am I arguing for something? What are the key words that I will use?
>
> **Structure:** What do my key words suggest about the structure of my paper? How does that structure work within the page limit I have chosen?
>
> **Audience:** Who is my audience? What do they know about this subject? What might need to be explained to them?
>
> **Sources:** What type of information will I need for this paper and where can I find it?

How Do You Gather Information?

What makes writing entertaining, informative, or persuasive is information—specific, relevant detail. If you try to write without gathering information, you end up skimming the surface of your subject, even if you already know something about it.

How you go about gathering information for your paper depends on your subject and your purpose for writing. Some topics, such as those involving a personal experience, require a memory search; other assignments, such as describing a particular place, require careful observation. Essays that convey information or argue particular positions often require gathering information through research.

Exploring Personal Experience and Observation   Even your most unforgettable experience has probably been forgotten in part. If you are going to re-create it for a reader, you will have to do some active searching among your memories. By focusing your attention, you can slowly recall more details. Ask yourself a series of questions about the chronology of the experience. For example, start with a particular detail and try to stimulate your memory: What happened just before? Just after? Who was there? Where did the experience take place? Why did it happen? When did it happen? How did it happen?

Descriptions, like every other form of writing, demand specific information, and the easiest way to gather details is to observe. Before you try to describe a person, place, or object, take some time to list specific details on a piece of paper. At first, record everything you notice. Do not worry about having too much, you can always edit later. At this stage, it is better to have too much than too little.

The next step is to decide what to include in your description and what to exclude. As a general principle, an effective written description does not try to record everything. The selection of detail should be governed by your purpose in the description. Ask yourself what you are trying to show or reveal. For what reason? What is particularly important about this person, place, or object? A description is not the verbal equivalent of a photograph or a tape recording.

Freewriting to Get Words Down   Putting words down on a page or a computer screen can be intimidating. Your editing instincts immediately want to take over: Are the words spelled correctly? Are the sentences complete? Do they contain mechanical or grammatical errors? Not only must you express your ideas in words, but suddenly those words must be the correct words.

If you translate thoughts into written words and at the same time edit those words, writing can seem impossibly difficult. Instead of allowing ideas to take shape through the words or allowing the writing to stimulate your thinking, you become fearful of committing anything to paper or a screen.

Writing can, however, stimulate thought. Every writer has experienced a time when an idea became clear only as it was written down. If your editing instincts can be turned off, you can use writing as a way of generating ideas.

Freewriting is an effective way to deal with this dilemma. Write without stopping for a fixed period of time; write for a period as short as 10 minutes or as long as an hour. Do not stop; do not edit; do not worry about mistakes. If you find yourself stuck for something to write, repeat the last word or phrase you wrote until a new thought comes to mind. You are looking for a focus point—an idea or a subject for a paper. You are trying to externalize your thinking into writing. What will emerge is a free association of ideas. Some will be relevant and some will be worthless. After you have ideas on paper, you can decide what is worth saving, developing, or simply throwing away.

Writing Daily in Journals and Blogs   A daily journal or blog can be an effective seedbed for writing projects. Such a journal is not a daily log of your activities (got up, went to class, had lunch) but rather a place where you record ideas, observations, memories, and feelings. Set aside a specific notebook or a particular file on your computer in which to keep your journal. Try to write for at least 10 minutes every day. Over a period of time, such as a semester, you will be surprised at how many ideas for papers or projects you will accumulate. When you are working on a paper, you might want to confine part of your daily journal entries to that particular subject. If your class uses blogs or posts responses online, pay attention to what your classmates suggest about your ideas.

Brainstorming and Mapping   Brainstorming is oral freewriting among a group of people jointly trying to solve a problem by spontaneously contributing ideas. Although brainstorming is by definition a group activity, it can be done by an individual writer. In the center of a blank sheet of paper, write down a key word or phrase that refers to your subject. Then in the space around that word, quickly jot down any ideas that come to mind. Do not write in sentences, just key words and phrases. Because you are not filling consecutive lines with words and because you have space in which the ideas can be arranged, this form of brainstorming often suggests structural relationships. You can increase the usefulness of such an idea generator by adding graphic devices such as circles, arrows, or connecting lines to indicate possible relationships among ideas.

Asking Formal Questions   One particularly effective way to gather information on any topic is to ask yourself questions about it. This allows you to explore the subject from a variety of angles. The secret to finding answers always lies in knowing the right questions to ask. A good place to start is with the list of questions presented here. Remember, though, not every question is appropriate for every topic.

Illustration

1. What examples of _____ can be found?
2. In what ways are these things examples of _____?
3. What details about _____ seem the most important?

Comparison and Contrast

1. To what is _____ similar? List the points of similarity.
2. From what is _____ different? List the points of difference.
3. Which points of similarity or difference seem most important?
4. What does the comparison or contrast tell the reader about _____?

Division and Classification

1. Into how many parts can _____ be divided?
2. How many parts is _____ composed of?
3. What other category of things is _____ most like?
4. How does _____ work?
5. What are _____'s component parts?

Process

1. How many steps or stages are involved in _____?
2. In what order do those steps or stages occur?

Cause and Effect

1. What precedes _____?
2. Is that a cause of _____?
3. What follows _____?
4. Is that an effect of _____?
5. How many causes of _____ can you find?
6. How many effects of _____ can you find?
7. Why does _____ happen?

Definition

1. How is _____ defined in a dictionary?
2. Does everyone agree about the meaning of _____?
3. Does _____ have any connotations? What are they?
4. Has the meaning of _____ changed over time?
5. What words are synonymous with _____?

Argument and Persuasion

1. How do your readers feel about _____?
2. How do you feel about _____?
3. What are the arguments in favor of _____? List those arguments in order of strength.
4. What are the arguments against _____? List those arguments in order of strength.

Finding Print and Online Sources   Chapter 10 offers detailed advice about how to go about gathering information for a paper using print and online sources. Be sure to read that chapter before you start a search for materials.

Most everyone looking for "quick" information simply goes to a computer to search an appropriate term or phrase. More often than not, Wikipedia turns up high on the list of retrieved sources. There is nothing wrong with such a strategy as long as you keep these cautions in mind:

1. Many instructors do not want you to use Wikipedia as a source for a paper.
2. Anyone can produce an impressive website that looks authoritative and reliable. Unless there is some scholarly, professional, or educational editorial oversight, you can never be sure that the information posted on a website is accurate.
3. Google (or any other search engine) turns up the "best" *matches* to your choice of key words and phrases, not necessarily the best sources. What are the best choices for words or phrases to search?

4. Your school's library has an online catalog of its holdings. But it probably also has a variety of online databases that allow access to articles in more scholarly journals, popular magazines, newspapers, and even government documents.

Interviewing   Print or electronic sources are not always available for a topic. In such a case, people often are a great source of information for a writer. Of course the people should have special credentials or knowledge about the writer's subject.

Interviewing requires special skills and tact. When you first contact someone to request an interview, always explain who you are, what you want to know, and how you will use the information. Remember that specific questions will produce more useful information than general ones. Take notes that you can expand later, or use a tape recorder or digital recorder. Keep attention focused on the information that you need, and do not be afraid to ask questions to keep your informant on the subject. If you plan to use direct quotations, make sure that the wording is accurate. If possible, check quotations with your source one final time.

How Do You Write a Thesis Statement?

Defining a Thesis Statement   The information-gathering stage of the writing process is the time to sharpen your general subject into a narrower topic. Subjects are broad, general ideas; for example, violence in video games. That subject is simply too large for an essay. You will need to narrow your focus by concentrating on a more precise issue. Consider a few possible approaches that the subject suggests:

- history of violence in video games
- vivid description of violence in a particular game
- classification of the types of violence depicted in video games
- comparison of the violence allowed in each of the ratings for video games
- analysis of why violent video games are so popular
- argument about whether or not violent video games stimulate violent behavior

You need to narrow your *subject* into a workable *topic*, that is, a more focused, more limiting statement. A topic limits a subject, narrowing its scope, suggesting a specific approach to the subject, and defining a particular purpose for the essay.

Subject: Violence in video games
Topic: Impact that violent video games have on behavior

The final step in the process is to move from a topic to a thesis. The word *thesis* is derived from a Greek word that means "placing," "position," or "proposition." When you formulate a thesis, you are defining your position on the subject. Because it represents your "final" position, a thesis is typically something that you develop and refine as you work on the paper. You begin with a tentative thesis (or *hypothesis*) and then allow your final position to emerge as you move through the stages of the writing process.

Remember that your thesis is a reflection of your purpose in writing. If you are working with an assigned topic, look for a verb in the assignment that suggests what your purpose is supposed to be. If you have chosen your own topic, make sure you have a purpose verb for your paper. If your purpose is to persuade your audience, your thesis will try to convince your readers to accept your position. If your purpose is to convey information to your readers, your thesis will forecast your main points and indicate how your paper will be organized.

Writing a Thesis Statement   When you have decided on your purpose, sharpened your general subject into a topic, and defined your position on that topic, you are ready to write a thesis statement. The process is simple. You write a thesis statement by linking together your topic and your position on that topic:

> **Subject:** Violent video games
> **Topic:** Impact that violent video games have on players' behavior
> **Thesis:** Violent video games desensitize players to violence, suggest
> that violence can be used to settle conflicts, and reward players for
> violent behavior.

Checklist for the Focusing Process

Ask yourself the following questions:

- ❏ What is my general subject?
- ❏ What is my specific topic within that general subject?
- ❏ What do I intend to do in my paper? What is my purpose?
- ❏ What is my position on that specific topic?

Checklist for an Effective Thesis

A thesis has these characteristics:

- ❏ Clearly signals the purpose of the paper
- ❏ States or takes a definite position, stating specifically what the paper will be doing
- ❏ Expresses that definite purpose and position in precise, familiar terms
- ❏ Is appropriate in scope for the paper's length
- ❏ Signals the structure that will follow in the paper

Notice that this thesis not only limits the scope of the paper and defines a precise position and purpose, it also signals that the body of the essay will have three parts arranged in a particular way.

Writing a Draft

Now it is time to write, because you have answered your key questions about the assignment or your proposed topic, you have thought about what the essay should do, you have gathered the information you will use in the paper, and you have a tentative thesis. Do not expect that this initial draft of the essay will be the final, ready-to-be-handed-in paper. Rather, consider this draft a work in progress—a first version of what will become the final, polished essay.

How Do You Structure Your Paper?

How Do You Organize the Middle?   No matter what their length, papers consist of three parts: an introduction, a body or middle, and a conclusion. The introduction generally ranges from one to two, or at most, three paragraphs. Conclusions are rarely longer than one paragraph. The body of the essay is thus the longest section of any paper. It is difficult, even impossible, to write an introduction or a conclusion until you know what it is that you are introducing or ending. Therefore, the place to begin with most essays is the middle. Always keep in mind your working thesis to ensure that you have a controlling idea. This idea will help you decide how to structure the body of your paper and what information is relevant.

The following organizational strategies suggest ways in which the middle of your paper might be arranged.

Strategy	Typical Body Arrangement
Narration	To tell a story or narrate an event or action • Chronological, from first to last • Flashbacks to rearrange time
Description	To record sense impressions • Visual, from side to side, front to back • Most obvious or important to least
Division	To break a whole into its component parts • Largest to smallest • Most important to least
Classification	To place similar items in categories or groups • Largest to smallest • Most important to least
Comparison	To find similarities between two or more items • Compare subject-by-subject (all of A to all of B) • Compare point-by-point (A point 1 to B point 1)

Strategy	Typical Body Arrangement
Contrast	To find difference between two or more items • Contrast subject-by-subject (all of A to all of B) • Contrast point-by-point (A point 1 to B point 1)
Process	To tell how to do something • First step, next step • Chronological order
Cause and Effect	To explain what caused something or what the effects of that something are • Forward and backward, linear order • Causes or effects arranged in order of time or importance
Definition	To offer an explanation of a word, concept, or event • Item placed in a class and added distinguishing features • Extended examples, explanation of how item works, comparison to something familiar
Argumentation	To offer logical reasons for a particular course of action or conclusion • Inductive • Deductive
Persuasion	To offer emotional reasons for a particular course of action or conclusion • Strongest to weakest • Weakest to strongest

How Do You Write an Introduction?   Do you always finish everything you start to read? Every newspaper or magazine article? Every piece of mail? Every book? The truth is, readers are far more likely to stop reading than they are to continue. You stop because you get distracted; you stop because you are bored by the subject or already know the information; you stop because you completely disagree with what the author is saying.

As a writer, remember that your readers are more likely to quit reading than to continue. No one thing is the key to keeping a reader interested. All the elements of good writing contribute: an interesting subject, valuable and accurate information, insightful analyses, clear organization, grammatically correct and varied sentences, and careful proofreading. Beginnings of essays are, however, especially important. Every paper needs a strong, effective introduction that will catch readers' attention and pull them in. Introductions are typically divided into two categories, reflecting the two goals that every introduction should have:

Hook—intended to "hook" readers and "pull" them into the body of the paper

Thesis—intended to state clearly and concisely the thesis or controlling idea of the paper

Introductions vary in length depending on the length of the paper that follows. They can be a single paragraph long or several paragraphs long. An effective introduction can consist of a hook and a thesis. Perhaps the first sentence, or even paragraph, is a hook; the later sentences or the last paragraph in the introduction might be the thesis. Note the fundamental differences between the two types in these examples from student essays.

The *hook introduction* is from an essay that contrasts two different search strategies to be used in a library's online catalog (Chapter 5). It appeals to the reader's self-interest and arouses curiosity: most of us probably never realized that more than one approach is necessary to locate books on any particular subject.

> **Hook**   The Cecil College Library has twenty books dealing with the death penalty, but unless you pay attention to the next couple of pages, you will never find all of them. Why? Because no single search strategy will lead you to all twenty books.

The *thesis introduction* is from an essay on the American "hobo" (Chapter 4), which explains where the term came from and what the factors were in American society that led to the creation of this huge group of people. The paragraph does not start with a vivid example or a startling statistic; instead, it gets right to the thesis.

> **Thesis**   Although homelessness and vagrancy might seem to be a distinctively modern phenomenon, the problem is probably less acute today (in terms of percentage of our total population) than it was at the turn of the twentieth century. At that time, a series of factors combined to create a large migratory population comprised almost exclusively of young males.

Your introduction is an extremely important part of your paper. Spend time in planning and polishing it. For specific suggestions on types of introductions, check the Glossary and Ready Reference at the back of this text.

How Do You Write a Conclusion?   Generally the conclusion is the last thing you write in a paper. Because it comes last and your time may be running short, a conclusion often gets the least amount of attention. You might revise your introduction a couple of times, trying to get it to reflect what is happening in the middle of your paper, but you may have time to write only one draft of your conclusion. (That happens to professional writers as well—see Nora Ephron's "Revision and Life" in Chapter 6.) Worse yet, sometimes the paper comes to an abrupt stop instead of achieving a sense of an ending, a closure. The introduction is the first impression that a reader gets of your paper, and the conclusion is the last impression. Every paper should have a planned conclusion. Do not just stop.

Conclusions can employ a variety of strategies depending on the length and nature of the paper. Typically, conclusions use one of three general strategies:

Purpose	Types of Conclusions
Entertain	End with the climactic moment or realization: the "end" of the story, the reason for telling the story or for describing something
Inform	End with a summary of the key points
Argue/Persuade	End with a call to action or for agreement on an issue

Langston Hughes in the narrative "Salvation" (Chapter 2) recounts an experience he had at a church revival meeting when he was 12. The narrative ends at a climactic moment, the "last moment" in the story. Hughes concludes by reflecting on the significance of that experience on the rest of his life:

> That night, for the last time in my life but one—I was a big boy twelve years old—I cried, I cried, in bed alone, and couldn't stop. I buried my head under the quilts, but my aunt heard me. She woke up and told my uncle I was crying because the Holy Ghost had come into my life, and because I had seen Jesus. But I was really crying because I couldn't bear to tell her that I had lied, that I had deceived everybody in the church, that I hadn't seen Jesus, and that now I didn't believe there was a Jesus any more, since he didn't come to help me.

David Bodanis in "What's in Your Toothpaste" (Chapter 4), a humorous, informational essay that identifies the ingredients in a typical tube of toothpaste, ends with a summary of the ingredients:

> So it's chalk, water, paint, seaweed, antifreeze, paraffin oil, detergent, peppermint, formaldehyde, and fluoride (which can go some way towards preserving children's teeth)—that's the usual mixture raised to the mouth on the toothbrush for a fresh morning's clean. If it sounds too unfortunate, take heart. Studies show that thoroughly brushing with just plain water will often do as good a job.

Conclusions to persuasive or argument essays often reveal what the authors see as the primary value that their position offers. Often that means that the conclusion will reaffirm the thesis of the essay or will urge readers to adopt a particular course of action or a particular belief. Katherine Porter in "The Value of a College Degree" (Chapter 9) argues, as her title suggests, for the value of getting an undergraduate degree. Her short, final paragraph emphasizes her point:

> While it is clear that investment in a college degree, especially for those students in the lowest income brackets, is a financial burden, the long-term benefits to individuals as well as to society at large, appear to far outweigh the costs.

In contrast, T. Colin Campbell, who argues for value of a vegan diet in "Cut Animal-Based Protein" (Chapter 9), defends his own dietary choices and suggests that readers should consider making a similar change:

> Based on the scientific evidence, and on the way I feel, I know beyond any doubt that I am better off for having changed my diet to whole and plant-based foods.

Plan a conclusion to your essay; try out different strategies. For additional advice on writing conclusions, consult the Glossary and Ready Reference at the back of this text.

How Do You Check the Structure of Your Paper?

The body of your essay needs to be organized coherently and logically. Sentences and paragraphs should be phrased in parallel forms and related to one another. Coordinate units are on the same level of hierarchy and are parallel in form. Subordinate units provide support or details for the unit under which they are placed.

The logical structure of your essay can be checked in several ways, but one of the easiest is to construct an outline. An outline is a visual display in which paragraphs and sentences are arranged on levels that reveal the relationships among them. The basic idea is to display the coordinate (equal) and the subordinate (unequal) structures. An abbreviated model looks something like this:

A. Topic sentence for Paragraph 1 (which is coordinate and equal to B)
  1. Support/detail (subordinate to A but coordinate to 2 and 3)
  2. Support/detail
  3. Support/detail
B. Topic sentence for Paragraph 2

The full form of an outline consists of coordinate and subordinate items that are labeled using Roman numerals (I, II, III), alphabet letters (A, a), and Arabic numbers (1, 2). Word-processing software can automatically create outlines for you.

Sometimes teachers and textbooks tell you to outline your paper before you begin drafting. It is a rare writer who can do so. Nevertheless, it is helpful if, as you draft your paper, you jot down each new idea and paragraph in a rough outline form to see if it fits in the evolving structure of the paper. An outline will reveal problems with the structure of both the paper as a whole and with individual paragraphs. ■

Checklist: Some Things to Remember About Writing a Draft

- ❑ Do not start writing before you have spent some time studying the assigned topic or defining a topic of your choice.
- ❑ Think about the number of pages you are to write. Is this a three- to four-page essay or a fifteen-page research paper? Can you write about this subject in that amount of space? You might need either to narrow your subject or make it larger.
- ❑ Plan a timeline for writing the paper. Allow sufficient time to move through the prewriting and writing stages. Try to avoid starting a paper the night before it is due. Ideally, try to have it finished at least a day early so that you will have time to revise it.
- ❑ Locate or create key words in the topic. What is it that you are to do? Key words are verbs such as *narrate, describe, explain, compare, contrast, analyze, argue.*
- ❑ Consider what those key words imply about the structure of your essay. How will the body of your essay be structured?
- ❑ Define a thesis or key idea for your paper. Write it out in a sentence and keep it before you as you begin to draft.
- ❑ Define your audience. How much do they already know about the subject? What will be the appropriate level of detail or explanation that you will need to provide?
- ❑ Gather information before you start to write. Once you begin writing, you may need to gather more, but do not start writing without having a sense of what will go into your paper.
- ❑ Plan a structure for the body of your essay. Try to outline it as you write to make sure that it is logically structured and developed.
- ❑ Write an introduction for your essay. If you start by writing an introduction before you write the body of the paper, go back once you have a complete draft and see if the introduction needs to be sharpened or focused.
- ❑ Allow time to write an effective conclusion for your paper. Do not just stop. Find a way to signal to your reader that the paper has closure.
- ❑ Make sure that your essay has a real title. No paper should ever be titled "Essay 1" or "Persuasive Essay."

How to Revise an Essay

LEARNING OBJECTIVES

In this section, you will learn how to
1. Recognize when an essay needs revision
2. Plan a revision strategy for your essay
3. Use the revision advice that other readers suggest
4. Practice proofreading skills

 Key Questions

UNDERSTANDING WHAT REVISION IS

What is involved in revising?

What are the steps in revising?

DEVELOPING YOUR OWN REVISING SKILLS

What is a revision log, and why is it important?

GETTING HELP FROM OTHER READERS

Why should you get help from your peers?

What can you expect from a writing center or writing tutor?

How should you prepare for a conference with your instructor?

MAKING SURE TO PROOFREAD

Why is proofreading important?

Isn't an error-free paper an "A" paper?

Understanding What Revision Is

What Is Involved in Revising?

The word *revision* literally means "to see again." Revision takes place after a draft of the whole paper or a part of it has been completed. Ideally, you revise after a period of time has elapsed and you have had a chance to get advice or criticism on what you wrote. Revision is quite different from proofreading. When you proofread, you are mostly looking for small things such as misspellings or typographical errors, incorrect punctuation, awkwardly constructed sentences, and undeveloped paragraphs. In a revision, on the other hand, you look at everything: from the larger issues (subject, thesis, purpose, audience), to the structure of paragraphs and sentences, and to smaller issues such as word choices and the paper's title. Everything in a paper should be scrutinized actively and carefully.

Revising does not occur only after a complete draft. In fact, many writers revise as they draft. They might write a sentence, then stop to change its structure, even erase it and start over; they might shift the order of sentences and paragraphs or even delete them altogether. In their search for the right words, the graceful sentence, and the clear paragraph, writers revise constantly.

When you are struggling to find the right word or the right sentence structure, you are probably not thinking much about the larger whole. Consequently, allowing time to elapse between drafts of your paper is important. You need to put the completed draft aside for a while so that you gain perspective on what you have written and read your paper objectively. Try to finish a complete draft at least one day before you hand in the paper. If circumstances prevent you from finishing a paper until an hour or two before class, you will not have a chance to revise. You will only be able to proofread.

What Are the Steps in Revising?

Begin with the Larger Issues The key to improving your writing is self-awareness. You have to look carefully and critically at what you have written, focus on areas that caused you the most problems, and work to correct the problem areas. Most writers can identify the key problems they faced in a particular paper or in writing in general, even though they might not know how to solve those problems. Knowing what causes your problems is the essential first step toward solving them.

When you analyze the first draft of an essay, begin by asking a series of specific questions. Start with the larger issues and work toward the smaller ones. Ideally, you should write out your answers because doing so forces you to have a specific response.

Length   **Is your paper long enough?** The specified length of a paper suggests the amount of space that you will need to develop and illustrate your thesis sufficiently. If your papers are consistently short, you have probably not included enough examples or illustrating details.

Is your paper too long? If your papers consistently exceed your instructor's guidelines, you have probably not sufficiently narrowed your subject or you have included too many details and examples. Of the material available to support, develop, and illustrate a thesis, some are more significant and relevant than the rest. Never try to include everything; rather, select the best, the most appropriate, and the most convincing.

Purpose   **Did you do what the assignment asked?** Look again at the assignment and circle the key words, verbs such as *analyze*, *argue*, *classify*, *compare*, *criticize*, *define*, *evaluate*, *narrate*, *describe*, *summarize*, and *recommend*. Such words tell you what your purpose should have been. Is that purpose clear in your paper?

Thesis   **What is the thesis of your paper?** Can you find a single sentence in your paper that states the position you have taken on your subject? If so, underline it. If not, write a one-sentence thesis statement. If you are unsure about what a thesis is, review the material in the Glossary and Ready Reference at the back of this text.

Structure   **Does your paper have a clear structure that is visible in how you paragraphed your paper?** Your paper must have a beginning (introduction), a middle (a series of body paragraphs), and an ending (conclusion). The introduction states the subject and thesis of the paper and tries to catch the reader's interest. The middle, or body, of the paper needs to have a coherent, logical structure that is revealed by how this section is paragraphed. The conclusion must bring a sense of an ending to the reader. Endings typically summarize, reinforce the thesis, or appeal to the reader to do something. A paper should never just stop.

Audience   **To whom are you writing?** In one sense, your answer is always your instructor. If class members share papers electronically or swap and critique papers in class, your peer readers are an important source of feedback. Did the assigned topic define an audience for the paper: peers, people who need this information, people trying to make some decisions? What does your audience already know about this subject? How much previous knowledge or experience do you assume your audience will have?

Sources   **What types of information were you to use in the paper?** Personal experiences or observations? Your own opinions? Factual information that you found in online or printed sources? Did you gather what you needed?

Always start by reseeing the larger issues. If your essay has serious problems with these larger issues, you will need to rethink what you have written. Cleaning up grammatical and writing errors will not "save" a paper that does not fulfill the assignment, lacks a thesis, has an unclear purpose, or ignores its audience.

Focus on Paragraphing You can check the structure of your essay by first looking at how you have paragraphed it. Remember, paragraphs reveal the structure of a paper and provide readers with places at which to rest. If you have only several paragraphs in a three-page essay, you have not clearly indicated the structure of your essay to your reader, or you have not developed a clear, logical organization. Likewise, a paper full of very short paragraphs probably is poorly developed. You might be shifting ideas too quickly, failing to provide supporting evidence and details. A good paragraph is meaty; a good essay is not a string of undeveloped ideas and bare generalizations.

A useful analytical tool for checking structure is outlining the body of the paper. An outline reveals main points and relationships among those points. Ideas, as an outline reveals, are either coordinate (equal) or subordinate (unequal). Outlining was discussed earlier in How to Write an Essay.

Paragraph structure	**Is each paragraph structured around a single idea?** Is there an explicit statement of that idea—often called a *topic sentence*? If so, underline it. If not, jot down in the margin the key word or words in that paragraph. Consider adding a sentence that states what that paragraph is about. Typically, such a sentence appears early in the paragraph as either the first sentence or the second sentence if the first sentence serves as a transition from the material in the previous paragraph.
Paragraph development	**Are the paragraphs in the body of the paper well developed with a series of details, support, and examples?** Outline each paragraph to reveal the coordinate and subordinate pattern. Does the outline reveal anything that is out of place?
Introduction	**Does the introduction indicate both the subject and thesis of the paper? Does it attempt to catch its reader's interest?** Remember that an introduction can be more than one paragraph, especially in a longer essay. The first paragraph might "hook" the reader; the second might contain the thesis statement. Check to see if your introduction is proportional to the rest of the paper; for example, a three-page paper should not have a one-page introduction. For suggestions, consult How to Write an Essay and the Glossary and Ready Reference at the back of this text.
Conclusion	**Does the paper really have a conclusion or did you just stop?** Conclusions are sometimes difficult to write because they are written last when time is often short. For suggestions, consult How to Write an Essay and the Glossary and Ready Reference at the back of this text.
Transitions	**Does the paper help the reader see transitions between ideas, sentences, and paragraphs?** If a paper is logically structured, it will have coherence. Nevertheless, the use of transitional expressions and transitional sentences will help your reader by providing signposts that direct the reader from one point to another. Such devices promote unity and

	coherence between paragraphs. For suggestions, consult the Glossary and Ready Reference at the back of this text.
Title	**Does the paper have a "real" title?** Every essay needs a title, not a descriptive phrase like "Essay 1" or "Argument Paper." An interesting, descriptive title is part of the attraction for readers. After all, no company ever sold its product with no name on the box or with a title like "Cereal" or "Automobile." Brainstorm some ideas; check them out with potential readers and ask for suggestions. For help with titles, consult the Glossary and Ready Reference at the back of this text.

Re-See Sentences and Word Choices Only after you have asked and answered questions about the larger elements of your essay should you consider questions dealing with style, grammar, and mechanics.

Sentence or fragment	**Is everything that you punctuated as a sentence—that is, with a beginning capital letter and an end mark such as a period—really a complete sentence?** Are any just fragments? If you are not sure of the difference, check the Glossary and Ready Reference at the back of this text. Fragments are acceptable in certain writing situations; if you are intentionally using a fragment for effect, check with your instructor first.
Sentence variety	**Have you used a variety of sentence types and lengths?** Check the Glossary and Ready Reference for an explanation. Ideally, your paper should have a mix of sentence types and a variety of lengths. Be particularly careful that you do not write strings of very short, simple sentences. They will make you sound either like a young, immature writer or like a writer addressing an elementary school audience.
Punctuation	**Is every mark of punctuation used correctly?** Check each mark. Is it the right choice for this place in the sentence? Every mark of punctuation has certain conditions under which it is used. A quick review of the major uses of each punctuation mark can be found in the Glossary and Ready Reference.
Misspellings	**Is every word spelled correctly?** Pronunciations and spellings do not always agree. Word-processing software will not pick up every misspelling. If you are uncertain about any word, or if you know that you have trouble with spelling, check the words about which you are uncertain in a dictionary.
Wrong words	**Are you certain what each word means?** Do you know the difference between *then* and *than*, *effect* and *affect*, *there*, *their*, *they're*?

Diction	**Are there any words or expressions that might be too informal or too colloquial?** These are words you might use in conversation with friends but not in academic writing. If you are using technical words, can you assume that your reader will know what they mean? The Glossary and Ready Reference provides some guidelines for problems with diction.

Developing Your Own Revising Skills

What Is a Revision Log, and Why Is It Important?

Keeping a log of writing problems you most often encounter is an excellent way of promoting self-awareness. Your log should include a wide range of writing problems, not just grammatical and mechanical errors. The log will help you keep track of the areas with which you know you have trouble and those that your instructor, peer readers, or writing tutors point out as needing improvement. Do you have a tendency to overparagraph? To stop rather than conclude? Do you have trouble with subject-verb agreement or with parallel structures? Do you keep misusing *then* and *than*? Each time you discover a problem or one is pointed out to you, list it in your log. Then, as you revise a paper, look back through your log to remind yourself of frequent problems and look closely for them in your current draft.

If a revision log seems like a lot of trouble, remember, only you can improve your writing. Improvement in writing, like improvement in any skill area, comes with recognizing problems that need attention and working to correct them.

Getting Help from Other Readers

Why Should You Get Help from Your Peers?

Most of the writing you do in college is aimed toward only one reader—your instructor. Writing just for an instructor has both advantages and disadvantages. A teacher is a critical reader who evaluates your paper by a set of standards, but a teacher is also a sympathetic reader, one who understands the difficulties of writing and is patient with problems writers have. Classmates, colleagues, and supervisors can be as critical as teachers, but less sympathetic.

Only in school do you have someone who will read everything you write and offer constructive criticism. After you graduate, your letters and reports will be read by many different readers, but you will no longer have a teacher to offer advice or a tutor to meet in conference with you. Instead, you will have to rely on your own analysis of your writing and on the advice of fellow workers. For these reasons, learning to use a peer reader as a resource in your revising process is extremely important. At first you might feel uncomfortable asking someone other than your instructor to read your papers, but after some experience, you will likely feel more relaxed about sharing. Remember, every reader is potentially a valuable resource for suggestions.

Often it is difficult to accept criticism, but if you want to improve your writing skills, you need someone to say, "Why not do this?" After all, you expect an athletic coach or a music teacher to offer criticism. Your writing instructor and other readers play the same role. The advice and criticism they offer is meant to make your writing more effective; it is not intended as personal criticism of you or your abilities.

Peer Editing   Many college writing courses include peer editing as a regular classroom activity. On a peer-editing day, students swap papers and critique one another's work, typically using a list of peer-editing guidelines. You don't have to do peer editing in class to get the benefits of such an activity. If your instructor approves, arrange to swap papers with a classmate outside of class, or ask a roommate or a friend to do a peer reading for you. If your class posts drafts and papers online, you have easy access to what others have written.

Regardless of how peer editings are arranged, several ground rules are important. First, remember that when you ask a peer to edit your paper, you are asking for advice and criticism. You cannot expect that your reader will love everything you have written. Second, peer editing is not proofreading. You should not ask your reader to look for misspelled words and missing commas. Rather, encourage your reader to react to the whole paper; keep your reader's attention focused on significant issues. Give your reader a checklist—a set of questions that reflect the criteria appropriate for evaluating this kind of paper. Third, you want a peer reader to offer specific and constructive criticism. To get that type of response, you need to ask questions that invite, or even require, a reader to comment in more than "yes" and "no" answers. For example, do not ask your reader, "Is the thesis clear?"; instead ask, "What is the thesis of this paper?" If your reader has trouble answering that question, or if the answer differs from your own, you know that this aspect of your paper needs more work.

Checklist of What to Ask for in Peer Editing

- ❑ Does the paper meet the requirements of the assignment?
- ❑ Does it have a clearly stated thesis?
- ❑ Does it have a clear organization reflected in how it is paragraphed?
- ❑ Is the content interesting? Clear? Informative? Persuasive?
- ❑ Does it have an effective introduction? A conclusion?
- ❑ How effective is the title of the paper?

Group Editing   Sharing your writing in a small group is another way to seek reader reaction. Such an editing activity can take place either inside or outside of the classroom. In either case, you can prepare for a group editing session in the same way. Plan to form a group of four or five students, and make a copy of your paper for each group member. If possible, distribute the copies or e-mail them before the group editing session so that each member has a chance to read and prepare comments for the discussion. Then follow these guidelines:

Before the Group Editing Session:

1. Read each paper carefully, marking or underlining the writer's main idea and key supporting points. Make any other notes about the paper that seem appropriate.
2. On a separate sheet, comment specifically on one or two aspects of the paper that most need improvement.

At the Group Editing Session:

1. When it is your turn, read your paper aloud to the group. You might become aware of problems as you read, so keep a pen or pencil handy to jot down notes.
2. When you are finished, tell the group members what you would like them to comment on.
3. Listen to their remarks and make notes. Feel free to ask members to explain or expand on their observations. Remember, you want as much advice as you can get.
4. Collect the copies of your paper and the sheets on which group members commented on specific areas that need improvement.

After the Group Editing Session:

1. Carefully consider both the oral and written comments of your group. You may not agree with everything that was said, but you need to weigh each comment. If the group members agree on a criticism, they are right, whether you agree with them or not.
2. Revise your paper. Remember that you are responsible for your own work. No one else—not your instructor, your peer editors, or your group readers—can or should tell you everything that you need to change.

Checklist of What to Expect in Group Editing

- ❏ Make sure everyone has a copy of your paper in advance.
- ❏ Ask specific questions of the group.
- ❏ Listen to what people say about your paper and take notes.
- ❏ Collect the written comments of other group members.
- ❏ Carefully consider every suggestion.
- ❏ Remember that you have obligations to help others in the same way.

What Can You Expect from a Writing Center or Writing Tutor?

Most colleges operate writing centers, writing labs, or writing tutor programs. Their purpose is to provide individual assistance to any student who has a question about a paper. They are staffed by trained tutors who want to help. In part, such services are intended to supplement the instruction that students receive in a writing class. Most writing teachers have too many students to be able to offer extensive help outside of class to everyone. These services also exist to provide advice to students who are writing papers for courses in disciplines where writing might be required but not discussed.

If you are having trouble with grammar or mechanics, if you consistently have problems with beginnings or middles or ends of papers, or if you are baffled by a particular assignment, do not be afraid to ask for help. Every writer can benefit from constructive advice or additional explanations, and writing centers and tutors exist to provide that help. Remember, though, that a writing tutor's job is to explain and to instruct. You do not drop your paper off at a writing center like you drop your automobile off at a garage. Your tutor will suggest ways that you can improve your paper or follow a particular convention. A tutor will not do the work for you.

Come to your appointment with a specific set of questions or problems. Why are you there? What do you want help with? What are the problem areas in your paper? What don't you understand about your instructor's comments? When you have a medical problem, you make an appointment with a medical professional to discuss a particular set of symptoms. A conference with a tutor should work in the same way.

Finally, keep some form of written record of your conference. Jot down what the tutor suggested or explained. Those notes will serve as a valuable reminder of what to do when you are revising a paper.

Checklist of How to Prepare for and Use Help from a Tutor

- ❑ Have a list of specific questions or problems.
- ❑ Ask for explanations of grammatical or mechanical problems.
- ❑ Take notes on what is said.
- ❑ Do not expect the tutor to "correct" your paper for you.

How Should You Prepare for a Conference with Your Instructor?

Your instructor in a writing class is always willing to talk with you about your writing. You can, of course, visit your instructor during scheduled office hours. In addition, many instructors, if their teaching schedules permit it, schedule a set of regular conference times spaced throughout the term or semester. Whatever the arrangement, a conference is an opportunity for you to ask questions about your writing in general or about a particular paper or problem.

Whether you have asked for the conference or the instructor has scheduled it as part of class requirements, several ground rules apply. As with a tutoring session, you should always come to a conference with a definite agenda and a specific set of questions. Writing out these questions is an excellent way to prepare for a conference. Generally, conferences are dialogues, so your active participation is expected. Do not be surprised, for example, if your instructor begins by asking you what you want to talk about. As time is always limited (remember your instructor might have to see dozens of students), you will not be able to ask about everything. Try to concentrate on the issues that trouble you the most.

Instructors consider conferences opportunities to discuss the larger issues of a paper: Is the thesis well defined? Is the structure as clear as it might be? Are there adequate transitions? Although your instructor may politely explain a troublesome grammatical or mechanical problem, do not expect the instructor to find and fix every mistake in your paper. A conference is not a proofreading session.

A conference is also not an oral grading of your paper. Grading a paper is a complicated task, one that frequently involves evaluating your essay in the context of the other papers from the class. As a result, your instructor cannot make a quick judgment. Do not ask about a grade.

As the conference proceeds, take notes about what is said. Do not rely on your memory. Those notes will constitute a plan for revising your paper.

Checklist of How to Prepare for and Use a Conference with Your Instructor

- ❏ Be prepared to identify what *you* want to talk about.
- ❏ Make a list of questions to ask.
- ❏ Take specific notes on what you need to do.
- ❏ Do not expect your teacher to identify every problem.
- ❏ Do not ask for a grade on the paper.

Making Sure to Proofread

Why Is Proofreading Important?

Everyone has had the comment "proofread!" written on a paper. The process of proofreading comes from printing terminology: a printer reads and corrects "proofs"—trial impressions made of pages of set type—before printing the job. You probably stared in dismay at obvious slips that somehow managed to escape your eye. Did you wonder why you were penalized for what were obviously just careless mistakes? Think about this question: Why do businesses and industries spend so much money making sure that their final written products are as free from errors as possible?

The answer focuses on audience perception of the writer (or the business). If a paper, letter, report, or advertisement contains even minor mistakes, these errors act as a form of "static" that interferes with the communication process. The reader's attention shifts away from the message to fundamental questions about the writer. A reader might wonder why you, the writer, did not have enough pride in your work to check it before handing it in. Even worse, a reader might question your basic competence as a writer and researcher. As the number of errors in proportion to the number of words rises, the reader's distraction grows. In college, such static can have serious consequences. Studies in New York city colleges, for example, revealed that readers would tolerate on average only five to six basic errors in a three-hundred-word passage before assigning a student to a remedial writing course. Careless mistakes are rhetorically damaging to you as a writer; they undermine your voice and authority.

After you have revised your paper thoroughly, you are ready for a final proofreading. The secret of proofreading is to read each word as you have written it. If you read too quickly, your mind corrects or skips over problems. Force yourself to read each word by moving a ruler or a piece of paper slowly down the page. Read aloud. When you combine looking at the page slowly with listening to the words, you increase your chances of catching mistakes that are visual (such as misspellings) and those that are aural (such as awkward constructions).

Misspellings are so common that they need special attention. Everyone misspells some words; even the most experienced writer, teacher, or editor has to check a dictionary for correct spelling of certain words.

Most misspellings can be eliminated if you do two things. First, recognize the kinds of words that you are likely to misspell. Do not assume that you know how to spell words that sound alike, such as *there* and *their* and *its* and *it's*. Second, once you have finished your paper, go back and check your spelling. Do not rely on your computer to catch everything: it will not tell you that you used *there* instead of *their*. Keep a dictionary handy and use it. If you know that you have a tendency to misspell words, look up every word that might be a problem.

Checklist of What to Look for When Proofreading

- ❑ Read each word of your paper aloud.
- ❑ Listen for awkward phrasing or passages that are difficult to read aloud.
- ❑ Check the spelling and meaning of words about which you are uncertain in a dictionary.
- ❑ Scrutinize each mark of punctuation. Is it used correctly?

- ❏ Watch for typographical errors where a letter is deleted or letters are transposed.
- ❏ Make sure your paper has a real title.

Isn't an Error-Free Paper an "A" Paper?

Although good, effective writing is mechanically and grammatically correct, you cannot reverse the equation. It is certainly possible to write a paper that has no "errors" but is still a poor paper. An effective paper fulfills the requirements of the assignment, has something interesting or meaningful to say, and provides specific evidence and examples rather than vague generalizations. Effective writing is a combination of many factors: appropriate content, focused purpose, clear organization, and fluent expression.

Although perfect grammar and mechanics do not make a perfect paper, such things are important. Minor errors are like static in your writing. Too many of them distract your reader and focus the reader's attention on your apparent carelessness instead of on your message. Minor errors can undermine your reader's confidence in you as a qualified authority. If you made errors in spelling or punctuation, for example, your reader might assume that you made similar errors in reporting information. So while revision is not just proofreading, proofreading should be a part of the revision process. ■

Checklist: Some Things to Remember About Revising

- ❏ Put your paper aside for a period of time before you attempt to revise it.
- ❏ Seek the advice of your instructor or a writing center tutor or the help of classmates.
- ❏ Reconsider your choice of topic. Were you able to treat it adequately in the space you had available?
- ❏ State your thesis in a sentence as a way of checking your content. Is everything in the paper relevant to that thesis?
- ❏ Check to make sure you have given enough examples to clarify your topic, to support your argument, or to make your thesis clear. Relevant specifics convince and interest a reader.
- ❏ Look through the advice given in each of the introductions to this text (How to Read an Essay, How to Write an Essay, How to Revise an Essay). Have you organized your paper carefully? Is its structure clear?
- ❏ Define your audience. To whom are you writing? What assumptions have you made about your audience? What changes are necessary to make your paper clear and interesting to that audience?
- ❏ Check the guidelines your instructor provided. Have you done what was asked? Is your paper too short or too long?

❑ Examine each sentence to make sure that it is complete and grammatically correct. Try for a variety of sentence structures and lengths.

❑ Look carefully at each paragraph. Does it obey the rules for effective paragraph construction? Do your paragraphs clearly indicate the structure of your essay?

❑ Check your word choice. Have you avoided slang, jargon, and clichés? Have you used specific words? Have you used appropriate words for your intended audience?

❑ Proofread one final time.

Writers at Work

LEARNING OBJECTIVES

In this section, you will learn how both student and professional writers

1. Plan a revision strategy using advice from peers
2. Select appropriate details and examples
3. Modify a draft to sharpen its focus and appeal to a reader

---

 Key Questions

A STUDENT WRITER

Tina Burton "The Watermelon Wooer"

Prewriting: Finding a Topic and Gathering Information

Drafting: First Draft

Revising: Second Draft

Revising: Final Draft

A PROFESSIONAL WRITER

Gordon Grice "Caught in the Widow's Web"

Prewriting: Finding a Topic and Gathering Information

Drafting: Next Drafts

Revising: Final Draft

When you have the time in which to plan, draft, and then revise an essay, the result will be considerably better than when you start and finish a paper the night before it is due. This process of prewriting, writing a draft, and then revising can be seen in the work of the two writers reproduced here. Tina Burton is a student writer producing a paper for a course; Gordon Grice is a professional writer who worked on his essay intermittently for more than two years. Despite those differences, both essays show how the writing process ideally works.

A Student Writer: Tina Burton's "The Watermelon Wooer"

Prewriting: Finding a Topic and Gathering Information

Tina's essay was written in response to a totally open assignment: she was asked to write an essay using examples. The paper was due in three weeks. The openness of the assignment proved initially frustrating to Tina. When she first began work on the essay, she started with a completely different topic than the one she eventually decided on.

On the weekend after she received the assignment, she went home to visit her parents. Her grandfather had died a few months before, and the family was sorting through some photographs and reminiscing about him. Suddenly she had the idea she wanted. She would write about her grandfather and her ambivalent feelings toward him. Once she had settled on this specific topic, she also determined her purpose (to inform readers about her grandfather and her mixed feelings, as well as to entertain through a vivid description of this unusual old man) and her audience (her instructor and peers). When Tina filled out answers to the questions her instructor had posed, she noted:

> **Subject:** My grandfather, a character sketch
> **Topic:** My ambivalent feelings about my grandfather—love and embarrassment
> **Purpose:** To inform my reader and to entertain
> **Audience:** My peers—we all have grandparents, and we often have ambivalent feelings toward them

Tina's first written work on the assignment was a list of about 30 things that she remembered about her grandfather. "The list had to be cut," Tina said, "so I marked off things that were too bawdy or too unbelievable. I wanted to portray him as sympathetic, but I was really afraid that the whole piece would come off as too sentimental or drippy."

At the next class meeting, the instructor set aside some time for prewriting activities. Students were encouraged to try either a freewriting or a brainstorming exercise. Tina did the brainstorming that appears above.

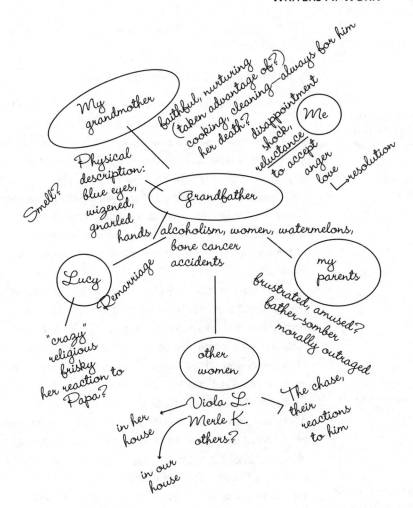

Drafting: First Draft

From here, Tina wrote a complete draft of her essay in one sitting. She had the most difficulty with the beginning of the essay. "I kept trying to describe him, but I found that I was including too much," she commented. The breakthrough came with the advice of two other students in the class. The first page of the first draft of Tina's essay follows. The comments were provided by Kathrine Varnes, a classmate.

Earlier Draft

The Watermelon Wooer

I have a personal dislike for this 3-word transition

some way to condense?

When someone you love dearly behaves in a manner that offends you, do you stop loving that person? Do you lose all respect for that person because you cannot forget the act (that you judged as repulsive?)(On the contrary), you might (eventually) fondly recall the once offensive behavior. (Perhaps,) In time, you might even understand why you found the behavior loathesome. Maybe, you will reach a point in time when you will be unable to think of your loved one without thinking of the once questionable behavior. Such is the case with my grandfather.

repulsive [?]

Eventually ?

so?

Before I tell the story of how my grandfather behaved in ways that I could neither understand nor tolerate, I must first (give some background information on) him. A wizened little man with dancing blue eyes and hands gnarled from years of carpentry work, "Papa" was a notorious womanizer and an alcoholic. Born and raised in Halifax County, Virginia, he spent most of his life building houses, distilling and selling corn liquor, and chasing women. After he and my grandmother had been married for thirty years or so, he decided to <u>curtail some of his wild behavior and treat her with more respect</u>. Actually, he remained faithful to her only after he discovered that she was ill and probably wouldn't be around to feed and nurture him for much longer. ~~So, as you can see,~~ my grandfather (does not) have a <u>spotless</u>, or even a remotely commendable (record of personal achievements.)

introduce?

both of these things? or respect by curtailing?

Use alternative diction to soften tone?

didn't

reputation

Revising: Second Draft

"Kathrine wanted me to condense and to find a way in which to jump right into the story," Tina noted. "She also said, 'You're trying to tell too much. Let the story tell itself. Try to think of one thing that might capture something essential or important about him.'" In a second peer edit, Tina sought the advice of Stephen Palley, another classmate. Stephen offered these comments on the first page of Tina's second draft.

The Watermelon Wooer

my grandfather never really (settled down)

characterize an essential part of his eccentricity intro?

Let me tell you a story about my grandfather ~~and, I guees, me see. I don't pretend to know whether my story will shook, offend, amuse, or bere~~. I only know that I feel the need to tell ~~the story,~~ *it* but eventually

For a time he
~~Before I tell the story of how my grandfather~~ behaved in ways that I could neither understand nor tolerate, I must first

(I see him now) Let me introduce

It's funny but when I think of my grandfather I think 1st of the way he smelled

introduce him. A wizened little man with ~~dancing blue eyes~~ and *smell?* hands ~~gnarled from years of carpentry work~~. "Papa" was a no-

Miller, ponies, fertilizer

torious womanizer and an alcoholic. Born and raised in Halifax County, Virginia, he spent most of his life building houses, distilling and selling corn liquor, and chasing women. After he and my grandmother had been married for thirty years or so, he decided to show her some respect by curtailing his wild behavior. Actually, he remained faithful to her only after he discovered that she was ill and probably wouldn't be around to feed and nurture him for much longer. Papa didn't have a spotless reputation.

"Stephen offered me quite a few helpful suggestions," Tina recalled, "but he also suggested something that I just didn't quite feel comfortable with." As you can see in the revised draft. Tina had queried Stephen about including her memories of scent. In a conversation, Stephen urged Tina to substitute memories of smells for memories of sights. In the end, though, Tina observed, "I just couldn't do what Stephen suggested."

Revising: Final Draft

Before the three weeks were over, Tina actually wrote five separate drafts of her essay. "Everything here is true," she said, "but I worried so much about what was included because I didn't want to embarrass anyone in my family."

"Throughout the process," she added, "I was also worried about my tone. I wanted it to be funny; I wanted my readers to like my grandfather and his watermelon adventures." As she moved toward her final draft, Tina was also able to write a thesis statement for her essay. Even though the essay is a humorous character sketch using narration and description, it still has a clearly stated thesis. Notice, however, that the thesis is placed not at the beginning of the essay but at the very end.

Thesis: The acts that troubled me eventually allowed me to glimpse the frail side of my grandfather, to see him as a human being possessed of fears and flaws rather than a cardboard ideal.

Reproduced here is Tina's final draft of her essay.

The Watermelon Wooer

I see him now, sprawled on our couch, clutching a frayed afghan, one brown toenail escaping his sock. His darting eyes are betraying his withered body.

Born and raised in backwoods Virginia, my grandfather spent most of his life building houses, distilling and selling corn liquor, and chasing women. After he and my grandmother had been married for thirty years or so, he decided to show her some respect by curtailing his wild behavior. Actually, he remained faithful to her only after he discovered that she was ill and probably wouldn't be around to feed and nurture him much longer. Papa didn't have a spotless reputation.

Because he'd been on the wagon for several years and hadn't had any affairs for the last ten years, my family thought that Papa would continue to behave in a "respectable" manner even after my grandmother died. I guess we were hoping for some sort of miracle. After my grandmother died in 1983, Papa became a rogue again: he insisted on reveling in wild abandon. When my father found out that Papa was drinking heavily again and crashing his car into mailboxes, houses, and other large obstacles, he asked Papa to move into our house. The fact that three of Papa's female neighbors had complained to the police about Papa's exposing himself probably had something to do with my father's decision.

The year that Papa lived with us rivaled the agony of Hell.

I was always Papa's favorite grandchild, his "gal," and I worshipped him from the time that I was old enough to spend summers with him on his farm. Until I saw him every day, witnessed for myself his sometimes lewd behavior and his odd personality quirks, I never really believed the stories about him that I had heard from my mother and father. Every morning, he baited my mother with comments like "the gravy's too thick," "my room's too cold," "your kids are too loud," and "the phone rings too often." Against my mother's wishes, he smoked in the house. In mixed company, he gleefully explained how to have sex in an inner tube in the ocean without getting caught and gave detailed physical descriptions of the women he'd had sex with. It surprised me how much my opinion of Papa changed in one year.

During this one year, Papa did many things that I thought were embarrassing and inexcusable. I came face-to-face with the "dark" side of his personality. One week after moving into my parents' home, Papa began to sneak the orange juice from the refrigerator and doctor it with Smirnoff's vodka. I knew he'd been pickling his brain with alcohol for years and that this was part of the disease, but he'd said that he'd gone dry. Besides, he was violating my father's most important rule: no alcohol in the house. I didn't know that his drinking was only the first of a long line of incredible acts.

The behaviors that ultimately endeared Papa to me, that made me forgive him his shortcomings, are also those which I recall with a great deal of sadness. These are the memories of him that I treasure, the stories that I will tell to my grandchildren when they are old enough to deal with graphic material. A year ago, I never would have believed that I could fondly remember, much less write about, these episodes.

For about a year, Papa engaged in what I refer to as the "watermelon affairs." Perhaps because he had lived on a vegetable farm for the majority of his life Papa had a special affinity for a wide variety of fruits and vegetables. Especially dear to him were watermelons. So, he assumed that other elderly people, particularly women, shared his proclivity for produce. One week after he moved into my parent's house, he embarked upon his mission—to woo with watermelons as many women as he could.

A shrewd man, possessed of a generous supply of common sense and watermelons, Papa decided to seduce a woman who lived very close to him. This woman happened to be my maternal grandmother who also lived in our house. Unaware of his lascivious intentions and bent on helping him assuage his grief over the loss of his wife, Grandmother Merle prepared special meals for Papa and spent long hours conversing with him about farming, grandchildren, and life in the "Old South." Merle assumed that the watermelons Papa brought to her were nothing more than a token of his appreciation for her kindness. When Papa grabbed a part of Merle that she preferred to remain untouched, these conversations came to an abrupt halt. Of course, we were mortified by his inappropriate behavior, but I suspect that my parents secretly were amused. While Papa's indiscretion with Merle was upsetting, at least no one other than members of my immediate family knew about the incident. His next romantic adventure earned him immediate notoriety in the neighborhood. One afternoon, huge watermelon in hand, he trotted over to visit Viola Lampson, a decrepit and cranky elderly woman with whom my family had been friendly for twenty years. Twenty minutes after Papa entered her house, the police came. Poor Viola was in a state of disrepair because my grandfather had been chasing her around her kitchen table demanding kisses. Fortunately, the policeman who arrived at the scene of the crime was quite understanding and polite; he advised my father to keep a careful watch on Papa at all times. My somber father was very embarrassed. Finally, we were all beginning to see the relationship between watermelons and women. He'd disappear with a watermelon and return with the police.

I was mortified by Papa's lecherous desire for other women. After all, wasn't he supposed to be grieving over the death of my grandmother, his wife of fifty years? I resigned myself to the fact that I never would love him or respect him in the manner that I once had. For a while, I avoided his company and refused to answer his frequent questions about why I was avoiding him. I didn't think about why he was behaving the way he was; I simply cast judgment on his behavior and shut myself off from him. Not until Papa remarried did I even try to understand his needs or his behavior.

Approximately one year after his wife died, Papa remarried. Finally, he found a woman who not only loved watermelon but also loved him and his frisky behavior. Lucy, often referred to as "crazy Lucy" by her neighbors who had heard her speak of miracle healings and visions of Christ, wed Papa and took him into her already jam-packed home. Amazingly, she convinced him to stop drinking and to refrain from molesting other women. She could not, however, convince Papa to "get the religion" as she called it. My family was nonplussed both by Papa's decision to remarry at age 77 and to stop drinking after all these years. We all were annoyed by the fact that Lucy convinced him to do in several months what we had been trying to get him to do for many years.

Not until I learned that Papa was dying of bone cancer did I try to understand why he needed to remarry and why I found that fact unbearable. Until this time, I harbored the feeling that Papa somehow was degrading the memory of my grandmother by remarrying. His attempted seductions of women disturbed me, but his decision to marry Lucy saddened me. Only after I spent many afternoons with Papa and Lucy did I realize that they truly loved each other. More importantly, I realized that Papa, devastated by his wife's death, was afraid to be alone in his old age. Perhaps sensing his illness, even though he knew nothing of its development at this time, he wanted to recapture some of his stamina, some of his youth. He really wasn't searching for someone to replace my grandmother: he simply wanted to have a companion to comfort him, to distract him from his grief.

Fortunately, I accepted Papa's actions and resolved my conflict with him before he died. Once again, I was his "gal" in spirit, and I even came to love and respect Lucy. Now, I find that I cannot conjure images of Papa without thinking of watermelons and his romantic escapades. The acts that once troubled me eventually allowed me to glimpse the frail side of my grandfather, to see him as a human being possessed of fears and flaws rather than a cardboard ideal.

A Professional Writer: Gordon Grice's "Caught in the Widow's Web"

Prewriting: Finding a Topic and Gathering Information

Gordon Grice began work on the essay "Caught in the Widow's Web" in a journal. He wrote a series of consecutive entries over a two-month period. This is not his usual way of working. He commented, "I rarely use this technique. I don't use it when I have a good idea of where I am going. Keeping a journal helps me when I don't really have a good subject in mind." He continued, "I kept this one while I was taking a nonfiction writing workshop, because I had to turn in pieces on deadline and didn't really know how to start."

Reproduced here are some of the original journal entries for the essay. Grice printed his entries in ink in a spiral-bound notebook. His revisions of those entries—made while he was keeping the journal—are preserved here. Crossed-out words are indicated by a line running through the word. Additions placed above or to the side of the cross-outs are reproduced here in brackets. As the entries show, writers often revise even as they first begin work on an essay.

Entry 1

1/16/93

The black widow has the ugliest web of any spider. The orb weavers ~~have~~ make
those seemingly delicate nets that poets have ~~turned~~ traditionally used as symbols
of imagination (~~Dickinson~~), order (~~Shakespeare~~), [and] perfection. The sheet-web
weavers make spiders weave crisp linens for the lawn [~~on the lawn~~] ~~some of these~~
~~have impressive looking underlayers and tunnels~~. But the widow makes messy-looking
tangles in the corners and bends of things and under logs and debris. Often the web
~~has~~ is littered with leaves. Beneath ~~the web~~ it lie the ~~corpses~~ husks of insect prey,
[their antenna stiff as gargoyle horns], cut loose and dropped; on them and the
surrounding ground are splashes of the spider's white ~~dung~~ [urine], which looks like
bird ~~urine~~ [guano] and smells of ammonia even at a distance of several feet. ~~If these~~
~~spiders this ground is biolog~~. This fetid material draws scavengers—ants, sow bugs,
crickets, roaches, and so on—which ~~walk into~~ become tangled in vertical strands of
~~web~~ [silk] reaching from the ground up into the web. The widow comes down and,
with a bicycling ~~motion~~ of the hind [pair of] legs, throws [gummy] ~~liquid~~ silk onto
this new prey.

> *Point of Comparison: Compare this entry with paragraphs 2 and 3 in
> "Caught in the Widow's Web."*

Entry 2

2/4/93

There is, of course, one pragmatic reason for fearing the widow.
These markings include a pair of triangles on the ventral side of the abdomen—the infamous "hourglass."
The widow's venom is, of course, a soundly pragmatic reason for fear. The venom contains a neurotoxin that produces chills, [sweats], vomiting, ~~and~~ fiery pain, ~~sometimes~~
[and] convulsions and death. ~~Death It is [And]~~ Occasionally ~~a person~~ [people] dies
from ~~the~~ widow bites ~~but less than the~~ Some researchers ~~have theorized~~ [hypothesized]
that the virulence of the venom was necessary for killing ~~scarab~~ beetles of the scarab
family. This family contains thousands of ~~beetles~~ [species], including the june bug and
the famous ~~Egyptian~~ dung beetle the Egyptians thought immortal. All the scarabs have
thick, strong bodies and [unusually] tough exoskeletons, and ~~these~~ many of them are
common prey for the widow.

> *Point of Comparison: Compare this entry with paragraphs 11 and 12 in
> "Caught in the Widow's Web."*

Drafting: Next Drafts

Grice moved from his journal entries to a first draft of the essay. In a conversation, Grice commented extensively on how the essay was revised.

When I started revising the black widow piece, I went to a junkyard with an empty mayonnaise jar and caught a widow. I kept her on my desk as I wrote. I kept observing interesting things I had never thought of putting in the piece before. If I'm writing about something I can't catch in a jar, I find some other way to research it. I hit the library or interview people. This helps me find interesting details that will fire up a boring draft.

I try to figure out what's working in a draft and what's not. I put it away for a while so I can get some distance on it. I get other people to criticize it. I don't trust anybody who likes everything I write or anybody who hates everything I write.

I analyze a draft like this: I want something interesting in the first sentence. Usually my first draft begins badly, so my job on revision is to decapitate the essay. I cut until I hit something interesting. Or I may find an interesting part somewhere else in the draft and move it to the beginning. I move things around a lot. If I get frustrated trying to keep it all straight on the computer, I print it out and sit on the floor with scissors rearranging things.

I look for long sections of exposition or summary and try to break these up with vivid examples or details. If some part is boring, I try to think of ways to make it into a story.

I fiddle with the sentences as I go. I try to cut all the passive voice verbs and all the *be* verbs. I strike filler words like *very*. If it doesn't sound right without the filler, I take that as a clue that something's wrong with the ideas themselves. I aim for the prose to sound simple, even if the ideas are complex.

Grice tried to get the revised draft published but with no success. He reflected: "I wasn't having any luck. I theorized that the opening wasn't catchy enough. I also thought that the piece didn't fit any magazine I could think of—it was too arty for a science magazine, and most of the essays I saw in literary journals had more personal material than I used."

A considerable amount of time elapsed: "I carried the piece around with me until I got the chance to work on it. I was substitute teaching a middle school shop class when I scribbled down a new opening." In the new opening, Grice describes having young widow spiders crawl all over his arms: "I thought the danger made it interesting." Grice sent off the essay—with its new opening—and it was immediately published in the *High Plains Literary Review* under the title "The Black Widow."

Revising: Final Draft

Grice's essay actually has three "final" forms. After the essay appeared in *High Plains Literary Review*, it was rewritten and reprinted in the large-circulation monthly magazine *Harper's*. Ironically, the new, more personal opening that Grice had written was cut and some other minor changes were made. Revision did not stop there, though, for the essay was later included in a collection of Grice's essays titled *The Red Hourglass: Inner Lives of the Predators* (1998). Commenting on that revision, he said, "It's five or six times longer, so I covered a lot of new material. For example, I developed the section about the widow's venom with some case studies. I added details and changed the overall shape of the essay. I changed word choices and sentence structures as well."

The draft reproduced here is the one that originally appeared in *Harper's* magazine.

Caught in the Widow's Web

GORDON GRICE

Gordon Grice earned his B.A. at Oklahoma State University and his M.F.A. at the University of Arkansas. Grice has published essays and poems in a wide range of literary magazines. His first collection of essays was The Red Hourglass: Lives of the Predators *(1998). The following essay, originally titled "The Black Widow," first appeared in the* High Plains Literary Review. *Grice reworked it for its appearance in* Harper's *magazine and then again for* The Red Hourglass. *The version reproduced here appeared in* Harper's. *His most recent book is* The Book of Deadly Animals *(2012).*

On Writing: *Widely praised for his precise and detailed attention to the "microworld," Grice has said, "Personal observation and experience are part of my approach to writing as a whole. I like to delve into the details and give my readers the feeling of being there and having their own hands in it."*

Before Reading

Connecting: How do you feel about spiders? To what do you attribute your reaction?

Anticipating: As you read, think about what the black widow symbolizes for Grice.

1   I hunt black widows. When I find one, I capture it. I have found them in discarded wheels and tires and under railroad ties. I have found them in house foundations and cellars, in automotive shops and toolsheds, in water meters and rock gardens, against fences and in cinder-block walls.

2   Black widows have the ugliest webs of any spider, messy looking tangles in the corners and bends of things and under logs and debris. Often the widow's web is littered with leaves. Beneath it lie the husks of consumed insects, their antennae stiff as gargoyle horns; on them and the surrounding ground are splashes of the spider's white urine, which looks like bird guano and smells of ammonia even at a distance of several feet.

3   This fetid material draws scavengers—ants, sow bugs, crickets, roaches, and so on—which become tangled in vertical strands of silk reaching from the ground up into the web. The widow climbs down and throws gummy silk onto this new prey. When the insect is seriously tangled but still struggling, the widow cautiously descends and bites it, usually on a leg joint. This is a killing bite; it pumps poison into the victim. As the creature dies, the widow delivers still more bites, injecting substances that liquefy the organs. Finally it settles down to suck the liquefied innards out of the prey, changing position two or three times to get it all.

4   Widows reportedly eat mice, toads, tarantulas—anything that wanders into that remarkable web. I have never witnessed a widow performing a gustatory act of that magnitude, but I have seen them eat scarab beetles heavy as pecans, carabid beetles strong enough to prey on wolf spiders, cockroaches more than an inch long, and hundreds of other arthropods of various sizes.

5   Many widows will eat as much as opportunity allows. One aggressive female I raised had an abdomen a little bigger than a pea. She snared a huge cockroach and spent several hours subduing it, then three days consuming it. Her abdomen swelled to the size of a largish marble, its glossy black stretching to a tight red-brown. With a different widow, I decided to see whether that appetite really was insatiable. I collected dozens of large crickets and grasshoppers and began to drop them into her web at a rate of one every three or four hours. After catching and devouring her tenth victim, this bloated widow fell from her web, landing on her back. She remained in this position for hours, making only feeble attempts to move. Then she died.

6   The first thing people ask when they hear about my fascination with the widow is why I am not afraid. The truth is that my fascination is rooted in fear.

7   I have childhood memories that partly account for this. When I was six my mother took my sister and me into the cellar of our farmhouse and told us to watch as she killed a widow. With great ceremony she produced a long stick (I am tempted to say a ten-foot pole) and, narrating her technique in exactly the hushed voice she used for discussing religion or sex, went to work. Her flashlight beam found a point halfway up the cement wall where two marbles hung together—one a crisp white, the other a shiny black. My mother ran her stick through the dirty silver web around them. As it tore it sounded like the crackling of paper in fire. The black marble rose on thin legs to fight off the intruder. My mother smashed the widow onto the stick and carried it up into the light. It was still kicking its remaining legs. Mom scraped it against the floor, grinding it into a paste. Then she returned for the white marble—the widow's egg sac. This, too, came to an abrasive end.

8   My mother's stated purpose was to teach us how to recognize and deal with a dangerous creature that we would probably encounter on the farm. But, of course, we also took away the understanding that widows were actively malevolent, that they waited in dark places to ambush us, that they were worthy of ritual disposition, like an enemy whose death is not sufficient but must be followed by the murder of his children and the salting of his land and whose unclean remains must not touch our hands.

9   The odd thing is that so *many* people, some of whom presumably did not first encounter the widow in such an atmosphere of mystic reverence, hold the widow in awe. Various friends have told me that the widow's bite is always fatal to humans—in fact, it almost never is. I have heard told for truth that goods imported from the Orient are likely to be infested with widows and that women with bouffant hairdos have died of widow infestation. Any contradiction of such tales is received as if it were a proclamation of atheism.

10   We project our archetypal terrors onto the widow. It is black; it avoids the light; it is a voracious carnivore. Its red markings suggest blood. The female's habit of eating her lovers invites a strangely sexual discomfort; the widow becomes an emblem for a man's fear of extending himself into the blood and darkness of a woman, something like the legendary Eskimo vampire that takes the form of a fanged vagina.

11   The widow's venom is, of course, a sound reason for fear. The venom contains a neurotoxin that can produce sweats, vomiting, swelling, convulsions, and dozens of other symptoms. The variation in symptoms from one person to the next is remarkable. The constant is pain. A useful question for a doctor trying to diagnose an uncertain case: "Is this the worst pain you've ever felt?" A "yes" suggests a diagnosis of a black widow bite. Occasionally people die from widow bites. The very young and the very old are especially vulnerable. Some people seem to die not from the venom but from the infection that may follow: because of its habitat, the widow carries dangerous microbes.

12   Researchers once hypothesized that the virulence of the venom was necessary for killing beetles of the scarabaeidae family. This family contains thousands of species, including the June beetle and the famous dung beetle that the Egyptians thought immortal. All the scarabs have thick, strong bodies and unusually tough exoskeletons, and many of them are common prey for the widow. The tough hide was supposed to require a particularly nasty venom. As it turns out, the venom is thousands of times more virulent than necessary for this purpose.

13   No one has ever offered a sufficient explanation for the dangerous venom. It provides no evolutionary advantages: all of the widow's prey would find lesser toxins fatal, and there is no particular benefit in killing or harming larger animals. A widow that bites a human being or other large animal is likely to be killed.

14   Natural selection favors the inheritance of useful characteristics that arise from random mutation and tends to extinguish disadvantageous traits. All other characteristics, the ones that neither help nor hinder survival, are preserved or extinguished at random as mutation links them with useful or harmful traits. Many people—even many scientists—assume that every animal is elegantly engineered for its ecological niche, that every bit of an animal's anatomy and behavior has a functional explanation. This assumption is false. Evolution sometimes produces flowers of natural evil—traits that are neither functional nor vestigial but utterly pointless.

15   We want the world to be an ordered room, but in a corner of that room there hangs an untidy web. Here the analytical mind finds an irreducible mystery, a motiveless evil in nature; here the scientist's vision of evil comes to match the vision of a God-fearing country woman with a ten-foot pole. No idea of the cosmos as elegant design accounts for the widow. No idea of a benevolent God is comfortable in a world with the widow. She hangs in her web, that marvel of design, and defies reason.   ■

QUESTIONS ON SUBJECT AND PURPOSE

1. Why is Grice so fascinated by black widow spiders? To what does he trace his fascination?
2. What particular aspects of the black widow spider does Grice focus on?
3. What does the spider symbolize to Grice?

QUESTIONS ON STRATEGY AND AUDIENCE

1. Explain why Grice begins with the simple sentence "I hunt black widows." What is the effect of that sentence?
2. Grice divides his essay into three sections through the use of additional white space (after paragraphs 5 and 10). How does that division reflect the structure of the essay?
3. What assumptions could Grice make about his audience and their attitudes toward spiders?

QUESTIONS ON VOCABULARY AND STYLE

1. In describing how his mother killed the spider, Grice writes, "With great ceremony she produced a long stick (I am tempted to say a ten-foot pole)" (paragraph 7). Why does he add the material in the parentheses?
2. What is the effect of labeling the spider a "voracious carnivore"? To what extent is that an accurate phrase?
3. Be prepared to define the following words: *fetid* (paragraph 3), *gustatory* (4), *malevolent* (8), *bouffant* (9), *voracious* (10), *carnivore* (10), *virulence* (12), *niche* (14), *vestigial* (14).

WRITING SUGGESTIONS

1. **Doing a Critical Analysis.** Grice has been called the "Stephen King" of nature writing. Look closely at his choice of words and use of figurative language and then analyze the impact these decisions have on how you react to the black widow spider.
2. **Journaling or Blogging.** Look closely at an object or a living thing in the natural world. Use a magnifying glass to observe details or carefully study a landscape. Record what you now see that you missed before.
3. **Practicing in a Paragraph.** Expand one of your observations into a descriptive paragraph. Try to make your reader see with you.

4. **Writing the Personal Essay.** Select a natural thing and in an essay describe it in such a way as to reveal a significance or meaning.

5. **Finding Reading Connections.** Compare Grice's choice of words and images with those in David Bodanis's "What's in Your Toothpaste?" (Chapter 4). How do these choices impact the reader emotionally?

6. **Exploring Links Online.** How do you react to spiders? On his website (deadlykingdom.blogspot.com), Grice has more stories about spiders—try "hobo spiders" for example. Why are so many people afraid of spiders?

7. **Writing the Research Paper.** Select another common living creature which arouses fear (e.g., great white sharks, snakes, bed bugs, jellyfish). In a formal research paper, blend a description of the creature with some of the myths and symbols that are attached to it. Formulate a thesis about why we react to this creature the way we do.

For Further Study

Focusing on Grammar and Writing. Look closely at the first five paragraphs of the essay. How are the vivid images created? To what extent does Grice use precise nouns, vivid verbs, and arresting details?

Working Together. Working in small groups, locate all the similes and metaphors that Grice uses in a block of paragraphs. Check the Glossary and Ready Reference for definitions of both terms.

Seeing Other Modes at Work. The essay makes extensive use of narration and process in its description of how the spider kills its prey and how his mother hunted the spider.

1 | Gathering and Using Examples

LEARNING OBJECTIVES

In this chapter, you will learn how to

1. Identify the importance of examples in your writing
2. Discover possible sources where examples can be found
3. Evaluate the appropriateness of each example
4. Arrange examples effectively in your essay
5. Create transitions between examples
6. Analyze readings that use examples

Key Questions

WRITING WITH EXAMPLES

Getting Ready to Write

How important are examples in your writing?

Where do you find your examples?

How do you gather examples from your experiences?

How do you gather examples from outside sources?

Writing

How many examples do you need?

How do you place examples in your essay?

Revising

Are your examples good choices?

How did you order or arrange your examples?

Did you make transitions as you moved from example to example?

Student Essay
   Frank Smite, "Looking for Love"

READING FOR EXAMPLES

In Prose
   Steven Pinker, from The Language Instinct

In Literature
   Bret Lott, "Night" (short story)

In a Visual
   Photographs of College Life

Writing with Examples

GETTING READY TO WRITE

How Important Are Examples in Your Writing?

Effective writing in any form depends on details and examples. Relevant details and examples make writing interesting, informative, and persuasive. If you try to write without gathering these essential specifics, you will be forced to skim the surface of your subject, relying on generalizations, incomplete and sometimes inaccurate details, and unsubstantiated opinions. Without specifics, even a paper with a strong, clearly stated thesis becomes superficial. For example, how convinced would you be by the following argument?

> In their quest for big-time football programs, American universities have lost sight of their educational responsibilities. Eager for the revenues and alumni support that come with winning teams, universities exploit their football players. They do not care if the players get an education. They care only that they remain academically eligible to play for four seasons. At many schools only a small percentage of these athletes graduate. Throughout their college careers they are encouraged to take easy courses and to put athletics first. It does not matter how they perform in the classroom as long as they distinguish themselves every Saturday afternoon. This exploitation should not be allowed to continue. Universities have the responsibility to educate their students, not to use them to gain publicity and to raise money.

Even if you agree with the writer's thesis, the paragraph does not go beyond the obvious. The writer generalizes—and probably distorts as a result. What the reader gets is an opinion unsupported by any evidence. For example, you might reasonably ask questions about the statement, "At many schools only a small percentage of these athletes graduate."

How many schools?
How small a percentage?
How does this percentage compare with that of nonathletes? After all, not everyone who starts college graduates.

To persuade your reader—even to interest your reader—you need specific information, details, and examples that illustrate the points you are trying to make.

Where Do You Find Your Examples?

You gather details and examples from your own experiences and observations or from research. In an essay based on personal experience, you draw from your memories and observations. Much of what you might be writing about, however, will require that you use research in printed or online sources, or interviews. When David Gutherson, for example, set out to write a magazine article about the Mall of America in Minneapolis, he drew from the facts contained within a prepared press kit. He chose to begin his essay with some of those facts in order to catch the reader's attention.

Last April, on a visit to the new Mall of America near Minneapolis, I carried with me the public-relations press kit provided for the benefit of reporters. It included an assortment of "fun facts" about the mall: 140,000 hot dogs sold each week, 10,000 permanent jobs, 44 escalators and 17 elevators, 12,750 parking places, 13,300 short tons of steel, $1 million in cash disbursed weekly from 8 automatic-teller machines. Opened in the summer of 1992, the mall was built on a 78-acre site of the former Metropolitan Stadium, a five-minute drive from the Minneapolis–St. Paul International Airport. With 4.2 million square feet of floor space—including twenty-two times the retail footage of the average American shopping center—the Mall of America was "the largest fully enclosed combination retail and family entertainment center in the United States."

As the examples in this chapter show, writers sometimes draw exclusively on their own experiences, as does Helen Keller in the selection from her autobiography. Bob Greene in "Cut" also interviewed other men about their reactions to being "cut." In contrast, for her essay "Why Looks Are the Last Bastion of Discrimination," Deborah L. Rhode did extensive research to document her assertions.

Regardless of where you find them, specific, relevant examples are important in everything you write. They add life and interest to your writing, and they illustrate or support the points you are trying to make.

How Do You Gather Examples from Your Experiences?

Where do you start when you want to narrate an experience that happened to you or describe something that you saw? You will spend some time remembering the event, sorting out the details of the experience, and deciding which example best supports the point you are trying to make. The best way to begin your memory and observation search is to consider the advice offered earlier in "How to Write an Essay" and to consider the resources available to you. Exploring a personal experience can involve a number of different activities:

Within Yourself	Outside
Probing memory	Seeing old photographs
Reexperiencing sense impressions	Talking with people
Revisiting places	Looking for material evidence

Many of the essays in this (and later chapters) begin with the writer's memories, experiences, and observations.

Links between Writing and Reading

	Source of examples
Bob Greene, "Cut"	Childhood memory, interviews
Helen Keller, "Acquiring Language"	Personal experiences
Rick Reilly, "Getting a Second Wind"	Someone else's experience

Even when writers add information from sources outside their own experiences, personal observation and experience might still play a significant role in shaping the essay.

How Do You Gather Examples from Outside Sources?

When you think about researching a subject, you might think only of going to the Web to search for appropriate sites or of going to a library to look for printed books and articles. As varied as these search methods are, you can also find information in many other ways:

Using Outside Sources   Interviewing people, conducting polls
                               Locating books and articles
                               Searching for Internet sites
                               Exploring media resources (such as film
                                    and music)
                               Performing an experiment or test

The experiences of other people can be excellent sources of information. Bob Greene, for example, recounts the experiences of four other men who were also cut from athletic teams when they were young. Many of the articles that appear in magazines and newspapers make extensive use of interviews rather than printed sources.

When you use information gathered from outside sources—whether those sources are printed or e-texts, websites, or interviews—it is important that you document those sources. Even though articles in newspapers and magazines do not provide the type of documentation that you find in a paper written for a college course, you are a student, not a reporter. Be sure to ask your instructor how you are to document quotations and paraphrases: Is it all right just to mention the sources in the text, or do you need to provide formal, parenthetical documentation and a list of works cited? Additional advice and samples can be found in Chapter 10: The Research Paper. Be sure to read that material before you hand in a paper that uses outside sources.

Links between Writing and Reading

	Source of examples
Bob Greene, "Cut"	Interviews with other men
Oscar Casares, "Fútbol?"	Interviews, observation, research
Deborah L. Rhode, "Why Looks"	Interviews, research

Prewriting Tips for Gathering Examples

1. Do not rush the example-gathering stage of your prewriting. Good writing depends on good examples, and quality is more important than quantity.

2. Remember that examples can be gathered from personal experience, from interviews with people, and from information in printed or online sources.

3. Choose examples for a reason: to support a point or a thesis. Does each example support the larger point you are trying to make?

4. Think about ways to order the examples in your essay. If you are narrating an event, will you use a chronological order or a flashback? If you are using examples to support an argument, will you start with the strongest example or end with it?

5. Plan an opening strategy for your essay. Maybe you will start with a vivid example, maybe with a statement of your thesis. Your opening paragraph is crucial; you will either catch your reader's attention or lose it.

WRITING

How Many Examples Do You Need?

Every writer's job would be much easier if there were a simple answer to the question of how many examples to use. Instead, the answer is "enough to interest or convince your reader." Sometimes one fully developed example might be enough. Advertisements for organizations such as Save the Children or the Christian Children's Fund often tell the story of a specific child who needs food and shelter. The single example, accompanied by a photograph, is enough to persuade many people to sponsor a child. At other times you might need to use many examples—appropriate, accurate, and convincing examples.

When you write from personal experience, your readers might not demand a great level of detail and accuracy in your examples. In "Cut," Bob Greene writes about how being cut from a junior high basketball team changed his life. To support his thesis and extend it beyond his own personal experience, Greene includes the stories of four other men who had similar experiences. But why give five examples? Why not three or seven? There is nothing magical about the number five. Green might have used five because he had that much column space in the magazine; nevertheless, the five lend credibility to Greene's thesis, or at least they create the illusion of credibility.

Proving the validity of Green's thesis would require a proper statistical sample. Only then could it be said with some certainty that the experience of being cut makes men superachievers later in life. In most writing situations, however, such thoroughness is not needed. If the details and examples are well chosen and relevant, the reader is likely to accept your assertions.

How Do You Place Examples in Your Essay?

Whether you use one example or many, examples alone do not make an essay. There is no such thing as an "exemplification essay." Examples are always subordinated to a thesis, an assertion, a story, an argument. Examples fill out the framework of an essay; they are the supporting evidence and the details that justify that thesis, assertion, story, or argument. Every essay, whether structured using narration, description, comparison and contrast, or any other rhetorical strategies used to organize information, uses examples. Without examples, an essay is just a bare framework of statements, opinions, and generalizations.

That initial framework is derived from one of the organizational strategies or patterns that you are using. In a narrative, details and examples are inserted into a chronological timeline; in a description, details and examples are added to a spatial pattern as the eye and ear move over the person, place, or landscape being described. The same procedure applies to each of the other organizational structures. A classification scheme is fleshed out with examples; a comparison demands that specific shared or differing examples and details be cited. Finally, in argument and persuasion, examples show that your position is the right and logical one to take.

Examples may be part of the beginning, middle, or end of an essay. An essay might begin with a particularly arresting example that is intended to catch readers' attention and draw them into the essay. If you are using an example as a "hook" for your introduction, begin with the example and place the essay's thesis or assertion either at the end of the opening paragraph or at the beginning of the next paragraph.

Examples make up a substantial part of the body of most essays. An extended example might occupy a whole body paragraph; smaller, shorter examples might be grouped into a single paragraph. Remember, though, that there is no reward for providing the greatest number of examples. The guiding principle is always quality and relevance, not quantity. The purpose

Links between Writing and Reading

Helen Keller, "Acquiring Language"	Her moment of insight
Bob Greene, "Cut"	Structure of five examples
Oscar Casares, "Fútbol?"	Closing example of the telephone call
Deborah L. Rhode, "Why Looks"	Unusual opening example

Drafting Tips for Using Examples

1. Look carefully at each example you plan to use. Is it completely relevant? Does it really prove the point that you want to make or support? Is it accurate and fair, or is it distorted?

2. Do you have enough examples? Too many? A single example is rarely enough to convince a reader of anything. On the other hand, a long list of examples can overwhelm your reader with unnecessary detail.

3. Are your examples specific? Or are they really just generalizations or unsubstantiated opinions? Do you provide facts? Statistics? Quotations? Or do you just assume that your readers will agree with you?

4. Are your examples subordinated to the larger point you are trying to make? Giving examples is not a goal in itself: rather, the examples are there to support or justify a larger goal. Examples must be proportional to the essay.

5. Have you provided clear transitional statements or markers as you move from one example to another? Your examples need to be connected in ways that make your essay flow smoothly.

of your essay is a deciding factor in how to order your examples. Rank examples on the basis of their prominence or importance. Generally arrange your examples in that order, either beginning or ending with the strongest and best example.

Sometimes you might end an essay with a relevant or emotional example. At the end of an essay, readers encounter the last of your message. A well-chosen example can be quite powerful.

REVISING

Are Your Examples Good Choices?

The examples you selected should meet specific criteria for the type of essay you are writing. In informational or persuasive writing, your examples must be accurate and unbiased. Look carefully at your examples. Are they fair? Accurate? Examples must also be relevant or important. Do they really support or clarify your assertion or thesis? Look at the examples you are using and number them in terms of their importance. Forget about those that are weak; use only your strongest examples. The number of examples you need depends on the length of your paper. A short paper, several pages in length, typically will not require as many examples as a many-paged research paper. Did you choose examples that are interesting or attention-getting? This is particularly important if you are starting or ending your essay with an example.

How Did You Order or Arrange Your Examples?

Now look at how you arranged your examples in your paper. You should then have arranged them in either descending order (the best comes first) or ascending order (the best comes last). That choice is yours: one order is not better or more correct than the other. The greatest danger in arranging examples in an essay comes when you start with a thesis or assertion and follow with a series of short examples that trail off into insignificance.

In some essays, because each example is different, you may be tempted to put each example into its own paragraph. The result may be a string of short, thin, poorly developed paragraphs. Look carefully at your essay. Count the number of paragraphs you have written. A three-page paper that has 20 short paragraphs needs to be revised: some examples can be deleted and other examples might be expanded. Do not assume that each example must be set off in a separate paragraph. Long, developed examples must be set off, but shorter, related examples can often be grouped under a topic sentence.

Did You Make Transitions as You Moved from Example to Example?

Check your essay to see if you have provided clear transition markers as you move from example to example. Transitional markers include words and phrases such as *for example, first, next, finally, also, on the other hand, in addition.* The Glossary and Ready Reference at the back of this text provides a fuller explanation and a more complete listing of such devices. Transitional devices, however, are no substitute for logical order and a clear sense of organization and purpose. Still, you need to help your reader see how all of these examples fit into the essay. A logical arrangement and transitional markers are like highway signs; they indicate to the reader what is coming and how it connects with what has already been covered in the essay.

Links between Writing and Reading

Bob Greene, "Cut"	Order of the examples
Rick Reilly, "Getting"	Transition in paragraph 9
Oscar Casares, "Fútbol?"	Use of "Speedy Gonzales" example
Deborah L. Rhode, "Why Looks"	Effectiveness of the examples

Revising Tips When Using Examples

1. If you are writing about yourself, it is especially important to keep your readers interested. They need to feel how significant this experience was. They need to become involved in the situation—to sympathize or empathize with what happened. Do not just tell them: show them. One way to do this is to dramatize the experience, to tell it as if it were happening at that moment.

2. Try different arrangements of the examples, sentences, and even paragraphs. Which order seems to work best?

3. How effective is your conclusion? Do you stop abruptly? Do you just repeat in slightly altered words what you said in your introduction? Remember the end of your essay—especially if you are arguing for something—is what will stay with your readers.

4. If you interviewed people in your research or used information from printed or online sources, make sure you punctuated your quotations properly and documented those sources.

5. Find someone to read your essay: a friend, roommate, classmate, or tutor in a writing center. Ask your reader for some constructive criticism and listen to what you hear.

Student Essay

First Draft

Frank Smite, recently divorced and recently returned to college, chose to work on an essay about the difficulties that older single or newly single people have in meeting people they can date. "Young college kids have it easy," Frank complained. "You are constantly surrounded by eligible people your own age. Try meeting someone when you're thirty-five, slightly balding, just divorced, and working all day." His first draft of the opening of his essay appears here:

My Search for Love

My wife and I separated and then quickly divorced a year ago. I figured that I would be able to forget some of the pain by returning to dating. At first, I was excited about the prospect of meeting new people. It made me feel young again. Besides, this time I'd be able to avoid the problems that led to my divorce. While I'm not exactly a male movie star—I'm thirty-five, a little overweight, kind of thin on the top, and have one daughter who I desperately miss seeing every day—I figured that romance was just around the corner.

It wasn't until I started to look for people to ask out that I realized how far away that corner was. Frankly, in my immediate world, there seemed to be no one who was roughly my age and unmarried. That's when I began to look at the various ways that people in my situation can meet people. I attended several meetings of the local Parents Without Partners group, but that didn't seem promising; I joined a computerized dating service; and, believe it or not, I started reading the "personals" in the newspaper.

Comments

When Frank came to revise his essay, he had his instructor's comments and the reactions of several classmates. Everyone agreed that he had an excellent subject and some good detail, but several readers were a little troubled by Frank's overuse of "I." One reader asked Frank if he could make his essay focus a little less on his own immediate experience and a little more on what anyone in his position might do. His instructor suggested that with the right type of revision, Frank might be able to publish his essay in the local newspaper— after all, she noted, many people are in the same situation. His instructor also suggested that Frank might eliminate the reference to his daughter and how much he misses her. Although those feelings are important, that is not where Frank wanted to center the essay. Frank liked the idea of sharing his experiences with a wider audience. His revised introduction—complete with a new title—follows.

Revised Draft

Looking for Love

Ask any single or divorced adult about the problems of meeting "prospective partners" and you are likely to get a litany of complaints and horrifying experiences. No longer can people rely on introductions from well-meaning friends. After all, most of those friends are also looking for love. Matchmaking has become big business— even, in fact, a franchised business.

Today the search for love takes many forms, from bar hopping, to organizations such as Parents Without Partners, to computerized and videotaped "search services," to singles groups organized around a shared concern (for example, those who are concerned about the environment or who love books). A little more desperate (and risky and certainly tacky) is the newspaper classified. Titled "Getting Personal" in my local newspaper, advertisements typically read like this one running today: "Single white female, pretty, petite blond, 40's ISO [in search of] WM [white male] for a perfect relationship (it does exist!)."

Checklist: Some Things to Remember About Using Examples

- ❑ Use details and examples—effective writing depends on them.
- ❑ For some subjects you can find the illustrations you need from your own experiences and observations. You will, however, probably need to work at remembering and gathering specifics.
- ❑ For some subjects you will need to do some type of research such as interviewing people, looking up material in your school's library, using the Internet and the Web to locate relevant documents and sites.
- ❑ Choose examples that are relevant and accurate. Quality is more important than quantity. Make sure your examples support your argument or illustrate the points you are trying to make. If you use an outside authority—an interview, a printed text, an electronic source— make sure that the source is knowledgeable and accurate. Remember also to document those sources.
- ❑ The number of details and examples you need necessarily varies. Sometimes one will do; sometimes you will need many. If you want your readers to do or to believe something, you must supply some evidence to gain their support or confidence.

Reading for Examples

Examples are essential to all types of writing: writers explain, entertain, analyze, and persuade by citing specific, relevant examples. Examples make writing vivid and interesting; examples provide evidence for your assertions. Without examples, there is just a framework, a skeletal outline of an essay. As you read, remember what you have learned about how to write with examples—that knowledge can help you as a reader.

- Examples do not provide a structure for an essay. They are inserted into essays to fill out a predetermined rhetorical strategy or organizational patterns. If you were to outline the essay, you would find that the examples support the assertions and are subordinated to the larger frame of the essay.
- Examples are organized; that is, the writer has planned the arrangement of examples in the essay or the paragraph. In an argument essay, for example, the strongest or best example might be placed first.
- Examples can be taken from personal experience or observation, but frequently they must be gathered using research such as interviews with knowledgeable people and printed or online sources.
- Examples must be accurate, relevant, and interesting. Each example should be judged by those tests.

IN PROSE

As you read this selection from Steven Pinker's *The Language Instinct: How the Mind Creates Language*, analyze how he uses examples to illustrate his assertions.

Topic sentence—the frame into which the examples will fit	For centuries people have been terrified that their programmed creations might outsmart them, overpower them, or put them out of work. The fear has been played out in fiction, from the medieval Jewish legend
Two examples—Golem and HAL support the initial assertion "for centuries"	of the Golem, a clay automaton animated by an inscription of the name of God placed in its mouth, to HAL, the mutinous computer of *2001: A Space Odyssey*. But when the branch of engineering called "artificial intel-
Examples of what computers can do supporting the fears people have. Number tasks are understandable; thinking tasks scary to people.	ligence" (AI) was born in the 1950s, it looked as though fiction was about to turn into frightening fact. It is easy to accept a computer calculating pi to a million decimal places or keeping track of a company's payroll, but suddenly computers were also proving theorems in logic and playing respectable chess. In the years follow-
Examples arranged chronologically (growth of problem solving)	ing there came computers that could beat anyone but a grand master and programs that outperformed most experts at recommending treatments for bacterial in-
Familiar examples from popular films. Example of what experts thought might be possible	fections and investing pension funds. With computers solving such brainy tasks, it seemed like only a matter of time before a C3P0 or a Terminator would be available from the mail-order catalogues; only the easy tasks remained to be programmed. According to legend, in the 1970s, Marvin Minsky, one of the founders of AI,
Topic sentence—frame	assigned "vision" to a graduate student as a seminar project.
Example—what a four-year-old can do that a computer cannot	But household robots are still confined to science fiction. The main lesson of thirty-five years of AI research is that the hard problems are easy and the easy
Example—seemingly smart robots are dumb	problems are hard. The mental abilities of a four-year-old that we take for granted—recognizing a face, lifting a pencil, walking across a room, answering a question—in fact solve some of the hardest engineering problems
Examples—questions that computers cannot answer (and a four-year-old probably could)	ever conceived. Do not be fooled by the assembly-line robots in the automobile commercials; all they do is weld and spray paint, tasks that do not require these clumsy Mr. Magoos to see or hold or place anything. And if you want to stump an artificial intelligence system, ask it questions like, Which is bigger, Chicago or a breadbox? Do zebras wear underwear? Is the floor likely to rise up and bite you? If Susan goes to the store, does her head

Examples—jobs that might be done by computers and jobs that cannot; ties back to the topic sentence of the previous paragraph

go with her? Most fears of automation are misplaced. As the new generation of intelligent devices appears, it will be the stock analysts and petrochemical engineers and parole board members who are in danger of being replaced by machines. The gardeners, receptionists, and cooks are secure in their jobs for decades to come.

QUESTIONS FOR ANALYSIS

1. How important are the examples in the paragraphs?
2. How are the examples arranged in each paragraph?
3. What roles do the examples play in the selection? For example, do they clarify points, extend the assertions, or create interest?
4. Where might Pinker have found his examples?

CRITICAL READING ACTIVITY

Outline the two paragraphs to reveal the relationships between the two topic sentences and the examples. Are the examples all subordinate to the topic sentences? Do the examples all coordinate with one another? What does the outline reveal about Pinker's use of examples?

IN LITERATURE

Bret Lott's very short story uses a single example to capture a painful reality. A father wakes up to hear what he thinks is his child breathing. It seems at first like an ordinary experience, but we quickly discover what that single example reveals.

Night

BRET LOTT

He woke up. He thought he could hear their child's breathing in the next room, the near-silent, smooth sound of air in and out.

He touched his wife. The room was too dark to let him see her, but he felt her movement, the shift of blanket and sheet.

"Listen," he whispered.

"Yesterday," she mumbled. "Why not yesterday," and she moved back into sleep.

He listened harder, though he could hear his wife's breath, thick and heavy next to him, there was beneath this the thin frost of his child's breathing.

The hardwood floor was cold beneath his feet. He held out a hand in front of him, and when he touched the doorjamb, he paused, listened again, heard the life of his child.

His fingertips led him along the hall and to the next room. Then he was in the doorway of a room as dark, as hollow as his own. He cut on the light.

The room, of course, was empty. They had left the bed just as their child had made it, the spread merely thrown over bunched and wrinkled sheets, the pillow crooked at the head. The small blue desk was littered with colored pencils and scraps of construction paper, a bottle of white glue.

He turned off the light and listened. He heard nothing, then backed out of the room and moved down the hall, back to his room, his hands at his sides, his fingertips helpless.

This happened each night, like a dream, but not.   ■

QUESTIONS FOR ANALYSIS

1. Who narrates the experience? What does that point of view contribute to the story?
2. At what point in the story do you realize what is happening?
3. Which of the descriptive details in the story seem most effective? Why?
4. What is the effect of the final sentence?

WRITING SUGGESTIONS

1. **Analysis.** How does the use of detail in this single detailed example capture and make vivid to the reader the emotion the father feels?
2. Lott does not tell us how the parents felt; he allows the single example of a nightly experience to reveal the loss that the father feels. Think about an emotion that you have had and try to capture that feeling in a single example. Possible starting points might include a life-changing event you experienced, the loss of something or someone; a discovery or realization.

IN A VISUAL

Information can often be displayed more efficiently through the use of visuals than through words. Textbooks, for example, make extensive use of visuals— tables, photographs, charts, diagrams—to help you understand complex information. Advertisements use photographs to catch your attention. During your junior and senior year in high school, when you were trying to pick a college or university, you probably received many catalogs and admission folders full of color photographs of the campus, the students, and the campus's facilities. Those images—and maybe others on the school's website—might have been influential in your final decision. The four photographs below appeared in one college's admission materials.

QUESTIONS FOR ANALYSIS

1. Why do you think each of these images was chosen? What do they seem to exemplify about the school?
2. Why might photographs be particularly effective in promoting a college or university to prospective students?

WRITING SUGGESTIONS

1. **Analysis.** A photographer posed or composed each of the images, deciding what would go into the image and what would not. Study each of the photographs. What do the images suggest about the school? What might be the thesis or purpose behind each of these photographs? How do these examples support that thesis? In an essay, analyze the content and significance of the images.
2. Given your college experiences so far, what images would you include if you were asked to write "an insider's guide to college life at——"? Using digital photographs that you include in your paper, write an essay that uses examples (and images) to reveal everyday life at your school and include captions for each of the images.

Cut

BOB GREENE

Bob Greene was born in Columbus, Ohio, in 1947 and received a B.J. from Northwestern University in 1969. A columnist and essayist, Greene is the author of Late Edition: A Love Story, *a tribute to the glory days of America's newspapers.*

On Writing: *Greene is, in many ways, a reporter of everyday events. He rarely tries to be profound but concentrates instead on human interest stories, the experiences that we all share. "Beyond entertaining or informing [my readers]," he has said, "the only responsibility I feel is . . . to make sure that they get to the last period of the last sentence of the last paragraph of the story. . . . I feel I have a responsibility to make the story interesting enough for them to read all the way through." In this essay from* Esquire, *a magazine aimed at a male audience, Greene relates the stories of five successful men who shared the experience of being "cut from the team." Does being cut, Greene wonders, make you a superachiever later in life?*

Before Reading

Connecting: Was there ever a time when you realized that you were not going to be allowed to participate in something that you wanted very much? Did someone tell you, "You're not good enough," or did you realize it yourself?

Anticipating: Writers recount personal experiences for some reason, and that reason is never just "here is what happened to me"; instead, writers focus on the significance of the experience. What significance does Greene see in these narratives?

1   ▌remember vividly the last time I cried. I was twelve years old, in the seventh grade, and I had tried out for the junior high school basketball team. I walked into the gymnasium; there was a piece of paper tacked to the bulletin board.

2   It was a cut list. The seventh-grade coach had put it up on the board. The boys whose names were on the list were still on the team; they were welcome to keep coming to practices. The boys whose names were not on the list had been cut; their presence was no longer desired. My name was not on the list.

3   I had not known the cut was coming that day. I stood and stared at the list. The coach had not composed it with a great deal of subtlety; the names of the very best athletes were at the top of the sheet of paper, and the other

members of the squad were listed in what appeared to be a descending order of talent. I kept looking at the bottom of the list, hoping against hope that my name would miraculously appear there if I looked hard enough.

4   I held myself together as I walked out of the gym and out of the school, but when I got home I began to sob. I couldn't stop. For the first time in my life, I had been told officially that I wasn't good enough. Athletics meant everything to boys that age; if you were on the team, even a substitute, it put you in the desirable group. If you weren't on the team, you might as well not be alive.

5   I had tried desperately in practice, but the coach never seemed to notice. It didn't matter how hard I was willing to work; he didn't want me there. I knew that when I went to school the next morning I would have to face the boys who had not been cut—the boys whose names were on the list, who were still on the team, who had been judged worthy while I had been judged unworthy.

6   All these years later, I remember it as if I were still standing right there in the gym. And a curious thing has happened: in traveling around the country, I have found that an inordinately large proportion of successful men share that same memory—the memory of being cut from a sports team as a boy.

7   I don't know how the mind works in matters like this; I don't know what went on in my head following that day when I was cut. But I know that my ambition has been enormous ever since then; I know that for all of my life since that day, I have done more work than I had to be doing, taken more assignments than I had to be taking, put in more hours than I had to be spending. I don't know if all of that came from a determination never to allow myself to be cut again—never to allow someone to tell me that I'm not good enough again—but I know it's there. And apparently it's there in a lot of other men, too.

8   Bob Graham, thirty-six, is a partner with the Jenner & Block law firm in Chicago. "When I was sixteen, baseball was my whole life," he said. "I had gone to a relatively small high school, and I had been on the team. But then my family moved, and I was going to a much bigger high school. All during the winter months I told everyone that I was a ballplayer. When spring came, of course I went out for the team.

9   "The cut list went up. I did not make the team. Reading that cut list is one of the clearest things I have in my memory. I wanted not to believe it, but there it was.

10   "I went home and told my father about it. He suggested that maybe I should talk to the coach. So I did. I pleaded to be put back on the team. He said there was nothing he could do; he said he didn't have enough room.

11   "I know for a fact that it altered my perception of myself. My view of myself was knocked down; my self-esteem was lowered. I felt so embarrassed; my whole life up to that point had revolved around sports, and particularly around playing baseball. That was the group I wanted to be in—the guys

on the baseball team. And I was told that I wasn't good enough to be one of them.

12   "I know now that it changed me. I found out, even though I couldn't articulate it at the time, that there would be times in my life when certain people would be in a position to say 'You're not good enough' to me. I did not want that to happen ever again.

13   "It seems obvious to me now that being cut was what started me in determining that my success would always be based on my own abilities, and not on someone else's perceptions. Since then I've always been something of an overachiever; when I came to the law firm I was very aggressive in trying to run my own cases right away, to be the lead lawyer in the cases with which I was involved. I made partner at thirty-one; I never wanted to be left behind.

14   "Looking back, maybe it shouldn't have been that important. It was only baseball. You pass that by. Here I am. That coach is probably still there, still a high school baseball coach, still cutting boys off the baseball team every year. I wonder how many hundreds of boys he's cut in his life?"

15 Maurice McGrath is senior vice-president of Genstar Mortgage Corporation, a mortgage banking firm in Glendale, California. "I'm forty-seven years old, and I was fourteen when it happened to me, and I still feel something when I think about it," he said.

16   "I was in the eighth grade. I went to St. Philip's School in Pasadena. I went out for the baseball team, and one day at practice the coach came over to me. He was an Occidental College student who had been hired as the eighth-grade coach.

17   "He said, 'You're no good.' Those were his words. I asked him why he was saying that. He said, 'You can't hit the ball. I don't want you here.' I didn't know what to do, so I went over and sat off to the side, watching the others practice. The coach said I should leave the practice field. He said that I wasn't on the team, and that I didn't belong there anymore.

18   "I was outwardly stoic about it. I didn't want anyone to see how I felt. I didn't want to show that it hurt. But oh, did it hurt. All my friends played baseball after school every day. My best friend was the pitcher on the team. After I got whittled down by the coach, I would hear the other boys talking in class about what they were going to do at practice after school. I knew that I'd just have to go home.

19   "I guess you make your mind up never to allow yourself to be hurt like that again. In some way I must have been saying to myself, 'I'll play the game better.' Not the sports game, but anything I tried. I must have been saying, 'If I have to, I'll sit on the bench, but I'll be part of the team.'

20   "I try to make my own kids believe that, too. I try to tell them that they should show that they're a little bit better than the rest. I tell them to think of themselves as better. Who cares what anyone else thinks? You know, I can almost hear that coach saying the words. 'You're no good.'"

21 Author Malcolm MacPherson *(The Blood of His Servants)*, forty, lives in New York. "It happened to me in the ninth grade, at the Yalesville School in Yalesville, Connecticut," he said. "Both of my parents had just been killed in a car crash, and as you can imagine, it was a very difficult time in my life. I went out for the baseball team, and I did pretty well in practice.

22   "But in the first game I clutched. I was playing second base; the batter hit a pop-up, and I moved back to catch it. I can see it now. I felt dizzy as I looked up at the ball. It was like I was moving in slow motion, but the ball was going at regular speed. I couldn't get out of the way of my own feet. The ball dropped to the ground. I didn't catch it.

23   "The next day at practice, the coach read off the lineup. I wasn't on it. I was off the squad.

24   "I remember what I did: I walked. It was a cold spring afternoon, and the ground was wet, and I just walked. I was living with an aunt and uncle, and I didn't want to go home. I just wanted to walk forever.

25   "It drove my opinion of myself right into a tunnel. Right into a cave. And when I came out of the cave, something inside of me wanted to make sure in one manner or another that I would never again be told I wasn't good enough.

26   "I will confess that my ambition, to this day, is out of control. It's like a fire. I think the fire would have pretty much stayed in control if I hadn't been cut from that team. But that got it going. You don't slice ambition two ways; it's either there or it isn't. Those of us who went through something like that always know that we have to catch the ball. We'd rather die than have the ball fall at our feet.

27   "Once that fire is started in us, it never gets extinguished, until we die or have heart attacks or something. Sometimes I wonder about the home-run hitters; the guys who never even had to worry about being cut. They may have gotten the applause and the attention back then, but I wonder if they ever got the fire. I doubt it. I think maybe you have to get kicked in the teeth to get the fire started.

28   "You can tell the effect of something like that by examining the trail you've left in your life, and tracing it backward. It's almost like being a junkie with a need for success. You get attention and applause and you like it, but you never quite trust it. Because you know that back then you were good enough if only they would have given you a chance. You don't trust what you achieve, because you're afraid that someone will take it away from you. You know that it can happen; it already did.

29   "So you try to show people how good you are. Maybe you don't go out and become Dan Rather; maybe you just end up owning the Pontiac dealership in your town. But it's your dealership, and you're the top man, and every day you're showing people that you're good enough."

30 Dan Rather, fifty-two, is anchor of the CBS *Evening News*. "When I was thirteen, I had rheumatic fever," he said. "I became extremely skinny and extremely weak, but I still went out for the seventh-grade baseball team at Alexander Hamilton Junior High School in Houston.

31   "The school was small enough that there was no cut as such; you were supposed to figure out that you weren't good enough, and quit. Game after game I sat at the end of the bench, hoping that maybe this was the time I would get in. The coach never even looked at me; I might as well have been invisible.

32   "I told my mother about it. Her advice was not to quit. So I went to practice every day, and I tried to do well so that the coach would be impressed. He never even knew I was there. At home in my room I would fantasize that there was a big game, and the three guys in front of me would all get hurt, and the coach would turn to me and put me in, and I would make the winning hit. But then there'd be another game, and the late innings would come, and if we were way ahead I'd keep hoping that this was the game when the coach would put me in. He never did.

33   "When you're that age, you're looking for someone to tell you you're okay. Your sense of self-esteem is just being formed. And what that experience that baseball season did was make me think that perhaps I wasn't okay.

34   "In the last game of the season something terrible happened. It was the last of the ninth inning, there were two outs, and there were two strikes on the batter. And the coach turned to me and told me to go out to right field.

35   "It was a totally humiliating thing for him to do. For him to put me in for one pitch, the last pitch of the season, in front of all the other boys on the team . . . I stood out there for that one pitch, and I just wanted to sink into the ground and disappear. Looking back on it, it was an extremely unkind thing for him to have done. That was nearly forty years ago, and I don't know why the memory should be so vivid now; I've never known if the coach was purposely making fun of me—and if he was, why a grown man would do that to a thirteen-year-old boy.

36   "I'm not a psychologist. I don't know if a man can point to one event in his life and say that that's the thing that made him the way he is. But when you're that age, and you're searching for your own identity, and all you want is to be told that you're all right . . . I wish I understood it better, but I know the feeling is still there." ■

QUESTIONS ON SUBJECT AND PURPOSE

1. Greene's "cuts" all refer to not making an athletic team. What other kinds of "cuts" can you experience?

2. It is always risky to speculate on an author's purpose, but why would Greene write about this? Why reveal to everyone something that hurt so much?

3. How might Greene have gone about gathering examples of other men's similar experiences? Why would they be willing to contribute? Would everyone who has been cut be so candid?

4. What can be said in the coaches' defense? Should everyone who tries out be automatically guaranteed a place on the team?

QUESTIONS ON STRATEGY AND AUDIENCE

1. Greene structures his essay in an unusual way. How can the essay be divided? Why give a series of examples of other men who were "cut"?

2. How many examples are enough? What if Greene had used two examples? Eight examples? How would either extreme have influenced your reaction as a reader?

3. Greene does not provide a concluding paragraph. Why?

4. Are you skeptical after you have finished the essay? Does everyone react to being cut in the same way? What would it take to convince you that these reactions are typical?

QUESTIONS ON VOCABULARY AND STYLE

1. How would you characterize the tone of Greene's essay? How is it achieved? Through language? Sentence structure? Paragraphing?

2. Why does Greene allow each man to tell his own story? Why not just summarize their experiences? Each story is enclosed in quotation marks. Do you think that these were the exact words of each man? Why?

3. What do *inordinately* (paragraph 6) and *stoic* (18) mean?

WRITING SUGGESTIONS

1. **Doing a Critical Analysis.** Greene structures his narrative essay in an unusual way: five short personal experiences; seemingly arranged in no particular order. In addition, the narrative has no framing introduction or conclusion. In an essay analyze the effectiveness of such an unusual structure.

2. **Journaling or Blogging.** Greene attributes enormous significance to a single experience; he feels that it literally changed his entire life. Explore some occasions when a disappointment seemed to change your life.

3. **Practicing in a Paragraph.** As children, we imagine ourselves as doing or becoming anything we want. Growing older, we realize that our choices are increasingly limited. Choose a time when you realized that a particular expectation or dream would never come true. Narrate that experience in a paragraph, making clear to your reader the significance of that realization.

4. **Writing the Personal Essay.** Describe an experience similar to Greene's. It could have happened in an academic course, in a school or community activity, on the job. We can be "cut" from almost anything. Remember to make your narrative vivid and to focus on the impact of that experience in your life.

5. **Finding Reading Connections.** Being "cut" in the context of sports implies that one lacked the necessary ability or skills to be competitive. Being "cut" (released, fired) in other contexts might actually be the result of discrimination or prejudice. Deborah L. Rhode, "Why Looks Are the Last Bastion of Discrimination" (this chapter) documents a number of cases where people were "cut" on the basis of their weight. What is the difference in effectiveness between citing some examples of discrimination (Rhode) and creating short narratives with quotations (Greene)?

6. **Exploring Links Online.** A number of websites offer perspectives on "cutting in sports." How could one of the scenarios Greene describes have been handled differently?

7. **Writing the Research Paper.** Is there any evidence from research studies about the psychological effects of such vivid rejections on young children? On teenagers? Locate both online and print sources and then using your research write an academic essay, with documentation, on such a practice.

For Further Study

Focusing on Grammar and Writing. Greene uses *and*s and *but*s to connect many sentences in his essay. We use both words more frequently in oral rather than written speech. Why might Greene use them in his essay? What cautions might be offered in using such words to link sentences together?

Working Together. Working in small groups, discuss what evidence Greene would need in order to "prove" his assertion that being cut makes you an overachiever in life. What is the strength and the weakness of the type of example that Greene uses as evidence?

Seeing Other Modes at Work. Each example in the essay is a narrative. How does Greene tell each story? To what extent are the narratives similar in structure? To what extent different?

Acquiring Language (from *The Story of My Life*)

HELEN KELLER

Helen Adams Keller was born in 1880 in Alabama. A precocious child, she started speaking when she was just six months old, walking at the age of one. At eighteen months, she fell ill with a high temperature. When she recovered. Keller had lost both her sight and hearing. In 1887 she began working with Anne Sullivan. The breakthrough moment in their relationship came in the scene Keller describes here when she first connected a word to its meaning. Keller worked for twenty-five years to learn to speak so others could understand her. Accompanied by Sullivan who helped her interpret texts and lectures, Keller graduated from Radcliff College in 1904. She wrote her first book, The Story of My Life, *in 1905. It was used as the basis for the play and film* The Miracle Worker.

*   *On Writing:* *Keller observed, "Trying to write is very much like trying to put a Chinese puzzle together. We have a pattern in mind which we wish to work out in words; but the words will not fit the spaces, or, if they do, they will not match the design."*

Before Reading

Connecting: Keller's autobiography was published in 1905. Over 100 years later, does her story seem relevant to you today? Why or why not?

Anticipating: What does Keller's experience here suggest about the link between language and thought? Does thought require language?

1   **T**he most important day I remember in all my life is the one on which my teacher, Anne Mansfield Sullivan, came to me. I am filled with wonder when I consider the immeasurable contrasts between the two lives which it connects. It was the third of March, 1887, three months before I was seven years old.

2   On the afternoon of that eventful day, I stood on the porch, dumb, expectant. I guessed vaguely from my mother's signs and from the hurrying to and fro in the house that something unusual was about to happen, so went to the door and waited on the steps. The afternoon sun penetrated the mass of honeysuckle that covered the porch, and fell on my upturned face. My fingers lingered almost unconsciously on the familiar leaves and blossoms which had just come forth to greet the sweet southern spring. I did not know what the future held of marvel or surprise for me. Anger and bitterness had preyed upon me continually for weeks and a deep languor had succeeded this passionate struggle.

3   Have you ever been at sea in a dense fog, when it seemed as if a tangible white darkness shut you in, and the great ship, tense and anxious, groped her way toward the shore with plummet and sounding-line, and you waited with beating heart for something to happen? I was like that ship before my education began, only I was without compass or sounding-line, and had no way of knowing how near the harbour was. "Light! Give me light!" was the wordless cry of my soul, and the light of love shone on me in that very hour.

4   I felt approaching footsteps. I stretched out my hand as I supposed to my mother. Some one took it, and I was caught up and held close in the arms of her who had come to reveal all things to me, and, more than all things else, to love me.

5   The morning after my teacher came she led me into her room and gave me a doll. . . . When I had played with it a little while, Miss Sullivan slowly spelled into my hand the word "d-o-l-l." I was at once interested in this finger play and tried to imitate it When I finally succeeded in making the letters correctly I was flushed with childish pleasure and pride. Running downstairs to my mother I held up my hand and made the letters for doll. I did not know that I was spelling a word or even that words existed; I was simply making fingers go in monkey-like imitation. In the days that followed I learned to spell in this uncomprehending way a great many words, among them *pin, hat, cup* and a few verbs like *sit, stand,* and *walk.*

But my teacher had been with me several weeks before I understood that everything has a name.

6   One day, while I was playing with my new doll, Miss Sullivan put my big rag doll into my lap also, spelled, "d-o-l-l" and tried to make me understand that "d-o-l-l" applied to both. Earlier in the day we had had a tussle over the words "m-u-g" and "w-a-t-e-r." Miss Sullivan had tried to impress upon me that "m-u-g" is *mug* and that "w-a-t-e-r" is *water*, but I persisted in confounding the two. In despair she had dropped the subject for the time, only to renew it at the first opportunity. I became impatient at her repeated attempts and, seizing the new doll, I dashed it upon the floor. I was keenly delighted when I felt the fragments of the broken doll at my feet. Neither sorrow nor regret followed my passionate outburst. I had not loved the doll. In the still, dark world in which I lived there was no strong sentiment or tenderness. I felt my teacher sweep the fragments to one side of the hearth and I had a sense of satisfaction that the cause of my discomfort was removed. She brought me my hat, and I knew I was going out into the warm sunshine. This thought, if a wordless sensation may be called a thought, made me hop and skip with pleasure.

7   We walked down the path to the well-house, attracted by the fragrance of the honeysuckle with which it was covered. Someone was drawing water and my teacher placed my hand under the spout. As the cool stream gushed over one hand she spelled into the other the word *water*, first slowly, then rapidly. I stood still, my whole attention fixed upon the motion of her fingers. Suddenly I felt a misty consciousness as of something forgotten—a thrill of returning thought; and somehow the mystery of language was revealed to me. I knew then that "w-a-t-e-r" meant the wonderful cool something that was flowing over my hand. That living word awakened my soul, gave it light, hope, joy, set it free! There were barriers still, it is true, but barriers that could in time be swept away.

8   I left the well-house eager to learn. Everything had a name, and each name gave birth to a new thought. As we returned to the house every object which I touched seemed to quiver with life. That was because I saw everything with the strange, new sight that had come to me. On entering the door I remembered the doll I had broken. I felt my way to the hearth and picked up the pieces. I tried vainly to put them together. Then my eyes filled with tears; for the first time I realized what I had done, and for the first time I felt repentance and sorrow.

9   I learned a great many new words that day. I do not remember what they all were; but I do know that mother, father, sister, teacher were among them—words that were to make the world blossom for me, "like Aaron's rod, with flowers." It would have been difficult to find a happier child than I was as I lay in my crib at the close of that eventful day and lived over the joys it had brought me, and for the first time I longed for a new day to come.   ■

QUESTIONS ON SUBJECT AND PURPOSE

1. What is so important to Keller about this particular experience?
2. In paragraph 2, Keller tells us that she had been feeling "anger and bitterness" followed by a "deeper languor." Why was she feeling this way? How does paragraph 3 help explain that feeling to us?
3. Keller's autobiography from which this is taken was published in 1905, some eighteen years after the experience described here. Why might she want to share her story with others?

QUESTIONS ON STRATEGY AND AUDIENCE

1. Blind and deaf, how could the six-year old experience the physical world? What do the details in her narrative tell us about the ability to perceive her world?
2. What might account for the difference between her actions in the two scenes with the doll (paragraphs 6 and 8)?
3. What might be so appealing to an audience about the story of Helen Keller?

QUESTIONS ON VOCABULARY AND STYLE

1. What is the literary device that Keller uses in paragraph 3?
2. When Keller observes that words made the "world blossom for me, 'like Aaron's rod, with flowers'" (paragraph 9), she is using two literary devices. What are they? To what does "Aaron's rod" refer–you might need to use the internet for an answer.
3. Be prepared to define the following words: *languor* (paragraph 2), *plummet* (3), *tussle* (6), *confounding* (6), *quiver* (8).

WRITING SUGGESTIONS

1. **Doing a Critical Analysis.** What role do sense impressions play in Keller's descriptions in this account? Being blind and deaf, and therefore unable to see or hear, how is she able to describe her world?
2. **Journaling or Blogging.** As children we all had moments in which an experience led to an important discovery or sudden realization. Explore your memories for suitable examples, realizing of course that our experiences were probably minor in comparison to Keller's.
3. **Practicing in a Paragraph.** Re-create one single moment or example using details that make the discovery and significance clear to a reader.
4. **Writing the Personal Essay.** Using the memories you explored in journaling and in the paragraph writing, re-create in detail for your reader that moment of discovery from your childhood.

5. **Finding Reading Connections.** Michael Jernigan, "Living the Dream" (Chapter 7), was severely injured and lost his sight to a roadside bomb in Iraq. Jernigan writes not about his blindness, but about his P.T.S.D. He observes that writing became a vent" for his frustration. In what way is writing important to both writers? What does it allow them to do?

6. **Exploring Links Online.** How do we, as children, acquire the ability to speak and to use language? How do scientists define the process of language acquisition in children?

7. **Writing the Research Paper.** The incredible success of Helen Keller can be contrasted with the story of "Genie," a feral-child, who came to the attention of authorities in 1970. What explains what happened to "Genie"? What exactly is a "feral" child?

For Further Study

Focusing on Grammar and Writing. Keller uses figurative language fairly often in this selection. How many examples are there and what does each simile or metaphor contribute to our understanding of what was happening and how significant it was?

Working Together. Working in small groups ask the students to list in two columns what Keller's experiences were like before she discovers the connection between the word "water" and what it signified.

Seeing Other Modes at Work. In its emphasis on the before and after, the selection is also an example of comparison and contrast.

Getting a Second Wind

RICK REILLY

Rick Reilly, named National Sportswriter of the Year eleven times, wrote for Sports Illustrated *from 1985 until 2007. For 10 years he wrote the "Life of Reilly" column, a weekly opinion essay. In 2008 he became a columnist and writer for ESPN. The author of a number of novels and collections of his columns, his newest book is* Sports from Hell *(2010), an account of his global search for the "stupidest sport" in the world. This essay appeared in* Sports Illustrated *in September 2007.*

On Writing: Commenting on his choice of subjects for his columns in Sports Illustrated, *Reilly observed: "I don't write about sports. I write about people who happen to be in sports. I write about human joy, sorrow, religion, and politics as it weaves itself through sports."*

Before Reading

Connecting: Are you already or would you consider identifying yourself as an organ donor? If not, why not?

Anticipating: What does the title of the story suggest to you? As you read, think about how the title relates to the story that Reilly is narrating.

1   **O**ne day five years ago bubbly, gorgeous soccer goalie Korinne Shroyer came home from eighth grade, found her father's revolver in his closet, and fired a bullet into her skull.

2   This is about the lives she saved doing it.

3   Out of a million kids you'd pick Korinne last to commit suicide. She was a popular kid in her class in Lynchburg, Virginia. But then she started feeling sad for no reason. Her parents took her to a therapist, who recommended Paxil. But one worry with Paxil is that it can give teenagers suicidal thoughts when they first start taking it. Korinne made it through ten days.

4   That bullet tore a hole in her father, Kevin, that you could drive an eighteen-wheeler through. Korinne was Kevin's best friend, the kid who would Rollerblade with him as he ran for hours, the kid who'd come with him to Orioles games and chat with him until his ears hurt. "I used to run all the time," says Kevin Shroyer, forty-six. "I loved it because it gave me time to think. But [after the suicide], thinking was the last thing I wanted to do."

5   Kevin, an investigator in the public defender's office, and his wife, Kristie, a hair stylist, were able to think one clear and brave and terrifying thought during the six days Korinne survived after the shooting. They decided to send out her organs like gifts.

6   Her green eyes would go in one direction, her glad heart another, her kidneys still another. Her liver and her pancreas went somewhere else, and her two good lungs—the ones that played the saxophone—went to a Gainesville, Georgia, man named Len Geiger, who was so close to dying that he was practically pricing caskets.

7   A runner and swimmer and nonsmoker, Geiger suddenly found one day that he only had enough breath for walking or talking, not both. Turns out he had genetic emphysema, also known as Alpha-1, and a lung transplant was his only hope for survival.

8   He was on his fifth year on the waiting list and "life wasn't worth living," he says, when Korinne pulled the trigger. Geiger received those two young lungs six days later in an operation at the University of Virginia Medical Center.

9   And that's where this story gets good.

10   Geiger, now forty-eight, went from 15 percent lung function to way above average for his age. He got his second wind and his second life. He was so grateful, he wrote Korinne's parents to say thank you. And that letter changed everybody's lives.

11   Korinne's parents wrote back, and Geiger asked to meet, and next thing you knew Geiger was at a bittersweet gathering that became soaked with every kind of tears.

12   The Shroyers and their other daughter, Kolby, now sixteen, gave Geiger a photo album of the girl whose life was now inside him. "She starts out as this beautiful baby," Geiger says. "Then she's a little girl in a Halloween costume. Then a gorgeous teenager. And then the pictures just stop. It was the saddest thing I've ever experienced."

13   Hours later the group was parting when Kristie said, "Len? Can I ask you a favor?" She walked over and stood before him.

14   "Anything," Geiger said.

15   "Can I put my hands on your chest for just a second?"

16   And she stood there, crying, as she felt her dead daughter breathe.

17   Kevin started to run again. And someone had a great idea. Why didn't he and Len run together? So they did. They ran an 8-K together, step for step, next to each other. One man's overflowing joy coming straight from the other's bottomless sorrow.

18   That whole run, Kevin never shut up. It was so unlike him that, at the end, Geiger asked him, "Why?"

19   "I had to," Kevin admitted, "because every time there was silence, I could hear Korinne breathing."

20   Next they ran a half-marathon, then a full one. By then, though, the steroids that Geiger had taken for years just to stay alive had damaged most of his joints, and he was running on two artificial hips. The best he could do was racewalk. At the seventeen-mile mark his hips were screaming. But he refused to quit.

21   It took them six hours and twenty-five minutes—with Shroyer matching him step by agonizing step—but they finished, hands clasped together, the three of them.

22   Kevin and Kristie aren't whole yet, but they're getting on with their lives. Geiger, meanwhile, is relishing his. He met a woman, Christina, married her, and they named their first baby after Korinne—Ava Corinne. Sometimes he stares at her, awed. "I know that without Korinne, I'm not here today and neither is Ava Corinne."

23   Sometimes life just takes your breath away, doesn't it?   ■

QUESTIONS ON SUBJECT AND PURPOSE

1. Korinne's organs changed or even saved the lives of a number of people. Reilly focuses only on one person. Why might he choose to tell the story of that one transplant?

2. The story could have ended at paragraph 21. Why might Reilly continue the story through paragraph 22?

3. How does the subject of this essay match the description (see On Writing) of what Reilly writes about?

QUESTIONS ON STRATEGY AND AUDIENCE

1. From what point of view is the story told? Who is telling the story?

2. What makes the opening of the essay so effective in catching the reader's attention and interest?

3. The essay originally appeared in *Sports Illustrated*. What assumptions can you make about Reilly's audience?

QUESTIONS ON VOCABULARY AND STYLE

1. What would you call the expression that is the title of the essay? To what does it refer?

2. What is unusual about the one-sentence paragraphs 2 and 9 and what do they signal about the essay?

3. What is the effect of using adjectives to modify the nouns in "her green eyes would go in one direction, her glad heart in another"? (paragraph 6).

WRITING SUGGESTIONS

1. **Doing a Critical Analysis.** What makes this essay so powerful and emotional? Why might a single example be more effective in moving its audience than several examples? Analyze the elements in this essay, such as point of view, selection of detail, choice of language, use of dialogue, that contribute to its emotional power.

2. **Journaling or Blogging.** The essay is typical of the columns that Reilly wrote for *Sports Illustrated*, focusing on "human joy and sorrow." Think about special people and their stories that you know. Brainstorm some possibilities that might be expanded into an essay.

3. **Practicing in a Paragraph.** Develop that idea above into a paragraph. Focus on a single revealing and emotional moment, perhaps using some dialogue rather than just a narrative or descriptive summary.

4. **Writing the Personal Essay.** Expand your paragraph into an essay. Remember that the story does not need to be sensational or unusual. Think of your story as illustrating something that is universal about human life and values.

5. **Finding Reading Connections.** Another perspective on organ donation can be found in Jennifer Kahn's "Stripped for Parts" (Chapter 6). In an essay compare and contrast the two views.

6. **Exploring Links Online.** Many websites offer detailed perspectives on teenage suicides. Why is suicide the second leading cause of death among college students?

7. **Writing the Research Paper.** Reilly mentions that Korinne started taking Paxil shortly before she took her own life. Research the links between anti-depressant medication (especially Paxil) and suicidal behavior. Using examples from your research, write an academic essay with appropriate documentation on the link.

For Further Study

Focusing on Grammar and Writing. Reilly uses clichés in the essay, although he often puts a twist on them so that they are appropriate for the context. How many clichés can you find in the essay?

Working Together. Working first independently, identify some of the distinctive features of Reilly's prose style. What is the "sound" of his voice and what creates that effect? Then pool your ideas as a class.

Seeing Other Modes at Work. The essay could easily be used as a persuasive argument for recruiting organ donors.

Ready for Some Fútbol?

OSCAR CASARES

Oscar Casares graduated from the University of Texas and worked in advertising before earning his M.F.A. from the University of Iowa's Writers' workshop. A native of Brownsville, Texas, the town from which the Potter Cowboys in the essay come, Casares writes short stories drawing on his years of growing up in the Rio Grande Valley. Brownsville, *a collection of short stories, appeared in 2003.*

"Ready for Some Fútbol?" was first published in Texas Monthly *in November 2006. It was included in* The Best American Sports Writing, 2007.

On Writing: *Talking about his choice of subjects for stories, Casares said: "I sort of feel my form of activism is that by showing Mexican-Americans involved in ordinary things as I have always seen them, by normalizing them, what I'm doing is sort of showing the humanity of the group."*

Before Reading

Connecting: Do you remember anytime in high school sports in which your school made banners or floats that made fun of the rival team? Was that any different than what happens at this game?

Anticipating: The event described in this essay was a high school state soccer championship game. What expectations might you have about a story that reports on a championship game?

1   **S**peedy Gonzales, the famous cartoon star of the fifties and sixties, has been in the news again lately. It seems the image of the "fastest mouse in all Mexico" was evoked recently at the boys' 5A state soccer championship,

pitting the nationally ranked Coppell Cowboys, from North Texas, against the Porter Cowboys, from Brownsville, the southernmost city on the U.S.-Mexico border. In an effort to belittle their opponents, the Coppell fans held up a poster showing Speedy Gonzales about to be squashed by a large shoe. The sign read STOMP ON BROWNVILLE! (and no, that's not a typo). When officials forced Coppell to remove the sign, the Porter fans continued cheering for their underdog team with the chant "*¡Sí se puede!*" ("Yes, we can!"), a call to action recovered from the era of Cesar Chavez's marches with the United Farm Workers of America. The Coppell fans answered this with their own chant of "USA! USA!" implying that the Porter players and their fans were not citizens of the United States. And when that didn't work, one of the fans called out, "You suck, you beaner!" In the end, though, their taunts were as effective as Sylvester the Cat's were on Speedy Gonzales, Porter won 2-1 in overtime.

2   Interestingly enough, this was all happening while Congress debated an immigration reform bill, including the possibility of a seven-hundred-mile wall along our southern border (one end of which would pass about a mile from Gladys Porter High School, my alma mater), and while hundreds of thousands of undocumented immigrants and their supporters marched in cities across the United States, also chanting "*¡Sí se puede!*" Soon several thousand National Guard troops would be deployed to assist the Border Patrol in certain areas, including South Texas.

3   What the Coppell fans and the players on the charged soccer field probably didn't realize was that their reaction toward a group they assumed was not American could hardly be counted as new. One of the most concentrated efforts to rid the country of illegal immigrants occurred in 1954, when the U.S. government officially passed Operation Wetback, a mandate to expel all illegal workers, particularly those from Mexico (as the name may have clued you in to). Led by the Immigration and Naturalization Service and aided by the municipal, county, state, and federal authorities, as well as the military, the operation resulted in a massive sweep of Mexican-American neighborhoods and random stops of "Mexican-looking" people.

4   A year earlier, when these bitter feelings were already escalating, Warner Bros. introduced a new cartoon character named Speedy Gonzales. The original Speedy debuted in a cartoon titled "Cat-Tails for Two," where his character looked more like a rat, mean and sleazy and with a gold tooth the animator must have thought would add a touch of realism. Speedy Gonzales then disappeared for a time, only to make a comeback in 1955 in what could be described as a more user-friendly version of the original drawing. Warner Bros. had fixed his teeth, worked on his English, expanded his wardrobe— from an old T-shirt, barely covering his privates, to white campesino pants and shirt, both finely pressed, and a red bandanna he kept neatly wound into what looked like a bow tie—and then added a bit of panache with the sombrero, worn slightly askew, that would soon become his trademark. Later that same year, Warner Bros. won the Academy Award for Best Short Subject with the cartoon *Speedy Gonzales*.

5   How strange then that the Coppell fans would choose to taunt their opponents with a poster of a mouse known for running circles around his enemies. What started out as mockery quickly turned into a self-fulfilling prophecy, as the little guy used his speed to even things out against a bigger, more physical competitor. Along the way, the Porter team would prove that the game amounted to more than just some name-calling. Because for all questions of nationality, this actually turns out to be the classic American story: underdog sports team from a small, remote town defies the odds and earns a bid to play in the championship game, where these players must now face a formidable opponent in a match that forces them to look inward if they hope to win.

6   Gladys Porter High School is located on International Boulevard, about two miles from the Gateway International Bridge, which crosses into Matamoros. The school is also a block from Southmost, historically one of the poorest areas of town, where at one time it was said that even the cops wouldn't go after dark. Locally, Porter was known as the school that couldn't win, in the classroom or on the playing field; it seemed the only people who believed in Porter were from Porter. The school has changed dramatically since I left some twenty years ago—it is now the district's magnet school for engineering and technology, and in 2003 the football team came close to capturing the district title—and it has gathered an almost cultlike following of fans, collectively known as the Porter Nation.

7   A few days before the big game, the Porter soccer players loaded their equipment onto the school bus that would take them the 370 miles from the border to Round Rock, just north of Austin, the site of the state championship. Now they just had to wait for the drug-detection dog to inspect the vehicle. The Brownsville Independent School District has a policy of bringing dogs to check any bus that is scheduled to leave the region; according to James Kizer, Porter's athletic coordinator, the searches are done to prevent any "surprises" later. The argument could be made that the inspections are in the best interest of the team and the school, as a preventive measure, should there be a player who decides to smuggle illegal drugs and run the risk of serious charges. But in a way, the searches are not so different from the ones the players would be subjected to if they were down the street at the bridge, trying to enter the United States from Mexico.

8   Once the team passed the inspection, it was clear to leave the area. That is, until the next inspection some ninety miles later, near the King Ranch. By law the bus driver was required to stop at the Border Patrol's Sarita checkpoint so federal agents and their drug-detection dogs could search the vehicle. To facilitate the process, the players wore special tags that identified them as student athletes en route to a competition. (These tags prevent the sort of incident that occurred earlier this year when another team made it through the checkpoint only for it to be discovered later that some of the passengers were not actually with the team and had slipped away from the bus during a stop, supposedly to make their way into Texas illegally.) The Porter players were used to stopping at the

checkpoint on their way to tournaments, including the semifinal match that had led to the championship game. Still, there is something disconcerting about being in your own country and having to identify yourself to a federal agent.

9   This time around, the Border Patrol agent happened to be female. As she boarded the bus, another agent led a dog around the perimeter of the vehicle. The players knew the drill: sit up in your seat and give the agent your full attention.

10   "Everybody U.S. citizens?" she asked, stepping into the aisle.

11   The coaches and players all nodded and said yes.

12   "Where are you coming from?" she asked.

13   "Brownsville," one of the nearby players answered.

14   "Which high school in Brownsville?"

15   "Porter."

16   "Hey," she said, "I went to Porter!"

17   After so many such inspections during the season, the players were more than happy to meet another member of the Porter Nation and hear her wish them luck. These warm feelings lasted only until the following afternoon, when they walked onto the field and fully realized the level of competition they were up against. The Coppell team was ranked second in the nation, with three of its players having already been recruited to play at the collegiate level. This was also Coppell's third straight year to compete in the state championship, including 2004, when it won the title. As if this weren't enough to contend with, there was also that Speedy Gonzales poster waving in the stands.

18   If Coppell fans noticed anything less than American about the Porter team, it might have been its style of play. Spectators in this country are used to watching the type of soccer showcased during the recent World Cup, which tends to be more physical (even when the players aren't giving each other head butts in the sternum). But Porter plays a faster-paced soccer that focuses on shorter passes, in what some people might describe as more of a Mexican style. It certainly isn't the kind of soccer most kids across suburbia grow up with. The quicker technique makes sense because of the smaller size of the players in the Rio Grande Valley. Porter's approach to the game is actually quite common in this region of Texas, as well as on the other side of the river, because until recently, crossing over to Matamoros was the only way for boys to play on leagues year-round.

19   These contrasting styles just added to what was already happening in the stands. As the game wore on and the tension grew, Porter coach Luis Zarate, who himself had grown up playing on both sides of the river before becoming a place kicker for the University of Houston, called a time-out to center his team and deal with the slurs. "Focus on your game. At the end of the day, people are going to be talking about who won the game, not about these other things," he said, probably in Spanish, since his players are bilingual and this is the common language of soccer along the border.

20   What Coach Zarate wanted more than anything was to impress upon his players that they had fought hard all season to make it to this final

game and had earned every right to be on the field. "You're here. You belong here!"

21   He repeated this until it began to sink in. "You're here. You belong here!" Here at the state championship, here in Texas, here in the United States. They had traveled all the way from Gladys Porter High School, in the shadows of a proposed anti-immigration wall, to the 5A state championship, and they were exactly where they should be. "You're here. You belong here!" His words held an immediacy, but they also managed to convey a message his players could carry with them off the soccer field.

22   Jorge Briones, described as "a scoring machine" by his coach, went on to make the two goals that won the game, and the Porter Cowboys became the first Rio Grande Valley team to win a 5A division title in any sport. The team returned to Brownsville to a hero's welcome. Everyone, from alumni dating back thirty years to local politicians, lined up to publicly offer his congratulations. What no one could offer the players, though, was a way to afford the $300 championship rings. The University Interscholastic League, the governing body for most high school athletics programs in the state, sets limits on what gifts a team can receive from its school or school district. Eventually, businesses came together to offer the players jobs at various car dealerships in town. Briones spent a couple weeks washing cars at Marroquin Auto Sales, a used-car dealership along the freeway, so he could earn the money for his state MVP ring.

23   When I called Coach Zarate on his cell phone, he and his team happened to be the guests of honor, along with a few Dallas Cowboys Cheerleaders, at the grand opening of the new Wal-Mart Supercenter in Brownsville. The store manager had just donated $1,000 to go toward the team's funds for next season. I spoke to Coach Zarate a few minutes before he asked if I wanted to talk to Briones. Then he turned to his star player and in Spanish told him there was a guy from a magazine who wanted to ask him some questions.

24   "Can I talk to him in Spanish?" I heard Briones ask.

25   "Sure," the coach said. "He's from down here."

26   Then Briones came on the line and I congratulated him, until it got so loud at the grand opening that he could hardly hear me. It sounded as if there were a pep rally going on.

27   "Can you wait a minute, sir?" he asked.

28   And then we both stayed on the line, listening to "The Star-Spangled Banner" playing in the background.   ■

QUESTIONS ON SUBJECT AND PURPOSE

1. What is the subject of the essay? How might this essay differ from a newspaper account of the championship game?

2. Paragraphs 7 through 16 deal with the bus ride and the two inspection stops that the Porter team must make. Why include these details?

3. What might Casares want to show or reveal in the essay?

QUESTIONS ON STRATEGY AND AUDIENCE

1. Casares acknowledges that Porter is his "alma mater" (paragraph 2). What is the effect of that disclosure?

2. Why might Casares have chosen to end the essay with the telephone conversation?

3. Presumably the essay was seen by many readers, the majority of whom are not Mexican American. How do you think that the audience might have reacted to the essay? What about the supporters of the Coppell team?

QUESTIONS ON VOCABULARY AND STYLE

1. What is ironic about displaying Speedy Gonzales, "the fastest mouse in all Mexico"?

2. Why might Casares choose to record the conversation between the Border Patrol agent and the team (paragraphs 9–16)?

3. Be prepared to define the following words: *deployed* (paragraph 2), *panache* (4), *askew* (4).

WRITING SUGGESTIONS

1. **Doing a Critical Analysis.** Casares's story would not have appeared on the sports pages of a newspaper. In an essay, analyze how Casares uses examples not just to report the results of a soccer match, but also to support a larger point about American society and prejudice.

2. **Journaling or Blogging.** Have you ever drawn criticisms or taunts from others based on your appearance, ethnic or racial identity, religious affiliation, sexual orientation, or socioeconomic status? Did you ever tease or make fun of someone? Explore a memory.

3. **Practicing in a Paragraph.** Expand your memory of that time into a paragraph. Focus on a single moment in which you were either the object of ridicule or when you engaged in such behavior. Focus on showing how you felt rather than simply telling what you felt.

4. **Writing the Personal Essay.** Gather a series of examples from different categories of taunts. Use the examples to alert your audience to the often unthinking remarks people make that reveal prejudice, disapproval, even hatred.

5. **Finding Reading Connections.** Stereotypes and prejudices are not just revealed in verbal abuse. How people react in certain situations also reveals their assumptions. Compare the reactions that Judith Ortiz Cofer in "The Myth of the Latin Woman" (Chapter 4) and Brent Staples in "Black Men and Public Space" (Chapter 7) encounter.

6. **Exploring Links Online.** Not every stereotype is negative; some are positive. Psychologists warn, though, that positive stereotypes are also dangerous and misleading. Explore other examples of positive, but misleading stereotypes.

7. **Writing the Research Paper.** How should you respond if someone taunts you or if you see someone being taunted? What reactions might be appropriate? Explore both Web and print sources that offer advice and present your conclusion in an academic essay with appropriate documentation.

For Further Study

Focusing on Grammar and Writing. Casares inserts material into the middle of sentences using a variety of punctuation: commas, parentheses, and dashes. Locate examples of each type and offer an explanation for why he chooses that particular way to punctuate the inserted information.

Working Together. Working together in small groups, compile a list of taunting behaviors you have encountered or observed at school. What might have led people to engage in such behavior? Was it intentionally malicious, thoughtless, or intended to be funny?

Seeing Other Modes at Work. The overall structure of the essay is a narrative that follows the Porter Cowboys from the point when they leave for the game until the point at which the town is celebrating their victory. To what extent might the essay also have a persuasive intention?

Why Looks Are the Last Bastion of Discrimination

DEBORAH L. RHODE

Deborah L. Rhode is a graduate of Yale and the Yale Law School. She clerked for Supreme Court Justice Thurgood Marshall before joining the faculty at Stanford University where she is the Ernest W. McFarland Professor of Law. The author or coauthor of over 20 books and many articles and editorials, she addresses this issue at length in her recent book, The Beauty Bias: The Injustice of Appearance in Life and Law, *Oxford UP, 2010.*

*   ***On Writing:*** *Writing about the origins of her research and writing on the role of appearance, Rhode commented: "It started with shoes. Like many American women, I have had more issues with appearance than I care to recall. Happily, however, I have landed in an occupation with undemanding standards. Academics are known for relentlessly unattractive apparel. I am a case in point."*

Before Reading

Connecting: Probably everyone at some point in their lives has encountered some form of discrimination or judgment based on their appearance. Do you remember a time when someone judged or criticized or made fun of some aspect of your appearance?

Anticipating: Is Rhode arguing for a change in our laws in order to prevent discrimination based on appearance?

1   In the 19th century, many American cities banned public appearances by "unsightly" individuals. A Chicago ordinance was typical: "Any person who is diseased, maimed, mutilated, or in any way deformed, so as to be an unsightly or disgusting subject . . . shall not . . . expose himself to public view, under the penalty of a fine of $1 for each offense."

2   Although the government is no longer in the business of enforcing such discrimination, it still allows businesses, schools and other organizations to indulge their own prejudices. Over the past half-century, the United States has expanded protections against discrimination to include race, religion, sex, age, disability and, in a growing number of jurisdictions, sexual orientation. Yet bias based on appearance remains perfectly permissible in all but one state and six cities and counties. Across the rest of the country, looks are the last bastion of acceptable bigotry.

3   We all know that appearance matters, but the price of prejudice can be steeper than we often assume. In Texas in 1994, an obese woman was rejected for a job as a bus driver when a company doctor assumed she was not up to the task after watching her, in his words, "waddling down the hall." He did not perform any agility tests to determine whether she was, as the company would later claim, unfit to evacuate the bus in the event of an accident.

4   In New Jersey in 2005, one of the Borgata Hotel Casino's "Borgata babe" cocktail waitresses went from a Size 4 to a Size 6 because of a thyroid condition. When the waitress, whose contract required her to keep an "hourglass figure" that was "height and weight appropriate," requested a larger uniform, she was turned down. "Borgata babes don't go up in size," she was told. (Unless, the waitress noted, they have breast implants, which the casino happily accommodated with paid medical leave and a bigger bustier.)

5   And in California in 2001, Jennifer Portnick, a 240-pound aerobics instructor, was denied a franchise by Jazzercise, a national fitness chain. Jazzercise explained that its image demanded instructors who are "fit" and "toned." But Portnick was both: She worked out six days a week, taught back-to-back classes and had no shortage of willing students.

6   Such cases are common. In a survey by the National Association to Advance Fat Acceptance, 62 percent of its overweight female members and 42 percent of its overweight male members said they had been turned down for a job because of their weight.

7   And it isn't just weight that's at issue; it's appearance overall. According to a national poll by the Employment Law Alliance in 2005, 16 percent of workers reported being victims of appearance discrimination more generally—a figure comparable to the percentage who in other surveys say they have experienced sex or race discrimination.

8   Conventional wisdom holds that beauty is in the eye of the beholder, but most beholders tend to agree on what is beautiful. A number of researchers have independently found that, when people are asked to rate an individual's attractiveness, their responses are quite consistent, even across race,

sex, age, class and cultural background. Facial symmetry and unblemished skin are universally admired. Men get a bump for height, women are favored if they have hourglass figures, and racial minorities get points for light skin color, European facial characteristics and conventionally "white" hairstyles.

9   Yale's Kelly Brownell and Rebecca Puhl and Harvard's Nancy Etcoff have each reviewed hundreds of studies on the impact of appearance. Etcoff finds that unattractive people are less likely than their attractive peers to be viewed as intelligent, likable and good. Brownell and Puhl have documented that overweight individuals consistently suffer disadvantages at school, at work and beyond.

10   Among the key findings of a quarter-century's worth of research: Unattractive people are less likely to be hired and promoted, and they earn lower salaries, even in fields in which looks have no obvious relationship to professional duties. (In one study, economists Jeff Biddle and Daniel Hamermesh estimated that for lawyers, such prejudice can translate to a pay cut of as much as 12 percent.) When researchers ask people to evaluate written essays, the same material receives lower ratings for ideas, style and creativity when an accompanying photograph shows a less attractive author. Good-looking professors get better course evaluations from students; teachers in turn rate good-looking students as more intelligent.

11   Not even justice is blind. In studies that simulate legal proceedings, unattractive plaintiffs receive lower damage awards. And in a study released this month, Stephen Ceci and Justin Gunnell, two researchers at Cornell University, gave students case studies involving real criminal defendants and asked them to come to a verdict and a punishment for each. The students gave unattractive defendants prison sentences that were, on average, 22 months longer than those they gave to attractive defendants.

12   Just like racial or gender discrimination, discrimination based on irrelevant physical characteristics reinforces invidious stereotypes and undermines equal-opportunity principles based on merit and performance. And when grooming choices come into play, such bias can also restrict personal freedom.

13   Consider Nikki Youngblood, a lesbian who in 2001 was denied a photo in her Tampa high school yearbook because she would not pose in a scoop-necked dress. Youngblood was "not a rebellious kid," her lawyer explained. "She simply wanted to appear in her yearbook as herself, not as a fluffed-up stereotype of what school administrators thought she should look like." Furthermore, many grooming codes sexualize the workplace and jeopardize employees' health. The weight restrictions at the Borgata, for example, reportedly contributed to eating disorders among its waitresses.

14   Appearance-related bias also exacerbates disadvantages based on gender, race, ethnicity, age, sexual orientation and class. Prevailing beauty standards penalize people who lack the time and money to invest in their appearance. And weight discrimination, in particular, imposes special costs on people who live in communities with shortages of healthy food options and exercise facilities.

15   So why not simply ban discrimination based on appearance?

16   Employers often argue that attractiveness is job-related; their workers' appearance, they say, can affect the company's image and its profitability. In

this way, the Borgata blamed its weight limits on market demands. Customers, according to a spokesperson, like being served by an attractive waitress. The same assumption presumably motivated the L'Oreal executive who was sued for sex discrimination in 2003 after allegedly ordering a store manager to fire a salesperson who was not "hot" enough.

17   Such practices can violate the law if they disproportionately exclude groups protected by civil rights statutes—hence the sex discrimination suit. Abercrombie & Fitch's notorious efforts to project what it called a "classic American" look led to a race discrimination settlement on behalf of minority job-seekers who said they were turned down for positions on the sales floor. But unless the victims of appearance bias belong to groups already protected by civil rights laws, they have no legal remedy.

18   As the history of civil rights legislation suggests, customer preferences should not be a defense for prejudice. During the early civil rights era, employers in the South often argued that hiring African Americans would be financially ruinous; white customers, they said, would take their business elsewhere. In rejecting this logic, Congress and the courts recognized that customer preferences often reflect and reinforce precisely the attitudes that society is seeking to eliminate. Over the decades, we've seen that the most effective way of combating prejudice is to deprive people of the option to indulge it.

19   Similarly, during the 1960s and 1970s, major airlines argued that the male business travelers who dominated their customer ranks preferred attractive female flight attendants. According to the airlines, that made sex a bona fide occupational qualification and exempted them from anti-discrimination requirements. But the courts reasoned that only if sexual allure were the "essence" of a job should employers be allowed to select workers on that basis. Since airplanes were not flying bordellos, it was time to start hiring men.

20   Opponents of a ban on appearance-based discrimination also warn that it would trivialize other, more serious forms of bias. After all, if the goal is a level playing field, why draw the line at looks? "By the time you've finished preventing discrimination against the ugly, the short, the skinny, the bald, the knobbly-kneed, the flat-chested, and the stupid," Andrew Sullivan wrote in the London Sunday Times in 1999, "you're living in a totalitarian state." Yet intelligence and civility are generally related to job performance in a way that appearance isn't.

21   We also have enough experience with prohibitions on appearance discrimination to challenge opponents' arguments. Already, one state (Michigan) and six local jurisdictions (the District of Columbia; Howard County, Md.; San Francisco; Santa Cruz, Calif.; Madison, Wis.; and Urbana, Ill.) have banned such discrimination. Some of these laws date back to the 1970s and 1980s, while some are more recent; some cover height and weight only, while others cover looks broadly; but all make exceptions for reasonable business needs.

22   Such bans have not produced a barrage of loony litigation or an erosion of support for civil rights remedies generally. These cities and counties each receive between zero and nine complaints a year, while the entire state of Michigan totals about 30, with fewer than one a year ending up in court.

23   Although the laws are unevenly enforced, they have had a positive effect by publicizing and remedying the worst abuses. Because Portnick, the aerobics

instructor turned away by Jazzercise, lived in San Francisco, she was able to bring a claim against the company. After a wave of sympathetic media coverage, Jazzercise changed its policy.

24   This is not to overstate the power of legal remedies. Given the stigma attached to unattractiveness, few will want to claim that status in public litigation. And in the vast majority of cases, the cost of filing suit and the difficulty of proving discrimination are likely to be prohibitive. But stricter anti-discrimination laws could play a modest role in advancing healthier and more inclusive ideals of attractiveness. At the very least, such laws could reflect our principles of equal opportunity and raise our collective consciousness when we fall short. ∎

QUESTIONS ON SUBJECT AND PURPOSE

1. Why are "looks" the last bastion of discrimination?
2. According to Rhode, how widespread is discrimination based on appearance?
3. Can you find a sentence or two in the essay that seems to sum up Rhode's purpose in writing the essay?

QUESTIONS ON STRATEGY AND AUDIENCE

1. Rhode begins her essay with a quotation from a 19th-century city ordinance. What type of an introduction is this to the essay? Is it effective?
2. Why might Rhode set a single sentence off as a paragraph (15)?
3. Rhode's essay appeared in the *Washington Post*, a national newspaper. In what ways might the place of publication and its audience have influenced the structure and appearance of the essay?

QUESTIONS ON VOCABULARY AND STYLE

1. What does the word "bastion" mean and why might Rhode use it in the title of the essay?
2. What is the expression "beauty is in the eye of the beholder" (paragraph 8) called?
3. Be prepared to define the following words: *bigotry* (paragraph 1), *bustier* (4), *invidious* (12), *exacerbates* (14), *bona fide* (19), *bordellos* (19), *civility* (20), *barrage* (22), *stigma* (24).

WRITING SUGGESTIONS

1. **Doing a Critical Analysis.** What is the role of examples in Rhode's essay? What types of examples are used? Are they convincing? Why or why not? What would happen if the examples were removed from the essay?
2. **Journaling or Blogging.** Do you ever find yourself stereotyping someone else on the basis of their physical appearance or their style of dress? Have you ever sensed that someone discriminated against you for similar reasons? Reflect on either type of experience.

3. **Practicing in a Paragraph.** Expand your journal entry into a paragraph. Be sure to give vivid details about the experience.

4. **Writing the Personal Essay.** For a personal essay, explore your own biases and prejudices. How and why do you react to a person's appearance? What is it that causes either a positive or negative reaction in you?

5. **Finding Reading Connections.** Are women more likely than men to be stereotyped or discriminated against on the basis of appearance? Judith Ortiz Cofer's "The Myth of the Latin Woman" (Chapter 4) offers a perspective on this question. What has been your experience?

6. **Exploring Links Online.** The effect of your physical appearance and style of dress apparently is more complicated in the business world than it might seem. Studies have shown that while being attractive was always an as-set to men, attractive women could face disadvantages in certain professions. Why would that be? Research the problem.

7. **Writing the Research Paper.** One's appearance can also be a matter of choice. Often young people will adopt a certain model—for example, Goth, biker, jock, punk, emo, geek—choosing certain types of clothing, hair or facial-hair styles, body art to conform to the stereotype. Why? Research the reasons for this or for the choice of a particular style. Be sure to provide documentation for your sources.

For Further Study

Focusing on Grammar and Writing. How many of Rhode's paragraphs begin with a topic sentence? What is the effect of those sentences on your reading experience?

Working Together. Divide into small groups (three to six, depending on the size of your class). Each group should take a block of the 24 paragraphs in the essay and discuss what type of documentation would be needed if this were an academic essay. You might also do the "Providing Documentation" exercise below.

Seeing Other Modes at Work. The essay shows cause and effect in its use of examples and also has elements of both persuasion and argumentation.

 Providing Documentation

Rhode's essay appeared in a newspaper which explains why none of the examples have the type of documentation you would need in an academic essay. Locate sources either online or in library databases that would provide documentation for each of the following examples. Do both a parenthetical citation and a list of works cited in either MLA or APA format as directed by your instructor.

1. The examples in paragraphs 4 through 6
2. The studies by Brownell, Puhl, and Etcoff cited in paragraph 9
3. Cevi and Gunnell's study mentioned in paragraph 11
4. Nikki Youngblood's experience in paragraph 13

Additional Writing Suggestions Using Examples

Examples are used to explain a concept or an assertion, to make a point vivid or interesting, or to support a thesis or argument. Examples can come from your own personal experiences or the experiences of others; from authorities or experts you interview; from newspaper, magazine, or online articles; from books or websites. Write an essay using examples to achieve one of the following purposes. You will have to narrow the topics and define a thesis for your paper.

Explain a Concept or Assertion

1. The "language" of text messaging
2. Conservative, liberal, libertarian, socialist
3. Courage
4. Success (how is it measured?), fame
5. Function or purpose of a college education
6. "Going green" or sustainability
7. Organic or natural
8. Best friend, friendship
9. Love, infatuation

Make a Point Vivid or Interesting

1. Dormitory life, roommates
2. Commuting
3. Campus parking, campus food
4. Parenthood
5. The date from hell, Internet dating
6. An achievement
7. Being an only or youngest or oldest child
8. An embarrassing moment
9. Part-time jobs, internships

Support a Thesis or Argument

1. Ban on cigarette smoking in public places
2. Using a cell phone or texting while driving
3. Popularity of Facebook, Twitter, YouTube, Pinterest
4. Changes in the driving age, purchase of alcohol
5. Performance-enhancing drugs for athletes
6. Importance of high grades in college
7. Distribution requirements for college graduation
8. Popularity of reality-based TV shows
9. Value of studying abroad or service learning

2 | Narration

LEARNING OBJECTIVES

In this chapter, you will learn how to

1. Recognize the elements essential to narration
2. Select appropriate details for your narrative
3. Create an effective structural order for those details
4. Write dialogue to make your narrative more vivid and interesting
5. Revise your narrative to make it more effective
6. Analyze readings that use narration

Key Questions

WRITING NARRATION

Getting Ready to Write

What is narration and what are its elements?

What are the common forms of narrative writing?

What do you write about if nothing ever happened to you?

What do you include in a narrative?

Writing

How do you structure a narrative?

How do you end a narrative?

How do you tell a narrative?

How do you write dialogue?

Revising

How do you revise a narrative?

Student Essay

　　Hope Zucker, *"The Ruby Slippers"*

READING NARRATION

In Prose

　　S. E. Schlosser, *"Blue Hen's Chicks"*

In Literature

　　Ron Wallace, *"Worry"* (short story)

In a Visual

　　"Turnabout is Fair Play" (visual narrative)

Writing Narration

GETTING READY TO WRITE

What Is Narration and What Are Its Elements?

> Once upon a time . . .
> Did you hear the one about . . . ?
> What did you two do last night?
> Well, officer, it was like this . . .
> What happened at the Battle of Gettysburg?

What follows each of those lines is a story or a narrative. All stories, whether they are personal experiences, jokes, novels, histories, films, or television serials, have the same essential ingredients: a series of events arranged in a chosen order and told by a narrator for some particular purpose.

On the simplest level, all stories are composed of three elements:

Plot	Beginning (the initiating action)
	Middle
	End (concluding action)

As these terms suggest, stories are told in time: the fundamental arrangement of those events is chronological. Stories, though, do not always begin at the beginning. The time order of events can be rearranged by using flashbacks. Stories can begin with the last event in the chronological sequence or with any event that occurs in the middle.

Stories also involve tellers, or narrators, who relate the story. The narrators of stories almost always tell the story themselves (using "I"—a first-person point of view) or tell the story as an observer ("she"/"he"/"it"—a third-person point of view).

Point of View	**First person** ("I was saved from sin when I was going on thirteen."—Langston Hughes's, "Salvation")
	Third person ("A runner and swimmer and nonsmoker, Geiger suddenly found one day he only had enough breath for walking or talking, not both." — Rick Reilly, "Getting a Second Wind")

Finally, stories have a purpose, a reason for being told, and that purpose controls the narrative and its selection of details. As you start to write a narrative, always ask yourself what point you are trying to make. Force yourself to finish the following statement:

Purpose	"I am telling this story because _____."

Any type of writing can use narration; it is not something found only in personal experience essays or in fiction. Narration can also be used as examples to support a thesis, as Bob Greene does in "Cut" (Chapter 1) by providing five personal narratives to support his assertion that being cut from an athletic team can make a person a superachiever later in life. Narration can also be found with description as in William Least Heat Moon's "Nameless, Tennessee" (Chapter 3) or underlying a persuasive argument as in Linda Lee's "The Case Against College" (Chapter 9). In fact, you can find examples of narration in readings throughout this text.

What Are the Common Forms of Narrative Writing?

In writing courses, the narratives you tend to produce come in several forms. Most common are personal experience narratives: you recount an experience that happened to you. You are the narrator; the event is more or less true (i.e., you might add a few minor details or rearrange some elements to make the story more interesting or more artful). Typically, you recount the experience to share with your reader an insight. It might be funny or serious, but either way, it must connect with your readers' experiences: it should be about something that is universal—a realization, a sudden understanding, an awareness the experience brought to you. Most of the essays in this chapter are personal experience narratives.

The second, less common, form of narrative in freshman writing courses is the "here-is-what-happened" narrative. Stories in newspapers and histories are good examples of this type of narrative. Writing such a narrative generally requires that you do some research. A newspaper reporter cannot write any news story without first gathering the facts. Factual or historical narratives are typically told by an omniscient narrator who is not part of the story; the stories are intended to inform a reader, to provide information. This type of narrative also occurs in process writing (see Chapter 6) when you are describing how something happens or works.

The third common form for narratives in writing courses is the story designed to entertain: a short story, a joke, or a tall tale. The story might be intended to scare us, to puzzle us, or to get us to think about a situation or a course of action. Typically, such narratives are fictionalized; that is, the author invents the characters and the plot.

What Do You Write About if Nothing Ever Happened to You?

Writing a personal narrative can pose some specific prewriting problems. It is easy to assume that the only things worth writing about are once-in-a-lifetime experiences—an heroic or death-defying act, a personal tragedy, an Olympic medal-winning performance. Few readers have been in a lockdown in prison (Evans Hopkins, "Lockdown"), and probably even fewer have visited famine-torn Africa (Tom Haines, "Facing Famine"). However, there is nothing extraordinary, for example, about the events Langston Hughes relates in "Salvation," even though Hughes's experience was a turning point in his life. Bob Greene in "Cut" (Chapter 1) narrates the kind of story—about being cut from a team—that is all too familiar to most readers; in one way or another, probably everyone has experienced a similar rejection and subsequent disappointment.

The secret to writing an effective personal narrative is twofold. First, you must tell your story in an organized manner, following the advice just outlined. Simply relating what happened, however, is not enough. Second, and equally important, you must reveal a purpose in your story. Purposes can be many. You might offer insight into human behavior or motivation; you might mark a significant moment in your life; you might reveal an awareness of what it is to be young and to have dreams; you might reflect on the precariousness of life and the inevitability of change and decay; you might even use your experience to argue, as Evans Hopkins does, for a change in social attitudes toward crime and punishment. However you use your narrative, make sure your story has a point, a reason for being, and make that reason clear to your reader.

What Do You Include in a Narrative?

> Just tell me what happened!
> Get to the punch line!

No one, probably not even your mother, wants to hear everything you did today. Readers, like listeners, want you to be selective, for some things are more important or more interesting than others. Historians review a mass of data and select what they will include and emphasize; they choose a place to begin and a place to end. Even in relating personal experiences, you must select and condense. Generally, you need to cut out the unnecessary, the uninteresting, and the redundant. What you include depends, of course, on what happened and, more importantly, on the purpose or meaning you are trying to convey.

Links between Writing and Reading

	Likely purpose
Lynn Bernardini, "Does This Date . . ."	Share an emotional moment
Tom Haines, "Facing Famine"	Evoke sympathy for and an understanding of famine
Evans Hopkins, "Lockdown"	Persuade audience of the impact of changes in prison sentencing and rehabilitation

Prewriting Tips for Writing Narrative

1. Before you start writing, set aside some time to brainstorm about your paper. If you are writing about a personal experience, you will discover that with time you will remember more and more details. Do you need to do research? Talk to people who were there? Gather information and take notes before you start to write.

2. Complete the following sentence: "I am narrating this story because. . . ." As you gather information, use your purpose statement to decide what to include and what to exclude.

3. Choose a point of view from which to tell the story. Personal narratives tend to be told in the first person ("I"); historical narratives and journalistic stories in the third person ("they," "he," "she").

4. Remember, your narrative must have a beginning, a middle, and an end, but stories do not have to be told in chronological order. You can flash back or forward in your narrative.

5. Look at the narratives in this chapter. Think about how each is organized. Do you see any strategies that might work in your essay?

WRITING

How Do You Structure a Narrative?

Time structures all narratives, although events need not always be arranged in chronological order. A narrative can begin at one point in time and then flash back to an earlier action or event. Langston Hughes's "Salvation" begins with a narrator looking back at an experience that occurred when he was 13, although the story itself is told in the order in which it happened. The most typical inversion is to begin at the end of the narrative and move backward in time to explain how that end was reached. More complex narratives may shift several times back and forth between incidents in the past or between the past and the present. Two cautions may be helpful: first, do not switch time too frequently, especially in short papers; second, make sure that any switches you make are clearly marked for your readers.

Remember as well that you control where your narrative begins and ends. For example, Evans Hopkins begins "Lockdown" with a predawn visit from two prison guards in armored vests and riot helmets; he does not begin with an account of the events that led to the lockdown or with the events that led to his imprisonment. Those details Hopkins fills in later, for they are not as dramatic or central to the points he is trying to make.

Writers frequently change or modify a personal experience in order to tell the story more effectively, heighten the tension, or make their purpose clearer. In her essay "On Keeping a Notebook," essayist and novelist Joan Didion remarks:

> I tell what some would call lies. "That's simply not true," the members of my family frequently tell me when they come up against my memory of a shared event. "The party was not for you, the spider was not a black widow, it wasn't that way at all." Very likely they are right, for not only have I always had trouble distinguishing between what happened and what merely might have happened, but I remain unconvinced that the distinction, for my purposes, matters.

Whenever you recall an experience, even if it happened last week, you do not necessarily remember it exactly as it occurred. The value of a personal narrative does not rest on relating the original experience with absolute accuracy. It does not matter, for example, whether the scene in Auntie Reed's church occurred exactly as Langston Hughes describes it years later. What does matter is that it could have happened as he describes it and that it is faithful to his purpose.

How Do You End a Narrative?

This question might seem to have a really simple answer: your narrative stops at the end of the moment or incident you are narrating. An ending, though, should reflect the reason or purpose for narrating a story. If you are telling a joke, for example, you end with the punch line in order to elicit laughter. In a story that focuses on the significance of the event in your life, you might want to lead up to the climactic moment of insight. Langston Hughes ("Salvation") does that in his final concluding paragraph where he explains the impact this experience had on the rest of his life. If you are using a narrative for a persuasive purpose, end by explaining what you want your reader to take away from the story. Evans Hopkins ("Lockdown") recounts his personal experience of a prison lockdown not just to share his feelings and experiences, but to trace the recent evolution in American attitudes toward prisons and prisoners and to suggest the consequences such attitudes have on the "young lives being thrown away." If you are using narrative to recount an historical event, end with a summary statement of the significance of that event. The short historical narrative—"Blue Hen's Chicks"—at the end of this introduction tells a story about an event during the American Revolution and concludes with a sentence that uses the narrative to explain why Delaware is today known as "The Blue Hen State." Your conclusion should reflect your purpose for telling this story.

How Do You Tell a Narrative?

Two things are especially important in relating your narrative. First, you must choose a *point of view* from which to tell the story. Personal experience narratives, such as those by Hughes, Choi, and Hopkins, are generally told in the first person: the narrator is an actor in the story. Historical narratives

Links between Writing and Reading

	Conclusions
Langston Hughes, "Salvation"	Significance of the event in his life
Tom Haines, "Facing Famine"	His emotional reaction to the event
Marguerite Choi, "The Suddenly Empty Chair"	Her purpose in writing the essay
Evans Hopkins, "Lockdown"	His concluding paragraph as persuasion

and narratives used as illustrations in a larger piece of writing are generally told in the third person. The historian or the reporter, for example, stands outside the narrative and provides an objective view of the actions described. Point of view can vary in one other way. The narrator can reveal only his or her thoughts (using what is known as a limited point of view), or the narrator can reveal what anyone else in the narrative thinks or feels (using the omniscient, or all-knowing) point of view.

Second, you need to decide whether you are going to *show* or *tell* or mix the two. Showing in a narrative involves dramatizing a scene and creating dialogue. Hughes re-creates his experience for the reader by showing what happened and by recording some of the conversation that took place the night he was "saved from sin." Telling, by contrast, means summarizing what happened. Showing makes a narrative more vivid, for it allows the reader to experience the scene directly. Telling allows you to include a greater number of events and details. Either way, selectivity is essential. Even when the experience being narrated took place over a short period of time, such as Hughes's experiences one evening at church, a writer cannot dramatize everything that happened. When an experience lasts four and a half months, as does the lockdown Hopkins describes, a writer could never summarize events on a day-to-day basis. Each writer selects the moments that best give shape and significance to the experience.

How Do You Write Dialogue?

Dialogue creates the illusion of speech, of verbal interaction among the characters in the narrative. It is an illusion because real conversation is longer, slower, and much more boring than written dialogue. You use dialogue when you create scenes in which your characters talk to one another. Dialogue is a way of dramatizing. It reveals characters; your readers can "hear" the characters and get a sense of their personalities from how they react and what they say. Creating small scenes with dialogue in your narrative increases its vividness. Instead of just telling the reader what happened, dialogue allows you to "show" what happened.

Writing effective dialogue in a narrative means recognizing when it can play an important role in your story. Use dialogue sparingly. Dialogue slows

Links between Writing and Reading

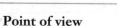

	Point of view
Ron Wallace, "Worry"	Third person ("she worried about people")
Lynn Bernardini, "Does This Date . . ."	First person ("I told my parents")
	Examples of the omission of time
Langston Hughes, "Salvation"	"Finally" (paragraph 6)
	"Now it was really getting late" (11)
Tom Haines, "Facing Famine"	Extra whi.te space after paragraphs (21 and 50)

down the action of a story, and too much dialogue can bring a narrative to a crawl. The purpose of dialogue is to reveal character or to generate tension, not to have characters summarize the events that are happening in the plot. In "Salvation," Hughes creates tension in his narrative by including four tiny scenes with dialogue—two are the appeals that the minister makes to him, one is his aunt's appeal, and one voices Westley's decision to fake being "saved." Hughes might have written, "My aunt begged me to be saved," a simple summary statement. Instead, he generates tension and makes the scene more vivid by having his aunt say, "Langston, why don't you come? Why don't you come and be saved? Oh, Lamb of God! Why don't you come?"

Short exchanges of dialogue are typically set off as if they were separate paragraphs and are "tagged" with something like "he said" or "she replied." Do not get too clever in the verbs used in the tags; they are only likely to distract the reader. The assumption behind dialogue is that speakers take turns. In an exchange of dialogue, you can omit the tags and even the quotation marks that typically are used to mark speech. Toward the end of his essay "Facing Famine," Haines records a conversation in which he tries to find the right English words to convey the feelings that the famine generates in those who suffer through it:

> Misery?
> Yes, Berhanu said calmly, that is a part of it.
> Emptiness? Yes, he said, that too.
> Anguish? Despair?
> His eyes sparkled at the connection.
> Anger? Yes.
> Frustration? Yes.
> Fear? No.
> Fear, Berhanu said, like sorry, was too light a word.
> Terror?
> Yes, Berhanu said, "terror" is a good word.

REVISING

How Do You Revise a Narrative?

Once you have a complete draft of your essay—not just a series of notes—always get feedback: from peer readers, from your instructor, from a writing center tutor. Listen carefully to what your readers say. If several readers see the same problem in your essay, they are right, even if you do not agree. Reconsider each choice that you have made; do not limit your revising to correcting obvious errors and changing an occasional word. Typically, your revision should be directed at three concerns:

- Pruning unnecessary detail
- Making structure clear
- Looking again at the difference between showing and telling

---

Links between Writing and Reading

	Use of showing and telling
Langston Hughes, "Salvation"	Sparse use of dialogue
Tom Haines, "Facing Famine"	Mixture that reveals the despair of the people
Evans Hopkins, "Lockdown"	Mixture in scene in paragraphs 17 to 27

Drafting Tips for Writing Narrative

1. Outline your narrative. Is the plot clear? Are there any places where your readers might have difficulty following the sequence of events?
2. Look carefully at any moment that you have dramatized. Does it add to the tension of your story? Does it reveal something about the characters and their reactions or feelings? Write a one-line justification for any scene you have included.
3. Check your use of point of view. Are you consistent throughout the essay or do you switch from first person to third?
4. Have you signaled the structure of your narrative to your reader? Do you need to introduce some type of typographical device (such as extra white space between blocks of paragraphs) to indicate that the story comes in sections?
5. Recruit readers for your draft, ask them questions, then follow their advice.

Pruning Unnecessary Detail   Remember that your narrative has a purpose; you have a reason for telling this story. Your purpose might be to entertain, to inform, to persuade, or a mixture of all three. On a separate sheet of paper write down your purpose statement and use that statement to test every detail you have included in your narrative. Think about how frustrated you become when someone tries to tell a joke and obscures the punch line. Think about how often you get impatient when people are relating what happened and include lots of unnecessary details. Prune details in your narrative that do not support or illustrate your purpose.

Making the Structure Clear   Narratives are told in time. They can be organized in a straightforward, chronological order, or they can manipulate time by flashing back or even forward. Remember that time changes can be puzzling to your reader unless you clearly signal them. Sometimes changing verb tenses—moving from past tense to present or present to future—is enough of a marker for your reader. More often, writers use a variety of typographical devices to mark such shifts: setting off a section that occurs at a different time by using extra white space before and after; numbering or lettering sections of the essay; or italicizing a section set in a different time. When you are getting advice from your readers, make sure to ask them if

Revising Tips When Writing Narratives

1. Look again at your essay's title. An informative, even catchy, title is a tremendous asset to an essay. If your title seems a little boring, brainstorm some other possibilities. Never title your paper "Narrative Essay," or "Essay," or "Essay #1"!

2. Remember to catch your reader's attention in the opening paragraphs. Look closely at your introduction. Ask a friend or classmate to read it. Does your reader want to continue or to quit?

3. Ask a reader to construct a timeline for what happened in your story. Is the plot clear and unambiguous? Do you ever shift time in the story? If so, is the shift clearly marked or signaled?

4. Look carefully at the dialogue. Does it sound plausible that characters might speak like this? Is it too long? Too wordy? Too formal? Remember, you are creating the illusion of speech rather than transcribing actual speech.

5. Look at your conclusion. How did you end? Did you lead up to a climactic moment or did you just end with a flat conclusion ("And so you can see why this experience was important to me.")? Compare how writers in this chapter end their narratives. You might be able to use similar strategies.

they were ever confused by the sequence of events in the story. A good test, for example, is to ask them to construct a chronological timeline for what happens. If they have problems or make mistakes, you know that you must revise the time changes in your essay.

Looking Again at the Difference between Showing and Telling   Most narratives benefit from having a mixture of showing (dramatizing) and telling (summarizing). Dramatizing a scene involves having the characters verbally interact through dialogue. Remember, though, to keep these scenes short and to choose only appropriate moments. Such scenes can add tension to a story, reveal a conflict among the characters, or show how characters interact. Ask yourself if there are moments in your narrative in which dramatization might be particularly effective. Do not have your characters speak in dialogue unless there is a clear and important reason for including that scene. Do not try to summarize what is happening in the story by having one character narrate events to another: "And so, Maria, remember that I told you yesterday that John took me out for dinner last night and we went to the restaurant where we saw his former girlfriend who dumped him three years ago."

Student Essay

First Draft

Hope Zucker decided to write about a powerful childhood memory—a pair of red shoes that became her "ruby slippers" and the key to the Land of Oz.

My New Shoes

When you are four years old anything longer than five minutes feels like eternity, so when the clerk told me and my mom that it would take three to four weeks for my new shoes to arrive, I was almost in tears. Since seeing *The Wizard of Oz,* I had thought of little else other than owning a pair of ruby slippers. My dreams were full of spinning houses, little munchkins, flying monkeys, and talking lions. All I wanted was to be Dorothy, and the shoe store had made a promise to find me a pair of red mary-janes which would hopefully take me to Munchkin Land and Oz.

For the next three weeks I made all the preparations I could think of in order to become Dorothy. It did not matter how convincing Judy Garland was because I knew in my heart that I was the true Dorothy. I sang "Somewhere Over the Rainbow" day and night, and I played dress up with an old light blue checked dress of my mother's. I even went as far as to carry my dog in a basket, but that did not work out too well. I had my mom braid my long brown hair, and after I insisted, she tied a light blue ribbon around each braid. I skipped wherever I went, and I even went as far as coloring part of our driveway with chalk to create my very own yellow brick road.

The only thing missing to my new persona was my ruby slippers. After my mother explained to me that three weeks really was not that far off in the future, I decided to help the store in their search for my red mary-janes. For a month I called the store everyday when I got home from preschool. Mr. Rogers and Big Bird could wait because there was nothing in the whole wide world that was more important than my red patent leather shoes. By the end of the month, the nice little old ladies at the store knew me by name and thought that I was the cutest child. Lucky for them, they did not have to put up with me.

Finally, after what seemed like years, the lady on the other side of the phone said that yes, my shiny red shoes had arrived. Now I had only to plead with my mother to get her to make a special trip into the city. After a few days of delay and a great deal of futile temper tantrums, my mom took me to the store. I could hardly contain my excitement. During the ride, I practiced the one and only line that only the real Dorothy could say, "There's no place like home." And of course, I clicked my beat up boondockers three times each time I recited my part. It was all practice for the real thing.

As we pulled into the parking lot, all the little old ladies inside the store waved to me as if they had been expecting me for days. I finally got to see my shoes, and they were as perfect as I knew they'd be. I was practically jumping out of my seat when she began to remove the stiff tissue paper surrounding my shoes, so rather than wait for her to fit my little feet into my slippers, I grabbed them from her and did it myself. They were the prettiest pair of shoes any girl could have!

For the next few weeks I was Dorothy and I'd stop everyone I'd see in order to prove it by tapping my heels together and saying, "There's no place like home." But soon my feet grew too big for my ruby slippers, and as I graduated into the next larger size, I no longer wanted to be Dorothy. As I grew up, so did my dreams. Cinderella, now she was someone to be! Yet, once again that phase, like the phases I am going through now, passed fairly quickly.

Comments

Hope made enough copies of her essay so that the whole class could read and then discuss it. After reading her essay to the class, Hope asked her classmates for their reactions. Several students suggested that she tighten her narrative, eliminating details that were not essential to the story. Most of their suggestions were centered in paragraphs 3 and 4. "Why mention Mr. Rogers and Big Bird?" someone asked. "I didn't want you to have to wait several days to pick them up, and I didn't want to be reminded of your temper," commented another. When Hope came to revise her draft, she used this advice. She also eliminated a number of clichés and made a significant change in the ending of the paper. Notice how much more effective the final version is as the result of these minor revisions.

Revised Draft

The Ruby Slippers

To a four-year old, anything longer than five minutes feels like eternity, so when the clerk told me and my mom that it would take three to four weeks for my new shoes to arrive, I was almost in tears. Since seeing *The Wizard of Oz*, I had thought of little else other than owning a pair of ruby slippers. My dreams were full of spinning houses, little munchkins, flying monkeys, and talking lions. All I wanted was to be Dorothy, and the shoe store had made a promise to find me a pair of red mary-janes which would hopefully take me to Munchkin Land and Oz.

For the next three weeks I made all the preparations I could think of in order to become Dorothy. It did not matter how convincing Judy Garland was because I knew in my heart that I was the true Dorothy. I sang "Somewhere Over the Rainbow" day and night, and I played dress up with an old light blue checked dress of my mother's. I even went as far as to carry my dog in a basket. My mom braided my long brown hair, and after I insisted, she tied a light blue ribbon around each braid. I skipped everywhere I went and colored part of our driveway with chalk to create my very own yellow brick road.

The only thing missing was my ruby slippers. After my mother explained that three weeks really was not that far off, I decided to help the store in their search for my red mary-janes. For a month I called the store everyday when I got home from preschool. By the end of the month, the ladies at the store knew me by name.

Finally, the woman on the other end of the phone said that yes, my shiny red shoes had arrived. I could hardly contain my excitement. During the ride, I practiced the one line that only the real Dorothy could say, "There's no place like home." And of course, I clicked my beat up loafers three times each time I recited that line. It was all practice for the real thing.

As we pulled into the parking lot, all the ladies inside the store waved to me as if they had been expecting me. I finally got to see my shoes, and they were as perfect as I had imagined. I was practically jumping out of my seat when she began to remove the stiff tissue paper surrounding my shoes, so rather than wait for her to fit my little feet into my slippers, I grabbed them from her and did it myself. They were the prettiest pair of shoes any girl could have!

For the next few weeks I was Dorothy and I'd stop everyone I'd see in order to prove it by tapping my heels together and saying, "There's no place like home." But soon my feet grew too big for my ruby slippers, and as I graduated into the next larger size, I no longer wanted to be Dorothy. As I grew up, so did my dreams.

Checklist: Some Things to Remember About Writing Narration

❑ Decide first why you are telling the reader *this* story. You must have a purpose clearly in mind.

❑ Choose an illustration, event, or experience that can be covered adequately within the space limitations you face. Do not try to narrate the history of your life in an essay!

❑ Decide on which point of view you will use. Do you want to be a part of the narrative or an objective observer? Which is more appropriate for your purpose?

❑ Keeping your purpose in mind, select the details or events that seem the most important or the most revealing.

❑ Arrange those details in an order—either a strict chronological one or one that uses a flashback. Keep your verb tenses consistent and signal any switches in time.

❑ Remember the differences between showing and telling. Which method will be better for your narrative?

Reading Narration

Every story is a narrative whether it is written in words or illustrated through visuals. All narratives—films, television shows, YouTube videos, jokes, short stories, novels, histories, news stories, personal narrative essays, biographies, autobiographies—share the same devices. As you read, remember what you have learned about how to write a narrative—that knowledge can help you as a reader.

• Narratives are told for a reason or purpose: they might be purely informational (here is what happened or how it happened); they might be entertaining (e.g., jokes are mini-narratives); they can be persuasive (a vivid story of what happened to someone can move you to action or empathy). As you read a narrative, ask yourself, why is the reader telling this story? Is there a thesis or obvious reason for the story?

• Narratives are structured in time. They might open with the first event in the chronological sequence or they might use flashbacks. You can always construct a timeline for a narrative.

• Narratives are always told by someone. The teller might be an objective, omniscient narrator (as in a history text or a newspaper story) or the teller might be an observer or a participant in the story. A guide to the types of point of view can be found in the Glossary and Ready Reference. Always ask yourself, who is telling this story and why might the author be using this point of view?

- Narratives are economical, that is, they do not tell or describe everything. As you read, ask yourself, What has the writer not told me and why might that information have been left out?
- Narratives frequently dramatize scenes within the story by using dialogue. Although dialogue can make the characters more vivid for the reader, dialogue also slows down the pace of the story. Does the narrative you are reading use dialogue? Why might the writer have chosen to render part of a scene in dialogue rather than just describe or summarize what happens?

IN PROSE

Every state has a nickname, and the origins of those nicknames are frequently related in a folktale, a short narrative that explains how the state or the people from the state acquired that name. Delaware has an unusual name—the Blue Hen State—and the University of Delaware mascot is, of course, a large blue hen. Here S. E. Schlosser recounts the folktale that explains how that name came about.

Blue Hen's Chicks

Opening sentence places the story in time and place

Character introduced, single sentence of dialogue—an exaggeration; they are only the "babies" of the hen at home

Story told chronologically

Application of story to the men

Final explanation of the nickname

<u>A Delaware man went to war during the American Revolution.</u> For entertainment, he brought with him two fighting cocks. When asked about these chickens, the soldier said slyly, "They are the chicks of a blue hen that I have at home."

Well, those cocks could fight. They were so fierce, they caused quite a stir among the men. It did not take long for the Delaware troops to begin boasting among the troops from the other states that they could outfight anyone, just like those famous fighting cocks. <u>"We're the Blue Hen's Chickens. We will fight to the end!"</u> became the theme of the Delaware troops. The other troops took to calling the men from Delaware "The Blue Hen's Chicks," and to this day, Delaware is known as the Blue Hen State.

QUESTIONS FOR ANALYSIS

1. Why might the narrative add the word "slyly" to describe how the soldier replies to the question?
2. Why might the speaker call his fighting cocks "chicks" of the hen he has at home?
3. What elements in the narration suggest that this is a folktale? How might a folktale differ from an historical fact?
4. From what point of view is the story narrated? Why that choice?

CRITICAL READING ACTIVITY

Identify the elements of narrative (e.g., plot, structure, character, setting, dialogue) used in the story and analyze how they each contribute to the effectiveness of the whole story.

IN LITERATURE

All stories—whether they are personal essays, imaginative fictions, journalistic reports, or histories—contain the same essential ingredients: a series of events arranged in an order structured through time recounted by a narrator for some purpose. Narratives can range from hundreds, even thousands, of pages to only a single paragraph. Ron Wallace's short story "Worry" is an example of what is called "microfiction," a genre that is limited to a maximum of 250 words.

Worry

RON WALLACE

1   **S**he worried about people; he worried about things. And between them, that about covered it.

2   "What would you think of our daughter sleeping around?" she said.

3   "The porch steps are rotting," he replied. "Someone's going to fall through."

4   They were lying in bed together, talking. They had been lying in bed together talking these twenty-five years. First about whether to have children, he wanted to (although the roof was going fast); she didn't (Down's syndrome, leukemia, microcephaly, mumps). Then, after their daughter was born, a healthy seven pounds eleven ounces ("She's not eating enough"; "The furnace is failing"), they talked about family matters, mostly ("Her friends are hoodlums, her room is a disaster"; "There's something about the brakes, the water heater's rusting out").

5   Worry grew between them like a son, with his own small insistencies and then more pressing demands. They stroked and coddled him; they set a place for him at the table; they sent him to kindergarten, private school, and college. Because he failed at nearly everything and always returned home, they loved him. After all, he was their son.

6   "I've been reading her diary. She does drugs. She sleeps around."

7   "I just don't think I can fix them myself. Where will we find a carpenter?"

8   Their daughter married her high school sweetheart, had a family, and started a health food store in a distant town. Although she recalled her childhood as fondly as anyone—how good her parents had been and how they worried for her, how old and infirm they must be growing, their house going to ruin—she rarely called or visited. She had worries of her own. ■

QUESTIONS FOR ANALYSIS

1. Other than paragraphing, what is the structural device that Wallace uses throughout the story?
2. Why are the people in the story never named?
3. In paragraph 5, a son is mentioned, Did the couple have a literal, that is real, son? What literary device in that paragraph signals the answer to that question?
4. What are the implications of the final line in the story, "She had worries of her own"?

WRITING SUGGESTIONS

1. **Analysis.** In an essay, analyze how the elements of narration (e.g., point of view, selection of detail, structure, dialogue, and even punctuation) contribute to the effect signaled by the word *worry*.
2. Often we find ourselves locked into repetitive patterns, small daily or weekly cycles that define us. Think about a pattern that you see in your own life. In a personal narrative essay, narrate that cycle for your readers. You can tell the story from either the first- or the third-person point of view. You can use some dialogue. Remember, though, to have a central purpose or idea that you wish to convey. Consider the following, as a possible starting point:
   a. A bad (or good) habit or behavior
   b. Situations in which you know how you will always react
   c. An endless topic of debate or disagreement

IN A VISUAL

A narrative tells a story. Generally, stories are told through words printed on a page; sometimes though stories are told through visuals or pictures printed on a page. Probably the most familiar printed visual narratives are comic

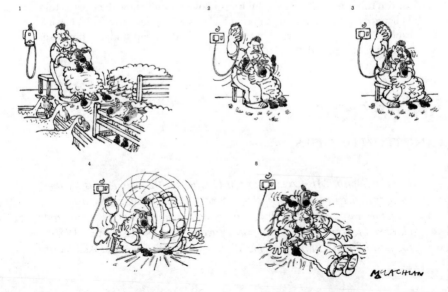

Ed McLachlan/Cartoon Stock

strips or graphic novels. The key moments in the story appear in separate pictures or panels. The reader moves from one image to another. As long as the images are arranged in a chronological order, they might not even need accompanying words. The reader fills in the gaps from her or his own imagination. Here in five scenes, meant to be read from left to right and from top to bottom, the artist visually narrates a story just in images—turnabout is fair play!

QUESTIONS FOR ANALYSIS

1. What do the individual illustrations correspond to in a story told just by words?
2. What kinds of stories can be illustrated? What kinds can be illustrated without using any captions or dialogue boxes?

WRITING SUGGESTIONS

1. **Analysis.** Study the five illustrations and identify what event it depicts in the story. How is it that you understand what is happening in the story without each step or action being described through words? What does this example suggest about the art of effective storytelling in a narrative? In an essay, analyze and assess the cartoon's effectiveness as an example of narration.
2. Imaging your future: Find a group of images—from magazines or online sources—that tell the story, as you imagine it, of the next 20 years of your life. What do you want to accomplish? Where do you want to be? What will your life be like? Use the images to illustrate an essay on how you imagine your future. Write captions for each of the illustrations and make sure that you depict each significant step in your story.
3. What makes for a good story? Select a television show episode, a narrative video on YouTube, or an illustrated children's book and study how the story is told. What goes into an effective, entertaining, or suspenseful narrative? In an essay, explore what can you learn about writing narratives from studying how visual narratives are created.

Salvation

LANGSTON HUGHES

Born in Joplin, Missouri, Langston Hughes (1902–1967) was an important figure in the Harlem Renaissance. He is best known for his jazz- and blues-inspired poetry, though he was also a talented prose writer and playwright. Among his writings are Simple Speaks His Mind *(1950), the first of four volumes of some of his best-loved stories, and* Ask Your

Mama: 12 Moods for Jazz *(1961), one of his later, angry collections of poetry fueled by emotions surrounding the civil rights movements. "Salvation" appeared in* The Big Sea: An Autobiography *(1940), which was published when Hughes was 38 years old and is a memoir of his early years, consisting of a series of short narratives focusing on events and people.*

On Writing: *Hughes once noted that, to him, the prime function of creative writing is "to affirm life, to yeah-say the excitement of living in relation to the vast rhythms of the universe of which we are a part, to untie the riddles of the gutter in order to closer tie the knot between man and God."*

Before Reading

Connecting: Was there a time in your teenage years when you were disappointed by someone or something?

Anticipating: No narrative recounts every minute of an experience. Writers must leave out far more than they include. What events connected with this experience does Hughes leave out of his narrative? Why?

1   I was saved from sin when I was going on thirteen. But not really saved. It happened like this. There was a big revival at my Auntie Reed's church. Every night for weeks there had been much preaching, singing, praying, and shouting, and some very hardened sinners had been brought to Christ, and the membership of the church had grown by leaps and bounds. Then just before the revival ended, they held a special meeting for children, "to bring the young lambs to the fold." My aunt spoke of it for days ahead. That night I was escorted to the front row and placed on the mourners' bench with all the other young sinners, who had not yet been brought to Jesus.

2   My aunt told me that when you were saved you saw a light, and something happened to you inside! And Jesus came into your life! And God was with you from then on! She said you could see and hear and feel Jesus in your soul. I believed her. I had heard a great many old people say the same thing and it seemed to me they ought to know. So I sat there calmly in the hot, crowded church, waiting for Jesus to come to me.

3   The preacher preached a wonderful rhythmical sermon, all moans and shouts and lonely cries and dire pictures of hell, and then he sang a song about the ninety and nine safe in the fold, but one little lamb was left out in the cold. Then he said: "Won't you come? Won't you come to Jesus? Young lambs, won't you come?" And he held out his arms to all us young sinners there on the mourners' bench. And the little girls cried. And some of them jumped up and went to Jesus right away. But most of us just sat there.

4   A great many old people came and knelt around us and prayed, old women with jet-black faces and braided hair, old men with work-gnarled

hands. And the church sang a song about the lower lights are burning, some poor sinners to be saved. And the whole building rocked with prayer and song.

5   Still I kept waiting to *see* Jesus.

6   Finally all the young people had gone to the altar and were saved, but one boy and me. He was a rounder's son named Westley. Westley and I were surrounded by sisters and deacons praying. It was very hot in the church, and getting late now. Finally Westley said to me in a whisper: "God damn! I'm tired o' sitting here. Let's get up and be saved." So he got up and was saved.

7   Then I was left all alone on the mourners' bench. My aunt came and knelt at my knees and cried, while prayers and song swirled all around me in the little church. The whole congregation prayed for me alone, in a mighty wail of moans and voices. And I kept waiting serenely for Jesus, waiting, waiting—but he didn't come. I wanted to see him, but nothing happened to me. Nothing! I wanted something to happen to me, but nothing happened.

8   I heard the songs and the minister saying: "Why don't you come? My dear child, why don't you come to Jesus? Jesus is waiting for you. He wants you. Why don't you come? Sister Reed, what is this child's name?"

9   "Langston," my aunt sobbed.

10   "Langston, why don't you come? Why don't you come and be saved? Oh, Lamb of God! Why don't you come?"

11   Now it was really getting late. I began to be ashamed of myself, holding everything up so long. I began to wonder what God thought about Westley, who certainly hadn't seen Jesus either, but who was now sitting proudly on the platform, swinging his knickerbockered legs and grinning down at me, surrounded by deacons and old women on their knees praying. God had not struck Westley dead for taking his name in vain or for lying in the temple. So I decided that maybe to save further trouble, I'd better lie, too, and say that Jesus had come, and get up and be saved.

12   So I got up.

13   Suddenly the whole room broke into a sea of shouting, as they saw me rise. Waves of rejoicing swept the place. Women leaped in the air. My aunt threw her arms around me. The minister took me by the hand and led me to the platform.

14   When things quieted down, in a hushed silence, punctuated by a few ecstatic "Amens," all the new young lambs were blessed in the name of God. Then joyous singing filled the room.

15   That night, for the last time in my life but one—for I was a big boy twelve years old—I cried. I cried, in bed alone, and couldn't stop. I buried my head under the quilts, but my aunt heard me. She woke up and told my uncle I was crying because the Holy Ghost had come into my life, and because I had seen Jesus. But I was really crying because I couldn't bear to tell her that I had lied, that I had deceived everybody in the church, that I hadn't seen Jesus, and that now I didn't believe there was a Jesus any more, since he didn't come to help me. ∎

QUESTIONS ON SUBJECT AND PURPOSE

1. Who narrates the story? From what point in time is it told?
2. What does the narrator expect to happen when he is to be saved? What does happen?
3. Why does the narrator cry at the end of the story?
4. What was Hughes's attitude toward his experience when it first happened? At the time he originally wrote this selection? How does the opening sentence reflect that change in attitude?

QUESTIONS ON STRATEGY AND AUDIENCE

1. Why did Hughes not tell the story in the present tense? How would doing so change the story?
2. How much dialogue is used in the narration? Why does Hughes not use more?
3. Why does Hughes blend telling with showing in the story?
4. How much time is represented by the events in the story? Where does Hughes compress the time in his narrative? Why does he do so?

QUESTIONS ON VOCABULARY AND STYLE

1. What is the effect of the short paragraphs (5, 9, and 12)? How does Hughes use paragraphing to help shape his story?
2. How much description does Hughes include in his narrative? What types of details does he single out?
3. What is the effect of the exclamation marks used in paragraph 2?
4. Try to identify or explain the following phrases: *the ninety and nine safe in the fold* (paragraph 3), *the lower lights are burning* (4), *a rounder's son* (6), *knickerbockered legs* (11).

WRITING SUGGESTIONS

1. **Doing a Critical Analysis.** Narratives are constructed in time. In an essay, analyze how Hughes manipulates time in retelling this experience to construct an artful and moving narrative.
2. **Journaling or Blogging.** Make a list of significant moments—both high and low points—that you remember from your early teenage years. Expand one of the moments.
3. **Practicing in a Paragraph.** We have all been disappointed by someone or something. Choose a particular moment from your past. Narrate that experience in a paragraph revealing what that experience meant to you at the time.
4. **Writing the Personal Essay.** Have you ever had an experience that changed your life? It does not need to be dramatic change—just a conviction that you will never do that again. Narrate the experience making sure you reveal what the significance of the experience was for you.
5. **Finding Reading Connections.** If Hughes was disappointed, Bernardini in "Does This Date Mean Anything to You" (this chapter) got what she had sought for so long. Compare the two experiences as they are re-created in the essays.

6. **Exploring Links Online.** In Hughes's poem "Theme for English B," he assumes the voice of a 22-year-old student writing a paper for an English course. At the time it was written, he was 47 years old. Similarly, the narrator in this story is 12, but the memoir was written when Hughes was in his late 30s. Compare the two narrators whom Hughes has created.

7. **Writing the Research Paper.** Is "Salvation" really autobiographical? Did Hughes really "lose" his faith as a result of this experience? Analyze in a research essay the significance (or insignificance) of this event in his life. Be sure to document information or direct quotations taken from source material.

For Further Study

Focusing on Grammar and Writing. Look first at the definitions in the Glossary and Ready Reference at the back of this book and then go through Hughes's essay and make a list of all the adjectives and adverbs he uses. Sometimes we assume that vividness in writing comes from using many adjectives and adverbs. Is that true here? What parts of speech create the vividness?

Working Together. Working in small groups, discuss how Hughes creates tension in his narrative. What devices does he use to keep the reader in suspense about the event's outcome?

Seeing Other Modes at Work. Hughes uses description to create a vivid sense of the place in which the experience occurs.

Does This Date Mean Anything to You?

LYNN BERNARDINI

Nursing was a second career for Lynn Bernardini. Her specialty was neonatal intensive care where, as she writes, "I help other women's babies survive." This essay was her first publication, originally appearing in the collection Intensive Care: More Poetry and Prose by Nurses *(2003).*

On Writing: *Asked about the essay, Bernardini simply said, "I wrote this true story of me from my heart."*

Before Reading

Connecting: Probably few readers have had an experience similar to Bernardini's. What is it, then, about the essay that invites readers to connect with her experience?

Anticipating: As you read the essay, do you expect that Bernardini will use her narrative to argue for a change in society's attitudes toward pregnant, unwed teenagers?

1   Twenty-three years ago, long before I became a registered nurse and began working in a neonatal intensive care unit, I gave my newborn son up for adoption.

2   My relationship with the baby's father was insignificant. We were both young and carefree, living only for the moment in the time of Woodstock, flower children, and the Vietnam War—certainly we were not suited for a lifelong relationship. But in 1970, unwed mothers were scorned, and homes for such mothers were common. When my parents learned of my pregnancy and my refusal to marry the baby's father, I was sent away.

3   Because living at the "Home" would be very expensive, I opted for my parents' less costly counter offer: I would live with a family and work for them, babysitting and housekeeping. A nineteen-year-old immature teenager, I was away from home for the first time, and strange things were happening to my body. The family was pleasant enough, the work was fair, and the kids were good. But I had shamed my parents, I was estranged from my friends, I was alone. And soon I would be abandoning my child.

4   I couldn't even do pregnancy correctly. Swollen, tired, and finally toxic with severe preeclampsia, I had to be hospitalized. The doctors told me I might die; even then, I didn't care. Fortunately, I met a social worker at the hospital clinic—she became my angel—and there was one OB nurse who really cared. These women talked to me, always remaining supportive and professional. But none of my family members came to visit. None of my friends were allowed to know. I had no significant other who cared. In two days, when l was discharged back to my "family," I realized that it was really just me and my baby—I had no one to cry to but him. I swore that he was not going to suffer for my mistakes.

5   A few mornings after my hospitalization, my contractions started. At first, I couldn't figure out what was happening—before this I'd only guessed what labor might be like. I tiptoed downstairs from my room and left a note on the kitchen table, hoping the woman of the family I lived with would find it. "After your kids and your husband are off in the morning," I wrote, "please come check on me and bring me back to the hospital." Sure enough, I would give birth eighteen hours later, but my temporary "mother" said she couldn't stay with me. Her kids were due home at 3 P.M.

6   Do you have any idea what labor feels like to a teenager in a room all alone? A nurse comes in for two minutes once an hour. There's nothing to do but lie on your back staring at a clock. A resident comes to check on you every two or three hours, asking the same monotone questions. When it gets dark outside, the demons of *Beowulf* come out: Women scream, people run, babies cry. I tried to breathe correctly, as I had learned in the classes that were given to us unwed mothers, but we'd also been told that true Lamaze wasn't possible. After all, they'd said, the fathers weren't involved, and a mother couldn't do Lamaze by herself. Now that I'm a nurse, I'm a strong believer: No one should ever go through the birth process alone.

7   As I labored, I heard fathers making happy phone calls in the hall. Nurses kept calling me by my mother's name, as if I were married. I just wanted them to call me by my first name. I wanted someone to be nice to me, rather than scowling every time they came into my cubicle. I didn't ask for anything; I thought if I was quiet and good, the nurses would like me. I only wanted some ice or to have someone sit by me in the chair. I hurt inside, I hurt outside. I hurt in my soul. But I was a clinic patient, not happily married and so, I told myself, I was getting what I deserved. Shame on me. This was the price I had to pay.

8   Of course, my water couldn't break when the resident was in the room. It broke when I was alone, and by the time someone answered my call bell, my knees were up and the baby's head was out. I heard nurses' voices yelling *Don't push, don't push* and felt someone shoving an anesthesia mask over my face as my stretcher was being pushed down the hall into a bright room. Then a doctor I'd never seen before was standing over me in a strange corridor and asking, "Why do you women always have to have babies so fast in the middle of the night?"

9   He'd delivered my baby boy, he explained, but he wasn't my doctor. And he advised me not to look at or hold my son. "It will be better that way. Just get back to your life, and I'll see you next year to do this all over again. Ladies like you always come back."

10   That morning I called the family I was staying with. I didn't phone my mother until later that afternoon; then all I said was, "It's over."

11   My hospital social worker came to visit and brought me an inexpensive bracelet made of violets—a gift, she said, from my son. She told me where my baby was if I wanted to see him. I did, and so we took that long walk.

12   He was in the nursery, over in the corner away from the viewing window with a sign on his bed: Do Not Show. The social worker, my angel, brought him to the window and unwrapped him. He was whole, beautiful, blond. He looked just like me. And he was just as alone. I knew what was right for him. I knew I was not to be his mother. I only wanted to hold him and hug him once to say good-bye.

13   My angel said she would be back the next day to bring me into the nursery to hold him, but I never saw her again. Overnight, I'd been assigned a new social worker who agreed with the doctor that I shouldn't see or hold my baby, that I should consider him dead.

14   I snuck back to the nursery twice. The first time I saw my baby alone, highlighted by the sun as if something from beyond was watching over him. The next time, he was gone. My arms would never hold or hug him. I'd never be able to ask him to understand or to forgive me.

15   I stayed with my assigned family for another month. When it was time for me to go home, I'd been away six months. I still have no idea where I was supposed to have been for that amount of time; my parents never said what they had told the neighbors. And no one asked.

16   Eight weeks later, my angel sent me the hospital birth certificate—my only keepsake and the only proof that my baby really existed. No pictures. No warm fuzzy blanket. No memories.

17   It took me years to like myself, to decide I was a good person, to under-stand that postpartum depression happens even when you don't bring a baby home. No one discussed any of this with me because, technically, I didn't *have* a baby. To most people, I had simply been on vacation.

18   For twenty-three years, I wondered. What ever happened to him? Where was he? Was he happy? Was he alive? What was he like? Every time I heard about a child being abducted, abused, or killed, I would think, *It could be him.*

19   In 1974, I married my friend and soul mate who knew all about my child. He understood that I would never go looking for this lost-to-me child. I'd given him life so he could make someone else's life whole. I wasn't going to ruin that by unexpectedly popping into his life.

20   "But," I told my husband, "if this child finds me, you'll have to accept him as you've accepted me."

21   "No problem," he said. He loved me.

22   Nevertheless, I worried that if I got pregnant again, some divine in-tervention might pay me back for what I'd done. When I did get pregnant, I worried the whole nine months. Would I have a miscarriage? Would I ever have another son? I had abandoned my firstborn and that made me, I once believed, a bad person. But lives change. Now I have a healthy family, a home, a career in a busy neonatal intensive care unit where I help other women's babies survive. I'm very good at what I do. And my husband and I have three sons: our own two and a special friend.

23   In August 1992, I received a phone call from an agency in New Haven.

24   "Does June 2, 1970, mean anything to you?" a woman asked. I hesitated for a long time. After all, this was a date I'd been told to forget by the judge when I'd signed the final adoption papers. That date meant everything to me, but society didn't want me to recognize it. How could I admit out loud to the stranger on the phone that my world had changed that day in 1970? I had grown up that day. I had become a mother that day, a hidden-away teenager who disgraced her family. That's the day every year that I cried uncontrol-lably. But no one was supposed to know.

25   "Does that date mean anything to you?" the voice repeated. If that call meant what I thought it meant, did I really want this? Did I want to explain my disgrace to my teenage-sons? Would this be a reason for others to blame me more than I'd blamed myself?

26   "Yes," I whispered to the stranger on the phone. "Yes, my wish has come true. On that date, I gave birth to a son."

27   Phyllis, the agency representative, explained that my son wanted to contact me. Two months later, I received a letter in which my son introduced himself and gave me a short history of his life. At last I knew: He was alive.

28   We met for the first time in May, 1993, just after Mother's Day. Fear of the unknown made me more nervous that day than on any other day in my life. Once again, I had to do this alone. We both had to do this alone.

29   I arranged to arrive at the restaurant first. My signal to him was that I would be reading a book. It was a good book—it helped me calm down. In fact, it was so good I suddenly realized there was a pair of shoes standing by

my table. Then I heard my name. This is it, I said to myself. Is he going to hate me, yell at me? What will he think of me?

30   I looked up to meet my son, my adult son. To my delight, he brought pictures from his mother, and I was able to watch him grow up in front of me. The similarities in our lives were eerie. His mother is a nurse. My husband and his father work for the same company. He has a sister with my first name. My husband and I once thought about buying a house down the street from his house. These facts—how close our lives had been all along—gave us chills.

31   We talked and laughed for a few hours. We agreed to keep in touch. And I finally got to give him a hug. It felt so good, that twenty-three-year-old touch. It had sparks.

32   When I told my children that they had a half brother, they accepted the news and couldn't wait to meet him. They told all their friends, and I too could at last speak out about a subject that had been taboo. I showed pictures to everyone: A twenty-three-year-old, a seventeen-year-old, and a fourteen-year-old, all going their own directions with their own lives, all their lives a part of mine.

33   I've explained to my two children that I am Bill's biological mother but not his mom, knowing they might not understand until they have children of their own. The wonderful lady who wanted him as much as I did, who was there for him through the good times, the bad times, and the sick times, is his mother. He turned out to be a good person, so I know she was a wonderful mother, comfortable enough with his love to guide him back to me.

34   I'd thought, after all these years, that attitudes toward mothers who opted for adoption had changed. But recently, after seeing how one teenage mom in our hospital was treated when she gave up her baby, my nightmares returned. Giving your baby away—a part of yourself—is a major decision, ideally made after much thought and consultation, both before and after the delivery. Holding the infant won't change a mother's mind. Taking pictures of her baby or having a lasting memento won't either. Some mothers need to smell, kiss, touch, and cry over their infants before they can let them go. They may want keepsakes, something to hold on to and look at in the days to come.

35   Knowing what I went through as a young unwed mother makes me kinder and more supportive of women who make the same difficult decision I made. And I know I've been blessed: I'm not his real mother, I'm his friend, the one who gave him life. But photos of my grown-up, adopted-away son now sit on my windowsill. I have his hugs every time we see each other. Knowing he won a "Beautiful Baby" contest makes me proud. Seeing how, growing up, he looked like my sons, makes me content. Noticing the family resemblance now among my sons warms my heart.

36   It's as if all the pieces have come together at last.   ∎

QUESTIONS ON SUBJECT AND PURPOSE

1. Bernardini met her son Bill in 1993. Based on what Bernardini includes in her narrative, what more recent event might have triggered the essay?
2. What does Bernardini mean when she explains to her other children that she is "Bill's biological mother but not his mom" (paragraph 33)?
3. Why might Bernardini have chosen to write about this experience so many years after it occurred?

QUESTIONS ON STRATEGY AND AUDIENCE

1. Bernardini opens with a one-sentence paragraph. What are the key narrative events that she introduces in that sentence?
2. From what point of view does Bernardini narrate her story?
3. As a reader, how do you react to the narrative? Was it moving? Why or why not? Did you expect it to have a more argumentative tone?

QUESTIONS ON VOCABULARY AND STYLE

1. What role does the question in the title play in the story?
2. What societal attitude is revealed by the delivering doctor's comments in paragraph 9?
3. Be prepared to define the following phrases and words: *neonatal* (paragraph 1), *estranged* (3), *preeclampsia* (4).

WRITING SUGGESTIONS

1. **Doing a Critical Analysis.** Time is the primary organizational pattern in any narrative. Along the timeline, the writer creates a series of scenes that reveal the unfolding action. In an essay, analyze the narrative structure that Bernardini uses in the essay and how it functions in creating an effective and moving story.
2. **Journaling or Blogging.** Brainstorm some moments from your memory in which you felt the special connection between yourself and one of your parents (remember that a parent does not need to be a birth parent).
3. **Practicing in a Paragraph.** Select one of those moments and expand it into a paragraph that re-creates that moment for the reader. Show, do not tell, its significance.
4. **Writing the Personal Essay.** Using a chronological timeline, create a series of scenes that reveal how that special connection evidenced itself over time.
5. **Finding Reading Connections.** Bernard R. Berelson in "The Value of Children" (Chapter 4) categorizes the reasons why people want children. Not everyone, though, wants or can keep a child. What might be some of the reasons? Explore the possible motivations.

6. **Exploring Links Online.** Not every reunion between birth parents and child is a positive experience. Locate some examples of different experiences and in an essay compare how other writers handle the reunion.

7. **Writing the Research Paper.** A recent study found that, in 2011, 36 percent of all births in the United States were to unmarried mothers. Bernardini notes that in 1970, "unwed mothers were scorned." Is the stigma attached to being an unwed mother a thing of the past? Research current attitudes toward single mothers giving birth and keeping their children.

For Further Study

Focusing on Grammar and Writing. How does Bernardini use paragraphing to shape and emphasize events in her narrative? What does this suggest about the role of paragraphs in a narrative?

Working Together. Divide up the essay and then work in small groups to identify all of the examples of prejudice, scorn, and even cruelty that Bernardini encountered. What is the effect of these examples?

Seeing Other Modes at Work. The essay makes extensive use of cause and effect in explaining why events happened as they did and the consequences that Bernardini felt as a result of her decision.

Facing Famine

TOM HAINES

Tom Haines grew up in the suburbs of Pittsburgh, Pennsylvania, and worked as a computer programmer in a bank after college. He took three months off to travel and never returned to his old job. He went to Berkeley for a journalism degree and spent the next 10 years as a news reporter. After a period as a freelance writer, he accepted a position as staff travel writer at the Boston Globe. *Haines has accumulated a number of awards for his travel writing, including Travel Journalist of the Year by the Society of Travel Writers. "Facing Famine" originally appeared in the* Boston Globe *in 2003.*

On Writing: Commenting on the role of the writer as a narrator in an essay such as this, Haines remarked: "If you have something to say compelling about yourself, fine, but it better be pretty compelling. . . . I think that the standard has to be pretty high when you introduce yourself into the story—not necessarily if you're doing this as a part of the narrative, such as 'I went there . . .; we went there . . .' in order to move the plot along, but more if you are making a point about your perceptions."

Before Reading

Connecting: American media regularly carry stories about famine in Africa. Famine, of course, is something that Americans have never experienced. Does Haines's essay make the famine "more real" to you as a reader than what you have seen or read elsewhere? If so, why? If not, why?

Anticipating: As you read, think about why Haines might be telling this story in this way. What might he want his readers to feel or to do after reading the essay? Can you find any evidence in the essay to support your conclusion?

1 **B**urtukan Abe braces against the hard mud wall as Osman, her two-year-old son, wails and wobbles on stick legs.

2 Are there others? I ask.

3 Yes, one, she says. A boy, one month old. He is inside.

4 There is no turning back. Through the low, narrow doorway, in the darkness that guards cool by day, heat by night, lies little Nurhusein.

5 May I see him?

6 This journey began weeks earlier, when yet another report described widespread drought and the threat of famine across much of Africa.

7 What can that life be like?

8 Travel often approaches boundaries of wealth and health. But what does it feel like to cross those boundaries and enter a place that is, everywhere, collapsing? What comes from knowing people who, with an empty grain basket or a thinning goat, edge closer to death?

9 The route led first to Addis Ababa, a highland capital, then east and south, down into rolling stretches of the Great Rift Valley. In the tattered town of Ogolcho, Berhanu Muse, a local irrigation specialist, agreed to serve as translator and guide.

10 A narrow road of rock headed south, through one village, then another, for one hour, then two.

11 In late afternoon, before evening wind lifted dirt from north to south, east to west, we stopped and parked near a hilltop. A man and woman collected grain from a tall stick bin on the corner of their rectangular plot of land.

12 Gebi Egato offered his hand from his perch inside the bin. Halima, his wife, smiled warmly, then carried a half-filled sack toward the family's low, round hut. Abdo, a three-year-old with determined eyes, barreled out the door.

13 I asked if we could stay.

14 "Welcome," Gebi said.

15 For four nights, a photographer and I would sleep here, beneath open sky, then wake to wander this village of one thousand people. We would step

into a schoolhouse, a clinic, and other thatch-roofed huts, including the one that held Nurhusein.

16   But that first afternoon, the village came to us. They were mostly old, all men, a group of perhaps two dozen. Many held walking sticks, one a long spear. One man said he would like to show us something: a hole, not too far, that used to hold water. The hole was shallow and wide, perhaps the size of a Boston backyard. It was empty, nothing but hard earth.

17   The men calmly debated how many months it had been since water filled the hole. Flies buzzed and jumped from eyelids to lips.

18   A young schoolteacher, a specialist in math and science, sat at my side, his legs crossed, hands in his lap.

19   "Thirst is thirst, hunger is hunger," he said.

20   Hours later, I awoke to a setting moon and could imagine this land as it long had been: Beneath my cot, wheat, barley, and teff shot from the ground. Birds swarmed tree branches, trading throaty, bubbling calls. Water pooled in ditches and holes. Thick green hedges framed the farmyard.

21   Gebi would describe to me what this can feel like. The land offers so much bounty, so much comfort, he said, that even when the sun is high and hot, you want to lie down on the earth, close your eyes, and sleep.

22   In the hut's outer room there is a low wooden bench, but little else. The food, furniture, even a grandmother and three uncles have gone.

23   Now five people remain: Burtukan, the mother, age nineteen; Abdurkedir Beriso, her husband, twenty-seven; Abduraman Beriso, his brother, sixteen. And the children, Osman and Nurhusein.

24   They have no animals, no money. Neighbors share hard bread and flour.

25   "I have nowhere to go," Abdurkedir told me. "I will die here."

26   From behind a curtain, in the hut's back room, I hear the rustle of blankets, a whimper, a soothing voice: sounds of a mother gathering a baby in her arms.

27   On our first morning, as nighttime hilltop sounds—a howling hyena, a barking dog, a farting donkey—gave way to those of dawn, we were outsiders, in the cool air, listening.

28   Beneath Gebi and Halima's thatch roof, Abdo squealed and pouted. Bontu, barely a year old, cried for breakfast.

29   Soon, with the fire made, the children fed, Halima strapped plastic canisters on the back of the family donkey and began to walk. Gebi followed with the ox.

30   Halima sauntered gracefully, as though out for a stroll. She crossed a parched soccer field to a footpath lined with huts. She greeted a woman walking toward her. They held hands and talked.

31   Farther along, in an empty cradle of land set back from the trail, a stack of branches and twigs covered a hole roughly twelve inches in diameter. Three times, the government had tried to dig a well in this village, which sits far from any river. The last time, a powerful machine made the narrow hole and bore in search of water. Villagers gathered and watched as earth spit upward. Then the drill bit broke, 820 feet underground. It was there still.

32   Halima walked on for more than an hour, then stopped in a spot of shade. She untied the canisters and knelt by a wide pond of muddy water. The pond teemed with salmonella, the root of typhoid fever, and parasites that thrive in intestines, infecting 70 percent of Adere Lepho's children.

33   Another young woman leaned at the pond's edge and filled every last ounce of space in her canister. She stuffed the spout with a plug of withered grass.

34   Hundreds of people came each day to this pond, the only water source for Adere Lepho and two neighboring villages, and carted home water to quench the thirst of thousands.

35   A month earlier, this pond, too, had been nearly empty. Then two days of heavy February rain filled it. How long would it last? Even village elders, men and women forty, forty-five, and fifty years old, had never seen this kind of drought.

36   Two years earlier, and two years before that, meager rains had fallen. Families had to sell animals, eat thinner harvests, and spend precious savings just to survive. But this was worse: the February downpour was the first time it had rained in nearly a year.

37   Late the next afternoon, rain fell. As the drops landed thick and heavy, men, women, and children took shelter in the low, open building that houses the village's grain mill. After three, maybe four minutes, the rain stopped.

38   Women heaved sacks of grain, some of them holding well-rationed harvests from years past, others gifts from farmland half a world away, onto a scale. Across the room, the mill owner sat alongside a conveyor belt spun by a howling generator, the only power in the village. The owner opened sacks into the mouth of a grinder that turned kernel to flour. Dust filled the air, sticking to hair and eyelashes.

39   Outside, dozens of men gathered beneath the branches of a wide tree.

40   Gebi Tola, elected leader of a local farmers' group, explained that the government had offered land for ten volunteers to move to another region. The government owns all land in Ethiopia. This resettlement program provided a rare chance.

41   The men, sitting on the ground in orderly rows, faced Tola. He explained that some plots of land were north, in a neighboring district. Most would be farther, three hundred miles to the west.

42   Voices rose. How can we know this land is good? one man asked. How can we trust that life will be better there?

43   Kedir Husein, a young father who had stood to ask many questions, stepped away from the group. He told me he had decided not to volunteer to leave.

44   "I am afraid," he said.

45   Nurhusein emerges, his head resting in the crook of his mother's left elbow.

46   A soft cotton blanket opens to shocks of slick, curly hair. Tiny fingers spread in the air. I touch Nurhusein's forehead, cool and smooth.

47   "He is beautiful," I say.

48   Nurhusein bleats softly. His lips often latch on to a dry breast. He has a small stomachache, Burtukan tells me.

49   The bleating rises then falls, just beyond the blanket's edge.

50   Nurhusein is already too wise. It is as if he knows.

51   Morning inside Gebi Egato's hut. Glowing coals. Boisterous children. Hearty porridge. A calf, head low, softly chewed its cud.

52   Shilla, the oldest at five, licked her fingers and pondered her favorite foods as Abdo crammed both hands full of porridge.

53   "Milk," she said. She raised her head and smiled. "And sugar."

54   Finished, Shilla and Abdo scrambled to waiting friends. Gebi and Halima took turns digging a wooden scoop deep into a jug decorated with shells.

55   Each bite brought more peril.

56   Gebi's tired cow and thirsty goats were giving little milk. The porridge was made from wheat that had been meant as seed for planting if the spring rains came. Neighbors with less were already selling cows and goats, driving prices down.

57   As the coals darkened, I asked how long the family could last.

58   Gebi told me that in two weeks the family's wheat would be gone. He would then sell his goats, then the cow. Then the ox and, finally, the donkey. He paused.

59   "Five months," he said.

60   Gebi, like most villagers a Muslim, said he was confident rain would come. Then he could partner his ox with that of a neighbor and together they could churn the dark, moist earth.

61   "We have seen so much hardship already, God will not add more," Gebi said. "I hope."

62   After breakfast, Gebi took the donkey and walked beneath the high sun for three hours. He crested three low ridges and crossed three shallow valleys. The first was carpeted in six inches of dust. The second traced the steep gorge of a dry creek. The third, staggered with acacia trees, opened widely toward the village of Cheffe Jilla.

63   A group of men, women, children, and donkeys swayed in the village's main square. White sacks of grain sat in lopsided piles. Gebi joined the hopeful and registered his name in a government office.

64   I saw Gebi Tola, the leader of Adere Lepho's farmers' association, standing beneath a tree. He told me families from his village would take home five hundred sacks of grain. But they could use a thousand. How do you judge the needy when a whole village is staggering?

65   He spoke quickly. A crowd of dozens, young, old, pressed in around us.

66   I asked Gebi how he felt.

67   "I feel sorry," he said.

68   I had grown used to stoicism. But sorry? I stepped aside with Berhanu, our translator. "Sorry" does not feel like the right word, I said.

69   In English, I explained, "sorry" often has a light sense. Sorry I stepped on your toe. Sorry I'm late for dinner. It is not something felt by someone watching his friends and neighbors beginning to starve.

70   Berhanu is a compassionate, intimate man. He raised his hand to his chin.

71   He told me that, in that case, "sorry" was not the word he meant.

72   The crowd moved in again and curious eyes followed our exchange.

73   I asked Berhanu to choose another English word that more closely matched the Oromigna word Tola had used.

74   He could not find an exact translation. I asked him to describe the feeling.

75   "Well," Berhanu said, "it is the feeling you have when something bad happens. Say, for example, when you lose your lovely brother. Is there a word in English for that?"

76   Misery?

77   Yes, Berhanu said calmly, that is part of it.

78   Emptiness? Yes, he said, that too.

79   Anguish, despair?

80   His eyes sparked at the connection.

81   Anger? Yes.

82   Frustration? Yes.

83   Fear? No.

84   Fear, Berhanu said, like sorry, was too light a word.

85   Terror?

86   Yes, Berhanu said, "terror" is a good word.

87   I stand before Nurhusein and start to cry.

88   Is it empathy? I have a ten-month-old son, a spirited boy with muscles across his back and a quick laugh.

89   Or am I crying from fear?

90   In the hot sun, looking from hut to hut, from face to face, the problem was always too vast.

91   I stare at Nurhusein. I cannot look again into his mother's eyes.   ■

QUESTIONS ON SUBJECT AND PURPOSE

1. Haines is a travel writer and the story appeared in the travel section of a newspaper. Is this the type of essay that you would expect to find in this section of a newspaper? Why or why not?

2. Where is this story taking place? In what part of the world?

3. Based on your reading experience, what purpose might Haines have had in writing the essay?

QUESTIONS ON STRATEGY AND AUDIENCE

1. Look carefully at the essay. In five places in the essay, Haines uses extra white space to mark divisions within the text. Locate those places.
2. Why is Haines so moved by the sight of the infant Nurhusein?
3. Who is Haines's audience? How does that audience influence the essay?

QUESTIONS ON VOCABULARY AND STYLE

1. How does its place of original publication (a newspaper) influence the paragraphing of the essay?
2. What is the effect of the passage in which Haines tries to find English words to describe the emotions that Gebi Tola felt (paragraphs 66–86)?
3. Be prepared to define the following words: *sauntered* (paragraph 30), *teemed* (32), *stoicism* (68), *empathy* (88).

WRITING SUGGESTIONS

1. **Doing a Critical Analysis.** Narratives typically use dialogue sparingly since it slows down the telling of the story. Why might Haines use so much dialogue? How is the dialogue related to the purpose of his narrative?
2. **Journaling or Blogging.** Do you have any emotional reaction to the essay? Do you feel indifferent? Concerned? Explore your reaction to the essay and why you feel that way.
3. **Practicing in a Paragraph.** Using the materials from the essay, write a paragraph in which you try to get readers to sponsor financially the infant Nurhusein.
4. **Writing the Personal Essay.** A single example puts a human face on a situation that cannot be achieved with just facts and statistics. Pick a painful social situation—for example, poverty, homelessness, chronic illness, old age, abuse—and put a human face on the problem. Interview someone or create a fictional character. Construct a narrative in which you use this one person to create empathy and understanding in your readers.
5. **Finding Reading Connections.** How might Peter Singer—"The Singer Solution to World Poverty" (Chapter 9)—react to the plight of the Ethiopian families in Haines's essay?
6. **Exploring Links Online.** Access images of the "Famine in East Africa" and compare the differences between a story told in words and a story told in photographs.
7. **Writing the Research Paper.** What are conditions like in Ethiopia today? Has anything improved or gotten worse? Using a variety of online and print sources, write a formal research paper on the problem. You might want to use a mix of photographs, statistics, and examples to make your paper more vivid and informative.

For Further Study

Focusing on Grammar and Writing. Haines uses a number of sentence fragments. Why? What is the effect that he is trying to achieve? Is the strategy effective?

Working Together. The essay originally appeared in a newspaper. The narrow-column format is why the essay has so many paragraphs. Working in small groups, select one of the sections of the essay and see how often one-sentence paragraphs might be combined into larger units.

Seeing Other Modes at Work. The essay includes description, cause and effect, and even elements of definition and persuasion.

The Suddenly Empty Chair

"MARGUERITE CHOI"

"Marguerite Choi" is a pseudonym. The article was published in the Chronicle of Higher Education *in April 2012. The author was identified only as a "visiting lecturer at a college in the southwestern United States."*

Before Reading

Connecting: Have you ever worried about a classmate or friend who seemed depressed?

Anticipating: What would you do if you knew that a fellow student was depressed?

1   **H**e only missed one day of class. As an instructor, when you look at your roster and see exemplary attendance, one day usually doesn't raise concern. But there's always that little voice in the back of your mind. The one that says, "This kid has record attendance. He's never missed a quiz or an assignment. E-mails when he's going to be late. Apologizes when he is. I hope he's OK."

2   Then you read the headline: "Student found dead on campus. Police investigating." And your heart sinks.

3   I cannot explain why, but I knew it was my student. I walked past his fraternity house later that morning. Police cars and TV-crew vans crowded the parking lot. From across the street I watched the dubious displays of grief and mourning from his brothers—young men, sitting sprawled out in tattered lawn chairs in the warm sunshine, some of them shirtless, circling a makeshift memorial of candles, flowers, and unsmoked cigars. Faces buried in their cellphones, the occasional smile, a pat on the back, a shaking of the head in apparent disbelief. He had killed himself several days before one of them noticed the smell and knocked on his door.

4   My judgment of them is a judgment of myself. I knew Geoffrey, as I'll call him here, but I did not know him. He was 19. That quiet student who floats in and out of the classroom. Asks the occasional question. Turns in

flawless work. Never misses a deadline. Scores well on quizzes. Dutifully collaborates with his group. We talked about Texas once. Compared notes on the Austin nightlife. How much I loved living there. How much he would like to. The small grin or smirk at my meager attempts at humor. Insignificant moments instructors share with their students.

5   What I did know about Geoffrey was that he seemed to be an anxious, high-strung young man. He would walk in, sit at his computer station, and fidget endlessly with the mouse, the keyboard, the monitor, his chair, his cellphone, the mouse again—making sure they were all in the correct position before proceeding to log in and begin his work. He was always clean-shaven, impeccably dressed regardless of whether he was wearing khakis and a dress shirt or a T-shirt and sweats. He wore a Polo baseball cap, and Ray-Bans.

6   Then came that one day he walked in with bloodshot eyes and stubble outlining his boyish complexion. He continued his morning ritual with precision. I chalked that one day up to the frat-boy nightlife. An all-night cram session. An argument with his girlfriend. I never asked if he was feeling OK.

7   I used to teach at the middle-school and high-school levels. As a public school teacher, I was trained to watch for warning signs. We were legally obligated and accountable for reporting questionable student behavior to an administrator or counselor. We were required to report suspected abuse to state officials. When a student does come on your radar, whether it is for aggressive behavior, suicidal notes, excessive absences, or even falling asleep in class, you stayed on it. They were minors under our care. You didn't want one to slip through the cracks.

8   At the college level, things are different. These are "adults" who can presumably take care of themselves. We don't meddle in their lives unless they write papers that encourage or display violent tendencies. There's no precedent for doing anything if the kid just looks tired or worn out.

9   I recently had a female student who fit that description. Normally jaunty, she came in to class one day looking downright haggard. When I asked her if she was OK, she broke down. She said she was going through some difficult times, but that she'd survive. I let it go at that. A week later she approached me to thank me for my concern. It turned out her parents were divorcing after 25 years of marriage. Being the eldest of seven siblings, she felt immense pressure. We talked for a few moments, and I offered to help in any way I could. She's looking better.

10   When the police confirmed Geoffrey's identity, I immediately contacted my department head to ask for some guidance, especially in dealing with informing the class the next day. His response reminded me of a line from Robert Frost: *"It couldn't be called ungentle, but how thoroughly departmental."* He told me to post the phone number and hours of operation for the student counseling center on the board at the beginning of class. He said he would "monitor the situation." I haven't heard from him since.

11   I was up all night. Considered canceling class. My attempt at a sober and restrained talk with my students the next morning failed miserably.

The moment I opened my mouth and said, "Some of you may have heard by now . . ." the tears that I had been stifling for two days started to flow.

12   I had not anticipated this. I couldn't tell if my students were more shocked by the news of Geoffrey's suicide or by this sudden eruption of emotion. I composed myself, apologized for my outburst, and told them to start the quiz. "*No one stands round to stare. It is nobody else's affair.*"

13   Geoffrey was my student. I was his instructor. I took this relationship too lightly. Students come and go. In all likelihood, nothing I could have said to him would have altered his fate. I tell myself this, but of course I don't believe it. Students come and go, but it's not supposed to be like this.

14   These young adults are not out of our realm of caring for their emotional, as well as intellectual, best interests. We are not here merely to disseminate information. We expect our students to care for themselves and each other; that expectation should be held for faculty and staff, as well. Geoffrey's death has taught me that my friendship, honesty, and compassion must extend far beyond the boundaries of my classroom. I care for my students. And they deserve to know that.   ■

QUESTIONS ON SUBJECT AND PURPOSE

1. What has prompted the essay? Is it just the sudden loss or something more as well?
2. In paragraphs 7 and 8, the author contrasts her experiences and sense of responsibility for her students on the middle and high school level with the college level. Why might she do so?
3. Can you find a sentence that seems to suggest what the author would like her readers to take away from the essay?

QUESTIONS ON STRATEGY AND AUDIENCE

1. Why might the essay begin with the sentence "He only missed one day of class"?
2. Why might the author include the detail in paragraph 9?
3. The *Chronicle of Higher Education* is a weekly publication for college and university faculty and administrators. It would not be read either by students or parents. How does that choice of audience seem to influence the essay?

QUESTIONS ON VOCABULARY AND STYLE

1. The essay contains a number of sentence fragments in paragraphs 4 and 6. Obviously they are used intentionally. Why?
2. What is the relationship between parallelism (see Glossary and Ready Reference) and those sentence fragments in paragraphs 4 and 6?
3. Be prepared to define the following words: *exemplary* (paragraph 1), *dubious* (3), *impeccably* (5), *jaunty* (9), *haggard* (9), *disseminate* (14).

WRITING SUGGESTIONS

1. **Doing a Critical Analysis.** How does the author handle time in the essay? Does the essay follow a chronological order? Are there flashbacks to earlier events? In an essay, analyze how time is manipulated in the essay and what effect that has on the essay.

2. **Journaling or Blogging.** Would you feel comfortable if one of your teachers asked you about how you were feeling? Or why you had missed class? Or why you seemed distracted? Reflect on that possibility.

3. **Practicing in a Paragraph.** If you knew someone who was depressed or was acting strangely, what should you do? In a paragraph, explore what response might be appropriate. Use a chronological order for a series of steps or actions that might be taken.

4. **Writing the Personal Essay.** What do you expect from your college instructors? Do you see them in the same way that you did middle and high school teachers? Do you expect them to just "disseminate information"? Do you expect them (or want them) to care for your "emotional, as well as intellectual, best interests" (paragraph 14)? Explore what you ideally want to happen in a college teaching environment.

5. **Finding Reading Connections.** How would you define the type or genre of this article? Compare it with Michael Jernigan's "Living the Dream" (Chapter 7) and to Libby Sander's "Colleges Confront a Gender Gap in Student Engagement" (Chapter 5). Is this article more like a blog entry than an essay that might appear in a magazine? In an essay, describe and define the structural and stylistic characteristics of this article.

6. **Exploring Links Online.** The allusions in paragraphs 10 and 12 are to the final four lines of Robert Frost's poem "Departmental." In what ways are the poem and this essay similar? Explore the connection in an essay.

7. **Writing the Research Paper.** Suicide is the second-leading cause of death among college students, accounting for about 1,100 deaths per year on campuses. The leading cause of death is accidents, including accidental overdoses, alcohol consumption, and automobile accidents. Why is the suicide rate so high? Research the problem and present your conclusion in a paper with appropriate documentation.

For Further Study

Focusing on Grammar and Writing. The essay contains a number of sentence fragments. Identify each one and then rewrite each to create a complete sentence. What keeps each fragment from being a complete sentence?

Working Together. Working in small groups, identify the elements in the essay that help readers understand how the writer's background and purpose influence how and what she writes.

Seeing Other Modes at Work. The essay makes use of a cause-and-effect pattern as well as it traces the stages of the author's reaction to the tragedy.

Lockdown

EVANS D. HOPKINS

A former inmate at Nottoway Correctional Center in Virginia and writer for the Black Panther Party, Evans Hopkins was paroled in 1997 after serving 16 years for armed robbery. He has published essays in the Washington Post, Nerve, *and* The New Yorker, *where this essay first appeared. His memoir,* Life After Life: A Story of Rage and Redemption, *was published in 2005.*

Before Reading

Connecting: What associations do you have with the words *prison* and *prisoner?*

Anticipating: Before you start to read, write down in a sentence or two how you feel about people sentenced to prison. For example, how should they be treated while they are in jail? Then read the essay.

1   I know something serious has happened when I wake up well before dawn to discover two guards wearing armored vests and riot helmets taking a head count. I'd gone to bed early this August evening, so that I might write in the early morning, as is my custom, before the prison clamor begins. So when I wake up I have no idea what was going down while I slept. But it's apparent that the prison is on "full lockdown status." At the minimum, we will be locked in our cells twenty-four hours a day for the next several days.

2   While lockdowns at Nottoway Correctional Center in Virginia are never announced in advance, I'm not altogether surprised by this one. The buzz among the eleven-hundred-man prison population was that a lockdown was imminent. The experienced prisoner knows to be prepared for a few weeks of complete isolation.

3   But I'm hardly prepared for the news I receive later in the day from a local TV station: two corrections officers and two nurses were taken hostage by three prisoners, following what authorities are calling "a terribly botched escape attempt" that included a fourth man. The incident was ended around 5:30 A.M. by a Department of Corrections strike-force team, with the hostages unharmed. However, according to authorities, eight of the rescuers, including the warden, were slightly wounded when a shotgun was discharged accidentally.

4   Oh, God, I think. Forget a few weeks. No telling how long we'll be on lock *now*. I try to take heart by telling myself, "It's nothing you haven't seen before, might as well take the opportunity to get the old typewriter pumpin', maybe even finish your book."

5   The idea that most people have of prison life consists of images from worst-case-scenario movies, or from news footage of local jails. Visitors to prison often comment on how surprised they are to see men moving around, without apparent restraint, having believed that prisoners are kept in their cells most of the time. In modern prisons, however, there is usually lots of orderly movement, as inmates go about the activities of normal life: working, eating, education, recreation, etc.

6   In a well-run institution, long lockdowns—where all inmate movement stops—are aberrations. Yet major institutions lock down regularly, for short periods, so that the prison can be searched for weapons and other contraband. Lockdowns are also called for emergencies, as this one has been at Nottoway, or, in fact, for any reason deemed necessary for security.

7   By the second week of the lockdown, one of our hot meals has been replaced with a bag lunch—four slices of bread, two slices of either cheese or a luncheon meat, and a small piece of plain cake or, more rarely, fruit. Since counsellors or administrative personnel must do most of the cooking, the lockdown menu usually consists of meals that require minimal culinary skills. Today we have chili-mac (an ungodly concoction of macaroni and ground beef), along with three tablespoons of anemic mixed vegetables and a piece of plain cake— all served on a disposable aluminum tray the size of a hard-cover book.

8   We have not yet been allowed out to shower, so I lay newspaper on the concrete floor and bathe at the sink. There is a hot water tap, in contrast to the cells at the now demolished State Penitentiary, in Richmond, where I served the first several years of my life sentence for armed robbery, and where I went through many very long lockdowns.

9   I have endured lockdowns in buildings with little or no heat; lockdowns during which authorities cut off the plumbing completely, so contraband couldn't be flushed away; and lockdowns where we weren't allowed out to shower for more than a month. I have been in prison since 1981, and my attitude has had to be "I can do time on the moon," if that is what's called for. So I'm not about to let this lockdown faze me. (Besides, I am in what is known as the "honor building," where conditions are marginally better.)

10   Around one o'clock in the morning, the three guards of the "shower squad" finally get around to our building. They have full riot gear on, and a Rottweiler in tow. One by one, we are handcuffed and escorted to the shower stalls at the center of the dayroom area. As I walk past the huge dog, I turn my head to keep an eye on it. The beast suddenly lunges against the handler's leash and barks at me with such ferocity that I actually feel the force of air on my face. I walk to the shower with feigned insouciance, but my heart is pumping furiously. I can forget sleeping for a while.

11   Back in the cell, I contemplate what's happening to this place. Information about the hostage incident has been trickling in. While the show of force

seems absurd to those of us here in the honor building, I have heard reports of assaults on guards in the cell houses of the main compound, where the treatment of the inmates is said to have been more severe. On the night of the original incident, some men in a section of one building refused to return to their cells, and in at least one section there was open rebellion—destruction and burning.

12   Today a memorandum from the warden is passed out, and the warden himself appears on a video broadcast on the prison's TV system. He announces that there will be no visitation until some time in October—about two months from now.

13   Other restrictions are to be imposed, he says, including immediate implementation of a new Department of Corrections guideline, stripping all prisoners of most personal property: televisions with screens larger than five and a half inches; any tape player other than a Walkman; nearly all personal clothing (jeans, nongray sweatsuits, colored underwear, etc.); and—most devastating for me—*all typewriters.*

14   I find this news disquieting, to say the least, and I decide to lie down, to try to get some sleep. This is difficult, as men are yelling back and forth from their cells, upset about this latest development. Many of them have done ten or fifteen years, like me, obeying all the rules and saving the meagre pay from prison jobs to buy a few personal items—items that we must now surrender.

15   I awaken in the night, sweating and feverish in the humid summer air. Sitting on the edge of my bed while considering my plight, I look at photographs of my family. My eyes rest on the school portrait of my son, taken shortly before he died from heart disease ten years ago, at age twelve. Sorrow overwhelms me, and I find myself giving in to grief, then to great, mournful sobs.

16   The tears stop as suddenly as they began. It has been years since I've wept so, and I realize that the grief has been only a trigger—that I am, by and large, really feeling sorry for myself. This is no good, if I'm to survive with my mind and spirit intact. I can't afford to succumb to self-pity.

17   This new day begins shortly after 8 A.M., when three guards come to my cell door. One of them says, "We're here to escort you to Personal Property. You have to pack up everything in your cell, and they will sort out what you have to send out, and what you can keep, over there."

18   He looks through the long, narrow vertical slot in the steel door and—seeing all the books, magazines, journal notebooks, and piles of papers I have stacked around the cell—shakes his head in disbelief. "Looks like you're gonna need a lot of boxes," he says. I have the accumulated papers, magazines, and books of a practicing freelance writer. The only problem is that my "office" is about as big as your average bathroom—complete with toilet and sink, but with a steel cot where your bathtub would be.

19   Now the new rules say twelve books, twelve magazines, twelve audiotapes. Period. And "a reasonable number of personal and legal papers." I wonder how much of all this stuff they will say is reasonable, when sometimes even I question the sanity of holding on to so much. But who knows *when* I'll be able to get to any files, manuscripts, books, and notes that I send

home? I finish packing after three hours, ending up with twelve full boxes. I sit and smoke a cigarette while waiting for the guards to return, and contemplate the stacked boxes filling the eight feet between the cot and the door. *Where are all the books, plays, and film scripts I dreamed of producing?*

20   As I walk to the property building, on the far side of the compound, the sun is bright, the sky is cloudless, and the air of the Virginia countryside is refreshing. I look away from the fortress-gray concrete buildings of the prison, and out through the twin perimeter fences and the gleaming rolls of razor wire, to note that the leaves of a distant maple have gone to orange. I realize that the season has changed since I was last out of the building.

21   I am accompanied by three guards. Two push a cart laden with my boxes, grumbling; the third, an older man I know, walks beside me, making small talk.

22   "Man, things are really changing here," this guard says. Lowering his voice so that the other two cannot hear him, he tells me that he considered transferring to work at another institution, but that the entire system is now going through similar changes.

23   Back in my cell, I don't have the energy to unpack the four boxes I've returned with. I am glad to have at least salvaged the part of the manuscripts I've worked on over the years.

24   I lie upon the bed like a mummy, feet crossed at the ankle and hands folded over my chest, and try to meditate. However, with my tape player gone (along with my television), I have no music to drown out the sounds coming from the cell house. A wave of defeat settles over me.

25   I think of what I've often told people who ask about my crime—that I got life for a robbery in which no one was hurt. I'll have to rephrase that from now on. If robbery can be said to be theft by force, I can't help but feel like I've just been robbed. And I've most certainly been *hurt*. Maybe that's the whole idea, I think—to injure us, eye for an eye.

26   Perhaps I should acknowledge that the lockdown—and, indeed, all these years—have damaged me more than I want to believe. But self-pity is anathema to the prisoner, and self-doubt is deadly to the writer.

27   I get up quickly, pull out a yellow pad and ballpoint from one of the boxes, and stuff spongy plugs in my ears to block out the noise. I know that if I don't go back to work immediately—on *something*—the loss of my typewriter may throw up a block that I'll never overcome.

28   Just before Christmas, the lockdown officially ends. The four and a half months have taken their toll on everyone. There have been reports of two or three suicides. Some inmates have become unhinged, and can be seen shuffling around, on Thorazine or something.

29   Things are far from being back to "normal operations." There is now the strictest control of *all* movement; attack dogs are everywhere and officers escort you wherever you go. The gym is closed, and recreation and visitation privileges have been drastically curtailed. At least the educational programs,

which were once touted as among the best in the state's prison system, are to resume again in the new year.

30　　On Christmas Eve, the first baked "real chicken on the bone" since summer is served. But the cafeteria-style serving line has been replaced with a wall of concrete blocks. Now the prisoner gets a standard tray served through a small slot at the end of the wall.

31　　As I hasten to finish my food in the allotted fifteen minutes, I look at the men from another building in the serving line. There is a drab sameness to the men, all dressed in the required ill-fitting uniform of denim jeans, blue work shirts, and prison jackets.

32　　I spot a friend of more than fifteen years, whom I haven't seen in months. I can only wave and call out a greeting, for as we are seated separately, "mingling" with men from another building is nearly impossible in the chow hall. "I'm a grandfather now," he shouts to me, beaming. "I've got some pictures to show you, when we get a chance." Then he remembers the strict segregation by building now, and his smile fades. He knows that I may never get a chance to see them.

33　　I notice a large number of new faces among the men in line. Most of them are black. Many are quite young, with a few appearing to be still in their teens.

34　　Such young men are a primary reason for the new lockdown policies, which are calculated largely to contain the "eighty-five-percenters"—those now entering Virginia's growing prison system, who must serve eighty-five percent of their sentences, under new, no-parole laws.

35　　Virginia, like most states and the federal government, has passed punitive sentencing laws in recent years. This has led to an unprecedented United States prison/jail population of more than a million six hundred thousand— about three times what it was when I entered prison, sixteen years ago. In the resulting expansion of the nation's prison systems, authorities have tended to dispense with much of the rehabilitative programming once prevalent in America's penal institutions.

36　　When I was sent to the State Penitentiary, in 1981, I was twenty-six— the quintessential angry young black male. However, there was a very different attitude toward rehabilitation at that time, particularly as regards education. I was able to take college courses for a number of years on a Pell grant. Vocational training was available, and literacy (or at least enrollment in school) was encouraged and increased one's chances for making parole.

37　　In the late seventies, there was a growing recognition that rehabilitation programs paid off in lower rates of recidivism. But things began to change a few years later. First, the highly publicized violence of the crack epidemic encouraged mandatory minimum sentencing. The throw-away-the key fever really took off in 1988, when George Bush's Presidential campaign hit the Willie Horton hot button, and sparked the tough-on-crime political climate that continues to this day. The transformation was nearly complete when President Clinton endorsed the concept of "three strikes you're out" in his

1994 State of the Union address. And when Congress outlawed Pell grants for prisoners later that year the message became clear: We really don't give a damn if you change or not.

38   Although the men are glad, after more than four months, to be out of their cells, there is little holiday spirit; it's just another day. Several watch whatever banality is on the dayroom TV screen. Most sit on the stainlesssteel tables and listlessly play cards to kill time, while others wait for a place at the table. Some wait to use one of two telephones, while others, standing around in bathrobes or towels, wait for a shower stall to become available.

39   Most of the men in this section of the building are in their forties or fifties, with a few elderly. It strikes me that for most of them prison has become a life of waiting: waiting in line to eat, for a phone call, the mail, or a visit. Or just waiting for tomorrow—for parole and freedom. For the older ones, with no hope of release, I suppose that they wait for the deliverance of death.

40   As I record the day in my notebook, I find myself thinking about my aunt's grandnephew—her adopted son. He was rumored to have been dealing drugs, and he was shot dead in the doorway of her home on Thanksgiving Day, just over a month ago; my father, who is seventy-five, was called to comfort her. With violence affecting so many lives, one can understand the desire—driven by fear—to lock away young male offenders. But considering their impoverished, danger-filled lives, I wonder whether the threat of being locked up for decades can really deter them from crime.

41   I understand the philosophy behind the increased use of long sentences and harsh incarceration. The idea is to make prison a secular hell on earth— a place where the young potential felon will fear to go, where the ex-con will fear to return. But an underlying theme is that "these people" are irredeemable "predators" (i.e., "animals"), who are without worth. Why, then, provide them with the opportunity to rehabilitate—or give them any hope?

42   Still, what really bothers me is knowing that many thousands of the young men entering prison now may never get the "last chance to change," which I was able to put to good use—in an era that, I'm afraid, is now in the past. And more disturbing, to my mind, are the long "no hope" sentences given to so many young men now—they can be given even to people as young as thirteen and fourteen. Although I personally remain eligible for parole— and in all likelihood will be released eventually—I can't help thinking of all the young lives that are now being thrown away. I know that if I had been born in another time I might very well have suffered the same fate. ■

QUESTIONS ON SUBJECT AND PURPOSE

1. How long does the lockdown last? How many specific days during that period does Hopkins write about?
2. At what point in the essay does Hopkins move away from his narrative account of the lockdown? What does Hopkins then do in the essay?
3. What objectives might Hopkins have in writing his essay?

QUESTIONS ON STRATEGY AND AUDIENCE

1. At times, Hopkins seems to talk to himself—even using quotation marks around his words, as in paragraph 4. Why? What is the effect of this strategy?
2. Hopkins uses white space to separate sections of the essay. How many divisions are there?
3. Whom might Hopkins imagine as his readers? To whom is he writing? How do you know?

QUESTIONS ON VOCABULARY AND STYLE

1. When the Rottweiler lunges at him, Hopkins writes, "I walk to the shower with feigned insouciance" (paragraph 10). What is the effect of his word choice?
2. Hopkins chooses to quote a few remarks that the guards make when he is asked to pack up his possessions (paragraphs 17, 18, and 22). Why?
3. Be prepared to define the following words: *clamor* (paragraph 1), *aberrations* (6), *insouciance* (10), *anathema* (26), *punitive* (35), *quintessential* (36), *recidivism* (37), *banality* (38).

WRITING SUGGESTIONS

1. **Doing a Critical Analysis.** Hopkins does not write about everything that happened during the lockdown period. In an essay, analyze his choice of moments or events to include. How do those choices relate to his purpose in the essay?
2. **Journaling or Blogging.** Think about personal experiences in your past that might be used to argue for a change in society's attitudes. Were you ever discriminated against, stereotyped, embarrassed, ridiculed? Did you ever do that to someone else? Make a list of possibilities.
3. **Practicing in a Paragraph.** Select one of the items on your list and in a paragraph narrate what happened. Then reflect on the damage or injustice reflected in that experience. Try to make your reader see the consequences of such behavior on society.
4. **Writing the Personal Essay.** Expand your paragraph into a personal essay. Your goal is to make the experience vivid for your reader and to signal the larger social issue that the experience reveals.
5. **Finding Reading Connections.** Hopkins raises the issue of whether prisons should merely house those who have committed crimes or also provide opportunities for rehabilitation. What about those in our society who are figuratively imprisoned? Lars Eighner in "My Daily Dives in the Dumpster" (Chapter 6) deals with the reality and the plight of those who are homeless. Do we have a moral obligation to help them?
6. **Exploring Links Online.** The Web has many poems and essays written by prisoners. Many of the essays offer insights into prison life. What is the "picture" of prison life that emerges from such essays?
7. **Writing the Research Paper.** What evidence is there to support or to refute the idea that prison can be a place for rehabilitation? Research the problems and then argue for or against providing educational or vocational opportunities to prisoners. Be sure to document your sources.

For Further Study

Focusing on Grammar and Writing. Under what circumstances do we use a dash (—) in writing? How does it differ from parentheses or commas? Look at how the dash is used in the essay. Using Hopkins's sentences as examples, write rules for its correct use in writing.

Working Together. Working in small groups, choose one substantial paragraph from the essay. What does Hopkins focus on in that paragraph? How does that one paragraph fit into the whole? Possible paragraphs to analyze include 7, 10, 20, 32, 39, and 40.

Seeing Other Modes at Work. In the last third of his essay, Hopkins moves from narration to reflection and then persuasion, trying to get his audience to realize the implications of denying prisoners opportunities for rehabilitation.

ADDITIONAL WRITING SUGGESTIONS FOR NARRATION

Narration is storytelling and it is used for a variety of purposes. Stories make us laugh and cry; understand and sympathize with situations we have never experienced; interpret the impact our experiences have had on us; move us to do or believe something. Some possible ideas are listed below.

Tell a Story

1. Write a several-paragraph-long joke that ends with a punch line.
2. Explain how your state got its nickname (or your school).
3. Narrate and explain the historical significance of a local place or event.
4. Tell a story about a campus legend or a famous or infamous graduate.
5. Select a current event and trace the actions that lead up to it.

Find Meaning in a Personal Experience

1. A moment of terror (or heartbreak, joy, embarrassment)
2. Hardest (best, worst, stupidest) decision I ever made
3. My greatest regret
4. I will never forget when . . .
5. I knew I was growing up when . . .
6. A loss or a disappointment

Tell a Story to Move Your Audience to an Action or Belief

1. Recycle (or conserve energy, water)
2. An encounter with sexual, racial, or ethnic discrimination or prejudice
3. Support or oppose the sale of automatic weapons (tobacco products, lottery tickets)
4. Ban on certain types of advertisements
5. Protest a campus policy

3 | Description

Writing Description

GETTING READY TO WRITE

What Is Description?

Description, like narration, is an everyday activity. You describe to a friend what cooked snails really taste like, how your favorite perfume smells, how your body feels when you have a fever, how a local band sounded last night, what you are wearing to the Halloween party. Description records and re-creates sense impressions by translating them into words.

Consider, for example, Darcy Frey's description of the playground on which Russell Thomas, a star basketball player at a Brooklyn, New York, high school, practices on an August evening:

> At this hour Russell usually has the court to himself; most of the other players won't come out until after dark, when the thick humid air begins to stir with night breezes and the court lights come on. But this evening is turning out to be a fine one—cool and foggy. The low, slanting sun sheds a feeble pink light over the silvery Atlantic a block away, and milky sheets of fog roll off the ocean and drift in tatters along the project walkways. The air smells of sewage and saltwater. At the far end of the court, where someone has torn a hole in the chicken wire fence, other players climb through and begin warming up.

Frey uses descriptive words and phrases to record sense impressions—sights and smells. Sensory details make it easy for the reader to create mentally a feeling and a visual impression for what it must have been like that evening on the basketball court at the project.

Translating sense impressions into words is not easy. When you have a firsthand experience, all of your senses are working at the same time: you see, taste, smell, feel, hear; you experience feelings and have thoughts about the experience. When you convey that experience to a reader or a listener, you can record only one sense impression at a time. Furthermore, sometimes it is difficult to find an adequate translation for a particular sense impression—how do you describe the smell of musk perfume or the taste of freshly squeezed orange juice?

Descriptions occur in all forms of writing. When you write a narrative, you include passages of description; when you compare and contrast two things, you describe both as part of that process; when you try to persuade an audience that strip mining destroys the landscape, you describe the abandoned mine site. Scientists write descriptions; writers create descriptions. Sometimes descriptions are a sentence long, sometimes a paragraph; sometimes an entire essay is composed of description.

Why Record Sense Impressions in Words?

Many types of sense impressions—smells, tastes, textures—cannot really be captured in any way except in words or in a physical re-creation of the original experiences. Sights and sounds, on the other hand, can be recorded in photographs and audio and video recordings. Indeed, at times a photograph or

Library of Congress Prints and Photographs Division
[Solomon D. Butcher/10966]

Nebraska State Historical Society Photograph

a video works much better than a verbal description. We cannot deny the power of the visual. Look, for example, at the following photograph of a sod house, probably taken in the Midwest in the 1880s. If we wanted to know what a settler's life was like on the Great Plains, if we wanted to experience the physical reality of that life, what better way than to study a group of photographs?

At the same time, though, words can do something that photographs never can. Photographs are static—a visual but unchanging moment captured in time. But what were the people in the photograph thinking? What were they feeling? What impression did the landscape leave on their minds and lives? What was it like to go to bed and wake up each morning in a sod house? How cold did it get in the winter? How wet and damp in the spring? What did it smell like? Descriptions in words should never attempt to capture a photographic reality. Instead, images are filtered through the mind of the writer—the writer evokes our feelings, our senses, our memories and emotions. The writer makes us feel that we are there. The writer of description records what she or he saw as important in the scene.

Translating sense impressions into words offers two distinct advantages. First, ideally, it isolates the most important aspects of the experience, ruling out anything else that might distract a reader's attention. Many things can be noticed in a scene, but what are the important ones on which the reader is to focus? Second, translating into words makes experiences more permanent. Sensory impressions decay in seconds, but written descriptions survive indefinitely and can be reaccessed each time they are reread.

How Do Objective and Subjective Description Differ?

Traditionally, descriptions are divided into two categories: objective and subjective. In objective description, you record details without making any personal evaluation or reaction. Few descriptions outside of science or technical writing, however, are completely objective. Instead of trying to include every detail, creating the verbal equivalent of a photograph, writers choose a few details carefully. That process of selection is determined by the writer's purpose and by the impression that the writer wants to create. In "The Day Nana Almost Flew," Alisa Wolf is stunned when her elderly Nana greets her at the door of her apartment:

> Since Nana had fussed over her appearance all of the years I'd known her, I was shocked when she opened the door to her apartment one afternoon snapped up in a housedress—the tops of her knee-high hose showing in the slit below the bottom snap, her toes crammed into stockings and black plastic slippers.

Wolf uses a few details about Nana's dress to capture the changes that dementia is having on her mind. Wolf is not interested in describing Nana's physical appearance and characteristics. She is creating an emotion, an impression.

In subjective description, you are free to interpret details for your reader; your choice of words and images can be suggestive, emotional, and value-loaded. Subjective descriptions frequently make use of figurative language—similes and metaphors that forge connections in the reader's mind. When Gordon Grice, in "Caught in the Widow's Web" (a descriptive essay found in Writers at Work), sees the debris that litters the ground under the spider's web, he uses a *simile* (a comparison that uses *like* or *as*) when he writes, "the husks of consumed insects, their antennae stiff as gargoyle horns." When Scott Russell Sanders, in "The Inheritance of Tools" (in this chapter), looks at his smashed thumbnail, he creates a *metaphor* (an analogy that directly identifies one thing with another) when he describes the wound as a "crescent moon" that "month by month. . . . rose across the pink sky of my thumbnail."

What Do You Include or Exclude from a Description?

Writing a description, like writing a narrative, involves selection. When you write a narrative, you have a purpose, a shaping focus, for the story. You strip away the unnecessary details and focus on the points or details that relate to your focus. The same principle holds true for writing a description. You cannot record every detail about a person, object, place, or landscape. How could you capture every aspect of anything? How could you include all that could be seen, or smelled, or heard, or felt? As you write description, stay focused on your purpose and be selective about the details you include.

Descriptions can serve a variety of purposes, but in every case it is important to make that purpose clear to your reader. Some description is done solely to record the facts, or to evoke an atmosphere. More often, description is used to support subjective purposes. Gordon Grice, in describing the black widow spider, is not trying to describe the spider as a scientist might. He uses description to emphasize the evil or malevolence that he sees embodied in the "flower of natural evil." The spider is more than just a physical thing; it becomes a symbol.

Ask yourself, "What am I trying to describe and why?" Write a purpose statement for your descriptive essay or even for a passage of description. Then use that purpose statement as a tool to measure the relevance or irrelevance of every detail that you are thinking about including.

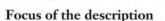

Links between Writing and Reading

	Focus of the description
Sonya Lea, "First Bath"	What descriptive details about the bath are included?
Alisa Wolf, "The Day Nana"	How do the details about Nana and the objects in her apartment create a unified impression of Nana?
William Least Heat Moon, "Nameless"	How much description can you find in the essay and what is described?
Adrienne Ross Scanlan, "The Queen"	What descriptive details about the bees does Scanlan include in her essay and how important are those details to the essay?
Scott Russell Sanders, "Inheritance"	Why does Sanders never describe his father? What does he do instead?

Prewriting Tips for Writing Description

1. Decide what you are going to describe in your essay—a person, a place, an object. Decide as well about length.
2. Make a list of the details that best describe your subject. Consider all of the senses. Which of the details are objective and which are subjective? Do you want to be as precise as possible or to create an atmosphere or emotion?
3. If possible, reexperience the place, person, or subject of your paper. Go and visit. Take notes. Listen. Look. Jot down details.
4. Once you have gathered details, write a purpose statement for your description. What are you trying to do? Create an emotion? Set a mood? Verbally photograph or record an event? Use that purpose statement to test each detail that you plan to include.
5. Remember that extended descriptions are static and may bore a reader. Be careful not to record too much detail.

WRITING

How Do You Describe an Object or a Place?

The first task in writing a description is to decide what you want to describe. As in every other writing task, if you make a good choice, the act of writing will be easier and probably more successful. Before you begin, keep two things in mind. First, there is rarely any point in describing a common object or place—something every reader has seen—unless you do it in a fresh and perceptive way. Probably most of Darcy Frey's readers had at least seen pictures of a project playground, but after reading his description, they come away with a sense of vividness—the passage evokes a mental picture of what it was like on the playground that evening.

Second, remember that your description must create a focused impression. Select details that contribute to your purpose; this will give you a way of deciding which details of the many available are relevant. Details in a description must be carefully chosen and arranged; otherwise, your reader will be overwhelmed or bored by an accumulation of irrelevancies.

How Do You Describe a Person?

Any time you read a narrative that contains a character, either real or fictional, you form a mental picture of the person, and that picture is generally not based on any physical description that the author has provided. In fact, in many narratives, authors provide only minimal description of the people involved. For example, if you look closely at the Thurmond Watts family in William Least Heat Moon's "Nameless, Tennessee," you will find almost no physical description of the people. Thurmond, we are told, is "tall" and "thin"—those are the only adjectives used to describe him. The rest of the family—his wife, Miss Ginny; his sister-in-law, Marilyn; and his daughter, Hilda—are not physically described at all. Nevertheless, we get a vivid sense of all four as people.

Why might that be so? Fictional characters or real people are created or revealed primarily through ways other than direct physical description. What a person does or says, for example, also reveals personality. The Wattses, in

---

Links between Writing and Reading

	How a place is described
William Least Heat Moon, "Nameless"	What does the author focus on in his description of the Wattses' store?
Adriene Ross Scanlan, "The Queen"	Why might Scanlan describe the yards and their flowers in such detail in the essay?
Scott Russell Sanders, "Inheritance"	What role does "building" things play in the essay?

Least Heat Moon's essay, are revealed by how they react, what they say, how their speech sounds, and what they consider to be important. These are the key factors in re-creating Least Heat Moon's experience for the reader.

In fact, descriptions of people should not try to be verbal portraits recording physical attributes in photographic detail. Decide what it is about the person that is worth describing. In all likelihood it will be something other than physical attributes. Once you know what that something is, you can then choose the details that best reveal or display the person.

How Do You Organize a Description?

You have a subject; you have studied it—either firsthand or in memory; you have decided on a reason for describing this particular subject; you have selected details that contribute to that reason or purpose. Now you need to organize your paragraph or essay. Descriptions, like narratives, have principles of order, although the principles vary depending on what sensory impressions are involved. When the primary descriptive emphasis is on

Links between Writing and Reading

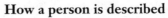

	How a person is described
Sonya Lea, "First Bath"	What aspects of her husband does Lea describe?
Alisa Wolf, "The Day Nana"	How does Wolf describe her grandmother through her actions and words?
William Least Heat Moon, "Nameless"	What role does dialogue have in creating character?

Links between Writing and Reading

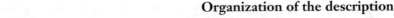

	Organization of the description
Sonya Lea, "First Bath"	How is the description organized in the story?
Alisa Wolf, "The Day Nana"	The essay describes a number of moments. What device organizes the descriptive details in the essay?
William Least Heat Moon, "Nameless"	How is the description of the interior of the store organized?
Adrienne Ross Scanlan, "The Queen"	Why might Scanlan describe in such detail the process of removing the queen from the compost hive?
Scott Russell Sanders, "Inheritance"	What is the principal organizing device in the essay?

Drafting Tips for Writing Description

1. Plan a structure for your essay. Does your description move spatially? From the most obvious to the least obvious? Does time underlie the structure of your description?

2. Look again at your purpose statement. Go through your essay and check each detail against that purpose.

3. Have you included too many details? Do parts of the paper seem too long, too crowded, too detailed?

4. Plan an opening for your paper. Think of at least three possible ways in which to begin. Write sample beginnings and ask friends to rate them.

5. Plan an ending for your essay. Think of several different ways to end. How do you know when you are finished? What will signal a conclusion to your reader?

---

seeing, the most obvious organization is spatial: from front to back, side to side, outside to inside, top to bottom, general to specific. The description moves as a camera would.

Other sensory experiences might be arranged in order of importance, from the most obvious to the least—the loudest noise at the concert, the most pervasive odor in the restaurant—or even in chronological order.

REVISING

How Do You Revise a Description?

Always try to finish a complete draft of your essay days before its due date. That will allow time to put the paper aside for awhile. When you come back to it, you will have a fresh perspective on what you have written. After you look again at the paper, you may be pleased with how good it seems, or you may realize that more work needs to be done. Try to get feedback from other readers. Ask for constructive advice; do not settle for empty responses such as "it's OK" or "I liked it." In writing descriptive passages or essays, problems tend to cluster around several key areas.

Avoiding Too Many Adjectives and Adverbs   You can create an image without providing a mountain of adjectives and adverbs—just as you can imagine what a character looks like without being told. One of the greatest dangers in writing a description is attempting to describe too much, trying to qualify every noun with at least one adjective and every verb with an adverb. Precise, vivid nouns and verbs will do most of the work for you.

Using Figurative Language Sparingly   Similes and metaphors can be powerful descriptive tools, but such figurative devices can present problems. Similes and metaphors add freshness and vividness to writing, and they help readers understand the unfamiliar by linking it to the familiar. Nevertheless, similes and metaphors are artificial language constructs that tend to call attention to themselves. The point to a description should not be to display your cleverness as a writer. You are describing something for a reason, a purpose, not to show off your verbal skills. Do not try to be too clever: on the other hand, do not use similes and metaphors that are nothing more than clichés. If a character in your essay does things in an unconventional way, do not write that she "marches to a different drummer"; if someone has no hair, do not write, he "was as bald as a billiard ball." Finally, do not write strings of similes and metaphors; use them sparingly.

Keeping Focused   An effective description is focused and tight. Never try to describe everything about a person, a scene, or an object; never feel compelled to include every possible sense impression. Descriptions can sprawl out of control, and because they are static, readers can easily get bored by the accumulation of descriptive detail. If you are describing a person, for example, do not give your reader several paragraphs of description—what the person looks like, what the person is wearing, what the person is thinking or feeling. Instead, put that person in motion: have the person do something, interact with someone, say lines of dialogue. Intermix descriptive details with action.

 ## Revising Tips for Writing Description

1. Check to see if you have used vivid nouns and verbs to carry most of the descriptive burden.
2. Consider whether you have been too heavy-handed in emphasizing the significance or importance that you see in the object of your description. Remember, you are trying to reveal significance; you are not lecturing on the "meaning" of your description.
3. Go through your essay and underline every descriptive detail. Are there too many? Are you trying to make the reader experience too much?
4. Find readers for your draft—a roommate, a classmate, a writing lab tutor. Ask your readers for honest advice. What did they like about your paper? What did they find tedious?
5. Look at your title again. Will it attract a reader or scare one away? Remember that "Descriptive Essay" is not an acceptable title.

Student Essay

Nadine Resnick chose to describe her favorite childhood toy, a stuffed doll named Natalie.

First Draft

Pretty in Pink

Standing in the middle of the aisle, staring up at the world as most children in nursery school do, something pink caught my eye. Just like Rapunzel in her high tower, there was a girl inside a cardboard and plastic prison atop a high shelf that smiled down at me. I pointed to the doll and brought her home with me that same day. Somehow I knew that she was special.

She was named Natalie. I do not know why, but the name just seemed perfect, like the rest of her. Natalie was less than twelve inches tall and wore a pink outfit. Her hands and grimacing face were made of plastic while the rest of her body was stuffed with love. She had brown eyes and brown hair, just like me, which peeked through her burgundy and pink-flowered bonnet. Perhaps the most unusual feature about her was that my mom had tattooed my name on her large bottom so that if Natalie ever strayed from me at nursery school or at the supermarket, she would be able to find me.

There was some kind of magic about Natalie's face. I think it was her grin from ear to ear. Even if I had played with her until she was so dirty that most of her facial features were hidden, Natalie's never-ending smile usually shone through. When I neglected her for days to play with some new toy and then later returned, her friendly smirk was still there. When I was left home alone for a few hours, her smile assured me that I need not be afraid. Natalie's bright smile also cheered me up when I was sick or had a bad day. And she always had enough hugs for me.

As I was growing up, Natalie and her beaming face could usually be found some-where in my room—on my bed, in her carriage, hiding under a pile of junk, and later piled in my closet with the rest of my other dolls and stuffed animals. When I got older, I foolishly decided that I no longer needed such childish toys. So I put Natalie and the rest of my stuffed animals in a large black plastic bag in a dark corner of the basement. I now realize that the basement really is not an honorable place for someone who has meant so much to me. But, I will bet that she is still smiling anyway.

Comments

Nadine had a chance to read her essay to a small group of classmates during a collaborative editing session. Everyone liked the essay and most of their suggested changes were fairly minor. For example, several people objected to her choice of the words *grimaced* and *smirk*, feeling that such words were not appropriate choices for a lovable doll. Another student, however, suggested a revision in the final paragraph. "It seems like you put her farther and farther away from you as you got older. Why don't you emphasize that distancing by having it occur in stages?" he commented. When Nadine rewrote her essay, she made a number of minor changes in the first three paragraphs and then followed her classmate's idea in the fourth paragraph.

Revised Draft

Natalie

Standing in the store's aisle, staring up at the world as most pre-school children do, something pink caught my eye. Just like Rapunzel in her high tower, a girl trapped inside a cardboard and plastic prison atop a high shelf smiled down at me. I pointed to the doll and brought her home with me that same day. Somehow I knew that she was special.

She was named Natalie. I do not know why, but the name just seemed perfect, like the rest of her. Natalie was less than twelve inches tall and wore a pink outfit. Her hands and smiling face were made of plastic while the rest of her body was plumply stuffed. Just like me, she had brown eyes and brown hair which peeked through her burgundy and pink-flowered bonnet. Perhaps her most unusual feature was my name tattooed on her bottom so that if Natalie ever strayed from me at nursery school or at the supermarket, she would be able to find me.

Natalie's face had a certain glow, some kind of magic. I think it was her grin from ear to ear. After I had played with her, no matter how dirty her face was, Natalie's never-ending smile still beamed through. When I neglected her for days to play with some new toy and then later returned, her friendly grin was still there. Years later, when I was old enough to be left home alone for a few hours, her smile assured me that I need not be afraid. Natalie's bright smile also cheered me up when I was sick or had a bad day. And she always had enough hugs for me.

As I was growing up, Natalie and her beaming face could usually be found somewhere in my room. However, she seemed to move further away from me as I got older. Natalie no longer slept with me; she slept in her own carriage. Then she rested on a high shelf across my room. Later she made her way into my closet with the rest of the dolls and stuffed animals that I had outgrown. Eventually, I decided that I no longer needed such childish toys, so I put Natalie and my other stuffed animals in a large black plastic bag in a dark cellar corner. Even though I abandoned her, I am sure that Natalie is still smiling at me today.

Checklist: Some Things to Remember About Writing Description

❏ Choose your subject carefully, make sure you have a specific reason or purpose in mind for whatever you describe.

❏ Study or observe your subject—try to see it or experience it in a fresh way. Gather details; make a list; use all your senses.

❏ Use your purpose as a way of deciding which details ought to be included and which excluded.

❏ Choose a pattern of organization to focus your reader's attention.

❏ Use precise, vivid nouns and verbs, as well as adjectives and adverbs, to create your descriptions.

Reading Description

Description records sense impressions: What can be seen, heard, felt, tasted. All descriptions, though, whether they are created with words or with visual images, are selective. The writer, the artist, the photographer selects details and arranges them to re-create an experience with a particular goal or purpose in mind. As you read, remember what you have learned about how to write a description—that knowledge can help you as a reader.

• Descriptions are written with a purpose in mind, and the details are chosen to reinforce that purpose. What the author includes and excludes are both important, and both choices are made with an eye to purpose.

• Descriptions can be either objective or subjective. A scientist attempting to describe something precisely produces an objective description. A writer trying to evoke an emotion in you through the description relies on subjective description.

• Descriptions are organized so that the reader can sense an order to the material. Sometimes that order follows a chronological pattern; sometimes it moves from the most obvious to the least obvious. Whatever the pattern, the organizational scheme orients the reader within the description.

• Descriptions frequently use figurative language, especially simile and metaphor, and capture a range of sense impressions.

IN PROSE

One of the most famous examples of subjective description comes from the opening paragraphs of Charles Dickens's *Bleak House* (1853). The novel is set in London, a city with muddy streets and polluted air from the coal-burning stoves, a city enveloped in fog. Dickens is not just describing a place, how-ever; he is creating a symbolic landscape. The mud, mire, and suffocating fog of the city reflect the London legal system and the eternal litigation of the Jarndyce estate case, which is as murky and miserable as the weather that Dickens describes in these paragraphs.

Opening sentence places the scene in the legal district; season is winter	London, Michaelmas Term lately over, and the Lord Chancellor sitting in Lincoln's Inn Hall. Implacable November weather. As much mud in the streets, as if the waters had but newly re-tired from the face of the earth, and it would not be wonderful
Extended Similes	to meet Megalosaurus, forty feet long or so, waddling like an elephantine lizard up Holborn Hill. Smoke lowering down from chimney pots, making a soft black drizzle, with flakes of soot in
Metaphor	it as big as full-grown snow-flakes—gone into mourning, one might imagine, for the death of the sun. Dogs, undistinguish-able in mire. Horses, scarcely better, splashed to their very blinkers. Foot passengers, jostling one another's umbrellas, in a general infection of ill-temper, and losing their foothold at street-corners, where tens of thousands of other foot passen-gers have been slipping and sliding since the day broke (if this day ever broke), adding new deposits to the crust upon crust of mud, sticking at these points tenaciously in the pavement, and
Metaphor	accumulating at compound interest.

QUESTIONS FOR ANALYSIS

1. Why might the description be placed in the month of November? Judging from the paragraph, what is the weather like then in London? Why November and not June?
2. Look closely at the sentence beginning "Smoke lowering down. . . ." How many different images does Dickens give us in that single sentence?
3. What is unusual about the phrase "a general infection of ill-temper"?
4. From what point of view is the description told? Why that choice?

CRITICAL READING ACTIVITY

List the examples of figurative language and unusual word choice that Dickens uses in the paragraph. How do these descriptive elements contribute to the literal and metaphoric atmosphere he is creating?

IN LITERATURE

Description is often intertwined with narration as it is in "Traveling to Town," a poem by Duane BigEagle that recalls a recurring experience during his childhood near the Osage Reservation in Oklahoma. As he explains in a note to the poem, "Monkey Ward" was the name many people used to refer to catalog merchandiser Montgomery Ward (once a competitor of Sears). As you read the poem, think about how sparse, but effective, the use of description is here.

Traveling to Town

DUANE BIGEAGLE

When I was very young,
we always went to town
in the flatbed wagon.
We'd leave as soon as the day's first heat
had stopped the mare's breath
from forming a cloud
in the air.
Kids sprawled in the back
among the dusty bushels
of corn and beans.
As we rode down main street,
the town revealed itself
backwards
for my sister and me to see.
We loved the brick and sandstone buildings
and the farmer's market
with its sawdust floor.
Best of all
was Monkey Ward
with its large wood paneled center room
and little wires
with paper messages
that flew back and forth
like trained birds.
We finally got to Safeway
where Grandma did the shopping
and Grandpa sat outside
on the brick steps in the sunlight
watching all the grandkids.

From a shady coolness
on the other side of the street
the ice cream store
would call to us
with its banging screen door.
Grandpa always had money for ice cream
and we'd ride home down main street
licking ice cream
watching the town reveal itself
backwards again
in afternoon sun.

QUESTIONS FOR ANALYSIS

1. The trip presumably takes an entire day. Out of the whole experience, what does BigEagle describe? Why these things?
2. Description doesn't always mean surrounding nouns with clusters of adjectives and verbs with adverbs. Focus on a detail or two in the poem that adds to the description. What does BigEagle do to make the detail seem vivid?
3. What is the overall impression that BigEagle seems to be trying to convey to his readers? How do the individual details contribute to that impression?
4. How is the description organized in the poem?

WRITING SUGGESTIONS

1. **Analysis.** The narrator in the poem is an adult who is remembering a recurring experience when he was "very young." In an essay, analyze how that time perspective works in the selection of descriptive details and their organization in the poem.
2. Describe an experience from your childhood or adolescence. Try to make the scene vivid to your readers through sense impressions. Notice that description often works best when it is sparsely done. Some possible places to start:

   a. An experience you had visiting your relatives in the summer or winter
   b. A special place that you regularly visited
   c. A moment of joy, of terror, of surprise

IN A VISUAL

Dickens's description of London reproduced above is subjective and symbolic. The photograph reproduced is an objective, visual record of how Mulberry Street in New York City looked on the day on which it was taken. Photographs capture a moment in time, visually. We cannot hear the noises or experience the smells, nor touch the objects and people depicted, but we can at least see what it was like to live in a densely populated city at the turn of the century.

QUESTIONS FOR ANALYSIS

1. What is present in this photograph that would not be present in a photograph of the same area taken today? What does the photograph reveal about urban life then?

2. Why might the photograph have been taken and then reproduced for others to see? What purpose might the photographer have had in capturing this particular scene?

WRITING SUGGESTIONS

1. **Analysis.** Identify the elements in the photograph that would be difficult to describe in words. Study how the photograph was composed. What do you notice about the angle from which it was taken? Why might the people be facing the camera? Does that influence your experience of the image? Analyze, in an essay, the photograph as an example of description.

2. What do you take photographs of—with your cellphone or a camera? Why do you take them and what do you do with them? Review the types of images that you have captured recently. What is the difference between having a visual record of an experience and recording a written account of an experience? Are some types of experiences suitable only for visuals? Write an essay about the role of visuals in your day-to-day life.

3. Newspapers concentrate on the printed word using only an occasional photograph. The Internet allows a newspaper to become more visually descriptive. Select a video or photographic feature from a newspaper's website and analyze what and how it contributes to your understanding of the story.

First Bath

SONYA LEA

Seattle-based Sonya Lea has written screenplays, essays, a novel, and has won a number of writing awards. Lea actively blogs and has published essays in magazines such as the Southern Review, Cold Mountain Review, *and the online* Brevity *where this essay first appeared in Fall 2012. Her husband is a cancer survivor.*

On Writing: *Commenting on this essay, Lea observed: "I began to write our memoir from the notes I made when I lived with my husband in a cancer hospital for three weeks. He was being treated with an aggressive surgery and chemotherapy, which had caused an anoxic insult, a brain injury in which his mind emptied his memories. . . . When we returned home, I wrote as a way to make sense of the events, and to release the trauma of that time and place."*

Before Reading

Connecting: Have you ever had to care for a loved one who is ill or who has had surgery?

Anticipating: Lea is describing a simple action; what makes her description so vivid?

1 **H**is shoulders hang low and his back is bowed. His body is forty pounds lighter than it was a few days ago, before the cancer surgery, before the blood loss that caused his mind to empty its memories. His is a body without strength, without vigor, without lust, without intention, without history. A body taken apart and reassembled, a body that has not settled into the space of gravity, a body that knows nothing about its own scars, crevices, grumbles.

2 "Would you like to bathe your husband in private?" Nurse Jen asks, and I walk across hard linoleum, and I come to his side, and I say, "Yes." She brings me a pink bowl filled with warm water where a bar of soap soaks. Nurse Jen lays out towels and a washcloth. She walks across the room and she pulls the curtain and she exits and the door closes fully behind her and the room is no longer open to the constant movement of others as it has been for the time we have been living in the cancer hospital.

3 My husband closes his eyes, and I take his hand in mine. The light of the new moon is in his thick fingers and large square hands. I squeeze the water from the cloth, rub across the soap, begin to make swirls in his palm, pressing into the flesh of the lifeline, stroking through each of the fingers. I lay the dry towel across his knees, and place his hand to rest there while I glide the cloth up his arm, softly caressing against the grain of his wispy black hair, smoothing over his wide shoulder. I lift his arm onto my shoulder

and I rub under as the silky soap makes a trail into the pit, dark curls slick with lather. Once I could lick there, swirling his hair in my tongue, breathing in his scent as if to memorize the salty musk. Now there is no odor, except of chemotherapy, the smell of ice on steel. His skin holds the fragrance of his first cancer treatment: a scalding mitomycin liquid, isolated from *Streptomyces lavendulae*, a 104 degree tumor-killer which they'd poured inside him while his organs lay on the table near his open body. I imagine the medicine binding to his cells, the sick cells dying, the dead cells pouring out of him, onto my cloth. I imagine the movement restoring his mind, the mind we will not know for six months hence has been permanently altered by an anoxic insult, a brain injury, a memory-eater.

4   I soak the cloth in water again, and rinse him, warm droplets sliding down his forearms where I hope to wake something that wants to live, where I hope to rouse some fire under the pallor. I dry the length of his arm, almost as big as half of me, and so weak it flops to his side without support. I rub down his broad back, pat his left arm and hand, touch the skin tenderly, walking around the pole that holds his IV lines, avoiding the tape and tubes near his wrist. I wash the dried blood near his chest tubes, move the water away from the tape down his middle, a wide bandage over two feet long, where his skin is quietly re-stitching. He is without his umbilicus, the part that connected him to his mama, the center that made him man, the place where my fingers found him in the dark. My hand travels down to clean his penis, and I gently swab around the catheter, my hand finding his testicles, holding their weight in the way I would if I'd wanted to make love. I wipe him with sweet strokes. I look up to his face. He opens his eyes. Tender, surrendered eyes. Tears fall down my chin at the dignity in his submission.

5   I wrap him in his clean gown, and lean him back into a fresh pillow and strap on the leg bands that will pulse his blood through the day and night, making the sound of wind, a measured music in our unsteady life.   ■

QUESTIONS ON SUBJECT AND PURPOSE

1. An "anoxic insult" (paragraph 3) occurs when the brain has suffered a complete lack of oxygen—a result of the blood loss that Lea mentions (paragraph 1). What have been the consequences of that event?
2. What is the focus of the essay?
3. Why might Lea have written the essay—that is, what seem to be her reasons for writing about the experience? Is it an objective description of her husband's surgery?

QUESTIONS ON STRATEGY AND AUDIENCE

1. In what verb tense does Lea write the essay? Why that choice?
2. How does Lea describe her husband's reaction to the bath?
3. What expectations might Lea have about her audience?

QUESTIONS ON VOCABULARY AND STYLE

1. Why might Lea begin the essay with the description of her husband's body after his surgery?
2. At the end of the essay, Lea writes of the inflating leg bands that force the circulation of blood through her husband's legs as "making the sound of wind, a measured music of our unsteady life." What figures of speech is she using?
3. Be prepared to define the following words: *pallor* (paragraph 4) and *umbilicus* (4).

WRITING SUGGESTIONS

1. **Doing a Critical Analysis.** Lea acknowledges that her piece is about her sensual experiences with her husband's changed body after his surgery. In an analysis, describe how Lea evokes sensual experience in the essay. Focus on her choice of words and her actions. How do those details make the essay so powerful emotionally?
2. **Journaling or Blogging.** Have you ever experienced the illness of a parent, grandparent, or sibling? What were your thoughts or reactions at the time—explore your memories.
3. **Practicing in a Paragraph.** In a descriptive paragraph, create one memory or scene. Maybe you were visiting someone in a hospital, helping someone do a task they are not capable of doing by themselves, realizing that something is now radically different.
4. **Writing the Personal Essay.** Lea focuses not on her husband in the essay, but upon describing what it was like to bathe the damaged body of someone she loves. Expand your paragraph into an essay and focus, as she does, on what you are feeling.
5. **Finding Reading Connections.** Sarah J. Lin in "Devotion" (Chapter 8) describes in graphic detail her reaction to the physical features and problems faced by a man named Sherman who had decided he loved her. Contrast her description with Lea's description of her husband. What emotions does each writer elicit from readers and how is that done?
6. **Exploring Links Online.** The Web is a rich source for stories of people dealing with a family member's cancer. Lea, in her essay, focuses on an action (bathing her husband). Find a story that focuses on objects (things, places) that recall that experience. Compare the two descriptive strategies in an essay.
7. **Writing the Research Paper.** Some evidence suggests that writing about traumatic events can produce beneficial physiological changes—emotional expressive therapy. Research the subject and then describe how this process might work in a formal paper with proper documentation.

For Further Study

Focusing on Grammar and Writing. Try rewriting a paragraph in the essay by changing the present tense verbs of the original to past tense verbs. Does that change your experience of the essay?

Working Together. To what extent does the essay also follow a process description? Working in groups, identify process elements in the description.

Seeing Other Modes at Work. The essay is also a narrative describing the bath from beginning to end.

The Day Nana Almost Flew

ALISA WOLF

Alisa Wolf has kept her writing practice going over 20 years of full-time work. As writer and editor, she has developed feature articles for consumer and trade magazines as well as marketing collateral and blog posts for a financial services firm. These projects have covered a wide range of subjects, from star gazing, to smoke-detector legislation, to investment portfolio construction. She earned an MFA from Vermont College, and she now develops and teaches adult education classes in fiction, memoir, and essay writing near her home in Medford, Massachusetts. Her work has appeared in Agni Online, Calyx, Cimarron Review, Concho River Review, The Legendary, Pisgah Review, Red Cedar Review, Reed Magazine, *and* Schuylkill Valley Journal.

On Writing: *Her grandmother once asked Wolf how she comes up with ideas. She laughed because getting ideas wasn't a problem. The hard part was choosing one that would sustain her curiosity, carry her through her doubts, and challenge her cherished views for however long it would take to finish. Wolf is currently working on a book of linked essays, tentatively titled, "This May Not Resolve as I Had Hoped."*

Before Reading

Connecting: Does Wolf's description remind you of a great grandparent or a grandparent?

Anticipating: Is the essay's focus on Nana or on the narrator? How can you tell?

1   **L**ast week, fourteen years after her death, Nana visited me in a dream, dressed not in one of the housedresses she'd worn exclusively in her final years, but in a blue worsted suit. As a young, single woman, Nana worked at an exclusive clothing store in downtown Boston, and she'd always been meticulous about her clothes. I was in my mid-twenties when she suggested that a little blouse and skirt might be more suitable for my job than the jerseys and jeans I wore when I visited her for lunch once every few weeks.

But no one I worked with at the group home dressed up, and the four mentally retarded women I supervised on the three-to-eleven shift changed their clothes after dinner from pants to pajamas. When I said I didn't see the point of buying anything I had to iron, Nana laughed.

• • •

2   Since Nana had fussed over her appearance all of the years I'd known her, I was shocked when she opened the door to her apartment one afternoon snapped up in a housedress—the tops of her knee-high hose showing in the slit below the bottom snap, her toes crammed into stockings and black plastic slippers. But as quickly as I registered my alarm, I pushed it away. After all, Nana didn't have to impress me. Besides, her hair, thick and white, gleamed with apparent good health, and her blue eyes shined behind pink-framed glasses; taking me in eagerly.

3   "Hello, dear. How is it outside?" Nana said.

4   "It's nice out," I said. I leaned down to hug her. She smelled of blossoms and talc.

5   She ushered me toward the small dining area, fragrant with the smells of chicken soup, roasted chicken, and noodle kugel issuing from her galley kitchen. The tabletop was padded thick with layers of cotton and topped off with a plastic covering that had a floral pattern on it, not unlike the pink-and-white flowers on Nana's housedress.

6   "How is it outside?" she asked again.

7   I gestured to the sun-streaked maple leaves filling the window. "It's still nice out, Nana."

8   I sat in my father's place at the head of the table. As always, a plate of challah covered with a linen napkin was set out. A salad of iceberg lettuce topped with sliced cucumbers, radishes, and tomatoes was also out, along with a half-gallon of Schweppes ginger ale.

9   "Would you like some ginger ale?" Nana asked.

10   "Thanks." I poured myself a glass and recapped the bottle.

11   Nana sat. Her eyes swept the table. "Would you like some ginger ale?" she asked again.

12   "Nana, I just took some."

13   Nana's laugh lit up like a flame that she quickly smothered out. "Ah, well," she said. She looked out toward the leaf-filled window and hummed a tune I'd only recently heard her sing. It was a Russian lullaby, a song from her childhood, she'd said on my last visit. She had no name for it, and she couldn't remember the words. I'd tried to learn the melody, singing "la la la" like she did, but the tune had slipped away from me as soon as I left her.

14   Nana leaned over the table and pulled back the plastic wrap over the salad. Then she went into the kitchen. She opened the refrigerator, lifted up jars, and plunked them back down, clanking and tinkling.

15   "Is everything okay in there, Nana?"

16   "I can't find the ginger ale," Nana said.

17   "Nana, it's right here." She came out of the kitchen and looked around, confused.

18   "Right here," I said.

19   "Do you want some ginger ale?" she asked. This time I didn't bother answering her.

• • •

20   I soon learned what should have been obvious—Nana was suffering from dementia. But I didn't connect her confusion with the disease until later when my father told me her doctor's diagnosis. In my defense, I'd never met anyone with dementia before, and I didn't recognize the symptoms. But I was also blinded by the comfort I took in the predictable rhythm of my visits with Nana. I'd been lulled by her conversational bits about the weather, the family, and veiled questions about my love life—to which I gave vague answers. Taking pleasure in being doted on, I allowed myself to dismiss earlier signs that she wasn't fully present. What's more, my visits with Nana provided me a refuge from my confusion about my life—who to love, where to find meaningful work, and how to manage my desires and fears—and I didn't want to see that the sanctuary she offered was about to go away.

• • •

21   After a meal Nana usually ushered me to the telephone table to call her sister Bessie, who had no children or grandchildren of her own. But on that day she didn't invite me to the nook outside the two bedrooms and bathroom, where she kept an ancient dial-up. It was made of metal and plated in black, its receiver a small barbell. She didn't heave it up, hook it on her shoulder, murmur the numbers as she dialed them, then say a few words to her sister before handing the phone to me. "It's Auntie Bessie," she'd whisper, as if my great-aunt didn't know I was there waiting to tell her that I was fine and that everyone in my family was too.

22   Since Nana didn't move toward the phone that day, I suggested we go out and walk to Bessie's apartment on Harvard Street, a ten-minute stroll. Nana put a white sweater on over the short sleeves of her housedress.

23   "Do you want to change into your shoes?" I asked.

24   "How is it out?"

25   "Fine, Nana," I said, and we went out into the sun.

• • •

26   When I was about ten years old, my mother disabused me of the notion that Nana had fled with my father's aunts and grandparents from a Russian *shtetl*, like the Jews hurrying out of ancient Egypt in the Passover story. In fact, Nana, her parents, and her siblings had immigrated decades before the Holocaust. For start-up capital, they'd brought their Eastern European recipes, which weren't written down. If I wanted to make Nana's dishes, the best way, my mother said, was to watch her do it.

27   I wasn't interested in stuffed cabbage, chopped liver, or sponge cake. So I asked Nana to make her creamy chocolate fudge. At my mother's stove during school vacation, Nana showed me how to bring butter, sugar, and evaporated milk to a boil. She dipped a wooden spoon into the syrup and then dribbled a bit into a glass of iced water. It turned instantly into a string of candy. When she dug it out, she rolled it between her fingers to check whether it had reached the soft-ball stage. Once it had, she took the pot off the heat, folded in melted chocolate, and then pulled a jar of marshmallow crème out of the cabinet. I glanced at the label and there, in print, was the recipe we were making. While we waited for the fudge to set, we watched *Days of Our Lives,* but I didn't follow the story. I was revising the myth of my old-world Nana, who wasn't so old-world after all.

28   Years later I went to Nana with a cassette recorder and a list of questions from a college oral history class. She didn't remember much about her village outside Vilnius or about her cross-Atlantic passage. Instead, she told me a story my father liked to tell. Once upon a time, when she'd worked as a sales girl, she held onto the quarter her mother gave her every day for lunch, saving up for the piano she'd buy once she married her yet unknown husband and had her own home. The clothing store didn't use price tags. Instead, Nana had bargained with her customers and was paid a commission. She added whatever else she managed to save to her lunch money, and eventually she bought an upright Vose, which was installed in her parlor after she married Pa. There she kept it dusted and shined so that her only son, my father, would one day play it. Years later my sister played it too.

29   My mother said the piano was a status symbol, a sign in Nana's mind of her refinement and good taste. But whatever else it might have been, it also represented the home and family she had wanted so badly that she'd been willing to skip lunches and go hungry. She'd been a passionate young woman once, like I was now. But she'd yearned for a husband and a home, whereas I ached to engage the world through work, ideas, and people with varied backgrounds and views. When I told her I was with a woman and wasn't interested in getting married, she looked at me the way she did when I came to see her in a wrinkled blouse.

30   "You're different," she said.

• • •

31   I crossed with Nana to the middle of the street and stepped up to a traffic island, green with summer grass and fragrant with plantings. I checked for traffic and then turned back to guide her on the rest of the way across. But Nana was looking in the direction we'd come. She spread her arms out like wings, tipped her head back to the sun, and laughed up at the sky. For a moment she became the girl she'd once been—in a pink dress, an expression of unguarded delight on her face.

32   I looked up too, squinting. "What's funny?" I said.

33   She cocked her head and, arms still spread, gave me a canny look. I had the bizarre notion that she was about to rise up onto her toes, lift off, and fly away. I felt alarmed, exactly as I would if I were hanging onto the hem of her dress, pulling her back to Earth.

34   Then she sat down.

35   "Nana, what's wrong? Are you tired?"

36   She looked up at me, recognition pouring back into her vacant expression. "Hello, dear. How is it out?" she said.

37   I took her by the hand and pulled her gently to her feet. I led her back across the street. We retraced our steps until we reached her modest brick apartment house. I guided her up the stairs and into her apartment. Then I called my father.

• • •

38   Over the following years Nana slipped slowly away. Soon, she stopped recognizing me. She mistook me on one visit to her nursing home for a social worker and, on another, for my father's wife. It was as if I'd veered so far from the outlines of the young woman she'd wanted me to be—the properly dressed career girl focused on furnishing a home, finding a husband, and having children—that I'd become a stranger. But hadn't I always kept a polite distance from Nana, pressing her for memories of the old days while volunteering little information about my own life?

39   In her nursing home's dining room, the aromas of her kugel and roasted chicken were replaced by the smell of baked, boiled, and fried food in large quantities, undercut with a whiff of something medicinal and the ubiquitous odor of urine. But I answered Nana's repeated questions about the weather and the family as I always had. When she was lucid and remembered to ask about my love life, I took a sip from a Styrofoam cup of tea with artificial sweetener and gave her my evasive reply. During lulls in what passed for conversation, she smoothed her housedress over her knees and hummed her Russian lullaby. I carried the tune out of the dining room with me, but it flew off the second I left the building. Though I strained to recall it, I had no luck. It was gone by the time I crossed the parking lot and started up my car.   ■

QUESTIONS ON SUBJECT AND PURPOSE

1. To what does the title refer?
2. Why might Wolf have chosen to write about her grandmother?
3. Is the essay about Nana or about the narrator's experience of Nana?

QUESTIONS ON STRATEGY AND AUDIENCE

1. What does Wolf describe about her Nana and what does she omit?
2. What is the role or purpose of the line of three spaced periods after paragraphs 1, 19, 20, 25, 30, and 37?
3. What expectations could Wolf have about her audience?

QUESTIONS ON VOCABULARY AND STYLE

1. How does Wolf "show" her readers Nana's decline rather than "telling" them what is happening?
2. When Wolf writes, "Nana's laugh lit up like a flame that she quickly smothered out" (paragraph 11), what figure of speech is she using?
3. Be prepared to define the following words: *worsted* (paragraph 1), *meticulous* (1), *challah* (6), *ubiquitous* (39).

WRITING SUGGESTIONS

1. **Doing a Critical Analysis.** Analyze how and why Wolf marks the passage of time in the essay. Why not simply describe her experiences in a linear fashion from earliest to last?
2. **Journaling or Blogging.** Explore your attitudes toward one of your grandparents. Make a list of descriptive details and typical behaviors.
3. **Practicing in a Paragraph.** Write a description of someone who is significantly older than you, preferably a grandparent. Try to visit your subject or at least talk with the person on the phone. Try to capture that person in your paragraph.
4. **Writing the Personal Essay.** Extend your paragraph into an essay. Use behavior, language, environment, and attitudes to reveal character. Use some dialogue rather than just relying on summary.
5. **Finding Reading Connections.** Lynn Bernardini in "Does This Date Mean Anything to You? (Chapter 2) uses a linear timeline with no flashbacks. In contrast, Wolf's essay involves movements back in time. Compare the two organizational strategies explaining why each is particularly appropriate.
6. **Exploring Links Online.** The Web has many stories about the impact of dementia or Alzheimer's on a family. Find another story that describes that experience. Compare the descriptive strategies that are used in the two essays.
7. **Writing the Research Paper.** According to the Alzheimer's Association (www.alz.org), the disease is the "6th leading cause of death in the United States and the 5th leading cause of death for those aged 65 and older. It is the only cause of death among the top 10 in America without a way to prevent it, cure it or even slow its progression." Using research, write a documented essay in which you describe the symptoms and the progression of the disease.

For Further Study

Focusing on Grammar and Writing. Wolf uses the dash a number of times in the essay. Look at each use and then draw some conclusions about when and why a dash should be used in writing.

Working Together. In describing her grandmother, Wolf selects a number of details. Working in small groups, choose one of the following details and discuss what it reveals about Nana: her clothes (paragraph 1), the questions about the ginger ale (6–19), the usual telephone call to Bessie (21), fudge making (27), the piano (29), the nursing home (39).

Seeing Other Modes at Work. Wolf obviously uses narrative to provide structure for her descriptions.

Nameless, Tennessee

WILLIAM LEAST HEAT MOON

William Least Heat Moon was born William Trogdon in Missouri in 1939 and earned a Ph.D. in English from the University of Missouri in 1973. Trogdon's father created his pen name in memory of their Sioux forefather. His books include Blue Highways: A Journey into America *(1982),* PrairyErth *(1991),* River-Horse: A Voyage Across America *(1999), and* Roads to Quoz: An American Mosey *(2008). The following essay is from* Blue Highways, *an account of Least Heat Moon's 14,000-mile journey through American backroads in a converted van called Ghost Dancing. Its title refers to the blue ink used by map publisher Rand McNally to indicate smaller, or secondary, roads.*

On Writing: *Asked about his writing, Least Heat Moon observed: "Woody Allen once said the hardest thing in writing is going from nothing to something. And I think he's right. I struggle so much getting that first draft down. My writing draws so much upon every bit that I am, that I feel drained when I finish a book, and it's years before I'm ready to write again."*

Before Reading

Connecting: If you could get in an automobile and drive off, and time, money, and responsibilities posed no obstacles, where would you go?

Anticipating: "Nameless, Tennessee" does more than just faithfully record everything Least Heat Moon saw while visiting the Wattses. The narrative has a central focus that controls the selection of detail. What is that focus?

1   **N**ameless, Tennessee, was a town of maybe ninety people if you pushed it, a dozen houses along the road, a couple of barns, same number of churches, a general merchandise store selling Fire Chief gasoline, and a community center with a lighted volleyball court. Behind the center was an open-roof, rusting metal privy with PAINT ME on the door, in the hollow of a nearby oak lay a full pint of Jack Daniel's Black Label. From the houses, the odor of coal smoke.

2   Next to a red tobacco barn stood the general merchandise with a poster of Senator Albert Gore, Jr., smiling from the window. I knocked. The door opened partway. A tall, thin man said, "Closed up. For good," and started to shut the door.

3   "Don't want to buy anything. Just a question for Mr. Thurmond Watts."

4   The man peered through the slight opening. He looked me over. "What question would that be?"

5   "If this is Nameless, Tennessee, could he tell me how it got that name?"

6   The man turned back into the store and called out, "Miss Ginny! Somebody here wants to know how Nameless come to be Nameless."

7   Miss Ginny edged to the door and looked me and my truck over. Clearly, she didn't approve. She said, "You know as well as I do, Thurmond. Don't keep him on the stoop in the damp to tell him." Miss Ginny, I found out, was Mrs. Virginia Watts, Thurmond's wife.

8   I stepped in and they both began telling the story, adding a detail here, the other correcting a fact there, both smiling at the foolishness of it all. It seems the hilltop settlement went for years without a name. Then one day the Post Office Department told the people if they wanted mail up on the mountain they would have to give the place a name you could properly address a letter to. The community met; there were only a handful, but they commenced debating. Some wanted patriotic names, some names from nature, one man recommended in all seriousness his own name. They couldn't agree, and they ran out of names to argue about. Finally, a fellow tired of the talk; he didn't like the mail he received anyway. "Forget the durn Post Office," he said. "This here's a nameless place if I ever seen one, so leave it be." And that's just what they did.

9   Watts pointed out the window. "We used to have signs on the road, but the Halloween boys keep tearin' them down."

10   "You think Nameless is a funny name," Miss Ginny said. "I see it plain in your eyes. Well, you take yourself up north a piece to Difficult or Defeated or Shake Rag. Now them are silly names."

11   The old store, lighted only by three fifty-watt bulbs, smelled of coal oil and baking bread. In the middle of the rectangular room, where the oak floor sagged a little, stood an iron stove. To the right was a wooden table with an unfinished game of checkers and a stool made from an apple-tree stump. On shelves around the walls sat earthen jugs with corncob stoppers, a few canned goods, and some of the two thousand old clocks and clockworks Thurmond Watts owned. Only one was ticking, the others he just looked at. I asked how long he'd been in the store.

12   "Thirty-five years, but we closed the first day of the year. We're hopin' to sell it to a churchly couple. Upright people. No athians."

13   "Did you build this store?"

14   "I built this one, but it's the third general store on the ground. I fear it'll be the last. I take no pleasure in that. Once you could come in here for a gallon of paint, a pickle, a pair of shoes, and a can of corn."

15   "Or horehound candy," Miss Ginny said. "Or corsets and salves. We had cough syrups and all that for the body. In season, we'd buy and sell blackberries and walnuts and chestnuts, before the blight got them. And outside, Thurmond milled corn and sharpened plows. Even shoed a horse sometimes."

16   "We could fix up a horse or a man or a baby," Watts said.

17   "Thurmond, tell him we had a doctor on the ridge in them days."

18   "We had a doctor on the ridge in them days. As good as any doctor alivin'. He'd cut a crooked toenail or deliver a woman. Dead these last years."

19   "I got some bad ham meat one day," Miss Ginny said, "and took to vomitin'. All day, all night. Hangin' on the drop edge of yonder. I said to Thurmond, 'Thurmond, unless you want shut of me, call the doctor.'"

20   "I studied on it," Watts said.

21   "You never did. You got him right now. He come over and put three drops of iodeen in half a glass of well water. I drank it down and the vomitin' stopped with the last swallow. Would you think iodeen could do that?"

22   "He put Miss Ginny on one teaspoon of spirits of ammonia in well water for her nerves. Ain't nothin' works better for her to this day."

23   "Calms me like the hand of the Lord."

24   Hilda, the Wattses' daughter, came out of the backroom. "I remember him," she said. "I was just a baby. Y'all were talkin' to him, and he lifted me up on the counter and gave me a stick of Juicy Fruit and a piece of cheese."

25   "Knew the old medicines," Watts said. "Only drugstore he needed was a good kitchen cabinet. None of them anteebeeotics that hit you worsen your ailment. Forgotten lore now, the old medicines, because they ain't profit in iodeen."

26   Miss Ginny started back to the side room where she and her sister Marilyn were taking apart a duck-down mattress to make bolsters. She stopped at the window for another look at Ghost Dancing. "How do you sleep in that thing? Ain't you all cramped and cold?"

27   "How does the clam sleep in his shell?" Watts said in my defense.

28   "Thurmond, get the boy a piece of buttermilk pie afore he goes on."

29   "Hilda, get some buttermilk pie." He looked at me. "You like good music?" I said I did. He cranked up an old Edison phonograph, the kind with the big morning-glory blossom for a speaker, and put on a wax cylinder. "This will be 'My Mother's Prayer,'" he said.

30   While I ate buttermilk pie, Watts served as disc jockey of Nameless, Tennessee. "Here's 'Mountain Rose.'" It was one of those moments that you know at the time will stay with you to the grave: the sweet pie, the gaunt man playing the old music, the coals in the stove glowing orange, the scent of kerosene and hot bread. "Here's 'Evening Rhapsody.'" The music was so heavily romantic we both laughed. I thought: It is for this I have come.

31   Feathered over and giggling, Miss Ginny stepped from the side room. She knew she was a sight. "Thurmond, give him some lunch. Still looks hungry."

32   Hilda pulled food off the woodstove in the backroom: home-butchered and canned whole-hog sausage, home-canned June apples, turnip greens, cole slaw, potatoes, stuffing, hot cornbread. All delicious.

33   Watts and Hilda sat and talked while I ate. "Wish you would join me."

34 "We've ate," Watts said. "Cain't beat a woodstove for flavorful cookin'."

35 He told me he was raised in a one-hundred-fifty-year-old cabin still standing in one of the hollows. "How many's left," he said, "that grew up in a log cabin? I ain't the last surely, but I must be climbin' on the list."

36 Hilda cleared the table. "You Watts ladies know how to cook."

37 "She's in nursin' school at Tennessee Tech. I went over for one of them football games last year there at Coevul." To say *Cookeville*, you let the word collapse in upon itself so that it comes out "Coevul."

38 "Do you like football?" I asked.

39 "Don't know. I was so high up in that stadium, I never opened my eyes."

40 Watts went to the back and returned with a fat spiral notebook that he set on the table. His expression had changed. "Miss Ginny's *Deathbook*."

41 The thing startled me. Was it something I was supposed to sign? He opened it but said nothing. There were scads of names written in a tidy hand over pages incised to crinkliness by a ball-point. Chronologically, the names had piled up: Wives, grandparents, a stillborn infant, relatives, friends close and distant. Names, names. After each, the date of the unknown finally known and transcribed. The last entry bore yesterday's date.

42 "She's wrote out twenty years' worth. Ever day she listens to the hospital report on the radio and puts the names in. Folks come by to check a date. Or they just turn through the books. Read them like a scrapbook."

43 Hilda said, "Like Saint Peter at the gates inscribin' the names."

44 Watts took my arm. "Come along." He led me to the fruit cellar under the store. As we went down, he said, "Always take a newborn baby upstairs afore you take him downstairs, otherwise you'll incline him downwards."

45 The cellar was dry and full of cobwebs and jar after jar of home-canned food, the bottles organized as a shopkeeper would: sausage, pumpkin, sweet pickles, tomatoes, corn relish, blackberries, peppers, squash, jellies. He held a hand out toward the dusty bottles. "Our tomorrows."

46 Upstairs again, he said, "Hope to sell the store to the right folk. I see now, though, it'll be somebody offen the ridge. I've studied on it, and maybe it's the end of our place." He stirred the coals. "This store could give a comfortable livin', but not likely get you rich. But just gettin' by is dice rollin' to people nowadays. I never did see my day guaranteed."

47 When it was time to go, Watts said, "If you find anyone along your ways wants a good store—on the road to Cordell Hull Lake—tell them about us."

48 I said I would. Miss Ginny and Hilda and Marilyn came out to say goodbye. It was cold and drizzling again. "Weather to give a man the weary dismals," Watts grumbled. "Where you headed from here?"

49 "I don't know."

50 "Cain't get lost then."

51 Miss Ginny looked again at my rig. It had worried her from the first as it had my mother. "I hope you don't get yourself kilt in that durn thing gallivantin' around the country."

52   "Come back when the hills dry off," Watts said. "We'll go lookin' for some of them round rocks all sparkly inside."

53   I thought a moment. "Geodes?"

54   "Them's the ones. The country's properly full of them."   ∎

QUESTIONS ON SUBJECT AND PURPOSE

1. At one point in the narrative (paragraph 30), Least Heat Moon remarks, "I thought: It is for this I have come." What does he seem to be suggesting? What is the "this" that he finds in Nameless?

2. Why do "Miss Ginny's *Deathbook*" (paragraph 40) and the "fruit cellar" (44) seem appropriate details?

3. What might have attracted Least Heat Moon to this place and these people? What does he want you to sense? Is there anything in his description and narrative that suggests how he feels about Nameless?

QUESTIONS ON STRATEGY AND AUDIENCE

1. After you have read the selection, describe each member of the Watts family. Describe the exterior and interior of their store. Then, carefully go through the selection and see how many specific descriptive details the author uses. List them.

2. What devices other than direct description does Least Heat Moon use to create the sense of place and personality? Make a list, and be prepared to tell how those devices work.

3. How is the narrative arranged? Is the order just spatial and chronological?

QUESTIONS ON VOCABULARY AND STYLE

1. Least Heat Moon attempts to reproduce the pronunciation of some words— for example, *athians* (paragraph 12), *iodeen* (21), and *anteebeeotics* (25). Make a list of all such phonetic spellings. Why does Least Heat Moon do this? Do you think he captures all of the Wattses' accent or just some part of it? Is the device effective?

2. Examine how Least Heat Moon uses dialogue in his description. How are the Wattses revealed by what they say? How much of what was actually said during the visit is recorded? Can you find specific points in the story where Least Heat Moon obviously omits dialogue?

3. Try to define or explain the following words and phrases: *horehound candy* (paragraph 15), *bolsters* (26), *buttermilk pie* (28), *incised to crinkliness by a ballpoint* (41), *weary dismals* (48), *gallivantin' around* (51).

WRITING SUGGESTIONS

1. **Doing a Critical Analysis.** Least Heat Moon describes the people in his story in large part by recording what they say and how they say it. In an essay, analyze how he uses dialogue to create and reveal the personalities of the Wattses.

2. **Journaling or Blogging.** Have you ever encountered or experienced a person, a place, or an event that seemed to be frozen in time? Try to recall a few such examples.

3. **Practicing in a Paragraph.** Every campus has a building or a location that has acquired a strange or vivid name (e.g., a cafeteria called "The Scrounge"). In a paragraph, describe such a place. Keep a central focus—you want to convey an atmosphere more than provide a photograph in words.

4. **Writing the Personal Essay.** Choose an unusual business in your town or city. In an essay describe the place. Make sure that you capture a central impression or thesis. Try to include both people and dialogue.

5. **Finding Reading Connections.** Tom Haines in "Facing Famine" (Chapter 1) also creates a vivid sense of character through the use of dialogue and description. Compare the descriptive techniques used by the two writers.

6. **Exploring Links Online.** Online travel magazines offer a wide assortment of essays on exciting things to do in North America—the food in New Orleans, blue grass festivals in North Carolina, canoeing in Maine, fishing in the Pacific Northwest. Select an essay and analyze how the writer evokes an atmosphere and captures your interest.

7. **Writing the Research Paper.** Least Heat Moon is fascinated by unusual names and often drives considerable distances to visit towns with names such as Dime Box and Liberty Bond. Choose an unusual place name (town, river, subdivision, topographical feature) from your home state and research the origin of the name. Write a formal research paper on the history of the name, documenting your sources.

For Further Study

Focusing on Grammar and Writing. Select a group of paragraphs from the essay and rewrite them using no dialogue. You could have your narrator summarize what was said. What is lost when the dialogue is removed?

Working Together. Working in small groups, divide the essay in blocks. Presumably, Least Heat Moon's visit lasted several hours. How much time is accounted for in the essay? Look for places where time is abridged or actions omitted. What does this reveal about artfully telling a story?

Seeing Other Modes at Work. The essay is also a narrative. How is the narrative structured?

The Queen and I

ADRIENNE ROSS SCANLAN

Adrienne Ross Scanlan's essays have appeared in Pilgrimage, Tiny Lights: A Journal of Personal Narrative, Tikkun, Under the Sun, *and many other online or print magazines and anthologies. She received a Seattle Arts Commission award, an Artist Trust Literature Fellowship, and is the nonfiction editor for the* Blue Lyra Review *(www.bluelyrareview.com). Her essay collection, "Turning Homeward: Restoring Nature in the Urban*

Wild," is circulating to agents and publishers. You can learn more about her work at www.adrienne-ross-scanlan.com.

On Writing: *Scanlan writes: "My work as a writer comes down to being alert to the place where I live and discovering questions in everyday moments. Being funny helps, too, if I can pull it off. I managed to do all three in 'The Queen and I' (at least I hope I did), making it one of my favorite essays."*

Before Reading

Connecting: How do you react to honey bees, bumblebees, hornets? Why do you react in that way? Fear? Curiosity?

Anticipating: By the end of the essay, can you explain why it might be acceptable to destroy a nest of wasps but not a nest of bees?

1   **F**ragile wings beat into a black-veined blur as the bees tried to fly through my bedroom window and back outside to the garden. The bees craved light. Once inside my room, the bees forgot how they had entered. Their evolution had left them unprepared for following summer light falling through glass windows. When a bee finally calmed down, I'd catch her in a glass teacup and release her outside, watching her fly to the orange nasturtiums like an infant kept too long from the breast. There was a certain *noblesse oblige* in my actions. If the bees were grateful they gave no sign. Off they went, without even the proverbial backward glance, to where the hot July days were sending sunlight falling in sharp, shining sheets over our tattered rose bushes and scraggly lawn.

2   I didn't release the bees out of a fondness for insects. I tolerated the spiders spreading their delicate webs in my bathroom corners. They were my allies, eating the flies and whatever else was wandering through my basement rooms. And how could anyone hate butterflies or ladybugs? For all the others it takes an act of sheer intellectual will to remember I share the same protein and DNA biochemistry as the creeping, crawling creatures I collectively ignore, dismissing them as bugs. If any insect could inspire some dim interest, it was bees.

3   A lay naturalist, I'm always eager for a good natural history book. Years ago, I picked up William Longgood's *The Queen Must Die*, an excellent introduction to the eccentricities of bees and beekeeping. Longgood's bees were honeybees. The bees exploring my scented candles, their fuzzy black bodies crowned with a yellow cap and tipped with a gold ring around their tails, were bumblebees. Pulling Longgood down from my library shelves, I read that:

4   *Bumblebees are . . . socially inclined but considered to be more primitive in development than honeybees. The female is impregnated in the fall and she alone survives the winter, snuggled into a hole in the earth. . . . Come spring . . . her offspring forms a working colony . . . they gather nectar while their mother devotes herself full time to laying eggs. . . .*

5   All too often, books serve as my guide into nature. Now I had creatures available for personal study. Was it pollinating behavior when a bumblebee arched her fuzzy body and rubbed her thin legs over the powdery remains of my Aurobindo Quiet Mind incense sticks? What was the function of the translucent droppings the bees left on the red and yellow wax hanging from my brass Hanukah menorahs? Not territory marking, that much I knew, for bumblebees use visual landmarks to find preferred foraging sites and once there don't monopolize feeding territories. The longer I watched the bumblebees, the more enchanted I became with their short, intricate lives. Without sugar to maintain energy, adult bees can die within a few hours, and in my rooms, they were dropping like flies. Losing even part of a day trapped in my bedroom was too long in a life that lasted two or so weeks.

6   Soon there were too many of them. Every morning, I'd pull out the teacup and get as many bees outside as I could. I'd cook breakfast, call clients and by mid-morning four, five, sometimes six or more bees would be buzzing, buzzing, *bizzing* above my shoulders.

7   Except they weren't only flying. Honeybees fly. Bumblebees fly and crawl: across the beige carpet in my home office, across the white linoleum in my bathroom (making it impossible for me to step out of the shower without first being sure nothing was moving between the bath mat and my slippers) and to my horror, across my bed.

8   *Noblesse oblige* collapsed before raw survival instinct. The spiders and I could share the same habitat thanks to mutually exclusive niches. The bumblebees were invading my space. I wanted them gone from my life. I just didn't want them killed.

9   All the environmentally responsible exterminators I called said the same thing. Honeybees could be removed by a beekeeper needing a new hive. Bumblebees were commercially worthless. They produced no honey or anything else that could be sold. Or at least nothing that could be *immediately* sold. Bumblebees are worth billions of dollars to North American farmers if only for their role in clover pollination. Here in Seattle, all the bees could pollinate were the ruby roses outside my bedroom window, the purple phlox and columbine draped in long wandering tendrils across our trellis. There was only one thing to do with bumblebees.

10   "We use a spray," the exterminators explained.

11   "What does it do?" I asked, as if I didn't know.

12   "It's made of chrysanthemums. It won't hurt you at all. Don't worry."

13   "What does it do to the bees?"

14   "Kills 'em. Kills 'em dead. But don't worry. It won't hurt you at all."

15   The exterminators insisted the bees were coming into the house from a hole in the outside walls. Inside the wall would be their nest. The only holes I found were where my window didn't quite meet the frame. Could the bees be nesting outside, I asked the exterminators, wriggling into my bedroom and then forgetting how to wriggle out? Highly unlikely, I was told, so I kept searching for the entry hole. While I didn't find any bees, I did discover a

hornet's nest hanging from our garage roof. If bees inspired mixed feelings, hornets were nothing but gleaming, ebony messengers of dread.

16   On a butterfly field trip the summer before, I'd made the mistake of wandering off into waist-high grasses. Suddenly, I had been surrounded by large, dark insects. As I tried to spot their field marks I felt a deep, searing sting followed by several more on my legs, and another on my arm. I stood frozen in an awful, primal fear before I threw my butterfly net into the air and raced from the hornets' nest hidden in the grass.

17   Standing in my driveway, I squinted into the bright sun to watch the hornets. How many times had I or my housemates opened the garage doors not knowing they were there? If the nest continued to grow, we would no longer be able to open the doors without bringing down an insect battle squadron.

18   Discouraged, I returned to my bedroom where the bees were buzzing with unfailing persistence against my window panes. The summer was razor hot and as short-lived as the bees. Outside my windows were marigolds with their ruffled petals, pink daisies, blood-crimson roses and ghostly white morning glories encircling the Douglas fir towering over our backyard. So many flowers waiting for bees. So many bees wanting nothing more than to wriggle their plump bodies into a flower's embrace, and then dart to the next encounter, the legs of these infertile female workers sticky with pollen that brought cross-fertilization to the flowers and food to their hive's young. It was a relationship as old as the flowers themselves extending back some 100 million years ago into the Cretaceous period.

19   It was then that bees and flowering plants developed their mutualistic relationship. Bees and other insects provided pollination, while plants reciprocated with nectar and other desired services. Bees are believed to have played a major role in the Cretaceous' explosive diversification of plant species. Regardless of which came first—the flowers or the bees—this longstanding relationship became so successful that now a majority of the world's flowering plants require insect pollination to reproduce. Watching the bees flit from our zucchini plants to the orange nasturtiums, I couldn't help but respect the erotic certainties of their lives.

20   Stepping carefully around the bees crawling across my rug, I glanced out the window to watch the hornets making their black darting flights. Knowledge is power, and power cuts both ways. Watching the ebony hornets gleaming in the sunlight, I wondered if knowledge wasn't power as much as it is intimacy. The more I learned about the bees, the closer I came to sharing their lives. No longer just some kind of a bug, the bees had become as real as I or my housemates and with as much right to go about their lives.

21   If I knew anything about the hornets shielded behind the fragile gray walls of their hive, I wouldn't be able to call in the exterminators. I'd have to surrender the garage, and then the driveway, the back yard and sooner or later my private basement entrance. I uneasily decided not to learn anything about hornets.

22   One of my housemates called suddenly from the back yard. He pointed towards our compost bin, his brown skin shining in the sunlight, excitedly crying: "Wasps! Wasps!"

23   *Great,* I thought as I walked outside. *Bees in the bedroom. Hornets in the garage. Wasps in the compost bin. What's next? Hordes of locusts? Plagues of grasshoppers?*

24   My housemate pointed to beneath a western red cedar's sheltering limbs. No one in the house knew how to care for compost. For years lawn clippings and weeds had been thrown in the plastic bin and forgotten. I frowned as I noticed the neat rows of diamond-shaped holes lining the bin's emerald green walls. There were no wasps in sight, but soon enough a bumblebee alighted on an opening, quickly disappearing inside. Another bee emerged from the same hole and took off for the daisies, followed by another bee. Hovering in the air was a bee eager to get into the bin.

25   *Foraging,* I thought, with quiet satisfaction. The bees were returning to the nest, their legs thick with pollen, while others were flying out to find food for the colony. More than finding the nest, I was seeing something completely new. I felt familiar gratitude for a world so worthy of curiosity.

26   Against all the exterminators' predictions, the bees were nesting outside, slipping through the cracks in my window frame. Every time I turned on my full-spectrum office lights the bees would circle my shoulders as I wrote grants for environmental education programs. As beleaguered as I felt, I still couldn't call in the exterminators with their green-trimmed jumpsuits and deadly chrysanthemum sprays.

27 A week later, a chance conversation at a folk dance introduced me to a local beekeeper.

28   "Removing the bees won't be a problem," she said with an easy smile and a shining confidence at the first mention of the word *bees.* "I'll get the nest and set them up in my garden. It's filled with flowers. They'll do fine."

29   "These aren't honeybees," I warned. "They're bumblebees. They're worthless to you."

30   My companion waved her hand nonchalantly. I glanced down at the dark yellow business card she gave me. Embossed in black ink was an illustration of an ebony-haired woman wearing a long Victorian gown not so very different from her own floral print dress. The woman gazed in seeming contentment at a hive encircled by bees. *Beauty and the Bees Honey,* read the card, *Sally Harris, Beekeeper.*

31   *Bees are bees to this woman,* I thought, *and she's one of them.*

32   "How much will it cost?"

33   "Nothing. But I'll need help," cautioned Sally as she sipped her ice water. She tugged her hand through thick black curls. "Someone will have to suit up to help capture them."

34   "Sure," I said, hoping the speed of my reply covered my inner cringing. Trapped in the sticky web of my own good intentions, I smiled weakly and said: "I can do that."

35 Sally came by late the next afternoon with an empty gallon yogurt container, trowels, hand hoes and two white beekeeper suits she placed on our weathered worm bin. I picked up the thin suit with dismay.

36   "I thought these were made out of canvas."

37   "Oh, no," Sally said with a smile as she slipped off her sandals. "Just cotton. That's usually thick enough."

38   "What do we wear under it?" I asked hopefully.

39   "This is fine," shrugged Sally, indicating our pastel tank tops and shorts. "But you'll need boots past your ankles to stuff the pants into."

40   I ran into my bedroom and pulled my hiking boots from my closet. I also pulled out my long-sleeved teal polypro shirt, making sure to zip up the neck after I yanked it on over my tank top. I tugged the matching pants on over my hiking shorts. At Sally's amazed stare when I returned, I said only: "If the bees don't get me, the heat will."

41   I stepped into the one-piece bee suit, flipped the black mesh hood over my head, and secured it with an intricate array of zippers and velcro. Completely impervious to the bees (or so I hoped), we advanced on the compost bin. The bin tipped over easily. A black, *buzzing* cloud of bees flew up, so many darting and circling that I couldn't count them. Sally pulled a three-pronged hand hoe through the bramble and brown leaves. She scooped bees and egg clusters into the yogurt container, closing it tightly as she said: "I'm not seeing a queen."

42   My heart sank. The colony wouldn't survive without the queen. All their collective lives were dedicated to keeping her alive and feeding the endless clutches of young she spewed out. If the queen was still in the compost it would only be a matter of time before the bees returned to my bedroom.

43   "Sally, we've got to find the queen," I insisted urgently. Sally calmly pulled back clumps of scratchy twigs and moldy brown leaves. The buzzing grew to a dull roar. Bees swooped, encircled our heads, darted between our arms and legs. Unlike honeybees, bumblebees don't die when they sting. I could be stung over and over again, enclosed by a thick ebony cloud of enraged bees. One bee droned louder than the others. I wanted to run but primal instinct rooted me in place. I swirled my eyes sideways. A bumblebee was perched on my hood not two inches from my left eye.

44   "I need to get away from the bees," I croaked, my voice leaden with fear.

45   Sally nodded unperturbed as she searched for the queen. I stepped from the cedar tree's shadows and back into the afternoon sunlight. It was only three feet but that was far enough for the bees. I was out of the orbit of their tattered hive and lost queen. I was beyond the range of their interest. I stood breathing hard, sweat clinging to my warm clothes, as drawn to the sunlight as the bees. Our worlds were so different. What the bees sensed so alien to what I saw and knew. The light we could share: that same distant warmth keeping us alive.

46   I let myself feel my terror as I stood still in the sunlight's brilliance. I could hide nothing in the light's illuminating safety. I walked back to Sally strangely unconcerned by the whirling bees.

47   Sally handed me the scratched yogurt container.

48   "I've looked everywhere," she said, "and still can't find any queens."

49   "Queens?" I stammered out. I stared at Sally in confused frustration. Successions in honeybee hives are fights to the death. Wild bee queens will kill in competitions over nest sites. "Queens? There's only one to a nest."

50   "That's honeybees. Bumblebee nests will sometimes have an old fertile queen and several virgin queens that haven't left to find their wintering sites.

51   "I don't want to hear this," I moaned.

52   "Look, there may be several queens in this nest, there may be just one. Either way, I haven't found any. She may be flying. We'll never catch her then."

53   "I thought queens only flew on their mating flights or when they swarmed," I said frowning, knowing that singular mating flight was a queen bee's initiation from virginity to lifelong motherhood. "Let me guess. That's honeybees, right?"

54   Sally nodded. "Want me to check the container in case I got a queen without realizing it?"

55   We put the yogurt container on the rickety picnic table. Carefully, Sally opened the lid.

56   "There she is!" Sally cried. She slammed the lid shut, giving me only a brief glimpse of a bee larger and more elongated than the plump fuzzy workers.

57   Sally left with the queen and what we hoped were enough workers to start the hive anew. A dozen or more bees circled their destroyed hive or dropped down to explore the moist brown darkness that had sheltered their queen. Within a few hours most had disappeared into the sunlight and the sweet embrace of irises and snapdragons. Some bees would be assimilated into a new hive, genetic outcasts working for the survival of another queen's line. Others would die soon, their legs sticky with pollen they no longer needed.

58   The hornets were soon gone, too. The next day, I came back from grocery shopping just as the exterminator was pulling out of our driveway. A single hornet circled where the nest used to be. Scraps of papery gray walls skittered in the late afternoon breeze. No sense of obligation could make me miss them.

59   I called Sally. She had placed the bees (". . . along with some leaf mulch so they'd feel at home . . .") under the rhododendron bushes in her front yard. Now bumblebees were buzzing and nuzzling flowers wherever she looked.

60   I walked out to the compost bin. There was no *buzzing* in my ears. Nothing small and black darted past me or glinted in the sunset glow. Relief mingled with sadness. Somewhere the bees from my garden were sinking into a gladiola or pink dahlia before daylight ebbed away. Now that I was no longer living with the bees I could appreciate their simple, unfailing perseverance. Life is short. And full of flowers.   ■

Author's Note: "The Queen and I" was written in the late 1990s, a seemingly halcyon time when honeybees and bumble-bees seemed as daily and abundant as flowers. In actuality, several wild bumblebee species were already declining in number and range, and by 2006–2007, Colony Collapse Disorder would deci-mate honeybee hives. Possible causes would include disease, loss of habitat, and pesticide exposure, even at the common dosages thought to be at nonfatal levels.

QUESTIONS ON SUBJECT AND PURPOSE

1. What might Scanlan mean when she writes, "I wondered if knowledge wasn't power as much as it is intimacy" (paragraph 20)?
2. Has Scanlan changed your view of bumblebees? Are you more interested? More sympathetic?
3. Why might she have written the essay? What might have been her motivation?

QUESTIONS ON STRATEGY AND AUDIENCE

1. The essay is divided into four parts using extra white space to signal that division. Why that division?
2. Why is she so sympathetic to be the bees and indifferent to the hornets (paragraph 21 and 58)?
3. What could Scanlan expect of her audience?

QUESTIONS ON VOCABULARY AND STYLE

1. When Scanlan describes the bee as flying to a flower "like an infant kept too long from the breast" (paragraph 1), what figure of speech is she using?
2. When she writes, "Trapped in the sticky web of my own good intentions" (paragraph 34), what figure of speech is she using?
3. Be prepared to define the following words or phrases: *noblesse oblige* (paragraph 1), *niches* (8), *reciprocated* (19), *beleaguered* (26), *nonchalantly* (30), *impervious* (41), *bramble* (41), *assimilated* (57), *perseverance* (60).

WRITING SUGGESTIONS

1. **Doing a Critical Analysis.** Scanlan uses figurative language, striking images, and poetic word choice in her essay. Analyze her use of these devices in her essay, focusing on what role they play in her descriptive technique.
2. **Journaling or Blogging.** Choose a living, common organism—a type of plant, an insect, a bird. It should be something that you have an opportunity to observe. Make a list of possibilities for a descriptive essay.
3. **Practicing in a Paragraph.** Choose one of the organisms on your list. Be specific in your choice—for example, poison ivy, marigolds, earthworms,

robins. Use your own powers of observation, but add as well information from both online and print sources.

4. **Writing the Personal Essay.** Flesh out your paragraph into an essay. Remember that a careful selection of vivid detail is the key to effective description. You are not writing the verbal equivalent of a photograph; you are revealing the life of the organism.

5. **Finding Reading Connections.** Gordon Grice in "Caught in the Widow's Web" (Writers at Work) describes in detail his encounters with the Black Widow spider. In an essay, compare the descriptive techniques of the two writers.

6. **Exploring Links Online.** Like to know more about bees and wasps and why they are so different? Using the Web, locate information and write a descriptive essay on their differences.

7. **Writing the Research Paper.** Bees are pollinators; wasps (a hornet is a type of wasp) are predators (feeding on insects). Bees are vitally important to agriculture and colonies/hives should not be exterminated. What about wasps, hornets, yellow jackets? Research one group of these insects and, in a documented essay, write a full description of its nature and habits.

For Further Study

Focusing on Grammar and Writing. Some words, sentences, and even the quotation are in italics. Why? What is the effect of this typographical device?

Working Together. Divide the essay into paragraph blocks and then, working in small groups, identify sentences, word choices, images, and figurative language that are particularly vivid or striking.

Seeing Other Modes at Work. The essay also uses narration, cause and effect, and process.

The Inheritance of Tools

SCOTT RUSSELL SANDERS

Born in Memphis, Tennessee, in 1945, Scott Russell Sanders received a Ph.D. from Cambridge University. Currently a professor of English at Indiana University, Sanders is a novelist, an essayist, and a science fiction writer. He has contributed fiction and essays to many journals and magazines and has published numerous books including A Private History of Awe *(2006).*

Sanders writes often about his childhood and his efforts to "ground" himself. In another of his collections of essays, Secrets of the Universe *(1991), Sanders describes growing up with an alcoholic father, noting that he "wants to drag into the light what eats at me—the fear, the guilt, the shame—so that my own children may be spared."*

> **On Writing:** *Commenting on the development of his writing style from academic prose to creative writing and essays, Sanders observed: "I flouted rules I learned about writing in school. I played with sound, strung images together line after line, flung out metaphors by the handful. Sin of sins, I even mixed metaphors, the way any fertile field will sprout dozens of species of grass and flower and fern. I let my feelings and opinions show. . . . I drew shamelessly on my own life. I swore off jargon and muddle and much. I wrote in the active voice."*

Before Reading

Connecting: Can you think of something that you learned how to do from a family member or friend?

Anticipating: In what ways is "The Inheritance of Tools" an appropriate title for the essay? What is the essay about?

1   **A**t just about the hour when my father died, soon after dawn one February morning when ice coated the windows like cataracts, I banged my thumb with a hammer. Naturally I swore at the hammer, the reckless thing, and in the moment of swearing I thought of what my father would say: "If you'd try hitting the nail it would go in a whole lot faster. Don't you know your thumb's not as hard as that hammer?" We both were doing carpentry that day, but far apart. He was building cupboards at my brother's place in Oklahoma; I was at home in Indiana putting up a wall in the basement to make a bedroom for my daughter. By the time my mother called with news of his death—the long distance wires whittling her voice until it seemed too thin to bear the weight of what she had to say—my thumb was swollen. A week or so later a white scar in the shape of a crescent moon began to show above the cuticle, and month by month it rose across the pink sky of my thumbnail. It took the better part of a year for the scar to disappear, and every time I noticed it I thought of my father.

2   The hammer had belonged to him, and to his father before him. The three of us have used it to build houses and barns and chicken coops, to upholster chairs and crack walnuts, to make doll furniture and book shelves and jewelry boxes. The head is scratched and pockmarked, like an old plowshare that has been working rocky fields, and it gives off the sort of dull sheen you see on fast creek water in the shade. It is a finishing hammer, about the weight of a bread loaf, too light, really, for framing walls, too heavy for cabinetwork, with a curved claw for pulling nails, a rounded head for pounding, a fluted neck for looks, and a hickory handle for strength.

3   The present handle is my third one, bought from a lumberyard in Tennessee down the road from where my brother and I were helping my father

build his retirement house. I broke the previous one by trying to pull sixteen-penny nails out of floor joists—a foolish thing to do with a finishing hammer, as my father pointed out. "You ever hear of a crowbar?" he said. No telling how many handles he and my grandfather had gone through before me. My grandfather used to cut down hickory trees on his farm, saw them into slabs, cure the planks in his hayloft, and carve handles with a drawknife. The grain in hickory is crooked and knotty, and therefore rough, hard to split, like the grain in the two men who owned this hammer before me.

4   After proposing marriage to a neighbor girl, my grandfather used this hammer to build a house for his bride on a stretch of river bottom in northern Mississippi. The lumber for the place, like the hickory for the handle, was cut on his own land. By the day of the wedding he had not quite finished the house, and so right after the ceremony he took his wife home and put her to work. My grandmother had worn her Sunday dress for the wedding, with a fringe of lace tacked on around the hem in honor of the occasion. She removed this lace and folded it away before going out to help my grandfather nail siding on the house. "There she was in her good dress," he told me some fifty-odd years after that wedding day, "holding up them long pieces of clapboard while I hammered, and together we got the place covered up before dark." As the family grew to four, six, eight, and eventually thirteen, my grandfather used this hammer to enlarge his house room by room, like a chambered nautilus expanding his shell.

5   By and by the hammer was passed along to my father. One day he was up on the roof of our pony barn nailing shingles with it, when I stepped out the kitchen door to call him for supper. Before I could yell, something about the sight of him straddling the spine of that roof and swinging the hammer caught my eye and made me hold my tongue. I was five or six years old, and the world's commonplaces were still news to me. He would pull a nail from the pouch at his waist, bring the hammer down, and a moment later the *thunk* of the blow would reach my ears. And that is what had stopped me in my tracks and stilled my tongue, that momentary gap between seeing and hearing the blow. Instead of yelling from the kitchen door, I ran to the barn and climbed two rungs up the ladder—as far as I was allowed to go—and spoke quietly to my father. On our walk to the house he explained that sound takes time to make its way through air. Suddenly the world seemed larger, the air more dense, if sound could be held back like any ordinary traveler.

6   By the time I started using this hammer, at about the age when I discovered the speed of sound, it already contained houses and mysteries for me. The smooth handle was one my grandfather had made. In those days I needed both hands to swing it. My father would start a nail in a scrap of wood, and I would pound away until I bent it over.

7   "Looks like you got ahold of some of those rubber nails," he would tell me. "Here, let me see if I can find you some stiff ones." And he would rummage in a drawer until he came up with a fistful of more cooperative nails. "Look at the head," he would tell me. "Don't look at your hands, don't look

at the hammer. Just look at the head of that nail and pretty soon you'll learn to hit it square."

8   Pretty soon I did learn. While he worked in the garage cutting dovetail joints for a drawer or skinning a deer or tuning an engine, I would hammer nails. I made innocent blocks of wood look like porcupines. He did not talk much in the midst of his tools, but he kept up a nearly ceaseless humming, slipping in and out of a dozen tunes in an afternoon, often running back over the same stretch of melody again and again, as if searching for a way out. When the humming did cease, I knew he was faced with a task requiring great delicacy or concentration, and I took care not to distract him.

9   He kept scraps of wood in a cardboard box—the ends of two-by-fours, slabs of shelving and plywood, odd pieces of molding—and everything in it was fair game. I nailed scraps together to fashion what I called boats or houses, but the results usually bore only faint resemblance to the visions I carried in my head. I would hold up these constructions to show my father, and he would turn them over in his hands admiringly, speculating about what they might be. My cobbled-together guitars might have been alien space-ships, my barns might have been models of Aztec temples, each wooden contraption might have been anything but what I had set out to make.

10   Now and again I would feel the need to have a chunk of wood shaped or shortened before I riddled it with nails, and I would clamp it in a vise and scrape at it with a handsaw. My father would let me lacerate the board until my arm gave out, and then he would wrap his hand around mine and help me finish the cut, showing me how to use my thumb to guide the blade, how to pull back on the saw to keep it from binding, how to let my shoulder do the work.

11   "Don't force it," he would say, "just drag it easy and give the teeth a chance to bite."

12   As the saw teeth bit down, the wood released its smell, each kind with its own fragrance, oak or walnut or cherry or pine—usually pine because it was the softest, easiest for a child to work. No matter how weathered and gray the board, no matter how warped and cracked, inside there was this smell waiting, as of something freshly baked. I gathered every smidgen of sawdust and stored it away in coffee cans, which I kept in a drawer of the workbench. When I did not feel like hammering nails I would dump my sawdust on the concrete floor of the garage and landscape it into highways and farms and towns, running miniature cars and trucks along miniature roads. Looming as huge as a colossus, my father worked over and around me, now and again bending down to inspect my work, careful not to trample my creations. It was a landscape that smelled dizzyingly of wood. Even after a bath my skin would carry the smell, and so would my father's hair, when he lifted me for a bedtime hug.

13   I tell these things not only from memory but also from recent observation, because my own son now turns blocks of wood into nailed porcupines, dumps cans full of sawdust at my feet and sculpts highways on the floor. He learns how to swing a hammer from the elbow instead of the wrist, how to lay his thumb beside the blade to guide a saw, how to tap a

chisel with a wooden mallet, how to mark a hole with an awl before starting a drill bit. My daughter did the same before him, and even now, on the brink of teenage aloofness, she will occasionally drag out my box of wood scraps and carpenter something. So I have seen my apprenticeship to wood and tools reenacted in each of my children, as my father saw his own apprenticeship renewed in me.

14   The saw I use belonged to him, as did my level and both of my squares, and all four tools had belonged to his father. The blade of the saw is the bluish color of gun barrels, and the maple handle, dark from the sweat of hands, is inscribed with curving leaf designs. The level is a shaft of walnut two feet long, edged with brass and pierced by three round windows in which air bubbles float in oil-filled tubes of glass. The middle window serves for testing if a surface is horizontal, the others for testing if a surface is plumb or vertical. My grandfather used to carry this level on the gun-rack behind the seat in his pickup, and when I rode with him I would turn around to watch the bubbles dance. The larger of the two squares is called a framing square, a flat steel elbow, so beat up and tarnished you can barely make out the rows of numbers that show how to figure the cuts on rafters. The smaller one is called a try square, for marking right angles, with a blued steel blade for the shank and a brass-faced block of cherry for the head.

15   I was taught early on that a saw is not to be used apart from a square: "If you're going to cut a piece of wood," my father insisted, "you owe it to the tree to cut it straight."

16   Long before studying geometry, I learned there is a mystical virtue in right angles. There is an unspoken morality in seeking the level and the plumb. A house will stand, a table will bear weight, the sides of a box will hold together only if the joints are square and the members upright. When the bubble is lined up between two marks etched in the glass tube of a level, you have aligned yourself with the forces that hold the universe together. When you miter the corners of a picture frame, each angle must be exactly forty-five degrees, as they are in the perfect triangles of Pythagoras, not a degree more or less. Otherwise the frame will hang crookedly, as if ashamed of itself and of its maker. No matter if the joints you are cutting do not show. Even if you are butting two pieces of wood together inside a cabinet, where no one except a wrecking crew will ever see them, you must take pains to insure that the ends are square and the studs are plumb.

17   I took pains over the wall I was building on the day my father died. Not long after that wall was finished—paneled with tongue-and-groove boards of yellow pine, the nail holes filled with putty and the wood all stained and sealed—I came close to wrecking it one afternoon when my daughter ran howling up the stairs to announce that her gerbils had escaped from their cage and were hiding in my brand new wall. She could hear them scratching and squeaking behind her bed. Impossible! I said. How on earth could they get inside my drum-tight wall? Through the heating vent, she answered. I went downstairs, pressed my ear to the honey-colored wood, and heard the *scritch scritch* of tiny feet.

18   "What can we do?" my daughter wailed. "They'll starve to death, they'll die of thirst, they'll suffocate."

19   "Hold on," I shouted, "I'll think of something."

20   While I thought and she fretted, the radio on her bedside table delivered us the headlines. Several thousand people had died in a city in India from a poisonous cloud that had leaked overnight from a chemical plant. A nuclear-powered submarine had been launched. Rioting continued in South Africa. An airplane had been hijacked in the Mediterranean. Authorities calculated that several thousand homeless people slept on the streets within sight of the Washington Monument. I felt my usual helplessness in face of all these calamities. But here was my daughter weeping because her gerbils were holed up in a wall. This calamity I could handle.

21   "Don't worry," I told her. "We'll set food and water by the heating vent and lure them out. And if that doesn't do the trick, I'll tear the wall apart until we find them."

22   She stopped crying and gazed as me. "You'd really tear it apart? Just for my gerbils? The *wall?*" Astonishment slowed her down only for a second, however, before she ran to the workbench and began tugging at drawers, saying, "Let's see, what'll we need? Crowbar. Hammer. Chisels. I hope we don't have to use them—but just in case."

23   We didn't need the wrecking tools. I never had to assault my handsome wall, because the gerbils eventually came out to nibble at a dish of popcorn. But for several hours I studied the tongue-and-groove skin I had nailed up on the day of my father's death, considering where to begin prying. There were no gaps in that wall, no crooked joints.

24   I had botched a great many pieces of wood before I mastered the right angle with a saw, botched even more before I learned to miter a joint. The knowledge of these things resides in my hands and eyes and the webwork of muscles, not in the tools. There are machines for sale—powered miter boxes and radial-arm saws, for instance—that will enable any casual soul to cut proper angles in board. The skill is invested in the gadget instead of the person who uses it, and this is what distinguishes a machine from a tool. If I had to earn my keep by making furniture or building houses, I suppose I would buy powered saws and pneumatic nailers; the need for speed would drive me to it. But since I carpenter only for my own pleasure or to help neighbors or to remake the house around the ears of my family, I stick with hand tools. Most of the ones I own were given to me by my father, who also taught me how to wield them. The tools in my work-bench are a double inheritance, for each hammer and level and saw is wrapped in a cloud of knowing.

25   All of these tools are a pleasure to look at and to hold. Merchants would never paste NEW NEW NEW! signs on them in stores. Their designs are old because they work, because they serve their purpose well. Like folksongs and aphorisms and the grainy bit of language, these tools have been pared down to essentials. I look at my claw hammer, the distillation of a hundred generations of carpenters, and consider that it holds up well

beside those other classics—Greek vases, Gregorian chants, *Don Quixote*, barbed fish hooks, candles, spoons. Knowledge of hammering stretches back to the earliest humans who squatted beside fires chipping flints. Anthropologists have a lovely name for those unworked rocks that served as the earliest hammers. *Dawn stones*, they are called. Their only qualification for the work, aside from hardness, is that they fit the hand. Our ancestors used them for grinding corn, tapping awls, smashing bones. From dawn stones to this claw hammer is a great leap in time, but no great distance in design or imagination.

26   On that iced-over February morning when I smashed my thumb with the hammer, I was down in the basement framing the wall that my daughter's gerbils would later hide in. I was thinking of my father, as I always did whenever I built anything, thinking how he would have gone about the work, hearing in memory what he would have said about the wisdom of hitting the nail instead of my thumb. I had the studs and plates nailed together all square and trim, and was lifting the wall into place when the phone rang upstairs. My wife answered, and in a moment she came to the basement door and called down softly to me. The stillness in her voice made me drop the framed wall and hurry upstairs. She told me my father was dead. Then I heared the details over the phone from my mother. Building a set of cupboards for my brother in Oklahoma, he bad knocked off work early the previous afternoon because of cramps in his stomach. Early this morning, on his way into the kitchen of my brother's trailer, maybe going for a glass of water, so early that no one else was awake, he slumped down on the linoleum and his heart quit.

27   For several hours I paced around inside my house, upstairs and down, in and out of every room, looking for the right door to open and knowing there was no such door. My wife and children followed me and wrapped me in arms and backed away again, circling and staring as if I were on fire. Where was the door, the door, the door? I kept wondering. My smashed thumb turned purple and throbbed, making me furious. I wanted to cut it off and rush outside and scrape away the snow and hack a hole in the frozen earth and bury the shameful thing.

28   I went down into the basement, opened a drawer in my workbench, and stared at the ranks of chisels and knives. Oiled and sharp, as my father would have kept them, they gleamed at me like teeth. I took up a clasp knife, pried out the longest blade and tested the edge on the hair of my forearm. A tuft came away cleanly, and I saw my father testing the sharpness of tools on his own skin, the blades of axes and knives and gouges and hoes, saw the red hair shaved off in patches from his arms and the backs of his hands. "That will cut bear," he would say. He never cut a bear with his blades, now my blades, but he cut deer, dirt, wood. I closed the knife and put it away. Then I took up the hammer and went back to work on my daughter's wall, snugging the bottom plate against a chalk line on the floor, shimming the top plate against the joists overhead, plumbing the studs with my level, making sure before I drove the first nail that every line was square and true. ■

QUESTIONS ON SUBJECT AND PURPOSE

1. What is the subject of Sanders's essay? Is it tools? His father's death?
2. Is Sanders's father or grandfather (or his children) ever described in the story? How are they revealed to the reader?
3. What "door" (paragraph 27) is Sanders searching for?
4. What exactly has Sanders inherited from his father?

QUESTIONS ON STRATEGY AND AUDIENCE

1. How does Sanders use time to structure his essay? Is the story told in chronological order?
2. What is the function of each of the following episodes or events in the essay?
   a. The sore thumb
   b. "A mystical virtue in right angles" (paragraph 16)
   c. The wall he was building
3. What expectations does Sanders seem to have about his audience?

QUESTIONS ON VOCABULARY AND STYLE

1. How much dialogue does Sanders use in the story? What does the dialogue contribute?
2. Throughout the essay, Sanders makes use of many effective similes and metaphors. Make a list of six such devices. What does each contribute to the essay? How fresh and arresting are these images?
3. Be able to define each of the following words or phrases: *plowshare* (paragraph 2), *sixteen-penny nails* (3), *chambered nautilus* (4), *rummage* (7), *lacerate* (10), *smidgen* (12), *plumb* (14), *miter* (24), *aphorisms* (25), *shimming* (28)

WRITING SUGGESTIONS

1. **Doing a Critical Analysis.** The death of Sanders's father triggers the essay, but the essay is not about his father. What is it about? In an essay, analyze what is being described in the essay and how it is described.
2. **Journaling or Blogging.** The word *inheritance* may suggest money or property bequeathed to a descendent. You can inherit many things that are far less tangible. Explore what you have inherited from someone in your family—a talent, an interest, an ability, an obsession.
3. **Practicing in a Paragraph.** Study the childhood scenes or episodes that Sanders includes in his essay—for example, calling his father to supper (paragraph 5), hammering nails (6–9), landscaping with sawdust (12). In a paragraph, re-create a similar experience from your childhood. Evoke sensory impressions for your reader—sight, sound, small, touch.
4. **Writing the Personal Essay.** Think about a skill, talent, or habit that you have learned from or share with a family member. In an essay, describe that inheritance and its effect on you.

5. **Finding Reading Connections.** The impact of a relative's death is also the subject of Alisa Wolf's "The Day Nana Almost Flew" (this chapter). Wolf also felt that she received an "inheritance" from her grandmother, although she does not use that term. Compare the impact that loss had on the two writers.

6. **Exploring Links Online.** Find an essay online about the loss of a parent or grandparent. Select one that uses a different descriptive strategy than Sanders, perhaps focusing on the loved one directly. In an essay, compare the two focusing on the detail that each writer selects for the descriptions.

7. **Writing the Research Paper.** The passing on of traditional crafts or skills is an important part of cultural tradition. Choose a society that interests you, and find a particular craft or skill that is preserved from one generation to another. It might also be something that has been preserved in your family's religious or ethnic heritage. In a formal research paper, document the nature of that craft or skill and the methods by which the culture has ensured its transmission.

For Further Study

Focusing on Grammar and Writing. Sanders often uses dashes to insert material into his sentences and to add material at their end. Study how he uses them and then write some rules for the use of the dash. What other marks of punctuation might Sanders have used in each case?

Working Together. Working in small groups, choose a block of paragraphs from the essay. Starting with a definition of simile and metaphor, how many examples can you find in that block? What do those images have in common?

Seeing Other Modes at Work. In addition to narration, Sanders uses comparison and contrast, particularly to draw the relationship between two generations of fathers and children.

ADDITIONAL WRITING SUGGESTIONS FOR DESCRIPTION

Descriptions always have a purpose—why are you describing this person place, or object? That purpose is never simply to capture objectively the word equivalent of a photograph. Descriptions are evocative. They reveal characters, and bring them to life for a reader. Descriptions capture a sense of place and what it means to you, the emotions and associations you have attached to it. Description allow readers to see objects in a new fresh way, thereby provoking thought and emotion. Keeping a purpose in mind, try one of the following topics.

Describe a Person

1. A friend or relative who made a difference in your life or is a personal hero for you

2. A great/horrible teacher/leader/coach

3. A child in great need—perhaps in another part of the world

4. You at an earlier age/ the "you" no one else knows

Describe a Place

1. A polluted landscape/walls covered with graffiti/a fantasy world
2. A popular campus or community location/a special childhood place
3. A scary place (evoke powerful emotions)
4. Your room or apartment (capture either the reality or the fantasy)

Describe an Object

1. A deserted landscape/an abandoned home or building/a vacant lot
2. A sentimental possession/a childhood possession
3. Something ordinary seen in a new and different way/an object with symbolic value
4. Something you really want

4 | Division and Classification

LEARNING OBJECTIVES

In this chapter, you will learn how to

1. Distinguish between division and classification
2. Choose an appropriate subject to be divided or classified
3. Define a purpose for your essay
4. Organize a subject into its appropriate and proportional parts
5. Construct parallel structures
6. Revise a division or classification to make it more effective
7. Analyze readings that use division and classification

Key Questions

WRITING DIVISION AND CLASSIFICATION

Getting Ready to Write

What is division?

What is classification?

How do you choose a subject to write about?

Writing

How do you divide or classify a subject?

How do you structure a division or classification essay?

Revising

How do you revise a division or classification essay?

Student Essay

Evan James, "Riding the Rails: The American 'Hobo'"

READING DIVISION AND CLASSIFICATION

In Prose

Mark Lester, from Grammar in the Classroom

In Literature

Aurora Levins Morales, "Child of the Americas" (poem)

In a Visual

Typical Brain/Einstein's Brain (cartoon)

Writing Division and Classification

GETTING READY TO WRITE

Division and classification are closely related methods of analysis. To remember the difference, ask yourself whether you are analyzing a single thing by dividing it into its constituent parts, or analyzing two or more things by sorting them into related categories.

What Is Division?

Division occurs when a single subject is subdivided into its parts. To cut a pizza into slices, to list the ingredients in a box of cereal, or to create a pie chart is to perform a division. The key is that you start with a single thing.

Writers can also divide a subject. In the following excerpt from a "chemistry primer" for people interested in cooking, Harold McGee uses division twice—first, to subdivide the atom into its smaller constituent particles and second, to subdivide the "space" within the atom into two areas (nucleus and shell):

> An atom is the smallest particle into which an element can be subdivided without losing its characteristic properties. The atom too is divisible into smaller particles, electrons, protons, and neutrons, but these are the building blocks of all atoms, no matter of what element. The different properties of the elements are due to the varying combinations of subatomic particles contained in their atoms. The Periodic Table arranges the elements in the order of the number of protons contained in one atom of each element. That number is called the atomic number.
>
> The atom is divided into two regions: the nucleus, or center in which the protons and neutrons are located, and a surrounding "orbit," or more accurately a "cloud" or "shell," in which the electrons move continuously. Both protons and neutrons weigh about 2000 times as much as electrons, so practically all of an atom's mass is concentrated in the nucleus.

Similarly, David Bodanis in "What's in Your Toothpaste?" uses division to structure a discussion of toothpaste; he analyzes its composition, offering some surprising insight into the "ingredients" we brush with every morning. Thomas Goetz in "Does the Pleasure of Lighting Up Outweigh the Consequences?" uses both division and process when he focuses on the moments in which Frank Kozik weighed the consequences of his cigarette smoking. Each stage marks a division in Kozik's life; each question is a key moment when he must decide whether the momentary experience is greater than the possible consequences.

Division, then, is used to show the components of a larger subject. Division helps the reader understand a complex whole by considering it in smaller units.

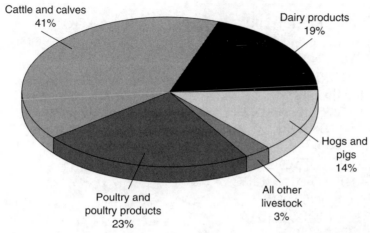

The ideal visual for division is a pie chart. A whole is divided into parts. Here, for example, is a U.S. Department of Agriculture chart on the value of livestock and poultry sold in the United States.
U.S. Department of Agriculture, National Agricultural Statistics Services.

What Is Classification?

Classification, instead of starting with a single subject and subdividing it into smaller units, begins with two or more items that are then grouped or classified into categories. Newspapers, for example, contain "classified" sections in which advertisements for the same type of goods or services are grouped or classified together.

A classification must have at least two categories. Depending on how many items you start with and how different they are, however, you may end up with quite a few categories. Consider the books in your school's library—they are arranged or classified in some way so that they can be easily found. Many schools use the Library of Congress Classification System, which organizes books by subject matter. The sciences, especially the biological sciences, make extensive use of classification. Remember the taxonomic classification you learned in high school biology? It begins by setting up five kingdoms (animals, plants, monera, fungi, and protista) and then moves downward to increasingly narrower categories (defined as phylum or division, class, order, family, genus, species).

Most classifications outside of the sciences are not as precisely and hierarchically defined. For example, E. B. White uses classification to discuss three different groups of people who make up New York City:

> There are roughly three New Yorks. There is, first, the New York of the man or woman who was born here, who takes the city for granted and accepts its size and its turbulence as natural and inevitable. Second, there is the New York of the commuter—the city that is devoured by locusts each day and spat

- A–GENERAL WORKS
- B–PHILOSOPHY, PSYCHOLOGY, RELIGION
- C–AUXILIARY SCIENCES OF HISTORY
- D–HISTORY (GENERAL) AND HISTORY OF EUROPE
- E–HISTORY: AMERICA
- F–HISTORY: AMERICA
- G–GEOGRAPHY, ANTHROPOLOGY, RECREATION
- H–SOCIAL SCIENCES
- J–POLITICAL SCIENCE
- K–LAW
- L–EDUCATION
- M–MUSIC AND BOOKS ON MUSIC
- N–FINE ARTS
- P–LANGUAGE AND LITERATURE
- Q–SCIENCE
- R–MEDICINE
- S–AGRICULTURE
- T–TECHNOLOGY
- U–MILITARY SCIENCE
- V–NAVAL SCIENCE
- Z–BIBLIOGRAPHY, LIBRARY SCIENCE, INFORMATION RESOURCES (GENERAL)

In the Library of Congress Classification System, books are first organized by "main classes" or by what we might call "subjects." Each class is assigned a letter of the alphabet. If you are familiar with the Library of Congress's system, you can browse the sections knowing that books on these subjects will be grouped together.

> out each night. Third, there is the New York of the person who was born somewhere else and came to New York in quest of something. Of these three trembling cities the greatest is the last—the city of final destination, the city that is a goal.

In this chapter, Bernard R. Berelson's classification of the reasons people want children is precisely and logically ordered. Notice how the organizational pattern is supported by the essay's title, "The Value of Children: A Taxonomical Essay," and by the headings.

Links between Writing and Reading

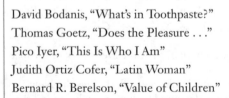

	Division or classification?
David Bodanis, "What's in Toothpaste?"	A whole subdivided into ingredients
Thomas Goetz, "Does the Pleasure . . ."	Series of decisions
Pico Iyer, "This Is Who I Am"	Two sides of self
Judith Ortiz Cofer, "Latin Woman"	Stereotypes of the "Latin woman"
Bernard R. Berelson, "Value of Children"	Reasons why people want children
Sue Shellenbarger, "The Peak Time"	Best times for specific tasks

How Do You Choose a Subject to Write About?

Division and classification are tools to help readers understand a subject. In that sense, part of the purpose of both is to inform readers. Readers will understand the whole better if they know how that whole can be divided, how it can be broken apart into small units. Similarly, if readers are faced with many "things," a classification scheme helps organize those things into more understandable and smaller categories. Think about the classified advertisements in a newspaper. If there were no structure or order to the

---

Links between Writing and Reading

	Purpose and audience
David Bodanis, "What's in Toothpaste?"	What is new or interesting about the topic?
Thomas Goetz, "Does the Pleasure . . ."	Why might this approach to health care be important today?
Pico Iyer, "This Is Who I Am"	Why might a reader care or what might be learned?
Judith Ortiz Cofer, "Latin Woman"	What does the reader learn?
Bernard R. Berelson, "Value of Children"	To whom is Berelson writing?
Sue Shellenbarger, "The Peak Times"	What value might this have for readers?

Prewriting Tips for Writing Division and Classification

1. Make a list of possible subjects for division and classification. Try out each idea on peer readers.
2. Consider what types of information you might need in order to divide or classify. Do you need to research the topic, or can you divide or classify with the information you already have?
3. Jot down a purpose statement for each possible topic. Why are you writing about this? Is your purpose purely informative? Does your topic have a persuasive value?
4. Think about your audience. What do they already know about your subject? Are you planning to tell them something that is obvious? Is your subject too complex or technical to handle in a short paper?
5. Brainstorm a tentative structure for the division and classification. That will help you as you gather and begin to organize the information.

advertisements, you would have to look through page after page to find the advertisements that relate to the specific subject for which you are looking.

Both division and classification impose order. The purpose of each is to make things clearer and more understandable. Naturally then, each of these methods of analysis should be clearly and logically structured.

That primary informative purpose also suggests care in choosing a topic. Consider how interesting or informative the subject might be to a reader. Avoid the obvious approach to the obvious topic. No subject is inherently bad, but if you choose to write about something obvious, find an interesting angle from which to approach it. Always ask, "Will my reader learn something or be entertained by what I plan to write?"

WRITING

How Do You Divide or Classify a Subject?

Both division and classification involve separation into parts—either dividing a whole into pieces or sorting many things into related groups or categories. As a writer, you have to find ways in which to divide or group the subject of your essay. Those ways can be objective and formal, such as the classification schemes used by biologists or by Bernard R. Berelson in "The Value of Children: A Taxonomical Essay," or they can be subjective and informal like Judith Ortiz Cofer in "The Myth of the Latin Woman." Either way, several tasks are particularly important.

Defining a Purpose   You subdivide or categorize for a reason or purpose, and your division or classification should be made with that end in mind. For example, Bernard R. Berelson in "The Value of Children" places people's reasons for wanting children into six categories: biological, cultural, political, economic, familial, and personal. His purpose is to explain the various factors that motivate people—all people, in all cultures, over all time—to want children. Berelson does not include, for example, a category labeled "accidental," for such a heading would be irrelevant to his stated purpose. There is a significant difference, after all, between why people *want* children and why people *have* children.

Making Your Classification or Division Complete   Your division or classification must be complete—you cannot omit pieces or leave items unclassified. How complete your classification will be depends on your purpose. Berelson, for example, sets out to be exhaustive, to isolate all the reasons people at any time and in every place have wanted children. As a result, he includes some categories that are essentially irrelevant for most Americans. Probably few Americans want or have children for political reasons, that is, because their government encourages them or forbids them to have children. In some societies or in certain times, however, political reasons have been important. Therefore, Berelson must include that category as well.

Using Parallelism   The categories or subdivisions you establish need to be parallel in form. In mathematical terms, the categories should share a lowest common denominator. A simple and fairly effective test for parallelism is to see whether your categories are all phrased in similar grammatical terms. Berelson, for example, defines his categories (the reasons for wanting children) in exactly parallel form:

> Biological
> Cultural
> Political
> Economic
> Familial
> Personal
> > Personal power
> > Personal competence
> > Personal status
> > Personal extension
> > Personal experience
> > Personal pleasure

Do not establish a catchall category that you label something such as "other." When Berelson is finished with his classification scheme, no reasons for wanting children are left out: everything fits into one of the six subdivisions. Finally, your categories or subdivisions should be mutually exclusive; that is, items should belong in only one category.

How Do You Structure a Division or Classification Essay?

The body of your division or classification essay will have as many parts as you have subdivisions or categories. Each subdivision or category can probably be treated in a single paragraph or in a group of related paragraphs. Bernard Berelson uses typographical devices (centered, numbered, boldface headings) to convey a clear sense of how his essay is organized. The headings promote clarity. Not every essay will be so evenly and perfectly divided.

Once you have decided how many subdivisions or categories you will have and how long each one will be, you have to decide how to order those parts or categories. Some subjects invite, imply, or even demand a particular order. For example, if you were classifying films using the ratings established by the motion picture industry, you would essentially have to follow the G, PG, PG-13, R, and NC-17 sequence; you could begin at either end, but it would not make sense to begin with one of the middle categories. Having an order underlying your division or classification can be a great help for both you and your reader. It allows you to know where to place each section, dictating the order you will follow. Bernard Berelson, for example, in "The Value of Children," arranges the reasons that people have children in an order that "starts with chemistry and proceeds to spirit" (paragraph 3). That is, he first deals with the biological reasons for wanting children and moves finally to the most spiritual of reasons—love.

Sometimes your subject does not demand a certain order and you must devise your organizational scheme. Judith Ortiz Cofer's "The Myth of the Latin Woman" uses narrative examples to establish and explore the common stereotypes of the "Latin woman" that she has encountered. Though the essay has a clear, chronological structure, Cofer analyzes the myth in sections of varying length.

Links between Writing and Reading

	Structure
David Bodanis, "What's in Toothpaste?"	What principle of order is used in subdividing the ingredients?
Thomas Goetz, "Does the Pleasure . . ."	How does the visual mirror the structure of the essay?
Pico Iyer, "This Is Who I Am"	Is the essay clearly divided between the two selves he is?
Judith Ortiz Cofer, "Latin Woman"	How does narrative help provide structure for the classification?
Bernard R. Berelson, "Value of Children"	What is the role and impact of the typographical devices in the structure of the essay?
Sue Shellenbarger, "The Peak Time . . ."	Do you see two types of order?

Drafting Tips for Writing Division and Classification

1. Look again at your subject and make sure that your approach is either division or classification.
2. Narrow your subject if necessary. Can your subject and your approach be handled in the amount of space you have available?
3. Make sure that the number of parts or categories in your essay is manageable. You cannot subdivide into a dozen pieces or a dozen categories and keep your paper a reasonable length. As a rough rule, in a two- to four-page essay, do not have more than six parts or categories.
4. Establish a logical organizational pattern. Once you have selected your subdivisions or categories, write each one on a separate index card. Reorder the cards several times to see how many arrangements might be possible.
5. Verify that your subdivisions or categories account for all or most of your subject. You should not have items that do not fit into your scheme.

REVISING

How Do You Revise a Division or Classification Essay?

A primary purpose for both division and classification is to help the reader analyze or organize information about a single topic or about a number of related items. It is vital, therefore, that the information be presented clearly and logically. When you have a draft of your essay and are beginning to revise, remember that the clarity and accuracy of your presentation are fundamental to an effective essay. Ask a peer reader, a writing tutor, or your instructor to look closely at those two issues. Does your paper make the subject or topic easier to understand? If your reader does not think so, you must address that problem.

When revising a division or classification essay, pay particular attention to the following areas: purpose, structure, proportional development, and parallelism.

Having a Clear Purpose Why have you chosen this particular subject? Check again to make sure that it is not so common or obvious that your readers are likely to be bored. Also, make sure that the subject is not so large or complicated that you cannot treat it adequately in the space you have available. Ask yourself again what your audience is likely to know about the topic, and be wary of either end of the spectrum—too much or too little knowledge. As you revise, look back to your purpose statement and use it to test what you have written.

Keeping the Analysis Logically Structured The order in which you present information in a division or classification is important. Do you move from the largest unit to the smallest, or in the other direction? The subdivisions or categories must be presented in an order that makes logical sense for the subject. You cannot jump around without a clear rationale. What principle have you used as you move from section to section? Is that principle clearly stated and consistently followed?

If your paper is logically structured and ordered, it will need only a minimum of stage or step markers (e.g., "first," "next") or transitional words or phrases ("the next category," "finally"). Coherence in a paper is best achieved by a clearly articulated, logical presentation of the material. For help with stage or step markers and transitional words and phrases, consult the Glossary and Ready Reference at the back of this text.

Making Categories or Parts Proportional Some of the subdivisions might represent a larger part of the whole than other subdivisions. Likewise, some of the categories in the classification might contain many more items than others. The principle of proportion does not mean that the parts must be equal in content. Rather, it means that you need to present each subdivision and each category in approximately the same amount of space. You should not give one category or subdivision a page and a half of your paper and another only three sentences.

Avoid subdividing or classifying in too great a detail. Your organizational scheme needs to account for the whole subject; that is, you should not have items that do not fit into your division or classification scheme. If you have a hundred objects on the table that you are placing into categories, your scheme must accommodate them all; you cannot have ten left over that do not fit into the scheme. Similarly, avoid catchall categories labeled "other" or "miscellaneous."

Checking for Parallelism One More Time   Subdivisions and categories need to be worded in parallel form; that is, they need to be cast into the same grammatical forms. Similar forms make it easy for the reader to see the relationships between the parts. Look back at the headings that are used in this chapter. The largest subdivisions are phrased in parallel form: "Getting Ready to Write," "Writing," and "Revising." At the next level, headings are all written as questions: "How do you . . .?" The third level of headings (where you are reading now) consists of identically structured clauses "having a clear purpose," "keeping the analysis," "making sure," and "checking for parallelism." Parallelism is an easy way to signal your paper's structure to your readers and an excellent way to promote clarity. Help with parallelism can be found in the Glossary and Ready Reference at the back of this text.

Revising Tips for Writing Division and Classification

1. Once you have a draft, write out a several-sentence summary of your essay. Ask some peers to read just that summary. Do they find your subject and approach interesting? Remember, there are no bad subjects, just bad approaches to subjects.
2. Look again at how you organized the body of your essay. Why did you begin and end where you did? Did you move from largest to smallest? Most important to least?
3. Have you accounted for everything in your division and classification? Is there anything that does not fall into the subdivisions or categories you have established?
4. Make sure you followed the principle of proportion.
5. Check the clarity of your order. Can your reader clearly tell when you have moved from one subdivision or category to another? Have you paragraphed the paper or added subheadings to make that structure clear? Have you used step markers or transitions? Is everything parallel in grammatical form?
6. Look again at your introduction. Have you tried to catch your reader's attention? Have you written a clear statement of what this paper is about and what your reader can expect to find in it?

Student Essay

Evan James chose to write his term paper for his introductory American studies course on the hobo in America. He read widely about the phenomenon, so he had plenty of information, but he was having trouble getting started and getting organized. He took his draft to the Writing Center.

First Draft

Hobos

Among the many social problems that the United States faced at the turn of this past century was that of the "hobo." My interest in hobos came about because of the book *The Ways of the Hobo* that we read. The term *hobo*, the dictionary says, was probably derived from the greeting "Ho! Beau!" commonly used by vagrants to greet each other, although other possibilities have been suggested as well. The number of hobos in the United States at the turn of the century was large because of soldiers returning from the Civil War and because increasing mechanization had reduced the number of jobs in factories and businesses. In fact, the unemployment rate in the late 1800s ran as high as 40% of the workforce. We think that unemployment rates of 6% are unacceptable today!

Actually hobos were careful about how they referred to themselves. Today, for example, we might use the words *hobo, tramp,* and *bum* interchangeably. I was surprised to learn that among the hobos themselves, the distinctions were clear. A hobo was a migrant worker, a tramp was a migrant nonworker, and a bum was a nonmigrant nonworker.

Comments

When the tutor asked about the problems Evan saw in his essay, Evan listed a couple: he thought the introduction was flat and boring and the essay didn't move smoothly from sentence to sentence ("I think I just jump around from idea to idea"). The tutor and Evan collaborated on a list of the qualities that make a good introduction. They also discussed how writers can group information and make transitions. In the process of revising, Evan found a stronger, more interesting way to begin, and he reparagraphed and developed his opening paragraphs to reflect an analysis both by division and by cause and effect.

Revised Draft

Riding the Rails: The American "Hobo"

Although homelessness and vagrancy might seem to be a distinctively modern phenomenon, the problem is probably less acute today (in terms of percentage of our total population) than it was at the turn of the twentieth century. At that time, a series of factors combined to create a large migratory population comprised almost exclusively of young males.

The Civil War was an uprooting experience for thousands of young men. Many left home in their teenage years, had acquired no job skills during their military service, and had grown accustomed to the nomadic life of the soldier—always on the move, living off the land, sleeping in the open. As the armies disbanded, many young men chose not to return home but to continue wandering the countryside.

Even if these former soldiers had wanted to work, few jobs were available to absorb the thousands of men who were mustered out. Increasingly, mechanization in the last decades of the 1800s brought the loss of jobs. In a world before unemployment benefits and social welfare, unemployment encouraged migration. The problem worsened in the 1870s when the country spiraled into a depression. Businesses failed, construction sagged, and the unemployment rate soared to an estimated 40%. Men, looking for work, took to the road.

Such men were called by a variety of names. One was *hobo*. The origin of that word is unknown. It has been suggested that *hobo* might be a shortened form of the Latin phrase *homo bonus* ("good man") or derived from the greeting "Ho! Beau!" commonly used among vagrants (dictionaries favor this suggestion). Other possibilities include a shortened form of the phrase "homeward bound" or "hoe boy," a term used in the eighteenth century for migrant farm workers.

Strictly speaking, not everyone who took to the road should be called a hobo. "Real" hobos were quick to insist on a series of distinctions. The words *hobo*, *tramp*, and *bum* were not interchangeable. By definition within the *hobo* community, the term *hobo* referred to a migrant worker, *tramp* to a migrant nonworker, and *bum* to a nonmigrant nonworker.

Obviously, the motives of the men traveling the road varied widely. Some were in search of work—migrant agricultural workers were an accepted fact by the turn of the century. Others were fleeing from the law, from family responsibilities, from themselves. Many were alcoholics; some were mentally impaired. All, though, were responding to a version of the American myth—the hope that a better future lay somewhere (geographically) ahead and that, meanwhile, the open road was the place to be. ∎

Checklist: Some Things to Remember About Writing Division and Classification

❏ In choosing a subject for division or classification, ask yourself, first, what is my purpose? and second, will my reader learn something or be entertained by my paper?

❏ Remember that your subdivision or classification should reflect your purpose; that is, the number of categories or parts is related to what you are trying to do.

❏ Make sure that your division or classification is complete. Do not omit any pieces or items. Account for everything.

❏ Take care that the parts or categories are phrased in parallel form.

❏ Avoid a category labeled something such as "other" or "miscellaneous."

❏ Remember to make your categories or subdivisions mutually exclusive.

❏ Once you have established your subdivisions, check to see whether there is an order implied or demanded by your subject.

❏ As you move from one subdivision to another, provide markers for the reader so that the parts are clearly labeled.

Reading Division and Classification

Division and classification are both used to impose order on a subject. Division breaks things apart into its constituent parts in an attempt to understand what it is, what is it composed of, how it works. Classification sorts information into related categories or groups making sense of a mass of objects or ideas. Both are common strategies for presenting information in a logical and easily understood way. As you read, remember what you have learned about how to write using division or classification—that knowledge can help you as a reader.

- Division and classification are used to present information in a clear and organized fashion. Their primary purpose is to inform and clarify, not to entertain or persuade.

- Division and classification involve either dividing a subject into its constituent parts or sorting things into related categories—making order where there appears to be chaos.

- The parts or categories in division and classification must allow for completeness. Nothing should be left over; you should be able to place every part within a division or classification of the broader subject.

- The parts or categories in division and classification must be arranged in a logical order.

- Division and classification make extensive use of parallelism (using the same grammatical structure for statements about related aspects of the parts or categories).

- Division and classification both lend themselves to visual displays and in fact might best be shown through a visual arrangement or device.

IN PROSE

The following selection is taken from Mark Lester's *Grammar in the Class-room* (1990), a college text intended for prospective teachers of grammar. Since the purpose of a textbook is to explain a subject to students, clarity of presentation is especially important. You do not demand to be entertained by a textbook; you expect to have the material presented as clearly and as simply as possible. Notice how Lester uses classification to explain how traditional grammar classifies sentences by purpose. Notice as well how Lester uses typographical devices and parallelism to promote the clarity and simplicity of the material.

Classifying Sentences By Purpose

Topic sentence—announces how the subject will be broken into categories

Typographical devices—spacing and numbering promote clarity

Parallelism
  a. Spacing
  b. Bold face
  c. Numbering
  d. Sentence structures
  e. Order of sentences
  f. Examples

Classification is complete

These are the only four ways in which sentences can be classified by purpose in traditional grammar

In traditional grammar, sentences are classified in a four-fold manner depending upon the purpose of the sentence. The following are the four types of sentences.

1. **Declarative:** A declarative sentence makes a statement. Declarative sentences are punctuated with a period.

    John went away.

2. **Imperative:** An imperative sentence gives a command or makes a request. Imperative sentences must have an understood *you* as subject. Imperative sentences may be punctuated with either a period or an exclamation point.

    Go away.
    Come here!
    Stop it!

3. **Interrogative:** An interrogative sentence asks a question. Interrogative sentences must be punctuated with a question mark.

    Did John go away?
    Where are you?

4. **Exclamatory:** An exclamatory sentence expresses strong feeling. Exclamatory sentences are declarative sentences with an exclamation point. Remember that imperative sentences can have exclamation points too.

The difference is that imperative sentences must always have an understood *you* as subject; exclamatory sentences can never have an understood you as subject. Exclamatory sentences must be punctuated with an exclamation point.

John went away!
Sally has no cavities!   ■

QUESTIONS FOR ANALYSIS

1. What is it about the presentation of this information that suggests it appeared in a textbook or reference work?
2. Why is this an example of classification rather than division?
3. What features of classification can you see in this selection?
4. Can you think of any other ways in which sentences might be classified? Think, for example, about the ways in which sentences can be structured.

CRITICAL READING ACTIVITY

What is the role of parallelism in this selection? How many examples can you find? Why might parallelism be an appropriate tool to use in classification?

IN LITERATURE

Like many Americans, Aurora Levins Morales sees in herself the different cultures and races that have made her "a child of the Americas." In her poem she uses division to analyze those diverse threads.

Child of the Americas

AURORA LEVINS MORALES

I am a child of the Americas,
a light-skinned mestiza of the Caribbean,
a child of many diaspora, born into this continent at a crossroads.

I am a U.S. Puerto Rican Jew,
a product of the ghettos of New York I have never known.
An immigrant and the daughter and granddaughter of immigrants.
I speak English with passion: it's the tone of my consciousness,
a flashing knife blade of crystal, my tool, my craft,

I am Caribeña, island grown. Spanish is in my flesh,
ripples from my tongue, lodges in my hips:
the language of garlic and mangoes,
the singing of my poetry, the flying gestures of my hands.
I am of Latinoamerica, rooted in the history of my continent:
I speak from that body.

I am not africa. Africa is in me, but I cannot return.
I am not taína. Taíno is in me, but there is no way back.
I am not european. Europe lives in me, but I have no home there.

I am new. History made me. My first language was spanlish
I was born at the crossroads
and I am whole.   ■

QUESTIONS FOR ANALYSIS

1. Why might Morales have titled her poem, "Child of the Americas"? Why the plural "Americas"?

2. How many different cultures does Morales identify as being a part of who she is? How does she order those cultures? Which is most predominant and why? What are the elements that she values?

3. What does Morales see as the contribution each culture has made to the person she is today?

4. Why does she assert in stanza 4 that she "cannot return," has "no way back," "has no home there"?

5. What might she mean by "I am new. History made me"?

WRITING SUGGESTIONS

1. **Analysis.** How does Morales use division as a structural device in the poem? Why is division an appropriate strategy given what the poem is about?

2. In one sense, everyone living in the United States is descended from immigrants. It is just a question of when our ancestors came over. Moreover, most people, like Morales, are a mixture of peoples from different cultures and races. Think about your own ancestry. Check with your grandparents or someone in your family who has traced the family's history. In an essay, explore your identity.

3. Most of us have different, even conflicting, elements in our personalities—that, we might argue, is what makes us interesting. Think about the defining elements/values/talents/behaviors/obsessions that combine in you. In an essay, separate those different elements.

IN A VISUAL

Division and classification are both strongly rooted in the visual. Division takes a single subject and breaks it into its parts. Visually, division is displayed by lists, tables, or pie charts. Classification takes many related items and sorts them into related groups. Visually, classification is usually displayed by charts that show how order can be imposed by displaying distinctions that can be made.

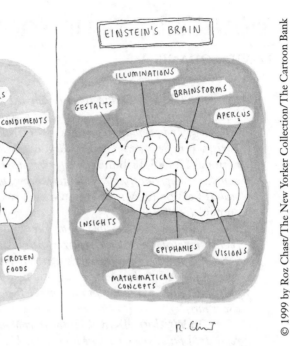

Cartoonist Roz Chast plays with both division and comparison in the juxtaposition of the typical brain with Einstein's brain. The typical brain is subdivided by the foods we eat; Einstein's, by his mental processes and experiences.

QUESTIONS FOR ANALYSIS

1. What is the basis for the division of sections of the two brains? Why food types in contrast to mental processes?
2. What is Chast suggesting about the difference between the two?
3. The cartoon is widely reproduced on posters. What might be appealing about the two images?

WRITING SUGGESTIONS

1. **Analysis.** How does the simplistic style of the cartoon and the labeling of subdivisions reflect the contrast that Chast is trying to make.
2. Look carefully at your Facebook page or your personal web page. Think about how the information is presented—photographs, messages, likes, comments, links to other pages. How would you describe this organization using a division pattern? What does the content suggest about you? In an essay, present your observations.
3. Locate print advertisements for a specific product used or consumed by people of your age. Locate at least 10 different advertisements for such a product (use different brands). Using those images, write an essay in which you classify the visual and textual approaches used in those advertisements.

What's in Your Toothpaste?

DAVID BODANIS

Raised in Chicago, David Bodanis earned a degree in mathematics from the University of Chicago and did postgraduate work in theoretical biology and population genetics. He traveled to London and then to Paris, where he began his journalism career as a copyboy at the International Herald Tribune. *Bodanis has a special talent for explaining complex concepts in simple, yet entertaining, language. His most recent book is* Passionate Minds: The Great Love Affair of the Enlightenment *(2006).*

This essay is excerpted from The Secret House *(1986). One reviewer noted: "The book explores the gee-whiz science that sits unnoticed under every homeowner's nose." If you are appalled to discover what is in your toothpaste, you ought to read Bodanis's account of some mass-produced ice cream that contains "leftover cattle parts that no one else wants."*

On Writing: *Asked about the start of his writing career, Bodanis replied: "I failed my writing exam at the University of Chicago, but it was fair. I didn't know how to write, didn't know the basics of structure." Later, he got a job at the* Herald Tribune *in Paris. "The people there taught practical writing. And I read books, and I felt that writing was a skill to learn, I never thought of it as a career."*

Before Reading

Connecting: Most of us are well aware of the toxic nature of some common products, but there are many others that we assume are safe and maybe even good for us. Think about the things that you use, eat, or drink every day. Which ones have you never worried about?

Anticipating: Is Bodanis being fair and objective in his essay? How can you judge?

1   Into the bathroom goes our male resident, and after the most pressing need is satisfied it's time to brush the teeth. The tube of toothpaste is squeezed, its pinched metal seams are splayed, pressure waves are generated inside, and the paste begins to flow. But what's in this toothpaste, so carefully being extruded out?

2   Water mostly, 30 to 45 percent in most brands: ordinary, everyday simple tap water. It's there because people like to have a big gob of toothpaste to spread on the brush, and water is the cheapest stuff there is when it comes

to making big gobs. Dripping a bit from the tap onto your brush would cost virtually nothing; whipped in with the rest of the toothpaste the manufacturers can sell it at a neat and accountant-pleasing $2 per pound equivalent. Toothpaste manufacture is a very lucrative occupation.

3   Second to water in quantity is chalk: exactly the same material that schoolteachers use to write on blackboards. It is collected from the crushed remains of long-dead ocean creatures. In the Cretaceous seas chalk particles served as part of the wickedly sharp outer skeleton that these creatures had to wrap around themselves to keep from getting chomped by all the slightly larger other ocean creatures they met. Their massed graves are our present chalk deposits.

4   The individual chalk particles—the size of the smallest mud particles in your garden—have kept their toughness over the aeons, and now on the toothbrush they'll need it. The enamel outer coating of the tooth they'll have to face is the hardest substance in the body—tougher than skull, or bone, or nail. Only the chalk particles in toothpaste can successfully grind into the teeth during brushing, ripping off the surface layers like an abrading wheel grinding down a boulder in a quarry.

5   The craters, slashes, and channels that the chalk tears into the teeth will also remove a certain amount of build-up yellow in the carnage, and it is for that polishing function that it's there. A certain amount of unduly enlarged extra-abrasive chalk fragments tear such cavernous pits into the teeth that future decay bacteria will be able to bunker down there and thrive; the quality control people find it almost impossible to screen out these errant super-chalk pieces, and government regulations allow them to stay in.

6   In case even the gouging doesn't get all the yellow off, another substance is worked into the toothpaste cream. This is titanium dioxide. It comes in tiny spheres, and it's the stuff bobbing around in white wall paint to make it come out white. Splashed around onto your teeth during the brushing it coats much of the yellow that remains. Being water soluble it leaks off in the next few hours and is swallowed, but at least for the quick glance up in the mirror after finishing it will make the user think his teeth are truly white. Some manufacturers add optical whitening dyes—the stuff more commonly found in washing machine bleach—to make extra sure that that glance in the mirror shows reassuring white.

7   These ingredients alone would not make a very attractive concoction. They would stick in the tube like a sloppy white plastic lump, hard to squeeze out as well as revolting to the touch. Few consumers would savor rubbing in a mixture of water, ground-up blackboard chalk, and the whitener from latex paint first thing in the morning. To get around that finicky distaste the manufacturers have mixed in a host of other goodies.

8   To keep the glop from drying out, a mixture including glycerine glycol—related to the most common car antifreeze ingredient—is whipped in with the chalk and water, and to give *that* concoction a bit of substance (all we really have so far is wet colored chalk) a large helping is added of gummy molecules from the seaweed *Chondrus Crispus*. This seaweed ooze spreads in among the chalk, paint, and antifreeze, then stretches itself in all directions

to hold the whole mass together. A bit of paraffin oil (the fuel that flickers in camping lamps) is pumped in with it to help the moss ooze keep the whole substance smooth.

9   With the glycol, ooze, and paraffin we're almost there. Only two major chemicals are left to make the refreshing, cleansing substance we know as toothpaste. The ingredients so far are fine for cleaning, but they wouldn't make much of the satisfying foam we have come to expect in the morning brushing.

10   To remedy that every toothpaste on the market has a big dollop of detergent added too. You've seen the suds detergent will make in a washing machine. The same substance added here will duplicate that inside the mouth. It's not particularly necessary, but it sells.

11   The only problem is that by itself this ingredient tastes, well, too like detergent. It's horribly bitter and harsh. The chalk put in toothpaste is pretty foul-tasting too for that matter. It's to get around that gustatory discomfort that the manufacturers put in the ingredient they tout perhaps the most of all. This is the flavoring, and it has to be strong. Double rectified peppermint oil is used—a flavorer so powerful that chemists know better than to sniff it in the raw state in the laboratory. Menthol crystals and saccharin or other sugar simulators are added to complete the camouflage operation.

12   Is that it? Chalk, water, paint, seaweed, antifreeze, paraffin oil, detergent, and peppermint? Not quite. A mix like that would be irresistible to the hundreds of thousands of individual bacteria lying on the surface of even an immaculately cleaned bathroom sink. They would get in, float in the water bubbles, ingest the ooze and paraffin, maybe even spray out enzymes to break down the chalk. The result would be an uninviting mess. The way manufacturers avoid that final obstacle is by putting something in to kill the bacteria. Something good and strong is needed, something that will zap any accidentally intrudant bacteria into oblivion. And that something is formaldehyde—the disinfectant used in anatomy labs.

13   So it's chalk, water, paint, seaweed, antifreeze, paraffin oil, peppermint, formaldehyde, and fluoride (which can go some way towards preserving children's teeth)—that's the usual mixture raised to the mouth on the toothbrush for a fresh morning's clean. If it sounds too unfortunate, take heart. Studies show that thorough brushing with just plain water will often do as good a job.   ■

QUESTIONS ON SUBJECT AND PURPOSE

1. Bodanis explains to the reader what toothpaste is composed of. Is his description objective? Could it appear, for example, in an encyclopedia?

2. After reading the essay, you might feel that Bodanis avoids certain crucial issues about the composition of toothpaste. Does he raise for you any questions that he does not answer?

3. What might Bodanis's purpose be? Is he arguing for something? Is he attacking something?

QUESTIONS ON STRATEGY AND AUDIENCE

1. How does Bodanis seem to arrange or order his division?
2. Bodanis gives the most space (three paragraphs) to chalk. Why? What is his focus in the section?
3. What could Bodanis expect about his audience?

QUESTIONS ON VOCABULARY AND STYLE

1. How would you characterize the tone of the essay?
2. Bodanis links most of the ingredients to their use in another product. Find these links, and be prepared to comment on the effect that these linkages have on the reader.
3. Be prepared to define the following words: *splayed* (paragraph 1), *extruded* (1), *lucrative* (2), *aeons* (4), *abrading* (4), *carnage* (5), *errant* (5), *finicky* (7), *dollop* (10), *gustatory* (11), *tout* (11), *intrudant* (12).

WRITING SUGGESTIONS

1. **Doing a Critical Analysis.** Bodanis's approach in the essay is humorous, even sensational or exaggerated. How does he create that tone? In an essay, analyze the elements in his writing that establish that tone.
2. **Journaling or Blogging.** Over a period of several days, keep a list of every product you use or consume—everything from a lip balm to cosmetics to cologne to mouthwash to chewing gum. Which ones would you like to know more about?
3. **Practicing in a Paragraph.** Select a common food and subdivide it into its constituent parts. Use the contents label on the package as the starting point. Present your division in a paragraph. Do not just describe the ingredients; develop an attitude or thesis toward what you find.
4. **Writing the Personal Essay.** Americans exhibit widely differing attitudes toward the food they eat. In an essay, classify the American eater from either a serious or comic point of view. Try to establish four to six categories.
5. **Finding Reading Connections.** In what ways are the tones of Bodanis's essay and Judy Brady's "I Want a Wife" (Chapter 8) similar? Analyze their writing strategies.
6. **Exploring Links Online.** Tempted to use one of those "energy shots or drinks" to get through that research paper or exam? Many articles on the ingredients in such drinks are available on the Web. In a documented essay, summarize for your peers what they are consuming.
7. **Writing the Research Paper.** Americans have become increasingly concerned about the additives that are put into food—for example, salt, high fructose corn syrup, MSG, trans fat, food dyes, sodium nitrate or nitrite, BHA. What types of additives are most common? Develop a classification scheme in a research paper to explain their presence. Be sure to document your sources.

For Further Study

Focusing on Grammar and Writing. Bodanis uses summary sentences to repeat or reinforce the points he is making—for example, in paragraphs 7, 8, 9, 12, and 13. What is the effect of such a strategy or repetition?

Working Together. Bodanis links the ingredients in toothpaste to other products in which they can be found. Divide into small groups and choose one of the ingredients he lists. How does he manage to shock the reader as he records each ingredient? Pay attention to word choice and analogy.

Seeing Other Modes at Work. The essay could easily be turned into a persuasive essay. What elements of persuasion are already there? What could be added?

Does the Pleasure of Lighting Up Outweigh the Consequences?

THOMAS GOETZ

Thomas Goetz has reported on media and business at the Village Voice *and at the* Wall Street Journal. *He was the executive editor at* Wired *magazine. Goetz has a Masters in Public Health from the University of California, Berkeley. This essay originally appeared in the February 2010 issue of* Wired *and is a part of his book* The Decision Tree: Taking Control of Your Health in the New Era of Personalized Medicine *(2010).*

Before Reading

Connecting: Do you use tobacco? Do you know someone who does? What would it take for you or that person to quit?

Anticipating: What is it that finally makes Kozik decide to quit smoking? What is so important about the consequences that he is facing then?

1   Frank Kozik knows how hard it is to quit smoking. He smoked for 39 years, off and on—and he's just 48 years old. You read that right: Kozik, a renowned poster designer since the heyday of alternative rock, has been smoking since he was 8 years old.

2   Like so many smokers, Kozik has quit several times. When he began bicycling in the 1980s, he kicked the habit for five years—until he

Frank's Decision Tree

Frank Kozik knew smoking could kill him but found the habit too pleasurable to quit for good, even though he had quit temporarily several times. Then a potentially immediate and drastic consequence caused him to reconsider his choices.

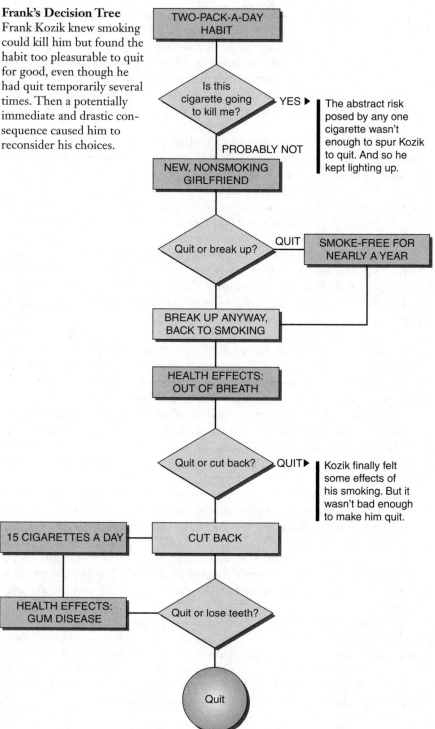

TWO-PACK-A-DAY HABIT

Is this cigarette going to kill me?

YES ▶ The abstract risk posed by any one cigarette wasn't enough to spur Kozik to quit. And so he kept lighting up.

PROBABLY NOT

NEW, NONSMOKING GIRLFRIEND

Quit or break up?

QUIT — SMOKE-FREE FOR NEARLY A YEAR

BREAK UP ANYWAY, BACK TO SMOKING

HEALTH EFFECTS: OUT OF BREATH

Quit or cut back?

QUIT ▶ Kozik finally felt some effects of his smoking. But it wasn't bad enough to make him quit.

15 CIGARETTES A DAY — CUT BACK

HEALTH EFFECTS: GUM DISEASE

Quit or lose teeth?

Quit

started seeing a woman who smoked. A few years later, when he started dating a more health-conscious woman, he quit again—only to resume after they broke up about a year later. Kozik has always been well aware of the risks—but he also knows the benefits. "Smoking is a really pleasurable thing," he says. "It's like a little high every time you light up. Of course, with every cigarette I also thought, 'Is this the one that's going to give me cancer?' But that was an abstract thought, and that little high was so much more real."

3   Kozik's description is spot-on. Of all our bad health habits, smoking is one of the worst of all possible worlds: It's among the least healthy and the hardest to stop. Half of all lifelong smokers will die of a smoking-related illness; nearly a third of all cancer deaths are caused by smoking. Very few health behaviors are so strongly associated with such lethal results. So what keeps smokers puffing away? Neurologically, smoking activates the mesocorticolimbic dopamine system in the brain, which drives the reward circuit, the motivational circuit, and the learning/memory circuit. (This means that smoking is a learned behavior, self-rewarding, and motivational all at the same time!) Each individual node in the smoker's decision tree pits an immediate tangible benefit against a longer-term abstract one.

4   This tension exemplifies the paradox of behavior change: We know what we are supposed to do, but we find all sorts of reasons not to do it. As a result, more than 85 percent of Americans don't eat enough fruits and vegetables, two-thirds are overweight—and 20 percent continue to smoke cigarettes. We don't lack for information. We lack for incentives.

5   For Kozik, those incentives finally started to register when he hit his mid-forties and he began to feel the effects of so many years of smoking. "All these health issues began to pop up," he says, and in early 2008, when he found it "harder to carry stuff up the stairs," he started to cut back from his two-pack-a-day habit to about 15 cigarettes a day.

6   But last year, Kozik faced a starker trade-off than a little shortness of breath. His dentist told him that smoking had severely aggravated his gums. If he didn't quit smoking, he was likely to start losing his teeth. "Right there, it became something real," Kozik says. "What do I value more: my teeth or smoking cigarettes? I mean, cancer was always this vague thing; you can't see your lungs. But you can see your teeth. It was a pretty clear decision." Kozik quit cold turkey last October and is resolved to never light up again.

7   "My entire life has been motivated by the possibility of what comes next," Kozik explains. "I'm a selfish person—we all are—and every decision I make comes down to which choice will benefit me more. But most of these choices are totally abstract, toward some idealized goal. Every once in a while, though, you'll hit a choice that's real. Having your teeth fall out is real. At that point, the value of a mild narcotic stimulant is zero." ■

QUESTIONS ON SUBJECT AND PURPOSE

1. What is the difference between a "real or tangible" benefit and an "abstract" one?
2. Why did Kozik continue to smoke knowing that it was not good for his health?
3. What does the subtitle of the book *The Decision Tree* indicate about Goetz's purpose in telling this story? See the headnote for the subtitle.

QUESTIONS ON STRATEGY AND AUDIENCE

1. How is the essay organized?
2. Why might smoking be a good example of how people can take control of their health?
3. Why might readers today be particularly interested in "taking control" of their health?

QUESTIONS ON VOCABULARY AND STYLE

1. In paragraph 3, Goetz encloses a sentence within parentheses. Why? What does that sentence do?
2. What would you call words and phrases such as *kicked the habit* (paragraph 2), *spot-on* (3), or *quit cold turkey* (5)?
3. Be prepared to define the following words: *lethal* (paragraph 3), *tangible* (3), *aggravated* (5).

WRITING SUGGESTIONS

1. **Doing a Critical Analysis.** In an essay, analyze the role that the graphic plays in your understanding of the essay. What does it contribute? If the story were told only in words, would it be as effective?
2. **Journaling or Blogging.** Do you have a "bad health habit"? What do you do (or don't do) that is negatively impacting your health?
3. **Practicing in a Paragraph.** Select one of your bad health habits (we all have some) and in a paragraph explore why you have difficulty changing or breaking that habit.
4. **Writing the Personal Essay.** Using the model provided in the essay and graphic, write a narrative that explains the decisions that you have been making and construct a graphic decision tree for dealing with your bad health habit.
5. **Finding Reading Connections.** To what extent is "fast food" consumption a "bad health habit"? Using the information in Maureen O'Hagan's "Kids Battle the Lure of Junk Food" (Chapter 7), explain the reasons why children are at such risk.
6. **Exploring Links Online.** The Centers for Disease Control and Prevention (cdc.gov) offers a fact-sheet guide to the "Health Effects of Cigarette Smoking." Given the widespread evidence of the dangers, why do young people continue to smoke? Using that information and interviews with friends who smoke, analyze the reasons they cite.

7. **Writing the Research Paper.** Bad health habits trigger or make worse a number of medical conditions such as obesity, heart attacks, strokes, diabetes, and STDs. Choose a condition that arises largely from bad decisions and, using online and print sources, write an essay that divides and analyzes the decisions that can lead to a solution.

For Further Study

Focusing on Grammar and Writing. How would you characterize the tone of the essay? Formal or informal? Technical or nontechnical? What evidence justifies your opinion?

Working Together. When we are young, we think that serious consequences of bad habits are years away. What kinds of motivation might a young person find to break a bad health habit? Working in small groups, suggest some possible strategies you might use to adapt Goetz's model for younger readers.

Seeing Other Modes at Work. The essay makes use of narration and cause and effect to trace Kozik's 39-year history of smoking.

READING THE "DECISION TREE" VISUAL

On his blog, Goetz comments about the "decision tree": "What's a decision tree? Well, basically it's a flow chart. So what does that have to do with health? The idea is this: Our health doesn't happen all at once; it's a consequence of years of choices—some large and some small—that combine to make up our health. Sometimes we've chosen wisely and we enjoy good health; sometimes we choose poorly and we suffer the consequences. A decision tree, then, is . . . a device that can make these decisions more explicit and more obviously something we are actually choosing—it's a way to externalize the choices that we otherwise make without much thought at all. Research shows that when we actually engage in a decision (when we think it through, even if just for a moment) we tend to make a better decision, defined both as one that we're more comfortable with in hindsight and one that potentially bodes a better outcome. By engaging with our health consciously and explicitly as a series of decisions, one leading to another, we can become 'smarter' and enjoy better health."

Study the decision tree carefully and answer the following questions:

1. What are the steps enclosed within the diamond shapes? What do they have in common?

2. What are the steps enclosed within the darker rectangles? Goetz refers to these as "inputs," that is, data that might affect health.

3. What are the steps enclosed within the lighter rectangles?

4. Why is there only one circle? What does that represent in the decision-making process?

5. What does the visual contribute to the reading experience? Why use it at all?

The Peak Time for Everything

SUE SHELLENBARGER

Sue Shellenbarger created and writes the Wall Street Journal's *column on "Work & Family," focusing on the conflict between work and family. The column has received seven major national awards. She is also the author of two books, the most recent of which was* The Breaking Point, *a study of the mid-life crisis in women. This column appeared in the* Journal *in September 2012.*

On Writing: *Shellenbarger originally thought she would teach writing, but, inspired by one of her teachers, she switched to journalism. As a columnist, she is able to work from home. The subject of her column, the conflict between work and family, is a reflection of her own experience. She commented: "It's very hard work, but being able to work from home allows me to work in between the kids' track meets and school conferences."*

Before Reading

Connecting: Have you ever noticed that some tasks are easier when they are done at a certain time during the day?

Anticipating: Thinking about the tasks that you must do on a regular basis as a student, what changes might you make in your schedule to match your work demands to your body's energy?

1   **C**ould you pack more into each day if you did everything at the optimal time?

2   A growing body of research suggests that paying attention to the body clock, and its effects on energy and alertness, can help pinpoint the different times of day when most of us perform our best at specific tasks, from resolving conflicts to thinking creatively.

3   Most people organize their time around everything but the body's natural rhythms. Workday demands, commuting, social events and kids' schedules frequently dominate—inevitably clashing with the body's circadian rhythms of waking and sleeping.

4   As difficult as it may be to align schedules with the body clock, it may be worth it to try, because of significant potential health benefits. Disruption of circadian rhythms has been linked to such problems as diabetes, depression, dementia and obesity, says Steve Kay, a professor of molecular and computational biology at the University of Southern California. When the body's master clock can synchronize functioning of all its metabolic, cardiovascular and behavioral rhythms in response to light and other natural stimuli, it "gives us an edge in daily life," Dr. Kay says.

5   When it comes to doing cognitive work, for example, most adults perform best in the late morning, says Dr. Kay. As body temperature starts to rise just before awakening in the morning and continues to increase through midday, working memory, alertness and concentration gradually improve. Taking a warm morning shower can jump-start the process.

6   The ability to focus and concentrate typically starts to slide soon thereafter. Most people are more easily distracted from noon to 4 p.m., according to recent research led by Robert Matchock, an associate professor of psychology at Pennsylvania State University.

7   Alertness tends to slump after eating a meal, Dr. Matchock found. Sleepiness also tends to peak around 2 p.m., making that a good time for a nap, says Martin Moore-Ede, chairman and chief executive of Circadian, a Stoneham, Mass., training and consulting firm.

8   Surprisingly, fatigue may boost creative powers. For most adults, problems that require open-ended thinking are often best tackled in the evening when they are tired, according to a 2011 study in the journal *Thinking & Reasoning*. When 428 students were asked to solve a series of two types of problems, requiring either analytical or novel thinking, their performance on the second type was best at non-peak times of day when they were tired, according to the study led by Mareike Wieth, an assistant professor of psychological sciences at Albion College in Michigan. (Their performance on analytical problems didn't change over the course of the day.) Fatigue, Dr. Wieth says, may allow the mind to wander more freely to explore alternative solutions.

9   Of course, everyone's body clock isn't the same, making it even harder to synchronize natural rhythms with daily plans. A significant minority of people operate on either of two distinctive chronotypes, research shows: Morning people tend to wake up and go to sleep earlier and to be most productive early in the day. Evening people tend to wake up later, start more slowly and peak in the evening.

10   Communicating with friends and colleagues online has its own optimal cycles, research shows. Sending emails early in the day helps beat the inbox rush; 6 a.m. messages are most likely to be read, says Dan Zarrella, social-media scientist for HubSpot, a Cambridge, Mass., Web marketing firm, based on a study of billions of emails. "Email is kind of like the newspaper. You check it at the beginning of the day," he says.

11   Reading Twitter at 8 a.m. or 9 a.m. can start your day on a cheery note. That's when users are most likely to tweet upbeat, enthusiastic messages, and least likely to send downbeat tweets steeped in fear, distress, anger or guilt, according to a study of 509 million tweets sent over two years by 2.4 million Twitter users, published last year in *Science*. One likely factor? "Sleep is refreshing" and leaves people alert and enthusiastic, says Michael Walton Macy, a sociology professor at Cornell University and co-author of the study. The cheeriness peaks about 1-1/2 hours later on weekends—perhaps because people are sleeping in, Dr. Macy says.

12   Other social networking is better done later in the day. If you want your tweets to be re-tweeted, post them between 3 p.m. and 6 p.m., when many people lack energy to share their own tweets and turn to relaying others' instead, Mr. Zarrella says. And posts to Facebook at about 8 p.m. tend to get the most "likes," after people get home from work or finish dinner. At that time of day, they're likely to turn to Facebook feeling less stressed. "You have less stuff to do and more time to give," says Mr. Zarrella.

13   Late-night drama can be found on Twitter, where emotions heat up just before bedtime, between 10 p.m. and 11 p.m., says Scott Andrew Golder, a Ph.D. candidate at Cornell University and co-author of the Twitter study. At that time, people tended to send more emotion-laden tweets, both positive and negative. Tired out by the workday, but also freed from its stresses and demands, people become "more alert and engaged, but also more agitated," Dr. Macy says.

14   When choosing a time of day to exercise, paying attention to your body clock can also improve results. Physical performance is usually best, and the risk of injury least, from about 3 p.m. to 6 p.m., says Michael Smolensky, an adjunct professor of biomedical engineering at the University of Texas, Austin, and lead author with Lynne Lamberg of "The Body Clock Guide to Better Health."

15   Muscle strength tends to peak between 2 p.m. and 6 p.m. at levels as much as 6% above the day's lows, improving your ability to grip a club or racquet. Another boost for physical strength comes from the lungs, which function 17.6% more efficiently at 5 p.m. than at midday, according to a study of 4,756 patients led by Boris Medarov, an assistant professor of medicine at Albany Medical College in New York.

16   Eye-hand coordination is best in late afternoon, making that a good time for racquetball or Frisbee. And joints and muscles are as much as 20% more flexible in the evening, lowering the risk of injury, Dr. Smolensky says.

17   These body rhythms hold true regardless of how much you've slept or how recently you've eaten. In a 2007 study at the University of South Carolina at Columbia, 25 experienced swimmers did six timed trials while sticking to an artificial schedule that controlled for variables like sleep, diet and other factors. The swimmers' performance still varied by time of day, peaking in the evening and hitting bottom at around 5 a.m.

18   Is there a best time to eat? To keep from packing on pounds, experts say, limit food consumption to your hours of peak activity. A study in *Cell Metabolism* last May linked disruptions of the body clock to weight gain. Researchers put two groups of mice on the same high-calorie diet. One group was allowed to eat anytime; the other group was restricted to eating only during an eight-hour period when they were normally awake and active. The mice that ate only while active were 40% leaner and had lower cholesterol and blood sugar.

19   While more research is needed on humans, Dr. Kay says, the research suggests that "we are not only what we eat, we are when we eat."   ■

QUESTIONS ON SUBJECT AND PURPOSE

1. What are "circadian rhythms?"
2. How do daily activities clash with "circadian rhythms of waking and sleeping"?
3. Why would this subject be particularly appropriate for a column that focuses on "work and family"?

QUESTIONS ON STRATEGY AND AUDIENCE

1. What organizational strategy is used in the essay?
2. Why might Shellenbarger end with a paragraph on the "best" time to eat?
3. What expectations might Shellenbarger have about her audience?

QUESTIONS ON VOCABULARY AND STYLE

1. Where does Shellenbarger get her information in the article? Why is there no formal documentation of those sources?
2. How effective is the first sentence of the essay? Did it catch your attention? Did it make you want to read on? Why or why not?
3. Be prepared to define the following words: *optimal* (paragraph 1) and *chronotypes* (9).

WRITING SUGGESTIONS

1. **Doing a Critical Analysis.** Look closely at each of the sources that Shellenbarger uses in the essay. How might she have gathered this information? Analyze the nature of the sources that she used. How is the credibility of the article's conclusions related to the research that has been done?
2. **Journaling or Blogging.** Do you have particular times during a day when you do certain kinds of activities? When do you feel most mentally sharp? Does it seem to matter what time of day you exercise?
3. **Practicing in a Paragraph.** Plan a change in your routine. For example, try confining your eating into the eight-hour period when you are most active, or move your exercise time until the later afternoon. In a paragraph, outline a change you will make and the reasons why.
4. **Writing the Personal Essay.** In an essay, divide your day into its typical stages. What is the normal pattern of each day during the school year? What does that schedule reveal about you and your work and play habits?
5. **Finding Reading Connections.** What possible connections might there be between Shellenbarger's subject and Mark Penn's in "Caffeine Crazies" (Chapter 7). Explore in an essay the possible connections between the two phenomena.
6. **Exploring Links Online.** Are you a morning person or an evening person? Find out more and take a quiz on the Web. What does research and your own experience as you get older tell you about your body's clock?

7. **Writing the Research Paper.** In paragraph 4, Shellenbarger suggests the connections between the disruption of the circadian rhythms and several diseases. Select one of the connections she mentions and explore the links that science and medicine have found. Be sure to document the research that you use.

For Further Study

Focusing on Grammar and Writing. If the essay appeared in an academic journal, all of Shellenbarger's sources would be documented in footnotes or in works cited. Study how she includes source information within the essay. What information does she include for each source and how is the information arranged?

Working Together. Working in small groups, gather information about the work and exercise habits of each person. How much agreement is there? Then share with the other groups, compiling a class profile.

Seeing Other Modes at Work. Within the general pattern of division in the essay, Shellenbarger also uses cause and effect.

This Is Who I Am When No One Is Looking

PICO IYER

Pico Iyer (1957–) was, as he writes, "born, as the son of Indian parents, in England, [and] moved to America at seven." One of the country's foremost travel writers, Iyer is the author of a number of books, including several about spiritual issues and his search for silence. His most recent book is The Man Within My Head *(2013). This essay was originally published in* Portland *magazine, a publication of the University of Portland, Oregon, in 2006.*

On Writing: *Iyer comments: "Writing should be an act of communication more than of mere self-expression—a telling of a story rather than a flourishing of skills. . . . Writing . . . should, ideally, be as spontaneous and urgent as a letter to a lover, or a message to a friend who has just lost a parent. And because of the ways a writer is obliged to tap in private the selves that even those closest to him never see, writing is, in the end, that oddest of anomalies: an intimate letter to a stranger."*

Before Reading

Connecting: Have you ever thought that the "real" you is someone that few, if any, people ever see?

Anticipating: Iyer is a global traveler who has written much about his experiences traveling. What is it that he is searching for on this "journey"?

1   **O**nce every three or four months, for much of my adult life now, I've gotten in my car in my mother's house in the dry hills of California, above the sea, and driven up the road, past the local yoga foundation, past the community of local sixties refugees, past the mock-Danish tourist town and the vineyards, past where Ronald Reagan used to keep his Western White House and where Michael Jackson sat imprisoned in his Neverland, past a lighthouse, past meadows of dormant cows, to another little room a thousand feet above the ocean, in the dry hills, where deer come out to graze at dusk and mountain lions come out, too, to stalk our urban fantasies.

2   There is a sign on the main highway down below—hanging from a large cross—and there is a saint's name on the door of the little room I enter, underneath the number. But the names are all forgotten here, especially my own, and when I step into the little "cell" than awaits me—narrow bed huddled up against one wall, closet and bathroom, wide blond-wood desk overlooking a garden that overlooks the sea—I really don't know or care what "Catholic" means, or hermitage, or monastery, or Big Sur.

3   There are crosses in this place, and hooded men singing the psalms at dawn (at noon, at dusk, at sunset), and there's a cross on the wall above the bed. But I go not because of all the trappings of the chapel I had to attend twice a day every school day of my adolescence, but in spite of it. I go to disappear into the silence.

4   My friends assume, I'm sure, that I go to the monastery to catch my breath, to be away from the phone, to drink in one of the most beautiful stretches of coastline in the world. What I can't tell them—what they don't want to hear—is that I go to the monastery to become another self, the self that we all are if only we choose to unpack our overstuffed lives and leave our selves at home.

5   In my cell I read novels in the ringing silence, and they are novels, often, of infidelity. In the best of them, the ones by Sue Miller, say, there is a palpable, quickening sense of the excitement of betraying others and your daily self in the world you know. I read these with recognition. This shadow story is as close to us as our dreams. All the great myths are about it, the stories of Shakespeare and Aeschylus and Homer are about it, as are our romance novels and our letters to Aunt Agony, but here in the monastery I'm committing a deeper infidelity, against the life I know and the values by which we are supposed to live. I am being disloyal in the deepest way to the assumptions of the daily round, and daring to lay claim to a mystery at the heart of me.

6   I step into my cell, and I step into the realest life I know. My secret life, as Leonard Cohen calls it, also happens to be my deepest and my best life. There is no will involved, no choice; this other world, and self, are waiting for me like the clothes I never thought to ask for.

7   I'm not a Benedictine monk, and I attend none of the services held day in, day out, four times a day, while I'm in my little room. If I make the mistake of attending one because of my longing to be good, my wish to pay,

in some way, the kind monks for making the silence available to me, I soon run out again. The presence of the fifteen kindly souls in hoods, singing, takes me back, somehow, to the world, the self I've come here to escape; the words in the psalms are all of war, and I notice which face looks kind and which one bitter.

8   No, the flight is to something much larger than a single text or doctrine. It's to—this the word I otherwise shy from—eternity. I step into a place that never changes, and with it that part of me, that ground in me, that belongs to what is changeless. There is a self at the core of us—what some call "Christ," others the "Buddha nature," and poets refer to as the immortal soul—that is simply part of the nonshifting nature of the universe. Not in any exalted way: just like the soil or sky or air. It does not fit into our everyday notions any more than sky fits into a bed. But I steal into this better world as into a secret love, and there, as in the best of loves, I feel I am known in a way I know is true.

9   Thomas Merton put this best, not because he was a Christian, or even because he was a monk, but because he fell in love with silence. And he made the pursuit of that real life his lifelong mission. He knew, he saw, that it was akin to the earthly love we feel, and that the heightening, the risking up to a higher place, the making sense of things—above all, the dissolution of the tiny self we know—when we fall in love is our closest approximation to this state, as certain drugs can give us an indication of what lies beyond. But it is only an approximation, a momentary glimpse, like snapshots of a sunset where we long to live forever.

10   I wouldn't call this a pilgrimage, because, as Merton says, again, I'm not off to find myself; only to lose myself. I'm not off in search of anything; in fact, only—the words sound fanciful—the sense of being found. You could say it's not a pilgrimage because there's no movement involved after I step out of my car, three hours and fifteen minutes north of my mother's house, and I don't pay any of the religious dues when I arrive. But all the movements and journeys I have taken around the world are underwritten, at heart, by this: this is who I am when nobody is looking. This is who I'm not, because the petty, struggling, ambitious "I" is gone. I am as still, as timeless as the plate of sea below me.

11   I keep quiet about this journey, usually because it sounds as strange to other people, or to myself, as a piece of silence brought to a shopping mall. If they have an equivalent—and they surely do, in meditation, in skydiving, in running, in sex—they will know what I'm talking of, and substitute their own terms; everyone knows at moments she has a deeper, purer self within, something that belongs to what stands out of time and space, and when she falls in love, she rises to that eternal candle in another, and to the self that is newly seen in her. But it belongs to a different order from the words we throw around at home. When we fall in love, when we enter a room with our beloved, we know that we can't really speak of it to anyone else. The point, the very beauty of it, is that it admits us into the realm of what cannot be said.

12   So when I come down to the monastery, I tell my friends that monks watch the film *A Fish Called Wanda* in the cloister. That most of the visitors are female, and very down to earth. The monks sell fruitcake and greeting cards and cassettes in the hermitage bookstore; they have Alcoholics Anonymous meetings once a week, and a sweet woman now lives on the property, helping care for the rooms. The monastery has a website and a fax number. There's a workout room in the "enclosure" for the monks; visiting it once, I came upon books by the Hollywood producer Robert Evans and by Woody Allen.

13   Everyone feels better when I assure them it's a mortal place, with regular human beings, balding, divorced, confused, with a mailing address I can send packages to. The infidelity sounds less glaring if I phrase it thus. But I can say all this only because I know I'm not talking about what I love and find; because this is the place where all seeking ends.   ■

QUESTIONS ON SUBJECT AND PURPOSE

1. Iyer reads novels in his cell about infidelity (paragraph 5), likening what he is doing to being unfaithful or disloyal. What does he mean?
2. At the end of the essay, Iyer confesses what he tells his friends about the monastery. Why, and in what sense is this also infidelity?
3. Relatively few people withdraw to monasteries for even brief stays. Iyer is not trying to promote the benefits from withdrawing from the world for a period of time. What, then, might be the reason he writes of his experience?

QUESTIONS ON STRATEGY AND AUDIENCE

1. What structural strategy does Iyer use in his opening paragraph?
2. What oppositions or divisions structure the essay?
3. How do Iyer's comments in On Writing shed light on this essay?

QUESTIONS ON VOCABULARY AND STYLE

1. Iyer is a travel writer who writes about the places he visits. Do you see any parallels between that type of writing and this essay?
2. In paragraph 5, Iyer mentions the "ringing silence"? How can silence ring?
3. What does the word *eternity* suggest to you? Is that word ever part of your thoughts?

WRITING SUGGESTIONS

1. **Doing a Critical Analysis.** In his essay, Iyer uses the metaphor of a journey. Where is he journeying to and why? In an essay, analyze how Iyer uses the metaphor as a structural device in the essay.
2. **Journaling or Blogging.** Have you ever just wanted to "get away from it all"? If you have, where did you want to go or what did you want to do instead? What exactly was the "it" from which you were trying to escape? If you have not felt that need, why not? Explore the concept in your journal or blog.

3. **Practicing in a Paragraph.** Is there some aspect of you that you do not readily share with others? In a paragraph, explore a sense of yourself as two different persons or as wearing two different faces. Who are those persons or faces?

4. **Writing the Personal Essay.** Part of the appeal of recreational drugs and alcohol probably has something to do with the needs about which Iyer is writing: to escape pressures, to obliterate self temporarily. In an essay, interview some peers and ask them how they deal with the pressures of life and school. Construct a classification scheme that lists the responses you found.

5. **Finding Reading Connections.** Iyer is able to "escape" from reality, but when the pain and wounds are more or less permanent, it is not easy to escape. Read Michael Jerigan's "Living the Dream" (Chapter 7). In an essay, contrast how each writer faces the present.

6. **Exploring Links Online.** George Santayana's "The Philosophy of Travel" can be found online. Compare Santayana's observations with Iyer's. Where do the two seem to agree? To disagree?

7. **Writing the Research Paper.** Travel agencies promote vacations as a way to escape. What they suggest as escapes, however, are quite different from what Iyer does. Research the escape vacations that are advertised on the Web. Construct a classification system that accounts for the major ways and destinations that are used to advertise an "escape" from the ordinary.

For Further Study

Focusing on Grammar and Writing. What is a *metaphor?* How many metaphors can you find in Lyer's essay?

Working Together. Split into pairs and interview one another about how each of you seeks to escape pressures. Do this a number of times to get a body of responses. Use the information as background for the essay topic listed under "Writing Suggestions."

Seeing Other Modes at Work. Iyer uses an underlying narrative to help structure the essay—from the trip up into the mountains in the opening paragraph to when he "comes down" from the monastery (paragraph 12).

The Myth of the Latin Woman: I Just Met a Girl Named Maria

JUDITH ORTIZ COFER

Judith Ortiz Cofer was born in Puerto Rico in 1952. Her family settled in Patterson, New Jersey, in 1954, but frequently returned to the island. Cofer is currently a professor of English and creative writing at the University of Georgia. She is the author of Woman in Front of the Sun: On Becoming a Writer *(2000).*

On Writing: Cofer *comments about living in and writing about two cultures: "The very term 'bilingual' tells you I have two worlds. At least now, they're very strictly separated, but when I was growing up it was a constant shift back and forth. I think my brain developed a sense of my world and my reality as being composed of two halves. But I'm not divided in them. I accept them, and I think they have basically been the difference that has allowed me to write things that are not like anybody else's."*

Before Reading

Connecting: Have you ever been treated as a stereotype? Have people ever expected certain things of you (good or bad) because of how you were classified in their eyes?

Anticipating: What expectations would you have of a "Latin woman"? Or a "Latin man"? Do those expectations coincide with those about which Cofer writes?

1   **O**n a bus trip to London from Oxford University where I was earning some graduate credits one summer, a young man, obviously fresh from a pub, spotted me and as if struck by inspiration went down on his knees in the aisle. With both hands over his heart he broke into an Irish tenor's rendition of "Maria" from *West Side Story*. My politely amused fellow passengers gave his lovely voice the round of gentle applause it deserved. Though I was not quite as amused, I managed my version of an English smile: no show of teeth, no extreme contortions of the facial muscles—I was at this time of my life practicing reserve and cool. Oh, that British control, how I coveted it. But "Maria" had followed me to London, reminding me of a prime fact of my life: you can leave the island, master the English language, and travel as far as you can, but if you are a Latina, especially one like me who so obviously belongs to Rita Moreno's gene pool, the island travels with you.

2   This is sometimes a very good thing—it may win you that extra minute of someone's attention. But with some people, the same things can make *you* an island—not a tropical paradise but an Alcatraz, a place nobody wants to visit. As a Puerto Rican girl living in the United States and wanting like most children to "belong," I resented the stereotype that my Hispanic appearance called forth from many people I met.

3   Growing up in a large urban center in New Jersey during the 1960s, I suffered from what I think of as "cultural schizophrenia." Our life was designed by my parents as a microcosm of their *casas* on the island. We spoke in Spanish, ate Puerto Rican food bought at the *bodega*, and practiced strict Catholicism at a church that allotted us a one-hour slot each week for mass, performed in Spanish by a Chinese priest trained as a missionary for Latin America.

4   As a girl I was kept under strict surveillance by my parents, since my virtue and modesty were, by their cultural equation, the same as their honor. As a teenager I was lectured constantly on how to behave as a proper *señorita*. But it was a conflicting message I received, since the Puerto Rican mothers also encouraged their daughters to look and act like women and to dress in clothes our Anglo friends and their mothers found too "mature" and flashy. The difference was, and is, cultural; yet I often felt humiliated when I appeared at an American friend's party wearing a dress more suitable to a semi-formal than to a playroom birthday celebration. At Puerto Rican festivities, neither the music nor the colors we wore could be too loud.

5   I remember Career Day in our high school, when teachers told us to come dressed as if for a job interview. It quickly became obvious that to the Puerto Rican girls "dressing up" meant wearing their mother's ornate jewelry and clothing, more appropriate (by mainstream standards) for the company Christmas party than as daily office attire. That morning I had agonized in front of my closet, trying to figure out what a "career girl" would wear. I knew how to dress for school (at the Catholic school I attended, we all wore uniforms), I knew how to dress for Sunday mass, and I knew what dresses to wear for parties at my relatives' homes. Though I do not recall the precise details of my Career Day outfit, it must have been a composite of these choices. But I remember a comment my friend (an Italian American) made in later years that coalesced my impressions of that day. She said that at the business school she was attending, the Puerto Rican girls always stood out for wearing "everything at once." She meant, of course, too much jewelry, too many accessories. On that day at school we were simply made the negative models by the nuns, who were themselves not credible fashion experts to any of us. But it was painfully obvious to me that to the others, in their tailored skirts and silk blouses, we must have seemed "hopeless" and "vulgar." Though I now know that most adolescents feel out of step much of the time, I also know that for the Puerto Rican girls of my generation that sense was intensified. The way our teachers and classmates looked at us that day in school was just a taste of the cultural clash that awaited us in the real world, where prospective employers and men on the street would often misinterpret our tight skirts and jingling bracelets as a "come-on."

6   Mixed cultural signals have perpetuated certain stereotypes—for example, that of the Hispanic woman as the "hot tamale" or sexual firebrand. It is a one-dimensional view that the media have found easy to promote. In their special vocabulary, advertisers have designated "sizzling" and "smoldering" as the adjectives of choice for describing not only the foods but also the women of Latin America. From conversations in my house I recall hearing about the harassment that Puerto Rican women endured in factories where the "boss-men" talked to them as if sexual innuendo was all they understood, and worse, often gave them the choice of submitting to their advances or being fired.

7   It is custom, however, not chromosomes, that leads us to choose scarlet over pale pink. As young girls, it was our mothers who influenced our

decisions about clothes and colors—mothers who had grown up on a tropical island where the natural environment was a riot of primary colors, where showing your skin was one way to keep cool as well as to look sexy. Most important of all, on the island, women perhaps felt freer to dress and move more provocatively since, in most cases, they were protected by the traditions, mores, and laws of a Spanish/Catholic system of morality and machismo whose main rule was: *You may look at my sister, but if you touch her I will kill you.* The extended family and church structure could provide a young woman with a circle of safety in her small pueblo on the island; if a man "wronged" a girl, everyone would close in to save her family honor.

8   My mother has told me about dressing in her best party clothes on Saturday nights and going to the town's plaza to promenade with her girlfriends in front of the boys they liked. The males were thus given an opportunity to admire the women and to express their admiration in the form of *piropos:* erotically charged street poems they composed on the spot. (I have myself been subjected to a few *piropos* while visiting the island, and they can be outrageous, although custom dictates that they must never cross into obscenity.) This ritual, as I understand it, also entails a show of studied indifference on the woman's part; if she is "decent," she must not acknowledge the man's impassioned words. So I do understand how things can be lost in translation. When a Puerto Rican girl dressed in her idea of what is attractive meets a man from the mainstream culture who has been trained to react to certain types of clothing as a sexual signal, a clash is likely to take place. I remember the boy who took me to my first formal dance leaning over to plant a sloppy, over-eager kiss painfully on my mouth; when I didn't respond with sufficient passion, he remarked resentfully: "I thought you Latin girls were supposed to mature early," as if I were expected to *ripen* like a fruit or vegetable, not just grow into womanhood like other girls.

9   It is surprising to my professional friends that even today some people, including those who should know better, still put others "in their place." It happened to me most recently during a stay at a classy metropolitan hotel favored by young professional couples for weddings. Late one evening after the theater, as I walked toward my room with a colleague (a woman with whom I was coordinating an arts program), a middle-aged man in a tuxedo, with a young girl in satin and lace on his arm, stepped directly into our path. With his champagne glass extended toward me, he exclaimed "Evita!"

10   Our way blocked, my companion and I listened as the man half-recited, half-bellowed "Don't Cry for Me, Argentina." When he finished, the young girl said: "How about a round of applause for my daddy?" We complied, hoping this would bring the silly spectacle to a close. I was becoming aware that our little group was attracting the attention of the other guests. "Daddy" must have perceived this too, and he once more barred the way as we tried to walk past him. He began to shout-sing a ditty to the tune of "La Bamba"— except the lyrics were about a girl named Maria whose exploits rhymed with her name and gonorrhea. The girl kept saying "Oh, Daddy" and looking at me with pleading eyes. She wanted me to laugh along with the others.

My companion and I stood silently waiting for the man to end his offensive song. When he finished, I looked not at him but at his daughter. I advised her calmly never to ask her father what he had done in the army. Then I walked between them and to my room. My friend complimented me on my cool handling of the situation, but I confessed that I had really wanted to push the jerk into the swimming pool. This same man—probably a corporate executive, well-educated, even worldly by most standards—would not have been likely to regale an Anglo woman with a dirty song in public. He might have checked his impulse by assuming that she could be somebody's wife or mother, or at least *somebody* who might take offense. But, to him, I was just an Evita or a Maria: merely a character in his cartoon-populated universe.

11   Another facet of the myth of the Latin woman in the United States is the menial, the domestic—Maria the housemaid or countergirl. It's true that work as domestics, as waitresses, and in factories is all that's available to women with little English and few skills. But the myth of the Hispanic menial—the funny maid, mispronouncing words and cooking up a spicy storm in a shiny California kitchen—has been perpetuated by the media in the same way that "Mammy" from *Gone with the Wind* became America's idea of the black woman for generations. Since I do not wear my diplomas around my neck for all to see, I have on occasion been sent to that "kitchen" where some think I obviously belong.

12   One incident has stayed with me, though I recognize it as a minor offense. My first public poetry reading took place in Miami, at a restaurant where a luncheon was being held before the event. I was nervous and excited as I walked in with notebook in hand. An older woman motioned me to her table, and thinking (foolish me) that she wanted me to autograph a copy of my newly published slender volume of verse, I went over. She ordered a cup of coffee from me, assuming I was the waitress. (Easy enough to mistake my poems for menus, I suppose.) I know it wasn't an intentional act of cruelty. Yet of all the good things that happened later, I remember that scene most clearly, because it reminded me of what I had to overcome before anyone would take me seriously. In retrospect I understand that my anger gave my reading fire. In fact, I have almost always taken any doubt in my abilities as a challenge, the result most often being the satisfaction of winning a convert, of seeing the cold, appraising eyes warm to my words, the body language change, the smile that indicates I have opened some avenue for communication. So that day as I read, I looked directly at that woman. Her lowered eyes told me she was embarrassed at her faux pas, and when I willed her to look up at me, she graciously allowed me to punish her with my full attention. We shook hands at the end of the reading and I never saw her again. She has probably forgotten the entire incident, but maybe not.

13   Yet I am one of the lucky ones. There are thousands of Latinas without the privilege of an education or the entrees into society that I have. For them life is a constant struggle against the misconceptions perpetuated by the myth of the Latina. My goal is to try to replace the old stereotypes with a much more interesting set of realities. Every time I give a reading, I hope the

stories I tell, the dreams and fears I examine in my work, can achieve some universal truth that will get my audience past the particulars of my skin color, my accent, or my clothes.

14   I once wrote a poem in which I called all Latinas "God's brown daughters." This poem is really a prayer of sorts, offered upward, but also, through the human-to-human channel of art, outward. It is a prayer for communication and for respect. In it, Latin women pray "in Spanish to an Anglo God/with a Jewish heritage," and they are "fervently hoping/that if not omnipotent,/at least He be bilingual." ■

QUESTIONS ON SUBJECT AND PURPOSE

1. What exactly is a stereotype? Where does the word *stereotype* come from?
2. What are the stereotypes or "myths" of the Latin woman that Cofer has experienced?
3. What is Cofer's announced goal in writing?

QUESTIONS ON STRATEGY AND AUDIENCE

1. At what point in time does the essay begin? Why does Cofer start with this example?
2. How does Cofer use time or chronology as a structural device in her essay?
3. Who does Cofer imagine as her reader? How can you tell?

QUESTIONS ON VOCABULARY AND STYLE

1. What does Cofer mean when she writes, "It is custom, however, not chromosomes, that leads us to choose scarlet over pale pink"?
2. What does *machismo* (paragraph 7) mean?
3. Be prepared to define the following words: *coveted* (paragraph 1), *microcosm* (3), *coalesced* (5), *innuendo* (6), *mores* (7), *regale* (10), *menial* (11), *faux pas* (12).

WRITING SUGGESTIONS

1. **Doing a Critical Analysis.** Cofer uses a personal experience narrative to illustrate the stereotypes that others have of the "Latin woman." She replaces "the old stereotypes with a much more interesting set of realities" (paragraph 13). In an essay, analyze how and why that strategy works so effectively.
2. **Journaling or Blogging.** Stereotypes are not limited to individuals from particular races or cultures. Stereotypes can be based on gender, age, physical appearance, hair or clothing styles, dialects. In your journal or blog, think about occasions when you have been stereotyped or when you have stereotyped someone else.
3. **Practicing in a Paragraph.** Take one of the stereotypes from above and, in a paragraph, describe how it evidenced itself in your attitudes or those of others.
4. **Writing the Personal Essay.** Expand your paragraph into an essay, exploring that stereotype as it was applied to you or to others. What aspects of

personality or behavior do people expect when they see you as a stereotype? What do you expect when you stereotype someone else? Classify those reactions and expectations.

5. **Finding Reading Connections.** Deborah L. Rhode, in "Why Looks Are the Last Bastion of Discrimination," (Chapter 1) offers a number of examples of stereotyping based on people's appearances and weight. Using both essays as background, discuss how and why we stereotype people—what might be our reasons? Offer a classification of those reasons.

6. **Exploring Links Online.** Research, on the Web, the public's reaction to homeless people. How do you feel when you see a homeless person? Do you see them as stereotypes? After reading the essay, analyze and classify your own reactions.

7. **Writing the Research Paper.** Select a culture (or some aspect of a culture) that seems to be widely misunderstood by most Americans. Research the cultural differences and present your findings in an essay. One excellent source of information would be interviews with students from other countries and cultures who are studying at your school.

For Further Study

Focusing on Grammar and Writing. Cofer uses parentheses in her writing. Look closely at her use of them and then construct some rules or suggestions for their use based on her sentences.

Working Together. Divide into small groups and then explain and analyze one of the following details: why men break into song when they see her; what Career Day revealed; why young men perform *piropos*; what the confrontation with the man and his daughter in the "classy" hotel revealed; how the essay concludes. What does each contribute to the essay?

Seeing Other Modes at Work. The essay uses narration to follow a Puerto Rican female from girlhood to adulthood.

The Value of Children: A Taxonomical Essay

BERNARD R. BERELSON

Bernard R. Berelson (1912–1979) was born in Spokane, Washington, and received a Ph.D. from the University of Chicago. He divided his time between the academic world and the world of international development assistance. In 1962, he joined the Population Council, eventually serving as its president until his retirement in 1974. Berelson published extensively on population policy and the prospects for fertility declines in developing countries.

Berelson's concern with population policy is obvious in this essay reprinted from the Annual Report *of the Population Council (1972). Using a clear scheme of classification, Berelson analyzes the reasons why people want children.*

Before Reading

Connecting: The phrase "the value of children" might seem a little unusual. What, for example, was your "value" to your parents? If you have children, in what sense do they have "value" to you?

Anticipating: Despite the many reasons for having or wanting children, people in many societies today consciously choose to limit the number of children that they have. How might Berelson explain this phenomenon?

1   **W**hy do people want children? It is a simple question to ask, perhaps an impossible one to answer.

2   Throughout most of human history, the question never seemed to need a reply. These years, however, the question has a new tone. It is being asked in a nonrhetorical way because of three revolutions in thought and behavior that characterize the latter decades of the twentieth century: the vital revolution in which lower death rates have given rise to the population problem and raise new issues about human fertility; the sexual revolution from reproduction; and the women's revolution, in which childbearing and -rearing no longer are being accepted as the only or even the primary roles of half the human race. Accordingly, for about the first time, the question of why people want children now can be asked, so to speak, with a straight face.

3   "Why" questions of this kind, with simple surfaces but profound depths, are not answered or settled; they are ventilated, explicated, clarified. Anything as complex as the motives for having children can be classified in various ways, and any such taxonomy has an arbitrary character to it. This one starts with chemistry and proceeds to spirit.

The Biological

4   Do people innately want children for some built-in reason of physiology? Is there anything to maternal instinct, or parental instinct? Or is biology satisfied with the sex instinct as the way to assure continuity?

5   In psychoanalytic thought there is talk of the "child-wish," the "instinctual drive of physiological cause," "the innate femaleness of the girl direct(ing) her development toward motherhood," and the wanting of children as "the essence of her self-realization," indicating normality. From

the experimental literature, there is some evidence that man, like other animals, is innately attracted to the quality of "babyishness."

6   If the young and adults of several species are compared for differences in bodily and facial features, it will be seen readily that the nature of the difference is apparently the same almost throughout the phylogenetic scale. Limbs are shorter and much heavier in proportion to the torso in babies than in adults. Also, the head is proportionately much larger in relation to the body than is the case with adults. On the face itself, the forehead is more prominent and bulbous; the eyes large and perhaps located as far down as below the middle of the face, because of the large forehead. In addition, the cheeks may be round and protruding. In many species there is also a greater degree of overall fatness in contrast to normal adult bodies. . . . In man, as in other animals, social prescriptions and customs are not the sole or even primary factors that guarantee the rearing and protection of babies. This seems to indicate that the biologically rooted releaser of babyishness may have promoted infant care in primitive man before societies ever were formed, just as it appears to do in many animal species. Thus this releaser may have a high survival value for the species of man.*

7   In the human species the question of social and personal motivation distinctively arises, but that does not necessarily mean that the biology is completely obliterated. In animals the instinct to reproduce appears to be all; in humans is it something?

The Cultural

8 Whatever the biological answer, people do not want all the children they physically can have—no society, hardly any woman. Everywhere social traditions and social pressures enforce a certain conformity to the approved childbearing pattern, whether large numbers of children in Africa or small numbers in Eastern Europe. People want children because that is "the thing to do"—culturally sanctioned and institutionally supported, hence about as natural as any social behavior can be.

9   Such social expectations, expressed by everyone toward everyone, are extremely strong in influencing behavior even on such an important element in life as childbearing and on whether the outcome is two children or six. In most human societies, the thing to do gets done, for social rewards and punishments are among the most powerful. Whether they produce lots of children or few and whether the matter is fully conscious or not, the cultural norms are all the more effective if, as often, they are rationalized as the will of God or the hand of fate.

The Political

10 The cultural shades off into political considerations: reproduction for the purposes of a higher authority. In a way, the human responsibility to perpetuate

---

*Eckhard H. Hess, "Ethology and Developmental Psychology," in Paul H. Musser, ed., *Carmichael's Manual of Child Psychology*, Vol. 1 (New York: Wiley, 1970), pp. 20–21.

the species is the grandest such expression—the human family pitted politically against fauna and flora—and there always might be people who partly rationalize their own childbearing as a contribution to that lofty end. Beneath that, however, there are political units for whom collective childbearing is or has been explicitly encouraged as a demographic duty—countries concerned with national glory or competitive political position; governments concerned with the supply of workers and soldiers; churches concerned with propagation of the faith or their relative strength; ethnic minorities concerned with their political power; linguistic communities competing for position; clans and tribes concerned over their relative status within a larger setting. In ancient Rome, according to the Oxford English Dictionary, the proletariat—from the root *proles*, for progeny—were "the lowest class of the community, regarded as contributing nothing to the state but offspring": and a proletaire was "one who served the state not with his property but only with his offspring." The world has changed since then, but not all the way.

The Economic

11 As the "new home economics" is reminding us in its current attention to the microeconomics of fertility, children are economically valuable. Not that that would come as a surprise to the poor peasant who consciously acts on the premise, but it is clear that some people want children or not for economic reasons.

12   Start with the obvious case of economic returns from children that appears to be characteristic of the rural poor. To some extent, that accounts for their generally higher fertility than that of their urban and wealthier counterparts: labor in the fields; hunting, fishing, animal care; help in the home and with the younger children; dowry and "bride-wealth"; support in later life (the individualized system of social security).

13   The economics of the case carries through on the negative side as well. It is not publicly comfortable to think of children as another consumer durable, but sometimes that is precisely the way parents do think of them, before conception: another child or a trip to Europe; a birth deferred in favor of a new car, the *n*th child requiring more expenditure on education or housing. But observe the special characteristics of children viewed as consumer durables: they come only in whole units; they are not rentable or returnable or exchangeable or available on trial; they cannot be evaluated quickly; they do not come in several competing brands or products; their quality cannot be pretested before delivery; they usually are not available for appraisal in large numbers in one's personal experience; they themselves participate actively in the household's decisions. And in the broad view, both societies and families tend to choose standard of living over number of children when the opportunity presents itself.

The Familial

14 In some societies people want children for what might be called familial reasons: to extend the family line or the family name; to propitiate the

ancestors; to enable the proper functioning of religious rituals involving the family (e.g., the Hindu son needed to light the father's funeral pyre, the Jewish son needed to say Kaddish for the dead father). Such reasons may seem thin in the modern, secularized society but they have been and are powerful indeed in other places.

15   In addition, one class of family reasons shares a border with the following category, namely, having children in order to maintain or improve a marriage: to hold the husband or occupy the wife; to repair or rejuvenate their marriage; to increase the number of children on the assumption that family happiness lies that way. The point is underlined by its converse: in some societies the failure to bear children (or males) is a threat to the marriage and a ready cause for divorce.

16   Beyond all that is the profound significance of children to the very institution of the family itself. To many people, husband and wife alone do not seem a proper family—they need children to enrich the circle, to validate its family character, to gather the redemptive influence of offspring. Children need the family, but the family seems also to need children, as the social institution uniquely available, at least in principle, for security, comfort, assurance, and direction in a changing, often hostile, world. To most people, such a home base, in the literal sense, needs more than one person for sustenance and in generational extension.

The Personal

17 Up to here the reasons for wanting children primarily refer to instrumental benefits. Now we come to a variety of reasons for wanting children that are supposed to bring direct personal benefits.

18   *Personal Power.* As noted, having children sometimes gives one parent power over the other. More than that, it gives the parents power over the child(ren)—in many cases, perhaps most, about as much effective power as they ever will have the opportunity of exercising on an individual basis. They are looked up to by the child(ren), literally and figuratively, and rarely does that happen otherwise. Beyond that, having children is involved in a wider circle of power:

19   In most simple societies the lines of kinship are the lines of political power, social prestige and economic aggrandizement. The more children a man has, the more successful marriage alliances he can arrange, increasing his own power and influence by linking himself to men of greater power or to men who will be his supporters. . . . In primitive and peasant societies, the man with few children is the man of minor influence and the childless man is virtually a social nonentity.*

20   *Personal Competence.* Becoming a parent demonstrates competence in an essential human role. Men and women who are closed off from other demonstrations of competence, through lack of talent or educational opportunity or

---

*Burton Benedict, "Population Regulation in Primitive Societies," in Anthony Ellison, *Population Control* (London: Penguin, 1970), pp. 176–77.

social status, still have this central one. For males, parenthood is thought to show virility, potency, *machismo*. For females it demonstrates fecundity, itself so critical to an acceptable life in many societies.

21   *Personal Status.* Everywhere parenthood confers status. It is an accomplishment open to all, or virtually all, and realized by the overwhelming majority of adult humankind. Indeed, achieving parenthood surely must be one of the two most significant events in one's life—that and being born in the first place. In many societies, then and only then is one considered a real man or a real woman.

22   Childbearing is one of the few ways in which the poor can compete with the rich. Life cannot make the poor man prosperous in material goods and services but it easily can make him rich with children. He cannot have as much of anything else worth having, except sex, which itself typically means children in such societies. Even so, the poor still are deprived by the arithmetic; they have only two or three times as many children as the rich whereas the rich have at least forty times the income of the poor.

23   *Personal Extension.* Beyond the family line, wanting children is a way to reach for personal immortality—for most people, the only way available. It is a way to extend oneself indefinitely into the future. And short of that, there is simply the physical and psychological extension of oneself in the children, here and now—a kind of narcissism: there they are and they are mine (or like me).

24
> *Look in thy glass and tell the face thou viewest,*
> *Now is the time that face should form another;*
> *But if thou live, remember'd not to be,*
> *Die single, and thine image dies with thee.*
>
>   —Shakespeare's Sonnets, III

25   *Personal Experience.* Among all the activities of life, parenthood is a unique experience. It is a part of life, or personal growth, that simply cannot be experienced in any other way and hence is literally an indispensable element of the full life. The experience has many profound facets: the deep curiosity as to how the child will turn out; the renewal of self in the second chance; the reliving of one's own childhood; the redemptive opportunity; the challenge to shape another human being; the sheer creativity and self-realization involved. For a large proportion of the world's women, there was and probably still is nothing else for the grown female to do with her time and energy, as society defines her role. And for many women, it might be the most emotional and spiritual experience they ever have and perhaps the most gratifying as well.

26   *Personal Pleasure.* Last, but one hopes not least, in the list of reasons for wanting children is the altruistic pleasure of having them, caring for them, watching them grow, shaping them, being with them, enjoying them. This reason comes last on the list but it is typically the first one mentioned in the casual inquiry: "because I like children." Even this reason has its dark side, as with parents who live through their children, often to the latter's distaste and

disadvantage. But that should not obscure a fundamental reason for wanting children: love.

27   There are, in short, many reasons for wanting children. Taken together, they must be among the most compelling motivations in human behavior: culturally imposed, institutionally reinforced, psychologically welcome. ■

QUESTIONS ON SUBJECT AND PURPOSE

1. What is "the value of children"? How many different values does Berelson cite?
2. Berelson gives positive, negative, and neutral reasons for wanting children. Is the overall effect of the essay positive, negative, or neutral?
3. Which of Berelson's reasons seem most relevant in American society today? Which seem least relevant?

QUESTIONS ON STRATEGY AND AUDIENCE

1. How does Berelson organize his classification? Can you find an explicit statement of organization?
2. Could the classification have been organized in a different way? Would that have changed the essay in any way?
3. How effective is Berelson's introduction? His conclusion? Suggest other ways in which the essay could have begun or ended.

QUESTIONS ON VOCABULARY AND STYLE

1. Berelson asks a number of rhetorical questions (see Glossary and Ready Reference). Why does he ask them? Does he answer them? Does he "ventilate," "explicate," and "clarify" them (paragraph 3)?
2. Describe the tone of Berelson's essay—what does he sound like? Be prepared to support your statement with some specific illustrations from the text.
3. Be prepared to define the following words: *taxonomy* (paragraph 3), *physiology* (4), *phylogenetic* (6), *bulbous* (6), *sanctioned* (8), *fauna and flora* (10), *demographic* (10), *consumer durable* (13), *propitiate* (14), *sustenance* (16), *aggrandizement* (19), *nonentity* (19), *machismo* (20), *fecundity* (20), *narcissism* (23).

WRITING SUGGESTIONS

1. **Doing a Critical Analysis.** In a classification, not only must the categories be clearly established, they must also be arranged in a logical or rhetorical order. In an essay, analyze how and why Berelson organizes the reasons why people want children.
2. **Journaling or Blogging.** In your journal or blog, explore the reasons why you do or do not want to have children. Would you choose to limit the number of children you have? Why or why not?

3. **Practicing in a Paragraph.** In a paragraph, classify the reasons for your decision about children. Focus on two or three reasons at most, and be sure to have some logical order to your arrangement.

4. **Writing the Personal Essay.** Few issues are so charged in American society today as abortion. In an essay, classify the reasons why people are either pro-choice or pro-life. Be objective. Do not write an argument for or against abortion or a piece of propaganda.

5. **Finding Reading Connections.** Tom Haines, in "Facing Famine," (Chapter 2) records the devastating effect that famine has on infants. Berelson classifies reasons why people want children, always assuming that those children can and will survive. In the face of such high infant mortality rates in areas of the world hit by famine or by civil wars, why might people not want to have children?

6. **Exploring Links Online.** What are the dire consequences that we are facing as a nation since our fertility rate has consistently fallen below the replacement rate? If, as Berelson points out, people want children for so many reasons, why are people not having children in America today?

7. **Writing the Research Paper.** Studies have shown that, as countries become increasingly industrialized, their population growth declines. In a research paper, explore how and why increasingly industrialized societies show decreased birth rates.

For Further Study

Focusing on Grammar and Writing. Berelson uses several different typographical devices (extra white space between paragraphs, bold face headings, indented italic headings) to structure his essay. How do such devices affect your reading experience?

Working Together. Starting as a class, come up with some items that could be sorted into a classification scheme—types of music, food, canned drinks, snacks. Once you have a list of subjects, divide into small groups and work on a classification system that would work for each of the subjects.

Seeing Other Modes at Work. Within each of the categories that he establishes, Berelson also uses cause and effect.

ADDITIONAL WRITING SUGGESTIONS FOR DIVISION AND CLASSIFICATION

Remember that division takes a whole and separates it into meaningful subdivisions. Classification takes many things and sorts them into categories as a means of ordering them and making them easier to understand. Both division and classification are done for a purpose, and both often make use of visual devices (e.g., charts or typographical devices) to help readers grasp the organizational pattern. Keeping a purpose in mind and using visuals if you wish, try writing about one of the following topics:

Division

1. Freshman class (as a whole) at your college or university
2. Way in which players on a team or in a band might be subdivided by roles
3. Organizational structure of a club or a business
4. Total cost of a year at your college or university/cost of a year for you (humorous)
5. Distribution of federal tax dollars
6. Composition (ingredients) of a prepared food that you regularly consume
7. Your stages in the writing process (try as a humorous essay)
8. A well-balanced meal (serious or humorous)
9. Responsibilities of your job (part-time or full-time)
10. Characteristics of your "ideal" job

Classification

1. Television talk or reality shows
2. Items found in a drawer, pocket, backpack, or purse
3. E-mails received
4. Excuses for bad behavior/lateness/missing class/not being prepared for class
5. Ways in which you waste time
6. Ways to procrastinate when you have to write a paper
7. Places to eat on campus or in town
8. People you regard as friends or enemies
9. Excuses for smoking or for not exercising more or eating less
10. Possible first-date activities

5 | Comparison and Contrast

LEARNING OBJECTIVES

In this chapter, you will learn how to

1. Distinguish between comparison and contrast
2. Find an appropriate subject for comparison and contrast
3. Identify the important points of similarity and difference
4. Construct an effective order for those points of similarity and difference
5. Employ appropriate analogies to clarify your analysis
6. Revise a comparison and contrast essay to increase its effectiveness
7. Analyze readings that use comparison and contrast

 Key Questions

WRITING COMPARISON AND CONTRAST

Getting Ready to Write

What is comparison and contrast?

How do you choose a subject?

Must you always find both similarities and differences?

Writing

How do you structure a comparison and contrast essay?

How do you use analogy, metaphor, and simile?

Revising

How do you revise a comparison and contrast essay?

Student Essay

   Alicia Gray, "Minimizing the Guesswork in a Library Search"

READING COMPARISON AND CONTRAST

In Prose

   John McPhee, from Oranges

In Literature

   Martin Espada, "Coca-Cola and Coco Frio" (poem)

In a Visual

   William Hogarth, "Beer Street" and "Gin Lane" (prints)

Writing Comparison and Contrast

GETTING READY TO WRITE

What Is Comparison and Contrast?

Whenever you decide between two alternatives, you engage in comparison and contrast. Which tablet is the best value or has the most attractive set of features? Which professor's section of Introductory Sociology should you register for in the spring semester? In both cases, you make a selection by comparing alternatives on a series of relevant points and then deciding which has the greatest advantages.

In comparison and contrast essays, subjects are set in opposition in order to reveal similarities and differences. Comparison involves finding similarities among two or more things, people, or ideas; contrast involves finding differences. Comparison and contrast writing tasks can involve then, three activities: emphasizing similarities, emphasizing differences, or emphasizing both.

Visual images can illustrate comparison and contrast. Look at the Venn diagram below, which shows two or more subjects that share some, but not all, things.

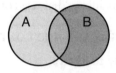

Comparison and contrast often involves visual displays of similarities and differences—things such as lists, tables, and charts—but it also occurs with just words. John Fischer uses comparison in this paragraph to emphasize the similarities between Ukrainians and Texans:

> The Ukrainians are the Texans of Russia. They believe they can fight, drink, ride, sing, and make love better than anyone else in the world, and if pressed will admit it. Their country, too, was a borderland—that's what Ukraine means—and like Texas it was settled by outlaws, horse thieves, land-hungry farmers, and people who hadn't made a go of it somewhere else. Some of these hard cases banded together, long ago, to raise hell and livestock. They called themselves Cossacks, and they would have felt right at home in any Western movie. Even today the Ukrainians cherish a wistful tradition of horsemanship, although most of them would feel as uncomfortable in a saddle as any Dallas banker. They still like to wear knee-high boots and big, furry hats, made of gray or Persian lamb, which is the local equivalent of the Stetson.

Fischer emphasizes only similarities. He tries to help his readers understand a foreign country by likening it to a place far more familiar to most Americans.

Henry Petroski, in his essay "The Gleaming Silver Bird and the Rusty Iron Horse," contrasts air travel and train travel, emphasizing their differences:

> The airplane lets us fly and forget. We are as gods, even in coach class, attended by young, smiling stewards and stewardesses who bring us food, drink, and entertainment. From the window of the airplane we marvel at the cities far beneath us, at the great land formations and waterways, and at the clouds. Political boundaries are forgotten, and the world is one. Everything is possible.
>
> Nothing is forgotten on the train, however. The right of way is strewn with the detritus of technology, and technology's disruptiveness is everywhere apparent. Outside the once-clean picture window of the train, which has probably slowed down to pass over a deteriorating roadbed under repair, one sees not heaven in the clouds but the graveyards of people and machines. One cannot help but notice how technology has changed the land and the lives of those who live beside the rails. The factory abandoned is a blight not easily removed; the neglected homes of myriad factory (and railroad?) workers are not easily restored.

Like every writing task, comparison and contrast is done to achieve a particular purpose. In practical situations, you use it to help make a decision. In academic situations, comparison and contrast allows you to analyze two or more subjects carefully and thoroughly on the basis of a series of shared similarities or differences.

How Do You Choose a Subject?

Many times, especially on examinations and papers for academic courses, the subject for comparison and contrast is chosen for you. On an economics examination you might be asked, "What are the main differences between the public and private sectors?" In political science you are to "compare the political platforms of the Republican and Democratic parties in the last

Links between Writing and Reading

	Comparison and contrast
William Zinsser, "The Transaction"	Contradictory answers to the same questions
Suzanne Britt, "Neat vs. Sloppy"	Comic exaggeration of two different stereotypes of people
Libby Sander, "Colleges Confront . . ."	Engagement of women vs. men
Michael Pollan, "The Consumer . . ."	One crop, two products
Meghan Daum, "Virtual Love"	Two "romances" with one person

election." At other times, however, you must choose your own subject for comparison and contrast.

When the choice is yours, several things are important. First, make sure that you choose subjects that have obvious similarities or differences. William Zinsser compares his writing process to Dr. Brock's; Suzanne Britt contrasts "sloppy" and "neat" people. Second, make sure that you have a reason for making the comparison and contrast. The objective is to reveal something new or important. Meghan Daum contrasts her relationships with the "virtual" and the "real" Pete. Although the romance flourished online, it dies instantly when they meet each other. Daum uses comparison and contrast to make a point not just about her relationship, but also about our needs and frustrations in trying to establish a meaningful relationship in contemporary society. She comments, "our need to worship somehow fuses with our need to be worshiped." Finally, concentrate your comparison and contrast on the important and significant points. Your goal is never to find as many points of comparison and contrast as possible.

Must You Always Find Both Similarities and Differences?

You can compare and contrast only if there is some basic similarity between two subjects: John Fischer compares two groups of people—Ukrainians and Texans; Henry Petroski compares two modes of transportation—the airplane and the railroad. There is no point in comparing two totally unrelated subjects; for example, the mind could be compared to a computer since both process information, but there would be no reason to compare a computer and a piece of fruit. Remember, too, that some similarities are obvious and hence are not worth writing about. It would be pointless for William Zinsser to observe that both he and Dr. Brock write on word processors, use dictionaries, or work best in a quiet room. Some similarities, however, are important and should be mentioned. Michael Pollan sees how excess corn production leads to two different epidemics.

Once you have chosen your subject, make a list of possible points of comparison and contrast. Be sure that those points are shared. Zinsser, for

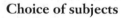

Links between Writing and Reading

	Choice of subjects
William Zinsser, "The Transaction"	Advice from a classic "informal guide" to writing
Suzanne Britt, "Neat vs. Sloppy"	Comic exploration of two stereotypes
Justin Pope, "MOOCs"	MOOCs vs. traditional classes
Michael Pollan, "The Consumer . . ."	Two products from corn
Meghan Daum, "Virtual Love"	Online dating and romance

Prewriting Tips for Writing Comparison and Contrast

1. Jot down ideas on subjects that might be compared or contrasted. Remember, comparison involves finding similarities among two or more things—typically things that initially appear to be different. Contrast involves finding differences among things that seem quite similar.

2. Under each possible subject, make a list of similarities or of differences. Do not worry about an order, just generate ideas.

3. Go back over your lists and make sure that the similarities or differences are important enough to write about. The idea is not to generate as many similarities or differences as possible, but to find interesting and significant points.

4. Narrow down to a possible topic and then explain in one sentence (a thesis) why you are making this comparison or contrast.

5. Check your list to see that all of the items on it are phrased in parallel form.

example, organizes his comparison and contrast around six questions. To each of the six, Zinsser gives first Dr. Brock's response and then his own. The contrast depends on the two responses to each of the six questions. If Brock had answered only one group of three and Zinsser a different group of three, the contrast would not have worked.

Be careful when you create analogies, similes, and metaphors. If you try to be too clever, your point will seem forced. But do not avoid such devices altogether. Used sparingly, these compressed comparisons can be evocative and effective.

WRITING

How Do You Structure a Comparison and Contrast Essay?

Comparison and contrast is not only an intellectual process, but it is also a structural pattern that can be used to organize paragraphs and essays. In comparing and contrasting two subjects, three organizational models are available.

Subject-by-Subject (all of subject A, then all of subject B)

SUBJECT A
    Point 1
    Point 2
    Point 3

SUBJECT B
   Point 1
   Point 2
   Point 3

The subject-by-subject pattern works best for short essays. All of subject A is treated in a paragraph or two; all of subject B is treated in another group of paragraphs. The points of comparison or contrast are presented in the same order and in the same grammatical form in each of the paragraphs. If your paper is fairly long and if the points of comparison and contrast are somewhat complicated, the subject-by-subject pattern might not be appropriate. In a longer, multipage paper, it is potentially more difficult for your reader to remember the analysis of subject A when reading the analysis of subject B.

Point-by-Point (point 1 in A, then point 1 in B)

SUBJECT A, POINT 1/ SUBJECT B, POINT 1
SUBJECT A, POINT 2/ SUBJECT B, POINT 2
SUBJECT A, POINT 3/ SUBJECT B, POINT 3

William Zinsser's comparison of his writing process with that of Dr. Brock's uses a point-by-point pattern of contrast. The two authors take turns responding to a series of six questions asked by students. The essay then follows a pattern that can be described as A1B1, A2B2, A3B3, A4B4, A5B5, A6B6. In replying to the fourth question, for example, about whether or not feeling "depressed or unhappy" will affect their writing, Brock and Zinsser reply:

> "Probably it will," Dr. Brock replied. "Go fishing. Take a walk."
> "Probably it won't," I said. "If your job is to write every day, you learn to do it like any other job."

The point-by-point, or alternating, pattern emphasizes the individual points of comparison or contrast rather than the subject as a whole. In college courses, students who use this pattern usually write a group of sentences or a paragraph for each point, alternating between subject A and subject B. If you use the alternating pattern, you must decide how to order your points—for instance, by beginning or by ending with the strongest or most significant.

In longer pieces of writing, authors typically mix the subject-by-subject and the point-by-point patterns. Such an arrangement provides variety and can make the points of comparison or contrast much more vivid for the reader.

Mixed Sequence (includes subject-by-subject and point-by-point)

SUBJECT A
   POINT 1
   POINT 2

SUBJECT B
   POINT 1
   POINT 2
SUBJECT A, POINT 3/ SUBJECT B, POINT 3

Much of the examination writing that you do in college probably should be organized in the subject-by-subject or point-by-point patterns, because these are the clearest structures for short responses. Many of the essays you encounter in magazines and newspapers use the mixed pattern in order to achieve flexibility and variety.

How Do You Use Analogy, Metaphor, and Simile?

Writing a comparison often involves constructing an analogy, that is, an extended comparison in which something complex or unfamiliar is likened to something simple or familiar. The reason for making the analogy is to help the reader more easily understand or visualize the more complex or unfamiliar subject. For example, if you are trying to explain how the hard disk on your computer is organized, you might use the analogy of a file cabinet. The hard disk, you write, is the file cabinet itself, which is partitioned into directories (the file drawers), each of which contains subdirectories (the hanging folders), which in turn contain the individual files (the manila folders in which the individual documents are stored). The way in which your software program displays your files (and the icons it uses) suggests this metaphor.

Analogies are also used to provide a new way of seeing something. J. Anthony Lukas, for example, explains his attraction to the game of pinball by an analogy:

> Pinball is a metaphor for life, pitting man's skill, nerve, persistence, and luck against the perverse machinery of human existence. The playfield is rich with rewards: targets that bring huge scores, bright lights, chiming bells, free balls, and extra games. But it is replete with perils, too: cul-de-sac, traps, gutters, and gobble holes down which the ball may disappear forever.

This analogy does not seek to explain the unfamiliar. Probably every reader has seen a pinball machine. Rather, the analogy invites the reader to see the game in a fresh way. The suggested similarity might help the reader understand why arcade games such as pinball have a particular significance or attraction.

Two common forms of analogy used frequently in writing are metaphor and simile. A *metaphor* identifies one thing with another. When Henry Petroski contrasts air travel and train travel, he uses metaphor—the airplane is a "silver bird" and the train is an "iron horse." A *simile*, as its name suggests, is also a comparison based on a point or points of similarity. A simile differs from a metaphor by using the word *like* or *as* to link the two things being compared. In a sense, a simile suggests, rather than directly establishes, the comparison. On the February morning when his father died, Scott Russell Sanders in "The Inheritance of Tools" (Chapter 3) saw that the ice "coated the windows like cataracts."

Links between Writing and Reading

	Primary organization of essay
William Zinsser, "The Transaction"	Point-by-point, but what is different about paragraphs 9 through 11?
Suzanne Britt, "Neat vs. Sloppy"	Subject-by-subject, "sloppy" then "neat"
Libby Sander, "Colleges Confront . . ."	Point-by-point
Michael Pollan, "The Consumer . . ."	Subject-by-subject—corn whiskey and corn syrup
Meghan Daum, "Virtual Love"	Subject-by-subject—"virtual" Pete then "real" Pete

REVISING

How Do You Revise a Comparison and Contrast Essay?

Comparison and contrast is intended to isolate similarities and differences between two or more subjects. It is a fundamental process by which the mind understands things. Like all writing tasks, comparison and contrast writing is done for a purpose—in this instance, to help the reader make a choice or to help the reader clarify and understand the subject. Although comparison and contrast writing can be funny and entertaining, generally it has a serious, informative purpose. For that reason, make sure your comparison and contrast essay is clearly and logically organized. When revising a comparison and contrast essay, pay particular attention to the following cautions: avoid the obvious and keep the analysis logically structured.

Avoiding the Obvious   Your paper needs to be both informative and interesting enough to hold your reader's attention. Do not compare and contrast points that are obvious. When John McPhee compares Florida and California oranges (see the heading Reading Comparison and Contrast), he focuses only on the differences that are important, explaining why oranges from two different states are so different. He contrasts them on the thickness of their skins, on their juiciness, and on the ease of peeling and separating segments. Readers tire easily of essays that offer only the obvious. Think again about what you have chosen to write. Ask a peer reader to assess your essay's interest. Does it tell readers only what they already know? Are the points of comparison and contrast significant or trivial? If there is a problem, you need to change your points of similarity or contrast or find a new subject.

Drafting Tips for Writing Comparison and Contrast

1. Decide on whether the best organizational strategy will be subject-by-subject, point-by-point, or a mix of the two. Plan the organizational strategy of your paper with an outline.

2. Decide on a rationale for ordering the points of comparison or contrast. What will come first and why? What will come last and why? Try different orders.

3. Rate each point of comparison or contrast. Is each one really significant or interesting? Eliminate any points that seem minor or trivial.

4. Check to see if your paragraphing in the essay reveals the structure of the essay. Can your reader clearly see your organizational plan?

5. Find a peer reader, tutor, or your instructor to read your draft. Ask for suggestions about how the paper might be improved. Consider each suggestion.

Keeping the Analysis Logically Structured   In addition to considering three organizational patterns (subject-by-subject, point-by-point, and mixed) in comparison and contrast writing, remember three organizational principles: The points of comparison and contrast must be (1) identical in both subjects, (2) taken in the same order, and (3) phrased in parallel grammatical form. You will guarantee a clear, organized, easily followed essay if you adhere to these three principles.

If you are using the subject-by-subject pattern, it is fairly easy to signal to your reader when you have finished one subject and started another. Typically, the essay will be divided by paragraphs in a way that marks the switch from one subject to another. If you are using the point-by-point or a mixed method, you will need to provide step or sequence markers for your reader to signal when you are moving to the next point. Have you called out the points (for example, *first, second, next, then*) or used transitional words or phrases to signal the transition?

Parallel structures—that is, items that are phrased in grammatically similar ways—are also important. Underline each of the points you are using. Have you cast those points in grammatical structures that are parallel in form?

Have you arranged the points of comparison and contrast in an order that makes sense? If the points are of the same relative importance, you can be flexible in ordering them. If the points can be arranged from greater to lesser significance, then you need to arrange them in a descending or an ascending order. Decide whether you want to start with the most significant difference or end with it.

Student Essay

As part of the library research paper unit in freshman English, Alicia Gray's class had been talking about searching their school's online library catalog for relevant books. The instructor had mentioned a number of times

---

Links between Writing and Reading

	Analogies, transitions, and arrangement
William Zinsser, "The Transaction"	Notice how paragraphing signals arrangement
Suzanne Britt, "Neat vs. Sloppy"	Analyze why there is no concluding paragraph
Justin Pope, "MOOCs"	Frame around the essay's core
Michael Pollan, "The Consumer . . ."	Notice transition in paragraph 6
Meghan Daum, "Virtual Love"	Notice use of analogies—similes and metaphors

---

 ## Revising Tips for Writing Comparison and Contrast

1. Assess the significance of your subject and your approach to it. Do not waste your reader's time on the obvious or the trivial.

2. Experiment with the paper's organizational strategy. Could it be arranged in another way? Could the points be put in a different order? Experiment with changes.

3. Look again at your introduction. Ask friends to read it. Does it make them want to keep reading? If not, rewrite your opening.

4. Honestly evaluate your conclusion. Did you just stop or did you really write a conclusion? Does your final paragraph seem to emphasize the points you are making in the essay? Does it reinforce your thesis?

5. Check your title. Every paper needs a real title—not something descriptive such as "Comparison and Contrast Essay." If necessary, write several other titles before choosing a final one.

that card catalogs could be searched for both subjects and keywords—the software program allowed for both. To give the students practice in both kinds of searches, Meghan, their instructor, gave them a worksheet to do for homework. On the way out of class, Alicia stopped and remarked to her instructor, "I always just do a keyword search," she said, "and it always seems like I find plenty of material. Since we have the capability to do a keyword search, isn't doing a subject search just unnecessary and even old-fashioned?" "Do the worksheet," Meghan replied. "Maybe you could compare and contrast the two methods for your essay, which is due next week." A week later, Alicia brought to class the following rough draft of her essay comparing keyword and subject searches.

First Draft

Subject vs. Keyword Searches

When it is time to start gathering information for your research paper in Freshman English, you will need to consult our Library's on-line catalog. The card catalog is a listing of the books that our library holds. Those books are cataloged, or listed, by author, title, subject, and keyword. Since normally we start by looking for books about our intended topic—rather than for specific titles by specific authors—we must start with either subject searches or keyword searches. What exactly is the difference between these two types of searches and how do you know when to use each?

When librarians refer to a "subject" search, they mean something quite specific and different from a "keyword." The term subject in library catalogs refers to a large listing of subject headings that are used by the Library of Congress to catalog a book. In fact, if you want to do a subject search in a library catalog, you don't start with the catalog itself. Instead you go to a multivolume series of books entitled the *Library of Congress Subject Headings*. Those books list alphabetically the various headings under which the Library of Congress files books. That listing is complete with cross-references, that is, with references to broader terms and to narrower, more specific terms. When catalogers at the Library of Congress look at new books, they do not just randomly assign a heading or a group of headings to the book, nor do they take the heading from a word in the book's title. Instead, they choose a heading or headings from the published list.

The principle behind the subject headings is to group related books under one heading. So instead of filing books about "the death penalty," "capital punishment," "death by lethal injection" under three separate subject headings, the Library of Congress uses a single subject heading ("capital punishment") and then provides cross-references from any other synonymous terms. The subject heading can also be followed by a whole series of other headings (for example, "capital punishment—history").

These other, more specific headings are very important because the Library of Congress always tries to assign the most specific subject heading to a book that it can. You never want to look under a large general heading if a more specific one is used. And how do you know if a more specific heading exists? You need to check the printed collection of headings currently in use. Subject headings impose a control on the vocabulary words used for headings.

In contrast, keyword searches look for words that are present somewhere in the book's record—typically in its title or subtitle, its author, its publisher. A keyword search retrieves information only when that word or group of words that you have entered appear in a record. That means there is no attempt at controlling the vocabulary. A book that had the phrase "the death penalty" somewhere in the title could be retrieved only if you typed in the keywords "death" and "penalty." A book on the same subject that used "capital punishment" would never appear—and keyword searches do not suggest related synonyms to you. Moreover, the presence of the keywords would not necessarily mean that the book would be about the "death penalty" in the sense of "capital punishment." The words could appear in the title of novel or a collection of poems; they could refer to vastly different and unrelated circumstances—"the death penalty in ancient Rome." And, if you don't indicate the relationship (for example, immediately next to each other) that the two (or more) terms are to have, you'll end up retrieving a mountain of records that have the terms "death" and "penalty" somewhere in the record (for example, "The Penalty of Life: The Death of John Sayce").

Keyword searches have an advantage in that they can be used to find the very specific words for which you might be looking. Maybe those words haven't yet been added to the subject headings. Since subject headings depend on printed lists, subject headings are slow to react to new fields of study or new technologies.

Comments

Alicia shared the opening paragraphs of her rough draft with a classmate during in-class peer editing. The instructor had asked the students to concentrate on the organizational pattern used in the body of the essay and on the introduction. After reading Alicia's paper, her partner Sara LaBarca offered some advice on revising the draft. "You have lots of information," she said, "but your main pattern of development is subject-by-subject except for the fifth paragraph where you switch to point-by-point. Maybe you should try doing more with the point-to-point; otherwise, by the time your readers come to the second half of your essay, they might forget the contrasts you established in the first half."

"I also think you need a strong introduction," she added. "You have a good thesis statement, but, well, frankly, I found the opening paragraph a little boring." Alicia tried to take Sara's advice and revised the opening of her essay and reorganized the body.

Revised Draft

Minimizing the Guesswork in a Library Search

The Cecil College Library has twenty books dealing with the death penalty, but unless you pay attention to the next couple of pages, you will never find most of them. Why? Because no single search strategy will lead you to all twenty books.

Looking for book sources is more complicated than you might think. A successful search will require two different types of searches—a subject and a keyword search. They are very different kinds of searches with different rules and results. But to maximize your sources for a quality research paper, you will need to know how to do both.

In both subject and keyword searches, you are looking for single words or phrases that will lead you to the books you need. Those subject or keyword terms come from two different places. The term *subject* in library catalogs refers to a large alphabetized listing of subject headings that are assigned by the Library of Congress when cataloging a book. You find an appropriate heading not by guessing as you stand at a computer terminal, but by looking in a multivolume series of books entitled *Library of Congress Subject Headings*. When catalogers at the Library of Congress look at new books, they do not just randomly assign a heading or a group of headings to the book, nor do they necessarily take the heading from a word in the book's title. Instead, they choose a heading or headings from the published list. A *keyword*, on the other hand, is a significant word, generally a noun, that is typically in a book's title or subtitle. Unlike a subject search where the categories are "controlled" (that is, someone has predetermined what subject headings will be used), a keyword search is, in one sense, guesswork. You think of an important word or phrase that might describe the topic about which you want information and you try that. Just like any time you guess, though, there are risks. A keyword search retrieves information only when that word or group of words that you have entered appears in a record.

"If I have the choice of having to look things up in a set of books or of just guessing, I'll guess," you might reply. But before you reject subject searches, consider the problem of synonyms—that is, words or phrases that mean roughly the same thing. A controlled subject search groups related books under one heading. So instead of filing books about "the death penalty," "capital punishment," and "death by lethal injection" under three separate subject headings, the Library of Congress uses a single subject heading ("capital punishment") and then provides cross-references from any other synonymous terms. In contrast, you can only retrieve a book in a keyword search if it has those specific words somewhere in its record. A book that had the phrase "the death penalty" somewhere in the title could be retrieved only if you typed in the keywords "death" and "penalty." A book on the same subject that used "capital punishment" would never appear, and keyword searches do not suggest related synonyms to you.

Moreover, the presence of the keywords would not necessarily mean that the book would be about the "death penalty" in the sense of "capital punishment." The words could appear in the title of a novel or a collection of poems; they could refer to vastly different and unrelated circumstances—"the death penalty in ancient Rome." And, if you don't indicate the relationship (for example, immediately next to each other) that the two (or more) terms are to have, you'll end up retrieving a mountain of records that have the terms "death" and "penalty" somewhere in the record (for example, "The Penalty of Life: The Death of John Sayce").

Keyword searches have some distinct advantages, however. Since subject searches are controlled, the Library of Congress tries to find existing appropriate terms under which to file books—even if they end up having to use more general terms. Although new subject headings are regularly added to the lists, emerging fields and technologies are rarely represented adequately in the subject headings. On the other hand, since keywords do not depend on any pre-existing published categories and since no one has tried to classify those keywords into categories, keywords can be the best way to look for books on new and emerging subjects. In that sense, a keyword can be far more precise (if you guess the right one!) than a subject heading.

Checklist: Some Things to Remember About Writing Comparison and Contrast

- ❏ Limit your comparison and contrast to subjects that can be adequately developed in a paragraph or an essay.
- ❏ Make sure that the subjects you are comparing and contrasting have some basic similarities. Make a list of similarities and differences before you begin to write.
- ❏ Decide why the comparison or contrast is important. What does it reveal? Remember to make the reason clear to the reader.
- ❏ Decide what points of comparison or contrast are the most important or the most revealing. In general, omit any points of comparison that would be obvious to anybody.
- ❏ Decide which of the three patterns of comparison and contrast best fits your purpose: subject-by-subject, point-by-point, or mixed.
- ❏ Remember to make clear to your reader when you are switching from one subject to another or from one point of comparison to another.

Reading Comparison and Contrast

Because comparison and contrast sets subjects in opposition in order to find similarities and differences, it is a way of thinking that we use every day. For example, any time we make a choice between items, we are using comparison and contrast. Because it is such a common tool, comparison and contrast offers a clear rhetorical structure to use in writing. That same knowledge of how it is done and how it is organized can be applied when reading a work that uses comparison and contrast. As you read these three selections, remember what you have learned about how to write comparison and contrast and see how that knowledge will help you as a reader.

- Comparison: find similarities among things that appear to be different. An analogy—likening an unfamiliar thing to a familiar one—is a form of comparison.
- Contrast: find differences among things that appear to be similar. Any time we look at the features of a service or a product before we purchase it, we are making a contrast.
- The primary purpose of comparison and contrast is to explain or clarify.
- Comparison and contrast has three possible organizational patterns. The subjects are treated one at a time (subject-by-subject), or the points of similarity and difference between the subjects are treated one at a time (point-by-point). In longer essays, a mixed pattern—a bit of both—is sometimes used.
- The points of comparison and contrast are typically arranged in an order that reflects their relative importance.
- The points of comparison and contrast are phrased in parallel form— identical grammatical forms.

IN PROSE

The following paragraph is taken from John McPhee's nonfiction book *Oranges*. McPhee is a writer fascinated by details, and *Oranges* contains just about everything you might ever want to know about the fruit. As McPhee indicates, domestically grown oranges typically come either from Florida or California. You might think first of the differences between seeded and unseeded (or navel) oranges, but as McPhee points out, the oranges grown in these two different climates differ significantly.

The paragraph focuses on points of contrast—the similarities are obvious: both are oranges

Florida
1. Tight skin
2. Heavy with juice
3. Harder to peel

An orange grown in Florida usually has a <u>thin and tightly fitting skin</u> and it is also <u>heavy with juice</u>. [Californians say that if you want to eat a Florida orange, you have to get into a bathtub first.] California oranges are <u>light in weight</u> and have <u>thick skins</u> that <u>break easily and come off in chunks.</u> The flesh inside is <u>marvelously sweet</u>, and the <u>segments almost separate themselves.</u> [In Florida, it is said that you can run over a California orange with a ten-ton truck and not even wet

California
1. Thicker skin
2. Not as juicy
3. Easier to peel

Comparison of growing conditions

Florida—abundant rain

California—irrigation

Comparison of amount of oranges grown

the pavement.] The differences from which these hyperboles arise will prevail in the two states even if the type of orange is the same. In arid climates, like California's, oranges develop a thick albedo, which is the white part of the skin. Florida is one of the two or three most rained-upon states in the United States. California uses the Colorado River and similarly impressive sources to irrigate its oranges, but of course irrigation can only do so much. The annual difference in rainfall between the Florida and California orange-growing areas is one million one hundred and forty-thousand gallons per acre. For years, California was the leading orange-growing state, but Florida surpassed California in 1942 and grows three times as many oranges now. California oranges, for their part, can safely be called three times as beautiful.   ■

QUESTIONS FOR ANALYSIS

1. What is it about the presentation of this information that suggests it appeared in a book intended for a general audience? What purpose might McPhee have in writing this?
2. Why is this an example of contrast rather than comparison?
3. Why might McPhee have chosen to set off two sentences within brackets? What do those sentences share? What is a hyperbole?
4. Write a topic sentence for this paragraph. Why didn't McPhee include a topic sentence?

CRITICAL READING ACTIVITY

What is the role of parallelism in this selection? How many examples can you find? Why might parallelism be an appropriate tool to use in comparison and contrast?

IN LITERATURE

Poet Martin Espada uses comparison and contrast to structure his poem "Coca-Cola and Coco Frío." As you read the poem, notice the points of comparison and contrast that Espada develops and think about what the comparison and contrast is intended to reveal.

Coca-Cola and Coco Frio

MARTIN ESPADA

On his first visit to Puerto Rico,
island of family folklore,
the fat boy wandered
from table to table
with his mouth open.
At every table, some great-aunt
would steer him with cool-spotted hands
to a glass of Coca-Cola.
One even sang to him, in all the English
she could remember, a Coca-Cola jingle
from the forties. He drank obediently, though
he was bored with this portion, familiar
from soda fountains in Brooklyn.

Then, at a roadside stand off the beach, the fat boy
opened his mouth to coco frio, a coconut
chilled, then scalped by a machete
so that a straw could inhale the clear milk.
The boy tilted the green shell overhead
and drooled coconut milk down his chin;
suddenly, Puerto Rico was not Coca-Cola
or Brooklyn, and neither was he.

For years afterwards, the boy marveled at an island
where the people drank Coca-Cola
and sang jingles from World War II
in a language they did not speak,
while so many coconuts in the trees
sagged heavy with milk, swollen
and unsuckled.

■

QUESTIONS FOR ANALYSIS

1. How does Espada organize his comparison and contrast in the poem? In what ways are the two drinks similar? In what ways are they different? How are those similarities and differences arranged in the poem?
2. What does the boy discover? How does the comparison and contrast lead to that discovery?
3. What image is developed in the final two lines of the poem? What is that image called? How is it also an example of comparison and contrast?
4. What is the significance of the word "unsuckled" in the final line? Who should consume the nourishment that the coconuts supply? Why?
5. What is it about the two drinks that catches Espada's attention? Why might he have written the poem? What might he be trying to reveal?

WRITING SUGGESTIONS

1. **Analysis.** How does Espada use comparison and contrast as a structural device in the poem? Why is comparison and contrast an appropriate strategy given what the poem is about?

2. Espada uses something from American popular culture to comment on the "island of [his] family folklore." Think about the conflicts you have experienced between how something is done in your culture and how it is done in another. The conflicts, for example, could result from differences in culture, in age, in religion, in value, in expectations, in social conventions, or in economic backgrounds. In an essay, compare and contrast such conflicts.

3. As of 2012, McDonald's operates restaurants in 119 different countries. How can an American icon be so successfully translated that it has world-wide appeal? What remains the same about the concept and the restaurants and what is different? Visit the McDonald's website.

IN A VISUAL

Comparison and contrast can be vividly displayed using visuals. Television commercials for medicines for acne or skin blemishes, weight-loss pills, and exercise regimens show us the "before" and "after" photographs. The "extreme makeovers" of people and houses so popular on television are, at their core, visual comparisons and contrasts—before and after. Comparison stresses similarities; contrast, differences. Visual comparison and contrast is typically intended to highlight differences.

Contrast as a visual strategy can clearly be seen in these two prints done by the English artist William Hogarth in 1751. Hogarth hoped that the prints would "reform some reigning Vices peculiar to the lower Class of

Courtesy of the National Library of Medicine

People." The particular vice in this case was the sale and consumption of gin. The two engravings are labeled Beer Street and Gin Lane. It is fairly obvious from the depictions that, for Hogarth, the consumption of beer, unlike the evils of the distilled spirit gin, led to a healthy and prosperous populace.

QUESTIONS FOR ANALYSIS

1. What are the points of contrast between the two?
2. How do the visual details and their arrangement differ in the two prints? How are they similar?
3. How effective do you think such a visual would be? Would it be more effective, for example, than simply a description in words?

WRITING SUGGESTIONS

1. **Analysis:** In an essay, analyze the two prints as visual propaganda for the evils of gin drinking in contrast to the consumption of beer.
2. Gather a series of advertisements that promote the same type of products to men and women (e.g., clothing, perfumes or cologne, beverages). What do the advertisements have in common? How are they different? What do they suggest about how advertisers market the same product to different genders? Using the visuals as your evidence, construct an essay in which you compare and contrast the images.
3. Select two television shows or two films that present essentially the same subject, but approach it from very different points of view. In an essay, compare and contrast how similar situations or stories can be rendered in quite different visual ways.

The Transaction: Two Writing Processes

WILLIAM ZINSSER

William Zinsser (1922–) has been an editor, critic, editorial writer, college teacher, and writing consultant. He is the author of many books including On Writing Well: An Informal Guide to Writing Nonfiction *(sixth edition, 1998), a textbook classic of which* The New York Times *wrote: "It belongs on any shelf of serious reference works for writers."*

On Writing: *As someone who earns his living as a writer, Zinsser sees writing as hard work. "The only way to learn to write," he has observed, "is to force yourself to produce a certain number of words on a regular basis." In an interview, he once remarked: "I don't think writing is an art. I think sometimes it's raised to an art, but basically it's a craft, like cabinet making or carpentry."*

Before Reading

Connecting: If you had to describe your writing process to a group of younger students, what would you say?

Anticipating: Why should writing seem so easy to Brock and so difficult to Zinsser? If he finds it so difficult, why does Zinsser continue to write?

1   **A** school in Connecticut once held "a day devoted to the arts," and I was asked if I would come and talk about writing as a vocation. When I arrived I found that a second speaker had been invited—Dr. Brock (as I'll call him), a surgeon who had recently begun to write and had sold some stories to magazines. He was going to talk about writing as an avocation. That made us a panel, and we sat down to face a crowd of students and teachers and parents, all eager to learn the secrets of our glamorous work.

2   Dr. Brock was dressed in a bright red jacket, looking vaguely bohemian, as authors are supposed to look, and the first question went to him. What was it like to be a writer?

3   He said it was tremendous fun. Coming home from an arduous day at the hospital, he would go straight to his yellow pad and write his tensions away. The words just flowed. It was easy. I then said that writing wasn't easy and wasn't fun. It was hard and lonely, and the words seldom just flowed.

4   Next Dr. Brock was asked if it was important to rewrite. Absolutely not, he said. "Let it all hang out," he told us and whatever form the sentences take will reflect the writer at his most natural. I then said that rewriting is the essence of writing. I pointed out that professional writers rewrite their sentences repeatedly over and over and then rewrite what they have rewritten.

5   "What do you do on days when it isn't going well?" Dr. Brock was asked. He said he just stopped writing and put the work aside for a day when it would go better. I then said that the professional writer must establish a daily schedule and stick to it. I said that writing is a craft, not an art, and that the man who runs away from his craft because he lacks inspiration is fooling himself. He is also going broke.

6   "What if you're feeling depressed or unhappy?" a student asked. "Won't that affect your writing?"

7   Probably it will, Dr. Brock replied. Go fishing. Take a walk. Probably it won't, I said. If your job is to write every day, you learn to do it like any other job.

8   A student asked if we found it useful to circulate in the literary world. Dr. Brock said he was greatly enjoying his new life as a man of letters, and he told several stories of being taken to lunch by his publisher and his agent

at Manhattan restaurants where writers and editors gather. I said that professional writers are solitary drudges who seldom see other writers.

9   "Do you put symbolism in your writing?" a student asked me.

10   "Not if I can help it," I replied. I have an unbroken record of missing the deeper meaning in any story, play or movie, and as for dance and mime, I have never had any idea of what is being conveyed.

11   "I *love* symbols!" Dr. Brock exclaimed, and he described with gusto the joys of weaving them through his work.

12   So the morning went, and it was a revelation to all of us. At the end Dr. Brock told me he was enormously interested in my answers—it had never occurred to him that writing could be hard. I told him I was just as interested in *his* answers—it had never occurred to me that writing could be easy. Maybe I should take up surgery on the side.

13   As for the students, anyone might think we left them bewildered. But in fact we probably gave them a broader glimpse of the writing process than if only one of us had talked. For there isn't any "right" way to do such personal work. There are all kinds of writers and all kinds of methods, and any method that helps you to say what you want to say is the right method for you. . . .   ■

QUESTIONS ON SUBJECT AND PURPOSE

1. Zinsser uses contrast to make a point about how people write. What is that point?
2. How effective is the beginning? Would the effect have been lost if Zinsser had opened with a statement similar to his final sentence?
3. What process do you use when you write? Does it help in any way to know what other people do? Why? Why not?

QUESTIONS ON STRATEGY AND AUDIENCE

1. Which method of development does Zinsser use for his examples? How many points of contrast does he make?
2. Would it have made any difference if Zinsser had used another pattern of development? Why?
3. How effective are the short paragraphs? Should they be longer?

QUESTIONS ON VOCABULARY AND STYLE

1. What makes Zinsser's story humorous? Try to isolate several aspects of humor.
2. Zinsser uses a number of parallel structures in his narrative. Make a list of them, and be prepared to show how they contribute to the narrative's effectiveness.
3. Be prepared to define the following words: *avocation* (paragraph 1), *bohemian* (2), *arduous* (3), *drudge* (8), *mime* (10), *gusto* (11).

WRITING SUGGESTIONS

1. **Doing a Critical Analysis.** Describe the tone of Zinsser's essay focusing on how his style, word choice, and narrating voice contribute to that tone. What is Zinsser trying to do in the essay and does his use of language achieve that end?

2. **Journaling or Blogging.** How do you feel about writing? Do you mind if other people read your writing? Is that a source of anxiety or pleasure? Explore those feelings.

3. **Practicing in a Paragraph.** Using the details provided by Zinsser, rewrite the narrative using a subject-by-subject pattern. Choose either writer, and put together his advice in a single paragraph. Be sure to write a topic sentence for the paragraph.

4. **Writing the Personal Essay.** Although writing instructors and textbooks offer one view of the writing process, the actual practices of writers vary. Plenty of essays get written at the last minute. In an essay, compare and contrast your typical writing behavior with the process outlined in this text.

5. **Finding Reading Connections.** Nora Ephron describes her writing and revising processes in "Revision and Life" (Chapter 6). Rewrite Zinsser's essay substituting Ephron's comments on writing in place of Dr. Brock's.

6. **Exploring Links Online.** The majority of writers tend to procrastinate when it is time to write. Using online sources, research the problem of writer's block. In an essay, offer advice to your peers on writing the college essay.

7. **Writing the Research Paper.** Compare the creative process of two artists— musicians, dancers, painters, actors—anyone involved in the creative arts in the past or in the present. Try to find interviews in which the artists talk about how they work. Be sure to document your sources.

For Further Study

Focusing on Grammar and Writing. Rewrite paragraph 12 in the essay using only simple sentences. What is the difference between your new paragraph and the one that Zinsser originally wrote?

Working Together. Divide into groups and reparagraph the essay. Is there general agreement on where the new paragraphing could occur? Do the changes make the essay more or less effective?

Seeing Other Modes at Work. Zinsser's essay is also a process narrative describing two views of the writing process step by step.

Neat People vs. Sloppy People

SUZANNE BRITT

Suzanne Britt was born in Winston-Salem, North Carolina, and currently teaches writing and literature courses at Meredith College in Raleigh, North Carolina. She has published essays in a number of newspapers and magazines and has published several collections of

essays and a college writing textbook, A Writer's Rhetoric *(1988).*
"Neat People vs. Sloppy People" first appeared in her collection Show
and Tell *(1983).*

Before Reading

Connecting: Are you a neat or a sloppy person? Sometimes a
little of both?

Anticipating: As you read, think about how Britt organizes her
essay. What types of structures does she use?

1   I've finally figured out the difference between neat people and sloppy
people. The distinction is, as always, moral. Neat people are lazier and
meaner than sloppy people.

2   Sloppy people, you see, are not really sloppy. Their sloppiness is merely
the unfortunate consequence of their extreme moral rectitude. Sloppy people
carry in their mind's eye a heavenly vision, a precise plan, that is so stupen-
dous, so perfect, it can't be achieved in this world or the next.

3   Sloppy people live in Never-Never Land. Someday is their métier.
Someday they are planning to alphabetize all their books and set up home
catalogs. Someday they will go through their wardrobes and mark certain
items for tentative mending and certain items for passing on to relatives of
similar shape and size. Someday sloppy people will make family scrapbooks
into which they will put newspaper clippings, postcards, locks of hair, and the
dried corsage from their senior prom. Someday they will file everything on
the surface of their desks, including the cash receipts from coffee purchases
at the snack shop. Someday they will sit down and read all the back issues of
The New Yorker.

4   For all these noble reasons and more, sloppy people never get neat.
They aim too high and wide. They save everything, planning someday to
file, order, and straighten out the world. But while these ambitious plans
take clearer and clearer shape in their heads, the books spill from the
shelves onto the floor, the clothes pile up in the hamper and closet, the
family mementos accumulate in every drawer, the surface of the desk is
buried under mounds of paper, and the unread magazines threaten to reach
the ceiling.

5   Sloppy people can't bear to part with anything. They give loving attention to every detail. When sloppy people say they're going to tackle the surface of a desk, they really mean it. Not a paper will go unturned; not a rubber
band will go unboxed. Four hours or two weeks into the excavation, the desk
looks exactly the same, primarily because the sloppy person is meticulously
creating new piles of papers with new headings and scrupulously stopping
to read all the old book catalogs before he throws them away. A neat person
would just bulldoze the desk.

6   Neat people are bums and clods at heart. They have cavalier attitudes toward possessions, including family heirlooms. Everything is just another dust-catcher to them. If anything collects dust, it's got to go and that's that. Neat people will toy with the idea of throwing the children out of the house just to cut down on the clutter.

7   Neat people don't care about process. They like results. What they want to do is get the whole thing over with so they can sit down and watch the rasslin' on TV. Neat people operate on two unvarying principles: Never handle any item twice, and throw everything away.

8   The only thing messy in a neat person's house is the trash can. The minute something comes to a neat person's hand, he will look at it, try to decide if it has immediate use and, finding none, throw it in the trash.

9   Neat people are especially vicious with mail. They never go through their mail unless they are standing directly over a trash can. If the trash can is beside the mailbox, even better. All ads, catalogs, pleas for charitable contributions, church bulletins, and money-saving coupons go straight into the trash can without being opened. All letters from home, postcards from Europe, bills, and paychecks are opened, immediately responded to, then dropped in the trash can. Neat people keep their receipts only for tax purposes. That's it. No sentimental salvaging of birthday cards or the last letter a dying relative ever wrote. Into the trash it goes.

10   Neat people place neatness above everything, even economics. They are incredibly wasteful. Neat people throw away several toys every time they walk through the den. I knew a neat person once who threw away a perfectly good dish drainer because it had mold on it. The drainer was too much trouble to wash. And neat people sell their furniture when they move. They will sell a La-Z-Boy recliner while you are reclining in it.

11   Neat people are no good to borrow from. Neat people buy everything in expensive little single portions. They get their flour and sugar in two-pound bags. They wouldn't consider clipping a coupon, saving a leftover, reusing plastic nondairy whipped cream containers, or rinsing off tin foil and draping it over the unmoldy dish drainer. You can never borrow a neat person's newspaper to see what's playing at the movies. Neat people have the paper all wadded up and in the trash by 7:05 A.M.

12   Neat people cut a clean swath through the organic as well as the inorganic world. People, animals, and things are all one to them. They are so insensitive. After they've finished with the pantry, the medicine cabinet, and the attic, they will throw out the red geranium (too many leaves), sell the dog (too many fleas), and send the children off to boarding school (too many scuff-marks on the hardwood floors). ■

QUESTIONS ON SUBJECT AND PURPOSE

1. Is Britt a neat or a sloppy person? How do you know?
2. If you are sloppy or neat, are you offended by anything in the essay? Do you regard this as an unfair criticism of you? Why or why not?
3. What might Britt's purpose be in writing the essay?

QUESTIONS ON STRATEGY AND AUDIENCE

1. How does Britt structure her essay? Is it subject-by-subject or point-by-point?
2. Is this essay comparison or contrast? Or both?
3. What can Britt assume about her audience? What does she expect of her audience?

QUESTIONS ON VOCABULARY AND STYLE

1. How would you describe the tone (see Glossary and Ready Reference) of the essay?
2. What is the effect of the repetition of the phrases "sloppy people" and "neat people" at the start of so many sentences in the essay?
3. Be prepared to define the following words: *rectitude* (paragraph 2), *métier* (3), *meticulously* (5), *scrupulously* (5), *cavalier* (6), *swath* (12).

WRITING SUGGESTIONS

1. **Doing a Critical Analysis.** Not everyone finds the essay funny. One reader commented: "The essay was painful to read, like a [Ku Klux] Klan pamphlet or a homophobic newsletter." How did you react to the essay? In a critical essay, analyze your response to the essay citing evidence from the text to support your position.
2. **Journaling or Blogging.** Brainstorm about some other possible pairings of people. Consider both serious topics and humorous ones.
3. **Practicing in a Paragraph.** Choose one of the topics from your journal or blog writing and explore it in a paragraph. Concentrate on a single point of comparison or contrast.
4. **Writing the Personal Essay.** Expand your paragraph into an essay. Compare or contrast a pairing of people on a numbers of points. Your approach can be either comic or serious.
5. **Finding Reading Connections.** Judy Brady's "I Want a Wife" (Chapter 8) uses a very similar tone in stereotyping the expectations of the husband. Normally, readers are likely to have negative reactions to stereotyping. In an essay, explore how both Britt and Brady use humor as a way to avoid those negative reactions from readers.
6. **Exploring Links Online.** Britt's position on neatness vs. sloppiness is clear. Using online sources, explore what other writers and researchers have concluded. Using the perspectives provided by your research, write an essay directed at a roommate or a friend who is either too neat or too sloppy.
7. **Writing the Research Paper.** What do we know about neatness or sloppiness? What makes a person one or the other? Is it just a behavior that can be changed or is it more deeply ingrained in personality? In a formal research paper with documentation, explore what is known about such behavior.

For Further Study

Focusing on Grammar and Writing. Look closely at the opening sentences in each of Britt's paragraphs. What role do these topic sentences play in the paragraph? How do they help you as a reader?

Working Together. Working in small groups, discuss the possibility of adding a third group—a group that exhibited some of the characteristics of both neat and sloppy. What might that section be like and would it add or detract from the essay?

Seeing Other Modes at Work. The essay also uses definition to show how sloppy and neat people react to similar situations.

Colleges Confront a Gender Gap in Student Engagement

LIBBY SANDER

Libby Sander is currently a staff writer for the Chronicle of Higher Education, *a publication targeted at college and university faculty and administrators. A former reporter for the* New York Times, *her work has also appeared in* Sports Illustrated. *Sander has an undergraduate degree from Bryn Mawr and a M.A. in journalism from Northwestern. This essay appeared in the* Chronicle *in October 2012.*

Before Reading

Connecting: What is the percentage of women and men currently enrolled at your school?

Anticipating: Before you start reading the essay, what differences, if any, would you expect in the ways that women and men differ in their engagement as students?

1   **F**or decades, women have enrolled in college in greater numbers than men, and, by many measures, have outperformed them in the classroom. But in recent years, as social scientists and student-affairs offices have focused on other differences between the genders, they have documented patterns that could explain how engagement influences student development.

2   The focus on gender is leading some colleges to try new approaches to interacting with their students. And it is also providing some fascinating—if often maddening—hints at how differently male and female students experience college.

3   Women tend to study abroad, volunteer in the community, and spend longer hours preparing for class, some experts have noted. Men spend more time playing video games, relaxing, and watching television. But men have more substantive engagements with their professors, are more likely to do undergraduate research, and tend to major in fields that steer them into better-paying jobs. And although women do many of the things that

researchers have identified as positive influences on a college experience, they also report higher levels of stress and lower levels of confidence than men.

4   Researchers continue to wrestle with those contrasts. How, they wonder, do such differences shape the way men and women experience college? The patterns prompt complex questions about the expectations that men and women internalize long before they even set foot on a campus.

5   "It's not necessarily that men are not engaged and that's bad, and women are very engaged and that's good. The real story is much more nuanced than that," says MaryAnn Baenninger, a scholar of gender and cognition and president of the College of Saint Benedict, a women's college in Minnesota. Saint Benedict has close ties to the all-male Saint John's University, sharing a curriculum and extracurricular activities with the institution six miles down the road.

6   Girls and boys are treated differently from the day they're born, Ms. Baenninger says, and the disparities playing out on college campuses say as much about how men and women are socialized before they get to campus as they do about what happens once they're there.

7   "They're different," she says. "But there is probably something to be learned from both the women and the men in terms of how they navigate in college."

8   Looking at student-engagement trends in the aggregate—men and women together—can mask some important differences between the genders, researchers say. Men and women, it turns out, tend to view college differently—and those differences often shape their willingness to get invested in academic pursuits and other activities.

9   Some colleges are trying to learn from the patterns. At Saint Benedict and Saint John's, academic awards used to be split evenly between women and men. (Women make up 52 percent of the two institutions' combined enrollment.) Then Ms. Baenninger advocated a survival-of-the-fittest approach. Now, she says, slightly fewer men receive awards: Phi Beta Kappa, for instance, is roughly 60 percent female.

10   "When left to their own devices in an academic environment, women are excelling," Ms. Baenninger says. But she's noticed that that doesn't always translate into professionally oriented tasks like career fairs, where men often schmooze more readily with prospective employers. The disconnect makes her wonder if the ideal lies somewhere between the women's academic gusto and the men's more laid-back approach.

11   "What good is Phi Beta Kappa if you don't know how to go through that job interview?" she asks. "And suppose you know how to go through that job interview—wouldn't it be great if you had Phi Beta Kappa on your résumé?"

12 When Demetri Morgan was a student at the University of Florida, he observed that his female friends were active on the campus and excelled academically as a way to assert themselves and find their footing at the large institution.

13   Not so for the guys. "That wasn't how they were defining themselves," he says. "Their social capital came from how many women they were sleeping with or how good they were at sports or what job they were aspiring to."

14   Today, Mr. Morgan, who graduated in 2011 and is now pursuing a master's degree in higher education and student affairs at Indiana University at Bloomington, sees a conflict between what he has learned from research on student engagement and what he has seen in his own life.

15   "I know plenty of guys who were only involved in the fraternity—and they weren't even really involved in that—and they're doing fine," he says. On many occasions, he'd get deep into discussions with other men about why it was important to get involved. They'd often meet his pleas with a pragmatic comeback: "If I'm here to get a degree, why are you talking to me about involvement?" he recalls them saying. "Sometimes I try to argue back about all the positive outcomes about engagement," he says. Other times, he felt they had a point: "I'm like, 'Yeah, you *are* here to get a degree.'"

16   Campuses of all stripes have struggled with how to draw in male students. Some, like Winona State University, in Minnesota, have men's centers. Others, like the University of Portland, tap into campus ministries to create groups like the League of Extraordinary Gentlemen. In some colleges, a course—like "Rock Music and American Masculinities," at Hobart and William Smith Colleges—has served as a magnet for male students and a platform for talking about masculinity.

17   Gar Kellom, director of student-support services at Winona State and a co-editor of *Engaging College Men: Discovering What Works and Why* (Men's Studies Press, 2010), has found that three simple approaches work best: Get men together in small groups to talk and hang out. Employ "pied pipers"— other young men whom male students are likely to look up to—to make those connections. And if figuring out what men need is still a mystery, just ask them.

18   The gender differences that make those tactics necessary tend to become evident early on, usually during students' first year of college, says Jillian Kinzie, associate director at the National Survey of Student Engagement, based at Indiana. At that time, survey results have shown, female students are participating at very different levels than male students are. The women are volunteering in the community, spending more time each week preparing for class, and caring for dependents; male students, meanwhile, spend more time relaxing and playing intramural sports.

19   Many of those trends equalize over time, Ms. Kinzie says. But she is troubled by other contrasts. Women work harder to meet expectations, spending more time on drafts of papers, say, before turning them in. But men spend more time interacting with faculty on research projects and other serious academic endeavors.

20   "Women are doing more of the things that are beneficial for them in college," says Linda J. Sax, a professor of higher education at the University of California at Los Angeles and one of the authors of *The Gender Gap in College* (Jossey-Bass, 2008). But the fact that men spend more time on leisure is "not necessarily a bad thing."

21   The diligence and motivation that many female students display, though, often belies a complicated vision of their own skills and abilities. Women appear to be harsher—or perhaps just more realistic—critics of themselves than men are.

22   In the 2011 freshman survey, administered each year by UCLA's Higher Education Research Institute, men claimed to be above average at certain skills at rates higher than women—in some cases, much higher. They saw themselves as above average in academic ability, popularity, mathematical ability, physical and emotional health, and in negotiating controversial issues, to name a few. In some cases, the gender disparities were more than 15 percentage points. (Women viewed themselves as "above average" more than men did in only a handful of categories, including artistic ability and "drive to achieve.")

23 Men and women also respond differently in academic settings. Women may spend more time revising papers and hitting the books, but the impact of academic engagement on students' overall success tends to be stronger for men, Ms. Sax says.

24   "We know that men spend less time studying. But we know that if we can increase their homework time, they're going to reap greater benefits," she says. "There's something about the academic engagement that's a bit more eye-opening for men than for women when it comes to their thinking about their place in the larger world."

25   Ms. Sax has found that interacting with professors is a powerful influence on how women view themselves. It can cut both ways, though. If women feel that faculty are taking them seriously, they tend to feel better about themselves. But if they think they're not being taken seriously, that impression can undermine their confidence.

26   Some scholars question the severity of the differences between the genders. Race and class have a far greater impact on students' academic success in college than does gender, says Richard Arum, one of the authors of *Academically Adrift: Limited Learning on College Campuses* (University of Chicago Press, 2011).

27   He believes the impact of engagement on learning might be overstated, or even misconstrued. Engagement is good for keeping students in college, he says, but while researching his book he found no evidence that students who were more socially engaged learned more. "In some cases," he says, "they learned less."

28   He found that the only differences between the genders were in grades—women had higher grade-point averages—and choice of major.

29   (Mr. Arum has had his own problems with engagement among male students: By the time he and his co-author went to press with *Academically Adrift*, the proportion of men in the sample had dwindled to 37 percent as male students dropped out. Today, as he continues research for a follow-up book, it's down even further, to 29 percent.)

30   Maybe increased social engagement would help more men stay in college, he concedes. "But it's not helping them learn."

31 With growth in female enrollment attributed in large part to an influx of women from previously underrepresented minority groups, it's men of color, researchers say, who are least likely to engage.

32   Mr. Morgan, the Indiana graduate student, has found that to be true. As an undergraduate at Florida and a self-described "involved guy," he wanted to understand why his fellow African-American male students held back. Under the auspices of his fraternity, he organized a group of black men to get together and talk about their experiences at the university.

33   The reason that black men didn't get involved, he learned, was that they didn't want to be seen as "gay" or nerdy. They also didn't want to seem white. After the discussion, Mr. Morgan says, he was angry. But he didn't know where to lay blame: On men, for hanging back? On the university, for not engaging them? On the women, whose energy the men saw as emasculating? "I was just confused," he says.

34   Some scholars and campus officials are grappling with similar dilemmas. But they do acknowledge that in other respects, the gender gap favors men. They still earn more than women, and they tend to dominate positions of power and prestige in government and the private sector. But Frank Harris III, an associate professor of postsecondary education at San Diego State University who has studied engagement among male college students for a decade, says that such eventual success doesn't let colleges off the hook now.

35   "Men are absolutely still more advantaged in society than are women," Mr. Harris says. "But I don't think that should be a reason for us not to do the work necessary to help men become better people."

36   The work that colleges do with men in their college years, he believes, could help them make better decisions later in life.

37   But first, colleges need men to show up.   ∎

QUESTIONS ON SUBJECT AND PURPOSE

1. What is meant by "student engagement"?
2. What are the major differences in how women and men experience college?
3. What particular factor makes it difficult to provide either a precise answer about why this occurs or how to remedy the problems?

QUESTIONS ON STRATEGY AND AUDIENCE

1. Sander writes, "Men and women . . . tend to view college differently—and those differences often shape their willingness to get invested in academic pursuits and other activities" (paragraph 8). In general, how do their views differ?
2. How does Sander identify and acknowledge the sources she uses in the essay?
3. Why would the *Chronicle of Higher Education* be an appropriate place of publication for such an essay?

QUESTIONS ON VOCABULARY AND STYLE

1. In paragraph 8, Sander uses the word "aggregate" and then follows it with a phrase set off in dashes. What is she doing?

2. Why might paragraph 29 be enclosed in parentheses?
3. Be prepared to define the following words: *nuanced* (paragraph 5), *schmooze* (10), *pragmatic* (15), *belies* (21), *misconstrued* (27), *auspices* (32).

WRITING SUGGESTIONS

1. **Doing a Critical Analysis.** Sander is writing to administrators and to faculty. What elements in the essay seem chosen for that particular audience? Contrast that presentation with what would be more appropriate if she were writing to an audience of undergraduates. How would the essay have to be different?

2. **Journaling or Blogging.** How would you characterize the differences between males and females at your school? Do you see the differences about which Sander writes?

3. **Practicing in a Paragraph.** In a paragraph, explore how accurately Sander's observations about women and men explain your own behavior and attitudes toward school.

4. **Writing the Personal Essay.** Did you see something similar to what Sander is describing when you were in high school? Did women and men "engage" in school, community, and social activities in different ways? In an essay, explore what you remember about your peers from high school.

5. **Finding Reading Connections.** Read Nick Schulz's "Hard Unemployment Truths About 'Soft' Skills" (How to Read and Then Analyze an Essay). Using the information provided by both essays, what job skills should both men and women be concerned about acquiring?

6. **Exploring Links Online.** Toward the end of the essay, Sander acknowledges that men of color are the least likely to engage. The College Board has done an extensive amount of research on this problem. Using information from their research, explore why there is such a difference between young women of color and young men of color.

7. **Writing the Research Paper.** Statistics show that by 2013 women will represented 57 percent of the undergraduate population in the United States. In 1970, women represented just 40 percent. Research the change—paying attention not only to why the percentage of women is growing, but also why the percentage of men is declining. Present your conclusions in a research paper with formal documentation.

For Further Study

Focusing on Grammar and Writing. Sander uses sources but acknowledges them parenthetically in her text. What advantage does such a form of documentation offer in an essay such as this?

Working Together. Working in small groups, ask students to interview peers not in your classroom. They should talk with 10 students about their attitudes and behavior toward school. Have them then discuss in class what they found. How accurate do these conclusions seem to be?

Seeing Other Modes at Work. The essay also uses elements of cause and effect.

MOOCs Gaining Popularity

JUSTIN POPE

A graduate of Princeton and Oxford University, Justin Pope is the national higher education reporter for the Associated Press. In 2010–11 he was a University of Michigan Knight-Wallace Journalism Fellow. You can follow him on Twitter at @JustinPopeAP.

Before Reading

Connecting: Before reading the essay, visit two websites: coursera.org and edX.org

Anticipating: What do you think might be, for you, the biggest advantages and drawbacks in enrolling in a MOOC?

1   In 15 years of teaching, University of Pennsylvania classicist Peter Struck has guided perhaps a few hundred students annually in his classes on Greek and Roman mythology through the works of Homer, Sophocles, Aeschylus and others—"the oldest strands of our cultural DNA."

2   But if you gathered all of those tuition-paying, in-person students together, the group would pale in size compared with the 54,000 from around the world who, this fall alone, are taking his class online for free—a "Massive Open Online Course," or MOOC, offered through a company called Coursera.

3   Reaching that broader audience of eager learners—seeing students in Brazil and Thailand wrestle online with texts dating back millennia—is thrilling. But he's not prepared to say they're getting the same educational experience.

4   "Where you have a back-and-forth, interrogating each other's ideas, finding shades of gray in each other's ideas, I don't know how much of that you can do in a MOOC," he said. "I can measure some things students are getting out of this course, but it's nowhere near what I can do even when I teach 300 here at Penn."

5   A year ago, hardly anybody knew the term MOOC. But the Internet-based courses offered by elite universities through Coursera, by a consortium led by Harvard and MIT called edX, and by others, are proving wildly popular, with some classes attracting hundreds of thousands of students. In a field known for glacial change, MOOCs have landed like a meteorite in higher education, and universities are racing for a piece of the action.

6   The question now is what the MOOCs will ultimately achieve. Will they simply expand access to good instruction (no small thing)? Or will they truly transform higher education, at last shaking up an enterprise that's

seemed incapable of improving productivity, thus dooming itself to ever-rising prices?

7   Much of the answer depends on the concept at the center of a string of recent MOOC announcements: course credit.

8   Credit's the coin of the realm in higher education, the difference between knowing something and the world recognizing that you do. Without it, students will get a little bit smarter. With it, they'll get smarter—and enjoy faster and cheaper routes to degrees and the careers that follow.

9   Students are telling the MOOC developers they want credit opportunities, and with a push from funders like the Bill and Melinda Gates Foundation, the MOOCs are trying to figure out how to get it to them.

10   "Initially, I said it'd be three years" before MOOCs began confronting the credit issue, said MIT's Anant Agarwal, president of edX, which launched only last May and has 420,000 students signed up this fall (Coursera is approaching 2 million). "It's been months."

11   But making MOOC courses credit-worthy brings challenges much harder than producing even the best online lectures, from entering a state-by-state regulatory thicket to assessment. How do you grade 100,000 essays? How do you make sure students in a coffee shop in Kazakhstan aren't cheating on quizzes?

12   Last Tuesday, Coursera, which offers classes from 34 universities, announced the American Council on Education would begin evaluating a handful of Coursera courses and could recommend other universities accept them for credit (individual colleges ultimately decide what credits to accept). Antioch University, Excelsior College, and the University of Texas system are already planning to award credit for some MOOCs.

13   Two days later, Duke, Northwestern, Vanderbilt and seven other prominent universities announced a consortium called Semester Online offering students at those institutions—and eventually others, though details aren't yet clear—access to new online courses for credit. These won't be giant classes, but the announcement is important because top colleges, generally stingy about accepting outside credit, are signaling they agree the technology can now replicate at least substantially some of the high-priced learning experience that takes place on campus.

14   The latest announcement will come Monday, and appears smaller but is potentially important: a first-of-its-kind partnership between edX, the MIT-Harvard consortium, and two Massachusetts community colleges. EdX's popular introductory computer science course from MIT will provide the backbone of a class at the community college—a key gateway to degree programs—with supplemental teaching and help from community college faculty on the ground.

15   This is where the rubber meets the road for transforming higher education. Community colleges are beset by waitlists (400,000 in California alone) and bottlenecks in important introductory courses, as well as low success rates. If scaled-up MIT-quality teaching can help with solving those problems, MOOCS could be truly revolutionary. Massachusetts Bay Community

College president John O'Donnell calls edX an invention comparable to Gutenberg's printing press.

16   Online classes have been around for going-on two decades, so what's the big-deal about MOOCs? Scale.

17   So far, online courses have offered convenience, but they generally haven't scaled up any more easily than traditional ones; somebody still has to grade the papers, and answer students' questions. One study found 93 percent of institutions charge the same or more for online courses as for in-person ones. No solving the college cost crisis there.

18   Molly Broad, president of the American Council on Education, refers to the "iron triangle" of higher education: cost, access, and quality. The assumption has always been it's a zero-sum game—you can improve any one of those only at the expense of the others. There's also the famous analogy of Princeton economists William Baumol and William Bowen from the 1960s, that college teaching is akin to a string quartet. No matter how technology improves, a string quartet simply can't be performed (well) by fewer people than in Beethoven's day. So the relative cost of college (and musical performance) will always rise, relative to other things where efficiency does improve.

19   If MOOCs solve the scale problem, they could upend those paradigms. But it isn't easy.

20   Take assessment. Multiple-choice online quizzes are simple enough, but on more open-ended assignments, MOOC students now are mostly grading each other's papers. When they have questions, they're mostly asking fellow students. "Crowd-sourced assessment" raises obvious questions. MOOC leaders are exploring artificial intelligence solutions but admit many aren't fully baked.

21   EdX's Agarwal even said his group is exploring a kind of rubric of "self-assessment." Asked if he had faith that, particularly in a course aspiring to credit-worthiness, students could really grade their own essays, he replied: "Faith? Yes. Certainty? No."

22   Cheating's another problem that suddenly matters with credit at stake. EdX is working with a testing company to arrange for proctored exams in centers around the world. Coursera says it will be easier for far-away students to let them wave an ID card and take a test in front of a webcam, proctored from afar. MOOCs won't offer those things for free. But they could cost much less than, well, the full string quartet.

23   Broad, of ACE, said MOOCs are promising, but her group will send faculty out to "kick the tires" and research whether online courses enrolling 150,000 can really be credit-worthy. They'll talk to both students who complete and those who drop out (at edX, 80 to 95 percent who sign up don't finish the work).

24   A likely outcome is more blended models like the Massachusetts experiment, where MOOCs provide the backbone and resources local institutions can't offer, but local institutions still handle the one-on-one and award the credit. Such models could be "the best of both worlds," said Coursera cofounder Daphne Koller. Versions are already in places as varied as San Jose State and the National University of Mongolia.

25   Struck, the Penn classicist, agrees courses like his will likely work best partnering with local institutions much closer to the students, at least when it comes to credit. Intro-level science classes are one thing, but it's just not feasible at a scale of 54,000 for a class like his.

26   Higher education involves both transmitting information and "experiential learning that changes a person," he said. For the latter, at least in his subject, the technology's not yet there.

27   "These characters of Greek and Roman myth are just full of gray, wonderfully instructive, fundamental grays that make us re-examine our own humanity," he said. "I don't know how much of that I can do with the MOOC." ■

QUESTIONS ON SUBJECT AND PURPOSE

1. What is a MOOC?
2. At this point, according to Pope, what is the model most likely to work for granting students credit for such online courses?
3. Does Pope seem biased in favor or against MOOCs or does he seem objective?

QUESTIONS ON STRATEGY AND AUDIENCE

1. Pope begins and ends with the example of Professor Peter Struck who had 54,000 students enrolled in his class on Greek and Roman mythology. Why frame the essay with this example?
2. What advantages do MOOCs offer students other than possibly lowering the cost of an education?
3. Do you think after reading the essay that you would be interested in taking courses online from consortiums such as Coursera or edX?

QUESTIONS ON VOCABULARY AND STYLE

1. What do you call expressions such as "a piece of the action" (paragraph 5) and "the coin of the realm" (8), "the rubber meets the road" (15), and "kick the tires" (23)?
2. When Pope writes "MOOCs have landed like a meteorite in higher education," what is the figure of speech he uses?
3. Be prepared to define the following words: *pale* (paragraph 2), *interrogating* (4), *glacial* (5), *consortium* (13), and *replicate* (13).

WRITING SUGGESTIONS

1. **Doing a Critical Analysis.** Pope remains objective about his subject; he does not reveal a particular bias. How does he achieve that sense of objectivity in the essay? Analyze his writing strategy, his word choice, and his examples.
2. **Journaling or Blogging.** Think about your own educational experiences, in high school and in college. In what types of classes (small, middle or large lecture, laboratory, online) did you seem to learn the most?
3. **Practicing in a Paragraph.** Contrast two different learning experiences that you have had, either in high school or in college. In what ways were they different?

4. **Writing the Personal Essay.** In an essay, reflect upon the advantages or disadvantages of the educational experience you are having right now. You might consider factors such as living on campus or commuting, large classes versus small, full time faculty versus adjuncts, the costs and the benefits.

5. **Finding Reading Connections.** The casebook material on college (Chapter 9) presents a variety of perspectives on a college education—most of which have nothing to do with cost. In light of one line of argument presented there, assess the likelihood that MOOCs will make a significant difference in higher education.

6. **Exploring Links Online.** Not everyone is enthusiastic about MOOCs. Using online sources, research the debate over the value and effectiveness of MOOCs. In an essay aimed at your peers, summarize either the reasons why or why not a student should enroll in a MOOC.

7. **Writing the Research Paper.** Since the year in which Pope's essay appeared (2012), what changes or developments have occurred in MOOCs? How are MOOCs faring in comparison to more regular classroom instruction? Present your update in a research paper with formal documentation.

For Further Study

Focusing on Grammar and Writing. Pope frequently uses dashes (—) in his writing. Look carefully at each use in the essay and write some rules on how and why the dash can be used in writing.

Working Together. Because Pope's essay appeared in narrow columns in an online newspaper (*Huffington Post*), the essay has many paragraphs. Which paragraphs in the essay could be put together to make one larger paragraph? **Seeing Other Modes at Work.** The essay has elements of cause and effect in part to explain why MOOCs exist.

The Consumer—A Republic of Fat

MICHAEL POLLAN

Michael Pollan, a former executive editor of Harper's Magazine, *is now the Knight Professor of Science and Environmental Journalism at University of California at Berkeley. His writing on food and agriculture has won many awards. His books include* The Omnivore's Dilemma *(2006), from which this selection is taken, and* In Defense of Food: An Eater's Manifesto *(2008). His most recent book is* Cooked: A Natural History of Transformation *(2013).*

> **On Writing:** *Commenting on the positions that he takes in his books, Pollan observed: "In my writing I've always been interested in finding places to stand, and I've found it very useful to have*

a direct experience of what I'm writing about." As a journalist, he noted: "Fairness forces you—even when you're writing a piece highly critical of, say, genetically modified food, as I have done—to make sure you represent the other side as extensively and as accurately as you possibly can."

Before Reading

Connecting: How many of the products that you eat and drink each day have high-fructose corn syrup as an ingredient? Carefully read labels for a day.

Anticipating: If you knew exactly how many calories were in a bag of snack food, a fast-food meal, or a bottled or fountain beverage, would it alter your eating habits? Do you ever look at the labels?

1   In the early years of the nineteenth century, Americans began drinking more than they ever had before or since, embarking on a collective bender that confronted the young republic with its first major public health crisis— the obesity epidemic of its day. Corn whiskey, suddenly superabundant and cheap, became the drink of choice, and in 1820 the typical American was putting away half a pint of the stuff every day. That comes to more than five gallons of spirits a year for every man, woman, and child in America. The figure today is less than one.

2   As the historian W. J. Rorabaugh tells the story in *The Alcoholic Republic*, we drank the hard stuff at breakfast, lunch, and dinner, before work and after and very often during. Employers were expected to supply spirits over the course of the workday; in fact, the modern coffee break began as a late-morning whiskey break called "the elevenses." (Just to pronounce it makes you sound tipsy.) Except for a brief respite Sunday morning in church, Americans simply did not gather—whether for a barn raising or quilting bee, corn husking or political rally—without passing the whiskey jug. Visitors from Europe—hardly models of sobriety themselves—marveled at the free flow of American spirits. "Come on then, if you love toping," the journalist William Cobbett wrote his fellow Englishmen in a dispatch from America. "For here you may drink yourself blind at the price of sixpence."

3   The results of all this toping were entirely predictable: a rising tide of public drunkenness, violence, and family abandonment, and a spike in alcohol-related diseases. Several of the Founding Fathers—including George Washington, Thomas Jefferson, and John Adams—denounced the excesses of "the Alcoholic Republic," inaugurating an American quarrel over drinking that would culminate a century later in Prohibition.

4   But the outcome of our national drinking binge is not nearly as relevant to our own situation as its underlying cause. Which, put simply, was this: American farmers were producing far too much corn. This was particularly true in the newly settled regions west of the Appalachians, where fertile,

virgin soils yielded one bumper crop after another. A mountain of surplus corn piled up in the Ohio River Valley. Much as today, the astounding productivity of American farmers proved to be their own worst enemy, as well as a threat to public health. For when yields rise, the market is flooded with grain, and its price collapses. What happens next? The excess biomass works like a vacuum in reverse: Sooner or later, clever marketers will figure out a way to induce the human omnivore to consume the surfeit of cheap calories.

5   As it is today, the clever thing to do with all that cheap corn was to process it—specifically, to distill it into alcohol. The Appalachian range made it difficult and expensive to transport surplus corn from the lightly settled Ohio River Valley to the more populous markets of the East, so farmers turned their corn into whiskey—a more compact and portable, and less perishable, value-added commodity. Before long the price of whiskey plummeted to the point that people could afford to drink it by the pint. Which is precisely what they did.

6   The Alcoholic Republic has long since given way to the Republic of Fat; we're eating today much the way we drank then, and for some of the same reasons. According to the surgeon general, obesity today is officially an epidemic; it is arguably the most pressing public health problem we face, costing the health care system an estimated $90 billion a year. Three of every five Americans are overweight; one of every five is obese. The disease formerly known as adult-onset diabetes has had to be renamed Type II diabetes since it now occurs so frequently in children. A recent study in the *Journal of the American Medical Association* predicts that a child born in 2000 has a one-in-three chance of developing diabetes. (An African American child's chances are two in five.) Because of diabetes and all the other health problems that accompany obesity, today's children may turn out to be the first generation of Americans whose life expectancy will actually be shorter than that of their parents. The problem is not limited to America: The United Nations reported that in 2000 the number of people suffering from overnutrition—a billion—had officially surpassed the number suffering from malnutrition—800 million.

7   You hear plenty of explanations for humanity's expanding waistline, all of them plausible. Changes in lifestyle (we're more sedentary; we eat out more). Affluence (more people can afford a high-fat Western diet). Poverty (healthier whole foods cost more). Technology (fewer of us use our bodies in our work; at home, the remote control keeps us pinned to the couch). Clever marketing (supersized portions; advertising to children). Changes in diet (more fats; more carbohydrates; more processed foods).

8   All these explanations are true, as far as they go. But it pays to go a little further, to search for the cause behind the causes. Which, very simply, is this: When food is abundant and cheap, people will eat more of it and get fat. Since 1977 an American's average daily intake of calories has jumped by more than 10 percent. Those two hundred calories have to go somewhere, and absent an increase in physical activity (which hasn't happened), they end up being stored away in fat cells in our bodies. But the important question is, Where, exactly, did all those extra calories come from in the first place? And the answer to that question takes us back to the source of almost all calories: the farm.

9   Most researchers trace America's rising rates of obesity to the 1970s. This was, of course, the same decade that America embraced a cheap-food farm policy and began dismantling forty years of programs designed to prevent overproduction. Earl Butz, you'll recall, sought to drive up agricultural yields in order to drive down the price of the industrial food chain's raw materials, particularly corn and soybeans. It worked: The price of food is no longer a political issue. Since the Nixon administration, farmers in the United States have managed to produce 500 additional calories per person every day (up from 3,300, already substantially more than we need); each of us is, heroically, managing to put away 200 of those surplus calories at the end of their trip up the food chain. Presumably the other 300 are being dumped overseas, or turned (once again!) into ethyl alcohol: ethanol for our cars.

10   The parallels with the alcoholic republic of two hundred years ago are hard to miss. Before the changes in lifestyle, before the clever marketing, comes the mountain of cheap corn. Corn accounts for most of the surplus calories we're growing and most of the surplus calories we're eating. As then, the smart thing to do with all that surplus grain is to process it, transform the cheap commodity into a value-added consumer product—a denser and more durable package of calories. In the 1820s the processing options were basically two: You could turn your corn into pork or alcohol. Today there are hundreds of things a processor can do with corn: They can use it to make everything from chicken nuggets and Big Macs to emulsifiers and nutraceuticals. Yet since the human desire for sweetness surpasses even our desire for intoxication, the cleverest thing to do with a bushel of corn is to refine it into thirty-three pounds of high-fructose corn syrup.

11   That at least is what we're doing with about 530 million bushels of the annual corn harvest—turning it into 17.5 billion pounds of high-fructose corn syrup. Considering that the human animal did not taste this particular food until 1980, for HFCS to have become the leading source of sweetness in our diet stands as a notable achievement on the part of the corn-refining industry, not to mention this remarkable plant. (But then, plants have always known that one of the surest paths to evolutionary success is by gratifying the mammalian omnivore's innate desire for sweetness.) Since 1985, an American's annual consumption of HFCS has gone from forty-five pounds to sixty-six pounds. You might think that this growth would have been offset by a decline in sugar consumption, since HFCS often replaces sugar, but that didn't happen: During the same period our consumption of refined sugar actually went up by five pounds. What this means is that we're eating and drinking all that high-fructose corn syrup *on top* of the sugars we were already consuming. In fact, since 1985 our consumption of all added sugars—cane, beet, HFCS, glucose, honey, maple syrup, whatever—has climbed from 128 pounds to 158 pounds per person.

12   This is what makes high-fructose corn syrup such a clever thing to do with a bushel of corn: By inducing people to consume more calories than they otherwise might, it gets them to really chomp through the corn surplus. Corn sweetener is to the republic of fat what corn whiskey was to the alcoholic republic. Read the food labels in your kitchen and you'll find that HFCS has

insinuated itself into every corner of the pantry: not just into our soft drinks and snack foods, where you would expect to find it, but into the ketchup and mustard, the breads and cereals, the relishes and crackers, the hot dogs and hams.

13   But it is in soft drinks that we consume most of our sixty-six pounds of high-fructose corn syrup, and to the red-letter dates in the natural history of *Zea mays*—right up there with teosinte's catastrophic sexual mutation, Columbus's introduction of maize to the court of Queen Isabella in 1493, and Henry Wallace's first F-l hybrid seed in 1927—we must now add the year 1980. That was the year corn first became an ingredient in Coca-Cola. By 1984, Coca-Cola and Pepsi had switched over entirely from sugar to high-fructose corn syrup. Why? Because HFCS was a few cents cheaper than sugar (thanks in part to tariffs on imported sugarcane secured by the corn refiners) and consumers didn't seem to notice the substitution.

14   The soft drink makers' switch should have been a straightforward, zero-sum trade-off between corn and sugarcane (both, incidentally, C-4 grasses), but it wasn't: We soon began swilling a lot more soda and therefore corn sweetener. The reason isn't far to seek: Like corn whiskey in the 1820s, the price of soft drinks plummeted. Note, however, that Coca-Cola and Pepsi did not simply cut the price of a bottle of cola. That would only have hurt profit margins, for how many people are going to buy a second soda just because it cost a few cents less? The companies had a much better idea: They would supersize their sodas. Since a soft drink's main raw material—corn sweetener—was now so cheap, why not get people to pay just a few pennies more for a substantially bigger bottle? Drop the price per ounce, but sell a lot more ounces. So began the transformation of the svelte eight-ounce Coke bottle into the chubby twenty-ouncer dispensed by most soda machines today.   ■

QUESTIONS ON SUBJECT AND PURPOSE

1.   What is Pollan comparing in this selection?
2.   Write or find a thesis statement for the selection.
3.   Judging from this selection, what do you think Pollan might want his audience to do?

QUESTIONS ON STRATEGY AND AUDIENCE

1.   How does Pollan structure his comparison?
2.   In paragraph 7, Pollan encloses information within a series of parentheses, often with internal semicolons. Why might he use the parentheses in this way? Why the semicolons? What effect is he trying to achieve by handling the structure of the paragraph in this way?
3.   Given both the subject and the word choices that Pollan makes, what assumptions might he have about his audience?

QUESTIONS ON VOCABULARY AND STYLE

1. Judging from the context in which the word is used, what does "toping" (paragraph 2) mean?
2. What is a "value-added commodity"?
3. Be prepared to define the following words: *bender* (paragraph 1), *respite* (2), *inaugurating* (3), *culminate* (3), *biomass* (4), *omnivore* (4), *surfeit* (4), *plummeted* (5), *nutraceuticals* (10), *svelte* (13).

WRITING SUGGESTIONS

1. **Doing a Critical Analysis.** Pollan uses both analogy and metaphor in the essay—what corn was to the Alcohol Republic, corn is to the Republic of Fat. Explain how that analogy and metaphor work in the essay and evaluate their effectiveness for making Pollan's argument.
2. **Journaling or Blogging.** Keep a list of every beverage you drink in a day. Next to each item, explain why you made that choice. Is there a pattern to how you choose your beverages?
3. **Practicing in a Paragraph.** In a paragraph, compare and contrast the nutritional value of two drinks that you consume on a regular basis.
4. **Writing the Personal Essay.** What exactly is the difference between high-fructose corn syrup and sugar? Compare and contrast the two sweeteners. Is one better for you than the other?
5. **Finding Reading Connections.** Maureen O'Hagan's "Kids Battle the Lure of Junk Food" (Chapter 7) offers another perspective on the rising rates of obesity, focusing on children. Compare and contrast the arguments of both writers in an essay. Which is more effective?
6. **Exploring Links Online.** Taxing nondiet drinks (the soda tax) has been proposed in many states and cities as a way of discouraging the consumption of soft drinks and thereby reducing obesity. The proposal has also been criticized widely. In an essay, using online sources, compare and contrast the two positions taken in this debate.
7. **Writing the Research Paper.** In paragraph 6, Pollan ends with a startling statistic reported by the United Nations in 2000: "The number of people suffering from overnutrition—a billion—has officially surpassed the number suffering from malnutrition—800 million." Have things changed since 2000? Research the problem and present your findings in an essay with formal documentation.

For Further Study

Focusing on Grammar and Writing. Pollan uses the colon (:) extensively in the selection. Locate each use and then explain why he chooses to use the colon in that particular way. What sentence structure underlies their use?

Working Together. Soft drinks were originally sold in 8-ounce glass bottles. In contrast, bottled soft drinks today rarely come in sizes smaller than 20 ounces. Do we drink more because the portions are larger? Working in small groups, brainstorm some possible strategies for getting people to reduce the quantity of what they drink.

Seeing Other Modes at Work. The essay also makes use of a cause and effect analysis.

Virtual Love

MEGHAN DAUM

Meghan Daum graduated from Vassar College and earned an M.F.A. at Columbia University. Her essays and articles have appeared in the New Yorker, *the* New York Times Book Review, GQ, Vogue *and* Self, *among others, and have been collected in* My Misspent Youth *(2001). "Virtual Love" first appeared in the* New Yorker. *Her most recent book is* Life Would Be Perfect If I Lived in that House *(2010).*

On Writing: *Asked about her writing, Daum commented: "The subjects that I find most fascinating concern ideas or events that have not only affected me personally but seem to resonate with the culture at large. Though I am often called a 'confessional' writer, I am less interested in 'confessing' than in using specific experiences as a tool for looking at more general or abstract phenomena in the world. The key to writing about yourself without falling into solipsism is to explore issues that transcend the merely personal and shed a new light on the experiences that many of us share. It also helps to have a sense of humor and respect for the absurdity of life by not taking yourself too seriously."*

Before Reading

Connecting: Do you think that it is possible to "fall in love" with someone whom you have never met face to face?

Anticipating: What is it about this "virtual" relationship that attracts Daum?

1   It was last November; fall was drifting away into an intolerable chill. I was at the end of my twenty-sixth year, and was living in New York City, trying to support myself as a writer, and taking part in the kind of urban life that might be construed as glamorous were it to appear in a memoir in the distant future. At the time, however, my days felt more like a grind than like an adventure: hours of work strung between the motions of waking up, getting the mail, watching TV with my roommates, and going to bed. One morning, I logged on to my America Online account to find a message under the

heading "is this the real meghan daum?" It came from someone with the screen name PFSlider. The body of the message consisted of five sentences, written entirely in lower-case letters, of perfectly turned flattery: something about PFSlider's admiration of some newspaper and magazine articles I had published over the last year and a half, something about his resulting infatuation with me, and something about his being a sportswriter in California.

2   I was engaged for the thirty seconds that it took me to read the message and fashion a reply. Though it felt strange to be in the position of confirming that I was indeed "the real meghan daum," I managed to say, "Yes, it's me. Thank you for writing." I clicked the "Send Now" icon, shot my words into the void, and forgot about PFSlider until the next day, when I received another message, this one headed "eureka."

3   "wow, it is you," he wrote, still in lower case. He chronicled the various conditions under which he'd read my few-and-far-between articles—a boardwalk in Laguna Beach, the spring-training pressroom for a baseball team that he covered for a Los Angeles newspaper. He confessed to having a crush on me. He referred to me as "princess daum." He said he wanted to have lunch with me during one of his two annual trips to New York.

4   The letter was outrageous and endearingly pathetic, possibly the practical joke of a friend trying to rouse me out of a temporary writer's block. But the kindness pouring forth from my computer screen was bizarrely exhilarating, and I logged off and thought about it for a few hours before writing back to express how flattered and "touched"—this was probably the first time I had ever used that word in earnest—I was by his message.

5   I am not what most people would call a computer person. I have no interest in chat rooms, newsgroups, or most Websites. I derive a palpable thrill from sticking a letter in the United States mail. But I have a constant low-grade fear of the telephone, and I often call people with the intention of getting their answering machines. There is something about the live voice that I have come to find unnervingly organic, as volatile as live television. E-mail provides a useful antidote for my particular communication anxieties. Though I generally send and receive only a few messages a week, I take comfort in their silence and their boundaries.

6   PFSlider and I tossed a few innocuous, smart-assed notes back and forth over the week following his first message. Let's say his name was Pete. He was twenty-nine, and single. I revealed very little about myself, relying instead on the ironic commentary and forced witticisms that are the conceit of so many E-mail messages. But I quickly developed an oblique affection for PFSlider. I was excited when there was a message from him, mildly depressed when there wasn't. After a few weeks, he gave me his phone number. I did not give him mine, but he looked it up and called me one Friday night. I was home. I picked up the phone. His voice was jarring, yet not unpleasant. He held up more than his end of the conversation for an hour, and when he asked permission to call me again I granted it, as though we were of an earlier era.

7   Pete—I could never wrap my mind around his name, privately thinking of him as PFSlider, "E-mail guy," or even "baseball boy"—began phoning

me two or three times a week. He asked if he could meet me, and I said that that would be O.K. Christmas was a few weeks away, and he told me that he would be coming back East to see his family. From there, he would take a short flight to New York and have lunch with me.

8   "It is my off-season mission to meet you," he said.

9   "There will probably be a snowstorm," I said.

10   "I'll take a team of sled dogs," he answered.

11   We talked about our work and our families, about baseball and Bill Clinton and Howard Stern and sex, about his hatred for Los Angeles and how much he wanted a new job. Sometimes we'd find each other logged on simultaneously and type back and forth for hours.

12   I had previously considered cyber-communication an oxymoron, a fast road to the breakdown of humanity. But, curiously, the Internet—at least in the limited form in which I was using it—felt anything but dehumanizing. My interaction with PFSlider seemed more authentic than much of what I experienced in the daylight realm of living beings. I was certainly putting more energy into the relationship than I had put into many others. I also was giving Pete attention that was by definition undivided, and relishing the safety of the distance between us by opting to be truthful instead of doling out the white lies that have become the staple of real life. The outside world—the place where I walked around avoiding people I didn't want to deal with, peppering my casual conversations with half-truths, and applying my motto "Let the machine take it" to almost any scenario—was sliding into the periphery of my mind.

13   For me, the time on-line with Pete was far superior to the phone. There were no background noises, no interruptions from "call waiting," no long-distance charges. Through typos and misspellings, he flirted maniacally. "I have an absurd crush on you," he said. "If I like you in person, you must promise to marry me." I was coy and conceited, telling him to get a life, baiting him into complimenting me further, teasing him in a way I would never have dared to do in person, or even on the phone. I would stay up until 3 A.M. typing with him, smiling at the screen, getting so giddy that when I quit I couldn't fall asleep. I was having difficulty recalling what I used to do at night. It was as if he and I lived together in our own quiet space—a space made all the more intimate because of our conscious decision to block everyone else out. My phone was tied up for hours at a time. No one in the real world could reach me, and I didn't really care.

14   Since my last serious relationship, I'd had the requisite number of false starts and five-night stands, dates that I wasn't sure were dates, and emphatically casual affairs that buckled under their own inertia. With PFSlider, on the other hand, I may not have known my suitor, but, for the first time in my life, I knew the deal: I was a desired person, the object of a blind man's gaze. He called not only when he said he would call but unexpectedly, just to say hello. He was protected by the shield of the Internet; his guard was not merely down but nonexistent. He let his phone bill grow to towering proportions. He told me that he thought about me all the time, though we both

knew that the "me" in his mind consisted largely of himself. He talked about me to his friends, and admitted it. He arranged his holiday schedule around our impending date. He managed to charm me with sports analogies. He didn't hesitate. He was unblinking and unapologetic, all nerviness and balls to the wall.

15   And so PFSlider became my everyday life. All the tangible stuff fell away. My body did not exist. I had no skin, no hair, no bones. All desire had converted itself into a cerebral current that reached nothing but my frontal lobe. There was no outdoors, no social life, no weather. There was only the computer screen and the phone, my chair, and maybe a glass of water. Most mornings, I would wake up to find a message from PFSlider, composed in Pacific time while I slept in the wee hours. "I had a date last night," he wrote. "And I am not ashamed to say it was doomed from the start because I couldn't stop thinking about you."

16   I fired back a message slapping his hand. "We must be careful where we tread," I said. This was true but not sincere. I wanted it, all of it. I wanted unfettered affection, soul-mating, true romance. In the weeks that had elapsed since I picked up "is this the real meghan daum?" the real me had undergone some kind of meltdown—a systemic rejection of all the savvy and independence I had worn for years, like a grownup Girl Scout badge.

17   Pete knew nothing of my scattered, juvenile self, and I did my best to keep it that way. Even though I was heading into my late twenties, I was still a child, ignorant of dance steps and health insurance, a prisoner of credit-card debt and student loans and the nagging feeling that I didn't want anyone to find me until I had pulled myself into some semblance of an adult. The fact that Pete had literally seemed to discover me, as if by turning over a rock, lent us an aura of fate which I actually took half-seriously. Though skepticism seemed like the obvious choice in this strange situation, I discarded it precisely because it was the obvious choice, because I wanted a more interesting narrative than cynicism would ever allow. I was a true believer in the urban dream: the dream of years of struggle, of getting a break, of making it. Like most of my friends, I wanted someone to love me, but I wasn't supposed to need it. To admit to loneliness was to smack the face of progress, to betray the times in which we lived. But PFSlider derailed me. He gave me all of what I'd never even realized I wanted.

18   My addiction to PFSlider's messages indicated a monstrous narcissism, but it also revealed a subtler desire, which I didn't fully understand at that time. My need to experience an old-fashioned kind of courtship was stronger than I had ever imagined. And the fact that technology was providing an avenue for such archaic discourse was a paradox that both fascinated and repelled me. Our relationship had an epistolary quality that put our communication closer to the eighteenth century than to the impending millennium. Thanks to the computer, I was involved in a well-defined courtship, a neat little space in which he and I were both safe to express the panic and the fascination of our mutual affection. Our interaction was refreshingly orderly, noble in its vigor, dignified despite its shamelessness. It was far removed from the

randomness of real-life relationships. We had an intimacy that seemed custom-made for our strange, lonely times. It seemed custom-made for me.

19   The day of our date, a week before Christmas, was frigid and sunny. Pete was sitting at the bar of the restaurant when I arrived. We shook hands. For a split second, he leaned toward me with his chin, as if to kiss me. He was shorter than I had pictured, though he was not short. He struck me as clean-cut. He had very nice hands. He wore a very nice shirt. We were seated at a very nice table. I scanned the restaurant for people I knew, saw none, and couldn't decide how I felt about that.

20   He talked, and I heard nothing he said. I stared at his profile and tried to figure out whether I liked him. He seemed to be saying nothing in particular, but he went on forever. Later, we went to the Museum of Natural History and watched a science film about storm chasers. We walked around looking for the dinosaurs, and he talked so much that I wanted to cry. Outside, walking along Central Park West at dusk, through the leaves, past the yellow cabs and the splendid lights of Manhattan at Christmas, he grabbed my hand to kiss me and I didn't let him. I felt as if my brain had been stuffed with cotton. Then, for some reason, I invited him back to my apartment. I gave him a few beers and finally let him kiss me on the lumpy futon in my bedroom. The radiator clanked. The phone rang and the machine picked up. A car alarm blared outside. A key turned in the door as one of my roommates came home. I had no sensation at all—only a clear conviction that I wanted Pete out of my apartment. I wanted to hand him his coat, close the door behind him, and fight the ensuing emptiness by turning on the computer and taking comfort in PFSlider.

21   When Pete finally did leave, I berated myself from every angle: for not kissing him on Central Park West, for letting him kiss me at all, for not liking him, for wanting to like him more than I had wanted anything in such a long time. I was horrified by the realization that I had invested so heavily in a made-up character—a character in whose creation I'd had a greater hand than even Pete himself. How could I, a person so self-congratulatingly reasonable, have been sucked into a scenario that was more akin to a television talk show than to the relatively full and sophisticated life I was so convinced I led? How could I have received a fan letter and allowed it to go this far?

22   The next day, a huge bouquet of FTD flowers arrived from him. No one had ever sent me flowers before. I forgave him. As human beings with actual flesh and hand gestures and Gap clothing, Pete and I were utterly incompatible, but I decided to pretend otherwise. He returned home and we fell back into the computer and the phone, and I continued to keep the real world safely away from the desk that held them. Instead of blaming him for my disappointment, I blamed the earth itself, the invasion of roommates and ringing phones into the immaculate communication that PFSlider and I had created.

23   When I pictured him in the weeks that followed, I saw the image of a plane lifting off over an overcast city. PFSlider was otherworldly, more a concept than a person. His romance lay in the notion of flight, the physics of gravity defiance. So when he offered to send me a plane ticket to spend

the weekend with him in Los Angeles I took it as an extension of our blissful remoteness, a three-dimensional E-mail message lasting an entire weekend.

24   The temperature of the runway at J.F.K. was seven degrees Fahrenheit. Our DC-10 sat for three hours waiting for deicing. Finally, it took off over the frozen city, and the ground below shrank into a drawing of itself. Phone calls were made, laptop computers were plopped onto tray tables. The recirculating air dried out my contact lenses. I watched movies without the sound and told myself that they were probably better that way. Something about the plastic interior of the fuselage and the plastic forks and the din of the air and the engines was soothing and strangely sexy.

25   Then we descended into LAX. We hit the tarmac, and the seat-belt signs blinked off. I hadn't moved my body in eight hours, and now I was walking through the tunnel to the gate, my clothes wrinkled, my hair matted, my hands shaking. When I saw Pete in the terminal, his face seemed to me just as blank and easy to miss as it had the first time I'd met him. He kissed me chastely. On the way out to the parking lot, he told me that he was being seriously considered for a job in New York. He was flying back there next week. If he got the job, he'd be moving within the month. I looked at him in astonishment. Something silent and invisible seemed to fall on us. Outside, the wind was warm, and the Avis and Hertz buses ambled alongside the curb of Terminal 5. The palm trees shook, and the air seemed as heavy and palpable as Pete's hand, which held mine for a few seconds before dropping it to get his car keys out of his pocket. He stood before me, all flesh and preoccupation, and for this I could not forgive him.

26   Gone were the computer, the erotic darkness of the telephone, the clean, single dimension of Pete's voice at 1 A.M. It was nighttime, yet the combination of sight and sound was blinding. It scared me. It turned me off. We went to a restaurant and ate outside on the sidewalk. We strained for conversation, and I tried not to care that we had to. We drove to his apartment and stood under the ceiling light not really looking at each other. Something was happening that we needed to snap out of. Any moment now, I thought. Any moment and we'll be all right. These moments were crowded with elements, with carpet fibers and automobiles and the smells of everything that had a smell. It was all wrong. The physical world had invaded our space.

27   For three days, we crawled along the ground and tried to pull ourselves up. We talked about things that I can no longer remember. We read the Los Angeles *Times* over breakfast. We drove north past Santa Barbara to tour the wine country. I felt like an object that could not be lifted, something that secretly weighed more than the world itself. Everything and everyone around us seemed imbued with a California lightness. I stomped around the countryside, an idiot New Yorker in my clunky shoes and black leather jacket. Not until I studied myself in the bathroom mirror of a highway rest stop did I fully realize the preposterousness of my uniform. I was dressed for war. I was dressed for my regular life.

28   That night, in a tiny town called Solvang, we ate an expensive dinner. We checked into a Marriott and watched television. Pete talked at me and

through me and past me. I tried to listen. I tried to talk. But I bored myself and irritated him. Our conversation was a needle that could not be threaded. Still, we played nice. We tried to care, and pretended to keep trying long after we had given up. In the car on the way home, he told me that I was cynical, and I didn't have the presence of mind to ask him just how many cynics he had met who would travel three thousand miles to see someone they barely knew.

29   Pete drove me to the airport at 7 A.M. so I could make my eight-o'clock flight home. He kissed me goodbye—another chaste peck that I recognized from countless dinner parties and dud dates. He said that he'd call me in a few days when he got to New York for his job interview, which we had discussed only in passing and with no reference to the fact that New York was where I happened to live. I returned home to frozen January. A few days later, he came to New York, and we didn't see each other. He called me from the plane taking him back to Los Angeles to tell me, through the static, that he had got the job. He was moving to my city.

30   PFSlider was dead. There would be no meeting him in distant hotel lobbies during the baseball season. There would be no more phone calls or E-mail messages. In a single moment, Pete had completed his journey out of our mating dance and officially stepped into the regular world—the world that gnawed at me daily, the world that fostered those five-night stands, the world where romance could not be sustained, because so many of us simply did not know how to do it. Instead, we were all chitchat and leather jackets, bold proclaimers of all that we did not need. But what struck me most about this affair was the unpredictable nature of our demise. Unlike most cyberromances, which seem to come fully equipped with the inevitable set of misrepresentations and false expectations, PFSlider and I had played it fairly straight. Neither of us had lied. We'd done the best we could. Our affair had died from natural causes rather than virtual ones.

31   Within a two-week period after I returned from Los Angeles, at least seven people confessed to me the vagaries of their own E-mail affairs. This topic arose, unprompted, in the course of normal conversation. I heard most of these stories in the close confines of smoky bars and crowded restaurants, and we all shook our heads in bewilderment as we told our tales, our eyes focused on some point in the distance. Four of these people had met their correspondents, by travelling from New Haven to Baltimore, from New York to Montana, from Texas to Virginia, and from New York to Johannesburg. These were normal people, writers and lawyers and scientists. They were all smart, attractive, and more than a little sheepish about admitting just how deeply they had been sucked in. Mostly, it was the courtship ritual that had seduced us. E-mail had become an electronic epistle, a yearned-for rule book. It allowed us to do what was necessary to experience love. The Internet was not responsible for our remote, fragmented lives. The problem was life itself.

32   The story of PFSlider still makes me sad, not so much because we no longer have anything to do with each other but because it forces me to

see the limits and the perils of daily life with more clarity than I used to. After I realized that our relationship would never transcend the screen and the phone—that, in fact, our face-to-face knowledge of each other had permanently contaminated the screen and the phone—I hit the pavement again, went through the motions of everyday life, said hello and goodbye to people in the regular way. If Pete and I had met at a party, we probably wouldn't have spoken to each other for more than ten minutes, and that would have made life easier but also less interesting. At the same time, it terrifies me to admit to a firsthand understanding of the way the heart and the ego are snarled and entwined like diseased trees that have folded in on each other. Our need to worship somehow fuses with our need to be worshipped. It upsets me still further to see how inaccessibility can make this entanglement so much more intoxicating. But I'm also thankful that I was forced to unpack the raw truth of my need and stare at it for a while. It was a dare I wouldn't have taken in three dimensions.

33   The last time I saw Pete, he was in New York, three thousand miles away from what had been his home, and a million miles away from PFSlider. In a final gesture of decency, in what I later realized was the most ordinary kind of closure, he took me out to dinner. As the few remaining traces of affection turned into embarrassed regret, we talked about nothing. He paid the bill. He drove me home in a rental car that felt as arbitrary and impersonal as what we now were to each other.

34   Pete had known how to get me where I lived until he came to where I lived: then he became as unmysterious as anyone next door. The world had proved to be too cluttered and too fast for us, too polluted to allow the thing we'd attempted through technology ever to grow in the earth. PFSlider and I had joined the angry and exhausted living. Even if we met on the street, we wouldn't recognize each other, our particular version of intimacy now obscured by the branches and bodies and falling debris that make up the physical world.   ∎

QUESTIONS ON SUBJECT AND PURPOSE

1. What is a "virtual" love?
2. In paragraph 18, Daum writes, "My need to experience an old-fashioned kind of courtship was stronger than I had ever imagined." How could an Internet romance be old-fashioned?
3. What is Daum saying or implying about "real" relationships in our society?

QUESTIONS ON STRATEGY AND AUDIENCE

1. What is the central contrast in Daum's essay?
2. The essay can be roughly divided into half. Where does the second half of the essay begin? What is the event that begins the second half?
3. Realistically, how large is Daum's audience? That is, to whom is she writing? How did you react to her essay?

QUESTIONS ON VOCABULARY AND STYLE

1. In paragraph 12, Daum writes: "I had previously considered cyber-communication an oxymoron." What is an *oxymoron*? What does she mean by that sentence?
2. Pete accuses Daum of being "cynical" (paragraph 28). What does that mean?
3. Be prepared to define the following words: *construed* (paragraph 1), *palpable* (5), *volatile* (5), *innocuous* (6), *conceit* (6), *periphery* (12), *unfettered* (16), *archaic* (18), *epistolary* (18), *berated* (21), *imbued* (27), *demise* (30), *vagaries* (31).

WRITING SUGGESTIONS

1. **Doing a Critical Analysis.** Daum's essay is an example of what is called "confessional journalism." It is not easy to write honestly about yourself and your experiences. Does the experience she describes seem "real" to you? Analyze how the use of point of view and detail creates or does not create a sense of truth in the essay.
2. **Journaling or Blogging.** Think of a time when you realized that a person you thought you knew suddenly seemed quite different. It could be a change for the better or the worse. What you are looking for is a contrast—a before and an after. Make a list of some moments of recognition.
3. **Practicing in a Paragraph.** Explore one of those before-and-after experiences in a paragraph.
4. **Writing the Personal Essay.** Expand your paragraph into an essay. You are working on a contrast—what you thought or assumed before and the reality that you discovered after.
5. **Finding Reading Connections.** On the basis of how he presents himself in "This Is Who I Am When No One is Looking" (Chapter 4), compare and contrast the personalities of Daum and Pico Iyer.
6. **Exploring Links Online.** Does Facebook provide just a random look at someone's life or an intentionally constructed presentation of self? In an essay, compare and contrast Facebook profile photos of some of your "friends."
7. **Writing the Research Paper.** The remarkable thing about Daum's "virtual" relationship was that neither person pretended to be different from who they were. Why do people often lie or misrepresent themselves on social media sites? Research the problem, documenting your sources.

For Further Study

Focusing on Grammar and Writing. At several points in the essay, Daum uses the same sentence structure: the final three sentences in paragraph 3; the first three sentences in paragraph 5; the final nine sentences in paragraph 14. What type of structure is she using and why?

Working Together. Divide into small groups and choose one of the following details from the story: the pieces of direct quotation (e.g., paragraphs 2, 8–10); the huge bouquet of flowers (22); the realization she is "dressed for war" (27);

Pete's move to New York City (concentrate on 30); her final dinner with Pete (33). What does each detail contribute to the essay?

Seeing Other Modes at Work. The essay is also a personal experience narrative following the relationship from its beginning to its end.

ADDITIONAL WRITING SUGGESTIONS FOR COMPARISON AND CONTRAST

Remember that comparison finds similarities while contrast finds differences. Regardless of which you are doing, also remember to focus on the significant and not the obvious or trivial. Have a reason or purpose for making this comparison or contrast.

COMPARISON

1. Playing a sport and working for a company or being in the military
2. A buffet in a restaurant and your school's undergraduate course offerings
3. Lessons learned as a child and adult experiences
4. Skateboarding and snowboarding or skiing
5. Something technical and something simple (develop an analogy)
6. A particular video game and life
7. Characteristics that achievers share (regardless of gender, race, or economic background)
8. Similarities among those who are seen by our culture as "celebrities" or "stars"
9. Qualities that make someone in our culture a "hero"
10. Life as a jungle and life as a beach

CONTRAST

1. Facebook and MySpace
2. Texting and telephone calls
3. Meat eaters and vegans
4. Early risers and late sleepers (humorous)
5. E-mailing and letter writing
6. Two different popular diet plans or two different types of exercise
7. Two gaming systems
8. Off-campus housing and dormitories
9. Two different types of music (e.g., rap and punk rock)
10. Your generation and your parents' or grandparents' generation

6 | Process

LEARNING OBJECTIVES

In this chapter, you will learn how to

1. Recognize what goes into a process description
2. Choose an appropriate and manageable subject for a process essay
3. Divide the process into clear steps or stages
4. Organize those steps or stages in their logical order
5. Revise a process essay to increase its effectiveness
6. Analyze readings that use process

Key Questions

WRITING PROCESS

Getting Ready to Write

What is process?

How do you choose a process subject?

Writing

How do you structure a process essay?

Revising

How do you revise a process essay?

Student Essay
    Julie Anne Halbfish, "How to Play Dreidel"

READING PROCESS

In Prose
    "Creamed Mouse" (recipe)

In Literature
    Janice Mirikitani, "Recipe" (poem)

In a Visual
    "Four-In-Hand" (diagram)

Writing Process

GETTING READY TO WRITE

What Is Process?

What do each of the following have in common?

> A recipe in a cookbook
> A textbook discussion of how the body converts food into energy and fat
> Directions on how to install a CD changer in your car
> An online explanation of why earthquakes occur

Each is a process analysis—either a set of directions for how to do something (make lasagna or install a CD changer) or a description of how something happens or is done (food is converted or the earth "quakes"). These two different types of process writing have two different purposes. The function of a set of directions is to allow the reader to duplicate the process. Several readings in this chapter offer advice or instructions on how to do something. Nicole Perlroth in "How to Devise Passwords That Drive Hackers Away" recommends a series of actions that you can take to make your online information safer. Richard Bolles in "The Internet: The 10% Solution" provides a comprehensive strategy by which you can more effectively search for a job.

Not every example of process is a set of directions about how to do something. Process can also be used to tell the reader how something happens or is made. Nora Ephron in "Revision and Life" describes her own revision process; Jennifer Kahn in "Stripped for Parts" describes the process through which organs are "harvested" from a dead donor for transplantation. Neither of these essays is meant to describe a process that we are to perform or imitate.

Links between Writing and Reading

	Nature of the process narrative
Nicole Perlroth, "How to Devise Passwords"	Steps to take
Sherry Simpson, "Tiny Masters"	How to write a personal essay
Lars Eighner, "My Daily Dives"	How he does it and what he has learned
Nora Ephron, "Revision and Life"	What the links are between life and revision
Richard Bolles, "The Internet"	How to search for a job
Jennifer Kahn, "Stripped for Parts"	How organs are "harvested" and the process of dying

How Do You Choose a Process Subject?

Choosing a subject is not a problem if you have been given a specific assignment, for example, to describe how a congressional bill becomes a law, how a chemistry experiment was performed, how to write an "A" paper for your English course. Often, however, you have to choose your own subject. Two considerations are crucial to that decision.

First, choose a subject that can be adequately described or analyzed in the space you have available. When Nora Ephron in "Revision and Life" traces her revision process, she isolates three decades of her life—her 20s, 30s, and 40s. She alternates paragraphs dealing with her evolving attitudes toward revision with paragraphs establishing links between revision and life. At 20, she revised nothing; at 40, she is increasingly drawn to revision. Ephron does not try to identify every change that occurred during these three decades. Instead, she confines her analysis to the major periods.

Second, in a process analysis, as in any other writing assignment, identify the audience to whom you are writing. What does that audience already know about your subject? Are you writing to a general audience, an audience of your fellow classmates, or a specialized audience? You do not want to bore your reader with the obvious, nor do you want to lose your reader in a tangle of unfamiliar terms and concepts. Your choice of subject and certainly your approach to it should be determined by your audience. Richard Bolles's essay on job-seeking strategies comes from a "job hunter's survival guide." Nicole Perlroth's "How to Devise Passwords That Drive Hackers Away" comes from a technology section of a major newspaper. Sherry Simpson's "Tiny Masters: An Artful Trick to Writing the Personal Essay" is aimed not at student writers, but at writing teachers. Identifying your audience—what they might be interested in, what they already know—will help in both selecting a subject and in deciding how or what to write about it.

Links between Writing and Reading

	Audience
Nicole Perlroth, "How to Devise Passwords"	Adults using computers and mobile devices
Sherry Simpson, "Tiny Masters"	Writing teachers
Lars Eighner, "My Daily Dives"	Surely not would-be dumpster divers
Nora Ephron, "Revision and Life"	College writers
Richard Bolles, "The Internet"	Adults seeking a job
Jennifer Kahn, "Stripped for Parts"	Everyone, but not likely to appeal to all, especially would-be organ donors

WRITING

How Do You Structure a Process Essay?

If you have ever tried to assemble something from a set of directions, you know how important it is that each step or stage in the process be clearly defined and properly placed in the sequence. Because process always involves a series of events or steps that must be done in proper order, the fundamental structure for a process paragraph or essay will be chronological (what occurs first in time).

Begin your planning by making a list of the various steps in the process. Once your list seems complete, arrange the items in the order in which they are performed or in which they occur. Check to make sure that nothing has been omitted or misplaced. If your process is a description of how to do or make something, check your arranged list by performing the process according to the directions you have assembled so far. This ordered list will serve as the outline for your process paper.

Converting your list or outline into a paragraph or an essay is the next step. Be sure that all the phrases on your outline have been turned into complete sentences and that any technical terms have been carefully explained. You will need some way of signaling to your reader each step or stage in the

 Prewriting Tips for Writing Process

1. Brainstorm some possible topics that lend themselves to a process narrative—how something is done, how to make something, the stages in which something occurred, or your plan for handling a situation.

2. Answer these questions: Why am I writing about this? What purpose do I have in mind? Am I trying to inform? Entertain? Persuade? Remember that an essay needs a purpose.

3. Define your audience and think about what they might already know about the subject. If your audience is very familiar with the subject, they are likely to be bored. If the subject is too technical or requires much prior knowledge, the audience will not understand.

4. Think about the steps or stages in the process that you are describing. Remember that you probably need between three and six. If the process involves fewer than three, it might be too simple to justify an essay; if it has more than six, it might be too complicated. This is not an unbreakable rule; use it for guidance.

5. Consider how your steps or stages might be ordered. Is there an obvious place at which to start? To end? What about the middle steps in the process?

process. On your list, you probably numbered the steps, but in your paragraph or essay you generally cannot use such a device. More commonly, process papers employ various types of step or time markers to indicate order. Step markers like *first*, *second*, and *third* can be used at the beginning of sentences or paragraphs devoted to each individual stage. Time markers like *begin*, *next*, *in three minutes*, or *while this is being done* remind the reader of the proper chronological sequence.

Links between Writing and Reading

	Structuring middles
Nicole Perlroth, "How to Devise Passwords"	Is there an order to the advice?
Sherry Simpson, "Tiny Masters"	What is the order in paragraphs 9–12?
Lars Eighner, "My Daily Dives"	What are the four parts of the essay?
Nora Ephron, "Revision and Life"	What role does time play in the essay's organization?
Richard Bolles, "The Internet"	How are the steps in the process ordered?
Jennifer Kahn, "Stripped for Parts"	What is the controlling pattern of organization?

Drafting Tips for Writing Process

1. Be sure to include each step necessary to perform or understand the process. Are those steps and stages in a logical or chronological order?
2. Have you clearly marked the steps or stages? Have you used sequence markers (e.g., *first*, *then*)? Have you put each stage in a separate paragraph?
3. Have you used any words or phrases that your audience might not understand? Be sure to provide a parenthetical definition after that word or phrase.
4. Check to see if your steps or stages are phrased in parallel form (for a definition see the Glossary and Ready Reference).
5. Once you have a complete draft, find someone who will read your essay and offer honest advice. Perhaps a classmate? Visit your school writing lab or center. Look for readers and listen to what they say.

REVISING

How Do You Revise a Process Essay?

Many writers revise as they write, and even if you do so, "re-see" your paper once again when you have a complete, finished draft. Ideally, you should allow some time to elapse between finishing the draft and looking again at what you have written. If you try to revise too soon, you may see what you want to see and not what you actually wrote. As you look again at your finished draft, remember that process is primarily written for an informative purpose. A how-to-do-it process essay is successful if the reader can reproduce the process you describe without error and with the same result. A here-is-how-it-works process narrative is intended to explain how something is done with no intention of having the reader reproduce the process. Either way, the key element in process writing is clarity.

When revising a process essay, pay particular attention to the following areas: choosing an interesting and manageable subject, checking for logical organization, and writing an appropriate beginning and ending.

Choosing an Interesting and Manageable Subject   Revision should always begin by looking critically at the essay as a whole. First ask yourself about your choice of subject. Was it too simple? Was it too complicated? Does your draft have three very short body paragraphs or twelve long ones? In either case, unless you have an unusual approach to a simple subject, your audience is likely to be bored. For example, a simple process such as how to make a peanut butter and jelly sandwich or how to put gasoline in your car is probably not a good choice. On the other hand, a complex process is likely to be too long and too detailed for an essay in a writing class.

Second, define your imagined reader. How much prior knowledge is the reader likely to have about your subject? Are you expecting too little or too much of your reader? If you have used technical words and concepts, make sure to provide definitions for them, enclosed with parentheses or set off with commas. Depending on your subject and what your instructor wants, you might want to use visuals in your essay. Often pictures are more effective than words in showing how something is done.

Third, assess again your purpose in the essay. Are you giving directions so the reader might be able to duplicate the process? Or are you trying to describe a process so the reader understands how it works?

Checking for Logical Organization   Because process essays are either directions on how to do something or descriptions of how something happens, they must be clearly organized into steps or stages. Think of the directions in a cookbook or a repair manual. The steps of the process must be arranged in a logical, and often chronological, order: first do this, then this, finally this. The steps in the process must be clearly marked off—by being placed in separate paragraphs or sentences, by the use of place and sequence markers (*first, next, finally*), or by numbering (*first* or 1.). Sometimes each step is illustrated with a diagram or a photograph.

The steps must then be arranged in the right order so that the process will work and will produce the same result each time. A good test of logical ordering is to ask a friend to follow the directions that you have given to see if they are clear, comprehensive, and in the right order.

Parallelism—that is, placing words, phrases, and clauses in the steps or sequence in a similar grammatical form—is extremely important in process writing.

Writing an Appropriate Beginning and Ending   Readers choose to read process essays when they need the information that the essay provides. If you are trying to add a double major or a minor, you are motivated to read how to do it. If you are learning about how a solar panel creates electricity, you are motivated to read about the process. Do not assume, however, that your reader will read regardless of what you say or how you say it. An introduction to a process essay identifies the subject, but it should try to catch readers' attention as well. In a sense, you are trying to persuade your readers to read your essay. What is important or interesting about this process? How will your readers benefit from knowing this?

Conclusions also pose challenges in process writing. Typically, you do not want simply to summarize the steps or stages in the process. That repetition would be boring and unnecessary. Instead, try suggesting what is important about this knowledge, why it might be useful, or what might be learned through studying the process.

Links between Writing and Reading

	Introductions and conclusions
Nicole Perlroth, "How to Devise Passwords"	Why the personal experience introduction?
Sherry Simpson, "Tiny Masters"	What strategy is used in the introduction?
Lars Eighner, "My Daily Dives"	What is the effect of the final sentence?
Nora Ephron, "Revision and Life"	How does the conclusion reflect the author's revising practice?
Richard Bolles, "The Internet"	What type of conclusion does the essay have?
Jennifer Kahn, "Stripped for Parts"	What about the introduction catches your attention?

Revising Tips for Writing Process

1. Use the feedback provided by a peer reader, your instructor, or a tutor to revise your essay.
2. Provide an answer to the following prompts: My purpose is? My intended audience is? My readers will be interested in this subject because?
3. Look again at your introduction and conclusion. Do you catch your readers' attention in your introduction? Do you have a clear statement of purpose? Does your conclusion simply repeat the steps or stages in the process?
4. Never underestimate the power of a good title. Write several titles for your paper. Ask friends to evaluate each one.
5. Remember to proofread one final time. See the advice on proofreading offered earlier in this text in How to Revise an Essay.

Student Essay

As part of her student-teaching assignment, Julie Anne Halbfish was asked by her cooperating teacher to write a set of directions on how to play dreidel, a game associated with the Jewish holiday Hanukkah. Most of the students in the seventh-grade class in which Julie was student-teaching had never played the game.

First Draft

How to Play Dreidel

A dreidel is a small top with four sides. On each side is a Hebrew letter. The letters correspond to the first letters in each word of the Hebrew phrase *"Nes gadol haya sham,"* which means "A great miracle happened there." That phrase refers to the military victory of the Maccabees over the Greeks and the story of the small jug of olive oil that burned for eight days. The corresponding Hebrew letters on the dreidel are called *nun* [נ], *gimel* [ג], *hay* [ה], and *shin* [ש].

Many people have heard the Hanukkah song "Dreidel," but most are unfamiliar with how to play the traditional children's game of the same name. The rules are actually quite simple.

To start the game, every player receives ten pieces of "money" (usually peanuts, candies, pennies, or anything else the players choose to play for) and a dreidel. Each player puts two pieces of money into the "pot" and then spins the dreidel. When the dreidel stops spinning, the letter that is on the side facing up determines how many pieces the player takes from or adds to the pot. If the dreidel lands on *nun*, the player takes nothing. If it lands on *gimel*, the player takes all of the pot. If the dreidel lands on *hay*, the player receives half of the pot. Finally, if the dreidel lands on *shin*, the player must put two additional pieces into the pot. After as many rounds of play as the players want, the game ends, and whoever has the most goodies is declared the winner. However, the reason so many people love this game is that everyone ends up with treats to enjoy, so nobody loses.

Comments

After Julie finished a draft of her essay, she showed her paper to Adam Helenic, a fellow classmate. At first, Adam simply praised the draft—"It's good; it's clear; it's fine, Julie." But Julie would not settle for simple approval. When pushed, Adam made several suggestions. Since many students have heard the dreidel song, he urged her somehow to work at least part of the song into the essay—maybe as an attention-getting introduction. He also suggested that she reorder paragraphs 1 and 2 and that she tighten up her prose in a number of places. When Julie revised her set of directions, she tried to incorporate all of the changes that Adam had suggested. Interestingly, when Julie set out to check her "facts" about the song and the game, she used the Web. She found a computerized Dreidel game that you might like to try; several are available online—for example, www.babaganewz.com/dreidel/dreidel.cfm.

Revised Draft

How to Play Dreidel

> I have a little dreidel,
> I made it out of clay.
> And when it's dry and ready,
> Oh, dreidel I shall play!
> It has a lovely body,
> With legs so short and thin.
> And when it gets all tired,
> It drops and then I win.

During Hanukkah, we often hear the "Dreidel" song, but most people have never actually played the traditional children's game to which the song refers. The game is quite simple, and since every player is sure to win something, dreidel is a popular Hanukkah game.

A dreidel is a small, four-sided top, traditionally made out of clay. On each side is a Hebrew letter. The letters correspond to the first letters in each word of the Hebrew phrase *"Nes gadol haya sham,"* which means "A great miracle happened there." That phrase refers to the military victory of the Maccabees over the Greeks and the story of the small jug of olive oil that miraculously burned for eight days. The corresponding Hebrew letters on the dreidel are called *nun* [נ], *gimel* [ג], *hay* [ה], and *shin* [ש].

To start the game, every player receives ten pieces of "money" (usually peanuts, candies, pennies, or anything else the players choose to play for) and a dreidel. Each player puts two pieces of money into the "pot" and then spins the dreidel. When the dreidel is spinning, the players are encouraged to sing a Hanukkah song or to shout *"Gimel!"* When the dreidel stops spinning, the letter that is on the side facing up determines how many pieces the player takes from or adds to the pot. If the dreidel lands on *nun*, the player takes nothing. If it lands on *gimel*, the player takes all of the pot. If the dreidel lands on *hay*, the player receives half of the pot. Finally, if the dreidel lands on *shin*, the player must put two additional pieces into the pot.

After as many rounds of play as the players want, the game ends, and whoever has the most goodies is declared the winner. Whether you win or not, no one really loses since everyone ends up with treats to enjoy.

Checklist: Some Things to Remember About Writing Process

❑ Choose a subject that can be analyzed and described within the space you have available.

❑ Remember that process takes one of two forms, reflecting its purpose: either to tell the reader how to do something or to tell the reader how something happens. Make sure you have a purpose clearly in mind before you start your paper.

❑ Identify your audience and write to that audience. Ask yourself: Will my audience be interested in what I am writing about? How much does my audience know about this subject?

❑ Make a list of the steps or stages in the process.

❑ Order or arrange the list, checking to make sure nothing is omitted or misplaced.

❑ Convert the list into paragraphs using complete sentences. Remember to define any unfamiliar terms or concepts.

❑ Use step or time markers to indicate the proper sequence in the process.

❑ Check your process one final time to make sure that nothing has been omitted. If you are describing how to do something, use your paper as a guide to the process. If you are describing how something happens, ask a friend to read your process analysis to see whether it is clear.

READING PROCESS

Every set of directions, or how-to-do-it, or how-it-is-done-or-produced is a process narrative. When we read a description of a process, we can expect to see several distinctive features:

- Process is always structured in time, from the first step to the last. In that sense, it is similar to a narrative or story, but unlike a narrative, process does not use flashbacks. That would only confuse the reader.
- The function of process is to allow a reader to duplicate the procedure or to understand the stages or steps. In that sense, process has a practical goal. It is effective only if the reader can follow it.
- To promote clarity, process frequently uses step or stage markers— first do this; then this. Typically, the steps or stages are numbered, or separated by extra space, or divided into paragraphs. The structure and how it is revealed on the printed page clearly emphasizes the steps.
- Process typically uses parallel structures—headings, sentences, and paragraphs are written so that they are grammatically similar in structure.
- Process is always conscious of its audience. Who is the intended audience? How much do they already know about the subject?

IN PROSE

Farley Moway, a Canadian author and conservationist, wrote many books about wildlife. In *Never Cry Wolf* (1963), he investigated the declining population of caribou. Through observation he established that the caribou were not being killed by wolves as many thought. In fact, wolves mainly ate field mice. He wrote, "I decided to experiment on myself by actually trying to live off these rodents—to see if it would provide a healthy lifestyle. If I could prove that it was possible for me to survive on a diet consisting only of mice, then I could make a conclusion that wolves too could survive off of mice only." Not surprisingly, Mowat found that the mice had "too many bones" and "a very dull flavor." As a solution, he then offered readers his recipe for creamed mouse (in French, *souis à la crème*)! The recipe, and then the steps to be followed preparing it, are as follows:

Souris à la crème (or Creamed Mouse)

One dozen fat mice

One cup white flour

One piece of sowbelly [pig belly—either salt pork or bacon]

Salt and pepper

Cloves

Ethyl alcohol [grain or drinking alcohol]

Skin, gut and wash some fat mice without removing their heads. Cover them in a pot with ethyl alcohol and marinate 2 hours. Cut a piece of salt pork or sowbelly into small dice and cook it slowly to extract the fat. Drain the mice, dredge them thoroughly in a mixture of flour, pepper, and salt, and fry slowly in the rendered fat for about 5 minutes. Add a cup of alcohol and 6 to 8 cloves, cover and simmer for 15 minutes. Prepare a cream sauce, transfer the sauteed mice to it, and warm them in it for about 10 minutes before serving.   ■

QUESTIONS FOR ANALYSIS

1. Why might the recipe be titled with the French phrase rather than the English?
2. What typographical devices does the text use to emphasize the steps or stages in the process? In a cookbook, how might those steps be marked?
3. How many examples of parallelism can you find in the recipe?
4. Do you think Mowat ever expected that any reader might try the recipe? Why then include it?

CRITICAL READING ACTIVITY

Look through your textbooks for this semester. Can you find examples of process narratives or analyses? Bring your examples to class to share.

IN LITERATURE

Janice Mirikitani, a third-generation Japanese American, uses process in her poem "Recipe." As the title and its list of "ingredients" suggest, the poem might at first seem like a set of directions that you would find in a magazine—"how to create the illusion of having round eyes." As you read the poem, think about how Mirikitani uses the elements of a process analysis to structure her poem.

Recipe

JANICE MIRIKITANI

Round Eyes
Ingredients: scissors, Scotch magic transparent tape.
eyeliner—water based, black.
Optional: false eyelashes.
Cleanse face thoroughly.
For best results, powder entire face, including eyelids.
(lighter shades suited to total effect desired)
With scissors, cut magic tape 1/16" wide, 1/4–1/2" long—depending
on length of eyelid.

Stick firmly onto mid-upper eyelid area
(looking down into handmirror facilitates finding adequate surface)
If using false eyelashes, affix first on lid, folding any excess lid over the
base of eyelash with glue.
Paint black eyeliner on tape and entire lid.
Do not cry.   ■

QUESTIONS FOR ANALYSIS

1. How do you think Mirikitani feels about "round" eyes? Is she trying simply to be describe how to create that illusion? Is her poem trying to be helpful?
2. How would you characterize the tone of the poem? What in the poem provides evidence for your viewpoint?
3. How does the process structure contribute to the poem's effect? What initial expectation do you have about the poem? Did that expectation change as you read the poem?
4. Is there anything in the "steps" of the process that seems unusual?
5. Why might she have chosen to title the poem "Recipe" rather than something more descriptive of its content?

WRITING SUGGESTIONS

1. **Analysis.** What makes this a poem and not a helpful set of instructions? Are there "poetic" effects in the poem? In an essay, analyze how and why Mirikitani creates a poem using a step-by-step process.
2. As this poem suggests, process does not have to be used in a simple, expository way. Mirikitani uses it to make a comment about a social issue, about cultural pressure and values. Explore a similar issue using a process model—either a set of directions or a description of how something works. Some possible topics include:
   a. Underage drinking or smoking.
   b. The desire to change your appearance (for example, hair coloring, body piercings, hair straightening or curling, plastic surgery, purging).
   c. The desire to conform to your peer group (for example, in behavior, dress, attitudes).

IN A VISUAL

Because process involves a series of steps or stages, it is typically represented through or accompanied by a series of photographs or drawings. Instructions on how to assemble or do something are often nothing more than a series of illustrations, like the example here. For men who need to wear neckties to work, tying a tie is a hurdle. Consider the five steps illustrated in the diagram below. Two mathematical physicists actually discovered at least 10 possibilities for a good necktie knot (most men are lucky to know one) and published their findings in one of the most distinguished science journals. When you look at the illustrations, it is easy to see why pictures are better than words! Just in case the diagram does not help you, you can find a written description of how to tie this knot (called a "four-in-hand" or simple knot) or watch a video of how to do it at www.ties-necktie.com/tie-knots-simple-knot-four-in-hand.php

QUESTIONS FOR ANALYSIS

1. Do you think you could tie a necktie using this diagram? Why or why not?
2. What visual devices does the artist use to make the steps in the process clear to a user?
3. Are any of the steps unclear, potentially confusing, or omitted?
4. Go to the website cited above and compare the three forms of process description—in words, in a diagram, in a video. Which is the most effective?

WRITING SUGGESTIONS

1. **Analysis:** A step-by-step process diagram is similar to the panel-by-panel narrative of a comic strip. What is the content of each diagram? What is important about the arrangement of the diagrams? What devices does the

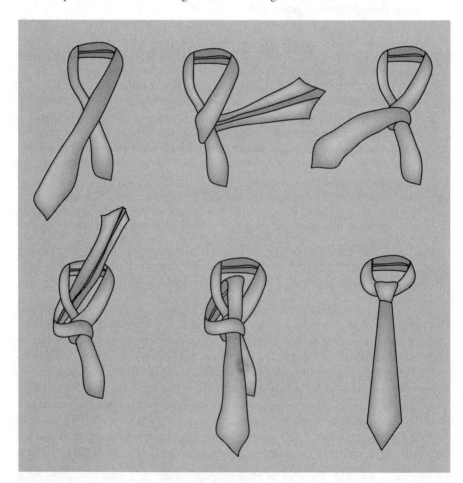

artist use to make the sequence clear and reproducible? In a short essay, analyze how this process diagram works and why showing (pictures) is more effective than simply telling (words).

2. Think of another process that is part of your everyday life. It should be something that requires a sequence of steps rather than just one or two; it should be something that you had to learn how to do, and perhaps have taught someone how to do. The process should be something that can be described in words, but also one which benefits from simple illustrations. In an essay, write a process narrative describing how it is done and accompany your essay with simple illustrations of the steps.

3. Television features a range of how-to-do-it shows, particularly for subjects such as home improvement, wood working, cooking. In contrast, other types of shows focus on accomplishment or competition rather than process, for example, shows about losing weight or dealing with family conflicts. In an essay, explore the difference between the two.

How to Devise Passwords That Drive Hackers Away

NICOLE PERLROTH

Nicole Perlroth is the technology reporter for the New York Times *covering cybersecurity and privacy. A graduate of Princeton with a M.A. in journalism from Stanford University, she was a deputy editor at* Forbes *covering venture capital and Web start-ups before joining the* Times. *She tweets at @nicoleperlroth.*

Before Reading

Connecting: Has your computer ever had a virus? How did you discover it?

Anticipating: What would be the safest things to do about your passwords for your computer, e-mail, online accounts?

1   **N**ot long after I began writing about cybersecurity, I became a paranoid caricature of my former self. It's hard to maintain peace of mind when hackers remind me every day, all day, just how easy it is to steal my personal data.

2   Within weeks, I set up unique, complex passwords for every Web site, enabled two-step authentication for my e-mail accounts, and even covered up my computer's Web camera with a piece of masking tape—a precaution that invited ridicule from friends and co-workers who suggested it was time to get my head checked.

3   But recent episodes offered vindication. I removed the webcam tape—after a friend convinced me that it was a little much—only to see its light turn green a few days later, suggesting someone was in my computer and watching. More recently, I received a text message from Google with the two-step verification code for my Gmail account. That's the string of numbers Google sends after you correctly enter the password to your Gmail account, and it serves as a second password. (Do sign up for it.) The only problem was that I was not trying to get into my Gmail account. I was nowhere near a computer. Apparently, somebody else was.

4   It is absurdly easy to get hacked. All it takes is clicking on one malicious link or attachment. Companies' computer systems are attacked every day by hackers looking for passwords to sell on auctionlike black market sites where a single password can fetch $20. Hackers regularly exploit tools like John the Ripper, a free password-cracking program that use lists of commonly used passwords from breached sites and can test millions of passwords per second.

5   Chances are, most people will get hacked at some point in their lifetime. The best they can do is delay the inevitable by avoiding suspicious links, even from friends, and manage their passwords. Unfortunately, good password hygiene is like flossing—you know it's important, but it takes effort. How do you possibly come up with different, hard-to-crack passwords for every single news, social network, e-commerce, banking, corporate and e-mail account and still remember them all?

6   To answer that question, I called two of the most (justifiably) paranoid people I know, Jeremiah Grossman and Paul Kocher, to find out how they keep their information safe. Mr. Grossman was the first hacker to demonstrate how easily somebody can break into a computer's webcam and microphone through a Web browser. He is now chief technology officer at WhiteHat Security, an Internet and network security firm, where he is frequently targeted by cybercriminals. Mr. Kocher, a well-known cryptographer, gained notice for clever hacks on security systems. He now runs Cryptography Research, a security firm that specializes in keeping systems hacker-resistant. Here were their tips:

7   FORGET THE DICTIONARY If your password can be found in a dictionary, you might as well not have one. "The worst passwords are dictionary words or a small number of insertions or changes to words that are in the dictionary," said Mr. Kocher. Hackers will often test passwords from a dictionary or aggregated from breaches. If your password is not in that set, hackers will typically move on.

8   NEVER USE THE SAME PASSWORD TWICE People tend to use the same password across multiple sites, a fact hackers regularly exploit. While cracking into someone's professional profile on LinkedIn might not have dire consequences, hackers will use that password to crack into, say, someone's e-mail, bank, or brokerage account where more valuable financial and personal data is stored.

9   COME UP WITH A PASS PHRASE The longer your password, the longer it will take to crack. A password should ideally be 14 characters or

more in length if you want to make it uncrackable by an attacker in less than 24 hours. Because longer passwords tend to be harder to remember, consider a passphrase, such as a favorite movie quote, song lyric, or poem, and string together only the first one or two letters of each word in the sentence.

10   OR JUST JAM ON YOUR KEYBOARD For sensitive accounts, Mr. Grossman says that instead of a passphrase, he will randomly jam on his keyboard, intermittently hitting the Shift and Alt keys, and copy the result into a text file which he stores on an encrypted, password protected USB drive. "That way, if someone puts a gun to my head and demands to know my password, I can honestly say I don't know it."

11   STORE YOUR PASSWORDS SECURELY Do not store your passwords in your in-box or on your desktop. If malware infects your computer, you're toast. Mr. Grossman stores his password file on an encrypted USB drive for which he has a long, complex password that he has memorized. He copies and pastes those passwords into accounts so that, in the event an attacker installs keystroke logging software on his computer, they cannot record the keystrokes to his password. Mr. Kocher takes a more old-fashioned approach: He keeps password hints, not the actual passwords, on a scrap of paper in his wallet. "I try to keep my most sensitive information off the Internet completely," Mr. Kocher said.

12   A PASSWORD MANAGER? MAYBE Password-protection software lets you store all your usernames and passwords in one place. Some programs will even create strong passwords for you and automatically log you in to sites as long as you provide one master password. LastPass, SplashData and AgileBits offer password management software for Windows, Macs and mobile devices. But consider yourself warned: Mr. Kocher said he did not use the software because even with encryption, it still lived on the computer itself. "If someone steals my computer, I've lost my passwords." Mr. Grossman said he did not trust the software because he didn't write it. Indeed, at a security conference in Amsterdam earlier this year, hackers demonstrated how easily the cryptography used by many popular mobile password managers could be cracked.

13   IGNORE SECURITY QUESTIONS There is a limited set of answers to questions like "What is your favorite color?" and most answers to questions like "What middle school did you attend?" can be found on the Internet. Hackers use that information to reset your password and take control of your account. Earlier this year, a hacker claimed he was able to crack into Mitt Romney's Hotmail and Dropbox accounts using the name of his favorite pet. A better approach would be to enter a password hint that has nothing to do with the question itself. For example, if the security question asks for the name of the hospital in which you were born, your answer might be: "Your favorite song lyric."

14   USE DIFFERENT BROWSERS Mr. Grossman makes a point of using different Web browsers for different activities. "Pick one browser for 'promiscuous' browsing: online forums, news sites, blogs—anything you don't consider important," he said. "When you're online banking or checking

e-mail, fire up a secondary Web browser, then shut it down." That way, if your browser catches an infection when you accidentally stumble on an X-rated site, your bank account is not necessarily compromised. As for which browser to use for which activities, a study last year by Accuvant Labs of Web browsers—including Mozilla Firefox, Google Chrome and Microsoft Internet Explorer—found that Chrome was the least susceptible to attacks.

15   SHARE CAUTIOUSLY "You are your e-mail address and your password," Mr. Kocher emphasized. Whenever possible, he will not register for online accounts using his real e-mail address. Instead he will use "throwaway" e-mail addresses, like those offered by 10minutemail.com. Users register and confirm an online account, which self-destructs 10 minutes later. Mr. Grossman said he often warned people to treat anything they typed or shared online as public record.

16   "At some point, you will get hacked—it's only a matter of time," warned Mr. Grossman. "If that's unacceptable to you, don't put it online."   ■

QUESTIONS ON SUBJECT AND PURPOSE

1. What is "malware"?
2. What is a "hacker"?
3. What clear purpose does the essay have?

QUESTIONS ON STRATEGY AND AUDIENCE

1. What is the point of view in the first three paragraphs?
2. Why might she begin the essay in this way?
3. What could Perlroth assume about her audience?

QUESTIONS ON VOCABULARY AND STYLE

1. What is a "passphrase" (paragraph 8)?
2. What typographical devices does Perlroth use to make the essay easier to read?
3. Be prepared to define the following words: *paranoid* (paragraph 1), *caricature* (1), *malicious* (4), *aggregated* (7), *dire* (8), *encrypted (11)*, *promiscuous* (14).

WRITING SUGGESTIONS

1. **Doing a Critical Analysis.** The advice given in the essay comes from two computer security experts, not from Perlroth. How does she integrate this information into the essay? How does she introduce the credentials of the two and how does she work quotations into her text? Analyze her use of sources in the text.
2. **Journaling or Blogging.** What warning signs would you expect to find if your computer or mobile device was infected? Brainstorm a list of possibilities.
3. **Practicing in a Paragraph.** What would you do if you discovered that your computer was infected with malware or a virus? Describe the steps you might take to correct the problem.

4. **Writing the Personal Essay.** What resources are available at your school to help you clean an infected computer? Before you write, check to make sure that you know exactly where to go. Write an essay aimed at your peers.

5. **Finding Reading Connections.** How do typographical devices help readers understand an essay's contents? In an essay, compare Perlroth's essay with Berelson's "The Value of Children" (Chapter 4) and Bolles's "The Internet: The 10% Solution" (this chapter).

6. **Exploring Links Online.** Not everyone agrees that you can devise passwords to prevent hacking. Using online sources, research other technologies that might replace the use of passwords. In an essay, describe how one of the proposed alternatives works.

7. **Writing the Research Paper.** How safe are your mobile devices like an iPhone or an Android? Research the problem. One expert, for example, notes, "All phones can be infected, no matter what operating system they run." In an essay, describe what might be done to make your mobile devices more secure. Be sure to document your sources.

For Further Study

Focusing on Grammar and Writing. Perlroth uses the dash (—) a number of times in the essay. How and why does she use that particular mark of punctuation?

Working Together. As homework, divide into groups and have each group spend some time exploring your school's resources for students with infected computers. How does your school protect its own computer system? Can you download an antivirus software for free? What online resources are available? Where on campus can you find help?

Seeing Other Modes at Work. The essay has persuasive elements as well, in that you are being urged to take these steps to avoid dangerous consequences.

Tiny Masters: An Artful Trick to Writing the Personal Essay

SHERRY SIMPSON

Sherry Simpson is a professor in the Department of Creative Writing and Literary Arts at the University of Alaska, Anchorage. She also teaches in the Rainier Writing Workshop, a low-residency M.F.A. program at Pacific Lutheran University. Simpson grew up in Juneau, Alaska, and attended the University of Alaska, Fairbanks, where she studied biology and journalism. She has published widely. This essay appeared in 2012 in the online journal Brevity.

__On Writing:__ Commenting on teaching writing, Simpson observed: "It's important to discover the possibilities in . . . drafts, and as *a mentor I like pointing to the places where doors open and the writer hasn't stepped through yet. My job is to ask questions. . . . I work best with students who are willing to ask questions of themselves rather than settling for what memory or opinion or ideology announces. With more experienced writers, I like focusing on the process of revision, from the sentence level to the driving ideas."*

Before Reading

Connecting: Before you read the essay, how would you define a "personal essay"?

Anticipating: As you read, does her definition of a "personal essay" seem different from what you expected?

1   **W**e've gone around the table introducing ourselves, and now comes the awkward moment when I sound a bit like a door-to-door salesman peddling an unfamiliar doohickey that costs too much and nobody really needs anyway.

2   "What is a personal essay?" I'll begin. Students start shifting uneasily in their seats. It's that word, essay. So scholarly, so stiff, so self-important. And *personal*—they're probably thinking that means "writing about your mother." I hurry through my notes.

3   "Let's not talk about what a personal essay is," I say. "Let's talk about what it can do." It opens a window into someone else's life and sensibility, I'll explain. Reveals something about the world that we didn't know. Engages us with a distinctive voice. Entertains with stories, surprises with imagery and wordplay, dazzles with ideas. Conveys a deeper meaning.

4   Now I can almost see thought balloons forming over their heads. *Meaning?* How are they supposed to find meaning? They don't even know what they'll write about yet. I have no idea what they'll write about. Now we're all feeling slightly nervous about the whole enterprise.

5   "Fortunately, we're not actually going to learn to be essayists," I'll announce. "We're going to become tiny masters."

6   That's when we can relax and start writing. Because it turns out—and this is true 100 percent of the time—we're all tiny masters of *something*.

7   The notion of tiny masters comes from author and *New Yorker* writer Susan Orlean, who once explained that she's most interested in writing about people who are masters of their "tiny domains." (She meant orchid thieves, 10-year-old boys, female bullfighters, Maui surfer girls, and The Shaggs, among others.) Adapting her approach to personal essays can help writers discover a rich subject near at hand—something they already know a lot about, something that interests them. It helps shift the focus from writing exclusively about the self to writing about knowledge, ideas and processes. As writers explore their mastery on the page, they instinctively begin playing with structure and making connections they never knew existed. Meaning begins emerging naturally from their drafts, pointing the way to future revisions.

8   This is how it works:

8a   • Make a list of 10 things of which you're a master. Include talents, skills, hobbies, qualities of character. I've created many lists over the years, and they surprise me every time: Making enchilada sauce. Building fires. Finding beach glass. Crossing rivers. Writing thank you notes. Collecting maps. Procrastinating. Teaching tricks to my dog.

8b   • Choose a mastery that appeals and free-write about it. Describe how to do it, when you learned it, what you accomplish, where you do it—whatever comes to mind.

8c   • Now write about a person connected with this mastery. Maybe it's the person who taught you how to do it, someone you've done it for, or someone who discouraged you from doing it. Include details that capture the person's personality or mannerisms.

8d   • Next, write about a particular scene or event that involves your mastery and/or your person. Look for opportunities to add dialogue and setting.

9   By this point, writers usually have created a rough but promising first draft, even if it's still in pieces. They've chosen something that's important to them without worrying about whether it's important enough. Stories, recollections, incidents and ideas start coalescing around their subject. Interrogating the draft reveals other connections and possibilities: Why this topic? What don't I know? What information or background would enlarge the story? Why do I even like doing this? What is this about? What is this about *really?*

10   The answer to that last question helps reveal meaning—not meaning that's imposed artificially, but meaning that surfaces as the story unfolds. Sarah realizes that she's not really writing about making pies. She's writing about breaking rules. Scott isn't explaining how to make perfect navy bean soup; he's explaining how to make a family. Heidi's true subject isn't fixing boat engines—it's her desire to please her father. Kellen is not just describing his pleasure in playing the drums at high school; he's reconciling himself to loving something he'll never be great at doing.

11   Once I've tricked students into drafting a personal essay, we can focus on the finer points of tightening sentences, incorporating reflection, and crafting strong openings and closings. Does the structure they instinctively chose suit the subject? We'll investigate alternatives. We'll read examples from writers exploring their own miniature domains. We'll figure out how to layer meaning by strengthening images and honing language.

12   By the time students are immersed in heavy revision, there will be no need to point out the obvious: They're all becoming tiny masters of the personal essay. ■

QUESTIONS ON SUBJECT AND PURPOSE

1. What is a "tiny master"?
2. According to Simpson, what can a personal essay "do"?
3. Ultimately, what Simpson is trying to uncover is the "meaning" that lies behind this mastery. What kind of "meaning" is she looking for?

QUESTIONS ON STRATEGY AND AUDIENCE

1. Why might Simpson indent paragraphs 8a through 8d?
2. Is there any part of her description of the process where you would like more explanation about how to do this?
3. To whom does Simpson seem to be writing?

QUESTIONS ON VOCABULARY AND STYLE

1. What is a "doohickey" (paragraph 1)?
2. Simpson uses contractions freely in her writing. What is a contraction? What is the effect created by using them? How does that fit the tone of the essay?
3. Be prepared to define the following words: *coalescing* (paragraph 9) and *honing* (11).

WRITING SUGGESTIONS

1. **Doing a Critical Analysis.** How would you characterize the tone of the essay? What elements in the writing and word choice create that tone? Is the tone appropriate for the subject?
2. **Journaling or Blogging.** Following the advice of Simpson, first make a list of 10 things of which you are a master.
3. **Practicing in a Paragraph.** Connect that mastery to a person who was, for you, connected in some way to it.
4. **Writing the Personal Essay.** Turn your paragraph into an essay focusing around scenes or events that involve both you and that person. As she suggests, describes the setting and use some dialogue.
5. **Finding Reading Connections.** The section in this text on "How to Write an Essay" offers advice on how to choose a topic of your own. Using what Simpson outlines, write an essay in which you incorporate and explain her ideas. Think of that essay as something that could then be added to that "How to Write" section.
6. **Exploring Links Online.** What is the most appropriate type of writing for a freshman English course? Not everyone agrees that is should be personal essays. Using online sources, describe another type of writing that should be used, instead.
7. **Writing the Research Paper.** What types of writing assignments would be best for high school students in order to prepare them for college-level work? Research the problem and in an essay with documentation present your findings.

For Further Study

Focusing on Grammar and Writing. The paragraphing in the essay seems a little unusual. Look at each of the paragraphs. What seems to be the rationale behind each paragraph?

Working Together. Divide into small groups and review the "personal essay" writing suggestions in any one of the chapters in this text. How many of the suggestions are similar to what Simpson is suggesting? Or is there another sense of the term "personal essay" that is reflected in those topics?

Seeing Other Modes at Work. The essay has elements of both definition (this is what a "personal essay" is) and persuasion.

My Daily Dives in the Dumpster

LARS EIGHNER

Born in 1948, Lars Eighner grew up in Houston, Texas. He attended the University of Texas at Austin but dropped out before graduation to do social work. In the mid-1980s, he lost his job as an attendant at a mental institution, which launched him on a three-year nightmare as a homeless person, with his dog, Lizbeth, as his companion. He later reworked these experiences as a book, Travels with Lizbeth *(1993), the final manuscript of which was written on a personal computer that Eighner found in a dumpster.*

On Writing: *Advice from Eighner's website: "The best thing you can do for your writing is to learn to revise effectively. Sure, some natural geniuses may never have to revise a word, but the number of writers who consider themselves geniuses must outnumber the true geniuses by a factor of a thousand. And yes, some writers who practice revision for a long time eventually learn to avoid most mistakes so that their first drafts do not need much revision. But everyone else needs to revise and revise and revise. Putting a work through a spelling checker or a grammar checker is not revision. . . . Revision means changing words and phrases and sometimes changing whole sentences and paragraphs. Almost everyone's writing needs this kind of revision."*

Before Reading

Connecting: If you came across someone "diving" into a dumpster, what assumptions would you be likely to make about that person?

Anticipating: One would hope that few of Eighner's readers will ever have to dive into dumpsters to survive. What then can readers learn from his essay?

1   **I** began Dumpster diving about a year before I became homeless.

2   I prefer the term "scavenging" and use the word "scrounging" when I mean to be obscure. I have heard people, evidently meaning to be polite, use the word "foraging," but I prefer to reserve that word for gathering nuts and berries and such, which I do also, according to the season and opportunity.

3   I like the frankness of the word "scavenging." I live from the refuse of others. I am a scavenger. I think it a sound and honorable niche, although if I could I would naturally prefer to live the comfortable consumer life, perhaps—and only perhaps—as a slightly less wasteful consumer owing to what I have learned as a scavenger.

4   Except for jeans, all my clothes come from Dumpsters. Boom boxes, candles, bedding, toilet paper, medicine, books, a typewriter, a virgin male love doll, change sometimes amounting to many dollars: All came from Dumpsters. And, yes, I eat from Dumpsters too.

5   There are a predictable series of stages that a person goes through in learning to scavenge. At first the new scavenger is filled with disgust and self-loathing. He is ashamed of being seen and may lurk around trying to duck behind things, or he may try to dive at night. (In fact, this is unnecessary, since most people instinctively look away from scavengers.)

6   Every grain of rice seems to be a maggot. Everything seems to stink. The scavenger can wipe the egg yolk off the found can, but he cannot erase the stigma of eating garbage from his mind.

7   This stage passes with experience. The scavenger finds a pair of running shoes that fit and look and smell brand-new. He finds a pocket calculator in perfect working order. He finds pristine ice cream, still frozen, more than he can eat or keep. He begins to understand: People do throw away perfectly good stuff, a lot of perfectly good stuff.

8   At this stage he may become lost and never recover. All the Dumpster divers I have known come to the point of trying to acquire everything they touch. Why not take it, they reason, it is all free. This is, of course, hopeless, and most divers come to realize that they must restrict themselves to items of relatively immediate utility.

9   The finding of objects is becoming something of an urban art. Even respectable, employed people will sometimes find something tempting sticking out of a Dumpster or standing beside one. Quite a number of people, not all of them of the bohemian type, are willing to brag that they found this or that piece in the trash.

10   But eating from Dumpsters is the thing that separates the dilettanti from the professionals. Eating safely involves three principles: using the senses and common sense to evaluate the condition of the found materials; knowing the Dumpsters of a given area and checking them regularly; and seeking always to answer the question, Why was this discarded?

11   Perhaps everyone who has a kitchen and a regular supply of groceries has, at one time or another, eaten half a sandwich before discovering mold on the bread, or has gotten a mouthful of milk before realizing the milk had

turned. Nothing of the sort is likely to happen to a Dumpster diver because he is constantly reminded that most food is discarded for a reason.

12   Yet perfectly good food can be found in Dumpsters. Canned goods, for example, turn up fairly often in the Dumpsters I frequent. All except the most phobic people would be willing to eat from a can even if it came from a Dumpster. I have few qualms about dry foods such as crackers, cookies, cereal, chips, and pasta if they are free of visible contaminates and still dry and crisp. Raw fruits and vegetables with intact skins seem perfectly safe to me, excluding, of course, the obviously rotten. Many are discarded for minor imperfections that can be pared away. Chocolate is often discarded only because it has become discolored as the cocoa butter de-emulsified.

13   I began scavenging by pulling pizzas out of the Dumpster behind a pizza delivery shop. In general, prepared food requires caution, but in this case I knew what time the shop closed and went to the Dumpster as soon as the last of the help left.

14   Because the workers at these places are usually inexperienced, pizzas are often made with the wrong topping, baked incorrectly, or refused on delivery for being cold. The products to be discarded are boxed up because inventory is kept by counting boxes: A boxed pizza can be written off; an unboxed pizza does not exist. So I had a steady supply of fresh, sometimes warm pizza.

15   The area I frequent is inhabited by many affluent college students. I am not here by chance; the Dumpsters are very rich. Students throw out many good things, including food, particularly at the end of the semester and before and after breaks. I find it advantageous to keep an eye on the academic calendar.

16   A typical discard is a half jar of peanut butter—though nonorganic peanut butter does not require refrigeration and is unlikely to spoil in any reasonable time. Occasionally I find a cheese with a spot of mold, which, of course, I just pare off, and because it is obvious why the cheese was discarded, I treat it with less suspicion than an apparently perfect cheese found in similar circumstances. One of my favorite finds is yogurt—often discarded, still sealed, when the expiration date has passed—because it will keep for several days, even in warm weather.

17   I avoid ethnic foods I am unfamiliar with. If I do not know what it is supposed to look or smell like when it is good, I cannot be certain I will be able to tell if it is bad.

18   No matter how careful I am I still get dysentery at least once a month, oftener in warm weather. I do not want to paint too romantic a picture. Dumpster diving has serious drawbacks as a way of life.

19   Though I have a proprietary feeling about my Dumpsters, I don't mind my direct competitors, other scavengers, as much as I hate the sodacan scroungers.

20   I have tried scrounging aluminum cans with an able-bodied companion, and afoot we could make no more than a few dollars a day. I can extract the necessities of life from the Dumpsters directly with far less effort than would be required to accumulate the equivalent value in aluminum.

Can scroungers, then, are people who *must* have small amounts of cash—mostly drug addicts and winos.

21   I do not begrudge them the cans, but can scroungers tend to tear up the Dumpsters, littering the area and mixing the contents. There are precious few courtesies among scavengers, but it is a common practice to set aside surplus items: pairs of shoes, clothing, canned goods, and such. A true scavenger hates to see good stuff go to waste, and what he cannot use he leaves in good condition in plain sight. Can scroungers lay waste to everything in their path and will stir one of a pair of good shoes to the bottom of a Dumpster to be lost or ruined in the muck. They become so specialized that they can see only cans and earn my contempt by passing up change, canned goods, and readily hockable items.

22   Can scroungers will even go through individual garbage cans, something I have never seen a scavenger do. Going through individual garbage cans without spreading litter is almost impossible, and litter is likely to reduce the public's tolerance of scavenging. But my strongest reservation about going through individual garbage cans is that this seems to me a very personal kind of invasion, one to which I would object if I were a homeowner.

23   Though Dumpsters seem somehow less personal than garbage cans, they still contain bank statements, bills, correspondence, pill bottles, and other sensitive information. I avoid trying to draw conclusions about the people who dump in the Dumpsters I frequent. I think it would be unethical to do so, although I know many people will find the idea of scavenger ethics too funny for words.

24   Occasionally a find tells a story. I once found a small paper bag containing some unused condoms, several partial tubes of flavored sexual lubricant, a partially used compact of birth control pills, and the torn pieces of a picture of a young man. Clearly, the woman was through with him and planning to give up sex altogether.

25   Dumpster things are often sad—abandoned teddy bears, shredded wedding albums, despaired-of sales kits. I find diaries and journals. College students also discard their papers; I am horrified to discover the kind of paper that now merits an A in an undergraduate course.

26   Dumpster diving is outdoor work, often surprisingly pleasant. It is not entirely predictable; things of interest turn up every day, and some days there are finds of great value. I am always very pleased when I can turn up exactly the thing I most wanted to find. Yet in spite of the element of chance, scavenging, more than most other pursuits, tends to yield returns in some proportion to the effort and intelligence brought to bear.

27   I think of scavenging as a modern form of self-reliance. After ten years of government service, where everything is geared to the lowest common denominator, I find work that rewards initiative and effort refreshing. Certainly I would be happy to have a sinecure again, but I am not heart-broken to be without one.

28   I find from the experience of scavenging two rather deep lessons. The first is to take what I can use and let the rest go. I have come to think that

there is no value in the abstract. A thing I cannot use or make useful, perhaps by trading, has no value, however fine or rare it may be. (I mean useful in the broad sense—some art, for example, I would think valuable.)

29   The second lesson is the transience of material being. I do not suppose that ideas are immortal, but certainly they are longer-lived than material objects.

30   The things I find in Dumpsters, the love letters and rag dolls of so many lives, remind me of this lesson. Many times in my travels I have lost everything but the clothes on my back. Now I hardly pick up a thing without envisioning the time I will cast it away. This, I think, is a healthy state of mind. Almost everything I have now has already been cast out at least once, proving that what I own is valueless to someone.

31   I find that my desire to grab for the gaudy bauble has been largely sated. I think this is an attitude I share with the very wealthy—we both know there is plenty more where whatever we have came from. Between us are the rat-race millions who have confounded their selves with the objects they grasp and who nightly scavenge the cable channels looking for they know not what.

32   I am sorry for them.   ∎

QUESTIONS ON SUBJECT AND PURPOSE

1. Is the subject of Eighner's essay simply how to "dive" into a dumpster? What other points does he make?
2. A substantial part of the essay deals with scavenging for food. Why does Eighner devote so much space to this?
3. What larger or more general lesson or truth does Eighner see in his experiences? For example, for whom does Eighner say he feels sorry at the end of the essay?

QUESTIONS ON STRATEGY AND AUDIENCE

1. In what ways does the essay use process as a writing strategy?
2. What are the "predictable stages" that a scavenger goes through?
3. What assumptions does Eighner make about his audience?

QUESTIONS ON VOCABULARY AND STYLE

1. Why does Eighner prefer the term *scavenging* to a more ambiguous or better-sounding term?
2. In what way is Eighner's final sentence ironic? Why might he choose to make it a separate paragraph?
3. Be prepared to define the following words: *niche* (paragraph 3), *stigma* (6), *pristine* (7), *bohemian* (9), *dilettanti* (10), *phobic* (12), *qualms* (12), *de-emulsified* (12), *affluent* (15), *proprietary* (19), *sinecure* (27), *transience* (29), *gaudy* (31), *bauble* (31), *sated* (31).

WRITING SUGGESTIONS

1. **Doing a Critical Analysis.** Eighner did "dumpster dive," but the essay also uses that activity as a metaphor. As a metaphor, what can this teach us about our values and activities? Analyze how Eighner uses that metaphor in the essay to say something that has universal application.

2. **Journaling or Blogging.** Suppose that suddenly you found yourself without a job or financial support from your family. Plan out in an ordered sequence what you would do to deal with the situation.

3. **Practicing in a Paragraph.** In a world in which many Americans, including college graduates, can find only low-paying jobs with no benefits, what advice would you offer to a young high school student today? Respond in a paragraph.

4. **Writing the Personal Essay.** What are your goals, objectives, aspirations in life? What are you doing right now to try to achieve those goals? In an essay, examine your directions and actions.

5. **Finding Reading Connections.** Look at the chart of "The 30 Occupations with the Largest Employment Growth, 2006–2016" in Chapter 9. In light of those statistics, what advice would you offer to your peers who are now in school? Or do you see those statistics as irrelevant in making career decisions? Explain.

6. **Exploring Links Online.** Using online sources, compile a list of realistic ways in which you and your classmates might help the homeless in your community.

7. **Writing the Research Paper.** As advice for those who are unemployed, prepare a guide to the resources available from local, state, and federal agencies. What steps need to be taken and in what order? Be sure to document your sources, including interviews.

For Further Study

Focusing on Grammar and Writing. Eighner uses both the semicolon (;) and the colon (:). On the basis of how he uses them in the essay, write a series of rules for the proper use of each mark.

Working Together. On his website, Eighner answers a student who asked him, "As a college student what advice could you give me to consume less and to not waste as much as the average American?" Working in small groups, come up with some possible advice for that student (and maybe for yourself).

Seeing Other Modes at Work. The essay has persuasive elements. If it were turned into a persuasive essay, what could be used and what might have to be deleted, changed, or expanded?

Revision and Life: Take It from the Top—Again

NORA EPHRON

Nora Ephron (1941–2012) graduated from Wellesley College and worked as a journalist and columnist for the New York Post, New York Magazine, *and* Esquire. *She was also a successful screenplay writer and director whose credits include* Sleepless in Seattle *(1993),* You've Got Mail *(1998), and* Julie and Julia *(2009). "Revision and Life," written in response to an invitation to participate in this textbook, was originally published in* The New York Times Book Review.

> **On Writing:** *When asked about the autobiographical influences of her first novel, Ephron replied: "I've always written about my life. That's how I grew up. 'Take notes. Everything is copy.' All that stuff my mother [also a writer] said to us."*

Before Reading

Connecting: When it comes to writing, what does the word *revision* suggest to you?

Anticipating: When Ephron observes, "A gift for revision may be a developmental stage," what does she mean?

1   I have been asked to write something for a textbook that is meant to teach college students something about writing and revision. I am happy to do this because I believe in revision. I have also been asked to save the early drafts of whatever I write, presumably to show these students the actual process of revision. This too I am happy to do. On the other hand, I suspect that there is just so much you can teach college students about revision; a gift for revision may be a developmental stage—like a 2-year-old's sudden ability to place one block on top of another—that comes along somewhat later, in one's mid-20s, say; most people may not be particularly good at it, or even interested in it, until then.

2   When I was in college, I revised nothing. I wrote out my papers in longhand, typed them up and turned them in. It would never have crossed my mind that what I had produced was only a first draft and that I had more work to do; the idea was to get to the end, and once you had got to the end you were finished. The same thinking, I might add, applied in life: I went pell-mell through my four years in college without a thought about whether I ought to do anything differently; the idea was to get to the end—to get out of school and become a journalist.

3 　　　Which I became, in fairly short order. I learned as a journalist to revise on deadline. I learned to write an article a paragraph at a time—and I arrived at the kind of writing and revising I do, which is basically a kind of typing and retyping. I am a great believer in this technique for the simple reason that I type faster than the wind. What I generally do is to start an article and get as far as I can—sometimes no farther in than a sentence or two—before running out of steam, ripping the piece of paper from the typewriter and starting all over again. I type over and over until I have got the beginning of the piece to the point where I am happy with it. I then am ready to plunge into the body of the article itself. This plunge usually requires something known as a transition. I approach a transition by completely retyping the opening of the article leading up to it in the hope that the ferocious speed of my typing will somehow catapult me into the next section of the piece. This does not work—what in fact catapults me into the next section is a concrete thought about what the next section ought to be about—but until I have the thought the typing keeps me busy, and keeps me from feeling something known as blocked.

4 　　　Typing and retyping as if you know where you're going is a version of what therapists tell you to do when they suggest that you try changing from the outside in—that if you can't master the total commitment to whatever change you want to make, you can at least do all the extraneous things connected with it, which make it that much easier to get there. I was 25 years old the first time a therapist suggested that I try changing from the outside in. In those days, I used to spend quite a lot of time lying awake at night wondering what I should have said earlier in the evening and revising my lines. I mention this not just because it's a way of illustrating that a gift for revision is practically instinctive, but also (once again) because it's possible that a genuine ability at it doesn't really come into play until one is older—or at least older than 25, when it seemed to me that all that was required in my life and my work was the chance to change a few lines.

5 　　　In my 30's, I began to write essays, one a month for *Esquire* magazine, and I am not exaggerating when I say that in the course of writing a short essay—1,500 words, that's only six double-spaced typewritten pages—I often used 300 or 400 pieces of typing paper, so often did I type and retype and catapult and recatapult myself, sometimes on each retyping moving not even a sentence farther from the spot I had reached the last time through. At the same time, though, I was polishing what I had already written: as I struggled with the middle of the article, I kept putting the beginning through the typewriter; as I approached the ending, the middle got its turn. (This is a kind of polishing that the word processor all but eliminates, which is why I don't use one. Word processors make it possible for a writer to change the sentences that clearly need changing without having to retype the rest, but I believe that you can't always tell whether a sentence needs work until it rises up in revolt against your fingers as you retype it.) By the time I had produced what you might call a first draft—an entire article with a beginning, middle and end—the beginning was in more like 45th draft, the middle in 20th, and the end was almost newborn. For this reason, the beginnings of my essays

are considerably better written than the ends, although I like to think no one ever notices this but me.

6   As I learned the essay form, writing became harder for me. I was finding a personal style, a voice if you will, a way of writing that looked chatty and informal. That wasn't the hard part—the hard part was that having found a voice, I had to work hard month to month not to seem as if I were repeating myself. At this point in this essay it will not surprise you to learn that the same sort of thing was operating in my life. I don't mean that my life had become harder—but that it was becoming clear that I had many more choices than had occurred to me when I was marching through my 20's. I no longer lost sleep over what I should have said. Not that I didn't care—it was just that I had moved to a new plane of late-night anxiety: I now wondered what I should have done. Whole areas of possible revision opened before me. What should I have done instead? What could I have done? What if I hadn't done it the way I did? What if I had a chance to do it over? What if I had a chance to do it over as a different person? These were the sorts of questions that kept me awake and led me into fiction, which at the very least (the level at which I practice it) is a chance to rework the events of your life so that you give the illusion of being the intelligence at the center of it, simultaneously managing to slip in all the lines that occurred to you later. Fiction, I suppose, is the ultimate shot at revision.

7   Now I am in my 40's and I write screenplays. Screenplays—if they are made into movies—are essentially collaborations, and movies are not a writer's medium, we all know this, and I don't want to dwell on the craft of screenwriting except insofar as it relates to revision. Because the moment you stop work on a script seems to be determined not by whether you think the draft is good but simply by whether shooting is about to begin: if it is, you get to call your script a final draft; and if it's not, you can always write another revision. This might seem to be a hateful way to live, but the odd thing is that it's somehow comforting; as long as you're revising, the project isn't dead. And by the same token, neither are you.

8   It was, as it happens, while thinking about all this one recent sleepless night that I figured out how to write this particular essay. I say "recent" in order to give a sense of immediacy and energy to the preceding sentence, but the truth is that I am finishing this article four months after the sleepless night in question, and the letter asking me to write it, from George Miller of the University of Delaware, arrived almost two years ago, so for all I know Mr. Miller has managed to assemble his textbook on revision without me.

9   Oh, well. That's how it goes when you start thinking about revision. That's the danger of it, in fact. You can spend so much time thinking about how to switch things around that the main event has passed you by. But it doesn't matter. Because by the time you reach middle age, you want more than anything for things not to come to an end; and as long as you're still revising, they don't.

10   I'm sorry to end so morbidly—dancing as I am around the subject of death—but there are advantages to it. For one thing, I have managed

to move fairly effortlessly and logically from the beginning of this piece through the middle and to the end. And for another, I am able to close with an exhortation, something I rarely manage, which is this: Revise now, before it's too late. ■

QUESTIONS ON SUBJECT AND PURPOSE

1. For Ephron, how are revision and life connected?
2. Why is fiction the "ultimate shot at revision" (paragraph 6)?
3. Is the essay about how to revise or about something else?

QUESTIONS ON STRATEGY AND AUDIENCE

1. How does Ephron structure her essay? What principle of order does she follow?
2. What might Ephron mean by her final sentence ("Revise now, before it's too late")?
3. It would have been a simple matter for Ephron to omit the references to this textbook (paragraphs 1 and 8). The *New York Times* audience, for example, would not be interested in knowing these details. Why might she have chosen to include these references in her essay?

QUESTIONS ON VOCABULARY AND STYLE

1. Have you ever heard the phrase "take it from the top—again"? In what context is it usually used? What might such a figure of speech be called?
2. Ephron refers to her strategy of retyping as a way of "catapulting" herself into the next section. Where does the verb *catapult* come from? What does it suggest?
3. Be prepared to define the following words: *pell-mell* (paragraph 2), *extraneous* (4), *exhortation* (10).

WRITING SUGGESTIONS

1. **Doing a Critical Analysis.** Ephron writes about finding a style or voice that sounds "chatty and informal" (paragraph 6). How would you describe her voice in the essay? What devices help create that tone?
2. **Journaling or Blogging.** What obstacles do you face when you try to revise something that you have written? Add to your list as you write each paper.
3. **Practicing in a Paragraph.** Formulate a thesis about Ephron's process of revision as she describes it. In a paragraph, support that thesis with appropriate evidence from the essay.
4. **Writing the Personal Essay.** On the basis of your own experience as a student writer, argue for or against *requiring* revision in a college writing course.
5. **Finding Reading Connections.** How would Zinsser and Dr. Brock in "The Transaction" (Chapter 5) react to Ephron's writing and revising habits? Compare the three writers.

6. **Exploring Links Online.** Want to know more about Ephron's writing habits? Using online sources, locate additional comments and advice that Ephron made about writing. On the basis of your research, sum up Ephron's advice about writing.

7. **Writing the Research Paper.** What role does revision play in the writing process of faculty and staff at your college or university? Interview a range of people and then, using notes and quotations from those interviews, write an essay about how these writers go about revising their writing. Be sure to include full documentation.

For Further Study

Focusing on Grammar and Writing. Information inserted into a sentence can be set off by commas, parentheses, or dashes. In paragraphs 5 and 6, Ephron uses all three marks. Do you see a reason for why she chose to punctuate each insertion or addition as she does?

Working Together. Working in small groups, discuss if and how each of you "revises" an essay. Are you willing to make major changes? Do you see revision as just changing words and correcting punctuation?

Seeing Other Modes at Work. Ephron uses division to structure the middle of her essay.

The Internet: The 10% Solution

RICHARD N. BOLLES

Richard Bolles wrote What Color Is Your Parachute? A Practical Manual for Job-Hunters and Career-Changers, *first published commercially in 1972 and now revised annually. Over the years,* What Color *has sold over 10 million copies, making it the best-selling book about searching for a job ever published. Translated into 20 languages, it is used in 26 countries throughout the world.*

*   **On Writing:** Commenting on his writing, Bolles observes, "I write as I speak. I use italics, pauses, numbers, words, and spaces between paragraphs in inconsistent ways throughout to convey the weight I intend for sentences, or the speed with which a particular sentence is read. In other words, I break rules, in order to serve a higher purpose: easy reading."*

Before Reading

Connecting: If someone asked you right now, "when you graduate, how do you plan to look for a job?", what would be your answer?

Anticipating: As the title suggests, Bolles is writing about using the Internet as a tool in a job search. According to Bolles, how important should the Internet be in anyone's job-search strategy?

1 **A** recent (3/27/09) NIELSEN Company study found that in the U.S. the average adult is spending eight and a half hours a day in front of a screen—be it a computer screen, cell phone screen, TV screen, DVDs, sports channels, video games, or whatever.

2 So naturally, when we are out of work, our instinct is to move to a screen for help: in this case, our computer screen and the Internet. In the U.S., at least three out of every four adults have access to the Internet.

3 How much does this help us find work? Statistics change over time, but past studies have shown that this results in a job for 10 out of every 100 job-hunters who try it. The other 90 have to turn elsewhere to locate those vacancies that do exist.

4 Still, if it works for you, you will thank your lucky stars for the Internet. So, I call this "the 10% Solution." It solves job-hunters' problems in 10% of cases; therefore it deserves 10% of every job-hunter's *time*, just in case. But not more than that. Unless you like beating your head against a brick wall.

5 Let's rehearse what we as job-hunters can find on the Internet:

6 The Internet is a place where employers go, to list *some* of their vacancies, but by no means *all*.

7 The Internet is a place where job-hunters go, to find those vacancies, or to hunt for employers regardless of known vacancies. It is also the place where job-hunters list their own availability, in case some bright-eyed employer is prowling the Internet—and notices.

8 And for completeness let us add: the Internet is also a place for *advice, career counseling, testing, researching* careers, industries, salaries, companies, or individuals who have the power to hire you, and actually *making contact* with people who may be able to do you some good (*networking*).

9 In this connection, I should mention that on the Internet there are free guides to the entire job-hunt process. In addition to my own website, **jobhuntersbible.com**, there are six sites I recommend as most comprehensive and helpful:

10 **www.job-hunt.org** run by Susan Joyce.

11 **www.jobstar.org** run by Mary Ellen Mort.

12 **www.rileyguide.com** run by Margaret F. Dikel.

13 **www.quintcareers.com** run by Dr. Randall Hansen.

14 **www.cacareerzone.org** run by the California Career Resource Network. Once you are on the home page, it gives you a choice between running the site under Text, Graphic, or Flash. Choose Graphic; I ran Flash, but it had serious hiccups at the time I tried it. Still, this site has nice self-tests, and much else. So, run it under Graphic, if Flash fails.

15 Now we turn to job-search.

16 **What should I know before I start my job-search on the Internet?**

17 In a word, *your target.* Many job-hunters "network" without any thought to what they're networking for. And when nothing works out, month after month, they express bewilderment.

18   "But I've been networking, just like everyone says I should!" they cry. I look at them, incredulous. "To what end?" I reply.

19   They wander like rudderless ships, drifting down the coast, carried briefly into any harbor they encounter, before being carried again out to sea. They have no destination; there is no city they are trying to reach. They're relying on plain blind Luck. *"Maybe I'll stumble across something that sounds interesting."* Yes, maybe you will. But most likely, you won't.

20   Having no clear target is the reason so many people are out of work during this brutal economic time.

21   So, before you go on the Internet define a target, a destination you are trying to reach. Write it down, and keep it at your elbow:

1. What kind of work are you looking for? What job-title specifically? *on or off the Internet.*
2. What industry or field are you looking for? *on or off the Internet.*
3. What section of the country are you looking for? *on or off the Internet.*
4. What kind of salary are you looking for? *on or off the Internet.*

22   If you can't answer these questions with words, close your eyes and try to visualize what kind of work would give you the greatest delight to do. Sometimes a picture is worth a thousand words. As they say.

23 **Okay, then what sites should I go to, to hunt for whatever vacancies employers have decided to post on the Internet?**

1. Omnibus Search Engines. These are sites which search for all the job listings on the Internet, thus saving you from having to go and visit each job-board, one by one.
   Examples: **Simplyhired.com**. This site claims to have over 5 million job listings, worldwide, as of 3/31/09.
   Indeed.com. This site claims to discover and index over 50 million jobs per year.
2. The Famous Job Boards.
   Examples: careerbuilder.com
   monster.com
   hotjobs.yahoo.com
3. Community Bulletin Boards.
   Example: craigslist.org
4. Niche Sites for Jobs in Specific Fields or Industries.
   To turn these up, for the industry that interests you, put the name of the industry and the word "jobs" into Google's search engine.

24   If you have no idea what industry you are hunting for, but you do know the basic building blocks of the job you are seeking, then put into your favorite search engine, such as Google, your skills, and field of interest (in one or three words) and see what industries these point to. Be specific. Not just your favorite skills— "writing researching speaking" —but skills and fields (for example) "writing renewable energy researching." That sort of narrowing down.

Example of a niche site: **dice.com**. This is for tech or IT jobs.

5. Social Networking Sites. Job-hunters are paying a lot of attention to these particular sites these days, inasmuch as over five million unemployed people are now 'networking': trying to meet as many people as they possibly can, because—well, that's what they've been told to do. Networking is 'hot.' That doesn't necessarily mean it will lead to a job.

25   These sites, like all the previous ones, may turn up jobs; but they particularly excel at turning up names of people. These sites help you look for people in your favorite industry; they may know of vacancies not being advertised as yet (thus comprising the so-called "hidden job market").

26   Anyway, if these sites have jobs, here is where they can be found:

27   **LinkedIn.com/jobs.** LinkedIn claims to be "the" professional network on the Web; certainly it is the most talked about. It has over 35 million members, in 170 industries, at this writing. 'Professional' doesn't mean white collar necessarily. Construction workers, for example, list themselves on this site; construction companies know that, and come here searching for them—when there's work to be had. There are similar sites to LinkedIn, notably **plaxo.com.** A complete list can be found at http://bit.ly/SC4l in Wikipedia.

28   **Twitterjobsearch.com.** Twitter has at least 6 million "users" who send "tweets." (Only 140 characters or spaces at a time, as you probably know.) Twistoridesktop.com allows you to search Twitter with keywords—or clusters of them—of your own choosing. Exectweets.com follows top business leaders; you can search by field or industry. WeFollow.com drills down into Twitter, and lets you search categories to see who's "twittering" from that category or industry. And there is also Twitdir.com; dir is short for "directory." Incidentally, TweetDeck.com is a wonderful way to organize your social contacts on the Internet.

29   **Jobs.MySpace.com.** MySpace has over 106 million members worldwide. It currently has the largest U.S. base among all the social networking sites, but that's predicted to change by January 2010, when Facebook will likely surpass it.

30   **Facebook.com.** There are over 20 applications you can use within Facebook to find a job; a nice list of them is to be found at

31   http://blog.bincsearch.com/?p=1108; Facebook currently has over 42 million U.S. members, over 175 million worldwide.

32   There! There are the five kinds of sites that you should explore, if you're looking for vacancies advertised on the Internet by employers.

33 Why doesn't the Internet work better at finding jobs?

34 It mostly has to do with the fact that job-hunters and employers like to look for each other, in almost exactly opposite ways. Resumes and the Internet are high on a job-hunter's preferred list; not necessarily on an employer's. You can see this from the following diagram:

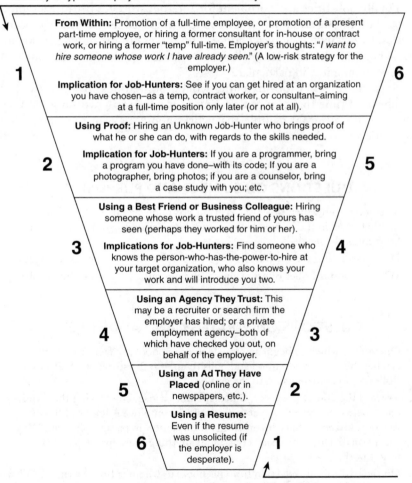

Many If Not Most Employers Hunt for Job-Hunters in the Exact Opposite Way from How Most Job-Hunters Hunt for Them

The Way a Typical Employer Prefers to Fill a Vacancy

1 / **6**
From Within: Promotion of a full-time employee, or promotion of a present part-time employee, or hiring a former consultant for in-house or contract work, or hiring a former "temp" full-time. Employer's thoughts: "*I want to hire someone whose work I have already seen.*" (A low-risk strategy for the employer.)

Implication for Job-Hunters: See if you can get hired at an organization you have chosen—as a temp, contract worker, or consultant—aiming at a full-time position only later (or not at all).

2 / **5**
Using Proof: Hiring an Unknown Job-Hunter who brings proof of what he or she can do, with regards to the skills needed.

Implication for Job-Hunters: If you are a programmer, bring a program you have done—with its code; If you are a photographer, bring photos; if you are a counselor, bring a case study with you; etc.

3 / **4**
Using a Best Friend or Business Colleague: Hiring someone whose work a trusted friend of yours has seen (perhaps they worked for him or her).

Implications for Job-Hunters: Find someone who knows the person-who-has-the-power-to-hire at your target organization, who also knows your work and will introduce you two.

4 / **3**
Using an Agency They Trust: This may be a recruiter or search firm the employer has hired; or a private employment agency—both of which have checked you out, on behalf of the employer.

5 / **2**
Using an Ad They Have Placed (online or in newspapers, etc.).

6 / **1**
Using a Resume: Even if the resume was unsolicited (if the employer is desperate).

The Way a Typical Job-Hunter Prefers to Fill a Vacancy

35 Besides this ironic fact illustrated by the above diagram, there is another.

36   When an employer comes on the Internet looking for someone to hire, they are essentially engaging in an activity called 'job-matching.'

37   Now, job-matching works by using job-titles.

38   And job-titles are, generally speaking, a big problem for the Internet. Not a big problem when you're looking for a job that has a simple title, such as "secretary," or "gardener," or "nurse," or "driver," or "waitress," or "mechanic," or "salesperson." Any of these should turn up a lot of matches.

39   But, you may be looking for a job that various employers call by differing titles, and that's an entirely different ballgame. If you guess wrongly about what they call the job you're looking for, then you and those employers will be like two ships passing in the night, on the Internet high seas. Your faithful, hardworking computer will report back to you in the morning: "No matches," when in fact there actually are. You just didn't guess correctly what title those employers are using. Oops!

40   Finally, job-titles are a problem for Internet searches because a typical job-board on the Internet may limit you to a prepared list of only two dozen job-titles, from which you must choose. This leaves out the other 20,000 job-titles that are out there in the work world—including, of course, the one that you are searching for, in particular.

41   So sure, Internet job-matching works. Sometimes. Beautifully. But know ahead of time that you can't count on it necessarily working for You. In the end, it's a big fat gamble that works about 10% of the time. It's a 10% solution to your problem.   ∎

QUESTIONS ON SUBJECT AND PURPOSE

1. The book from which this essay is taken was published in 2009. What economic factors in the United States during this period suggested that such a book might be needed?

2. How does Bolles use the phrase "The 10% Solution" to tie his essay together?

3. What caution is Bolles offering about relying on the Internet to find a job?

QUESTIONS ON STRATEGY AND AUDIENCE

1. One way in which to begin an essay is to use a "hook," a fact or story that catches the readers' attention and pulls them into the story. How effective is Bolles's hook introduction to the essay?

2. Toward the end of the essay, Bolles includes a visual displaying the differences between how employers and would-be employees look to fill a job vacancy. He could have included the information in paragraph form. Why use a visual? Does the visual contribute anything that a prose paragraph might not?

3. On the basis of this selection from his book, to whom is Bolles writing? What expectations does he seem to have about his audience?

QUESTIONS ON VOCABULARY AND STYLE

1. Check the Glossary and Ready Reference in the back of this book for the definition of a "cliché". Can you find clichés in the essay?
2. What device of figurative language does Bolles use in the opening sentence of paragraph 19?
3. Be prepared to define the following words: *incredulous* (paragraph 18), *omnibus* (23), *niche* (23).

WRITING SUGGESTIONS

1. **Doing a Critical Analysis.** In "On Writing," Bolles explains that he breaks the rules of formal writing in order to make his book easier to read. Do those devices make the essay easier to read? How are they related to his purpose in the essay?
2. **Journaling or Blogging.** Jobs require certain skills—technical and interpersonal (the ability to interact effectively with other people). At this point in your education, you might not have many technical skills, but what are your "people" skills? Make a list.
3. **Practicing in a Paragraph.** Identify one internship (paid or volunteer) that you might apply for right now. Your college's placement office will be able to help you locate some possibilities. In a paragraph, explain how your "people" skills qualify you for that position.
4. **Writing the Personal Essay.** In an essay, offer advice on how an undergraduate at your school could find and apply for internship positions related to a major or possible career.
5. **Finding Reading Connections.** Read Nick Schulz's "Hard Unemployment Truths About 'Soft' Skills" (How to Read and Then Analyze an Essay). In an essay, offer advice to your peers about how to improve their "soft" skills and why that is important.
6. **Exploring Links Online.** The Web has many sites that offer advice on finding an internship. Not everyone agrees on the best strategies. Using multiple online sources, compile some practical advice for your peers.
7. **Writing the Research Paper.** Whenever you apply for a job, even a summer job or an internship, it is important to have a resume. Advice on compiling one can be found in print and online sources. Research the form and the strategies used in an effective resume and then write an essay telling readers how to construct one. Be sure to document your sources.

For Further Study

Focusing on Grammar and Writing. Bolles makes frequent use of the semicolon in his writing. Semicolons require certain grammatical requirements for their correct use. Using Bolles's examples, what are those requirements?

Working Together. Working in small groups, brainstorm about how a first-year college student might find a summer job that would be related to a major or possible career interest.

Seeing Other Modes at Work. Although Bolles uses process, the essay has persuasive elements as well. Identify those elements in the essay.

Stripped for Parts

JENNIFER KAHN

A graduate of Princeton and the University of California, Berkeley, Jennifer Kahn is a writer and a contributing editor to magazines such as Wired *and* National Geographic. *In 2003, she was awarded a journalism fellowship from the American Academy of Neurology; in 2004, the CASE-UCLA media fellowship in neuroscience. "Stripped for Parts" first appeared in* Wired *in 2003.*

> **On Writing:** *Commenting on the essay, Kahn noted: "It was one of those stories that turn out to be dramatically different from the original assignment. Basically, I'd been sent out to find out what was new in the world of transplant surgery: the standard 'hooray for scientific progress' tale. Instead I was struck by how fragile the organ recovery process was. . . . In the end the piece was quite controversial; there were a lot of angry letters from people who accused me of discouraging donation."*

Before Reading

Connecting: What do you know about organ donations? Are you an organ donor? Many states allow this designation to be placed on a driver's license.

Anticipating: What surprises you the most in the essay?

1 **T**he television in the dead man's room stays on all night. Right now the program is *Shipmates*, a reality-dating drama that's barely audible over the hiss of the ventilator. It's 4 AM, and I've been here for six hours, sitting in the corner while three nurses fuss intermittently over a set of intravenous drips. They're worried about the dead man's health.

2 To me, he looks fine. His face is slack but flush, he breathes steadily, and his heart beats like a clock, despite the fact that his lungs have recently begun to leak fluid. The nurses roll the body from side to side periodically so that the liquid doesn't pool. At one point, a white plastic vest designed to clear the lungs inflates and begins to vibrate violently—as if some invisible person has seized the dead man by the shoulders and is trying to shake him awake. The rest of the time, the nurses consult monitors and watch for signs of cardiac arrest. When someone scratches the bottom of the dead man's foot, it twitches.

3 None of this is what I expected from an organ transplant. When I arrived last night at this Northern California hospital I was prepared to see a fast-paced surgery culminating in renewal: the mortally ill patient restored to glorious health. In all my preliminary research on transplants, the dead

man was rarely mentioned. Even doctors I spoke with avoided the subject, and popular accounts I came across ducked the matter of provenance altogether. In the movies, for instance, surgeons tended to say it would take time to "find" a heart—as though one had been hidden behind a tree or misplaced along with the car keys. Insofar as corpses came up, it was only in anxious reference to the would-be recipient whose time was running out.

4   In the dead man's room, a different calculus is unfolding. Here the organ is the patient, and the patient a mere container, the safest place to store body parts until surgeons are ready to use them. It can be more than a day from the time a donor dies until his organs are harvested—the surgery alone takes hours, not to mention the time needed to do blood tests, match tissue, and fly in special surgical teams for the evisceration. And yet, a heart lasts at most six hours outside the body, even after it has been kneaded, flushed with preservatives, and packed in a cooler. Organs left on ice too long tend to perform poorly in their new environment, and doctors are picky about which viscera they're willing to work with. Even an ailing cadaver is a better container than a cooler.

5   These conditions create a strange medical specialty. Rather than extracting this man's vitals right away, the hospital contacts the California Transplant Donor Network, which dispatches a procurement team to begin "donor maintenance": the process of artificially supporting a dead body until recipients are ready. When the parathyroid gland stops regulating calcium, key to keeping the heart pumping, the team sends the proper amount down an intravenous drip. When blood pressure drops, they add vasoconstrictors, which contract the blood vessels. Normally the brain would compensate for a decrease in blood pressure, but with it out of commission, the three-nurse procurement team must take over.

6   In this case, the eroding balance will have to be sustained for almost 24 hours. The goal is to fool the body into believing that it's alive and well, even as everything is falling apart. As one crew member concedes, "It's unbelievable that all this stuff is being done to a dead person."

7   Unbelievable and, to me, somehow barbaric. Sustaining a dead body until its organs can be harvested is a tricky process requiring the latest in medical technology. But it's also a distinct anachronism in an era when medicine is becoming less and less invasive. Fixing blocked coronary arteries, which not long ago required prying a patient's chest open with a saw and spreader, can now be accomplished with a tiny stent delivered to the heart on a slender wire threaded up the leg. Exploratory surgery has given way to robot cameras and high-resolution imaging. Already, we are eyeing the tantalizing summit of gene therapy, where diseases are cured even before they do damage. Compared with such microscale cures, transplants—which consist of salvaging entire organs from a heart-beating cadaver and sewing them into a different body—seem crudely mechanical, even medieval.

8   "To let an organ reach a state where the only solution is to cut it out is not progress; it's a failure of medicine," says pathologist Neil Theise of NYU. Theise, who was the first researcher to demonstrate that stem cells can

become liver cells in humans, argues that the future of transplantation lies in regeneration. Within five years, he estimates, we'll be able to instruct the body to send stem cells to the liver from the store that exists in bone marrow, hopefully countering the effects of a disease like hepatitis A or B and letting the body heal itself. And numerous researchers are forging similar paths. One outspoken surgeon, Richard Satava from the University of Washington, says that medicine is only now catching on to the fundamental lesson of modern industry, which is that when our car alternator breaks, we get a brand new one. Transplantation, he argues, is a dying art.

9   Few researchers predict that human-harvested organs will become obsolete anytime soon, however; one cardiovascular pathologist, Charles Murry, says we'll still be using them a century from now. But it's reasonable to expect—and hope for—an alternative. "I don't think anybody enjoys recovering organs," Murry says frankly. "You tell yourself it's for a good cause, which it is, a very good cause, but you're still butchering a human."

10   Intensive care is not a good place to spend the evening. Tonight, the ward has perhaps 12 patients, including a woman who moans constantly and a deathly pale man who reportedly jumped out the window of a moving Greyhound bus. The absence of clocks and the always-on lights create a casino-like timelessness. In the staff lounge, which smells of stale pizza, a lone nurse corners me and describes watching a man bleed to death ("He was conscious. He knew what was happening"), and announces, sotto voce, that she knows of South American organ brokers who charge $60,000 for a heart, then swap it for a baboon's.

11   Although I don't admit it to the procurement team, I've grown attached to the dead man. There's something vulnerable about his rumpled hair and middle-aged body, naked save a waist-high sheet. Under the hospital lights, everything is exposed: the muscular arms gone flabby above the elbow; the legs, wiry and lean, foreshortened under a powerful torso. It's the body of a man in his fifties, simultaneously bullish and elfin. One foot, the right, peeps out from the sheet, and for a brief moment I want to hold it and rub the toes that must be cold—a hopeless gesture of consolation.

12   Organ support is about staving off entropy. In the moments after death, a cascade of changes sweeps over the body. Potassium diminishes and salt accumulates, drawing fluid into cells. Sugar builds up in the blood. With the pituitary system offline, the heart fills with lactic acid like the muscles of an exhausted runner. Free radicals circulate unchecked and disrupt other cells, in effect causing the body to rust. The process quickly becomes irreversible. As cell membranes grow porous, a "death gene" is activated and damaged cells begin to self-destruct. All this happens in minutes.

13   When transplant activists talk about an organ shortage, it's usually to lament how few people are willing to donate. This is a valid worry, but it eclipses an important point, which is that the window for retrieving a viable organ is staggeringly small. Because of how fast the body degrades once the heart stops, there's no way to recover an organ from someone who dies at home, in a car, in an ambulance, or even while on the operating table.

In fact, the only situation that really lends itself to harvest is brain death, which means finding an otherwise healthy patient whose brain activity has ceased but whose heart continues to beat—right up until the moment it's taken out. In short, victims of stroke or severe head injury. These cases are so rare (approximately 0.5 percent of all deaths in the US) that even if everybody in America were to become a donor, they wouldn't clear the organ wait lists.

14   This is partly a scientific problem. Cell death remains poorly understood, and for years now, cadaveric transplants have lingered on a research plateau. While immunosuppressants have improved incrementally, transplants proceed much as they did 20 years ago. Compared with a field like psychopharmacology, the procedure has come to a near-standstill.

15   But there are cultural factors as well. Medicine has always reserved its glory for the living. Even among transplant surgeons, a hierarchy exists: Those who put organs into living patients have a higher status than those who extract them from the dead. One anesthesiologist confesses that his peers don't like to work on cadaveric organ recoveries. (Even brain-dead bodies require sedation, since spinal reflexes can make a corpse "buck" in surgery.) "You spend all this time monitoring the heartbeat, the blood pressure," the anesthesiologist explains. "To just turn everything off when you're done and walk out. It's bizarre."

16   Although the procurement team will stay up all night, I break at 4:30 AM for a two-hour nap on an empty bed in the ICU. The nurse removes a wrinkled top sheet but leaves the bottom one. Doctors sleep like this all the time, I know, catnapping on gurneys, but I can't shake the feeling of climbing onto my deathbed. The room is identical to the one I've been sitting in for the past eight hours, and I'd prefer to sleep almost anywhere else—in the nurses' lounge or even on the small outside balcony. Instead, I lie down in my clothes and pull the sheet up under my arms.

17   For a while I read a magazine, then finally close my eyes, hoping I won't dream.

18   By morning, little seems to have changed, except that the commotion of chest X-rays and ultrasounds has left the dead man's hair more mussed. On both sides of his bed, vital stats scroll across screens: oxygen ratios, pulse, blood volumes.

19   All of this vigilance is good, of course: After all, transplants save lives. Every year, thousands of people who would otherwise die survive with organs from brain-dead donors; sometimes, doctors say, a patient's color will visibly change on the operating table once a newly attached liver begins to work. Still—and with the possible exception of kidneys—transplants have never quite lived up to their initial promise. In the early 1970s, few who received new organs lasted even a year, and most died within weeks. Even today, 22 percent of heart recipients die in less than four years, and 12 percent reject a new heart within the first few months. Those who survive are usually consigned to a lifetime regime of costly immunosuppressive drugs, some with debilitating side effects. Recipients of artificial hearts traditionally fare the worst, alongside those who receive transplants from animals. Under the

circumstances, it took a weird kind of perseverance for doctors operating in 1984 to suggest sewing a walnut-sized baboon heart into a human baby. And there was grief, if not surprise, when the patient died of a morbid immune reaction just 21 days later.

20   By the time we head into surgery, the patient has been dead for more than 24 hours, but he still looks pink and healthy. In the operating room, all the intravenous drips are still flowing, convincing the body that everything's fine even as it's cleaved in half.

21   Although multiorgan transfer can involve as many as five teams in the OR at once, this time there is only one: a four-man surgical unit from Southern California. They've flown in to retrieve the liver, but because teams sometimes swap favors, they'll also remove the kidneys for a group of doctors elsewhere— saving them a last-minute, late-night flight. One of the doctors has brought a footstool for me to stand on at the head of the operating table, so that I can see over the sheet that hangs between the patient's head and body. I've been warned that the room will smell bad during the "opening," like flesh and burning bone—an odor that has something in common with a dentist's drill. Behind me, the anesthesiologist checks the dead man's mask and confirms that he's sedated. The surgery will take four hours, and the doctors have arranged for the score of Game Five of the World Series to be phoned in at intervals.

22   I've heard that transplant doctors are the endurance athletes of medicine, and the longer I stand on the stool, the better I understand the comparison. Below me, the rib cage has been split, and I can see the heart, strangely yellow, beating inside a cave of red muscle. It doesn't beat forward, as I expect, but knocks anxiously back and forth like a small animal trapped in a cage. Farther down, the doctors rummage under the slough of intestines as though through a poorly organized toolbox. When I tell the anesthesiologist that the heart is beautiful, he says that livers are the transplants to watch. "Hearts are slash and burn," he shrugs, adjusting a dial. "No finesse."

23   Two hours pass, and the surgeons make progress. Despite the procurement team's best efforts, however, most of the organs have already been lost. The pancreas was deemed too old before surgery. One lung was bad at the outset, and the other turned out to be too big for the only matching recipients—a short list given the donor's rare blood type. At 7 this morning, the heart went bust after someone at the receiving hospital suggested a shot of thyroid hormone, shown in some studies to stimulate contractions—but even before then, the surgeon had had second thoughts. A 54-year-old heart can't travel far—and this one was already questionable—but the hospital may have thought this would improve its chances. Instead, the dead man's pulse shot to 140, and his blood began circulating so fast it nearly ruptured his arteries. Now the heart will go to Cryolife, a biosupply company that irradiates and freeze-dries the valves, then packages them for sale to hospitals in screw-top jars. The kidneys have remained healthy enough to be passed on—one to a man who will soon be in line for a pancreas, the other to a 42-year-old woman.

24   Both kidneys have been packed off in quart-sized plastic jars. Originally, the liver was going to a nearby hospital, but an ultrasound suggested it

was hyperechoic, or probably fatty. On the second pass, it was accepted by a doctor in Southern California and ensconced in a bag of icy slurry.

25   The liver is enormous—it looks like a polished stone, flat and purplish—and with it gone, the body seems eerily empty, although the heart continues to beat. Watching this pumping vessel makes me oddly anxious. It's sped up slightly, as though sensing what will happen next. Below me, the man's face is still flushed. He's the one I wish would survive, I realize, even though there was never any chance of that. Meanwhile, the head surgeon has walked away. He's busy examining the liver and relaying a description over the phone to the doctor who will perform the attachment. Almost unnoticed, an aide clamps the arteries above and below the heart, and cuts. The patient's face doesn't move, but its pinkness drains to a waxy yellow. After 24 hours, the dead man finally looks dead.

26   Once all the organs are out, the tempo picks up in the operating room. The heart is packed in a cardboard box also loaded with the kidneys, which are traveling by Learjet to a city a few hundred miles away. Someday, I'm convinced, transporting organs in coolers will seem as strange and outdated as putting a patient in an iron lung. In the meantime, transplants will survive: a vehicle, like the dead man, to get us to a better place. As an assistant closes, sewing up the body so that it will be ready for its funeral, I get on the plane with the heart and the kidneys. They've become a strange, unhealthy orange in their little jars. But no one else seems worried. "A kidney almost always perks up," someone tells me, "once we get it in a happier environment."   ■

QUESTIONS ON SUBJECT AND PURPOSE

1. What did Kahn expect to see at an organ transplant operation?
2. Why does Kahn get on the airplane with the heart and kidneys at the end of the story?
3. Having read the essay, have you changed your attitude toward organ donation? Do you think that Kahn wants to change your opinion?

QUESTIONS ON STRATEGY AND AUDIENCE

1. Why might Kahn have titled the essay "Stripped for Parts"? What associations do you have with that phrase?
2. How effective is the opening paragraph? Does it make you want to keep reading?
3. What could Kahn assume about her audience?

QUESTIONS ON VOCABULARY AND STYLE

1. How is the story told or narrated to the reader? How else might the story have been told?
2. How would you describe the tone of the essay?
3. Be prepared to define the following words: *culminating* (paragraph 3), *provenance* (3), *evisceration* (4), *viscera* (4), *anachronism* (7), *sotto voce* (10), *elfin* (11), *entropy* (12), *debilitating* (19), *morbid* (19), *slough* (22), *hyperechoic* (24), *ensconced* (24).

WRITING SUGGESTIONS

1. **Doing a Critical Analysis.** Kahn injects herself into the essay by using a first-person narration. How does her choice of point of view contribute to the impact of the essay? Analyze that choice and evaluate its effectiveness.

2. **Journaling or Blogging.** Why is this side of organ donation—the harvesting—ignored? How do you feel about the whole process? Record your feelings.

3. **Practicing in a Paragraph.** What would you want to happen to your body and organs if you were in a fatal accident?

4. **Writing the Personal Essay.** How do you make a "living" will? Why would anyone, especially a young person, want one? In an essay intended for your peers, describe the process of making such a will.

5. **Finding Reading Connections.** Rick Reilly's "Getting a Second Wind" (Chapter 1) offers a moving story about an organ transplant. A casebook on organ donation can also be found in Chapter 9. In an essay using all of these texts, present the case for or against organ donation.

6. **Exploring Links Online.** Many myths and misconceptions are associated with organ donation. As you talk with friends and relatives, do they believe any of these myths? In an essay, target a particular audience (such as the young or older adults) and offer reasons why they should be organ donors.

7. **Writing the Research Paper.** Kahn quotes a stem-cell researcher who "argues that the future of transplantation lies in regeneration" (paragraph 8). What is the state of stem-cell research now? Will we be able to regenerate organs rather than transplanting them? Research the issue and describe in a research paper the process by which scientists think that this might be possible.

For Further Study

Focusing on Grammar and Writing. Kahn makes extensive use of the dash in the essay. Classify the ways and the grammatical situations in which the dash is used in the essay.

Working Together. Working in groups, divide the essay into groups of paragraphs and then rewrite a group so that the "I" is replaced by an omniscient third person. What happens to the story as a result?

Seeing Other Modes at Work. The essay is a narrative with elements of description and cause and effect (in the description of why and how the body breaks down so quickly).

ADDITIONAL WRITING SUGGESTIONS FOR PROCESS

Process writing falls into two categories based on purpose. One type tells the reader how to do or make something. It assumes that the reader wishes to duplicate the process. The second type describes how something works or happened. It assumes that the reader wants to know how or why the process works. With either type of process writing, visual devices are often helpful and occasionally even indispensable.

How-To-Do-It

1. How to choose the cell phone plan that is best for you
2. How to fail a course (humorous) / how to earn an "A"
3. How to choose a major / locate a summer job / an internship
4. How to find a good roommate / break up with a partner
5. How to lose weight / get in shape / train for a sports event
6. How to change a tire / change the oil in your car
7. How to persuade your parents to allow you to study abroad
8. How to control your Facebook habit
9. How to conquer your fear of public speaking

How-It-Works

1. How does text messaging work / cell phone?
2. How do air bags work / GPS systems / Skype / Twitter?
3. How do you increase muscle size / get great abs?
4. How does alcohol make you drunk?
5. How is oil refined / biofuels?
6. How do Web search engines work?
7. How do cattle contribute to global warming?
8. How does aspirin work?
9. How can fiber optics transmit information?

7 | Cause and Effect

LEARNING OBJECTIVES

In this chapter, you will learn how to

1. Identify what is a cause and what is an effect
2. Choose an appropriate and manageable subject for a cause-and-effect analysis
3. Assess the relevant importance of each cause or effect
4. Arrange causes or effects in a logical order in your paper
5. Revise a cause-and-effect analysis to increase its effectiveness
6. Analyze readings that use cause and effect

 Key Questions

WRITING CAUSE AND EFFECT

Getting Ready to Write

What is cause and effect?
How do you write a cause-and-effect analysis?
How do you choose a subject?
How do you isolate and evaluate causes and effects?

Writing

How do you structure a cause-and-effect analysis?

Revising

How do you revise a cause-and-effect essay?

Student Essay

Katie McCarthy, *"Why Are Tattoos So Popular?"*

READING CAUSE AND EFFECT

In Prose

"Immediate Effects of Alcohol on the Body"

In Literature

Ellie Schoenfeld, *"Barbie's Little Sister"* (poem)

In a Visual

"Polar Bear Adrift" (photograph)

Writing Cause and Effect

GETTING READY TO WRITE

What Is Cause and Effect?

It is a rainy morning and you are late for class. You have an accident while driving to campus in an automobile with faulty brakes. Considering the circumstances, the accident might be attributable to a variety of causes:

> You were driving too fast.
> Visibility was poor.
> Roads were slippery.
> The brakes did not work properly.

Visually, cause and effect can be displayed in what are called "fishbone" diagrams, tools used to analyze and display possible causes. If we used a fishbone diagram to analyze your accident, it might look like this:

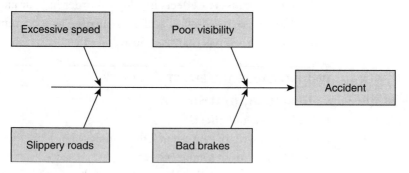

The diagram could also branch out further since the accident, in turn, could produce a series of consequences or effects:

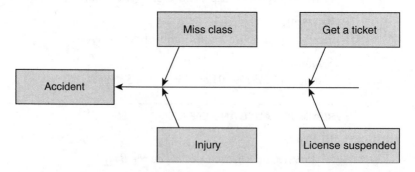

Causes and effects can be either immediate or remote with reference to time. The lists regarding the hypothetical automobile accident suggest only immediate causes and effects, things that could be most directly linked in time to the accident. Another pair of lists of more remote causes and effects could be compiled—for example, your brakes were faulty because you did not have the money to fix them, or because of your accident, your insurance rates will go up.

Causes and effects can be either primary or secondary with reference to their significance and importance. If you had not been in a hurry and driving too fast, it might not have mattered that the visibility was poor, the roads were slippery, or your brakes were faulty. Similarly, if you or someone else had been injured, the other consequences would have seemed insignificant in comparison.

In some instances, causes and effects are linked in a causal chain: if you were driving too fast and tried to stop on slippery roads with inadequate brakes, each of those causes is interlinked in the inevitable accident. Likewise, the accident means that you will get a ticket, that ticket carries points again your license, your license could as a result be suspended, and either way your insurance rates will certainly increase.

How Do You Write a Cause-and-Effect Analysis?

Cause-and-effect analyses are intended to reveal the reasons why something happened or the consequences of a particular occurrence. James Paul Gee, in "Games, Not Schools, Are Teaching Kids to Think," attributes the poor performance of American education to ineffective and misguided learning strategies. Andres Martin in "On Teenagers and Tattoos" explores some of the reasons why tattoos and body piercings appeal to adolescents. In "Kids Battle the Lure of Junk Food," Maureen O'Hagan isolates some of the complicated causes that lie behind childhood obesity. Brent Staples in "Black Men and Public Space" uses his own experiences as an urban night walker to explore the effects that he, as a young black male, has on those who share the streets with him. Mark Penn in "Caffeine Crazies" analyzes why Americans of all ages are consuming ever larger quantities of caffeinated beverages. Finally, Michael Jernigan in his blog post "Living the Dream" details the effects that he experiences from his Post Traumatic Stress Disorder.

Cause-and-effect analyses can also be used to persuade readers to do or believe something. Andres Martin's analysis of body marking and teenagers is written for an audience of clinicians who work with adolescents. His analysis is also persuasive for he suggests that such markings provide a point of contact with patients and offer insights into their perceptions of self and reality. Brent Staples's experience as an urban night walker challenges all of us when we realize how quickly and easily we form stereotypes—a young, large black man dressed casually on an urban street at night must be dangerous, must be someone to avoid.

How Do You Choose a Subject?

In picking a subject to analyze, first remember the limits of your assignment. The larger the subject, the more difficult it will be to do justice to it. Trying to analyze the causes of the Vietnam War or the effects of technology

Links between Writing and Reading

	Possible purpose/audience interest
John Paul Gee, "Games, Not Schools"	A plan to reform education?
Andres Martin, "Teenagers and Tattoos"	Published in a journal for adolescent psychiatrists, why might this article have a broader appeal?
Maureen O'Hagan, "Kids Battle"	How widespread is this problem?
Brent Staples, "Black Men"	Why might an audience be interested in this article? (It was originally published in a magazine whose audience was women.)
Mark Penn, "Caffeine Crazies"	Between energy drinks and coffee, who doesn't consume caffeine each day?
Michael Jernigan, "Living the Dream"	Who might be reading the "Home Fire" blog?

in 500 words is an invitation to disaster. Second, make sure that the relationships you see between causes and effects are genuine. The fact that a particular event preceded another does not necessarily mean that the first caused the second. In logic, this error is labeled *post hoc, ergo propter hoc* (after this, therefore because of this). If a black cat crossed the street several blocks before your automobile accident, that does not mean that the cat was a cause of the accident.

How Do You Isolate and Evaluate Causes and Effects?

Before you begin to write, take time to analyze and, if necessary, research your subject thoroughly. Remember to consider all of the major factors involved in the relationship. Relatively few things are the result of a single cause, and rarely does a cause have a single effect.

Depending on your subject, your analysis could be based on personal experience, thoughtful reflection and examination, or research. John Paul Gee's research is in literacy and digital learning. Brent Staples draws on his own personal experiences and those of a fellow black journalist. Michael Jernigan blogs on a site that features American veterans talking about postwar life and reflects on how he lives with Post Traumatic Stress Disorder. Other writers rely on research. Maureen O'Hagan conducted extensive interviews with children, parents, and experts to explain why solving the problem of childhood obesity will not be easy. Andres Martin specializes in adolescent psychiatry, and his analysis depends on his experience with patients and his knowledge of the published research. Finally, Mark Penn gathers and documents his

Links between Writing and Reading

	Basis for the analysis
John Paul Gee, "Games, Not Schools"	Research
Andres Martin, "Teenagers and Tattoos"	Personal observation of patients and research
Maureen O'Hagan, "Kids Battle"	Interviews
Brent Staples, "Black Men"	Personal experience—his and a friend's
Mark Penn, "Caffeine Crazies"	Wide range of studies and statistics
Michael Jernigan, "Living the Dream"	Personal experience

 ## Prewriting Tips for Writing Cause and Effect

1. Choose a subject that can be analyzed within the amount of space that you have available.
2. Decide whether you are exploring causes or effects. In a short paper, it probably is not possible to do both.
3. Make a list of possible causes or effects. Test each item on your list to make sure that it is a likely cause or effect. Remember, just because something happens before or after your subject does not necessarily mean that it is a cause or effect.
4. Rank the causes or effects in terms of their significance. Typically, you are not asked to analyze all of the possible causes or effects. Focus on the most important ones. In a short paper, you will probably not treat more than three to five causes or effects.
5. Remember your audience. How much do they already know about your subject? Will your analysis be too complex and technical? Will it be too obvious? Either extreme presents problems.

findings on Americans' love of caffeine from a variety of sources, all of which he cites.

Once you have gathered a list of possible causes and effects, the next step is to evaluate each item. Any phenomenon can have many causes or many effects, so you will have to select the explanations that seem the most relevant or most convincing. Rarely should you list every cause or every effect you can find. Generally, choose the causes and effects that are immediate and primary, although the choice is always determined by your purpose.

WRITING

How Do You Structure a Cause-and-Effect Analysis?

By definition, causes precede effects, so a cause-and-effect analysis involves a linear or chronological order. In most cases, structure your analysis to reflect that sequence. If you are analyzing causes, typically you begin by identifying the subject you are trying to explain; then you move to analyze its causes. If you are analyzing effects, typically you begin by identifying the subject that produced the effects; then you move to enumerate or explain what those effects were.

A cause-and-effect analysis can also go in both directions. In trying to explain the popularity of caffeinated drinks, Mark Penn looks first at some causes: the 24/7 wakefulness of American life, the greater sense of pressure, the premium we put on being energetic. The last section of the essay, though, traces effects: what are the positive and negative effects that caffeine has on our health.

Within these patterns, you face one other choice. If you are listing multiple causes or effects, how do you decide in what order to treat them? That arrangement depends on whether the reasons or consequences are linked in a chain. If they happen in a definite sequence, arrange them in an order to reflect that sequence—normally a chronological order (this happened, then this, and finally this). This linear arrangement is similar to what you do in a process narrative except that your purpose here is to answer the question *why* rather than *how*. In "Black Men and Public Space," Brent Staples follows a chronological pattern of development. He begins with his first experience as a night walker in Chicago and ends with his most recent experiences in Brooklyn. The essay includes a brief flashback as well to his childhood days in Chester, Pennsylvania. As he is narrating his experience, Staples explores

Links between Writing and Reading

	Organizing middles
John Paul Gee, "Games, Not Schools"	What role do topic sentences play?
Andres Martin, "Teenagers and Tattoos"	What is the role of the subheadings in the essay?
Maureen O'Hagan, "Kids Battle"	How is the essay structured into sections?
Brent Staples, "Black Men"	What organizational device ensures continuity in the essay?
Mark Penn, "Caffeine Crazies"	What are the causes of the exploding popularity of caffeinated drinks?
Michael Jernigan, "Living the Dream"	What are the effects of PTSD on American veterans?

Drafting Tips for Writing Cause and Effect

1. Plan a middle for your essay. How are you going to arrange the causes and effects? Which comes first in the body of your paper; which comes last? Are you moving from most important to least? From the chronologically first to last?

2. Place each cause or effect in a separate paragraph. Make sure the paragraph is more than one sentence long. Explain or develop each cause or effect so that the reader can clearly understand your analysis.

3. Write a purpose statement for your essay as it is developing. What are you trying to explain in the paper? Why might the reader want this knowledge? Identifying a need or interest in your prospective reader always suggests strategies by which you can begin your essay.

4. Think about the extent to which your draft is objective and factual and to what extent it is subjective and argumentative. How likely are your readers to agree with what you attribute to cause and what to effect? Have you done research to support your analysis? Cause-and-effect essays are often difficult to write simply from preexisting knowledge or from simple observation and reflection.

5. Draft an introduction and a conclusion to the essay that appeal to your reader's need for the information. Why would the reader want to have this information?

the reasons why people react as they do when they encounter him at night on a city street. At the same time, Staples analyzes the impact or effects that their reactions have had on him.

However, multiple causes and effects are not always linked in time. If the causes or effects that you have isolated are not linked in a chain of time, you must find another way in which to order them. They could be arranged from immediate to remote, for example. When the degree of significance or importance varies, the most obvious structural choice would be to move from the primary to the secondary or from the secondary to the primary. Before you establish any sequence in your analysis, study your list of causes or effects to see whether any principle of order is evident—chronological, spatial, immediate to remote, primary to secondary. If you see some logical order, follow it.

REVISING

How Do You Revise a Cause-and-Effect Essay?

Your success in any paper always depends on your readers. If your readers like it, if they feel that it was worth reading, if it taught them something they wanted to know or persuaded them to agree with you, then you have succeeded. Unless your readers agree, it does not matter if you think that your paper is clear and interesting. For that reason, when you are revising, always seek feedback from your readers. Perhaps in your writing class you have regular opportunities to read each other's papers, either in hard copy or online, and offer advice. Maybe your school has a writing center or writing tutors you can visit; maybe your instructor has the time to read a first draft and suggest possible revisions. If so, take advantage of those readers. Ask them specific questions; ask for their criticisms and suggestions. If such situations are not part of the formal structure of your class, ask a roommate or a friend to read your essay. Then pay attention to what he or she says.

A cause-and-effect essay is primarily explanatory and informative. It explains the reasons or causes for why something happened or the consequences or effects that come from whatever happened. The best cause-and-effect analyses are based on thoughtful analysis coupled with research. The worst cause-and-effect analyses grow only out of subjective, biased, unsubstantiated opinions. If you are sick, you want accurate, objective medical advice. What caused my illness? What are the likely side effects of this course of treatment?

When revising a cause-and-effect essay, play particular attention to the following areas: retesting your subject, concentrating on the important, checking for logical organization, and beginning and ending appropriately.

Retesting Your Subject   Once you have a draft of your essay, look again at your subject. Ask yourself two questions and answer each honestly. First, were you able to develop adequately your subject in the space that you had available, or were you forced to skim over the surface? Some subjects are simply too large and too complicated to be analyzed in three or four pages. Second, were you objective and accurate in what you identified as causes and effects? The world, and especially the Web, is full of bogus explanations for what caused this or what the effects of that have been. Sometimes people intentionally mislead by parading their own biases and opinions as objective facts. Readers want accurate and reliable information and analyses.

Not every subject needs research. Sometimes personal experience is adequate; sometimes we can thoughtfully and insightfully analyze a situation. Even then, though, our response is based on knowledge that has been acquired only through our own experiences. Try to check your personal knowledge against what others have experienced or written about. You always want your analysis to be based on accurate information.

Concentrating on the Important   You will never be given an essay assignment that says "find all of the causes or all of the effects" of something. In some instances, causes and effects are many. Think about the lists of possible side effects that accompany any over-the-counter or prescription drug. Often the lists are paragraphs long. Similarly, many illnesses can result from a complex series of causes, some interacting in causal chains. In a typical writing situation, however, you need to concentrate on the major causes and effects.

Once you have identified those causes or effects, number them in the order of their significance or importance. Depending on the length of your paper—is it a "regular" essay or a term or research paper?—choose to discuss only the most important.

Checking for Logical Organization   Look again at how you have arranged either the causes or the effects in the body of your paper. A typical organizational strategy is to put the main cause or the main effect first and then to move down the list in descending order of importance. You could move in the opposite direction, building to your strongest or most forceful cause or effect, but there would be no logical reason to place the most important cause or effect in the middle of the list. Causes and effects can also be listed in a chronological order, especially if there is a causal chain (this happens, which leads to this, which then leads to this). Other possible organizational strategies might also be appropriate, for example, from the most visible effect to the least visible. Whatever order you choose should be a conscious and thoughtful act on your part, and you should be able to defend your choice to any critic.

Another aspect of logical organization is proportion. Treat your causes or effects in paragraphs or paragraph blocks of roughly the same length. You do not want to start off with a long, detailed paragraph and then have the rest of the essay trail off into a series of ever-shorter, thinner paragraphs.

Logical organization grows out of careful, intentional arrangement of your analysis, but transitional devices can also play an important role. As you move from one cause or effect to another, make sure that you signal that move to readers. Develop each cause or effect in a separate paragraph, and start each paragraph with an explanatory statement of how this fits into what has gone before. Use parallelism and transitional phrases or markers; think of these devices as road signs for your readers to tell them what to expect ahead. For help and advice on using such devices, consult the Glossary and Ready Reference at the back of this text.

Beginning and Ending   Your teacher is the only reader who *has* to read your essay. Your introduction needs to catch your readers' attention and pull them into the paper. Think about why your readers would want to read an essay about this subject. What value does it hold for them? How curious might they be about the subject? What will you help them understand? Your introduction needs to be an inviting bridge between the world of your readers and the essay. Of course you will explain your thesis and your purpose for writing about this subject. Try to suggest as well, however, what is of particular interest or importance about this subject and to provoke the curiosity of readers.

Every paper needs a conclusion. Never simply stop because you have run out of time. In a short paper, a conclusion does not need to summarize the causes or effects that you have just described. They are fresh in your readers' minds. Try instead to end by stressing the significance of your analysis

Links between Writing and Reading

	Introductions/conclusions
John Paul Gee, "Games, Not Schools"	How effective is the introduction?
Andres Martin, "Teenagers and Tattoos"	What is the function of the essay's conclusion?
Maureen O'Hagan, "Kids Battle"	What is the effect of the conclusion?
Brent Staples, "Black Men"	What is the effect of the strategy used in the introduction?
Mark Penn, "Caffeine Crazies"	Why begin with the example of bottled water?
Michael Jernigan, "Living the Dream"	Why does the blog post begin and end like a letter?

 ## Revising Tips for Writing Cause and Effect

1. Reexamine your subject. Have you been able to treat your subject adequately in the space that you have available? Do you need to narrow the subject in any way? Or is your subject too narrow to begin with?

2. Look critically at the body of your essay. Are the paragraphs substantial in length? Are they roughly proportional to one another in length? Your essay should not consist of many very short paragraphs or a couple of very long paragraphs and some very short paragraphs.

3. Evaluate your transitions. Have you provided clear transitions from one paragraph or section to another? Have you used transitional expressions or time and place markers to indicate that you are moving from one cause or effect to another?

4. Examine your conclusion. Does it just repeat the words of your opening paragraph in a slightly different way? Does it build a bridge between your subject and your reader, pointing out what is interesting or important about the subject?

5. Make a list of potential problems that you sense in your essay. These may be grammatical or mechanical, or they might be structural. Take your list and a copy of your paper to your school's writing center or to a writing tutor and ask for help. See if your instructor has the time—perhaps during office hours—to critique your draft.

and how it may help readers understand the subject. Look at the conclusions that the six writers provided for their essays in this chapter. More concluding strategies for papers can be found in the Glossary and Ready Reference at the back of this text.

Student Essay

For a cause-and-effect essay, Katie McCarthy chose to analyze some of the reasons why so many young people get tattoos and piercings. She interviewed some of her classmates and did some online research.

First Draft

Tattoos and body piercings have become a common fad in our society. According to the Pew Research Center, the total number of Americans who have at least one tattoo is currently over 45 million people. Of these, 36 percent of U.S. adults ages 18 to 25 have at least one tattoo, while 40 percent of U.S. adults ages 26 to 40 have at least one tattoo.

As more people ink their bodies or pierce them in areas other than the soft ear lobe, the common question is "why?" Many students feel that the tattoo has a personal meaning and message that is important to them. One student with numerous tattoos said they all represented significant times in his life. He wants people to be able to see who he is when they first encounter him, which is why he put the tattoos in obvious places. He also sees tattoos as a way to illustrate that every person has a story. The tattoo on his right arm, a music note, illustrates his love for music and his dedication to achieving his dream of one day being successful in the music business.

Other students said they had tattoos and/or piercings because it was an act of rebellion. They were able to get the tattoo or piercing without parental permission. Some did it because their parents simply said that they couldn't. Others got it because it was the first thing they were able to do without authorization from their parents. Some got the piercings because they knew it would annoy their parents.

All of those who had tattoos or piercings also realized the negative stigma that goes along with having them. The students found that many people regarded tattoos and piercings as unprofessional in the workplace. They also realized that some people associated tattoos with gangs. However, most of the students tended to put their tattoos in discrete places so that they would not be visible when they dressed for work. Those who had facial piercings or piercings that were visible stated that they would take out the piercings when they sought a full-time job.

Comments

Katie had a conference with her instructor who noticed some issues with her essay. Since the statistics and much of the first draft dealt with tattoos rather than piercings, he encouraged her to focus just on tattoos. He also told Katie to document the source for any statistics she used in her text and to put a "works cited" at the end of her essay as well.

Katie also had a few awkwardly worded sentences. The instructor discussed with Katie how to solve the problems in some of these sentences. He pointed, for example, to the sentence, "He wants people to be able to see who he is when they first encounter him, which is why he put the tattoos in obvious places." The instructor encouraged her to revise the sentence, by making it into two sentences. Katie also lacked supporting evidence in her third paragraph. He suggested that she add some examples of why students felt that they were rebelling against parents, and what the consequences were in doing so. Since the draft stopped abruptly rather than coming to a conclusion, Katie was also encouraged to add at least a summary ending to the essay. She also added a title.

Revised Draft

Why Are Tattoos So Popular?

Tattoos have become a common fad in our society. According to the Pew Research Center, the total number of Americans who have at least one tattoo is currently over 45 million people. Of these 45 million Americans, 36 percent of U.S. adults ages 18 to 25 have at least one tattoo, while 40 percent of U.S. adults ages 26 to 40 have at least one tattoo ("Tattoo Statistics").

As more people get tattoos, the obvious question is, why? Several students feel that the tattoo contains personal meanings and messages that are important to them. Josh, a student at the University of Delaware, has several tattoos located all over his body. He stated that the numerous tattoos represent significant times in his life. "I wanted others to form a first impression of me based on my tattoos," he said. By placing the tattoos in strategically obvious places, people who were curious about their meaning could then approach him. Josh, an avid musician, has a tattoo of a music note on his right arm to remind him that he can one day achieve his dream of becoming successful in the music business. "Every person has a story," Josh said. "You can just see mine a little clearer through my tattoos." Chelsea placed a single word—"fly"—on the side of her body. She decided to get this particular tattoo as a reminder that sometimes you just need to step back from a situation and find peace and calmness. "I don't have tattoos to look cool or please other people; they're my form of art," Chelsea said.

For some, tattoos are an act of rebellion. They were able to get the tattoos without parental permission. However, all said their parents were not comfortable with their tattoos because they felt that it was unprofessional in the workplace. Many parents also associated tattoos with gangs and felt uncomfortable with their children having them. However, most of the students said that they purposely placed the tattoos in discrete places so that they were not visible.

According to a 2008 poll, 16 percent of those with tattoos suffer "tattoo remorse" (Tuttle). Stephan, for example, explained that he got the tattoos when he was younger because it was the popular thing to do. However, after starting a professional job, he realized that the tattoo was a fad that he had simply out-grown. It can cost several thousand dollars to have each tattoo removed and the process is very painful.

While tattoos are not necessarily permanent, no one should get a "tat" without carefully considering the image and its placement. You can change your hairstyle and your clothing as you mature, but you live with the tattoos you chose when you were a quite different and less mature person.

Works Cited

"Tattoo Statistics." www.statisticbrain.com. *Statistic Brain*, 23 July 2012. Web. 19 Jan. 2013.

Tuttle, Brad. "The Rise of Tattoo Remorse: Heavy Cost to Erase What's Often an Impulse Decision." www.businesstime.com. *Time*, 8 Sept. 2011. Web. 19 Jan. 2013.   ■

Checklist: Some Things to Remember About Writing Cause and Effect

❑ Choose a topic that can be analyzed thoroughly within the limits of the assignment.

❑ Decide on a purpose: are you trying to explain or to persuade?

❑ Determine an audience. For whom are you writing? What does your audience already know about your subject?

❑ Analyze and research your subject. Remember to provide factual support wherever necessary. Not every cause-and-effect analysis can rely on unsupported opinion.

❑ Be certain that the relationships you see between causes and effects are genuine.

❑ Concentrate your efforts on immediate and primary causes or effects rather than on remote or secondary ones. Do not try to list every cause or every effect that you can.

❑ Begin with the cause and then move to effects, or begin with an effect and then move to its causes.

❑ Look for a principle of order to organize your list of causes or effects. It might be chronological or spatial, for example, or it might move from immediate to remote or from primary to secondary.

❑ Remember that you are explaining why something happens or what will happen. You are not just describing how.

Reading Cause and Effect

A cause-and-effect analysis is intended either to explain how something came about or what consequences follow from the action. It explores connections in a logical and structured way that can be revealed in a formal outline. It can be used in exposition to explain or in persuasion to convince readers of the rightness or wrongness of an action or decision. As you read, remember what you have learned about how to write using cause and effect and how that knowledge might help you as a reader.

- An analysis of cause explains why something happens or how it came about. An analysis of effect explains the consequences that come from an event or situation.
- Causes and effects are related to the event by factors other than the time of their occurrence. A rainstorm right after you washed your car was not caused by your action.
- Cause-and-effect analyses tend to concentrate either on causes or on effects rather than attempting to do both.
- Causes and effects vary in importance and in timing. Some are primary and some are secondary; some are immediate and others are remote.
- Causes and effects are logically organized, typically moving from first to last, most important to least, immediate to remote.
- Cause-and-effect analyses employ transitions and parallelism to signal to the reader the structure of the analysis.

IN PROSE

College textbooks must present accurate information in readable and easily understood language. As a result, they offer excellent examples of informative writing. This example, taken from Rebecca Donatelle's popular *Access to Health*, explains why some college students feel the painful effects of a night of partying.

Immediate Effects of Alcohol

The most dramatic effects produced by ethanol occur within the central nervous system (CNS). The primary action of the drug is to reduce the frequency of nerve transmissions and impulses at synaptic junctions. This reduction of nerve transmissions results in a significant depression of CNS functions, with resulting decreases in respiratory rate, pulse rate, and blood pressure. As CNS depression deepens, vital functions become noticeably depressed. In extreme cases, coma and death can result.

Alcohol is a diuretic, causing increased urinary output. Although this effect might be expected to lead to automatic dehydration (loss of water), the body actually retains water, most of it in the muscles or in the cerebral tissues. This is because water is usually pulled out of the cerebrospinal fluid (fluid within the brain and spinal cord), leading to what is known as mitochondrial dehydration at the cell level within the nervous system. Mitochondria are miniature organs within the cells that are responsible for specific functions. They rely heavily upon fluid balance. When mitochondrial dehydration occurs from drinking, the mitochondria cannot carry out their normal functions, resulting in symptoms that include the "morning-after" headaches suffered by some drinkers.

Alcohol irritates the gastrointestinal system and may cause indigestion and heartburn if taken on an empty stomach. Long-term use of alcohol causes repeated irritation that has been linked to cancers of the esophagus and stomach. In addition, people who engage in brief drinking sprees during which they consume unusually high amounts of alcohol put themselves at risk for irregular heartbeat or even total loss of heart rhythm, which can cause disruption in blood flow and possible damage to the heart muscle. ■

QUESTIONS FOR ANALYSIS

1. What device does the writer use to make sure the reader understands the meaning of medical terms?
2. How is the explanation structured? How does the paragraphing help in making that structure clear?
3. How does the analysis help you to understand what happens when you consume alcohol?
4. What assumptions does the writer seem to make about potential readers?

CRITICAL READING ACTIVITY

Do a formal outline for the passage. What does that reveal about its structure and organization?

IN LITERATURE

Ellie Schoenfeld's poem "Barbie's Little Sister" playfully uses a cause-and-effect structure in order to comment on the image and values that are embodied in Barbie's "little sister Aurora." Aurora's fictional activities and behavior do not reflect the cultural "ideal" that Barbie and her friends and family are meant to project. As you read, think about the image that Mattel is creating for its popular dolls and the millions of young girls who play with them.

Barbie's Little Sister

ELLIE SCHOENFELD

Barbie's little sister
Aurora
got sent away to reform school
when she was thirteen.

Mattel brought her back complete
with wheat germ, a VW love bus
and a recipe for sesame dream bars.

But she never caught on.

Didn't go for the vanity
table or the bubble head.

Thought Barbie was repressed
and Ken was a nerd
so she hit the road
with his cousin Jeremy.

They went to demonstrations
wore love beads
and got matching tattoos.

Finally Mattel stopped marketing her,
didn't think she'd make
a good role model.   ∎

QUESTIONS FOR ANALYSIS

1. What is it about the fictional activities of Aurora that make her a "bad" role model?

2. Schoenfeld implies that Mattel regards Barbie as a "good" role model for young girls. What does that entail? How would "good" be defined?

3. What does Schoenfeld mean when she writes that Aurora "didn't go for the vanity table or the bubble head"?

4. What reaction might Schoenfeld be trying to evoke in her readers?

WRITING SUGGESTIONS

1. **Analysis.** What assumption is Schoenfeld making about her readers' knowledge of Barbie and her world? Why can she make that assumption? What does that imply about the power of marketing, especially marketing to young children and their parents? In an essay, analyze the role that our assumptions/knowledge about Barbie play in the poem.

2. It is difficult to be aware of the pressures generated by popular culture yet alone to be able to deal with them. How are you influenced by what you see around you—by images in magazines, in advertisements, in films, in music, in television? To what extent are those images a problem? Do they ever make you do things that you shouldn't, feel bad about yourself, or feel pressured to change and conform? Explore in an essay one aspect of the influence of popular culture on your life. Possible points of departure include:
    a. Your physical self—size, proportions, weight, appearance
    b. Your values and expectations in life—how do you measure success? Happiness?
    c. Your possessions—what role do they play in your life?

IN A VISUAL

A photographic image is static; it captures or freezes one moment in time. Cause and effect involves a change over time. Photographic images can, however, suggest a cause and effect relationship. It is the viewer who sees the image,

Alexander/Fotolia

who supplies the necessary causal links, in order to read the image as an example of cause and effect. For example, look at the image above. Do you see it just as a funny animal picture? Or does some causal connection immediately come to mind? What is it and why do you think that? Would you read the image in the same way if it were a bird perched on the small chunk of floating ice?

QUESTIONS FOR ANALYSIS

1. What is it about the image that makes it both comic and tragic?
2. Does the bear's posture influence your reading of the image?
3. Do you attribute an emotion to the bear? Why or why not?
4. What can you surmise about where the photograph was taken?

WRITING SUGGESTIONS

1. **Analysis.** Obviously the image was not posed. The photographer captured what she or he saw. What is it about the image—its composition, its location—that suggests that it is more than a cute photograph of an animal taken in its natural environment? In an essay, analyze what it is about the image that suggests or implies a cause-and-effect pattern.

2. Choose a cause-and-effect issue/situation about which you feel strongly—for example, water pollution, garbage disposal, animal rights, working conditions, water shortages. Go to Google Images and locate four to six images that could be used to accompany your essay.

3. A really successful television show and film always begets imitators. Select a type of television show (e.g., reality, crime drama, celebrity "watches," adult cartoon) or film (e.g., vampires, alien invasions, catastrophic disaster), and analyze in an essay the possible reasons for the popularity of the format or subject.

Games, Not Schools, Are Teaching Kids to Think

JAMES PAUL GEE

James Paul Gee is the Mary Lou Fulton Presidential Professor of Literacy Studies at Arizona State University and affiliated with the Games, Learning, and Society group at the University of Wisconsin–Madison. Gee has written and lectured widely on psycholinguistics, discourse analysis, sociolinguistics, bilingual education, and literacy. Two of his recent books related to this essay are What Video Games Have to Teach Us About Learning and Literacy *(2nd ed. 2007) and* The Anti-Education Era: Creating Smarter Students through Digital Learning *(2013).*

On Writing: *Gee observed: "Writing systems are cultural inventions. Some writing systems are closely tied to speech (e.g., alphabets) and others are not (e.g., logograms). Unlike speech, in the case of writing systems, production (writing) is less common and more restricted than is consumption (reading). It is normal for people to be better at reading than writing and even the ability to read has rarely been universal in societies. The ability to write has never been."*

Before Reading

Connecting: Do you play videogames? If so, what do you think you learn from them?

Anticipating: Videogames and their content are often criticized. As you read the essay, do you find Gee's assertions persuasive?

1   **T**he US spends almost $50 billion each year on education, so why aren't kids learning? Forty percent of students lack basic reading skills, and their academic performance is dismal compared with that of their foreign counterparts. In response to this crisis, schools are skilling-and-drilling their way "back to basics," moving toward mechanical instruction methods that rely on line-by-line scripting for teachers and endless multiple-choice testing. Consequently, kids aren't learning how to think anymore—they're learning how to memorize. This might be an ideal recipe for the future Babbitts of the world, but it won't produce the kind of agile, analytical minds that will lead the high tech global age. Fortunately, we've got *Grand Theft Auto: Vice City* and *Deus X* for that.

2   After school, kids are devouring new information, concepts, and skills every day, and, like it or not, they're doing it controller in hand, plastered

to the TV. The fact is, when kids play videogames they can experience a much more powerful form of learning than when they're in the classroom. Learning isn't about memorizing isolated facts. It's about connecting and manipulating them. Doubt it? Just ask anyone who's beaten *Legend of Zelda* or solved *Morrowind*.

3   The phenomenon of the videogame as an agent of mental training is largely unstudied; more often, games are denigrated for being violent or they're just plain ignored. They shouldn't be. Young gamers today aren't training to be gun-toting carjackers. They're learning how to learn. In *Pikmin*, children manage an army of plant-like aliens and strategize to solve problems. In *Metal Gear Solid 2*, players move stealthily through virtual environments and carry out intricate missions. Even in the notorious *Vice City*, players craft a persona, build a history, and shape a virtual world. In strategy games like *WarCraft III* and *Age of Mythology*, they learn to micromanage an array of elements while simultaneously balancing short- and long-term goals. That sounds like something for their resumes.

4   The secret of a videogame as a teaching machine isn't its immersive 3-D graphics but its underlying architecture. Each level dances around the outer limits of the player's abilities, seeking at every point to be hard enough to be just doable. In cognitive science, this is referred to as the "regime of competence principle," which results in a feeling of simultaneous pleasure and frustration—a sensation as familiar to gamers as sore thumbs. Cognitive scientist Andy diSessa has argued that the best instruction hovers at the boundary of a student's competence. Most schools, however, seek to avoid invoking feelings of both pleasure and frustration, blind to the fact that these emotions can be extremely useful when it comes to teaching kids.

5   Also, good videogames incorporate the principle of expertise. They tend to encourage players to achieve total mastery of one level, only to challenge and undo that mastery in the next, forcing kids to adapt and evolve. This carefully choreographed dialectic has been identified by learning theorists as the best way to achieve expertise in any field. This doesn't happen much in our routine-driven schools, where "good" students are often just good at "doing school."

6   How did videogames become such successful models of effective learning? Game coders aren't trained as cognitive scientists. It's a simple case of free-market economics: If a title doesn't teach players how to play it well, it won't sell well. Game companies don't rake in $6.9 billion a year by dumbing down the material—aficionados condemn short and easy games like *Half Life: Blue Shift* and *Devil May Cry 2*. Designers respond by making harder and more complex games that require mastery of sophisticated worlds and as many as 50 to 100 hours to complete. Schools, meanwhile, respond with more tests, more drills, and more rigidity. They're in the cognitive-science dark ages.

7   We don't often think about videogames as relevant to education reform, but maybe we should. Game designers don't often think of themselves as learning theorists. Maybe they should. Kids often say it doesn't feel like

learning when they're gaming—they're much too focused on playing. If kids were to say that about a science lesson, our country's education problems would be solved. ■

QUESTIONS ON SUBJECT AND PURPOSE

1. According to Gee what strategies do designers of videogames use that are effective teaching tools?
2. In contrast, according to Gee, what learning strategies are schools using?
3. After reading the essay and the biographical headnote, what purpose might Gee have in writing the essay?

QUESTIONS ON STRATEGY AND AUDIENCE

1. What does Gee see as responsible for the "forty percent of students [who] lack basic reading skills"?
2. What preconceptions about videogames does Gee think his audience has?
3. On the basis of the vocabulary and the sentence structures that Gee uses what assumptions might be making about his audience?

QUESTIONS ON VOCABULARY AND STYLE

1. What does the phrase "immersive 3-D graphics" (paragraph 4) mean? Could you paraphrase that?
2. What is the effect of including the names of so many videogames in the essay?
3. Be prepared to define the following words: *denigrated* (paragraph 3), *stealthily* (3), *immersive* (4), *dialectic* (5), *aficionados* (6).

WRITING SUGGESTIONS

1. **Doing a Critical Analysis.** By closely analyzing the detail, the word choice, the structure of the essay, define the audience that Gee seems to have in mind.
2. **Journaling or Blogging.** If you had to list three times in your life—and not just your school life—when you learned something, what were those three occasions? Make a list and write a sentence for each explaining what it was that you learned and why you learned it.
3. **Practicing in a Paragraph.** Select one of your examples and develop it into a paragraph. Describe what you did and explain why that was a learning experience.
4. **Writing the Personal Essay.** Look again at your list and then abstract from it a list of reasons why these were learning experiences. In a cause and effect analysis explore what makes an experience an effective learning strategy.
5. **Finding Reading Connections.** Libby Sander in "Colleges Confront a Gender Gap in Student Engagement" (Chapter 5) points to some significant differences between males and females in "engagement" in college. Might there be a connection between what Sander sees and Gee's point?

6. **Exploring Links Online.** Would using videogames strategies improve the quality of education in U.S. classrooms? Using online sources, research how widely accepted or criticized such an idea is.

7. **Writing the Research Paper.** Gee notes that 40% of U.S. students lack basic reading skills. Research that statistic and the causes that are typically cited as responsible for that number. Remember to document your sources.

For Further Study

Focusing on Grammar and Writing. Look carefully at the opening sentence of each paragraph. What role does that sentence play in signaling the content of the paragraph?

Working Together. Working in small groups brainstorm some suggestions about how Gee's points might be presented to a school board or to the administration at your college or university.

Seeing Other Modes at Work. The essay also show elements of persuasion/argumentation and comparison and contrast.

On Teenagers and Tattoos

ANDRES MARTIN

Andres Martin received his M.D. from the Universidad Nacional Antonoma de Mexico in 1990. He is currently a professor and medical director of the Child Psychiatric Inpatient Service at Yale University. He specializes in inpatient child and adolescent psychiatry and psychopharmacology. A widely known authority, he is the author of many professional publications. "On Teenagers and Tattoos" was first published in the Journal of Child and Adolescent Psychiatry *in 1997.*

Before Reading

Connecting: Do you have any tattoos or piercings? How many? How old were you when you got each?

Anticipating: Martin suggests reasons why adolescents get tattoos and piercings. Do you recognize any of these reasons as ones that motivated you or a friend to get either a tattoo or a piercing?

> The skeleton dimensions I shall now proceed to set down are copied verbatim from my right arm, where I had them tattooed: as in my wild wanderings at that period, there was no other secure way of preserving such valuable statistics.
>
> —MELVILLE, *MOBY DICK*

1 **T**attoos and piercing have become a part of our everyday landscape. They are ubiquitous, having entered the circles of glamour and the mainstream of fashion, and they have even become an increasingly common feature of our urban youth. Legislation in most states restricts professional tattooing to adults older than 18 years of age, so "high end" tattooing is rare in children and adolescents, but such tattoos are occasionally seen in older teenagers. Piercings, by comparison, as well as self-made or "jailhouse" type tattoos, are not at all rare among adolescents or even among school-age children. Like hairdo, makeup, or baggy jeans, tattoos and piercings can be subject to fad influence or peer pressure in an effort toward group affiliation. As with any other fashion statement, they can be construed as bodily aids in the inner struggle toward identity consolidation, serving as adjuncts to the defining and sculpting of the self by means of external manipulations. But unlike most other body decorations, tattoos and piercings are set apart by their irreversible and permanent nature, a quality at the core of their magnetic appeal to adolescents.

2 Adolescents and their parents are often at odds over the acquisition of bodily decorations. For the adolescent, piercing or tattoos may be seen as personal and beautifying statements, while parents may construe them as oppositional and enraging affronts to their authority. Distinguishing bodily adornment from self-mutilation may indeed prove challenging, particularly when a family is in disagreement over a teenager's motivations and a clinician is summoned as the final arbiter. At such times it may be most important to realize jointly that the skin can all too readily become but another battleground for the tensions of the age, arguments having less to do with tattoos and piercings than with core issues such as separation from the family matrix. Exploring the motivations and significance [underlying] tattoos (Grumet, 1983) and piercings can go a long way toward resolving such differences and can become a novel and additional way of getting to know teenagers. An interested and nonjudgmental appreciation of teenagers' surface presentations may become a way of making contact not only in their terms but on their turfs: quite literally on the territory of their skins.

3 The following three sections exemplify some of the complex psychological underpinnings of youth tattooing.

Identity and the Adolescent's Body

4 Tattoos and piercing can offer a concrete and readily available solution for many of the identity crises and conflicts normative to adolescent development. In using such decorations, and by marking out their bodily territories, adolescents can support their efforts at autonomy, privacy, and insulation. Seeking individuation, tattooed adolescents can become unambiguously demarcated from others and singled out as unique. The intense and often disturbing reactions that are mobilized in viewers can help to effectively keep them at bay, becoming tantamount to the proverbial "Keep Out" sign hanging from a teenager's door.

5   Alternatively, feeling prey to a rapidly evolving body over which they have no say, self-made and openly visible decorations may restore adolescents' sense of normalcy and control, a way of turning a passive experience into an active identity. By indelibly marking their bodies, adolescents can strive to reclaim their bearings within an environment experienced as alien, estranged, or suffocating or to lay claim over their evolving and increasingly unrecognizable bodies. In either case, the net outcome can be a resolution to unwelcome impositions: external, familial, or societal in one case; internal and hormonal in the other. In the words of a 16-year-old girl with several facial piercings, and who could have been referring to her body just as well as to the position within her family: "If I don't fit in, it is because I say so."

Incorporation and Ownership

6 Imagery of a religious, deathly, or skeletal nature, the likenesses of fierce animals or imagined creatures, and the simple inscription of names are some of the time-tested favorite contents for tattoos. In all instances, marks become not only memorials or recipients for dearly held persons or concepts: they strive for incorporation, with images and abstract symbols gaining substance on becoming a permanent part of the individual's skin. Thickly embedded in personally meaningful representations and object relations, tattoos can become not only the ongoing memento of a relationship, but at times even the only evidence that there ever was such a bond. They can quite literally become the relationship itself. The turbulence and impulsivity of early attachments and infatuations may become grounded, effectively bridging oblivion through the visible reality to tattoos.

7   Case Vignette: "A," a 13-year-old boy, proudly showed me his tattooed deltoid. The coarsely depicted roll of the dice marked the day and month of his birth. Rather disappointed, he then uncovered an immaculate back, going on to draw for me the great "piece" he envisioned for it. A menacing figure held a hand of cards: two aces, two eights, and a card with two sets of dates. "A's" father had belonged to Dead Man's Hand, a motorcycle gang named after the set of cards (aces and eights) that the legendary Wild Bill Hickock had held in the 1890s when shot dead over a poker table in Deadwood, South Dakota. "A" had only the vaguest memory of and sketchiest information about his father, but he knew he had died in a motorcycle accident: The fifth card marked the dates of his birth and death.

8   The case vignette also serves to illustrate how tattoos are often the culmination of a long process of imagination, fantasy, and planning that can start at an early age. Limited markings, or relatively reversible ones such as piercings, can at a later time scaffold toward the more radical commitment of a permanent tattoo.

The Quest of Permanence

9 The popularity of the anchor as a tattoo motif may historically have had to do less with guild identification among sailors than with an intense longing

for rootedness and stability. In a similar vein, the recent increase in the popularity and acceptance of tattoos may be understood as an antidote or counterpoint to our urban and nomadic lifestyles. Within an increasingly mobile society, in which relationships are so often transient—as attested by the frequencies of divorce, abandonment, foster placement, and repeated moves, for example—tattoos can be a readily available source of grounding. Tattoos, unlike many relationships, can promise permanence and stability. A sense of constancy can be derived from unchanging marks that can be carried along no matter what the physical, temporal, or geographical vicissitudes at hand. Tattoos stay, while all else may change.

10   Case Vignette: A proud father at 17, "B" had had the smiling face of his 4-month-old baby girl tattooed on his chest. As we talked at a tattoo convention, he proudly introduced her to me, explaining how he would "always know how beautiful she is today" when years from then he saw her semblance etched on himself.

11   The quest for permanence may at other times prove misleading and offer premature closure to unresolved conflicts. At a time of normative uncertainties, adolescents may maladaptively and all too readily commit to a tattoo and its indefinite presence. A wish to hold on to a current certainty may lead the adolescent to lay down in ink what is valued and cherished one day but may not necessarily be in the future. The frequency of self-made tattoos among hospitalized, incarcerated, or gang-affiliated youths suggests such motivations: A sense of stability may be a particularly dire need under temporary, turbulent, or volatile conditions. In addition, through their designs teenagers may assert a sense of bonding and allegiance to a group larger than themselves. Tattoos may attest to powerful experiences, such as adolescence itself, lived and even survived together. As with Moby Dick's protagonist, Ishmael, they may bear witness to the "valuable statistics" of one's "wild wanderings": those of adolescent exhilaration and excitement on the one hand; of growing pains, shared misfortune, or even incarceration on the other.

12   Adolescents' bodily decorations, at times radical and dramatic in their presentation, can be seen in terms of figuration rather than disfigurement, of the natural body being through them transformed into a personalized body (Brain, 1979). They can often be understood as self-constructive and adorning efforts, rather than prematurely subsumed as mutilatory and destructive acts. If we bear all of this in mind, we may not only arrive at a position to pass more reasoned clinical judgment, but become sensitized through our patients' skins to another level of their internal reality.

REFERENCES

Brain, R. (1979). *The decorated body*. New York: Harper & Row.

Grumet, G. W. (1983). Psychodynamic implications of tattoos. *American Journal of Orthopsychiatry*, 53, 482–92.

QUESTIONS ON SUBJECT AND PURPOSE

1. In what ways are tattoos and piercings different from hairstyles or clothing fads?
2. According to Martin, what is the typical parental reaction to such markings?
3. What purpose might Martin have in the essay? Before you answer this, define his audience (see question 3 in Strategy and Audience below).

QUESTIONS ON STRATEGY AND AUDIENCE

1. What is the effect on the reader of subdividing the text with additional white space and providing headings for the subsections?
2. What is the effect of including the two "case vignettes" (paragraphs 7 and 10)?
3. Who does Martin imagine as his audience, and what evidence can you cite to support your answer?

QUESTIONS ON VOCABULARY AND STYLE

1. What is the significance of the quotation from Melville's *Moby Dick*, which prefaces the essay?
2. What does the presence of documented sources in the essay suggest?
3. Be prepared to define the following words: *ubiquitous* (paragraph 1), *affront* (2), *demarcated* (4), *tantamount* (4), *nomadic* (9), *vicissitudes* (9), *maladaptively* (11), *volatile* (11).

WRITING SUGGESTIONS

1. **Doing a Critical Analysis.** Obviously the essay was not written for a general audience. How could the essay be recast if it were to be published in a magazine aimed at parents of teenage children? What changes would you have to make and why? In an essay, analyze why those changes would be more appropriate for that new audience.
2. **Journaling or Blogging.** Do you have body markings? Why did you do so? If not, why have you made that choice?
3. **Practicing in a Paragraph.** In a paragraph, perhaps drawing on your own experiences or those of friends, analyze two potential effects of having such body markings.
4. **Writing the Personal Essay.** Interview a substantial number of friends who have body markings. Why did they get them? What were the reasons or causes? What have been effects of having these marks? In an essay, write about the causes or the effects that they report.
5. **Finding Reading Connections.** The student essay in the opening of this chapter deals with the same subject. What does it add to the discussion of why body markings are so common?
6. **Exploring Links Online.** Employers can refuse to hire anyone with visible tattoos and/or piercings. You can find a large number of online articles about this. What can be the effects of such markings on your job prospects? Explore the subject in an essay.

7. **Writing the Research Paper.** Martin identifies some of the reasons why young people make such "surface representations." Explore the link in the other direction: what are the effects—physical, psychological, cultural—of such markings? In a research paper with formal documentation, analyze what research tells us about these effects.

For Further Study

Focusing on Grammar and Writing. What types of transitional devices does Martin use in his essay to move from one cause or reason to another?

Working Together. Working in small groups, divide the essay into blocks of paragraphs. What evidence in each block reveals Martin's understanding of his audience?

Seeing Other Modes at Work. In addition to cause and effect, Martin is also trying to persuade his readers to see how important it is to know why people mark their bodies.

Kids Battle the Lure of Junk Food

MAUREEN O'HAGAN

Maureen O'Hagan is a reporter for the Seattle Times. *She was a Knight-Wallace Journalism Fellow at the University of Michigan and has won many national, state, and regional journalism awards for her work. In 2004, she was a finalist for the Pulitzer Prize in Public Service. This essay appeared in the* Pacific Northwest Magazine, *available online at the* Seattle Times, *in 2011 and was reprinted in* The Best Food Writing 2012 *(Boston: Da Capo, 2012).*

Before Reading

Connecting: Do you feel the "lure" of junk food? Be honest. What attracts you?

Anticipating: O'Hagan's essay is not about "fast food," but about "junk food." What types of foods could be labeled as "junk" and why?

1   **N**athan Stoltzfus has a problem.

2   It starts first thing in the morning, when he catches five or 10 minutes of TV just before heading out the door to Northshore Junior High. "There's these commercials for Cookie Crisp cereal or Pop-Tarts," he says. "They show some really happy kid eating them."

3   Over at school, he makes his way to homeroom as the smell of French toast drifts from the cafeteria.

4   At lunchtime, he sees a sign over the ice cream and cookies. It says, "Treat yourself today." He tries to focus on his veggie-filled sandwich. But invariably, one of his buddies will jump up for another run through the lunch line. "Who wants to come with me to get some cookies?" the kid'll ask.

5   To Nathan, this innocent question is a trap. As the heaviest kid at the table, he tells himself, keep your eyes on the veggies. But he also wants to fit in. "It's very tempting," Nathan says. "You feel like you almost have to do it in order to be friends."

6   Now, Nathan's just 14, but he's no slouch. He's articulate, creative, has a good group of friends and seems to take time to think about what he's doing. He's dedicated, too, singing for years with the Northwest Boychoir.

7   He's also been overweight for most of his life. To him, it feels like a curse.

8   And the pressure never subsides. There's the school's annual pie day to celebrate "pi"; there's the group Slurpee runs after school; the torment of his skinny brother devouring Oreos; the weekend trips to the mall. "A couple weeks ago, there was like 16 of us. One of the guys said, 'Oh my gosh you have to try this ice cream,'" he recalls.

9   What's a kid to do?

10   Right now, leaders here are trying hard to help. In the past decade, local agencies have been awarded at least $53 million in grants and other funding to combat obesity—most of it in the past year. They've enlisted hundreds of partners in this effort, and they're using some of the most newfangled approaches.

11   Within the next year, for example, they'll have spent at least $1.8 million getting healthy produce into corner stores. In the next two years, another $276,000 will be spent on building school gardens. Money will go to rejigger P.E. curriculums, train cafeteria workers and try to get kids to walk to school.

12   Still, all this effort will miss one of the biggest battlegrounds of all: what's going on inside Nathan's head.

13   "Treat yourself today," the sign in the cafeteria commands. Just say no, Nathan tries to tell himself. Let's call this the Temptation Complication.

14   It's a problem for Nathan. It's a problem for tens of thousands of overweight kids in Washington. And it's a problem for all of us.

15   It'll take a lot more than school gardens to dig our way out of this one.

16 People who work on childhood obesity often talk about how different the world was a generation ago. When she was a kid, University of Washington researcher Donna Johnson told me, soda was a special treat. Now, sugar-sweetened beverages are just a few quarters away, in the school vending machine. In surveys of Washington adolescents, about 40 percent said they drank at least one soda yesterday.

17   When he was a kid, former FDA Commissioner David Kessler says, there weren't coffee shops on every corner selling super-duper, fat-and-sugar, grande frappa-yummies. There wasn't the cacophony of chips and cookies at every gas station.

18   When I was a kid, I recall, we ate pretty much what our parents ate. Now, vast product lines are designed just for youngsters: the Go-Gurts and Lunchables and drink pouches. Experts say more new food products are introduced each year for kids than for adults. And guess what: Studies show kid food has more sugar than the adult version.

19   And don't even get me started on the "fruit leathers" and "fruit snacks" with nary a drop of juice. "When I was a kid," snickers Margo Wootan, director of nutrition policy at the Center for Science in the Public Interest, "they were called jelly beans."

20   This special kid food is sold on special TV stations created just for kids by special advertising execs who study youth culture as if they were researching a doctoral thesis.

21   Meanwhile, kids are noshing practically nonstop. "Your product doesn't have to be for a meal anymore," says Laurie Demeritt, president of the Bellevue market-research firm the Hartman Group. "Now there are 10 different 'eating occasions' throughout the day."

22   What we have here is a supply problem. Food is everywhere. That means temptation is everywhere. If Nathan makes healthy choices half the time, it's probably not enough.

23   But the Temptation Complication has another layer, one that's older than Go-Gurt and Nickelodeon and Mountain Dew. It has to do with biology.

24 Patsy Treece says her daughter, Hannah, has a "face that radiates kindness." She's right. Her eyes are a beautiful brown; her smile shines. At age 13, Treece says, Hannah's the kind of kid who'll stop to help if someone gets hurt on the playground.

25   She also has an appetite that won't quit.

26   At dinner, she'll ask for seconds, even thirds. "I'm really, really hungry," she explains.

27   Well, maybe not hungry exactly.

28   "It's just that if I see something good," she sighs, "I automatically pick it up and eat it." Like a lot of us, she gets pleasure from food. But afterward, she also feels pain.

29   Hannah's twin brother is slim and athletic, but her mom is also overweight. Treece has tried different diets with Hannah. She's tried sports. Delay. Portion control, using 100-calorie snack packs. "She'll have a couple of them," Treece says.

30   Don't even mention Flamin' Hot Cheetos. "She would kill somebody to get a package of those," Treece says. "It's almost like a compulsion." No kidding. Remember the old ad campaign, "Betcha can't eat just one"? That was Lay's Potato Chips. The same company makes Hannah's Cheetos.

31   Some people simply *can't* stop. There's science to prove it, says former FDA Commissioner Kessler.

32   Here's a guy who fought Big Tobacco. He's a doctor; he knows what's healthful. Yet until recently, he could come undone over a chocolate-chip cookie. "I have suits in every size," he says ruefully.

33   Our desire to eat doesn't originate in the stomach, really. We're wired to crave salt, sugar and fat, Kessler says. You see it in laboratory rats, too. They'll brave the possibility of electric shocks to keep eating their junk food. Even *bacteria* swim to sugar.

34   There's more.

35   "We used to think people were lazy or it was a question of willpower," Kessler explains. "I can now show you the (brain) scans. The vast majority of people who have a hard time controlling their eating have excessive activation of the brain's emotional core."

36   When you eat things like cookies or Cheetos you get an immediate reward. You feel good. Your brain actually changes when you eat that stuff, Kessler explains. The neurocircuitry gets rewired. Stumble across a "food cue"—maybe an ad for cereal, or the smell of French toast—and suddenly, your brain lights up. Your thoughts slip into those newly laid tracks and can't get off, like the way your skis follow along in a cross-country trail. Your brain, Kessler says, gets "hijacked." And the new pathway is reinforced further. Scientists say it's not exactly that we're addicted to food, but it sure is an awful lot like that.

37   Problem is, these food cues are everywhere. "We're living in a food carnival," Kessler says.

38   So we're not just fighting temptation like Nathan. We're battling our very biology, that automatic response that makes Kessler crumble at the thought of cookies and Hannah unshakable in the face of orangey-red salt.

39   Let's call this the Cheeto Compulsion. Betcha can't eat just one.

40 Hilary Bromberg, strategy director at the Seattle brand/communications firm Egg, says they sometimes put clients through a little exercise: *Talk about your food history.* "They enter almost a trance state," she says. "They say, my grandmother made me this, or my mother made me this. There's this visceral attachment."

41   Eating, in other words, isn't some sort of clinical calculation of calories. Most people aren't thinking, *Gee, I better have carrots instead of cake because I didn't get my five servings of vegetables today.* "Food is a source of sensual pleasure," Bromberg explains. "The emotions around food are profound." She's saying this as a marketing maven. She's also saying this as someone who studied cognitive neuroscience at Harvard and MIT.

42   Nathan's mother, Susan Stoltzfus, knows this, too. "Food has been that comfort or that source of consolation or that sense of belonging," she says. It's immediate, too—unlike losing weight, which requires forgoing that sense of pleasure over and over and over. "How do you live for that delayed gratification?" she wonders.

43   Nathan and Hannah might not explain it the same way. But they understand. Food is pleasure. Food is family, culture and tradition. Food is love.

44   Let's call this the Comfort Connection. And I'm willing to bet it's within arm's reach right now.

45   Marlene Schwartz, a clinical psychologist at Yale University, suggested a little experiment. Ask a roomful of people, *Who thinks junk-food marketing works?* All the hands will go up.

46   Ask, *does it work on you?* The hands will vanish.

47   "I think people decide, once it's in their pantry, it's no longer junk food," she says. Talk about getting inside your head. These marketing guys can put an idea in there and you don't even know it.

48   And it's growing even more sophisticated. Food producers have long hired experts to survey thousands of consumers at once. But in the past decade or so, the behind-the-scenes work has become even more stunning in its scope and highly particular in its findings. Some of the topics food marketers have studied recently: mother/daughter baking rituals; parents' stress level on car trips; the habits of kids at sporting events; how preschoolers are using their parents' smartphones; the traits of parents who are strict versus parents who are more permissive—and what it all means for their kids' eating habits. There's an entirely new genre of marketing and advertising firms, in fact, that focus on youth culture.

49   Meanwhile, in the past decade or two, says Demeritt of the Bellevue market-research firm, food-marketing companies also started going directly into people's homes. Shopping with them. Asking detailed personal questions. It's called ethnographic research, and it's being done in many cases by social anthropologists. Hordes of psychologists have been enlisted, as well, to better get inside consumers' heads.

50   The result is that marketers know exactly how families eat, what they eat and why. They know what makes them keep coming back, even when they know it's probably less nutritious.

51   Take Go-Gurt, for instance. It's one of the most successful kid foods ever. Moms are doling it out for breakfast, yet it's got more sugar per ounce than Coke. Yoplait sells $129 million worth of this stuff a year. Unnatural-hued goo in a squeezable tube!

52   How did Go-Gurt come to be? Really good research. In phone interviews, typical consumers would say breakfast was a sit-down, family affair. But when General Mills hired an anthropologist to spend time with ordinary families, she discovered they were actually eating on the go. A niche was identified: Families could use something portable. And squeezable yogurt was born.

53   It appeals to a kid's taste buds for sure. But the makers of Go-Gurt aren't selling that, per se. They're selling fun, coolness. Remember Kessler and the way food activates the emotional core? Bingo.

54   The opportunities to hit that emotional core are greater than ever. Advertisers can reach kids on their own cable channels. They can reach them on the Internet—for a lot less money. At the same time, they'll learn even more about them. Marketers know the search terms consumers enter, the information they put on social-networking sites, the pages they view and countless other metrics. Companies are prohibited from collecting personal data on users less than 13 without parental permission, but a *Wall Street Journal*

investigation found even youngsters' online activities were being tracked, and in some cases offered for sale to advertisers. "Youth in 2010 will be the first generation in the post-digital economy the retailer will know by name," one marketing report said last year.

55   Check it out. There are Go-Gurt pages on Facebook. Go-Gurt videos on YouTube. There's even a Go-Gurt game. Betcha can't quit at one.

56 Last December, Demeritt's firm conducted a nationally representative survey about weight issues. Forty-two percent of people said childhood obesity is a big problem. But among the same people, only 3 percent agreed it was a problem in *their* family. "It shows you why people don't really do anything about weight," she says.

57   Other studies have found that most people aren't driven by a desire to be healthy. Instead, they judge their own weight in relation to their peers. If your peers are heavy, there's less motivation to reduce. As it turns out, we have a lot of heavy peers.

58   And look what we're up against: the Temptation Complication, the Cheeto Compulsion, the Comfort Connection.

59   Then there's the sheer firepower of food producers. "I remember a honcho at the CDC looked at me and said, 'They're way smarter than we are, and they have more money,'" the UW's Johnson recalls. She spends a lot of time nowadays thinking about the food environment, how it's easier to get Cheetos than it is to get an apple. But even if apples were everywhere, I ask her, would Nathan choose them? Would Hannah forgo her Cheetos? That's a tough one, she says.

60   "Most of us," she says sadly, "are going to choose fat and salt and sugar over foods that don't have those things in them." It's biology. It's culture.

61   Then she thinks, what if apples were made to seem more appealing? "It's not like Madison Avenue is inherently evil, right?" she muses. "If we could harness that . . . oh, man. . . . Think of the potential of what they could sell." ■

QUESTIONS ON SUBJECT AND PURPOSE

1. The word that O'Hagan uses in her title is "lure." Why that word? To what is she referring?
2. What is the "temptation complication"?
3. What might O'Hagan want her readers to learn from reading her essay?

QUESTIONS ON STRATEGY AND AUDIENCE

1. What is the "Cheeto Compulsion"?
2. The final two paragraphs include a quotation from a researcher. How do those paragraphs make you feel about this problem?
3. To whom is O'Hagan writing? Who seems to be her primary audience?

QUESTIONS ON VOCABULARY AND STYLE

1. At several points, O'Hagan repeats a version of "Betcha can't eat just one." Where did that saying come from?
2. At a number of points in the essay, O'Hagan introduces extra white space between groups of paragraphs. Why?
3. Be prepared to define the following words: *rejigger* (paragraph 11), *cacophony* (17), *nary* (18), *noshing* (21), *visceral* (40), *maven* (41), and *niche* (52).

WRITING SUGGESTIONS

1. **Doing a Critical Analysis.** O'Hagan includes two narrative examples in her essay: Nathan Stoltzfus and Hannah Treece. What role do these two stories play in the argument she is making?
2. **Journaling or Blogging.** As an adult, do you have junk food addictions? Do they arise out of your childhood? What is it that you cannot eat "just one" of?
3. **Practicing in a Paragraph.** Analyze one specific junk food weakness. In a cause analysis, suggest what it is about that one thing that "lures" you.
4. **Writing the Personal Essay.** Think about the food choices that you make each day. What do you choose to eat and why? Are your choices made deliberately or just by what is available? In an essay, analyze your daily eating habits.
5. **Finding Reading Connections.** Deborah L. Rhode in "Why Looks Are the Last Bastion of Discrimination" (Chapter 1) discusses some of the effects of obesity in hiring decisions. What are the effects for children? Do they encounter similar forms of discrimination?
6. **Exploring Links Online.** O'Hagan concentrates on some of the "causes" of childhood obesity. What about its effects? The Defense Department estimates that "one in four young adults is too overweight to enlist." In an essay, explore some of the effects of obesity on young adults.
7. **Writing the Research Paper.** In paragraph 56, O'Hagan cites a study in which 42% of people said childhood obesity was a significant problem, but only 3% felt it was a problem in their family. Research this disparity. What accounts for it? What are the consequences of such a belief?

For Further Study

Focusing on Grammar and Writing. O'Hagan's essay does not contain parenthetical references, footnotes, or a list of works/people cited. How does she handle documentation in the essay?

Working Together. The essay has many paragraphs in part because it was originally published in the column format of an online supplement to a newspaper. Working in groups, identify blocks of paragraphs that could be combined together and explain why.

Seeing Other Modes at Work. The essay also makes extensive use of narration.

Black Men and Public Space

BRENT STAPLES

Born in Chester, Pennsylvania, Brent Staples graduated from Widener University in 1973 and earned a Ph.D. in psychology from the University of Chicago in 1982. He worked for the Chicago Sun-Times *as a reporter before moving to the* New York Times *in 1985. In 1994 he published a memoir,* Parallel Time: Growing Up in Black and White, *which tells the story of his childhood in Chester, a mixed-race, economically declining town. The book focuses on his younger brother, a drug dealer who died of gunshot wounds at age 22.*

"Black Men and Public Space" was originally published in Ms. *(1986) magazine under the title "Just Walk on By: A Black Man Ponders His Power to Alter Public Space." In revised and edited form, it was reprinted in* Harper's *(1986) with the current title.*

On Writing: *In* Parallel Time, *Staples describes how, in his early 20s, he began to explore his voice as a writer: "I was carrying a journal with me everywhere. . . . I wrote on buses and on the Jackson Park el—though only at the stops to keep the writing legible. I traveled to distant neighborhoods, sat on the curbs, and sketched what I saw in words. Thursday meant free admission at the Art Institute. All day I attributed motives to people in paintings, especially people in Rembrandts. At closing time, I went to a nightclub in The Loop and spied on the patrons, copied their conversations, and speculated about their lives. The journal was more than 'a record of my inner transactions.' It was a collection of stolen souls from which I would one day construct a book."*

Before Reading

Connecting: What precautions do you take if you have to walk at night in public spaces?

Anticipating: Why does Staples whistle melodies from classical music when he walks at night? What effect does that particular "cowbell" have on people?

1   **M**y first victim was a woman—white, well dressed, probably in her early twenties. I came upon her late one evening on a deserted street in Hyde Park, a relatively affluent neighborhood in an otherwise mean, impoverished section of Chicago. As I swung onto the avenue behind her, there seemed to be a discreet, uninflammatory distance between us. Not so. She cast back a worried glance. To her, the youngish black man—a broad six feet two inches with a beard and billowing hair, both hands shoved into the pockets of a bulky

military jacket—seemed menacingly close. After a few more quick glimpses, she picked up her pace and was soon running in earnest. Within seconds she disappeared into a cross street.

2   That was more than a decade ago. I was twenty-two years old, a graduate student newly arrived at the University of Chicago. It was in the echo of that terrified woman's footfalls that I first began to know the unwieldy inheritance I'd come into—the ability to alter public space in ugly ways. It was clear that she thought herself the quarry of a mugger, a rapist, or worse. Suffering a bout of insomnia, however, I was stalking sleep, not defenseless wayfarers. As a softy who is scarcely able to take a knife to a raw chicken—let alone hold one to a person's throat—I was surprised, embarrassed, and dismayed all at once. Her flight made me feel like an accomplice in tyranny. It also made it clear that I was indistinguishable from the muggers who occasionally seeped into the area from the surrounding ghetto. That first encounter, and those that followed, signified that a vast, unnerving gulf lay between nighttime pedestrians—particularly women—and me. And I soon gathered that being perceived as dangerous is a hazard in itself. I only needed to turn a corner into a dicey situation, or crowd some frightened, armed person in a foyer somewhere, or make an errant move after being pulled over by a policeman. Where fear and weapons meet—and they often do in urban America—there is always the possibility of death.

3   In that first year, my first away from my hometown, I was to become thoroughly familiar with the language of fear. At dark, shadowy intersections, I could cross in front of a car stopped at a traffic light and elicit the *thunk, thunk, thunk, thunk* of the driver—black, white, male, or female—hammering down the door locks. On less traveled streets after dark, I grew accustomed to but never comfortable with people crossing to the other side of the street rather than pass me. Then there were the standard unpleasantries with policemen, doormen, bouncers, cabdrivers, and others whose business it is to screen out troublesome individuals *before* there is any nastiness.

4   I moved to New York nearly two years ago and I have remained an avid night walker. In central Manhattan, the near-constant crowd cover minimizes tense one-on-one street encounters. Elsewhere—in SoHo, for example, where sidewalks are narrow and tightly spaced buildings shut out the sky—things can get very taut indeed.

5   After dark, on the warrenlike streets of Brooklyn where I live, I often see women who fear the worst from me. They seem to have set their faces on neutral, and with their purse straps strung across their chests bandolier-style, they forge ahead as though bracing themselves against being tackled. I understand, of course, that the danger they perceive is not a hallucination. Women are particularly vulnerable to street violence, and young black males are drastically overrepresented among the perpetrators of that violence. Yet these truths are no solace against the kind of alienation that comes of being ever the suspect, a fearsome entity with whom pedestrians avoid making eye contact.

6   It is not altogether clear to me how I reached the ripe old age of twenty-two without being conscious of the lethality nighttime pedestrians attributed

to me. Perhaps it was because in Chester, Pennsylvania, the small, angry industrial town where I came of age in the 1960s, I was scarcely noticeable against a backdrop of gang warfare, street knifings, and murders. I grew up one of the good boys, had perhaps a half-dozen fistfights. In retrospect, my shyness of combat has clear sources.

7   As a boy, I saw countless tough guys locked away; I have since buried several, too. They were babies, really—a teenage cousin, a brother of twenty-two, a childhood friend in his mid-twenties—all gone down in episodes of bravado played out in the streets. I came to doubt the virtues of intimidation early on. I chose, perhaps unconsciously, to remain a shadow—timid, but a survivor.

8   The fearsomeness mistakenly attributed to me in public places often has a perilous flavor. The most frightening of these confusions occurred in the late 1970s and early 1980s, when I worked as a journalist in Chicago. One day, rushing into the office of a magazine I was writing for with a deadline story in hand, I was mistaken for a burglar. The office manager called security and, with an ad hoc posse, pursued me through the labyrinthine halls, nearly to my editor's door. I had no way of proving who I was. I could only move briskly toward the company of someone who knew me.

9   Another time I was on assignment for a local paper and killing time before an interview. I entered a jewelry store on the city's affluent Near North Side. The proprietor excused herself and returned with an enormous red Doberman pinscher straining at the end of a leash. She stood, the dog extended toward me, silent to my questions, her eyes bulging nearly out of her head. I took a cursory look around, nodded, and bade her good night.

10   Relatively speaking, however, I never fared as badly as another black male journalist. He went to nearby Waukegan, Illinois, a couple of summers ago to work on a story about a murderer who was born there. Mistaking the reporter for the killer, police officers hauled him from his car at gunpoint and but for his press credentials would probably have tried to book him. Such episodes are not uncommon. Black men trade tales like this all the time.

11   Over the years, I learned to smother the rage I felt at so often being taken for a criminal. Not to do so would surely have led to madness. I now take precautions to make myself less threatening. I move about with care, particularly late in the evening. I give a wide berth to nervous people on subway platforms during the wee hours, particularly when I have exchanged business clothes for jeans. If I happen to be entering a building behind some people who appear skittish, I may walk by, letting them clear the lobby before I return, so as not to seem to be following them. I have been calm and extremely congenial on those rare occasions when I've been pulled over by the police.

12   And on late-evening constitutionals I employ what has proved to be an excellent tension-reducing measure: I whistle melodies from Beethoven and Vivaldi and the more popular classical composers. Even steely New Yorkers hunching toward night-time destinations seem to relax, and occasionally they even join in the tune. Virtually everybody seems to sense that a mugger

wouldn't be warbling bright, sunny selections from Vivaldi's *Four Seasons*. It is my equivalent of the cowbell that hikers wear when they know they are in bear country.   ■

QUESTIONS ON SUBJECT AND PURPOSE

1. What does Staples mean by the phrase "public space"? In what way is he capable of altering it?
2. What types of evidence does Staples provide to illustrate his point—that black men can alter public space?
3. What purpose might Staples have had in writing the essay?

QUESTIONS ON STRATEGY AND AUDIENCE

1. In addition to cause and effect, what other structure is at work in the essay?
2. When the essay was first published, it was entitled "Just Walk on By." When it appeared in a slightly revised form, it was retitled, "Black Men and Public Space." What is the effect of the change in title?
3. The essay first appeared in *Ms.* magazine. What assumptions could Staples have had about his initial audience?

QUESTIONS ON VOCABULARY AND STYLE

1. What is the effect of Staples's opening sentence in the essay? Why does he write "my first victim"?
2. In paragraph 5, Staples writes the phrase "on the warrenlike streets of Brooklyn." What is a *warren?* To what does the term usually refer? Can you think of another word or phrase that Staples could have used instead that might be more vivid to most readers?
3. Be prepared to define the following words: *discreet* (paragraph 1), *dicey* (2), *errant* (2), *taut* (4), *warrenlike* (5), *bandolier* (5), *solace* (5), *entity* (5), *bravado* (7), *ad hoc* (8), *cursory* (9), *skittish* (11), *congenial* (11), *constitutionals* (12).

WRITING SUGGESTIONS

1. **Doing a Critical Analysis.** In an essay, analyze how Staples ensures continuity in his essay. Is it held together by chronology or by the logical development of an idea or an awareness?
2. **Journaling or Blogging.** Have you ever been frightened in a public space? Explore your memories or recent experiences. What happened? How did you feel?
3. **Practicing in a Paragraph.** Select one of the experiences you listed above and narrate that experience in a paragraph. How and why did you react? Was your fear justified?
4. **Writing the Personal Essay.** We all provoke reactions from people who do not know us. Sometimes we even try to provoke a reaction by how we dress or act or speak. Describe your image and behavior and then analyze how and why people react to you as a result.

5. **Finding Reading Connections.** Judith Ortiz Cofer's "The Myth of the Latin Woman" (Chapter 4) describes how people have reacted to her. Compare the reactions that the two provoke in others. To what extent might the reactions differ because of the authors' genders?

6. **Exploring Links Online.** What additional prejudices do young black men face today? Has anything changed since the original publication of "Black Men and Public Space" in 1986? Research the problem online.

7. **Writing the Research Paper.** Research the problem of assault or mugging in your own community or your own college campus. What are your chances of being a victim? Where and when is it most likely to happen? Your school's security office will have statistics. Provide documentation for your sources.

For Further Study

Focusing on Grammar and Writing. Staples often uses vivid verbs in telling his story. What do those verbs suggest about how to create a vivid story or description?

Working Together. Staples's introduction seems more appropriate for a magazine targeted at women rather than men. Working in small groups, recast the opening paragraphs so they are aimed at a male audience.

Seeing Other Modes at Work. Staples uses both narration and description in the essay as well.

Caffeine Crazies

MARK J. PENN

Mark J. Penn is the president of Penn, Schoen and Berland Associates, a polling firm, and worldwide CEO of Burson-Marsteller, a public relations company. He served as chief strategist and pollster for the 2008 presidential campaign of Hillary Rodham Clinton. His clients have included former President Bill Clinton and Microsoft's Bill Gates. Penn graduated from Harvard where he served as city editor for the school's newspaper, the Harvard Crimson. *This essay is taken from his book* Microtrends *(rev. ed. 2007). Penn defined a microtrend as "a small but growing group of people, who share an intense choice or preferences, that . . . has sometimes been missed or undercounted by the companies, marketers, policymakers." With his coauthor, E. Kinney Zalesne, he has been writing an online column titled "Microtrends" in the* Wall Street Journal *since December 2008.*

> **On Writing:** *In a 2009 column, Penn commented on the growing popularity of blogging. He wrote: "The best studies we can find say that we are a nation of over 20 million bloggers, with 1.7 million*

*profiting from the work, and 452,000 of those using blogging as their
primary source of income. . . . This could make us the most noisily opin-
ionated nation on earth. The Information Age has spawned many new
professions, but blogging could well be the one with the most profound
effect on our culture."*

Before Reading

Connecting: Stop and think: How many caffeinated drinks
(coffee, tea, colas, energy drinks) have you had today?

Anticipating: Why do you think caffeinated drinks are so
popular in American society? If you drink them, why?

1   **P**erhaps the most obvious trend in America is the vast and increasing consumption of bottled water.

2   In the early 1980s, the idea of paying for bottled water, instead of taking
it perfectly free from the tap, was laughable. But these days, you almost never
see anyone—from athletes to blue-collar workers to business executives—
without their little brand-name H_2Os. As of 2004, Americans drank over
twenty-three gallons of bottled water per person per year—almost ten times
the amount we drank in 1980. In 2006 alone, sales of Coca-Cola's Dasani and
PepsiCo's Aquafina (both of which, by the way, come from local tap water)
grew by more than 20 percent, putting them both on the list of top ten
refreshment beverages in the United States.

3   Add some vitamins, minerals, flavors, and/or fizzies to our water, and
we leap even higher. According to consumer surveys, people drink bottled
water because they think it is cleaner, healthier, and safer than tap water—
and if the bottlers add something "useful" to it like vitamins or minerals,
we're even happier. According to the Beverage Marketing Association, in
2006, beverages with "functional benefits" grew at two to three times the rate
of conventional beverages.

4   But while some of us are seeking the purity of bottled water, others have
gone in the opposite direction, driving the high-caffeine drink to new heights
of profit. The totally artificial, stimulus-producing, murky brown stuff that
couldn't be more different from water in taste, texture, and packaging. As
of 2007, almost 6 in 10 Americans drink a cup of coffee every day, up from
under half just three years ago. At-work coffee drinkers are nearly 1 in 4, up
from only 1 in 6 in 2003. Starbucks revenues *alone* grew from $1.7 billion in
1999 to a phenomenal $5.3 billion in 2004.

5   Coffee shops say they're getting espresso customers as young as 10 and 11.
Even church groups lure youth in with coffeehouse-like atmospheres—complete
with coffee.

6   And, of course, carbonated soft drinks are towering over other American beverages—at a staggering 52 gallons per person per year. According to a 2005 study, soft drinks are now the leading source of calories in the average American diet, accounting for almost 1 in every 10 calories consumed. (In the early 1990s, the leading calorie source was white bread.)

7   Even tea sales have more than tripled since the early 1990s. And innovators are launching new caffeinated breakfast products—like "Buzz Donuts" and "Buzzed Bagels." In case it was too much work to ingest your morning carbs and your morning caffeine in two separate mouthfuls.

8   Indeed, some people in America will give up the social aspect, and the flavor, of coffees and colas—if they can just have the caffeine straight. By far the fastest-growing beverages in 2006 were energy drinks, like Red Bull and Monster. Your basic 12-ounce can of Coke has 34 milligrams of caffeine. Red Bull has 80. Rockstar Zero Carb has 120. The new "Censored" Energy Drink—known until May 2007 as "Cocaine"—has 280.

9   In 2006, nearly 200 new such energy drinks hit the shelves, propelling the industry to 50 percent growth and nearly $4 billion in sales. From virtual obscurity just a couple years ago, Red Bull now ranks number seven in U.S. refreshment beverage company revenues, well ahead of Ocean Spray and just a notch or two behind Kraft Foods (which makes Country Time, Crystal Light, Kool-Aid, and Capri Sun). Apparently, Red Bull is the third-largest source of beverage profits in convenience stores across the U.S.

10   And no one thinks this trend is easing. In 2007, both PepsiCo and Coca-Cola are launching drinks with two to three times the caffeine content of their regular brands.

11   Yes, even back when I was in college in the 1970s, kids took No-Doz to cram the night before a big exam. But No-Doz has only 100 milligrams of caffeine per tablet, at most. What's a little 100 mg pill compared to Cocaine (the formerly named drink), at almost three times that dose? Indeed, the combination of high pressure to perform, lackluster judgment, and easy availability of caffeine is causing teens and young adults to drive the hyper-consumption of hyper-caffeinated drinks. According to a three-year study of calls to a Chicago Poison Center released in October 2006, the average age of caffeine overdosers—many of whom required hospitalization and, in some cases, intensive care—was 21.

12   Why the caffeine craziness? What is all the raging buzz for *buzz*?

13   Part of it, of course, is the 24/7 wakefulness of American life. From round-the-clock shopping and entertainment, to round-the-world colleagues and clients, life in America today is a rest-less frenzy. Americans already sleep an average of 25 percent less per night than we did 100 years ago, and so to some degree we are trying to make up for it with beverages turbo-packed with caffeine. Today's students, especially, feel themselves to be under more pressure to excel than students of prior generations—and with late nights out, 24-hour convenience stores, and little adult supervision, more and more of them are going Caffeine Crazy.

14   Another reason for the surge in booster drinks is that energy is at an all-time premium in American culture. For a population that is as old as it's ever been, we value vim, vitality, and vigor like never before. Gym memberships are soaring, especially among seniors. Plastic surgery—to make us look younger, at least—is on the rise. Viagra use, between 1998 and 2002, grew over 200 percent among men aged 46–55—and *over 300 percent* among men aged 18–45. Can it be that regular human performance is simply not enough these days? Many of us want to be super-alert, super-charged, and super-men. And if Red Bull, or a venti latte, can get us there—even if we're 12 years old, or if it's our third such drink that day—so be it.

15   The health effects of the Caffeine Crazy trend are worrisome. It is well documented that caffeine, especially in high doses, can cause insomnia, anxiety, headaches, stomach problems, cardiac arrhythmias, and weight gain—especially if lashed to sugary soft drinks and caramel macchiatos. The quest for super-energy, ironically, can weigh us down.

16   It's even worse for children, who may be the fastest-growing subgroup of caffeine consumers. Not only are American kids already becoming obese at alarming rates, but a child who drinks one can of caffeinated soda apparently experiences the same effects as an adult who drinks four cups of coffee. While the full effects of energy drinks like Red Bull have yet to be determined, some countries—like France, Norway, and Denmark—have outlawed them entirely because of alleged links to sudden deaths.

17   Of course, some will rise to defend caffeine's impact on health. It can make athletes more alert, especially if they are not regular users; and many a drowsy driver has probably stayed alive thanks to coffee. Caffeine has been linked to lower Alzheimer's rates, less diabetes, fewer gallstones, lower rates of Parkinson's, and less colon cancer. It is also said to support the delivery of other vitamins or healing agents (which is why there are surprisingly high quantities of caffeine in over-the-counter pain relievers). One study says caffeine grows brain cells, potentially improving memory and the ability to learn. Another study says it cures male baldness (although you need something like sixty cups a day to make it work, so scientists are working on creams that let you just smear it right onto your scalp).

18   Americans are becoming big drinkers overall. Our poor little kidneys don't know what to make of all the increased hydration and dehydration. (Since 1980, the average American's beverage consumption has grown by an astounding 30 gallons per year—putting pressure on not just our personal plumbing systems, but on the nation's in general.) But Americans are not consuming more alcohol; that consumption has dropped since 1980. They are looking for a very different sort of buzz—drinks that pick them up, not drinks that bring them down. In today's 24/7 world, it should not be a surprise that more and more of them are reaching for caffeine. How else will they be able to stay awake longer hours, or multitask all the time? So hold the martini and pass the Monster; it's time to set up caffeine bars where stimulus-hungry Americans can mix and mingle around their common interest—staying awake.

SOURCES

All statistics on bottled water, soft drink, alcohol, and overall beverage consumption come from U.S. Census Bureau, Statistical Abstract of the US: 2007, Table 201, "Per Capita Consumption of Selected Beverages by Type: 1900–2004."

Information on sales of Dasani and Aquafina, drinks with "functional benefits," and energy drinks, comes from March 8, 2007, press release of the Beverage Marketing Corporation, accessed April 2007, at www.beveragemarketing .com/news2.htm.

Coffee-drinking statistics are reported in Reuters, "More Adults Prefer Daily Cup of Coffee," citing the 2006 National Coffee Drinking Trends report, March 3, 2007; and Tammy Joyner, "Innovators Come Up with Ways to Get Daily Jolt," Cox News Service, February 16, 2007. The latter article also provided the information about caffeine-laden food.

Starbucks growth statistics were cited in "Gourmet Coffee Popping Up in Unexpected Places," Associated Press, May 2, 2005.

The study on soft drinks being the leading source of American caloric intake was reported in Shari Roan, "Less than Zero," *Los Angeles Times*, November 27, 2006.

Tea sales data come from "Steaming Ahead, America's Tea Boom," *Economist*, July 8, 2006.

More information about energy drinks can be found in Michael Mason, "The Energy Drink Buzz Is Unmistakable," *New York Times*, December 12, 2006.

The Chicago poison center study was reported by an October 16, 2006, American College of Emergency Physicians press release, "Caffeine Abuse Among Young People Discovered in Examination of Poison Center Calls," accessed April 2007, at www.acep.org/webporta/Newsroorn/NR/ general/2006/101606b.htm.

For more on Americans' sleeping habits, see the 2002 Sleep in America poll, conducted by the National Sleep Foundation, accessed April 2007, at www.sleep-deprivation.com/.

The Viagra data come from "Younger Men Lead Surge in Viagra Use, Study Reveals," *Medical News Today*, August 6, 2004.   ∎

QUESTIONS ON SUBJECT AND PURPOSE

1. Despite the title and the opening sentence, Penn covers a number of closely related topics in the essay. Read the entire essay and then identify the broad subject of his essay.
2. Does "Caffeine Crazies" seem like an appropriate title for the essay? Why or why not?
3. How does this subject fit into what Penn calls a "microtrend"?

QUESTIONS ON STRATEGY AND AUDIENCE

1. How does Penn use the cause-and-effect structure in the essay?
2. What is the role of the opening sentence in paragraph 4?
3. Given the statistics that Penn cites in his essay, what could we assume about his intended audience?

QUESTIONS ON VOCABULARY AND STYLE

1. Penn uses statistics; he does not quote authorities. Articles in newspapers and magazines typically use interviews and quotations from identified experts. What is the rhetorical difference between the two options? Is one strategy more convincing than another?

2. Paragraph 12 consists of two short sentences that are phrased as rhetorical questions (see Glossary for a definition). Why might Penn do this?

3. Be prepared to define the following words: *ingest* (paragraph 7), *vim* (14), *arrhythmias* (15).

WRITING SUGGESTIONS

1. **Doing a Critical Analysis.** What is the nature and role of documentation in this cause-and-effect essay?

2. **Journaling or Blogging.** Penn begins his essay with the popularity of bottled water. Do you buy bottled water? Why not bring tap water from home or your dorm in a reusable container? Reflect on your choice.

3. **Practicing in a Paragraph.** Do you drink caffeinated drinks? When and why? If not, why do you avoid them?

4. **Writing the Personal Essay.** Beginning with the Working Together activity below, select a subject that could be called a "microtrend"—a product or activity that is growing in popularity among your peers. Avoid the obvious. In an essay, describe the phenomenon and then analyze the reasons why it seems to be so popular.

5. **Finding Reading Connections.** In this chapter, Maureen O'Hagan in "Kids Battle the Lure of Junk Food" does a similar analysis on the dairy product called "Go-Gurt." Caffeine, tobacco, and alcohol can be addictive. Can advertising create something at least somewhat similar? Explore the links in an essay.

6. **Exploring Links Online.** Using online sources, research the scientific facts (rather than "myths") about the effects of caffeine. In a cause-and-effect essay, summarize what science knows.

7. **Writing the Research Paper.** As Penn points out, the growth in coffee marketing and consumption has been phenomenal. Research how coffee sellers have revolutionized the marketing and sales of their products. What does the growth in expensive coffees and complex, sweetened coffee-based drinks say about our culture?

For Further Study

Focusing on Grammar and Writing. Look at the first sentences in each of Penn's paragraphs. What role do they play in the paragraph and in the essay?

Working Together. Penn argues that business opportunities abound whenever a new trend emerges in society. Working in small groups, brainstorm a list of other products, activities, and interests that seem to be growing in popularity among your peers.

Seeing Other Modes at Work. Penn's essay shows an effective choice and use of examples.

USING DOCUMENTATION: READING AND WRITING

1. Penn provides a list of sources for the factual information used in the essay. Why would documentation be important in this essay?

2. In a conventional essay, each of the statistics used would have had a footnote or endnote. Why might Penn choose not to use footnotes, but to just include a list of sources? In his book, the list of sources does not immediately follow the essay; it comes in an appendix at the back of the book.

3. **For Practice with Documentation.** Select one or more of Penn's paragraphs and, using the information provided in the list of sources, write more formal footnotes and endnotes. Then convert the list of sources provided here into a more formal bibliography or list of works cited. Be sure to use the proper MLA or APA style for both.

Living the Dream

MICHAEL JERNIGAN

Michael Jernigan blogged for the New York Times *in a regular feature originally called "Home Fires," blogs written by men and women who had returned from military service. The project continues now under the title "At War: Notes from the Front Lines." In its biographical statement about Jernigan, the paper wrote: "Michael Jernigan served in 2004 with Easy Company, Second Battalion, Second Marine Regiment in Mahmudiya, Zadon, and Falluja [Iraq], where he was severely injured and blinded by a roadside bomb. He was medically retired from the Marine Corps in December 2005." In 2012, Jernigan graduated with a degree in history from the University of South Florida and now works for Southeastern Guide Dogs, Inc., as a community outreach coordinator. This post originally appeared on October 2009.*

Video: Jernigan and his father are featured in a six-minute video that can be found on YouTube. Made for Learning Ally, a nonprofit that produces audio books for the blind, the video was awarded a 2008 Platinum Award by the Association of Marketing and Communications Professionals. Jernigan was also featured in the HBO documentary "Alive Day Memories: Home from Iraq," hosted by James Gandolfini.

On Writing: *Interviewed on the radio program "Talk of the Nation" on NPR in 2007, Jernigan said: "It's a good thing to find a positive vent for your frustrations, for all the emotions that you're feeling. You know, for me, it was writing. For a lot of people, it's doing music or painting or anything like that."*

Before Reading

Connecting: Have you heard of P.T.S.D.? Could you define it? What do you expect to discover about P.T.S.D. when you read this?

Anticipating: This is a "post" or an entry in a blog that appeared regularly on the website of *the New York Times*. As you read, think about how this piece of writing differs from a story that might appear elsewhere in the newspaper.

1   **G**reetings again from the Sunshine State.

2   As I mentioned in my first post I would like to bring some awareness to an issue facing many of us returning war veterans. Post Traumatic Stress Disorder (P.T.S.D.) is a monster that war veterans have been facing since the beginning of armed conflict. In a nutshell, it is the stress brought on by a traumatic event. I understand that it is more complicated than that but I would like to keep it as simple as possible for our purposes here.

3   I am living with P.T.S.D., and I am thriving in some respects and having problems in others. In this and future posts I plan to use myself and my experiences as examples.

4   Post-traumatic stress can manifest itself in many different ways. It is usually brought on by a trigger mechanism, or what some might call a catalyst. It can be something very minor that can be easily controlled or it can be so large that it has life altering circumstances.

5   So what do I mean when I say I am both thriving and having problems at the same time? Well, I can tell you that in school I am thriving. I have been back for a couple of years now and continue to pull a 3-plus grade point average every semester. It is in other parts of my life that I am struggling.

6   My relationship with my wife has been strained because of the way I react to certain things; my relationship with my stepson has suffered as well. I have quick reactions full of emotion that are not checked before they come out. In many cases they are very aggressive and quite counterproductive. I am impatient in numerous situations and become frustrated easily. To top it all off I often have to overcome bouts of anxiety, especially when I am outside my house. I do well in social situations but I find them physically taxing. I have been receiving help with all of these problems and I am improving at a good rate. My wife and I have worked hard to help me overcome a lot of these symptoms.

7   One of the most common problems facing our war veterans when we return home is drug and alcohol abuse. We turn to these to escape from emotions. I drank heavily when I returned home. I would drink to the point that I would pass out at night. I would do this because I could not sleep. I could not sleep because there were a healthy wave of emotions that I refused to face. What made sleep hard was the P.T.S.D. in conjunction with a traumatic brain injury. When I would finally sleep I had to deal with some strange and horrific dreams.

8   I would have dreams that most people would be scared by. I was scared, too, especially when I would have the same dream more than once. One of the strangest dreams took place in Iraq. We would be returning from a foot

patrol at night. It was as if I were looking through a set of night vision goggles. There were two gates that we would have to come through at our forward operating base (F.O.B.). I can remember gaining access through the first gate but then not being able to enter the inner part of the base until daybreak. Since we could not get back to our hooches we would decide to sleep under the gun line (155-millimeter howitzers), something that would not be done for safety purposes. Just when I would be drifting off to sleep the gun line would open up. It was at that point that I would awake for real. I was never able to go back to sleep after that.

9   There were dreams that were both strange and violent. In one of them, I was in the spare bedroom of a condominium that I had rented before I enlisted. When I lived there the only thing in this room was my gun cabinet with all of my rifles and shotguns in it. During my dream I was in this room waist deep in stuffed animals. Someone would enter the room (I could never identify the person) and attack me. We would be fighting in this room. At a certain point in the fight I would gain the advantage. I would bend over this individual and bite his throat out. It was always bloody. Just then I would wake up.

10   One of the hardest dreams to deal with came back many times. It was one of the scariest in my mind. It took place in Iraq as well. I can remember being on patrol in Mahmudiya. That is the town that I was wounded in. I was always on patrol with a group of Marines. At some point in the dream I would become separated from my patrol. Iraq can be a scary place to find yourself alone in. It got worse. I cannot remember how, but I would lose my rifle (a good Marine does not lose his weapon). I would see a small kid scampering off with my rifle and follow him. I was terrified of returning back to base without my rifle. The kid would enter a building and I knew that I would have to follow him into the building. Keep in mind that I am defenseless. When I would enter the building I always encountered hand to hand combat with a few different individuals at one time. I would always defeat those attacking me. I can remember that I also would find a number of weapons that had once belonged to Marines—pistols, rifles and shotguns. To my dismay I would never find my rifle.

11   I would see the kid again and chase him one more time. I always wound up chasing him into another building and encountering more and more hand to hand combat situations. I would always find more weapons but never mine. I always picked up the weapons that I would find and bring them with me before I gave pursuit to that kid again. This cycle would never end. I would thrash around in my bed until I would wake up hot and sweating. I could never get back to sleep and was quite disturbed by this dream.

12   While I was in Washington D.C. I started to make significant progress on many different fronts. I found a counselor there named Carey Smith, a disabled veteran from the Vietnam War. He has been through what I have. He began to teach me how to interpret my dreams in a positive way. I know that this can be hard to do. When he first told me I was very hesitant. As he explained it to me I started to understand what he was talking about.

13   We came to the conclusion that the dreams were my mind's way of rec-onciling problems I had. They usually dealt with some guilt I had over one thing or another. In many of these situations, I would have no way of making things better, so my brain would do it for me in my sleep. Once I grasped this concept the dreams became much easier to deal with. I would then wake up in the middle of the night and be able to tell myself that there was nothing wrong and return to sleep. It is great. Currently, I am not dealing with any harsh dreams. I use the term "harsh" because I no longer see these dreams as bad but as healthy and productive.

14   One of the things that I am learning as I am living with P.T.S.D. is that these feelings can be dealt with positively, that these different symptoms do not have to control my life. I am doing my best to live my life and be happy. There is no magic pill that will make things better. By facing the dif-ficult emotions and learning how to positively react to them my life becomes easier. The emotions are still there—they will probably never go away. But when I face them sober and head on I can live my good dreams and not be controlled by the difficult ones.

Semper Fidelis,
Mike Jernigan
■

QUESTIONS ON SUBJECT AND PURPOSE

1. What are the effects of P.T.S.D. about which Jernigan writes?
2. Jernigan titles this entry "Living the Dream." To what does that seem to refer? How is that title related to the subject and the analysis that occurs in the entry?
3. What purposes might Jernigan have in writing this blog?

QUESTIONS ON STRATEGY AND AUDIENCE

1. In what ways does a blog post differ in form or in content from a personal essay you might write in a course?
2. More than half of the essay deals with specific dreams that Jernigan has. In what ways are those dreams similar?
3. Whether you are a veteran who has experienced P.T.S.D., someone who knows a person who suffers from it, or simply an interested reader, what expectations do you have as you begin the essay? Would those expectations differ if this were an article written from a clinical point of view?

QUESTIONS ON VOCABULARY AND STYLE

1. Throughout the entry, Jernigan makes extensive use of the first-person pronoun ("I"). How is that appropriate for this type of writing?

2. It is never easy to describe "tone" in an essay. Look at the definition given in Glossary and Ready Reference at the back of this book and then try to find some words that describe the tone of the blog.

3. Be prepared to define the following words or phrases: *traumatic* (paragraph 2), *bouts* (6), "*hooches*" (8), and "*semper fidelis*" (the salutation).

WRITING SUGGESTIONS

1. **Doing a Critical Analysis.** We might not think of blog writing as something we would do in a college composition course or something that a teacher might grade. In an essay, identify the elements of blog writing that you see in this piece, explaining how they differ from a more conventional paper assignment.

2. **Journaling or Blogging.** Not everyone feels comfortable writing a personal blog. It is one thing to write in a diary that no one sees except yourself and quite another to allow anyone to read your blog on the Web. Would you be willing to blog about your life and feelings? About some things but not others? Jot down a response in your journal.

3. **Practicing in a Paragraph.** In a paragraph, analyze your response to your journal assignment. What are the reasons why you would or would not be willing to write about yourself? What do you see as the effects, either positive or negative, about such a decision?

4. **Writing the Personal Essay.** The subjects of our dreams often reveal the stresses in our lives. Do you have subjects or situations about which you regularly dream? Using a similar approach as Jernigan, give some examples of your dreams and see if you can identify the causes that underlie your examples. Is there a consistent pattern that manifests the same type of fears or anxieties?

5. **Finding Reading Connections.** The symptoms of P.T.S.D. are not limited to wounded military veterans. Any traumatic experience can produce symptoms and the symptoms can come and go. Consider the experiences described in Bob Greene's "Cut" (Chapter 1) or in Marguerite Choi's "The Empty Chair" (2). Although both of these experiences are much less traumatic than Jernigan's, what common elements do you see as the writers recount their experiences? Explore the connections in an essay.

6. **Exploring Links Online.** Using online sources, locate additional blogs about P.T.S.D. What insights into the disorder do these blogs offer? Why might they be written as blogs rather than as articles published in newspapers or magazines?

7. **Writing the Research Paper.** Given the increasing access to technology, it is not surprising that so many soldiers stationed in Iraq and Afghanistan have blogged about their experiences. Jernigan also notes that writing helps him vent his frustrations (On Writing above). What do we know about the effect of creative expression (writing, painting, performing) on dealing with any type of traumatic experience?

For Further Study

Focusing on Grammar and Writing. Can you find any words, expressions, or cliches in the blog that seem more likely to occur in conversation rather than in a written essay? What is the effect of such things on your reading experience?

Working Together. Working in small groups, discuss why it is important for those who have not experienced combat to read a blog like this. What is the effect likely to be on its readers? On you?

Seeing Other Modes at Work. Jernigan notes in paragraph 3 that he is using his experiences as "examples." What is the role of examples in this post?

ADDITIONAL WRITING SUGGESTIONS FOR CAUSE AND EFFECT

Cause-and-effect analyses move backward or forward in time: you are either analyzing the reasons why something happened or the consequences that arise from it. Most cause-and-effect essays in writing courses focus on one direction rather than trying to explore both. Typically cause-and-effect analyses are intended to be informative, although they can also be entertaining and persuasive. Remember to keep your audience in mind. What do they already know about the subject? Do not attempt anything too simple or too obvious, but do not tackle complex and technical subjects in the space of a few pages. Always consider as well why anyone might be interested in reading your paper.

1. Why are cell phones so popular? So "essential"? What is the effect of "instant" communication in our society?

2. Why do people purchase and wear an article of clothing that advertises a product? They are, after all, walking advertisements. Why does a particular brand of anything become so desirable?

3. Why is blogging so popular? What might account for that popularity? What has been the effect of the many blogs in cyberspace?

4. Why is college so expensive? What have you come to expect from your college in terms of services, amenities, programs, and facilities?

5. Why are some people willing to risk or sacrifice their lives for the safety of others?

6. What are the causes of our culture's obsession with the "ideal" body for women or men? What are the effects of this obsession?

7. Why is YouTube so popular? What impact does it have on us and our culture?

8. What accounts for the popularity of certain sports, the growth of "extreme" sports?

9. Why are medical costs so high? What is the effect of these costs on the availability of healthcare options to many Americans?

10. What accounts for the popularity of electronic devices such as the iPod? The BlackBerry? What is the effect of such devices on our lives?

11. Why is oil so expensive? What will be the long-term impact of high prices on how and what Americans drive? How might high prices influence future housing patterns in the United States?

12. What has shaped your expectations of the personal "future" that you want?

13. What explains the growing interest in "organic" products? What is the impact of that interest on the agricultural industry in the United States?

14. Why are Americans so interested in self-help books and videos? What does this say about us and our culture?

8 | Definition

LEARNING OBJECTIVES

In this chapter, you will learn how to

1. Distinguish between denotation and connotation in writing a definition
2. Select appropriate details to include in a definition
3. Choose an appropriate structure for arranging those details
4. Assess and adjust to an audience's previous knowledge of the subject
5. Write an effective introduction and conclusion
6. Analyze readings that use definition

Key Questions

WRITING DEFINITION

Getting Ready to Write

What is definition?

What is the difference between denotation and connotation?

How much do you include in a definition essay?

Writing

How do you structure a definition essay?

Revising

How do you revise a definition essay?

Student Essay

Sherry Heck, "In*fall*ible"

READING DEFINITION

In Prose

Columbia Electronic Encyclopedia, "ADHD"

In Literature

Jamaica Kincaid, "Girl" (short story)

In a Visual

"Seeing Yourself" (photograph)

Writing Definition

GETTING READY TO WRITE

What Is Definition?

> **def • i • ni • tion** (def' ə nish'ən) *n.* [ME *diffinicioun* < OR
> *definition* & ML *diffinitio*, both < L *difinitio*] 1 a defining
> or being defined 2 a statement of what a thing is 3 a
> statement of the meaning of a word, phrase, etc.

On the midterm examination in your introductory economics class, only the essay question remains to be answered: "What is capitalism?" You are tempted to write the one-sentence definition you memorized from the glossary of your textbook and dash from the room. But it is unlikely that your professor will react positively or even charitably to such a skimpy (and rote) response. Instead, you realize your answer must be an extended definition, one that explains what factors were necessary before capitalism could emerge, what elements are most characteristic of a capitalistic economy, how capitalism differs from other economic systems, how a capitalistic economy works, how capitalism is linked to technology and politics. You need a narrative, a division, a comparison and contrast, a process, and a cause-and-effect analysis all working together to provide a full definition of what is a very complex term.

When you are asked to define a word, you generally do two things. First, you provide a dictionary-like definition, normally a single sentence. Second, if the occasion demands, you provide a longer, extended definition, analyzing the subject and giving examples or details. If you write an essay and use technical or specialized words that might be unfamiliar to your reader, you

---

Links between Writing and Reading

	Why does this need a definition?
Sarah J. Lin, "Devotion"	How do actions define "devotion"?
Judy Brady, "I Want a Wife"	Why isn't "a woman married to a man" enough of a definition of wife?
Mark Bittman, "Eating Food"	Why do we need to know what "organic" really means?
Jhumpa Lahiri "My Two Lives"	Why does she feel she has two lives?
Amy Tan, "Mother Tongue"	What does the title suggest about the subject?
MediaSmarts, "Little Princesses"	Are there dangers in promoting this stereotype?

SIPRESS

"I'd like to take a moment to define what I mean by 'defining moment.'"

include a parenthetical definition: "Macroeconomics, the portion of economics concerned with large-scale movements such as inflation and deflation, is particularly interested in changes in the GDP, or gross domestic product."

What Is the Difference between Denotation and Connotation?

Definitions can be denotative, connotative, or a mixture of the two. Dictionary definitions are denotative; that is, they offer a literal and explicit definition of a word. A dictionary, for example, defines the word *prejudice* as "a judgment or opinion formed before the facts are known; a preconceived idea." In most cases, however, a single sentence is not enough to give a reader a clear understanding of the word or concept.

Many words have more than just literal meanings; they also carry connotations, either positive or negative, and these connotations may make up part of an extended definition. For example, in 1944, when the United States was at war with both Germany and Japan, E. B. White was asked to write about the "meaning of democracy" for the Writers' War Board. White's one-paragraph response goes beyond a literal definition to explore the connotations and associations that surround the word *democracy*:

> Surely the Board knows what democracy is. It is the line that forms on the right. It is the don't in Don't Shove. It is the hole in the stuffed shirt through which the sawdust trickles; it is the dent in the high hat. Democracy is the

recurrent suspicion that more than half of the people are right more than half of the time. It is the feeling of privacy in the voting booths, the feeling of communion in the libraries, the feeling of vitality everywhere. Democracy is the score at the beginning of the ninth. It is an idea which hasn't been disproved yet, a song the words of which have not gone bad. It's the mustard on the hot dog and the cream in the rationed coffee. Democracy is a request from a War Board, in the middle of a morning in the middle of a war, wanting to know what democracy is.

Democracy was, to White, not simply a form of government, but a whole way of life.

Most writing situations, especially those you encounter in college, require extended definitions. The reading selections in this chapter define a variety of subjects, and they suggest how differently extended definitions can be handled. Sarah J. Lin defines "devotion" by describing actions. Judy Brady defines the word "wife" through the many associations that people have with that word. Mark Bittman tells us what the word "organic" really means when it is applied to food. Jhumpa Lahiri explains why it is difficult for her to answer the question, "what am I?" Amy Tan explores a definition of the phrase *mother tongue*, based on her own mother's Chinese-inflected English. Finally, the writer for MediaSmarts explores the associations and stereotypes connected with the "little princess" image.

How Much Do You Include in a Definition Essay?

Every word, whether it refers to a specific physical object or to the most theoretical concept, has a dictionary definition. Whether that one-sentence definition is sufficient depends on why you are defining the word. Complex words and words with many nuances and connotations generally require a fuller definition than a single sentence can provide. Moreover, one-sentence definitions often contain other words and phrases that need to be defined.

For example, if you were asked, "What is a wife?" you could reply, "a woman married to a man." Although that definition is accurate, it does not convey any sense of what such a relationship might involve. Judy Brady's "I Want a Wife" defines the word by showing what men (or some men at least) expect in a wife. Brady divides and lists a wife's many responsibilities—things expected of her by an actual or potential husband. Brady's essay, comically overstated as it is, offers a far more meaningful definition of the term *wife* than any one-sentence dictionary entry. Her intention surely was to reveal inequality in marriage, and she makes that point by listing a stereotypical set of male expectations.

Writing a definition is a fairly common activity in college work. In your literature course, you are asked to define the romantic movement; in art history, the baroque period; in psychology, abnormal behavior. Since a single-sentence definition can never do justice to such complicated terms, an extended definition is necessary. In each case, the breadth and depth of your knowledge is being tested; your professor expects you to formulate a definition that accounts for the major subdivisions and characteristics of the subject.

Links between Writing and Reading

	From where does the information come?
Sarah J. Lin, "Devotion"	Personal experience
Judy Brady, "I Want a Wife"	Anything other than observation?
Mark Bittman, "Eating Food"	What are the main sources of information?
Jhumpa Lahiri, "My Two Lives"	Personal experience?
Amy Tan, "Mother Tongue"	Experience and observation?
MediaSmarts, "Little Princesses"	Why are sources cited in essays?

 ## Prewriting Tips for Writing Definition

1. Once you have chosen or been assigned a word, phrase, or concept to define, write a short dictionary definition of it.
2. Write a purpose statement for your paper: "My purpose in this essay is to. . . ." Use that statement as a way of testing your developing draft.
3. Describe your intended audience. How much do they know about this term? Is it technical? Complicated? Will you need to provide parenthetical definitions of other words or phrases as you are defining?
4. Determine whether visuals—diagrams, photographs, sketches—will be helpful. Check with your instructor to see if you can include such things in your essay.
5. Remember that a definition essay involves an extended definition— that is, you must add appropriate details and examples. What types of details or examples will help fill out your definition?

Your purpose is two-fold: to convince your professor that you have read and mastered the assigned materials, and to select among them and organize them, often adding some special insight of your own, into a logical and coherent response.

WRITING

How Do You Structure a Definition Essay?

Sentence definitions are relatively easy to write. You first place a word in a general class ("A wife is a *woman*") and then add any distinguishing features that set it apart from other members of the class ("married to a man"). However, the types of definitions you are asked to write in college are generally much more detailed than dictionary entries. How, then, do you get from a single sentence to a paragraph or an essay?

Extended definitions do not have a structure peculiar to themselves. That is, when you write a definition, you do not have a predetermined structural pattern as you do with comparison and contrast, division and classification, process, or cause and effect. Instead, when you construct definitions, you use all of the various strategies in this book. Sarah J. Lin's definition of "devotion" depends on a series of actions that she wishes she would have been capable of. Mark Bittman offers a denotative definition of the term "organic" that corrects many of the associations we have with that word. In her definition of a wife, Judy Brady uses division to organize the many types of responsibilities demanded of a wife. Jhumpa Lahiri and Amy Tan use narration as a vital part of their definition. The writer of "Little Princesses" defines a particular gender stereotype promoted for young girls.

Once you have chosen a subject for definition, think first about its essential characteristics, steps, or parts. What examples would best define the subject? Then plan your organization by seeing how those details can be presented most effectively to your reader. If you are breaking a subject into its parts, use definition or possibly even process. If you are defining by comparing your subject to another, use comparison and contrast. If your subject is defined as a result of some causal connection, use a cause-and-effect structure. Definitions can also involve narration, description, and even persuasion. The longer the extended definition, the greater the likelihood that your paper will involve a series of structures.

Links between Writing and Reading

	How does the definition work?
Sarah J. Lin, "Devotion"	How is the personal experience organized?
Judy Brady, "I Want a Wife"	Denotation or connotation or both?
Mark Bittman, "Eating Food"	What's the difference between the denotation and the connotations of the word "organic"?
Jhumpa Lahiri, "My Two Lives"	When does defining by a single culture become difficult or impossible?
Amy Tan, "Mother Tongue"	Is there an academic definition of *mother tongue*?
MediaSmarts, "Little Princesses"	Denotation or connotation or both?

Drafting Tips for Writing Definition

1. Look at the list of details and examples that you have gathered as preparation for writing. Can you sort them into structural categories as a first step in planning an organization for your essay? For example, do any involve comparison and contrast? Division or classification, cause or effect? Narration or description? Process?

2. Make sure you have considered all the connotations of the word or concept that you are defining. Readers have associations with terms that are not necessarily part of the terms' denotative definitions.

3. Think about your audience's prior knowledge about this subject. Does your essay involve technical concepts or specialized knowledge that will need to be explained?

4. Remember, like every essay, your definition paper needs an introduction, a body or middle, and a conclusion. As you write, jot down an outline of the developing structure. Middles are the longest and most complicated.

5. Plan at least two different introductions to your essay: make one a straightforward explanation of what you are defining; make the other more reader-friendly.

REVISING

How Do You Revise a Definition Essay?

You look for a definition of a word or concept in a dictionary or an encyclopedia to find out what it means—you need the information to understand the word or concept. You expect to come away with a clear understanding of the meaning. If you are confused by other terms used in the definition, or if the information presented is not clear, logical, and easily understood, then your needs have not been met. All definitions, including the extended definition essays that you write in academic courses, must meet the tests of clarity and comprehension. As you are revising your definition essay, enlist the help of other readers, especially peer readers. After they have read your paper, ask them to rephrase the definition in their own words. Have they understood what you are trying to explain? Ask them to identify any words or phrases that they do not understand or cannot define themselves. Address all potential problems as you revise your draft.

When revising a definition essay, pay particular attention to audience, organization, and the beginning and ending of your essay.

Paying Attention to Your Audience Look again at your statement of intended audience and your readers' responses. Have you adequately and clearly defined your subject? Have you used words readers will understand? If your definition contains technical words and phrases, make sure they are defined in context for your readers. You can do so in two ways. First, you can insert a parenthetical definition (enclosed either within a pair of commas or within parentheses) after the word or phrase—for example, "hyperactivity (feelings of restlessness, fidgeting, or inappropriate activity when one is expected to be quiet)." Second, you can include a definition or an example in the sentence without enclosing it in commas or parentheses—for example, "Hyperactivity refers to feelings of restlessness, fidgeting, or inappropriate activity (running, wandering) when one is expected to be quiet."

Checking Organization   Your essay needs a clear organizational structure. Outline your draft to see if the sections of the essay fit together in a way that is easy to follow. Broadly speaking, definition essays can be organized either inductively or deductively. In an inductive organization, you could begin with a sentence definition and then expand that definition by using examples, developing contrasts, explaining cause and effect, or by any of a number of other strategies. You could also invert the pattern to a deductive structure: your examples and details come first, leading then to a sentence definition placed near the end of your essay.

As you move from section to section, make sure you clearly signal to your reader what follows. For instance, write topic sentences that introduce the subject to be covered in the next paragraph or section. Or subdivide your text using typographical devices such as centered headings, numbered sections, or extra white space. If your extended definition makes use of any of the other strategies discussed in this text—for example, comparison, contrast, process—review the advice in that chapter as you revise what you have written.

Beginning and Ending   Writing the middle of any essay is generally easier than writing either the beginning or the ending, but a good definition essay needs both a strong introduction and a strong conclusion. When you consult a dictionary or a textbook for a definition, you expect it to be clear, concise, and informative. When you read an extended definition in a magazine or on a website, you expect it to also be interesting, to reach out and pull you into the piece. In extended definitions that you write for courses, try to find a reader-friendly way to begin. Avoid opening sentences that begin like these: "According to Webster's dictionary, ADHD is defined as . . ." or "ADHD is when. . . ." Instead, can you start with an example? With an interesting fact or quotation? Can you begin with a provocative statement? In a writing class, your reader is typically reading because the subject and the approach are readable and interesting, not because he or she needs the information.

Similarly, resist the temptation to end your essay with a simple repetition of the short definition of your subject or with a paraphrase of the opening of your essay. Do not just stop your essay either, providing no sense of closure. Your reader needs to feel that the essay is now over—it has reached its logical and appropriate conclusion. Study some of the endings that the writers in this chapter use for their essays. You can also check the Glossary and Ready Reference at the back of this text for additional suggestions on effective conclusions.

Links between Writing and Reading

	Beginning and ending
Sarah J. Lin, "Devotion"	What strategy is used in the last paragraph?
Judy Brady, "I Want a Wife"	How effective is the final sentence as a conclusion to the essay?
Mark Bittman, "Eating Food"	Why begin the essay with statistics?
Jhumpa Lahiri, "My Two Lives"	What important information is given in the opening sentence?
Amy Tan, "Mother Tongue"	In what way is the opening example (paragraph 3) appropriate for the subject of the essay?
MediaSmarts, "Little Princesses"	Why might the essay begin with a question?

Revising Tips for Writing Definition

1. Ask a peer or a classmate to read your essay and to comment on the clarity of your definition. Does your reader understand all of the words and concepts you have used in your definition?

2. Check the body of your essay again. Do you see a clear organizational pattern? If you have used any of the other strategies discussed in this book, check the relevant chapters for advice on how to structure and develop each one.

3. Make sure your structure is clear. Have you clearly signaled transitions as you move from section to section in your essay? Have you written topic sentences for each section? Have you included any typographical devices—for example, subheadings, extra white space, numbered sections—to signal the structure of the paper?

4. Evaluate your examples. Have you provided enough examples or details to support your generalizations? Are your examples and details really helpful in defining your subject? Are they all relevant?

5. Look carefully at your essay's title. A title is a part of the appeal of an essay. "Essay #5" or "Definition Essay" are simply not titles.

Student Essay

Sherry Heck's essay started from a simple set of directions: "Write an extended definition of a word of your choice." Sherry's approach to the assignment, however, was very different from everyone else's in the class. In her purpose statement, Sherry wrote, "I wanted to inform a general audience in an amusing way of the connotations and associations that accrue to the word *fall*. I got the idea while thumbing through a dictionary looking for words!" Her first draft reads as follows.

First Draft

Falling

When you were four years old, covered in scrapes and bruises, the word fall was probably too familiar. Perhaps you went exploring, discovering the creek in the woods, and following it to its falls. Summers would end too quickly and fall would arrive, and Mom would send you off to school.

You mastered the art of walking, yet it remained all too easy to fall over yourself in front of your peers. The popular kids would laugh, sending you to fall into the wrong crowd. As you sprayed graffiti triumphantly, you fell into agreement with your friends that this was the best way to slander the principal.

Then one day, you are sitting in school and you feel someone's glance fall on you. You fall silent and stare back. Soon you find yourself falling for that special someone, and you fall in love. Eventually, you have a huge falling out with that person. Your friends have long abandoned you, leaving you no one to fall back on. Your spirits fall, and you feel like the fall guy around your old peers.

Eventually, out of school, you fall into a good job, and you are able to fall out of your trance. Determined not to fall short of your career goals, you fall into line with society. Events seem to fall into place. The pace of the job speeds up, and several people fall out of the rat race. Their jobs fall to you, tripling your workload. It is difficult not to avoid falling from power, and your life's plans begin to fall through.

Alone, rejected, and jobless, you begin to blame your misfortunes on the root of all evil, the fall of Adam and Eve. Life continues, and you ponder this thought until your friends begin to fall off. Your face falls at the thought of your own fall. Your bones are weak, and falling means more than a scraped knee. Your blood pressure falls more easily. These physical worries all disappear when one day, after feeling a free-fall sensation, you fall asleep, peacefully, forever.

Comments

Sherry met with her instructor, Nathan Andrews, to go over her preliminary draft. He encouraged her to watch that she not repeat phrases—for example, in the fourth paragraph, Sherry had repeated *fall out* twice. After they had brainstormed some additional *fall* phrases, he encouraged her to search for more in the dictionaries in her school's library. He also suggested that she underline each *fall* phrase so that the reader could more easily see the wordplay. In her revised essay, Sherry was able to add a number of new examples.

Revised Draft

Infallible

When you were four years old, covered in scrapes and bruises, the word fall was probably too familiar. Perhaps you went exploring, discovering the creek in the woods, and following it to its falls. Summers would end too quickly and fall would arrive, and Mom would send you off to school.

You mastered the art of walking, yet it remained all too easy to fall all over yourself in front of your peers. The popular kids would laugh, sending you to fall in with the wrong crowd. As you sprayed the graffiti triumphantly, you fell in agreement with your friends that this was the best way to slander the principal. Your behavior was leading you to fall afoul of the law.

Then one day, you are sitting in school and you feel someone's glance fall on you. You fall silent and stare back. Soon you find yourself falling for that special someone, and you fall in love. Eventually, you have a huge falling out with that person. The relationship falls apart. Your friends have long abandoned you, leaving you no one to fall back on. Your cries for help fall on deaf ears. Your spirits fall, and you feel like the fall guy around your old peers.

Eventually, out of school, you fall over backwards to get a good job, and you are able to fall out of your trance. Your love life has fallen by the wayside. Determined not to fall short of your career goals, you fall into line with society. Events seem to fall into place. The pace of the job speeds up, and several people fall on their faces. Their jobs fall to you, tripling your workload. You fall behind in your work. It is difficult not to avoid falling from power, and your life's plans begin to fall through.

Alone, rejected and jobless, you begin to blame your misfortunes on the root of all evil, the Fall of Adam and Eve. Life continues, and you ponder this thought until your friends begin to fall off. Your face falls at the thought of your own fall. Your bones are weak, and falling means more than a scraped knee. Your blood pressure falls more easily. These physical worries all disappear when one day, after feeling a free-fall sensation, you fall asleep, peacefully, forever.

Checklist: Some Things to Remember About Writing Definition

- ❑ Choose a subject that can be reasonably and fully defined within the limits of your paper. That is, make sure it is neither too limited nor too large.
- ❑ Determine a purpose for your definition.
- ❑ Spend time analyzing your subject to see what its essential characteristics, steps, or parts are.
- ❑ Write a dictionary-type definition for your subject. Do this even if you are writing an extended definition. The features that set your subject apart from others in its general class reveal what must be included in your definition.
- ❑ Choose examples that are clear and appropriate.
- ❑ Decide which of the organizational patterns will best convey the information you have gathered.
- ❑ Be careful about beginning with a direct dictionary definition. There are usually more effective and interesting ways to announce your subject.

Reading Definition

What is it? That is a question you ask—consciously or unconsciously—every time you encounter something new or something you do not understand. You consult a dictionary to understand unfamiliar words you encounter; you expect that textbooks will clearly explain and define technical concepts. Definition can be pretty straightforward for simple subjects but fairly complex and extended for more complicated subjects. As you read, remember what you have learned about how to write a definition and how that knowledge might help you as a reader.

- A sentence definition places a word in a general class ("a chronic, neurologically based syndrome") and then adds distinguishing features that set it apart from other members of the class ("characterized by any or all of three types of behaviors").
- A definition essay is an extended definition in which additional information or details are added to clarify or explain further the subject.
- Definitions must take into consideration the prior knowledge of readers. A technical or complicated subject is likely to require parenthetical definitions of other words and phrases. An effective definition is measured by its clarity in explaining the subject to its readers.
- The primary purpose of a definition essay is to provide its readers with information. Clarity and logical organization are essential.
- Definitions make use of a range of possible organizational strategies: they might provide examples; classify or divide the subject; use process, narration, or description; compare or contrast the essay topic with a topic that helps clarify the definition; or separate causes and effects. Definition has no single structural pattern that is always used; it is a composite of other patterns employed together.

IN PROSE

The National Institute of Mental Health estimates that two to three percent of children in the United States have ADHD (attention deficit hyperactivity disorder). One of the most common childhood disorders, this means that in a typical classroom at least one child has ADHD. Read the following definition from the online Columbia Electronic Encyclopedia.

Dictionary definition Definition describes behaviors	Attention deficit hyperactivity disorder (ADHD), formerly called hyperkinesis or minimal brain dysfunction, a chronic, neurologically based syndrome characterized by any or all of three types of behavior: hyperactivity, distractibility, and impulsivity.
Each behavior is then defined	Hyperactivity refers to feelings of restlessness, fidgeting, or inappropriate activity (running, wandering) when one is expected to be quiet; distractibility to heightened distraction by irrelevant sights and sounds or carelessness and inability to carry simple tasks to completion; and impulsivity to socially inappropriate speech (e.g., blurting out something without thinking) or striking out.
Although the behaviors can be commonly found, in ADHD they are consistent and do not fluctuate	Unlike similar behaviors caused by emotional problems or anxiety, ADHD does not fluctuate with emotional states. While the three typical behaviors occur in nearly everyone from time to time, in those with ADHD they are excessive, long-term, and pervasive and create difficulties in school, at home, or at work. ADHD is usually diagnosed before age seven. It is often accompanied by a learning disability. ■

QUESTIONS FOR ANALYSIS

1. What strategies are used to provide a definition of the term?
2. In the selection, what is the role of the information enclosed within parentheses?
3. How is the definition structured?
4. Judging from the information provided, who is most likely to have ADHD?
5. What assumptions does the author seem to have about her or his audience?

CRITICAL READING ACTIVITY

Write a formal outline for the definition. What does that reveal about its structure and principle of organization?

IN LITERATURE

Jamaica Kincaid (born Elaine Cynthia Potter Richardson) uses definition in her short story "Girl." As you read the story, think about how the story is an example of definition. What is being defined in the story and how?

Girl

JAMAICA KINCAID

Wash the white clothes on Monday and put them on the stone heap; wash the color clothes on Tuesday and put them on the clothesline to dry; don't walk barehead in the hot sun; cook pumpkin fritters in very hot sweet oil; soak your little clothes right after you take them off; when buying cotton to make yourself a nice blouse, be sure that it doesn't have gum on it, because that way it won't hold up well after a wash; soak salt fish overnight before you cook it; is it true that you sing benna in Sunday school?; always eat your food in such a way that it won't turn someone else's stomach; on Sundays try to walk like a lady and not like the slut you are so bent on becoming; don't sing benna in Sunday school; you mustn't speak to wharf-rat boys, not even to give directions; don't eat fruits on the street—flies will follow you; *but I don't sing benna on Sundays at all and never in Sunday school*; this is how to sew on a button; this is how to make a buttonhole for the button you have just sewed on; this is how to hem a dress when you see the hem coming down and so to prevent yourself from looking like the slut I know you are so bent on becoming; this is how you iron your father's khaki shirt so that it doesn't have a crease; this is how you iron your father's khaki pants so that they don't have a crease; this is how you grow okra—far from the house, because okra tree harbors red ants; when you are growing dasheen, make sure it gets plenty of water or else it makes your throat itch when you are eating it; this is how you sweep a corner; this is how you sweep a whole house; this is how you sweep a yard; this is how you smile to someone you don't like too much; this is how you smile to someone you don't like at all; this is how you smile to someone you like completely; this is how you set a table for tea; this is how you set a table for dinner; this is how you set a table for dinner with an important guest; this is how you set a table for lunch; this is how you set a table for breakfast; this is how to behave in the presence of men who don't know you very well, and this way they won't recognize immediately the slut I have warned you against becoming; be sure to wash every day, even if it is with your own spit; don't squat down to play marbles—you are not a boy, you know; don't pick people's flowers—you might catch something; don't throw stones at blackbirds, because it might not be a blackbird at all; this is how to make a bread pudding; this is how to make doukona; this is how to make pepper pot; this is how to make a good medicine for a cold; this is how to make a good medicine to throw away a child before it even becomes a child; this is how to catch a fish; this is how to throw back a fish you don't like, and that way something bad won't fall on you; this is how to bully a man; this is how a man bullies you; this is how to love a man, and if this doesn't work there are other ways, and if they don't work don't feel too bad about giving up; this is how to spit up in the air if you feel like it, and this is how to move quickly so that it doesn't fall on you; this is how to make ends meet; always squeeze bread to make sure it's fresh; *but what if the baker won't let me feel the bread?*; you mean to say that after all you are really going to be the kind of woman who the baker won't let near the bread? ■

QUESTIONS FOR ANALYSIS

1. Why might Kincaid entitle her story "Girl"? If you were trying to write a title that reflected the content of the story, what might that title be?
2. What is "benna"? You will probably need to look up the word on the Web.
3. Presumably the speaker in the story is the girl's mother. How would you characterize her tone in the story? Why might she be passing on this range of advice? How would you feel if your mother or father talked to you in this way?
4. Why are two sentences in the story printed in italics?
5. What is being defined in the story, and by whom?

WRITING SUGGESTIONS

1. **Analysis.** The story consists of a string of sentences of advice separated with semicolons. Kincaid chose to not subdivide or paragraph the story. Why? What does this arrangement contribute to what the story is about? In an essay, analyze the relationship between the form of the story and its content.
2. Kincaid's story is similar in approach to Judy Brady's "I Want a Wife" (in this chapter) in that both define terms through cataloguing expectations or responsibilities. Suppose that your mother or father had a similar conversation with you, what would they say to you about being a daughter/woman/wife or a son/man/husband? In an essay, offer a definition based on what you sense as their expectations of you. Do not try to imitate Kincaid's structure.
3. Definitions can do many things. In part, they tell us what something is. We look up a word or a phrase in a dictionary or encyclopedia so that we understand it. Definitions, though, can also suggest or offer new perspectives on the familiar; they can allow us to see things in a fresh way. Write a definition in which you offer a creative way of capturing the term, a new way of seeing it. Consider the following suggestions as possibilities:
   a. A part of the human body
   b. A common, useful object—such as a hairbrush, a computer mouse, a pen, a pair of glasses or contacts, a digital watch, a camera phone, a ceiling fan
   c. A term connected with being a student—dropping or adding a course, auditing, being a "work study" student, cramming for an exam, group projects, internships, service learning

IN A VISUAL

When you need a definition of a word or a concept, you look in a dictionary—online or print. Often, dictionaries also provide images or pictures as well. When the word or concept is a concrete noun, for example, an illustration is a more effective way of defining a word than a sentence-long description. On the other hand, when the word is an abstract noun, such as *economy*, or an adverb such as *slowly*, or a verb such as *seemed*, an image is often impossible.

Complex words and concepts often resist simple definitions. If someone asks "Who are you?" you might define yourself in many ways—for example, by age, gender, nationality, genealogical descent, status or position. Visual definitions of self can take a number of forms. In a sense, your Facebook page is a form of self-definition done by displaying your interests, friends, photographs and videos, music links. Your sense of "self," though, can be misleading—to others (consider the risks posed by certain types of personal photographs posted on your Facebook page!) and even to you. Consider this

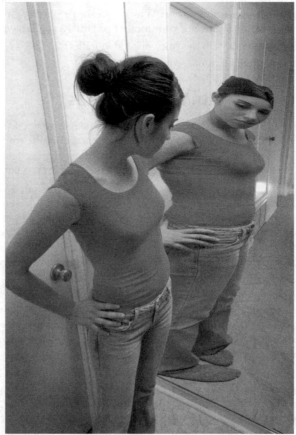

Ted Foxx/Alamy

photograph of a young woman seeing herself in a mirror—one way in which everyone defines self. What she sees is not what we see—her sense of self is symbolically distorted by the mirror.

QUESTIONS FOR ANALYSIS

1. Why might the image be a young woman? Why not a young man? Why not an older person?
2. What is the difference between what we see in the image and what she sees? Is this just someone looking into a distorting mirror?
3. Why might the figure be tilting her head?
4. Why might the figure be dressed as she is? Is that significant in some way?

WRITING SUGGESTIONS

1. **Analysis:** How does the composition of the photograph contribute to its effect? What is the implied sense of self-definition that we see? Speculate in an essay on what thesis the photographer might have for the image and analyze how that is achieved in the image.
2. Take a photograph of your personal space—for example, your bedroom or dorm room. What does that space, and the objects that occupy it, say about you? How does the image and its contents define you? Remember that how you see it and how someone else sees it can be very different. Ask some friends—of both genders—to "read" your image. In an essay, explore how the photograph defines you and include the photograph.
3. Businesses try to create a brand image, a self-definition in a sense. That intended image can be seen in the company's advertisements, the products or services it markets, even the appearance of its employees. Select a company—for example, a fast-food chain, a fashion company, a sports equipment manufacturer—and look at how it represents itself to the public. Using images from print and online sources, describe in an essay the self-definition that the company is projecting and speculate on why.

Devotion

SARAH J. LIN

Sarah J. Lin was born and raised in New York City. A graduate of Binghamton University and Colorado State University (M.F.A.), she has been an editor, a copywriter, and a teacher of writing. Lin has blogged online about food and restaurants and writes short stories and essays. This essay first appeared in the online journal Brevity *(Brevitymag.com) in Summer 2010.*

> **On Writing:** Lin commented, *"Creating and editing are two different processes. You must ignore one to immerse yourself fully in the other."*

Before Reading

Connecting: Have you ever regretted how you treated someone?

Anticipating: If you faced a situation like the one Lin describes, how would you have reacted?

1 **W**here I grew up in Queens, New York City, there was a boy living in the house across the street. His name was Sherman. Somewhere, there is a photo of the two of us from the day I turned seven: I am in a yellow dress and a yellow birthday hat, running down the drive way with friends; he is standing in the background, watching. He is tall, lurching, awkward; his small, sloped eyes are magnified behind the thick lenses of his brown glasses. On his face is a gummy and lopsided smile.

2 All through my childhood and adolescence, Sherman called my family's house two or three times a day, hoping to engage whomever picked up the receiver in conversation. He never wanted to hang up. He invited my family to his birthday party every year, came heaving up our driveway whenever he saw one of us outside, and once a week he asked my older brother and me to come over for microwaved White Castle cheeseburgers and to hang out in his bedroom. Sometimes we went, and sometimes we didn't.

*

3 When I was twelve years old, a boy named Sherman decided he loved me. Sherman was nine years older than me and had been born with Down syndrome, an unfortunate effect of his father's exposure to the chemical Agent Orange during the Vietnam War. For nearly all of his life, Sherman wore a hearing aid and depended on crutches and a wheelchair for mobility.

4 Puberty had thickened his body and turned his belly into a potbelly; his skin had inflamed with red pustules of acne and then scarred. Sherman's laugh was guttural and so was his speech. He repulsed me, but my feelings did not sway his devotion. Whenever he saw me he gripped me in a number of uncomfortable, humiliating embraces, and no matter what I told him, he stubbornly insisted that I was his girlfriend. The very idea made me indignant. But Sherman thought I was his; he believed this for years.

*

5 I was twenty-eight years old when my neighbor Sherman passed away. His body had weakened from strokes and organ failure until, on a sunny morning in early October, his heart gave out for good. He was thirty-seven.

6   I had last seen Sherman a year earlier, as he lay in a metal bed resembling a crib, his body wasted, his eyes blind. His skin was soft and swollen from medications and lack of exercise; his fingers were pale and groping. Since I moved out of my parents' house, I had not gone to see him, so I had not understood or witnessed his deterioration. But now I entered his bedroom, moving gingerly around the stacks of adult diapers and pill bottles. I breathed through my mouth to avoid the smell of disinfectant that permeated the room.

7   I stayed for an hour, and during that time a live-in nurse assisted him with defecation. I waited in the living room, pretending I couldn't hear him. When I went to say goodbye, his hand reached up from the crib, seeking contact with mine. "I love you," he said. He wanted me to stay. Would I?

8   "It was nice to see you," I said. I ignored his words. I took my hand away from his and went up the stairs and out of his house.

*

9   I've narrated exactly what happened and still I am not absolved.

*

10   This is what I wish were true: I treated his affection for me with grace and humility. I did not embarrass him; I was not embarrassed. I made him feel respected and whole. During an afternoon in his bedroom, I ignored the smells and my discomfort, came close enough to the bed so that Sherman could reach me. I held his hand until he fell asleep. I was not a monster, no.   ■

QUESTIONS ON SUBJECT AND PURPOSE

1. In what way is this a definition of "devotion"?
2. What might Lin mean when she says, "I am not absolved."
3. What purpose or purposes might Lin have had in writing the essay?

QUESTIONS ON STRATEGY AND AUDIENCE

1. Why might Lin withhold the information that Sherman was born with Down syndrome until paragraph 3?
2. How does Lin structure and divide her essay?
3. What expectations might Lin have of her audience?

QUESTIONS ON VOCABULARY AND STYLE

1. Why might Lin have chosen to use a one-sentence paragraph (9)?
2. What is the effect of the descriptive details in paragraphs 4 and 6?
3. Be prepared to define the following words: *pustules* (paragraph 4) and *guttural* (4).

WRITING SUGGESTIONS

1. **Doing a Critical Analysis.** At points, Lin withholds information in the essay allowing the reader to discover gradually both the situation and how she came to feel about her own reactions. Describe and analyze how that strategy works in the essay.

2. **Journaling or Blogging.** We define our relationships with others not by words, but by our actions. Make a list of words that are used to define the quality of a relationship (e.g., loving, compassionate, concerned, nurturing) and next to each add a defining action.

3. **Practicing in a Paragraph.** Take one of the words from your list and develop a definition for it by describing the actions that would characterize it.

4. **Writing the Personal Essay.** Connect your paragraph definition to an experience with someone in your past. Maybe you were embarrassed or uncomfortable; maybe you simply did not know how to react. In retrospect, though, you would now act differently than you originally did. Describe how you treated someone and then how you wish you had acted.

5. **Finding Reading Connections.** Sonja Lea in "First Bath (Chapter 3) depicts a scene that reveals devotion. In an essay, compare her reactions to Lin's.

6. **Exploring Links Online.** Using online sources, research the characteristics of a person with Down Syndrome.

7. **Writing the Research Paper.** One of the goals of the disability rights movement and the Americans with Disabilities Act (ADA) is to get Americans to understand what it means to have a disability. How is a disability defined? In a documented research paper, explore the varying definitions of that term.

For Further Study

Focusing on Grammar and Writing. Lin uses both the colon (:) and the semicolon (;). Study her use of the marks and then explain how you would know which mark to use and when.

Working Together. Working in small groups, brainstorm a list of words that you could use for the journal/blog exercise.

Seeing Other Modes at Work. The essay also uses a chronological narrative pattern and comparison and contrast.

I Want a Wife

JUDY BRADY

Judy Brady was born in 1937 in San Francisco, California, and received a B.F.A. in painting from the University of Iowa. As a freelance writer, Brady has written essays on topics such as union organizing, abortion, and the role of women in society. Currently an activist focusing on issues related to cancer and the environment, she has edited several books on the subject, including One in Three: Women with Cancer Confront an Epidemic *(1991).*

    Brady's most frequently reprinted essay is "I Want a Wife," *which originally appeared in* Ms. *magazine in 1971. After examining the stereotypical male demands in marriage, Brady concludes, "Who* wouldn't *want a wife?"*

Before Reading

Connecting: In a relationship, what separates reasonable needs or desires from unreasonable or selfish ones?

Anticipating: What is the effect of the repetition of the phrase "I want a . . ." in the essay?

1   **I** belong to that classification of people known as wives. I am a Wife. And, not altogether incidentally, I am a mother.

2   Not too long ago a male friend of mine appeared on the scene fresh from a recent divorce. He had one child, who is, of course, with his ex-wife. He is obviously looking for another wife. As I thought about him while I was ironing one evening, it suddenly occurred to me that I, too, would like to have a wife. Why do I want a wife?

3   I would like to go back to school so that I can become economically independent, support myself, and, if need be, support those dependent upon me. I want a wife who will work and send me to school. And while I am going to school I want a wife to take care of my children. I want a wife to keep track of the children's doctor and dentist appointments. And to keep track of mine, too. I want a wife to make sure my children eat properly and are kept clean. I want a wife who will wash the children's clothes and keep them mended. I want a wife who is a good nurturant attendant to my children, who arranges for their schooling, makes sure that they have an adequate social life with their peers, takes them to the park, the zoo, etc. I want a wife who takes care of the children when they are sick, a wife who arranges to be around when the children need special care, because, of course, I cannot miss classes at school. My wife must arrange to lose time at work, and not lose the job. It may mean a small cut in my wife's income from time to time, but I guess I can tolerate that. Needless to say, my wife will arrange and pay for the care of the children while my wife is working.

4   I want a wife who will take care of my physical needs. I want a wife who will keep my house clean. A wife who will pick up after me. I want a wife who will keep my clothes clean, ironed, mended, replaced when need be, and who will see to it that my personal things are kept in their proper place so that I can find what I need the minute I need it. I want a wife who cooks the meals, a wife who is a good cook. I want a wife who will plan the meals, do the necessary grocery shopping, prepare the meals, serve them pleasantly, and then do the cleaning up while I do my studying. I want a wife who will

care for me when I am sick and sympathize with my pain and loss of time from school. I want a wife to go along when our family takes a vacation so that someone can continue to care for me and my children when I need a rest and change of scene.

5   I want a wife who will not bother me with rambling complaints about a wife's duties. But I want a wife who will listen to me when I feel the need to explain a rather difficult point I have come across in my course of studies. And I want a wife who will type my papers for me when I have written them.

6   I want a wife who will take care of the details of my social life. When my wife and I are invited out by my friends, I want a wife who will take care of the babysitting arrangements. When I meet people at school that I like and want to entertain, I want a wife who will have the house clean, will prepare a special meal, serve it to me and my friends, and not interrupt when I talk about the things that interest me and my friends. I want a wife who will have arranged that the children are fed and ready for bed before my guests arrive so that the children do not bother us. I want a wife who takes care of the needs of my guests so that they feel comfortable, who makes sure that they have an ashtray, that they are passed the hors d'oeuvres, that they are offered a second helping of the food, that their wine glasses are replenished when necessary, that their coffee is served to them as they like it. And I want a wife who knows that sometimes I need a night out by myself.

7   I want a wife who is sensitive to my sexual needs, a wife who makes love passionately and eagerly when I feel like it, a wife who makes sure that I am satisfied. And, of course, I want a wife who will not demand sexual attention when I am not in the mood for it. I want a wife who assumes the complete responsibility for birth control, because I do not want more children. I want a wife who will remain sexually faithful to me so that I do not have to clutter up my intellectual life with jealousies. And I want a wife who understands that *my* sexual needs may entail more than strict adherence to monogamy. I must, after all, be able to relate to people as fully as possible.

8   If, by chance, I find another person more suitable as a wife than the wife I already have, I want the liberty to replace my present wife with another one. Naturally I will expect a fresh, new life; my wife will take the children and be solely responsible for them so that I am left free.

9   When I am through with school and have a job, I want my wife to quit working and remain at home so that my wife can more fully and completely take care of a wife's duties.

10   My God, who *wouldn't* want a wife?   ■

QUESTIONS ON SUBJECT AND PURPOSE

1. In what way is this essay a definition of a wife? Why does Brady avoid a more conventional definition?

2. Is Brady being fair? Is there anything that she leaves out of her definition that you would have included?

3. What purpose might Brady have been trying to achieve?

QUESTIONS ON STRATEGY AND AUDIENCE

1. How does Brady structure her essay? What is the order of the development? Could the essay have been arranged in any other way?
2. Why does Brady identify herself by her roles—wife and mother—at the beginning of the essay? Is that information relevant in any way?
3. What assumptions does Brady have about her audience (readers of *Ms.* magazine in the early 1970s)? How do you know?

QUESTIONS ON VOCABULARY AND STYLE

1. How does Brady use repetition in the essay? Why? Does it work? What effect does it create?
2. How effective is Brady's final rhetorical question? Where else in the essay does she use a rhetorical question?
3. Be prepared to define the following words: *nurturant* (paragraph 3), *hors d'oeuvres* (6), *replenished* (6), *monogamy* (7).

WRITING SUGGESTIONS

1. **Doing a Critical Analysis.** Brady's point in the essay—inequality in marriage—could have been made using many perspectives: a personal experience, an objective analysis, a statistical or ethnographic study of many marriages. In an essay, analyze why Brady might have chosen to make her point in this way.
2. **Journaling or Blogging.** What are you looking for in a possible spouse or partner? Brainstorm a list of wants and expectations. Rank them according to their priority for you.
3. **Practicing in a Paragraph.** Using the list from above, write a paragraph definition of the kind of person you seek for a committed relationship.
4. **Writing the Personal Essay.** Select a word that names a central role in human relationships, such as *lover, friend, father, mother, sister, brother* or *grandparent.* Define that word in an essay by showing what such a person does or should do.
5. **Finding Reading Connections.** Compare the definitions of a girl/woman offered in Brady, in Schoenfeld's "Barbie's Little Sister" (Chapter 7), and MediaSmarts' "Little Princesses and Fairy Tale Stereotypes" (this Chapter).
6. **Exploring Links Online.** Using online sources, write an essay in which you describe and define the stereotypical husband.
7. **Writing the Research Paper.** What does it mean to be a wife in another culture? Choose at least two other cultures and research those societies' expectations of a wife. Interviews might be a good source of information. Using your documented research, write an essay offering a comparative definition of *wife.*

For Further Study

Focusing on Grammar and Writing. The most distinctive stylistic feature of Brady's essay is the repetition of "I want a wife who. . . ." Normally, no one would ever advise you to repeat the same sentence structure and words again and again. How is this sentence appropriate for the point that Brady is trying to make?

Working Together. Working in small groups, brainstorm ideas for an essay titled "I Want a Husband." Compile lists of duties, responsibilities, and stereotypes.

Seeing Other Modes at Work. Throughout the essay, Brady uses division to organize the "duties" of a wife.

Eating Food That's Better for You, Organic or Not

MARK BITTMAN

Mark Bittman writes about food for the New York Times Magazine *and does an opinion column for the* New York Times. *The author of a number of award-winning cookbooks, his* How to Cook Everything *has sold more than 1 million copies. He has frequently appeared on the* NBC Today Show. *This essay appeared in a weekend edition of the* Times.

On Writing: *In an interview with the Institute of Culinary Education in 2012, Bittman was asked about the editorial columns he writes. He replied, "The op-ed column, that's straight from the heart; that's what I want to say. I see it as an advocacy position and I see it as a call to action. It's not just describing a problem; I try to say what needs to be done about it. It all is geared to that thing that I just said, of discouraging the consumption of bad food—there's a lot to write about that—and encouraging the consumption of good food—there's a lot to write about that."*

Before Reading

Connecting: When you see the word "organic" applied to food, what associations do you have? What are you expecting?

Anticipating: What the biggest surprise about the government's definition of "organic"?

1   In the six-and-one-half years since the federal government began certifying food as "organic," Americans have taken to the idea with considerable enthusiasm. Sales have at least doubled, and three-quarters of the nation's grocery stores now carry at least some organic food. A Harris poll in October 2007 found that about 30 percent of Americans buy organic food at least on occasion, and most think it is safer, better for the environment and healthier.

2   "People believe it must be better for you if it's organic," says Phil Howard, an assistant professor of community, food and agriculture at Michigan State University.

3   So I discovered on a recent book tour around the United States and Canada.

4   No matter how carefully I avoided using the word "organic" when I spoke to groups of food enthusiasts about how to eat better, someone in the audience would inevitably ask, "What it I can't afford to buy organic food?" It seems to have become the magic cure-all, synonymous with eating well, healthfully, sanely, even ethically.

5   But eating "organic" offers no guarantee of any of that. And the truth is that most Americans eat so badly—we get 7 percent of our calories from soft drinks, more than we do from vegetables; the top food group by caloric intake is "sweets"; and one-third of nation's adults are now obese—that the organic question is a secondary one. It's not unimportant, but it's not the primary issue in the way Americans eat.

6   To eat well, says Michael Pollan, the author of "In Defense of Food," means avoiding "edible food-like substances" and sticking to real ingredients, increasingly from the plant kingdom. (Americans each consume an average of nearly two pounds a day of animal products.) There's plenty of evidence that both a person's health—as well as the environment's—will improve with a simple shift in eating habits away from animal products and highly processed foods to plant products and what might be called "real food." (With all due respect to people in the "food movement," the food need not be "slow," either.)

7   From these changes, Americans would reduce the amount of land, water and chemicals used to produce the food we eat, as well as the incidence of lifestyle diseases linked to unhealthy diets, and greenhouse gases from industrial meat production. All without legislation.

8   And the food would not necessarily have to be organic, which, under the United States Department of Agriculture's definition, means it is generally free of synthetic substances; contains no antibiotics and hormones; has not been irradiated or fertilized with sewage sludge; was raised without the use of most conventional pesticides; and contains no genetically modified ingredients.

9   Those requirements, which must be met in order for food to be labeled "U.S.D.A. Organic," are fine, of course. But they still fall short of the lofty dreams of early organic farmers and consumers who gave the word "organic" its allure—of returning natural nutrients and substance to the soil in the same proportion used by the growing process (there is no requirement that this be done); of raising animals humanely in accordance with nature (animals must be given access to the outdoors, but for how long and under what conditions is not spelled out); and of producing the most nutritious food possible (the evidence is mixed on whether organic food is more nutritious) in the most ecologically conscious way.

10   The government's organic program, says Joan Shaffer, a spokeswoman for the Agriculture Department, "is a marketing program that sets standards

for what can be certified as organic. Neither the enabling legislation nor the regulations address food safety or nutrition."

11   People don't understand that, nor do they realize "organic" doesn't mean "local." "It doesn't matter if it's from the farm down the road or from Chile," Ms. Shaffer said. "As long as it meets the standards it's organic."

12   Hence, the organic status of salmon flown in from Chile, or of frozen vegetables grown in China and sold in the United States—no matter the size of the carbon foot print left behind by getting from there to here.

13   Today, most farmers who practice truly sustainable farming, or what you might call "organic in spirit," operate on small scale, some so small they can't afford the requirements to be certified organic by the government. Others say that certification isn't meaningful enough to bother. These farmers argue that, "When you buy organic you don't just buy a product, you buy a way of life that is committed to not exploiting the planet," says Ed Maltby, executive director of the Northeast Organic Dairy Producers Alliance.

14   But the organic food business is now big business, and getting bigger. Professor Howard estimates that major corporations now are responsible for at least 25 percent of all organic manufacturing and marketing (40 percent if you count only processed organic foods). Much of the nation's organic food is as much a part of industrial food production as midwinter grapes, and becoming more so. In 2006, sales of organic foods and beverages totaled about $16.7 billion, according to the most recent figures from Organic Trade Association.

15   Still, those sales amounted to slightly less than 3 percent of overall food and beverage sales. For all the hoo-ha, organic food is not making much of an impact on the way Americans eat, though, as Mark Kastel, co-founder of The Cornucopia Institute, puts it: "There are generic benefits from doing organics. It protects the land from the ravages of conventional agriculture," and safeguards farm workers from being exposed to pesticides.

16   But the questions remain over how we eat in general. It may feel better to eat an organic Oreo than a conventional Oreo, but, says Marion Nestle, a professor at New York University's department of nutrition, food studies and public health, "Organic junk food is still junk food."

17   Last week, Michelle Obama began digging up a patch of the South Lawn of the White House to plant an organic vegetable garden to provide food for the first family and, more important, to educate children about healthy, locally grown fruits and vegetables at a time when obesity and diabetes have become national concerns.

18   But Mrs. Obama also emphasized that there were many changes Americans can make if they don't have the time or space for an organic garden.

19   "You can begin in your own cupboard," she said, "by eliminating processed food, trying to cook a meal a little more often, trying to incorporate more fruits and vegetables."

20   Popularizing such choices may not be as marketable as creating a logo that says "organic." But when Americans have had their fill of "value-added" and overprocessed food, perhaps they can begin producing and consuming

more food that treats animals and the land as if they mattered. Some of that food will be organic, and hooray for that. Meanwhile, they should remember that the word itself is not synonymous with "safe," "healthy," "fair" or even necessarily "good." ■

QUESTIONS ON SUBJECT AND PURPOSE

1. According to the United States Department of Agriculture, how is the word "organic" defined when applied to food?
2. What were the "lofty" dreams that were originally associated with the term "organic"?
3. In the process of defining at length what "organic" means when applied to food, what other purpose might he have for the essay?

QUESTIONS ON STRATEGY AND AUDIENCE

1. Bittman quotes seven different people in his essay. Why might he use these quotations?
2. What is the value of having a logo like "organic" when you are marketing a food?
3. The essay appeared as an article in a Sunday edition of the *New York Times*. What assumptions could Bittman make about his audience?

QUESTIONS ON VOCABULARY AND STYLE

1. Why might Bittman have titled the essay in this way? What does the title emphasize?
2. Grammatically, what would you call "All without legislation" (paragraph 7)?
3. Be prepared to define the following words: *synonymous* (paragraph 4), *irradiated* (8), *allure* (9), *sustainable* (13), *ravages* (15).

WRITING SUGGESTIONS

1. **Doing a Critical Analysis.** What is the difference between an "opinion" and a "factual" informative essay? How would you classify this? In an essay, analyze the devices that Bittman uses that justify your conclusion.
2. **Journaling or Blogging.** How important to you is eating "real," healthy food? Do you make smart choices each day? Keep notes on the choices you make over several days.
3. **Practicing in a Paragraph.** On the basis of your notes, how would you define your diet? In a paragraph, using some specific examples, characterize your eating habits.
4. **Writing the Personal Essay.** In an essay aimed at an audience of your contemporaries, outline what a healthy diet would be. How would it be defined? What would it include? What would it exclude?
5. **Finding Reading Connections.** A perfect pairing is with the two essays in the casebook "Is a Vegan Diet Healthier Than a Balanced Diet?" in Chapter 9. What exactly is the difference between the value of animal proteins and plant proteins? In an essay define the two terms and explain why one might be better than another.

6. **Exploring Links Online.** Now that you know how the word "organic" is defined by the Department of Agriculture, what about the word "natural"? In a definition essay, explore the technical definition of that term along with the connotations that we associate with it when it appears on food labels.

7. **Writing the Research Paper.** One important advantage to organic foods that researchers agree on is the reduction or elimination of certain pesticides. This makes organic foods safer for those who grow and harvest it as well as those who consume it. What is a pesticide and how do the most dangerous ones work?

For Further Study

Focusing on Grammar and Writing. After each authority quoted (with the exception of First Lady Michelle Obama), Bittman adds an identifying title. How does he set off these titles within his sentences?

Working Together. For its length, the essay has a number of paragraphs, probably occasioned by its publication in a newspaper. Working in small groups, decide how the essay could be re-paragraphed. Which paragraphs could be combined? Would additional words need to be added?

Seeing Other Modes at Work. The essay has a persuasive purpose as well. A thesis for such a purpose can be seen in the final paragraph.

My Two Lives

JHUMPA LAHIRI

Jhumpa Lahiri was born in London and grew up in Rhode Island. A graduate of Barnard College in New York City, she earned three M.A. degrees (English, creative writing, and comparative studies in literature and the arts) and a Ph.D. from Boston University. Her books include the Pulitzer-prize–winning collection of stories Interpreter of Maladies *(1999); the novel* The Namesake *(2003), made into a film with the same title (2006); and the collection of stories* Unaccustomed Earth *(2008).*

On Writing: *When asked about writing, Lahiri observed: "Even now in my own work, I just want to get it less—get it plainer. When I rework things I try to get it as simple as I can."*

Before Reading

Connecting: All Americans are the descendants of immigrants— it is just a question of when our ancestors came to this country. What do you know about your ancestors? From where and when did they come to this country? If you are uncertain, why is that question difficult for you to answer?

Anticipating: How does Lahiri's sense of her self-definition change over time?

1   I have lived in the United States for almost 37 years and anticipate growing old in this country. Therefore, with the exception of my first two years in London, "Indian-American" has been a constant way to describe me. Less constant is my relationship to the term. When I was growing up in Rhode Island in the 1970s I felt neither Indian nor American. Like many immigrant offspring I felt intense pressure to be two things, loyal to the old world and fluent in the new, approved of on either side of the hyphen. Looking back, I see that this was generally the case. But my perception as a young girl was that I fell short at both ends, shuttling between two dimensions that had nothing to do with one another.

2   At home I followed the customs of my parents, speaking Bengali and eating rice and dal with my fingers. These ordinary facts seemed part of a secret, utterly alien way of life, and I took pains to hide them from my American friends. For my parents, home was not our house in Rhode Island but Calcutta, where they were raised. I was aware that the things they lived for—the Nazrul songs they listened to on the reel-to-reel, the family they missed, the clothes my mother wore that were not available in any store in any mall—were at once as precious and as worthless as an outmoded currency.

3   I also entered a world my parents had little knowledge or control of; school, books, music, television, things that seeped in and became a fundamental aspect of who I am. I spoke English without an accent, comprehending the language in a way my parents still do not. And yet there was evidence that I was not entirely American. In addition to my distinguishing name and looks, I did not attend Sunday school, did not know how to ice-skate, and disappeared to India for months at a time. Many of these friends proudly called themselves Irish-American or Italian-American. But they were several generations removed from the frequently humiliating process of immigration, so that the ethnic roots they claimed had descended underground whereas mine were still tangled and green. According to my parents I was not American, nor would I ever be no matter how hard I tried. I felt doomed by their pronouncement, misunderstood and gradually defiant. In spite of the first lessons of arithmetic, one plus one did not equal two but zero, my conflicting selves always canceling each other out.

4   When I first started writing I was not conscious that my subject was the Indian-American experience. What drew me to my craft was the desire to force the two worlds I occupied to mingle on the page as I was not brave enough, or mature enough, to allow in life. My first book was published in 1999, and around then, on the cusp of a new century, the term "Indian-American" has become part of this country's vocabulary. I've heard it so often that these days, if asked about my background, I use the term myself, pleasantly surprised that I do not have to explain further. What a difference from my early life, when there was no such way to describe me, when the most I could do was to clumsily and ineffectually explain.

5   As I approach middle age, one plus one equals two, both in my work and in my daily existence. The traditions on either side of the hyphen dwell

in me like siblings, still occasionally sparring, one outshining the other depending on the day. But like siblings they are intimately familiar with one another, forgiving and intertwined. When my husband and I were married five years ago in Calcutta we invited friends who had never been to India, and they came full of enthusiasm for a place I avoided talking about in my childhood, fearful of what people might say. Around non-Indian friends, I no longer feel compelled to hide the fact that I speak another language. I speak Bengali to my children, even though I lack the proficiency to teach them to read or write the language. As a child I sought perfection and so denied myself the claim to any identity. As an adult I accept that a bicultural upbringing is a rich but imperfect thing.

6   While I am American by virtue of the fact that I was raised in this country, I am Indian thanks to the efforts of two individuals. I feel Indian not because of the time I've spent in India or because of my genetic composition but rather because of my parents' steadfast presence in my life. They live three hours from my home; I speak to them daily and see them about once a month. Everything will change once they die. They will take certain things with them—conversations in another tongue, and perceptions about the difficulties of being foreign. Without them, the back-and-forth life my family leads, both literally and figuratively, will at last approach stillness. An anchor will drop, and a line of connection will be severed.

7   I have always believed that I lack the authority my parents bring to being Indian. But as long as they live they protect me from feeling like an impostor. Their passing will mark not only the loss of the people who created me but the loss of a singular way of life, a singular struggle. The immigrant's journey, no matter how ultimately rewarding, is founded on departure and deprivation, but it secures for the subsequent generation a sense of arrival and advantage. I can see a day coming when my American side, lacking the counterpoint India has until now maintained, begins to gain ascendancy and weight. It is in fiction that I will continue to interpret the term "Indian-American," calculating that shifting equation, whatever answers it may yield. ■

QUESTIONS ON SUBJECT AND PURPOSE

1. As a child, why did Lahiri feel that she was neither Indian nor American?
2. Why does Lahiri feel that, as she grows older, she will see her "American side" gain "ascendancy and weight"?
3. What has been the role of writing in Lahiri's attempt to deal with the separation between the two worlds in which she lived?

QUESTIONS ON STRATEGY AND AUDIENCE

1. Although the essay makes use of comparison and contrast and definition, what is the controlling narrative structure that holds the essay together?
2. What is it that Lahiri is trying to define in the essay?
3. Readers do not need to be Indian-American to connect with the feelings that Lahiri has. What is potentially universal about the experience and conflict that she describes?

QUESTIONS ON VOCABULARY AND STYLE

1. Lahiri compares the two traditions in which she has grown up [Indian and American] to siblings: "The traditions on either side of the hyphen dwell in me like siblings" (paragraph 5). What is this figure of speech called? How are these traditions like siblings?
2. Lahiri expects that, once her parents have died, her sense of self-definition will change. "The back-and-forth" will "approach stillness" and "an anchor will drop" (paragraph 6). What is this figure of speech called?
3. Be prepared to define the following words: *fluent* (paragraph 1), *dal* (2), *cusp* (4), *sparring* (5).

WRITING SUGGESTIONS

1. **Doing a Critical Analysis.** The essay describes the difficulty that Lahiri has had in defining her identity—is she Indian, American, Indian-American? That self-definition has been evolving. In an essay, analyze how Lahiri blends definition, comparison and contrast, narration and example to trace that evolving sense of identity.
2. **Journaling or Blogging.** Lahiri writes that growing up she felt that she was "shuttling between two dimensions that had nothing to do with one another." Have you ever had a similar experience? Explore some possible examples from your life—they might be ethical, racial, social, geographic, economic, generational, or cultural.
3. **Practicing in a Paragraph.** Expand your experience into a paragraph. Concentrate on a single experience and allow it to reveal something about how it challenged or confirmed your sense of identity.
4. **Writing the Personal Essay.** In an interview, Lahiri explained her difficulty with the question "Where are you from?" Her feeling, she writes, was that "there was no single place to which I fully belonged." In an essay, explore the extent to which place plays a crucial role in your sense of self-definition.
5. **Finding Reading Connections.** Amy Tan in "Mother Tongue" (this chapter) moves between two worlds as she deals with her mother. In what ways do Tan and Lahiri have a similar experience with self-identity?
6. **Exploring Links Online.** Using online sources, explore the ways in which cultural identity can be defined. Then, in an essay define your cultural identity.
7. **Writing the Research Paper.** In the essay Lahiri refers to her identity as involving a hyphen, for example, "Indian-American." The term "hyphenated American" has been in use for a considerable period of time. In a documented research essay, trace the history of this phrase.

For Further Study

Focusing on Grammar and Writing. Lahiri makes use of figurative language in a number of places in the essay. Identify each use and label it as a simile or metaphor.

Working Together. Working in small groups, select examples of figurative language from the essay and then discuss how each works in the essay. What does each contribute?

Seeing Other Modes at Work. The essay makes extensive use of comparison and contrast.

Mother Tongue

AMY TAN

Born in Oakland, California, in 1952 to Chinese immigrants, Amy Tan graduated from San Jose State University with a double major in English and linguistics and an M.A. in linguistics. Tan did not write fiction until 1985, when she began the stories that would become her first and very successful novel, The Joy Luck Club *(1989), also a popular film. Tan's children's book* The Chinese Siamese Cat *(1994) is the basis for the daily animated television series,* Sagwa, The Chinese Siamese Cat *(PBS). Her most recent novel is* Saving Fish From Drowning *(2005).*

On Writing: Asked about her writing, Tan responded: "I welcome criticism when I'm writing my books. I want to become better and better as a writer. I go to a writer's group every week. We read our work aloud." In another interview she commented, "I still think of myself, in many ways, as a beginning writer. I'm still learning my craft, learning what makes for a good story, what's an honest voice."

Before Reading

Connecting: How sensitive are you to the language that you use or your family uses? Are you ever conscious of that language? Are you ever embarrassed by it? Are you proud of it?

Anticipating: In what ways does the language of Tan and her mother "define" them in the eyes of others?

1   I am not a scholar of English or literature. I cannot give you much more than personal opinions on the English language and its variations in this country or others.

2   I am a writer. And by that definition, I am someone who has always loved language. I am fascinated by language in daily life. I spend a great deal

of my time thinking about the power of language—the way it can evoke an emotion, a visual image, a complex idea, or a simple truth. Language is the tool of my trade. And I use them all—all the Englishes I grew up with.

3   Recently, I was made keenly aware of the different Englishes I do use. I was giving a talk to a large group of people, the same talk I had already given to half a dozen other groups. The nature of the talk was about my writing, my life, and my book, *The Joy Luck Club*. The talk was going along well enough, until I remembered one major difference that made the whole talk sound wrong. My mother was in the room. And it was perhaps the first time she had heard me give a lengthy speech, using the kind of English I have never used with her. I was saying things like, "The intersection of memory upon imagination" and "There is an aspect of my fiction that relates to thus-and-thus"—a speech filled with carefully wrought grammatical phrases, burdened, it suddenly seemed to me, with nominalized forms, past perfect tenses, conditional phrases, all the forms of standard English that I had learned in school and through books, the forms of English I did not use at home with my mother.

4   Just last week, I was walking down the street with my mother, and I again found myself conscious of the English I was using, the English I do use with her. We were talking about the price of new and used furniture and I heard myself saying this: "Not waste money that way." My husband was with us as well, and he didn't notice any switch in my English. And then I realized why. It's because over the twenty years we've been together I've often used that same kind of English with him, and sometimes he even uses it with me. It has become our language of intimacy, a different sort of English that relates to family talk, the language I grew up with.

5   So you'll have some idea of what this family talk I heard sounds like, I'll quote what my mother said during a recent conversation which I videotaped and then transcribed. During this conversation, my mother was talking about a political gangster in Shanghai who had the same last name as her family's, Du, and how the gangster in his early years wanted to be adopted by her family, which was rich by comparison. Later, the gangster became more powerful, far richer than my mother's family, and one day showed up at my mother's wedding to pay his respects. Here's what she said in part:

6   "Du Yusong having business like fruit stand. Like off the street kind. He is Du like Du Zong—but not Tsung-ming Island people. The local people call putong, the river east side, he belong to that side local people. That man want to ask Du Zong father take him in like become own family. Du Zong father wasn't look down on him, but didn't take seriously, until that man big like become a mafia. Now important person, very hard to inviting him. Chinese way, came only to show respect, don't stay for dinner. Respect for making big celebration, he shows up. Mean gives lots of respect. Chinese custom. Chinese social life that way. If too important won't have to stay too long. He come to my wedding. I didn't see, I heard it. I gone to boy's side, they have YMCA dinner. Chinese age I was nineteen."

7   You should know that my mother's expressive command of English belies how much she actually understands. She reads the *Forbes* report, listens to *Wall Street Week*, converses daily with her stockbroker, reads all of Shirley MacLaine's books with ease—all kinds of things I can't begin to understand. Yet some of my friends tell me they understand 50 percent of what my mother says. Some say they understand 80 to 90 percent. Some say they understand none of it, as if she were speaking pure Chinese. But to me, my mother's English is perfectly clear, perfectly natural. It's my mother tongue. Her language, as I hear it, is vivid, direct, full of observation and imagery. That was the language that helped shape the way I saw things, expressed things, made sense of the world.

8   Lately, I've been giving more thought to the kind of English my mother speaks. Like others, I have described it to people as "broken" or "fractured" English. But I wince when I say that. It has always bothered me that I can think of no way to describe it other than "broken," as if it were damaged and needed to be fixed, as if it lacked a certain wholeness and soundness. I've heard other terms used, "limited English," for example. But they seem just as bad, as if everything is limited, including people's perceptions of the limited English speaker.

9   I know this for a fact, because when I was growing up, my mother's "limited" English limited *my* perception of her. I was ashamed of her English. I believed that her English reflected the quality of what she had to say. That is, because she expressed them imperfectly her thoughts were imperfect. And I had plenty of empirical evidence to support me: the fact that people in department stores, at banks, and at restaurants did not take her seriously, did not give her good service, pretended not to understand her, or even acted as if they did not hear her.

10   My mother has long realized the limitations of her English as well. When I was fifteen, she used to have me call people on the phone to pretend I was she. In this guise, I was forced to ask for information or even to complain and yell at people who had been rude to her. One time it was a call to her stockbroker in New York. She had cashed out her small portfolio and it just so happened we were going to go to New York the next week, our very first trip outside California. I had to get on the phone and say in an adolescent voice that was not very convincing, "This is Mrs. Tan."

11   And my mother was standing in the back whispering loudly, "Why he don't send me check, already two weeks late. So mad he lie to me, losing me money."

12   And then I said in perfect English, "Yes, I'm getting rather concerned. You had agreed to send the check two weeks ago, but it hasn't arrived."

13   Then she began to talk more loudly. "What he want, I come to New York tell him front of his boss, you cheating me?" And I was trying to calm her down, make her be quiet, while telling the stockbroker, "I can't tolerate any more excuses. If I don't receive the check immediately, I am going to have to speak to your manager when I'm in New York next week." And sure enough, the following week there we were in front of this astonished

stockbroker, and I was sitting there red-faced and quiet, and my mother, the real Mrs. Tan, was shouting at his boss in her impeccable broken English.

14　　We used a similar routine just five days ago, for a situation that was far less humorous. My mother had gone to the hospital for an appointment, to find out about a benign brain tumor a CAT scan had revealed a month ago. She said she had spoken very good English, her best English, no mistakes. Still, she said, the hospital did not apologize when they said they had lost the CAT scan and she had come for nothing. She said they did not seem to have any sympathy when she told them she was anxious to know the exact diagnosis, since her husband and son had both died of brain tumors. She said they would not give her any more information until the next time and she would have to make another appointment for that. So she said she would not leave until the doctor called her daughter. She wouldn't budge. And when the doctor finally called her daughter, me, who spoke in perfect English—lo and behold—we had assurances the CAT scan would be found, promises that a conference call on Monday would be held, and apologies for any suffering my mother had gone through for a most regrettable mistake.

15　　I think my mother's English almost had an effect on limiting my possibilities in life as well. Sociologists and linguists probably will tell you that a person's developing language skills are more influenced by peers. But I do think that the language spoken in the family, especially in immigrant families which are more insular, plays a large role in shaping the language of the child. And I believe that it affected my results on achievement tests, IQ tests, and the SAT. While my English skills were never judged as poor, compared to math, English could not be considered my strong suit. In grade school I did moderately well, getting perhaps B's, sometimes B-pluses, in English and scoring perhaps in the sixtieth or seventieth percentile on achievement tests. But those scores were not good enough to override the opinion that my true abilities lay in math and science, because in those areas I achieved A's and scored in the ninetieth percentile or higher.

16　　This was understandable. Math is precise; there is only one correct answer. Whereas, for me at least, the answers on English tests were always a judgment call, a matter of opinion and personal experience. Those tests were constructed around items like fill-in-the-blank sentence completion, such as, "Even though Tom was _____, Mary thought he was _____." And the correct answer always seemed to be the most bland combinations of thoughts, for example, "Even though Tom was shy, Mary thought he was charming," with the grammatical structure "even though" limiting the correct answer to some sort of semantic opposites, so you wouldn't get answers like, "Even though Tom was foolish, Mary thought he was ridiculous." Well, according to my mother, there were very few limitations as to what Tom could have been and what Mary might have thought of him. So I never did well on tests like that.

17　　The same was true with word analogies, pairs of words in which you were supposed to find some sort of logical, semantic relationship—for example, "*Sunset* is to *nightfall* as _____ is to _____." And here you would be presented with a list of four possible pairs, one of which showed the same kind of relationship: *red* is to *stoplight*, *bus* is to *arrival*, *chills* is to *fever*, *yawn* is to *boring*. Well, I could never think that way. I knew what the tests were asking, but I could not block out of my mind the images already created by the first pair, "*sunset* is to *nightfall*"—and I would see a burst of colors against a darkening sky, the moon rising, the lowering of a curtain of stars. And all the other pairs of words—*red, bus, stoplight, boring*—just threw up a mass of confusing images, making it impossible for me to sort out something as logical as saying: "A sunset precedes nightfall" is the same as "a chill precedes a fever." The only way I would have gotten that answer right would have been to imagine an associative situation, for example, my being disobedient and staying out past sunset, catching a chill at night, which turns into feverish pneumonia as punishment, which indeed did happen to me.

18   I have been thinking about all this lately, about my mother's English, about achievement tests. Because lately I've been asked, as a writer, why there are not more Asian-Americans represented in American literature. Why are there few Asian Americans enrolled in creative writing programs? Why do so many Chinese students go into engineering? Well, these are broad sociological questions I can't begin to answer. But I have noticed in surveys—in fact, just last week—that Asian students, as a whole, always do significantly better on math achievement tests than in English. And this makes me think that there are other Asian-American students whose English spoken in the home might also be described as "broken" or "limited." And perhaps they also have teachers who are steering them away from writing and into math and science, which is what happened to me.

19   Fortunately, I happen to be rebellious in nature and enjoy the challenge of disproving assumptions made about me. I became an English major my first year in college, after being enrolled as pre-med. I started writing nonfiction as a freelancer the week after I was told by my former boss that writing was my worst skill and I should hone my talents toward account management.

20   But it wasn't until 1985 that I finally began to write fiction. And at first I wrote using what I thought to be wittily crafted sentences, sentences that would finally prove I had mastery over the English language. Here's an example from the first draft of a story that later made its way into *The Joy Luck Club*, but without this line: "That was my mental quandary in its nascent state." A terrible line, which I can barely pronounce.

21   Fortunately, for reasons I won't get into today, I later decided I should envision a reader for the stories I would write. And the reader I decided upon was my mother, because these were stories about mothers. So with this reader in mind—and in fact she did read my early drafts—I began to write stories using all the Englishes I grew up with: the English I spoke to my mother, which for lack of a better term might be described as "simple"; the English she used with me, which for lack of a better term might be described as "broken"; my translation of her Chinese, which could certainly be described as "watered down"; and what I imagined to be her translation of her Chinese if she could speak in perfect English, her internal language, and for that I sought to

preserve the essence, but neither an English nor a Chinese structure. I wanted to capture what language ability tests can never reveal: her intent, her passion, her imagery, the rhythms of her speech and the nature of her thoughts.

22   Apart from what any critic had to say about my writing, I knew I had succeeded where it counted when my mother finished reading my book and gave me her verdict: "So easy to read." ■

QUESTIONS ON SUBJECT AND PURPOSE

1. What does the title "Mother Tongue" suggest?
2. How many subjects does Tan explore in the essay?
3. How does Tan feel about her mother's "tongue"?

QUESTIONS ON STRATEGY AND AUDIENCE

1. In paragraph 6, Tan quotes part of one of her mother's conversations. Why?
2. After paragraphs 7 and 17, Tan uses additional space to indicate divisions in her essay. Why does she divide the essay into three parts?
3. Tan notes in paragraph 21 that she thinks of her mother as her audience when she writes stories. Why?

QUESTIONS ON VOCABULARY AND STYLE

1. How would you characterize Tan's tone (see the Glossary and Ready Reference for a definition) in the essay?
2. In paragraph 20, Tan quotes a "terrible line" she once wrote: "That was my mental quandary in its nascent state." What is so terrible about that line?
3. Be prepared to define the following words: *belies* (7), *empirical* (9), *benign* (14), *insular* (15), *semantic* (16), *hone* (19), *quandary* (20), *nascent* (20).

WRITING SUGGESTIONS

1. **Doing a Critical Analysis.** Tan is writing about what linguists call "code-switching," the practice of adjusting our language depending on the context and audience. We do it all the time, talking to friends in one way, to a potential employer in another. Analyze how Tan uses "all the Englishes I grew up with" (paragraph 2) in her essay.
2. **Journaling or Blogging.** Reflect on the extent to which your language (word choice, pronunciation, dialect, second-language skills) is influenced by your parents, your education, your geographical location, your peers.
3. **Practicing in a Paragraph.** Using the information you gathered above, write a paragraph in which you define your "mother tongue." Define the influences that have shaped both what you say and how you say it.
4. **Writing the Personal Essay.** Expand your paragraph into an essay. As your audience changes (e.g., friends, teachers, people in authority, employers, parents), what changes do you make in your English?
5. **Finding Reading Connections.** Deborah L. Rhode in "Why Looks Are the Last Bastion of Discrimination" (Chapter 1) focuses on physical appearance.

To what extent can your spoken "English" also be a source of discrimination? Reflect on the links between the two essays.

6. **Exploring Links Online.** Puzzled about "code switching"? Search the phrase on YouTube and watch some video clips of examples. Pair that with online sources that deal with this term. Why must you be able to "code switch" to be successful?

7. **Writing the Research Paper.** Tan suggests that a certain type or dialect of English is the language of power, that if you use it, people in authority will listen and respect you. That English is sometimes referred to as "edited American English." Research the features of this English and, in a documented essay, offer a definition aimed at an audience of your peers.

For Further Study

Focusing on Grammar and Writing. Tan occasionally writes an extremely long sentence (e.g., the final sentences in paragraphs 3, 9, 13, 14, 17 and the next to last sentence in 21). How can Tan write such a long sentence and still achieve clarity? Analyze how these sentences are constructed.

Working Together. Working in small groups, choose one of the following topics and examine its role in the essay: the introduction (paragraphs 1 and 2); the transcription of her mother's conversation (6); the meeting with the stockbroker (10–13); the CAT scan (14); the verbal sections of achievement tests (16 and 17).

Seeing Other Modes at Work. Tan uses classification at several points in the essay to talk about the "different Englishes" that she uses.

Little Princesses and Fairy Tale Stereotypes

BACKGROUNDER, MEDIASMARTS

MediaSmarts defines itself as "a Canadian not-for-profit charitable organization for digital and media literacy . . . [whose] vision is that children and youth have the critical thinking skills to engage with media as active and informed digital citizens." It maintains an extensive website with materials for teachers and has provided "digital and media literacy programs and resources for Canadian homes, schools and communities since 1996."

Before Reading

Connecting: Do you think you are still susceptible to gender stereotypes? What type of costume, for example, would you choose for a Halloween party?

Anticipating: Is there any reason that parents should be concerned about the impact of the "little princess" stereotype?

1 ■t's a question that most parents of young daughters face: "Has she hit the 'princess phase' yet?" Not all parents are upset by this; many happily buy their girls princess costumes, toys, and accessories ranging from shoes to purses, all in pink. Some, though, despair of the powerful gender stereotyping this delivers to young girls and each new piece of princess gear can be a source of conflict.

2   The source of much of this princess culture is Disney, and in 2009 the studio extended its reach by introducing its first African-American princess, Tiana, in the animated film *The Princess and the Frog*. Princesses are big business for Disney. Since 2000, when the company began to tie together all the merchandising for any of its characters who might conceivably be called "princesses," the line has become one of the company's biggest earners. Disney's Andy Mooney, who spearheaded the creation of the princess line, told the *New York Times* that he got the idea from seeing girls at Disney on Ice shows who were dressed in non-Disney princess costumes, and in the years since, the company has pushed the line into almost every imaginable aspect of a child's life, from beddings to Band-Aids to lip balm.

3   Not surprisingly, the marketing of Princess Tiana began well in advance of the movie's December premiere: more than 45,000 dolls based on the character had already been sold by mid-November, while actors portraying her were already performing in "Tiana's Showboat Jubilee" at Disneyland and Disney World.

4   The creation of Princess Tiana would seem to be an attempt to expand into the one market as yet untouched by princesses: African-American girls. The official list of Disney princesses includes, along with born princess Snow White and married-to-royalty Cinderella, two entirely nonroyal characters, Mulan and Pocahontas, who are Chinese and Native respectively. The last two characters, though, rarely appear on merchandise—less, perhaps, due to their ethnic origin than the fact that neither fits well with the "princess aesthetic"; in their movies, Pocahontas appears in tolerably realistic (if somewhat revealing) Native garb, while Mulan actively rejects feminine attire in order to masquerade as a male soldier. Tiana, though, is carefully crafted to fit the princess mold, with an hourglass figure, many glamorous dresses, and even a tiara. Of course, she spends much of the movie in the shape of a frog, but that's not the image that will adorn lunchboxes everywhere.

5   Is this necessarily a bad thing, though? After all, princesses—whether born to royalty at the beginning of a story or married into it by the end— have been fairy-tale protagonists for hundreds of years; the characters of Cinderella and Snow White long predate their Disney incarnations. The appeal of princesses is not hard to see: the unearned wealth and privilege of being a princess makes it a close parallel to classic boys' fantasies of being demigods or orphans rocketed at birth from a distant planet. Where the male and female versions diverge is that, while boys imagine gaining powers and abilities from their special status, being a princess brings girls wealth, beauty, and romance. It's not surprising, then, that many parents are concerned about just what gender roles their daughters are being trained to play.

6   One common feature of the many articles on this phenomenon is that young girls resist any criticism or alteration of their princesses. In an article in the *Los Angeles Times*, Rosa Brooks writes of failing to convince her daughters that princesses are more likely to end up at a guillotine than a fairy-tale wedding; and Tracee Sioux, who writes a blog titled *The Girl Revolution*, describes her unsuccessful efforts to steer her daughter away from princesses. Nor can girls be easily swayed by stories that try to subvert the classic princess: "Frogs and snails and feminist tales: Preschool children and gender," a 1989 study by Bronwyn Davies, found that both boys and girls tend to reject stories that attempt to alter the traditional gender roles found in fairy tales.

7   Is it really gender roles that children are so attached to, or is it the fairy-tale narratives on which they are experts? A recent article by Karen Wohlwend, "Damsels in Discourse: Girls Consuming and Producing Identity Texts Through Disney Princess Play," finds that while children engaging in "media play" with princess characters feel a strong loyalty to the original narratives, they are not averse to changing things like the gender of secondary characters (turning Prince Charming into a princess, for instance) or making the protagonist more active, especially if that means giving themselves a larger and more entertaining role to play. (One of the girls in Wohlwend's study finds a way to involve a comatose Sleeping Beauty in a swordfight.)

8   The children in Wohlwend's study, though, are kindergarteners; though they might have been exposed to quite a lot of princess-related media by this age, they're still in the early stages of forming gender identities. As girls get older, the worrying aspects of princess culture—the passivity, consumerism, and so on—may become more and more confining. As Lyn Mikel Brown, coauthor of *Packaging Girlhood*, writes, the issue is not princess play but the sheer dominance of princess culture: "When one thing is so dominant, then it's no longer a choice: it's a mandate, cannibalizing all other forms of play. There's the illusion of more choices out there for girls, but if you look around, you'll see their choices are steadily narrowing." Her coauthor, Sharon Lamb, points out as well that the road travelled by princesses is a narrow one, leading to the hypersexualized roles now being sold to 'tween and teen girls: "There's a trap at the end of that rainbow, because the natural progression from pale, innocent pink is not to other colors. It's to hot, sexy pink—exactly the kind of sexualization parents are trying to avoid."

9   Disney is certainly aware of the gender issues underlying the "Disney Princess" line, and is walking a fine line between making movies that are girly without being too girly: after the disappointing box-office performance of *The Princess and the Frog*, which was ascribed to the unwillingness of boys to see a movie with the word "princess" in the title, the title of the upcoming *Rapunzel* was changed to a more gender-neutral *Tangled* and the male lead made more prominent. Even if the marketing of the film is designed to appeal to boys, though, you can be sure that Rapunzel will be added to the roster of Disney Princesses and her face plastered on hundreds of licensed products (all pink, of course): the studio now has a policy of only making movies that

can be spun off into brands, which means that in the long run how well the Rapunzel toothbrushes and bed sheets sell will be more important than how the movie performs.

10   How should parents deal with the arrival of the "princess phase"? One option is simply to say "no"—something parents should never be afraid to do. But an outright ban may backfire by making all things princess even more desirable. What may be more effective is to make sure that girls (and boys) are also exposed to more positive female role models. There are many children's books with strong female characters; kids' movies with good female leads can be harder to find, but the anime produced by Studio Ghibli—such as *Kiki's Delivery Service* and *My Neighbor Totoro*—is a good place to start.

11   Most important is that parents engage with their children's media and be ready to discuss the images and events they see. Don't be confrontational, but ask questions: do you think you can really change an angry person into a nice person, like Belle does to the Beast? Is it worth it to give up your voice and your family for a boy, the way Ariel does? If Mulan spends most of her movie dressed as a boy, why is she in girls' clothes on the merchandising? Why do you think Disney changed the title of "Rapunzel"? There may be no escaping the "princess phase," but teaching kids to view media critically can help make sure your princess doesn't grow up expecting a handsome prince—or a fairy godmother—to solve all her problems. ■

QUESTIONS ON SUBJECT AND PURPOSE

1. What are the associations connected with the "little princess" stereotype?
2. In paragraph 8, a writer comments on the "road" traveled by princesses is a "narrow" one. According to that writer, where does the road lead?
3. What seems to be the purpose of the essay?

QUESTIONS ON STRATEGY AND AUDIENCE

1. What is the role of the sources and quotations included in the text?
2. Does it seem likely that playing with princesses will make little girls expect, when they grow up, that "a handsome prince" or a "fairy godmother" will solve their problems?
3. Who is the intended audience for the essay?

QUESTIONS ON VOCABULARY AND STYLE

1. Four of the paragraphs in the essay begin by asking a question. Why might the writer use this strategy?
2. How would you describe the tone of the essay? What creates or contributes to that tone?
3. Be prepared to define the following words: *tiara* (paragraph 4), *averse* (7), *comatose* (7), *anime* (10).

WRITING SUGGESTIONS

1. **Doing a Critical Analysis.** How is the essay structured? Given both where the essay originally appeared and its intended audience, what is appropriate about that structure?

2. **Journaling or Blogging.** Think back to your childhood, what types of toys did you gravitate to? Make a list. What appealed to you about those toys?

3. **Practicing in a Paragraph.** Looking at your list, did you conform to a gender stereotype or did you resist it? In a paragraph, focus on what your toys and activities revealed about you.

4. **Writing the Personal Essay.** How would you define "masculinity" or "femininity"? Do not write about your own gender. What associations do you have with those words? What would be their defining characteristics?

5. **Finding Reading Connections.** Explore the links among Janice Mirikitani's "Recipe" (Chapter 6), Ellie Schoenfeld's "Barbie's Little Sister" (Chapter 7), and Jamaica Kincaid's "Girl" (this chapter).

6. **Exploring Links Online.** Using online sources, research the impact that a toy such as G.I. Joe has on young boys. What does he suggest about masculinity?

7. **Writing the Research Paper.** Elizabeth Sweet, in her research, found that, in 1975, very few toys were "explicitly marketed according to gender, and nearly 70 percent showed no markings of gender whatsoever." Today, however, she notes that "finding a toy that is not marketed either explicitly or subtly (e.g., through use of color) by gender has become incredibly difficult." In a time when gender equality is more of an issue than ever, why would toys be so clearly gender differentiated? In a researched and documented essay, explore this phenomenon.

For Further Study

Focusing on Grammar and Writing. Look closely at the first sentences in each of the paragraphs. What role do they play in the paragraph and in the essay?

Working Together. As a prewriting exercise for suggestion 4 above, form two groups by gender, asking males to brainstorm their associations with the term "femininity" and females, "masculinity." After each group has compiled a list, then switch lists.

Seeing Other Modes at Work. The essay makes extensive use of cause and effect as well.

USING DOCUMENTATION: READING AND WRITING

1. The essay references a number of sources. What does the presence of those references and quotations contribute to the essay?

2. Why might the author not have used conventional documentation (footnotes, works cited) for those references?

3. **For Practice with Documentation.** Using the information provided in the essay and then doing an online search, construct more formal footnotes or endnotes. Create as well a formal bibliography or a list of works cited. Be sure to use the proper MLA or APA style for both.

ADDITIONAL WRITING SUGGESTIONS FOR DEFINITION

When we come across a word or phrase that is not familiar, we consult a dictionary, either in print or online. As necessary and as helpful as dictionaries are, however, entries are typically limited to a single sentence. Often, we need an extended definition, one that provides both denotation and connotation, explains the term in great depth, and offers a series of examples. Definition essays offer just that—extended definitions that potentially draw upon all of the writing strategies examined in this text. The following suggestions invite you to write an extended definition of a complex term.

1. How would you define a *terrorist?* An *insurgent?* Can a terrorist ever be seen by another culture as a *martyr?*
2. What exactly does the Bill of Rights mean when it says, "the right to bear arms"?
3. What is the difference between an *idol* and a *hero?*
4. How would you define *adulthood?* Would it be any different than how your parents might define it?
5. What does *being disrespected* mean? What would be the necessary conditions under which one might feel "dissed"?
6. How would you define *success?*
7. What constitutes *plagiarism?* How does the law define the term? Can you plagiarize common knowledge? Does plagiarism occur only when you reproduce someone else's work word for word?
8. What did the phrase the "separation of church and state" mean when it was written into the U.S. Constitution?
9. What is *patriotism?* How is it manifested? What kinds of action might be labeled *unpatriotic?*
10. What is, or was, the "American Dream"?
11. How would you define the term *marriage?*
12. When you were younger, what did it mean "to be going out" with someone? What does it mean now?
13. Define a particular type or style of music—rock, rap, punk, heavy metal, alternative rock.
14. What does the term *free trade* mean? What are the conditions under which it operates? In what sense is it "free"?
15. Pick a word that you and your friends use frequently, a word whose meaning is not likely to be found in a dictionary. Write a definition of the term and provide examples of how and when it might be used or applied.

9 | Argument and Persuasion

LEARNING OBJECTIVES

In this chapter, you will learn how to
1. Distinguish between argument and persuasion
2. Match your argument to your intended audience
3. Link your thesis and your evidence logically
4. Recognize and reply to your opposition
5. Revise an argumentative or persuasive essay to increase its effectiveness
6. Analyze readings that use argument and persuasion

Key Questions

WRITING ARGUMENT AND PERSUASION

Getting Ready to Write

What is the difference between arguing and persuading?

What do you already know about arguing and persuading?

How do you analyze your audience?

What does it take to convince a reader?

Writing

How do you connect your thesis and your evidence in an argument?

How do you make sure that your argument is logical?

How do you structure an argument?

Revising

How do you revise an argumentative or persuasive essay?

Student Essay

   Morgan Murphy, "A Not So Simple Solution"

READING ARGUMENT AND PERSUASION

In Prose

   "Parents Need Our Help"

In Literature

   Wilfred Owen, "Dulce et Decorum Est" (poem)

In a Visual

   James Montgomery Flagg, "I Want You" (poster)

Writing Argument and Persuasion

GETTING READY TO WRITE

We live in a world of persuasive messages—billboards, advertisements in newspapers and magazines, commercials on television and radio, pop-ups and advertisements on nearly every website, signs on storefronts, bumper stickers, T-shirts and caps with messages, and manufacturers' logos prominently displayed on clothing. Advertisements demonstrate a wide range of persuasive strategies. Sometimes they appeal to logic and reason—they ask you to compare the features and price of one car with those of any competitor and judge for yourself. More often, though, they appeal to your emotions and feelings.

What Is the Difference between Arguing and Persuading?

Argument and persuasion share two important qualities. First, both start with a thesis, a statement of purpose or position. The word *thesis* is derived from a Greek word that means "placing," "position," or "proposition." Second, both seek to move an audience to a particular course of action—to do something or to believe something. Sometimes a distinction is made between argument and persuasion: *argument* seeks to win over an audience by appealing to reason; *persuasion*, on the other hand, works by appealing to an audience's emotions, feelings, prejudices, and beliefs. Rarely, however, do you find one strategy without some elements of the other. As a result, the words are generally linked together, as they are in the title of this chapter.

Links between Writing and Reading

	Thesis or claim—can you locate the full statement in the text?
Katherine Porter, "Value of College"	College education is worth its costs.
Linda Lee, "Case Against College"	Not everyone needs college.
Michael Dillingham, "Steroids, Sports"	Steroid use is a form of cheating.
Pete du Pont, "Have a Heart"	Buying and selling organs will alleviate the shortage.
T. Colin Campbell, "Cut Animal-Based Protein"	Cut animal protein.
Nancy Rodriguez, "It's a Question of Balance"	Eat a balanced diet.
Singer, "Singer Solution"	Any money not needed for necessities should be given away.

Links between Writing and Reading

	Source of evidence or data
Katherine Porter, "Value of College"	Where does she find her statistics?
Linda Lee, "Case Against College"	How persuasive is her personal example?
Michael Dillingham, "Steroids, Sports"	How does Dillingham's training lend credibility to his argument?
Pete du Pont, "Have a Heart"	Why might the essay start with statistics?
T. Colin Campbell, "Cut Animal-Based Protein"	What role does personal experience play?
Nancy Rodriguez, "It's a Question of Balance"	What research does she cite?
Singer, "Singer Solution"	Is the analogy convincing? How important is it in the argument?

Argument and persuasion always seek to convince an *audience* to do or to believe something. They never simply entertain or inform; rather, they create logical or emotional appeals to achieve an intended goal. The effectiveness of an essay of argument or persuasion lies in whether the reader agrees with the writer's position or performs some type of requested action. The cleverest, most artistic and amusing advertisement is a failure if it does not "sell" the product. On the other hand, arguments exist because there are at least two sides to the issue. You try to persuade an audience to accept your point of view or to perform or endorse the action that you request by supplying evidence. That evidence, as we will see, can be quite varied. However, no matter how reliable and extensive your evidence, that alone may not get your audience to agree with you. Your goal, then, is to convince them of the validity and reasonableness of your position.

What Do You Already Know About Arguing and Persuading?

Perhaps you have not thought about your extensive experience in constructing arguments and in persuading an audience. Every time you try to convince someone to do or to believe something, you argue and persuade.

Consider a hypothetical example. You are concerned about your father's health. He smokes cigarettes, avoids exercise, is overweight, and works long hours in a stressful job. Even though you are worried, he is completely unconcerned and has always resisted the family's efforts to change his ways. Your task is to persuade him to change or modify his lifestyle, and doing so involves making the dangers clear, offering convincing reasons for change, and urging specific action.

Fresco Michael Mirrorpix/Newscom

People tend to associate argument with reason and factual evidence and to associate persuasion with emotional appeals. Salespeople are persuaders, as are those who use the "soapbox" approach.

Establishing the dangers is the first step, and you have a wide range of medical evidence from which to draw. That evidence involves statistics, testimony or advice from doctors, and case histories of men who have suffered the consequences of years of abusing or ignoring their health. From that body of material, you select the items that are most likely to get through to your obstinate father. He might not be moved by cold statistics citing life-expectancy tables for smokers and nonexercisers, but he might be touched by the story of a friend his age who suffered a heart attack or stroke. The evidence you gather and use becomes a part of the convincing reasons for change that you offer in your argument. If your father persists in ignoring his health, he is likely to suffer some consequences. You might, at this point, include emotional appeals in your strategy. If he is not concerned about what will happen to him, what about his family? What will they do if he dies?

We will assume you got your father to realize and acknowledge the dangers inherent in his lifestyle and to understand the reasons why he should make changes. What remains is to urge specific action. In framing a plan for that action, consider your audience. If you urge your father to stop smoking immediately, join a daily exercise class, go on a thousand-calorie-a-day diet, and find a new job, chances are that he will think your proposal too drastic even to try. Instead, you might urge a moderate plan, one that phases in changes over a period of time and offers compromises.

How Do You Analyze Your Audience?

An essay of argument and persuasion, unlike any other type of writing described in this text, has a special purpose—to persuade its audience. Because you want your reader to agree with your position or act as you urge, you need to analyze your audience carefully before you start to write. Try to answer each of the following questions:

- Who are my readers?
- What do they already know about this subject?
- How interested are they likely to be?
- How impartial or prejudiced are they going to be?
- Is my subject one that strongly challenges their lifestyle or their ethical or moral beliefs and values?
- What values do my readers share with me?
- What types of evidence are most likely to be effective with them?
- Is my plan for requested agreement or action reasonable?

Your argumentative strategy should always reflect an awareness of your audience. Look again at the hypothetical case of the unhealthy father. It is obvious that some types of evidence would be more effective than others and that some solutions or plans for action would be more reasonable and therefore more acceptable than others.

Another important consideration in any argument is to anticipate your audience's objections and be ready to answer them. Debaters study both sides of an argument so that they can effectively counter any opposition. In arguing about abortion, for example, the right-to-life advocate has to be prepared to deal with subjects such as abnormal fetuses or pregnancies that resulted from rape or incest. The pro-choice advocate must face questions about when life begins and when the rights of the unborn might take precedence over the mother's rights.

What Does It Take to Convince a Reader?

In some cases, nothing will persuade your reader. For example, if you are arguing for legalized abortion, you will never convince a reader who believes that an embryo is a human being from the moment of conception.

Abortion to that reader will always be murder. It is extremely difficult to argue any position that is counter to your audience's moral or ethical values. You will also find it difficult to argue a position that is counter to your audience's normal patterns of behavior. For example, you could reasonably argue that your readers ought to stop at all stop signs and obey the speed limit. However, the likelihood of persuading your audience to always do these two things—even though not doing so means breaking the law—is slim.

Links between Writing and Reading

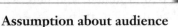

	Assumption about audience
Katherine Porter, "Value of College"	Aimed at parents? Children? Educators?
Linda Lee, "Case Against College"	Aimed at parents or children?
Michael Dillingham, "Steroids, Sports"	Who is his audience? Athletes? Coaches?
Pete du Pont, "Have a Heart"	Does du Pont assume his audience will be sympathetic or hostile to his argument?
T. Colin Campbell, "Cut Animal-Based Protein"	Why might his position be more difficult to argue?
Nancy Rodriguez, "It's a Question of Balance"	Why might her audience be sympathetic to her position?
Singer, "Singer Solution"	Does he really expect his audience to do this?

These cautions are not meant to imply that you should only argue "safe" subjects or that winning is everything. Choose a subject about which you feel strongly; present a fair, logical argument; express honest emotion; but avoid distorted evidence or inflammatory language. Even if no one is finally persuaded, at least you have offered a clear, intelligent explanation of your position.

In most arguments, you have two possible types of support: you can supply factual evidence, and you can appeal to your reader's values, assumptions, and beliefs. Suppose you are arguing that professional boxing should be banned because it is dangerous. Your readers may or may not accept your premise, but they would expect you to support your assertion. Your first task would be to gather evidence. The strongest evidence is factual—statistics dealing with the number of fighters each year who are fatally injured or mentally impaired. You might quote appropriate authorities—physicians, scientists, former boxers—on the risks connected with professional boxing. You might relate several instances of boxing injuries or even a single example of a particular fighter who was killed or permanently injured while boxing. You might describe in detail how blows affect the human body or brain; you might trace the process by which a series of punches can inflict permanent brain damage. You might catalog the effects that years of physical punishment can produce in the human body. In your argument, you might use some or all of this factual evidence. Your job as a writer is to gather the most accurate and most effective evidence and present it in a clear and orderly way.

You can also appeal to your reader's emotions and values. You could argue that a sport in which a participant can be killed or permanently injured is not a sport at all. You could argue that the object of a boxing match—to render one's opponent unconscious or too impaired to continue—is different in kind from any other sport and not one that we, as human beings, should condone, let alone encourage. Appeals to values can be extremely effective.

Effective argumentation generally involves appealing to both reason and emotion. It is often easier, however, to catch your reader's attention through an emotional appeal. Demonstrators against vivisection, the dissecting of animals for laboratory research, display photographs of the torments suffered by these animals. Organizations that fight famine throughout the world show photographs of starving children. Advertisers use a wide range of persuasive tactics to touch our fears, our anxieties, our desires. But the type of argumentative writing that you are asked to do in college or in your job rarely allows for only emotional evidence.

One more factor is crucially important in persuading readers. You must sound (and be) fair, reasonable, and credible to win the respect and approval of your readers. Readers distrust arguments that use unfair or inflammatory language, faulty logic, and biased or distorted evidence.

Prewriting Tips for Writing Argument and Persuasion

1. Consider your choice of subject in light of the proposed length of the paper. Can you adequately cover the topic within the space available?

2. Analyze your audience. What assumptions or ideas do they already have about this subject? How likely are they to agree or disagree with you?

3. Anticipate your audience's objections to your argument. Make a list of the possible points of disagreement and think of how you might counter their criticisms.

4. Remember that you need specific, accurate information to argue convincingly. Most arguments need more than unsubstantiated personal opinions.

5. Write a specific statement of the action or reaction you want from your audience. Keep that in mind as you write.

WRITING

How Do You Connect Your Thesis and Your Evidence in an Argument?

Stephen Toulmin, a British philosopher, developed a simplified model for argument in the 1950s that is widely used in speech and communication, as well as in writing. Toulmin's model of an argument consists of three essential parts that could be visually displayed in the following way:

The **claim**	The **data**
(the thesis)	(the evidence or support for the claim or thesis)

connected by
The **warrant**
(the assumptions, values, and common beliefs that connect the claim/thesis and the data/evidence)

It is relatively easy to recognize claims or theses, because they are explicitly stated in a thesis statement. Similarly, identification of data or evidence poses no difficulty, as data are explicitly provided. The warrants, on the other hand, are more puzzling, especially because they are often not explicitly stated in the written or oral argument. In addition, any argument might have more than one unwritten or unspoken warrant, and a writer and readers might have different warrants! Essays of argument are not commonly constructed around the Toulmin model (unless a teacher asks that an essay be divided into claim, data, and warrant). Rather, the Toulmin model is used for analysis—in preparing an argument and in reading an argument.

What then is the value of warrants, if they are unspoken, unwritten, and variable? It is important for you as a writer to realize what you are basing your argument on, just as it is important for your audience to understand the link you are making between your thesis and your evidence. When you and your audience share warrants, you are more likely to be convincing to your readers. The warrants serve as a common ground for agreement. Consider an example from a presidential election:

Claim:	Candidate A is not fit to be President because he is not patriotic.
Data:	Candidate A did not serve in the military.
	Candidate A refuses to wear a flag pin in his lapel.
Possible warrants:	Patriots would wear flag pins.
	Anyone who would not wear a flag pin is unpatriotic.
	Military service is the only way in which to demonstrate patriotism.

Why is Toulmin's model important when writing and reading arguments? Because it asks you to consciously identify how the claim and evidence are connected.

How Do You Make Sure That Your Argument Is Logical?

Logic, or reason, is crucial to an effective argument. Try to avoid logical fallacies or errors. When you construct your argument, make sure that you avoid the following common mistakes:

- *Ad hominem argument* (literally, to argue "to the person"): criticizing a person's position by criticizing his or her personal character. If an underworld figure asserts that boxing is the manly art of self-defense, you do not counter his argument by claiming that he makes money by betting on the fights.

- *Ad populum argument* (literally, to argue "to the people"): appealing to the prejudices of your audience instead of offering facts or reasons. You do not defend boxing by asserting that it is part of the American way of life and that anyone who criticizes it is a communist who seeks to undermine our society.

- *Appeal to an unqualified authority:* using testimony from someone who is unqualified to give it. In arguing against boxing, your relevant authorities would be physicians or scientists or former boxers—people who have had some direct experience. You do not quote a professional football player or your dermatologist.

- *Begging the question:* assuming the truth of whatever you are trying to prove. "Boxing is dangerous, and because it is dangerous, it ought to be outlawed." The first statement ("boxing is dangerous") is the premise you set out to prove, but the second statement uses that unproved premise as a basis for drawing a conclusion.

- *Either-or:* stating or implying that there are only two possibilities. Do not assert that the two choices are either to ban boxing or to allow this brutality to continue. Perhaps other changes might make the sport safer and hence less objectionable.

- *Faulty analogy:* using an inappropriate or superficially similar analogy as evidence. "Allowing a fighter to kill another man with his fists is like giving him a gun and permission to shoot to kill." The analogy might be vivid, but the two acts are much more different than they are similar.

- *Hasty generalization:* basing a conclusion on evidence that is atypical or unrepresentative. Do not assert that every boxer has suffered brain damage just because you can cite a few well-known cases.

- *Non sequitur* (literally, "it does not follow"): arriving at a conclusion not justified by the premises or evidence. "My father has watched many fights on television; therefore, he is an authority on the physical hazards that boxers face."

- *Oversimplification:* suggesting a simple solution to a complex problem. "If professional boxers were made aware of the risks they take, they would stop boxing."

How Do You Structure an Argument?

If you are constructing an argument based on a formal, logical progression, you can use either *inductive* or *deductive* reasoning. An *inductive argument* begins with specific evidence and moves to a generalized conclusion that accounts for the evidence. The writer assumes the role of detective, piecing together the evidence in an investigation and only then arriving at a conclusion. An inductive structure is often effective because it can arouse the reader's interest, or even anger, by focusing on examples. If your thesis is likely to be rejected immediately by some readers, an inductive strategy can be effective, because it hides the thesis until the readers are involved in your argument.

In contrast to an inductive argument, a *deductive argument* starts with a general truth or assumption and moves to provide evidence or support. Here the detective announces who the murderer is and then proceeds to show us how she arrived at that conclusion. Linda Lee in "The Case Against College" signals her thesis even in her title. Two paragraphs into the essay, Lee makes her argumentative, and provocative, assertion: "Not everyone needs a higher education." In the rest of her essay, Lee provides the support that leads to her conclusion, drawing from statistics and from her own experience with her son. A deductive argument immediately announces its thesis, so it runs the risk of instantly alienating a reader, especially if it is arguing for something about which many readers might disagree.

The simplest form of a deductive argument is the *syllogism*, a three-step argument involving a major premise, a minor premise, and a conclusion. Few essays—either those you write or those you read—can be reduced to a syllogism. Our thought patterns are rarely so logical; our reasoning rarely so precise. Although few essays state a syllogism explicitly, syllogisms do play a role in shaping an argument. For example, a number of essays in this textbook begin with the same syllogism, even though it is not directly stated:

Major premise:	All people should have equal opportunities.
Minor premise:	Minorities are people.
Conclusion:	Minorities should have equal opportunities.

Despite the fact that a syllogism is a precise structural form, do not assume that a written argument will imitate it—that the first paragraph or group of paragraphs will contain a major premise; the next, a minor premise; and the final, a conclusion. Syllogisms can be basic to an argument without being the framework on which it is constructed in the same way that arguments have warrants even though the warrants are not explicitly stated.

No matter how you structure your argument, one final consideration is important: end your paper decisively. The purpose of argument and persuasion is to get a reader to agree with your position or to act in a particular way.

> ## Drafting Tips for Writing
> ## Argument and Persuasion
>
> 1. Look carefully at the structure of your essay. Did you begin with a position and then provide evidence (deductive order) or did you begin with examples and then draw a conclusion (inductive order)? Why did you choose that order?
> 2. Within that inductive or deductive order, have you placed your strongest points first or last? Why did you choose that arrangement?
> 3. Details—accurate, factual, logical—are vital to making an argument effective. Do your details meet those criteria?
> 4. Avoid distorted or inflammatory language or examples.
> 5. Document all information and quotations taken from sources, otherwise you are plagiarizing.

REVISING

How Do You Revise an Argumentative or Persuasive Essay?

Argument and persuasion are particularly reader oriented. That is, the goal of argument and persuasion is not simply to inform or to entertain readers; rather, the goal is to convince readers to commit to a certain course of action or to agree with (or at the very least to understand) the writer's stand on the issue or subject. Argument presumes that there is at least one other side, that disagreement already exists about the subject. Persuasion suggests that readers can be brought into agreement with the writer's position.

Readers typically approach argument and persuasion with some preformed opinions; they are not generally completely neutral about the subject. In some cases, readers will not actively resist a point of view, even if they will not commit to the desired course of action. For example, surely few people in the United States believe that smoking tobacco is healthy. Those who smoke might not disagree with an essay meant to persuade smokers to stop, but that does not mean they will stop. Habit and addiction can be far stronger than logical argument or emotional appeal. On subjects that touch on deeply held religious or ethical beliefs, many readers will never be persuaded to accept an argument that runs counter to those beliefs. If your readers believe in intelligent design, they will never accept your argument that evolution is the only answer to the origins of human life.

Because argument and persuasion seek to engage an audience in particular ways, it is especially important to involve readers in the revising stage of your essay. Aim to enlist a minimum of several readers, ideally readers who do not agree with you or who will not agree just to please or get rid of you. Ask them to react to your argument. Do they agree with you? Why or why not? Is this a subject about which they could be open-minded? What is your strongest argument? What is your weakest? What might it take to convince them that even if you are not right, you have articulated a position that they can understand and respect?

When writing an argumentative or persuasive essay, pay particular attention to the following areas: understanding and respecting your opposition, being honest and fair, and ending forcefully.

Understanding and Respecting Your Opposition   In planning, writing, and revising argument and persuasion, you need to be aware of the other sides to your argument that can exist. Debaters prepare by being able to argue either side of an issue; lawyers in a courtroom have to anticipate and be ready to counter arguments made by their adversaries. As you write and revise, you must decide which points you have to concede and which points can be refuted. Anytime you are arguing, remember to anticipate the objections and counterarguments of those who will disagree with you.

Being Honest and Fair   Everyday of your life you are surrounded by attempts at persuasion and argument. Little children throw temper tantrums because they are not getting what they want; a television political advertisement denounces the untrustworthiness and seemingly criminal behavior of the opposition; a print commercial implies that the "good" life lies in owning this particular car or watch or drinking this expensive brand of vodka; a salesperson and the manager try to close the deal by pressuring you. In much of such argument and persuasion, the goal is winning—winning by any means, no matter how unscrupulous, deceitful, or biased. That is never the goal of argumentative or persuasive writing in college. As you review your draft, look again at the nature of the evidence you are presenting and the language that

Links between Writing and Reading

	Conclusion
Katherine Porter, "Value of College"	How does Porter end and why?
Linda Lee, "Case Against College"	How does the essay end and why at that particular place?
Michael Dillingham, "Steroids, Sports"	What action does he call for?
Pete du Pont, "Have a Heart"	How effective are the final sentences?
T. Colin Campbell, "Cut Animal-Based Protein"	What is the focus of the final paragraph?
Nancy Rodriguez, "It's a Question of Balance"	What concessions are made in the final paragraph?
Singer, "Singer Solution"	What does Singer really want his audience to do?

Revising Tips for Writing Argument and Persuasion

1. Ask some peer readers to evaluate honestly your position in the paper. Do they agree or disagree with you? Why?
2. Have you acknowledged and confronted the arguments that might be used against your position?
3. Check the list of logical fallacies or errors in this chapter. Have you avoided each of these in your essay?
4. Have you provided a clear organizational pattern? Have you arranged your points in an effective order and signal transitions?
5. What do you want your reader to do at the end of your essay? Are you urging a course of action or a change of understanding?

you have used. Is the information accurate and fair? Is your language free from inflammatory words and phrases?

Ending Forcefully   Conclusions to essays of argument and persuasion are especially important. Your conclusions complete the stand or position that you have been advocating, and they are what remains in your readers' mind. If you are urging readers to commit to a particular course of action (e.g., to register and then vote), you need to end with a specific request or call to action. If you are trying to get readers to agree with your position, you need to remind them again of what that position is and why they should agree with you.

Student Essay

Morgan Murphy decided to tackle a subject vital to every college student and parent—the high cost of education and the increasing amount of student debt. Morgan read an online article that suggested that students should go to community college for two years, then transfer to a four-year institution, and to take online courses at "cheap" universities. Morgan disagreed, and wrote a first-draft counterargument. She chose to focus just on the first part of the proposed solution: live at home and attend a local two-year community college and then transfer to a four-year school.

First Draft

A Not So Simple Solution

Aaron Broadus in "A Simple Solution on Student Loans" argues that students should take advantage of local community colleges where tuitions are more affordable and living costs can be minimized by commuting. However, Broadus fails to acknowledge that often students who attend community colleges end up staying longer in college and increasing their debt because some of their credits do not transfer to the four-year college that they wish to attend. In this economy, a college degree is essential to finding a job, and many times students find themselves having to go on to a master's program in order to make themselves marketable. Unlike community colleges, four-year schools also offer more opportunities for students to get involved with clubs and activities that pertain to their major and future careers. Four-year institutions can provide students with more research opportunities, as well as different classroom experiences, because they have the finances and resources to do so. Because of the plethora of opportunities, students are able to grow and develop more fully in the classroom setting.

The "college experience" is also important. By attending a four-year school starting at the age of 18, students are forced to grow and become independent. Most community colleges do not have dorms and if you are living at home, it is more difficult to become self-sufficient and resourceful since you continue to rely on your parents. A simple task such as doing laundry and cooking allows students to become less reliant on their parents and offers them an opportunity to grow. Skills such as time management and self sufficiency are learned through these experiences and students can apply those skills to future jobs as well as everyday life.

Comments

Morgan had a conference with her writing instructor to discuss some issues with her first draft. One of the first things that the instructor noticed was the organization of the essay. The instructor encouraged Morgan to create a more unified essay by putting similar talking points together and creating a clear and concise structure. The instructor also reminded Morgan to provide appropriate documentation for the essay she cites.

Finally, Morgan was encouraged to develop her points more clearly. She was asked to provide more information about the topics that she had discussed in her essay such as economical advantages, academic advantages, as well as the "college experience." By providing more information for the three points, her essay would support her opinion more effectively.

Revised Draft

A Not So Simple Solution

Aaron Broadus in "A Simple Solution on Student Loans" argues that students should take advantage of local community colleges where tuitions are more affordable and living costs are minimized by commuting. Although community colleges are vital for students who truly have limited financial resources, there are potential drawbacks to his strategy of attending a local community college in order to avoid accumulating debt. Often students who attend community colleges end up staying longer in college since some of their credits do not transfer to the four-year college they wish to attend. Four-year schools often have students beginning a core curriculum as early as their freshman year. Many two-year colleges offer only what are considered "general requirements" and therefore students are already at a disadvantage when transferring to a new school. If a student is interested in a technical major or a major with many requirements and prerequisites, transferring in after two years at a community college might mean an extra semester or year to finish the degree.

Four-year schools also offer more opportunities for students to get involved with clubs and activities related to their major and future careers. They can also provide students with more research opportunities as well as different classroom experiences because they have more resources and financial support than two-year colleges. Because of the abundance of opportunities, students are able to grow and develop more fully in the classroom setting while learning skills that are pertinent to their future careers. Many four-year schools encourage students even as early as their sophomore year to work with faculty on research projects.

Getting away from home to have the "college experience" is also an important factor when attending a four-year school. Especially if students are not commuting from home, four-year schools allow students to become more independent and rely less on their parents. Simple tasks such as doing laundry and cooking offer students an opportunity to grow. Skills such as time management and self sufficiency are also learned when given independence, and with these experiences students can apply them to future jobs as well as everyday life. Living on a college campus also provides a much greater exposure to students from other parts of the country and the world. Part of a college education is an increased exposure to a global perspective.

Two-year colleges have a vital role to play in higher education and it is an ever-expanding role. No one wants to graduate with a massive debt, but under certain circumstances, it might be a better investment to choose a more expensive alternative. If two-year colleges offer real financial savings, four-year schools offer a wider range of educational and living experiences.

Work Cited

Broadus, Aaron. "A Simple Solution on Student Loans." www.insidehighered.com.
    Inside Higher Ed, 6 July 2012. Web. 19 Jan. 2013.

Checklist: Some Things to Remember About Writing Argument and Persuasion

❑ Choose a subject that allows for the possibility of persuading your reader. Avoid emotionally charged subjects that resist logical examination.

❑ Analyze your audience. Who are your readers? What do they already know about your subject? How are they likely to feel about it? How impartial or prejudiced are they going to be?

❑ Make a list of the evidence or reasons you will use in your argument. Analyze each piece of evidence to see how effective it might be in achieving your end.

❑ Honest emotion is fair, but avoid anything that is distorted, inaccurate, or inflammatory. Argue with solid, reasonable, fair, and relevant evidence.

❑ Avoid the common logical fallacies listed in this chapter.

❑ Make a list of all the possible counterarguments or objections your audience might have. Think of ways in which you can respond to those objections.

❑ Decide how to structure your essay. You can begin with a position and then provide evidence, or you can begin with the evidence and end with a conclusion. Which structure seems to fit your subject and evidence better?

❑ End forcefully. Conclusions are what listeners and readers are most likely to remember. Repeat or restate your position. Drive home the importance of your argument.

Reading Argument and Persuasion

The effectiveness of argument or persuasion can be measured by its success in convincing readers or bringing them to action. In our daily world, that success typically means that consumers bought the product or they voted for the candidate or the issue you were promoting. In college writing, however, the goal is not always action but often understanding. Effective argument and persuasion is founded on evidence, on logic and reason, on the integrity and commitment of the writer. In effective college writing, the end does not justify the means. As you read, remember what you have learned about how to write an argumentative and persuasive essay and how that knowledge might help you as a reader:

• Essays of argument and persuasion always have a specific goal, typically to get readers to commit to a course of action (to register and vote) or to understand more fully (and hopefully to agree with) the writer's position.

• Because they are goal-driven, essays of argument and persuasion involve a thorough understanding of what the audience already knows

and feels about the subject. If your position on the subject runs counter to the audience's deeply held beliefs (moral, religious, ethical), your
argument is not likely to convince any reader. You can, however, at
least make your position known.

- Argument and persuasion must take into consideration objections or
  counterarguments that the other side would offer. You cannot ignore
  the opposition. Your essay must concede certain points; it must refute
  others.

- Argumentative and persuasive essays in college writing require
  convincing reasons and evidence. Typically, you need to support your
  position with facts or quotations or logical reasoning. This is especially
  true if positions on the subject are debatable.

- Arguments are clearly and logically organized in one of two patterns:
  in a deductive pattern, the position or stand is stated first and the
  reasons or evidence follow; in an inductive pattern, evidence comes
  first and the position or stand follow.

- Argument and persuasion in college writing should not resort to
  inflammatory, emotional, or biased language or evidence. The goal is
  never to win at all costs.

IN PROSE

One of the most common forms of persuasive writing is editorial or opinion
writing. Generally rather short in length, and sometimes occurring orally
rather than in print, these pieces take one side of a debatable issue, arguing for
that one point of view. Of course, the opinions they express are right; the opposition is clearly wrong and, of course, never heard from in the essay. The length
of the pieces, along with their intentional focus on their position, means that
arguments are not balanced, evidence is minimal, and emotional words and
phrases are often used. The editorial reproduced below appeared in *USA Today*,
a newspaper with a national circulation. It was written by the then governor of
Illinois who was defending new legislation that prohibited the sale or rental of
excessively violent or sexually explicit video games to children. The impact
of such videos on children has been widely studied and some studies suggest
not negative effects, but positive ones—an example can be found in John Paul
Gee's "Games, Not Schools, Are Teaching Kids to Think" (Chapter 7).

Parents Need Our Help

1   When I was growing up, my parents used to worry if I was hanging out with the
wrong kids in the neighborhood. Today, parents have even more to worry about: instead
of playing basketball at the schoolyard, our children are spending their afternoons at the
controls of a Sony PlayStation simulating acts of murder, dismemberment, decapitation
and sexual seduction.

2   Games such as Grand Theft Auto and Halo 2 use the same techniques the U.S. military uses to train our soldiers to kill the enemy. Another game, JFK Reloaded, re-enacts the assassination of the late president. As a parent, this is the last thing I want my 8-year-old exposed to.

3   But the truth is that 92% of children between the ages of 2 and 17 are playing video games—and it's taking a toll on them.

4   A recent study at Iowa State University tied playing video games with an area of the brain directly linked to extreme behavioral disorders. Another study found that kids who play violent games have lower test scores. As one parent told me, we're "compet-ing with video games for the minds and souls of our children." From what I can tell, the video games are winning.

5   That's why—as both a parent and a governor—I was delighted we passed legisla-tion last week making Illinois the first state in the nation to prohibit the sale or rental of excessively violent or sexually explicit video games to children under 18.

6   We don't let our kids buy cigarettes. We don't let them buy alcohol. We don't let children purchase pornography. So why should we let them purchase video games that we know can cause them long-term harm?

7   Many retailers will argue that they don't sell these kinds of games to kids. But a study by the Federal Trade Commission found that 69% of teenage boys were able to purchase violent and sexually explicit games without permission from their parents. I don't believe we should ever put profits ahead of what's best for our children.

8   I know that some interest groups don't like the idea of limiting anything. But when it comes to our children and their well-being, how about a little common sense? Telling kids they can purchase violent and sexually explicit video games sends the wrong message and reinforces the wrong values.

9   Parents deserve a fighting chance. It's our responsibility to give it to them.   ■

QUESTIONS FOR ANALYSIS

1. The essay makes frequent use of the word "parents." The writer mentions that he is a "parent" as well with an 8-year-old. What is the intended effect of such references? Who is the writer imagining as his audience?

2. Why make the contrast in the opening paragraph—this is what it used to be like, and this is what children do now? Who responds to appeals such as that?

3. What is the effect of the descriptions of the video games in paragraph 2?

4. The evidence in paragraph 4 references, in one sentence each, two studies. One is identified as coming from Iowa State University, the second is simply identified as "recent." The third example is a quotation from a parent. How persuasive is the evidence? Who is likely to be persuaded by these references?

5. How effective is the analogy—we don't let kids buy cigarettes, or alcohol, or pornography, so why allow them to buy video games?

CRITICAL READING ACTIVITY

Persuasion often uses emotional appeals, rather than logical ones, to capture an audience's attention and agreement. In an essay, analyze the variety of emotional devices, including word choice, the writer uses in this editorial.

IN LITERATURE

British poet Wilfred Owen served as a soldier during World War I. Over 8.5 million soldiers died in that war; on a single day, the British lost more than 57,000 soldiers. The third leading cause of death was poison gas, used by both sides during the war. Owen's title is taken from the Latin quotation from Horace, cited at the end of the poem, which translates "it is sweet and fitting to die for one's country." As you read the poem, think about whether Owen agreed with Horace.

Dulce et Decorum Est

WILFRED OWEN

Bent double, like old beggars under sacks,
Knock-kneed, coughing like hags, we cursed through sludge,
Till on the haunting flares we turned our backs,
And towards our distant rest began to trudge.

Men marched asleep. Many had lost their boots,
But limped on, blood-shod. All went lame, all blind;
Drunk with fatigue; deaf even to the hoots
Of gas-shells dropping slowly behind.

Gas! GAS! Quick, boys! An ecstasy of fumbling,
Fitting the clumsy helmets just in time,
But someone still was yelling out and stumbling
And flound'ring like a man in fire or lime.—
Dim through the misty panes and thick green light,
As under a green sea, I saw him drowning.

If in some smothering dreams, you too could pace
Behind the wagon that we flung him in,
And watch the white eyes writhing in his face,
His hanging face, like a devil's sick of sin,
If you could hear, at every jolt, the blood
Come gargling from the froth-corrupted lungs
Obscene as cancer, bitter as the cud
Of vile, incurable sores on innocent tongues.—
My friend, you would not tell with such zest
To children ardent for some desperate glory,
The old lie: Dulce et decorum est
        Pro patria mori.

QUESTIONS FOR ANALYSIS

1. How many examples of simile can you find in the poem? What does each contribute to the poem?
2. In the second stanza, what is happening to the men's sense perceptions? Why?
3. Why does the third stanza begin as it does? What is Owen trying to capture?
4. Why does Owen describe the man as "drowning"? How is that image carried over to the fourth stanza? How did the poison gas kill?
5. In using a quotation from a Roman writer that is not translated into English, what assumption is Owen making about his readers?
6. What purpose might Owen have had in writing the poem? Who might he have been trying to persuade? What might he have wanted his reader to see, feel, or understand?

WRITING SUGGESTIONS

1. **Analysis.** In the last section of the poem, Owen focuses on the agonizing death of a single soldier. Is describing the death of a single soldier an effective strategy? Why might Owen choose to focus on just one example and not on many? In an essay, analyze how Owen describes that one death and how that strategy is connected to his persuasive purpose in the poem.
2. Living as we do in a world full of advertisements, we are surrounded by persuasion—buy this, do this. Choose a social or moral issue about which you have strong feelings and then, using a single extended example, try to persuade your audience to agree with you and/or to do something. Consider the following possibilities:

   a. The plight of the homeless in the United States
   b. Dangers of addiction or at-risk behaviors
   c. Genetic engineering

IN A VISUAL

You are surrounded each day with hundreds of examples of visual argumentation and persuasion—advertisements. Sometimes advertisements appeal to reason, citing specific facts and statistics to buttress their claims. Other times, advertisements use subtle, persuasive appeals: if you wear this cologne or perfume, you will be irresistible; if you drive this automobile, you will be a rugged adventurer or an important professional. You might think that you see through these claims, but consumers respond to these visual appeals; otherwise, companies would stop advertising in such ways.

Visuals are also used to persuade people to commit to a certain course of action or to believe in or support a particular cause. Bumper stickers, posters, even T-shirts announce political and social agendas. In times of national conflict, advertisements enlist support and participation. Consider this famous U.S. army recruitment poster created by artist James Montgomery Flagg during World War I and later revived during World War II. From 1917 through 1918, over four million copies of the poster were printed.

QUESTIONS FOR ANALYSIS

1. The figure in the poster is "Uncle Sam." Who was Uncle Sam? And why might Flagg have chosen to use this symbol?

2. Why is the figure looking at the viewer and pointing his finger? Why is "You" emphasized (in the original it was printed in red ink)?

3. Flagg said that he used his own face as a model to avoid having to find someone else. He aged the face and added the white goatee. Why make Uncle Sam look like this—that is, as a stern, older man with white hair and goatee? Why not a younger man?

4. Why might Flagg have chosen these words for the message? Why not something like "Enlist now" or "Join the War effort"?

5. The poster has been referred to as "the most famous poster in the World" and copies could be seen in every town in the United States. What made the poster so popular and, presumably, so effective?

WRITING SUGGESTIONS

1. **Analysis:** What is persuasive about this image? Four million copies of it were printed during World War I to stimulate enlistment—and it worked. For it to have been so effective, what assumptions about his audience and their motivations must Flagg have had? In an essay, analyze the image as an example of persuasion.

2. How do the armed services promote enlistment in the 21st century? Is a static image, such as a poster, enough? Must it be a video? Look for advertisements targeted at young men and women (e.g., "Army Strong"). Select one and in an essay, analyze its persuasive elements and its assumptions about its audience. Include a copy of the visual with your essay.

3. Find two print advertisements that represent contradictory positions on the same issue, for example, legalized gambling, gun control, conflicts between personal freedoms and government regulations. In an essay, analyze how each side uses the techniques of argument and persuasion to advance its position and discredit the opposition.

Debate Casebook: Is College for Everyone and Just How Valuable Is a College Education?

College costs (tuition, room and board, fees, and books) are increasing substantially each year. Low-cost loan programs have been sharply cut back. Students are forced to borrow large amounts of money that they will have difficulty repaying. Those who do finish their degrees often have difficulty finding an appropriate job. These realities have forced many students and parents to weigh the benefits of a two-year or four-year college education. Schools that provide technical job training are flourishing as a more affordable and more realistic alternative.

The selections in this casebook highlight a number of issues. The two essays debate the "value" of a college education. Porter's essay is objective and scholarly, citing substantial evidence provided by a number of research studies; Lee's essay is subjective and draws on her experience with her son. Lee argues, for example, that the benefit or value of a college education depends upon the student's attitude and seriousness. Because of the difference in their approaches, their conclusions can be equally valid.

The data provided in the table "The 30 Occupations with the Largest Employment Growth, 2006–2016" from the U.S. Bureau of Labor Statistics raises other issues. Only six of the thirty "growth" occupations require a four-year college degree. How do we justify sending 70 percent of our high school graduates to college when many will end up underemployed?

The forum conducted by *the Chronicle of Higher Education* and excerpted here offers a series of perspectives on attending college from experts in public policy and education. They respond to a series of provocative questions including "Who Should and Shouldn't Go to College?"; "How Much Does Increasing College-Going Rates Matter to Our Economy and Society?"; "Economists Have Cited the Economic Benefits That Individual Students Derive From College. Does That Still Apply?" and "At What Point Does the Cost of College Outweigh the Benefits?" Some of their assertions and conclusions will stimulate widespread debate.

Before Reading

Connecting: Was there ever a debate in your family or in your mind about whether it was worthwhile to attend a college or a university? Did you consider other alternatives?

Anticipating: Should people be discouraged from attending a college? Shouldn't everyone have a chance? Is past performance in high school always a good guide to how someone will do in college? Is it fair that college is most accessible to those who have the most financial resources?

The Value of a College Degree

KATHERINE PORTER

This essay originally appeared in the ERIC Clearinghouse on Higher Education in 2002.

1   The escalating cost of higher education is causing many to question the value of continuing education beyond high school. Many wonder whether the high cost of tuition, the opportunity cost of choosing college over full-time employment, and the accumulation of thousands of dollars of debt is, in the long run, worth the investment. The risk is especially large for low-income families who have a difficult time making ends meet without the additional burden of college tuition and fees.

The Economic Value of Higher Education

2 In order to determine whether higher education is worth the investment, it is useful to examine what is known about the value of higher education and the rates of return on investment to both the individual and to society.

3   There is considerable support for the notion that the rate of return on investment in higher education is high enough to warrant the financial burden associated with pursuing a college degree. Though the earnings differential between college and high school graduates varies over time, college graduates, on average, earn more than high school graduates. According to the Census Bureau, over an adult's working life, high school graduates earn an average of $1.2 million; associate's degree holders earn about $1.6 million; and bachelor's degree holders earn about $2.1 million (Day and Newburger, 2002).

4   These sizeable differences in lifetime earnings put the costs of college study in realistic perspective. Most students today—about 80 percent of all students—enroll either in public 4-year colleges or in public 2-year colleges. According to the U.S. Department of Education report, Think College Early, a full-time student at a public 4-year college pays an average of $8,655 for in-state tuition, room and board (U.S. Dept. of Education, 2000). A full-time student in a public 2-year college pays an average of $1,359 per year in tuition (U.S. Dept. of Education, 2000).

5   These statistics support the contention that, though the cost of higher education is significant, given the earnings disparity that exists between those who earn a bachelor's degree and those who do not, the individual rate of return on investment in higher education is sufficiently high to warrant the cost.

Other Benefits of Higher Education

6 College graduates also enjoy benefits beyond increased income. A 1998 report published by the Institute for Higher Education Policy reviews the individual benefits that college graduates enjoy, including higher levels of saving, increased personal/professional mobility, improved quality of life for their offspring, better consumer decision making, and more hobbies and leisure activities (Institute for Higher Education Policy, 1998). According to a report published by the Carnegie Foundation, non-monetary individual benefits of higher education include the tendency for postsecondary students to become more open-minded, more cultured, more rational, more consistent and less authoritarian; these benefits are also passed along to succeeding generations (Rowley and Hurtado, 2002). Additionally, college attendance has been shown to "decrease prejudice, enhance knowledge of world affairs and enhance social status" while increasing economic and job security for those who earn bachelor's degrees (Ibid.)

7   Research has also consistently shown a positive correlation between completion of higher education and good health, not only for oneself, but

also for one's children. In fact, "parental schooling levels (after controlling for differences in earnings) are positively correlated with the health status of their children" and "increased schooling (and higher relative income) are correlated with lower mortality rates for given age brackets" (Cohn and Geske, 1992).

The Social Value of Higher Education

8 A number of studies have shown a high correlation between higher education and cultural and family values, and economic growth. According to Elchanan Cohn and Terry Geske (1992), there is the tendency for more highly educated women to spend more time with their children; these women tend to use this time to better prepare their children for the future. Cohn and Geske (1992) report that "college graduates appear to have a more optimistic view of their past and future personal progress."

9   Public benefits of attending college include increased tax revenues, greater workplace productivity, increased consumption, increased workforce flexibility, and decreased reliance on government financial support (Institute for Higher Education Policy, 1998).

College Attendance Versus College Completion

10 In their report, "College for All? Is There Too Much Emphasis on Getting a 4-Year College Degree?" Boesel and Fredland estimate that around 600,000 students leave 4-year colleges annually without graduating. These noncompleters earn less than college graduates because they get fewer years of education. More surprising, they tend to earn less than or the same amount as 2-year college students who have as much education. Furthermore, 2-year college students show about the same gains in tested cognitive skills for each year of attendance as 4-year college students. Students at 4-year colleges also pay more in tuition and are more likely to have student loan debts than 2-year students (Boesel and Fredland, 1999, p. viii). The authors conclude that high school graduates of modest ability or uncertain motivation—factors that increase their chances of leaving college before graduation—would be well-advised to consider attending 2-year, instead of 4-year, colleges. If they did, they would probably realize the same earnings and cognitive skill gains at lower cost and with less debt. In order to maximize the return on their time and monetary investment, students who do choose to enroll in 4-year colleges should do everything in their power to graduate (Boesel and Fredland, 1999, p. ix).

Conclusion

11 While it is clear that investment in a college degree, especially for those students in the lowest income brackets, is a financial burden, the long-term benefits to individuals as well as to society at large, appear to far outweigh the costs.

REFERENCES

Boesel, D., & Fredland, E. (1999). College for all? Is there too much emphasis on getting a 4-year college degree? Washington, DC: U.S. Department of Education, Office of Educational Research and Improvement, National Library of Education.

Cohn, E., & Geske, T. G. (1992). Private Nonmonetary Returns to Investment in Higher Education. In W. Becker & D. Lewis, *The Economics of American Higher Education*. Boston, MA: Kluwer Academic Publishers.

The College Board. (2001). *Trends in Student Aid 2001*. New York: The College Board.

Day, J. C., & Newburger, E. C. (2002). The Big Payoff: Educational Attainment and Synthetic Estimates of Work-Life Earnings. (Current Population Reports, Special Studies, P23-210). Washington, DC: Commerce Dept., Economics and Statistics Administration, Census Bureau. [On-Line]. Available: http://www.census.gov/prod/2002pubs/p23-210.pdf

Institute for Higher Education Policy (1998). *Reaping the Benefits: Defining the Public and Private Value of Going to College*. The New Millennium Project on Higher Education Costs, Pricing, and Productivity. Washington, DC: Author.

Rowley, L. L., & Hurtado, S. (2002). *The Non-Monetary Benefits of an Undergraduate Education*. University of Michigan: Center for the Study of Higher and Postsecondary Education.

Schultz, T. W. (1961). Investment in Human Capital. *American Economic Review*, 51: 1–17.

U.S. Department of Education (2001). Digest of Education Statistics 2001. [On-Line]. Available: http://nces.ed.gov/pubs2002/digest2001/tables/PDF/table170.pdf

U.S. Department of Education (2000). Think College Early: Average College Costs. [On-Line]. Available: http://www.ed.gov/offices/OPE/thinkcollege/early/parents/college_costs.htm

Wolfe, B. L. (1994). External Benefits of Education. *International Encyclopedia of Education*. Oxford; New York: Pergamon Press.   ∎

QUESTIONS ON SUBJECT AND PURPOSE

1. Porter does not limit her argument to the financial benefits of a four-year education. What other benefits does she cite?
2. Are you convinced by her argument? Why or why not?
3. What does the range of benefits to the family and society that Porter cites suggest about her purpose in the essay?

QUESTIONS ON STRATEGY AND AUDIENCE

1. What typographical devices does Porter use in the essay and why?
2. What is the effect on the readers of the parenthetical citations of authorities and the list of references?
3. How might Porter have defined her audience? How can you tell?

QUESTIONS ON VOCABULARY AND STYLE

1. How would you describe the tone of the essay?
2. What difference in point of view do you notice between Porter's essay and Lee's essay?
3. Be prepared to define the following words: *warrant* (paragraph 3), *disparity* (5), *cognitive* (10).

WRITING SUGGESTIONS

1. **Doing a Critical Analysis.** Porter uses specific information from a number of sources then identified in "References." Analyze how Porter uses these sources in her argumentation strategies in the essay.
2. **Journaling or Blogging.** Why did you come to college? What role did your parents have in that decision? Make a list of reasons and reflect on them.
3. **Practicing in a Paragraph.** Identify and then explain what you see as the primary reason you came to college. Be honest.
4. **Writing the Personal Essay.** A younger sibling, relative, or friend is uncertain about attending college. In a persuasive essay, either encourage or discourage that person drawing on your experiences and those of your peers.
5. **Finding Reading Connections.** One strategy for reducing the costs of college are the online college courses described by Justin Pope in "MOOCs Gaining Popularity" (Chapter 5). Considering your own experience as a college student, argue for or against MOOCs as a partial alternative to classroom education.
6. **Exploring Links Online.** Are you borrowing money for college? Should you choose a community college, a less expensive school, or online alternatives? Using online sources, argue for or against choosing a college on the basis of cost.
7. **Writing the Research Paper.** Although Porter provides much evidence to support the economic benefit of a four-year college education, she does not argue for the value of attending an expensive prestigious school as opposed to a lower-cost one. Does the type of college you attend produce a greater economic benefit? Research that question and in an essay with documentation argue your position.

For Further Study

Focusing on Grammar and Writing. How does Porter document her sources in the essay? How would that change if the essay appeared in a popular magazine?

Working Together. The essay begins and ends with a thesis-driven paragraph. The essay could have wide appeal but would need some changes for a new audience. Working in small groups, brainstorm other ways in which to begin and end the essay.

Seeing Other Modes at Work. In outlining the various categories that can be used to organize the benefits of a four-year college education, Porter uses classification.

The Case Against College

LINDA LEE

This essay first appeared in *Family Circle* magazine in 2001.

1   **D**o you, like me, have a child who is smart but never paid attention in class? Now it's high school graduation time. Other parents are talking Stanford this and State U. that. Your own child has gotten into a pretty good college. The question is: Is he ready? Should he go at all?

2   In this country two-thirds of high school graduates go on to college. In some middle-class suburbs, that number reaches 90 percent. So why do so many feel the need to go?

3   America is obsessed with college. It has the second-highest number of graduates worldwide, after (not Great Britain, not Japan, not Germany) Australia. Even so, only 27 percent of Americans have a bachelor's degree or higher. That leaves an awful lot who succeed without college, or at least without a degree. Many read books, think seriously about life and have well-paying jobs. Some want to start businesses. Others want to be electricians or wilderness guides or makeup artists. Not everyone needs a higher education.

4   What about the statistics showing that college graduates make more money? First, until the computer industry came along, all the highest-paying jobs *required* a college degree: doctor, lawyer, engineer. Second, on average, the brightest and hardest-working kids in school go to college. So is it a surprise that they go on to make more money? And those studies almost always pit kids with degrees against those with just high school. An awful lot have additional training, but they are not included. Ponder for a moment: Who makes more, a plumber or a philosophy major?

5   These are tough words. I certainly wouldn't have listened to them five years ago when my son was graduating from high school. He had been smart enough to get into the Bronx High School of Science in New York and did well on his SATs. But I know now that he did not belong in college, at least not straight out of high school.

6   But he went, because all his friends were going, because it sounded like fun, because he could drink beer and hang out. He did not go to study philosophy. Nor did he feel it incumbent to go to class or complete courses. Meanwhile I was paying $1,000 a week for this pleasure cruise.

7   Eventually I asked myself, "Is he getting $1,000 a week's worth of education?" Heck no. That's when I began wondering why everyone needs to go to college. (My hair colorist makes $300,000 a year without a degree.) What about the famous people who don't have one, like Bill Gates (dropped out of Harvard) and Walter Cronkite (who left the University of Texas to begin a career in journalism)?

8   So I told my son (in a kind way) that his college career was over for now, but he could reapply to the Bank of Mom in two years if he wanted to go back. Meanwhile, I said, get a job.

9   If college is so wonderful, how come so many kids "stop out"? (That's the new terminology.) One study showed only 26 percent of those who began four-year colleges had earned a degree in six years. And what about the kids who finish, then can't find work? Of course, education is worth a great deal more than just employment. But most kids today view college as a way to get a good job.

10   I know, I know. What else is there to do? Won't he miss the "college experience?" First off, there are thousands of things for kids to do. And yes, he will miss the college experience, which may include binge drinking, reckless driving and sleeping in on class days. He can have the same experience in the Marine Corps, minus the sleeping in, and be paid good money for it and learn a trade and discipline.

11   If my son had gone straight through college, he would be a graduate by now. A number of his friends are, and those who were savvy enough to go into computers at an Ivy League school walked into $50,000-a-year jobs. But that's not everyone. An awful lot became teachers making half that. And some still don't know what they want to do.

12   They may, like my son, end up taking whatever jobs they can get. Over the last two years, he's done roofing, delivered UPS packages and fixed broken toilets. His phone was turned off a few times, and he began to pay attention to details, like the price of a gallon of gasoline.

13   But a year ago he began working at a telecommunications company. He loves his work, and over the last year, he's gotten a raise and a year-end bonus. He tells me now he plans to stay there and become a manager.

14   So, just about on schedule, my son has had his own graduation day. And although I won't be able to take a picture of him in cap and gown, I couldn't be any more proud. He grew up, as most kids do. And he did it, for the most part, in spite of college.   ∎

QUESTIONS ON SUBJECT AND PURPOSE

1. How does Lee feel about a college education? What reservations does she have? Under what circumstances does she have reservations?

2. The essay appeared in a June issue of *Family Circle* magazine, probably on sale by late May. How is that timing reflected in the essay?

3. What purpose might Lee have had in the essay?

QUESTIONS ON STRATEGY AND AUDIENCE

1. Judging just from the first sentence of the essay, to whom do you think Lee is writing?

2. Can you find a thesis statement in the essay? Where is it?

3. The essay originally appeared in *Family Circle* magazine. Have you ever seen *Family Circle*? Who is the audience for the magazine?

QUESTIONS ON VOCABULARY AND STYLE

1. What is the effect of opening the essay with a question and of addressing the reader as "you"?

2. How would you define the tone of Lee's essay? Is it formal or informal? Conversational?

3. Be prepared to define the following words: *incumbent* (paragraph 6) and *savvy* (11).

WRITING SUGGESTIONS

1. **Doing a Critical Analysis.** Lee writes using the first person ("I"), citing as her evidence her own experience with her son. How effective and sound is this strategy?

2. **Journaling or Blogging.** Why did you come to college? Were you expected to? Did you expect to? Did you consider other, noncollege options? Jot down your memories about making that decision.

3. **Practicing in a Paragraph.** Do you agree or disagree with Lee's argument? In a paragraph, respond to that argument. Focus on your own experience.

4. **Writing the Personal Essay.** Whether you agree with Lee or not, write a rebuttal to her essay—something like "The Case for College." Write to an audience of parents.

5. **Finding Reading Connections.** Libby Sander in "Colleges Confront a Gender Gap in Student Engagement" (Chapter 5) writes about how students engage with their college experience in quite different ways. What connection(s) might be made between these two essays?

6. **Exploring Links Online.** If you had a choice, would you commute to college or live at home? Using online sources, see what others have argued.

7. **Writing the Research Paper.** Lee cites a study that claims only "26 percent of those who began four-year college had earned a degree in six years." Why do so many students take more than four years to complete an undergraduate degree? What is the statistic for your school? Write a research paper aimed at the incoming freshman class at your school, persuading them to make efficient use of their college experience.

For Further Study

Focusing on Grammar and Writing. Remembering the audience to whom she is writing, how effective is Lee's introduction? Why might she delay her thesis statement, choosing instead to begin with a question?

Working Together. Working in small groups, debate whether a college education is a "right" or a "privilege." How would you react if your parents did what Lee did to her son?

Seeing Other Modes at Work. Lee makes use of cause and effect in her essay, as well as narration in relating her son's experiences.

The 30 Occupations with the Largest Employment Growth, 2006–2016

Occupation	Employment 2006	2016	Percent Change	Most Significant Training Required
Registered nurses	2,505,000	3,092,000	23.5	Associate degree
Retail salespersons	4,477,000	5,034,000	12.4	Short-term on the job
Customer service	2,202,000	2,747,000	24.8	Moderate-term on the job
Food workers, preparation and serving, including fast food	2,503,000	2,955,000	18.1	Short-term on the job
Office clerks, general	3,200,000	3,604,000	12.6	Short-term on the job
Personal and home care aides	767,000	1,156,000	50.6	Short-term on the job
Home health aides	787,000	1,171,000	48.7	Short-term on the job
Postsecondary teachers	1,672,000	2,054,000	22.9	Doctoral degree
Janitors and cleaners, except maids and household cleaners	2,387,000	2,732,000	14.5	Short-term on the job
Nursing aides, orderlies, attendants	1,447,000	1,711,000	18.2	Postsecondary vocational
Bookkeeping, accounting, auditing clerks	2,114,000	2,377,000	12.5	Moderate-term on the job
Waiters, waitresses	2,361,000	2,615,000	10.8	Short-term on the job
Child care workers	1,388,000	1,636,000	17.8	Short-term on the job
Executive secretaries, administrative assistants	1,618,000	1,857,000	14.8	Work experience
Computer software engineers	507,000	733,000	44.6	Bachelor's degree
Accountants, auditors	1,274,000	1,500,000	17.7	Bachelor's degree
Landscaping, groundskeeping workers	1,220,000	1,441,000	18.1	Short-term on the job
Elementary school teacher, except special education	1,540,000	1,749,000	13.6	Bachelor's degree
Receptionists, information clerks	1,173,000	1,375,000	17.2	Short-term on the job
Truck drivers, heavy and tractor-trailer	1,860,000	2,053,000	10.4	Moderate-term on the job
Maids, housekeeping cleaners	1,470,000	1,656,000	12.7	Short-term on the job

(*continued*)

The 30 Occupations with the Largest Employment Growth, 2006–2016
(*Continued*)

Occupation	Employment 2006	2016	Percent Change	Most Significant Training Required
Security guards	1,040,000	1,216,000	16.9	Short-term on the job
Carpenters	1,462,000	1,612,000	10.3	Long-term on the job
Management analysts	678,000	827,000	21.9	Bachelor's or higher, plus work experience
Medical assistants	417,000	565,000	35.4	Moderate-term on the job
Computer systems analysts	504,000	650,000	29.0	Bachelor's
Maintenance and repair workers, general	1,391,000	1,531,000	10.1	Moderate-term on the job
Network systems and data communications analysts	262,000	402,000	53.5	Bachelor's
Food preparation workers	902,000	1,040,000	15.3	Short-term on the job
Teacher assistants	1,312,000	1,449,000	10.4	Short-term on the job

READING AND INTERPRETING DATA

A table is an arrangement of data in rows and columns. Its purpose is to allow users to examine a large amount of factual information and to make comparisons on a number of different points. This table from the U.S. Bureau of Labor Statistics describes the 30 largest-growing occupations in the United States for the period from 2006 to 2016, showing the predicted growth in terms of the number of jobs, the percentage of growth over the next 10 years, and the typical training that is required for the job. Imagine how difficult it would be to provide all of this information in prose and how difficult it would be to make comparisons. This table is just a prediction; a changing economic climate in the United States could certainly alter the predictions. Study the table carefully and answer the following questions:

1. What is the nature of the jobs that seem to offer the greatest growth potential? The smallest? Could they be classified into groups?
2. How many of the jobs require postsecondary education? Why so few?
3. What are the limitations of such a table? For example, just citing projected numbers ignores what other factors?
4. Would you be willing to make a decision about higher education based on this table? About your career choice? Why or why not?

5. In what types of arguments might the evidence from the table be used? In what types would it be irrelevant?

6. What does the table suggest about American society in the 21st century?

7. Construct a one-sentence thesis that reflects the data and then list the evidence that you would cite to support it.

Using Data in Writing

1. Define a context (a situation and an audience) where the information in the table might be used to construct an argument. Write a several-paragraph essay that integrates some of the data into your argument.

2. How might Katherine Porter have used the table in her argument? Write several paragraphs in which you acknowledge the information from the table but point out what other evidence it omits.

3. How might Linda Lee have used some of the information in the table in her essay? Rewrite a section of Lee's essay inserting examples drawn from the table.

PERSPECTIVES FOR ARGUMENT: "ARE TOO MANY STUDENTS GOING TO COLLEGE?"

In November 2009, the *Chronicle of Higher Education*, a newspaper for college and university administrators and others connected with postsecondary education, published a forum in response to the provocative question, "Are Too Many Students Going to College?" The *Chronicle* prefaced the responses by observing: "With student debt rising and more of those enrolled failing to graduate in four years, there is a growing sentiment that college may not be the best option for all students." The newspaper asked nine experts connected with higher education to respond to six questions, selections from their responses appear below.

Who Should and Shouldn't Go to College?

Charles Murray [scholar at the American Enterprise Institute]: It has been empirically demonstrated that doing well (B average or better) in a traditional college major in the arts and sciences requires levels of linguistic and logical/mathematical ability that only 10 to 15 percent of the nation's youth possess. That doesn't mean that only 10 to 15 percent should get more than a high-school education. It does mean that the four-year residential program leading to a B.A. is the wrong model for a large majority of young people.

Marty Nemko [career counselor]: All high-school students should receive a cost-benefit analysis of the various options suitable to their situations: four-year college, two-year degree program, short-term career-prep program, apprenticeship program, on-the-job training, self-employment, the military. Students with weak academic records should be informed that, of freshmen at "four year" colleges who graduated in the bottom 40 percent of their high-school class, two-thirds won't graduate even if given eight and a half years. And that even if such students defy the odds, they will likely graduate with a low GPA and a major in low demand by employers. A college should not admit a student it believes would more wisely attend another institution or pursue a noncollege postsecondary option. Students' lives are at stake, not just enrollment targets.

How Much Does Increasing College-Going Rates Matter to Our Economy and Society?

Marty Nemko [career counselor]: Increasing college-going rates may actually hurt our economy. We now send 70 percent of high school graduates to college, up from 40 percent in 1970. At the same time, employers are accelerating their offshoring, part-timing, and temping of as many white-collar jobs as possible. That results in ever more unemployed and underemployed B.A.s. Meanwhile, there's a shortage of tradespeople to take the Obama infrastructure-rebuilding jobs. And you and I have a hard time getting a reliable plumber even if we're willing to pay $80 an hour—more than many professors make.

Marcus A. Winters [senior fellow at the Manhattan Institute]: Increasing college-attendance rates in the United States is essential to reducing income inequality and maintaining our stature as a world economic leader. Our economic dominance in the second half of the 20th century was directly related to our educational dominance. The United States was the first nation to provide basic education to all people regardless of their income.

Economists Have Cited the Economic Benefits That Individual Students Derive from College. Does That Still Apply?

Daniel Yankelovich [public policy expert]: It applies more than ever. With the disappearance of virtually all highly paid, low-skill jobs, the only way that most Americans can fulfill their aspirations for middle-class status is through acquiring a higher-education credential and the skills that go with it. From a practical standpoint, the credential is more important than specific skill sets. Employers know that they are able to train qualified employees in specialized skills. For most employers, "qualified" means having core skills like the ability to read, write, think clearly, and bring a strong work ethic to the task. It is those core skills (and virtues) that higher education warrants.

Marcus A. Winters [senior fellow at the Manhattan Institute]: Those who argue that the bachelor's degree has lost its luster in the labor market are ignoring empirical evidence to the contrary. As of 2005, after accounting for the differences between those who go to college and those who do not, the premium for a year of college education was about 13 to 14 percent of an individual's weekly wage. Employers clearly value the general knowledge and work ethic that a student acquires in college. It is important to note that the benefits of attending college are found both across and within professions. Blue-collar workers benefit nearly as much as white-collar workers from a year of college education. That is, going to college makes you a better plumber than you would have been otherwise. Why? One reason might be that college imparts nonacademic, social skills that can benefit blue-collar workers, who often must interact with customers and clients who are themselves college-educated.

At What Point Does the Cost of College Outweigh the Benefits?

Sandy Baum [Senior policy analyst for the College Board]: That is a question that will have a different answer for different individuals. First, the benefits of going to college are much broader and deeper than the financial return. If the question is how much is worth spending, the answer depends on career goals and alternative options. But it is clear that, at current college prices, and considering existing financial aid, continuing their education after high school makes sense for most people who are motivated to do so, even if that requires postponing a portion of the payment in the form of loans.

Sandy Baum [Senior policy analyst for the College Board]: We have a moral obligation as a society to create the opportunity for as many students as possible to go to college if they are so motivated. We have a moral obligation to make the financial aspects of college attendance manageable and to ensure that students get the financial, academic, and social supports necessary for success. Doing the morally right thing also means doing the smart thing for our general economic and social well-being.

DEVELOPING AN ARGUMENT FROM A THESIS

Each of the paragraphs in the forum opens with a thesis statement—an assertion about the subject that defines the stance or position that the writer takes. Obviously, the experts do not agree; their theses represent conflicting responses to the questions. In argument, a thesis must then be supported by evidence. The stronger, the more persuasive the evidence, the more likely that a reader will agree with the position.

1. Of the theses presented here, with which do you agree? With which do you disagree? Why? What are the strengths and weaknesses of each?
2. The positions here are a single paragraph long. What types of evidence might you find to further support the positions each writer takes?
3. Which positions might be supported by material taken from either the two essays or the table of data in this casebook?

CONSTRUCTING AN ARGUMENT USING MULTIPLE SOURCES

Using the material provided in this casebook, construct an essay in which you argue for one side or the other on the following issues. Use material from the four sources provided here, making sure that you quote correctly and that you document your sources using parenthetical citations and a list of works cited (examples and guidelines can be found in Chapter 10).

A. Only the academically gifted should attend college.
   Everyone ought to have a chance at a college education regardless of their high school academic record.

B. College ought to focus on specific skill sets necessary in the workplace.
   College should focus on a broader knowledge base stressing core skills like "the ability to read, write, think clearly, and bring a strong work ethic to the task."

C. A large body of college-educated citizens is vital to our economic welfare as a nation.
   What our nation needs is more people with specific skill sets, not more people with academic degrees.

D. We have a moral obligation as a nation to provide a college education for everyone who is motivated to seek one.
   Given the job growth that our nation will see in the next decades, we have a moral obligation to encourage students to seek other job-training experiences rather than choosing to go to college.

Debate Casebook: Are Performance-Enhancing Drugs Cheating?

Asterisks in the record books, forfeited Olympic medals, international bans from sports participation, federal investigations, college and even high school athletes increasingly using and abusing performance-enhancing drugs—each year brings new revelations about the role that drugs are playing in sports at all levels. Should they be banned or just more carefully monitored? Is this cheating or just an enhanced level of athletic conditioning? The debate is more complicated than we might imagine. The selections in this casebook highlight a number of issues. In the full essay, Dillingham, a professional football team physician, argues that using such drugs "creates an unfair advantage for those who take them, and this breaks the social contract athletes have implicitly agreed to: We are going to have a fair contest." But in a short extract, Yuhas asks: *Isn't it hypocritical of a society obsessed with pills to argue that putting "something in your body that makes you more competitive in your livelihood . . . is somehow morally corrupt"?*

Before Reading

Connecting: Do you see using a performance-enhancing drug as a form of "cheating"? Is there a difference between a drug that makes you more mentally alert, or thinner, and a drug that makes you physically stronger?

Anticipating: Knowing the side effects and the consequences of taking performance-enhancing drugs, why would an athlete do so? Why would a high school or college athlete do so? Should either group be protected from taking such risks?

Steroids, Sports, and the Ethics of Winning

MICHAEL DILLINGHAM

Michael Dillingham, M.D., specializes in orthopaedics and sports medicine. He was a team physician for the NFL's San Francisco 49ers. The essay appeared on the website of the Markkula Center for Applied Ethics, Santa Clara University.

1   Why, ethically, does the use of steroids in sports bother us? The medical issues are fairly straightforward. The use of anabolic steroids increases the athlete's chance of getting liver cancer. Heavy or prolonged use can cause psychological and emotional problems—so-called "steroid rage."

2   Men will have testicular atrophy and libido problems, and women will have abnormal periods and changes in their normal hormonal balance.

3   Because steroids enable heavy lifting, tendon tears and osteoarthritis are common ailments. I could tell you about guys who do what their bodies weren't designed to do—such as benching 400 pounds—and by the time they are 35, they cannot lift their arms.

4   So, why do people use them? The answer to that question is also straightforward. They make you bigger, faster, and stronger. And they work perfectly well in anybody who's training heavily.

5   Should athletes be allowed to make this trade-off? Many say, "It hurts only me, so why does society care?"

6   Society cares because steroid use is a form of cheating. Since steroids work so well, they create an unfair advantage for those who take them, and this breaks the social contract athletes have implicitly agreed to: We are going to have a fair contest. There are things we can and cannot do. Even if

there were a safe performance-enhancing substance, if it weren't available to everybody, using it would still be cheating.

7   Unfortunately, steroids are still ubiquitous, and one of the problems is that we let people use them. Society loves sports and tends to look the other way when they become dangerous. We tolerate boxing, where you have two guys beating each other's brains out; we tolerate sports that have severe life-time side effects like some elements of track and field.

8   The conspirators in this are everywhere—coaches, institutions, even some parents. We see parents who are in complete denial when their kids—college athletes with eating disorders—have stress fractures of their tibias or patellas because their bones are fragile from anorexia. The parents are living through the children's achievements, so it's very difficult to break this pattern.

9   Steroid use is part of this whole youthful delusion that says, "If I just do this for a period of my life, I'll be fine. I'll smoke until I'm older; I'll only binge drink in college; I'll be anorexic or bulimic so I can run, and then I'll stop being that way and I'll go on and have a wonderful life."

10   That's playing Russian roulette, which is not a game I think we want to encourage. The only things that work to discourage doping are testing and penalties. You can talk about personal responsibility until you're blue in the face, but to stop steroid use, testing is necessary. Cocaine and steroids have ceased to be big problems in professional football because of testing.

11   In most other professional sports, the inmates are running the asylum. There is no effective testing, and the penalties are pitiful. If Congress pushes this issue, and if professional sports and unions stop obstructing, and if some of the professionals get busted, we may get somewhere. I'm hopeful.   ∎

QUESTIONS ON SUBJECT AND PURPOSE

1. What reasons does Dillingham give for not using such drugs?
2. What is particularly dangerous about performance-enhancing drugs such as steroids when used by young athletes?
3. What would Dillingham like to see happen?

QUESTIONS ON STRATEGY AND AUDIENCE

1. The headnote explains Dillingham's qualifications for writing on such a topic. Does that information influence in any way your reaction to his argument?
2. The essay appears on a website. Search its title and you can find the original. How does seeing it there explain why Dillingham paragraphs the essay in this way?
3. The website is devoted to "applied ethics." What does that phrase mean? What does that imply about its audience?

QUESTIONS ON VOCABULARY AND STYLE

1. In paragraph 9, why might Dillingham enclose the possible replies that young users might make in quotation marks?
2. What is the expression "the inmates are running the asylum" (paragraph 11) called? What do you think it means?
3. Be prepared to define the following words and phrases: *testicular atrophy* (paragraph 2), *libido* (2), *ubiquitous* (7), *tibia* (8), *patella* (8).

WRITING SUGGESTIONS

1. **Doing a Critical Analysis.** How effective is Dillingham's argument? Analyze the quality of his evidence, logic, and language.
2. **Journaling or Blogging.** To cheat is to have an unfair advantage. Reflect on times when you either cheated or considered cheating. Do the ends ever justify the means?
3. **Practicing in a Paragraph.** Expand upon your journal entry by describing an instance in which you decided either to cheat or not to cheat.
4. **Writing the Personal Essay.** The Educational Testing Service has done studies on cheating among high school and college students. Among those who admit to cheating, they rationalize their actions by saying, "It's a victimless crime"; "it's OK if you don't get caught"; "everybody does it"; "it makes up for unfair tests"; "I didn't have a chance to study." In an essay in which you argue against cheating, respond to those rationalizations.
5. **Finding Reading Connections.** To what extent is the use of performance-enhancing drugs for athletics or academics a form of addiction? What connections could be made with Mark Penn's "Caffeine Crazies" (Chapter 7)?
6. **Exploring Links Online.** Using online sources, research the use of drugs, such as "addy" or adderall as an aid to academic performance. In an essay, argue for or against the use of "study drugs."
7. **Writing the Research Paper.** How widespread is the use of performance-enhancing drugs or steroids in high school athletes? In a researched and documented essay, argue for (or against) bans on such drugs.

For Further Study

Focusing on Grammar and Writing. Dillingham makes use of the dash (—) in his essay. What seems to be the rule or rules governing the use of this mark?

Working Together. Is there a valid analogy between cheating in sports and cheating in school? Divide into small groups and debate how appropriate that analogy is.

Seeing Other Modes at Work. The essay also contains elements of cause and effect.

PERSPECTIVES FOR ARGUMENT: IS USING PERFORMANCE-ENHANCING DRUGS "FAIR"?

Steve Yuhas, a columnist and a radio talk-show host at KOGO 600 AM in San Diego, California, dubbed "Uniquely Conservative Talk Radio™," in "Steroid Scandal Overblown and Hypocritical" published at www.politics .com in 2004:

> Popping a pill or injecting yourself with steroids, although harmful to the individual in the long run, does not make a person more athletically talented than anyone else. Yes, they can become stronger and their biceps may grow to the size of a normal person's thigh, but that doesn't make them able to hit a small ball with a thin bat and it certainly doesn't make a football player throw more accurately or kick the ball through the uprights with more precision.
>
> For all the blather about the immorality of steroids or other performance enhancing drugs it is amazing that it is perfectly acceptable to drink champagne or smoke celebratory cigars after winning a game played by the same people now caught up in the "scandal" of behavior that fills the stands and doesn't affect anyone except the individual using the substance. There seems to be a sliding scale of morality involved in steroids that is absent from any other substance. Popping a pill to render a child more productive in school or to make a fat person thin is great; sucking the fat out of a woman's behind or injecting a forehead with botox is simply cosmetic upkeep, but put something in your body that makes you more competitive in your livelihood and it is somehow morally corrupt. . . .

Sharon Ryan, Ph.D., Department of Philosophy at West Virginia University, in the August 2008 article titled "What's So Bad About Performance Enhancing Drugs?," published in the collection of essays *Football and Philosophy*, ed. by Michael W. Austin (Lexington, U. of Kentucky, 2008): "Due to economic circumstances or even luck, some athletes have better nutrition, 'natural' supplements, coaches, trainers, nutritionists, information, lawyers, and equipment than others do. Some athletes have more free time to train than others do. Some athletes are naturally smarter, faster, and stronger than others are. All athletes, whether or not they use PEDs, are not 'playing on a level playing field' and that is . . . unfair."

David Fairchild, Ph.D., Professor Emeritus of Philosophy at Indiana University-Purdue University at Fort Wayne, in "Of Cabbages and Kings: Continuing Conversation on Performance Enhancers in Sport," from the *Proceedings of the International Symposium for Olympic Research* in February 1992: "[T]he use of performance enhancers is cheating because it violates constitutive rules of the activity. Since such use is cheating, it is wrong and we should expect the disqualification of competitors who are caught doping. This conclusion is established through a simple and straightforward argument. Cheating is the deliberate, knowing, and voluntary violation of certain constitutive rules in order to gain a competitive advantage."

DEVELOPING AN ARGUMENT FROM A THESIS

Each of the selections above opens with a thesis statement—an assertion about the subject that defines the stance or position that the writer takes. Obviously, the writers do not agree; their theses represent conflicting responses to the questions. In argument, a thesis must then be supported by evidence. The stronger, the more persuasive the evidence, the more likely that a reader will agree with the position.

1. Of the theses presented here, with which do you agree? With which do you disagree? Why? What are the strengths and weaknesses of each?
2. How does the argument advanced by Yuhas differ from the others? How effective does it seem to be? Are you persuaded by analogies?
3. The positions here are represented by short selections. What types of evidence might you find to further support the positions each writer takes?

CONSTRUCTING AN ARGUMENT USING MULTIPLE SOURCES

Using the material provided in this casebook, construct an essay in which you argue for one side or the other on the following issues. Use material from the sources provided here, making sure that you quote correctly and that you document your sources using parenthetical citations and a list of works cited (examples and guidelines can be found in Chapter 10).

A. Performance-enhancing drugs should be banned from all athletic competition.
  As long as athletes know the medical risks involved, performance-enhancing drugs are acceptable in professional sports.
B. Winning is everything and worth whatever the cost.
  Using performance-enhancing drugs is cheating and immoral.
  Using performance-enhancing drugs is no different than having cosmzetic surgery.

Debate Casebook: What Are the Ethical Issues Surrounding Human Organ Harvesting and Donation?

As of early 2013, according to the statistics maintained by the United Network for Organ Sharing, the list of those awaiting an organ transplant numbered 127,601. [You can update that statistic by visiting their website at www.unos.org]. That number is more than four times larger than the number of transplants done in all of 2012. In short, many people die each year because organs are not available. The only legal source of human organs in the United States are those willingly donated, often by living family members, or those removed with permission from people who have died under special circumstances. For some background on the circumstances, read Rick Reilly's "Getting a Second Wind" (Chapter 1) and Jennifer Kahn's "Stripped for Parts" (Chapter 6).

The shortage of donors, and particularly of donors who die under the conditions in which organs can be harvested, has led to proposals to allow living donors to sell or be compensated for giving up a healthy organ. You can sacrifice a limited number of organs in the human body and still potentially live a normal life. Obviously this does not include your heart or your brain, but you can function without one of your two kidneys; you could give up one lung and a portion of your liver. However, under the federal National Organ Transplant Act (1984, amended 1988 and 1990) and the states' Uniform Anatomical Gift Act of 2007, it is illegal to sell your organs. Still, people have tried: kidneys were briefly advertised on both Craigslist and eBay.

Even though selling organs is illegal in the United States, it has been done even in this county on the black market. For example, a Brooklyn rabbi was arrested and charged in 2009 with trafficking in human organs by offering a kidney for sale for $160,000 that he had bought from an Israeli for $10,000. People desperate for money and people in desperate need for a healthy organ (particularly a kidney) create a potential for abuse. Selling organs is also an international business, leading to what is called "transplant tourism." What about harvesting organs from criminals who received the death penalty? In 2009, the Chinese government acknowledged that two-thirds of the organ donations in that country came from executed prisoners. Not surprisingly, the ethical issues surrounding organ harvesting, sale, donation, and transplantation are many and complex.

The selections in this casebook focus on a number of issues. The first essay, "Have a Heart—but Pay Me for It," written by former Delaware governor Pete du Pont, argues that the organ shortage should be addressed by offering donors various forms of compensation. Two additional short selections introduce other issues. Michael Potts and Paul A. Bryne in an extract with the provocative title "Is It Morally Right for Physicians to Kill Their Patients That Good May Come?" argue against harvesting organs from "brain dead" or "cardiac dead" patients. Sally Satel in a short selection from "Body Part Recipients Should Not Be Selected on Moral Grounds" reflects on how in the past a lucky recipient was chosen, raising the question, should "good organs go to bad people"?

A final section in this casebook suggests a wide range of related topics that you could investigate when preparing an argumentative or persuasive research paper on an aspect of the ethics and morality of organ donation and transplantation.

Before Reading

Connecting: Most states have some type of organ donor registration typically connected with and indicated on a driver's license. Have you registered as an organ donor? Do you carry that designation, for example, on your driver's license? Why or why not?

Anticipating: Does the subject of organ harvesting and transplantation raise any questions or problems for you? Should you be able to sell a body part? Would you buy one if your life were at stake?

Have a Heart—but Pay Me for It

PETE DU PONT

This essay originally appeared in the *San Diego Union-Tribune*, September 29, 1997.

1 There are currently about 45,000 people [in 1997] waiting for a humanorgan transplant. About 3,000 of them will die on that waiting list because a suitable transplant organ will not become available in time. The short supply of organs has recently led to some overt attempts to ration them in a way that would be more beneficial to society.

Rationing Organs

2 For example, the United Network for Organ Sharing (UNOS) has altered its guidelines for those needing a liver transplant so that those with acute liver problems get priority. Those with a chronic liver condition like hepatitis or cirrhosis (which could be the result of alcohol abuse) cannot rise above the second level in priority status.

3   In addition, the legislature in the state of Washington recently passed legislation—which the governor vetoed for being too vague—that would prohibit those on Death Row from receiving "lifesaving health care procedures" such as an organ transplant. Now the Cleveland Clinic is being accused of removing organs before some patients are legally dead.

4   Instead of looking for new ways to ration organs or take them prematurely, we should ask how we can increase the supply of organs so that doctors are not forced to decide who lives and who dies. The answer is to compensate donors for their organs. Unfortunately, doing so is currently against the law. That's because the National Organ Transplant Act

(1984) prohibits "any person to knowingly acquire, receive or otherwise transfer any human organ for valuable consideration for use in human transplantation."

5   As a result, altruism is the only legal motive for individuals or their surrogates to donate their organs. But while altruism is a noble motive, it is seldom a compelling one. Economic theory clearly recognizes that when demand for a good or service is high, its price will increase until the supply and demand reach an equilibrium. If the price is prohibited from rising, a shortage will occur because people will not provide a product when the price is too low.

6   Thus, permitting donors to receive some type of compensation for their organs would help alleviate our organ-shortage problem. Opponents of a market for organs immediately conjure up images of strange people selling off body parts. But a market for organs could develop in a number of ways: Some would be more open and direct, while others might be indirect and incorporate the concerns of some of those who oppose compensation.

Several Approaches to Compensation

7 We could, for example:

8   +Permit a donor pool. Dr. Robert M. Sade, a surgeon and professor of medicine at the Medical University of South Carolina, and his colleagues have proposed to create an in-kind market for organs. Every adult would be given the option of joining the Transplant Recipient and Donor Organization (TRADO). Membership would require permission to have your organs removed at death, and only those joining would be permitted to receive a transplanted organ. Those who chose not to join would be electing for standard medical care, short of transplantation. Thus, the only way to receive an organ while living would be to have given permission to have your organs taken at death.

9   +Permit people to receive after-death compensation. A person wanting to become an organ donor would simply contract with an organ-donor organization, which would compensate the deceased's estate for each organ successfully harvested. The compensation could be in a variety of forms. A hospital or organ-donor network might pay part or all of a donor's burial expenses, for example.

10   Such a provision might encourage lower-income people who could not afford life insurance to sign up for the program as a way to provide for their funeral costs. (A similar provision has been supported by an article in the *Journal of the American Medical Association*.)

11   +Contribute funds to the donor's designated charity—a hospital, university, or social services agency. Let people sell whatever they want, when they want. The most open and market-oriented approach would be to let anyone who wanted to sell one or more organs do so. Thus, if someone needed a

kidney and was willing to pay for one, a compatible donor could provide the recipient with a kidney for the market-set price.

12   A variation on this proposal would let people sell their organs now at a discounted price for harvesting after death. There are obvious dangers in this approach that would need more thought before it is adopted. The pressures on people unable to make knowledgeable decisions might be prohibitive.

A Market for Organs Would Save Lives

13 The point is, there are ways to encourage people to donate their organs to help others live. These mechanisms would increase the supply of organs, the waiting lines and needless deaths would decrease if not disappear, and donors and recipients would have more choices. While opponents to these proposals want more organs, they don't want a market for organs. Paternalistically, they impose their values on everyone else. And with regard to organ availability, while paternalism lives, people die. ■

QUESTIONS ON SUBJECT AND PURPOSE

1. Can you identify one sentence that explicitly states du Pont's position in the argument?
2. The title of the essay could be potentially misleading. Suggest another title that might describe the position du Pont takes more accurately.
3. What compensation alternatives does du Pont suggest?

QUESTIONS ON STRATEGY AND AUDIENCE

1. Allowing for the fact that the statistics that du Pont quotes in the opening paragraph are out of date, what role do they have in the argument?
2. In paragraphs 7 and 9, du Pont cites two sources that have made proposals similar to his. What is the effect of such citations?
3. What is du Pont assuming about his audience?

QUESTIONS ON VOCABULARY AND STYLE

1. What is the expression "have a heart" called? Does this seem like an appropriate phrase to use in the title?
2. In the final two sentences of the essay, du Pont uses a form of the word "paternalism" twice. What does that word mean in this context? What might be another synonym for that word in this context?
3. Be prepared to define the following words: *overt* (paragraph 1) and *altruism* (5).

WRITING SUGGESTIONS

1. **Doing a Critical Analysis.** Analyze du Pont's choice of words in the essay. Are those choices appropriate for his newspaper audience?

2. **Journaling or Blogging.** Du Pont mentions a plan that would have prohibited death row inmates from receiving "lifesaving health care procedures" (paragraph 3). Jot down your thoughts on this issue, keeping in mind that some death row inmates have been later found innocent.

3. **Practicing in a Paragraph.** Expand your journal thoughts into a paragraph focusing on a single aspect of the issue from either point of view.

4. **Writing the Personal Essay.** Argue for or against a proposal to prohibit death row inmates from receiving organ transplants.

5. **Finding Reading Connections.** How persuasive do you find Rick Reilly's "Getting a Second Wind" (Chapter 1)? Evaluate the strategies used by du Pont and Reilly in recruiting potential donors.

6. **Exploring Links Online.** Someday instead of transplantation, doctors will be able to grow new organs. Use online sources to research this possible option. Argue for or against such a development.

7. **Writing the Research Paper.** Given the shortage of available donors and the high need, rationing must happen. Someone must decide who lives and who dies. The United Network for Organ Sharing (www.unos.org) has established criteria, "How the Transplant System Works," for these decisions. Argue for or against those criteria.

For Further Study

Focusing on Grammar and Writing. Du Pont uses both parentheses and dashes (—) in his essay. What is the role of the two marks and how do they differ in their use?

Working Together. Working in small groups, plan a persuasive print advertisement that employs one of the three alternative compensation strategies that du Pont cites.

Seeing Other Modes at Work. The essay uses division to organize the possible alternatives for compensation.

ADVERTISEMENT PROMOTING ORGAN DONATION

TELL US NOW

that you want to be an

organic donor! ♥

Brandon's decision to be a donor gave life to five others.

Last year, 22% of Michigan donors and 33% of Michigan transplant recipients were ethnic minorities.

♥ Donor

Brandon Spight
Organ Donor
Detroit, MI

Writing Suggestions

1. **Analysis:** The advertisement is intended to promote organ donation. How persuasive do you find it? Analyze the choice of the image and the accompanying copy in assessing its effectiveness.

2. In an essay cast as a proposal to an organ donor campaign, suggest another approach to increasing organ donation. Describe your strategy in the essay and why you think it would be effective. Construct a mockup using images from the Internet and your proposed copy to accompany your paper.

PERSPECTIVES FOR ARGUMENT: WHAT MORAL ISSUES DOES TRANSPLANTATION RAISE

Michael Potts and Paul A. Bryne: "Is It Morally Right for Physicians to Kill Their Patients That Good May Come?" originally appeared in *The Internet Journal of Law, Healthcare, and Ethics* in 2009.
    Note: The preceding essay does not raise the issue of harvesting organs from those who have been pronounced as having suffered brain or heart (cardiac) death. This selection raises that issue.

Is it ever morally right for doctors to kill their patients when the patients would be allowed to die anyway and when such killing would yield great benefit to others? We do not believe so. We will assume, for the sake of argument, that the following statements are true: (1) "brain dead" organ donors are not truly dead, (2) organ donors "by cardiac death" are not truly dead, (3) organ donation is the direct cause of death of these donors, and (4) the benefits for others from organ donation are significant, including extended life and improved lifestyle for organ recipients.

The fundamental problem with killing patients for their organs (or for any other utilitarian end) has to do with the fundamental nature of medical practice. . . . Central to the practice of medicine, as Edmond Pellegrino and David Thomasma point out, is, at the most fundamental level, a relationship between the patient and the physician, a relationship oriented toward healing. The patient comes to a healthcare practitioner for help with illness; the physician (or other healthcare practitioner) has both the knowledge and power to protect and preserve the life of the patient. This end of medicine ("healing") implies certain moral principles intrinsic to medicine, one of which is the principle of nonmaleficence, "do no harm." Harming a patient, since it violates the healing relationship between patient and physician, is fundamentally inimical to the practice of medicine.[1]

---

[1] Pellegrino, Edmund D. and David C. Thomasma. *A Philosophical Basis of Medical Practice.* New York: Oxford University Press, 1981.

Developing an Argument from a Thesis

1. How many theses could be developed from the argument advanced here? Write out each possible thesis. What evidence would you need in order to support each of those theses? How would you gather it?

2. What are the implications of these theses in relation to organ transplantation? Under what circumstances might organ transplantation occur?

3. Write an essay in which you either support or reject the position represented here with additional information and evidence.

Sally Satel: "The God Committee: Should Criminals Have Equal Access to Scarce Medical Treatments?," originally appeared in the online journal *Slate* [www.slate.com] on June 17, 2008.

Note: The United Network for Organ Sharing details the "Organ Placement Process" as it operates today: "The match list of potential recipients is ranked according to objective medical criteria (i.e., blood type, tissue type, size of the organ, medical urgency of the patient) as well as time already spent on the waiting list and distance between donor and recipient."

There was a time . . . when character did determine access to scarce treatment. In devising a way to select patients, physicians imagined that the public preferred to think of decision makers as wise stewards of scarce resources. In 1962, Seattle's Swedish Hospital established what later came to be called the "God Committee." Formally known as the Admissions and Policy Committee of the Seattle Artificial Kidney Center at Swedish Hospital, its task was to decide which terminal patient would get access to scarce dialysis machines, or artificial kidneys, as they were called then. . . . The Seattle committee was composed of seven lay people—a lawyer, a minister, a housewife, a state government official, a banker, a labor leader, and a surgeon who served as a "doctor-citizen"—and was among the earliest instances, if not the first, of physicians bringing nonprofessionals into the realm of clinical decision making. The members, all unpaid, insisted on anonymity. They considered the prospective patient's marital status, net worth, nature of occupation, extent of education, church attendance, number of dependents (the more kids or dependent relatives, the better the chance of being chosen), and potential to resume work. They struggled with the ultimate question of who should be saved: the person who contributes the most to society or the one whose death would impose the greatest burden on society, in the form of children left without care or resources.

Developing an Argument from a Thesis

1. Should character determine access to organ transplantation? Organs are rationed. As the du Pont essay suggests, under some circumstances, right now an organ might be denied to someone who is an adequate medical match. Write a thesis that argues in favor or against the concept of a "God committee."

2. What types of evidence would you provide in order to develop these two theses? What are the implications of either position? For example, should donors or donors' families be allowed to specify the type of person who might receive an organ? Would this increase organ donation?

3. Write an essay in which you either support or reject changing the criteria by which an organ recipient is chosen.

ADDITIONAL RESEARCH TOPICS FOR ARGUMENT

1. If it is legal in the United States to sell your blood, or your eggs, or your sperm, why are you not allowed to sell an organ? What difference, if any, is there between these cases? Is this a case of government infringing on the rights of the individual?

2. Should organs be taken from prisoners who have been executed? Should that be a choice that the prisoner makes? Should compensation be involved? If so, who profits? The government? The surviving descendants?

3. Should death-row inmates be offered life imprisonment if they donate a healthy organ? The Indiana University Center for Bioethics has a detailed collection of resources on Death Row Organ Donations at www.bioethics.iu.edu/body.cfm?id=79. Such a proposal has been made in at least one state in this country.

4. Should more efforts be placed on prevention of organ failure? Would preventive measures—for example, such things as increasing cardiac health, decreasing the use of products such as alcohol and tobacco, keeping diabetes under control, reducing obesity—have any impact on this problem?

5. The desperate poverty in which many people around the world live has fostered what is referred to as "transplant tourism." Someone who is willing to sell an organ (almost always a kidney) is paid a sum of money and sent to a hospital/clinic in another country where the organ is removed and then transplanted into a needy recipient willing to compensate the donor and cover all of the medical expenses. Is this ethical?

6. Should more research money be directed to the development of artificial organs? Does the research so far suggest that artificial organs might be a possible solution for the problem?

7. Should more research money be directed to xenotransplantation (the transplantation of organs from other animal species into humans)? Research here has concentrated on organs and tissue taken from pigs since they are biochemically similar to human organs.

8. Should more research be directed at "growing" new organs primarily from stem cells? What are the moral and ethical issues involved in such an idea?

9. What is the likelihood that donating an organ might ultimately compromise your own health in the future? Can you really give up a kidney or a lung or a part of your liver and suffer no medical compromises?

Debate Casebook: Is a Vegan Diet Healthier Than a Balanced Diet?

Perhaps because we have such an abundance of available food, Americans worry about their weights, their diets, and the foods they consume. We all know that "fast food," sugar-laden beverages, and processed meats are not good for us. Bad diets and obesity cut life expectancies and drive up the cost of medical insurance, prescription drugs, and medical care. Can we, should we, change what we eat? Should we become "vegans," people who eat no meat or dairy products? Or should we simply be more careful in balancing our food choices?

The *Wall Street Journal* asked two scientists to debate the issue. Vegans currently make up about 2% of the U.S. population; roughly 60% of Americans eat red meat regularly and 71%, dairy products. T. Colin Campbell, a retired professor of nutritional studies at Cornell, argues the benefits of a vegan diet. Nancy Rodriguez, a professor of nutritional sciences at University of Connecticut, urges a balanced diet.

Before Reading

Connecting: Have you ever considered becoming a vegan? Why or why not?

Anticipating: Did either writer convince you? If you plan to continue making your regular food choices, what would it take to get you to change your mind?

Cut Animal-Based Protein

T. COLIN CAMPBELL

This essay originally appeared in the *Wall Street Journal*, September 18, 2012.

1   I was raised on a dairy farm. I milked cows until starting my doctoral research over 50 years ago at Cornell University in the animal-science department. Meat and dairy foods were my daily fare, and I loved them.

2   When I began my experimental research program on the effects of nutrition on cancer and other diseases, I assumed it was healthy to eat plenty

of meat, milk and eggs. But eventually, our evidence raised questions about some of my most-cherished beliefs and practices.

3   Our findings, published in top peer-reviewed journals, pointed away from meat and milk as the building blocks of a healthy diet, and toward whole, plant-based foods with little or no added oil, sugar or salt.

4   My dietary practices changed based on these findings, and so did those of my family. So, what is this evidence that has had such an impact on my life?

5   In human population studies, prevalence rates of heart disease and certain cancers strongly associate with animal-protein-based diets, usually reported as total fat consumption. Animal-based protein isn't the only cause of these diseases, but it is a marker of the simultaneous effects of multiple nutrients found in diets that are high in meat and dairy products and low in **plant-based** foods.

Trojan Horse

6 Historically, the primary health value of meat and dairy has been attributed to their generous supply of protein. But therein lay a Trojan horse.

7   More than 70 years ago, for example, casein (the main protein of cow's milk) was shown in experimental animal studies to substantially increase cholesterol and early heart disease. Later human studies concurred. Casein, whose properties, it's important to note, are associated with other animal proteins in general, also was shown during the 1940s and 1950s to enhance cancer growth in experimental animal studies.

8   Casein, in fact, is the most "relevant" chemical carcinogen ever identified; its cancer-producing effects occur in animals at consumption levels close to normal—strikingly unlike cancer-causing environmental chemicals that are fed to lab animals at a few hundred or even a few thousand times their normal levels of consumption. In my lab, from the 1960s to the 1990s, we conducted a series of studies and published dozens of peer-reviewed papers demonstrating casein's remarkable ability to promote cancer growth in test animals when consumed in excess of protein needs, which is about 10% of total calories, as recommended by the National Research Council of the National Academy of Sciences more than 70 years ago.

9   One of the biggest fallacies my opponent presents is that a diet including meat and dairy products is the most efficient way of giving the body the nutrients it needs with a healthy level of calories. Plant-based foods have plenty of protein and calcium along with far greater amounts of countless other essential nutrients (such as anti-oxidants and complex carbohydrates) than meat and dairy.

10   Higher-protein diets achieved by consuming animal-based foods increase the risks of cancer, cardiovascular diseases and many similar ailments, caused by excess protein and other unbalanced nutrients as well.

11   It's also worth noting that the government recommendations for certain population groups to increase their protein and iron consumption come from the U.S. Department of Agriculture, an agency long known to be subservient to the meat and dairy industries.

12   The dairy industry has long promoted the myth that milk and milk products promote increased bone health—but the opposite is true. The evidence is now abundantly convincing that higher consumption of dairy is associated with higher rates of bone fracture and osteoporosis, according to Yale and Harvard University research groups.

Pain Relief

13 Some of the most compelling evidence of the effects of meat and dairy foods arises when we stop eating them. Increasing numbers of individuals resolve their pain (arthritic, migraine, cardiac) when they avoid dairy food. And switching to a whole-food, plant-based diet with little or no added salt, sugar and fat, produces astounding health benefits. This dietary lifestyle can prevent and even *reverse* 70% to 80% of existing, symptomatic disease, with an equivalent savings in health-care costs for those who comply.

14   This treatment effect is broad in scope, exceptionally rapid in response (days to weeks) and often, lifesaving. It cannot be duplicated by animal-based foods, processed foods or drug therapies.

15   By contrast, any evidence that low-fat or fat-free-dairy foods reduce blood pressure is trivial compared with the lower blood pressure obtained and sustained by a whole-foods, plant-based diet.

16   Based on the scientific evidence, and on the way I feel, I know beyond any doubt that I am better off for having changed my diet to whole and plant-based foods. ■

QUESTIONS ON SUBJECT AND PURPOSE

1. What is the difference between a vegan and a vegetarian?
2. Campbell begins and ends with a first-person reference ("I"). Why?
3. Do you think that Campbell really expects to persuade his readers to change their diet?

QUESTIONS ON STRATEGY AND AUDIENCE

1. Why might Campbell begin the essay with references to his farming background?
2. On what basis does Campbell dismiss government recommendations about protein and iron consumption (paragraph 11)?
3. How might the essay's place of publication—*The Wall Street Journal*—a daily business newspaper, influence its content or style?

QUESTIONS ON VOCABULARY AND STYLE

1. Why does Campbell choose parentheses, rather than dashes (—), to enclose information in paragraphs 7, 9, 13, and 14?
2. What does he mean when he writes, "But therein lay a Trojan horse"?
3. Be prepared to define the following words: *carcinogen* (paragraph 8), *subservient* (11), *osteoporosis* (12).

WRITING SUGGESTIONS

1. **Doing a Critical Analysis.** How effective are Campbell's argumentation/persuasion strategies? Evaluate them in a critique of his essay.

2. **Journaling or Blogging.** How does a diet consisting of "whole, plant-based foods with little or no added oil, sugar or salt" (paragraph 3) sound to you? Jot down your reactions.

3. **Practicing in a Paragraph.** How motivated are you to change your diet? You do not have to become a vegan, but rather just make healthier decisions about your food and drink choices. Think of one persuasive reason that might motivate you and explore it.

4. **Writing the Personal Essay.** In an essay aimed at your peers, persuade them to make changes in their food and drink choices. Use reasons that they are most likely to find persuasive.

5. **Finding Reading Connections.** Maureen O'Hagan in "Kids Battle the Lure of Junk Food" (Chapter 7) outlines some of the challenges that children face in making food choices. How might Campbell approach the temptations that O'Hagan mentions? What would he tell children and parents?

6. **Exploring Links Online.** Can athletes stay competitive if they eat a vegan diet? Using online sources as research, in an essay, answer that question.

7. **Writing the Research Paper.** Campbell's "most compelling evidence" for a vegan diet is the health changes it can bring about. He writes, "This dietary lifestyle can prevent or even *reverse* 70% to 80% of existing, symptomatic diseases" (paragraph 13). Research that statistic and in a documented essay, present your argument either affirming or rejecting that claim.

For Further Study

Focusing on Grammar and Writing. What is the effect of introducing personal experience into the essay? Does it strengthen or weaken his argument? Assess that writing strategy.

Working Together. What lies behind the food choices that college students make? Working in small groups, explore how and why you make these food and drink decisions. Are you more worried about health issues or weight issues, or neither?

Seeing Other Modes at Work. The essay makes use of a cause-and-effect structure.

It's a Question of Balance

NANCY RODRIGUEZ

This essay originally appeared in the *Wall Street Journal*, September 18, 2012.

1   **F**or years a wealth of scientific research has supported the idea that healthy nutrition begins with a balanced diet consisting of the basic food groups: fruits, vegetables, grains *and* protein and dairy.

2   Each group offers nutrients that are essential to our health. Experts agree that the most important thing to remember when considering a vegetarian or vegan lifestyle is that essential nutrients removed from the diet with the elimination of meat or dairy need to be obtained from other foods.

3   Individuals who stop eating meat and dairy products are at risk of not getting enough calcium, vitamin D, protein, vitamin B_{12}, zinc and iron in their diets—all nutrients that come mostly from food products derived from animals.

4   What happens then? Insufficient calcium and vitamin D can compromise bone structure. Lack of zinc can hinder growth in children. B_{12} and iron assist production of red blood cells, which deliver oxygen throughout the body. Proteins are essential for building and maintaining muscle and keeping our brains healthy. And animal proteins provide all the essential amino acids, nutrients our bodies cannot make on its own.

Calorie Efficiency

5 Including dairy and meat in a balanced diet can be an important way to get essential nutrients without excess calories—a key consideration given concerns about our overweight and undernourished nation. Our average daily consumption of dairy products, for example, provides more than half of the recommended daily amount of calcium and vitamin D in our diets, for only one-tenth of the calories. A three-ounce serving of beef has less than 10% of the calories in a typical 2,000-calorie-a-day diet while supplying more than 10% of the daily value for 10 essential nutrients.

6   Contrary to popular belief, Americans aren't eating too much protein. According to Economic Research Service data from the U.S. Department of Agriculture, the daily caloric contribution of flour and cereal products increased by about 200 calories per person from 1970 to 2008, compared with only a 19-calorie increase from meat, eggs and nuts.

7   The Dietary Guidelines (the U.S. government's science-based nutritional recommendations, compiled and issued every five years) have noted that some Americans need more protein, and that adequate consumption of iron and B_{12} (both found in lean meat) is a concern for specific population groups. The Dietary Guidelines are founded on evidence-based, peer-reviewed scientific literature, and take into account the entire body of research, not just a single study.

8   Proponents of a vegan diet paint a grim picture of the effects of animal protein on human health. But the effects of powdered, isolated casein on rats tells us very little about what traditionally consumed forms of milk will do to humans. And it tells us nothing that can be generalized to all "animal nutrients." Casein is one of many proteins found in milk and is recognized around the world for its nutritional quality.

9   It is simply untrue to suggest that animal protein causes cancer. The American Cancer Society, along with other leading health organizations, emphasizes that the effects of foods and nutrients need to be considered in the context of the total diet. Research from many sources shows that other factors, such as not smoking, responsible alcohol consumption, maintaining a healthy weight and regular physical activity, are much more important to reducing cancer risk than eating or avoiding any individual food.

10   There is scientific evidence that low-fat or fat-free dairy and lean meat, as part of a balanced diet, produce specific health benefits such as reducing blood pressure. Fat-free, low-fat and reduced-fat options are widely available, as are lactose-free milk and milk products. Many of the most popular beef cuts are lean, including top sirloin, tenderloin, T-bone steak and 95% lean ground beef.

Calcium Question?

11 Finally, contrary to my opponent's assertions, dairy's role in strengthening bones has long been established by the nutrition and science community. Don't take just the Dietary Guidelines' word. Dozens of randomized, controlled, clinical trials—the gold standard in research—have demonstrated that calcium and dairy products contribute to stronger bones. These trials far outweigh any observational studies which, by their very design, cannot show a causal relationship between eliminating meat and dairy foods and a subsequent improvement in health.

12   Government and public health organizations around the globe encourage daily consumption of dairy foods to promote good health and help prevent disease. We all have emotional and cultural connections to various foods; many of us have opinions on what to eat, how much and why. But appreciating the science behind nutrition helps us make smart choices about the best way to feed ourselves and the world.   ■

QUESTIONS ON SUBJECT AND PURPOSE

1. Campbell never references Rodriguez's argument in his essay. Has Rodriguez read Campbell's argument?
2. What is the key problem that Rodriguez cites with a vegan diet?
3. Is it easier to argue for a balanced diet than a vegan diet? Why or why not?

QUESTIONS ON STRATEGY AND AUDIENCE

1. Rodriguez never refers to herself or her personal experience. Does that influence your reaction to her argument?
2. What is the function of paragraph 4 in her argument?
3. What concessions to her readers does Rodriguez make in her final paragraph?

QUESTIONS ON VOCABULARY AND STYLE

1. What is "calorie efficiency"?
2. What does the phrase a "balanced diet" mean to you?
3. What does the phrase "the gold standard in research" (paragraph 11) mean?

WRITING SUGGESTIONS

1. **Doing a Critical Analysis.** Rodriguez is responding to Campbell's essay. Analyze how she counters his arguments and the types of evidence that she uses in doing so.
2. **Journaling or Blogging.** How balanced is your diet? Do you make a conscious attempt to eat foods from each group every day? Reflect on your daily food choices.
3. **Practicing in a Paragraph.** Could you "improve" your diet? In a paragraph, persuade yourself (or someone else) to make better food choices each day.
4. **Writing the Personal Essay.** Many people skip breakfast even though science and medicine tells you that is wrong. In an essay, explain to your readers why it is important to eat breakfast—and the right kind of breakfast— each day.
5. **Finding Reading Connections.** Americans, as Mark Penn in "Caffeine Crazies" (Chapter 7) argues, love caffeine. How does caffeine fit into either a vegan or balanced diet? In an essay, argue for or against the consumption of caffeine.
6. **Exploring Links Online.** Diet recommendations always include exercise recommendations. What is the relationship between diet and exercise? Use online sources for your argument and then, in an essay on weight control/loss, argue for or against the need for combining diet and exercise.
7. **Writing the Research Paper.** The newest recommendation for healthy eating is the Mediterranean Diet. What is this and why does it seem to work so well? In a documented research paper, present the argument for this diet.

For Further Study

Focusing on Grammar and Writing. Look carefully at the first sentence in each of Rodriguez's paragraphs. What do you call these sentences and what role do they play in her essay?

Working Together. Working in small groups, list first the arguments that Campbell advances for a vegan diet and then the counter arguments that Rodriguez offers.

Seeing Other Modes at Work. The essay uses elements of both definition and cause and effect.

Debate Casebook: Are You Willing to Save a Child's Life?

Many children throughout the world have no access to medical care or to vaccinations that would prevent deadly childhood diseases. Many children die each day from malnutrition and from contaminated water supplies. As someone who lives in the most prosperous country in world, what obligation do you have to help those children in need? Peter Singer in "The Singer Solution to World Poverty" suggests that your moral obligation is extremely high. Another writer takes issue with Singer's argument.

Before Reading

Connecting: How much money do you contribute annually to organizations seeking to care for children in need throughout the world?

Anticipating: As you read, think about whether Singer's essay has persuaded you to change your own behavior. Why or why not?

The Singer Solution to World Poverty

PETER SINGER

Peter Singer (1946–), born in Australia, is Ira W. DeCamp Professor of Bioethics at the University Center for Human Values at Princeton. A prolific author on a wide range of ethical issues, Singer has been referred to as "maybe the most controversial [ethicist] alive. . . . [and] certainly among the most influential." His most recent book is The Life You Can Save: Acting Now to End World Poverty *(2009). This essay originally appeared in* the New York Times Magazine *in a slightly longer version.*

> *On Writing: In an interview, Singer had this to say about the effects of argument: "I think we are (mostly) rational beings and rational argument does move people to action particularly when it gets them to see that what they are doing is inconsistent with other beliefs that they have and other values that they have that are important to them."*

1   In his 1996 book, *Living High and Letting Die*, the New York University philosopher Peter Unger presented an ingenious series of imaginary examples designed to probe our intuitions about whether it is wrong to live well without giving substantial amounts of money to help people who are hungry, malnourished, or dying from easily treatable illnesses like diarrhea. Here's my paraphrase of one of these examples:

2   Bob is close to retirement. He has invested most of his savings in a very rare and valuable old car, a Bugatti, which he has not been able to insure. The Bugatti is his pride and joy. In addition to the pleasure he gets from driving and caring for his car, Bob knows that its rising market value means that he will always be able to sell it and live comfortably after retirement. One day when Bob is out for a drive, he parks the Bugatti near the end of a railway siding and goes for a walk up the track. As he does so, he sees that a runaway train, with no one aboard, is running down the railway track. Looking farther down the track, he sees the small figure of a child very likely to be killed by the runaway train. He can't stop the train and the child is too far away to warn of the danger, but he can throw a switch that will divert the train down the siding where his Bugatti is parked. Then nobody will be killed—but the train will destroy his Bugatti. Thinking of his joy in owning the car and the financial security it represents, Bob decides not to throw the switch. The child is killed. For many years to come, Bob enjoys owning his Bugatti and the financial security it represents.

3   Bob's conduct, most of us will immediately respond, was gravely wrong. Unger agrees. But then he reminds us that we too have opportunities to save the lives of children. We can give to organizations like UNICEF or Oxfam America. How much would we have to give one of these organizations to have a high probability of saving the life of a child threatened by easily preventable diseases? (I do not believe that children are more worth saving than adults, but since no one can argue that children have brought their poverty on themselves, focusing on them simplifies the issues.) Unger called up some experts and used the information they provided to offer some plausible estimates that include the cost of raising money, administrative expenses, and the cost of delivering aid where it is most needed. By his calculation, $200 in donations would help a sickly two-year-old transform into a healthy six-year-old—offering safe passage through childhood's most dangerous years. To show how practical philosophical argument can be, Unger even tells his readers that they can easily donate funds by using their credit card and calling one of these toll-free numbers: (800) 367-5437 for UNICEF; (800) 693-2687 for Oxfam America.

4   Now you too have the information you need to save a child's life. How should you judge yourself if you don't do it? Think again about Bob and his Bugatti. . . .

5   If you still think that it was very wrong of Bob not to throw the switch that would have diverted the train and saved the child's life, then it is hard to see how you could deny that it is also very wrong not to send money to one

of the organizations listed above. Unless, that is, there is some morally important difference between the two situations that I have overlooked.

6   Is it the practical uncertainties about whether aid will really reach the people who need it? Nobody who knows the world of overseas aid can doubt that such uncertainties exist. But Unger's figure of $200 to save a child's life was reached after he had made conservative assumptions about the proportion of the money donated that will actually reach its target.

7   One genuine difference between Bob and those who can afford to donate to overseas aid organizations but don't is that only Bob can save the child on the tracks, whereas there are hundreds of millions of people who can give $200 to overseas aid organizations. The problem is that most of them aren't doing it. Does this mean that it is all right for you not to do it?

8   Suppose that there were more owners of priceless vintage cars—Carol, Dave, Emma, Fred, and so on, down to Ziggy—all in exactly the same situation as Bob, with their own siding and their own switch, all sacrificing the child in order to preserve their own cherished car. Would that make it all right for Bob to do the same? To answer this question affirmatively is to endorse follow-the-crowd ethics—the kind of ethics that led many Germans to look away when the Nazi atrocities were being committed. We do not excuse them because others were behaving no better.

9   We seem to lack a sound basis for drawing a clear moral line between Bob's situation and that of any reader of this article with $200 to spare who does not donate it to an overseas aid agency. These readers seem to be acting at least as badly as Bob was acting when he chose to let the runaway train hurtle toward the unsuspecting child. In the light of this conclusion, I trust that many readers will reach for the phone and donate that $200. Perhaps you should do it before reading further.

*

10   Now that you have distinguished yourself morally from people who put their vintage cars ahead of a child's life, how about treating yourself and your partner to dinner at your favorite restaurant? But wait. The money you will spend at the restaurant could also help save the lives of children overseas! True, you weren't planning to blow $200 tonight, but if you were to give up dining out just for one month, you would easily save that amount. And what is one month's dining out compared to a child's life? There's the rub. Since there are a lot of desperately needy children in the world, there will always be another child whose life you could save for another $200. Are you therefore obliged to keep giving until you have nothing left? At what point can you stop?

11   Hypothetical examples can easily become farcical. Consider Bob. How far past losing the Bugatti should he go? Imagine that Bob had got his foot stuck in the track of the siding, and if he diverted the train, then before it rammed the car it would also amputate his big toe. Should he still throw the switch? What if it would amputate his foot? His entire leg?

12   As absurd as the Bugatti scenario gets when pushed to extremes, the point it raises is a serious one: only when the sacrifices become very significant

indeed would most people be prepared to say that Bob does nothing wrong when he decides not to throw the switch. Of course, most people could be wrong; we can't decide moral issues by taking opinion polls. But consider for yourself the level of sacrifice that you would demand of Bob, and then think about how much money you would have to give away in order to make a sacrifice that is roughly equal to that. It's almost certainly much, much more than $200. For most middle-class Americans, it could easily be more like $200,000.

13   Isn't it counterproductive to ask people to do so much? Don't we run the risk that many will shrug their shoulders and say that morality, so conceived, is fine for saints but not for them? I accept that we are unlikely to see, in the near or even medium-term future, a world in which it is normal for wealthy Americans to give the bulk of their wealth to strangers. When it comes to praising or blaming people for what they do, we tend to use a standard that is relative to some conception of normal behavior. Comfortably off Americans who give, say, 10 percent of their income to overseas aid organizations are so far ahead of most of their equally comfortable fellow citizens that I wouldn't go out of my way to chastise them for not doing more. Nevertheless, they should be doing much more, and they are in no position to criticize Bob for failing to make the much greater sacrifice of his Bugatti.

14   At this point various objections may crop up. Someone may say, "If every citizen living in the affluent nations contributed his or her share, I wouldn't have to make such a drastic sacrifice, because long before such levels were reached the resources would have been there to save the lives of all those children dying from lack of food or medical care. So why should I give more than my fair share?" Another, related objection is that the government ought to increase its overseas aid allocations, since that would spread the burden more equitably across all taxpayers.

15   Yet the question of how much we ought to give is a matter to be decided in the real world—and that, sadly, is a world in which we know that most people do not, and in the immediate future will not, give substantial amounts to overseas aid agencies. We know too that at least in the next year, the United States government is not going to meet even the very modest United Nations–recommended target of 0.7 percent of gross national product; at the moment it lags far below that, at 0.09 percent, not even half of Japan's 0.22 percent or a tenth of Denmark's 0.97 percent. Thus, we know that the money we can give beyond that theoretical "fair share" is still going to save lives that would otherwise be lost. While the idea that no one need do more than his or her fair share is a powerful one, should it prevail if we know that others are not doing their fair share and that children will die preventable deaths unless we do more than our fair share? That would be taking fairness too far.

16   Thus, this ground for limiting how much we ought to give also fails. In the world as it is now, I can see no escape from the conclusion that each one of us with wealth surplus to his or her essential needs should be giving most of it to help people suffering from poverty so dire as to be life-threatening.

That's right: I'm saying that you shouldn't buy that new car, take that cruise, redecorate the house, or get that pricy new suit. After all, a thousand-dollar suit could save five children's lives.

17   So how does my philosophy break down in dollars and cents? An American household with an income of $50,000 spends around $30,000 annually on necessities, according to the Conference Board, a nonprofit economic research organization. Therefore, for a household bringing in $50,000 a year, donations to help the world's poor should be as close as possible to $20,000. The $30,000 required for necessities holds for higher incomes as well. So a household making $100,000 could cut a yearly check for $70,000. Again, the formula is simple: whatever money you're spending on luxuries, not necessities, should be given away.

18   Now, evolutionary psychologists tell us that human nature just isn't sufficiently altruistic to make it plausible that many people will sacrifice so much for strangers. On the facts of human nature, they might be right, but they would be wrong to draw a moral conclusion from those facts. If it is the case that we ought to do things that, predictably, most of us won't do, then let's face that fact head-on. Then, if we value the life of a child more than going to fancy restaurants, the next time we dine out we will know that we could have done something better with our money. If that makes living a morally decent life extremely arduous, well, then that is the way things are. If we don't do it, then we should at least know that we are failing to live a morally decent life—not because it is good to wallow in guilt but because knowing where we should be going is the first step toward heading in that direction.

19   When Bob first grasped the dilemma that faced him as he stood by that railway switch, he must have thought how extraordinarily unlucky he was to be placed in a situation in which he must choose between the life of an innocent child and the sacrifice of most of his savings. But he was not unlucky at all. We are all in that situation.   ■

QUESTIONS ON SUBJECT AND PURPOSE

1. Singer labels himself a "utilitarian" philosopher. How does he explain what that means?

2. Is there any limit for Singer to how much money one ought to give away for overseas aid?

3. What type of response do you think that Singer hopes for from his audience? Expects from his audience?

QUESTIONS ON STRATEGY AND AUDIENCE

1. How effective is the analogy to Bob and his Bugatti?

2. The text of the essay is separated after paragraph 9 by a centered asterisk (*). What division does this indicate in the essay itself?

3. What assumptions could Singer make about his audience?

QUESTIONS ON VOCABULARY AND STYLE

1. What is an analogy? Does Singer use analogy in his argument?
2. What is the effect of including the telephone numbers for UNICEF and Oxfam America in the essay?
3. Be prepared to define the following words: *ingenious* (paragraph 1), *altruistic* (18), *arduous* (18).

WRITING SUGGESTIONS

1. **Doing a Critical Analysis.** Singer's purpose is persuasive, but the essay uses a variety of other strategies as well. Identify other rhetorical patterns in the essay and analyze their role in the essay's persuasive goal.
2. **Journaling or Blogging.** For a week, make a detailed list of how you spend your money. At the end of the week, make some notes on your spending habits.
3. **Practicing in a Paragraph.** What did your notes reveal? In a paragraph, explore your values and either defend or criticize your behavior.
4. **Writing the Personal Essay.** Singer cites the example of how a two-hundred-dollar donation can "help transform a sickly two-year-old into a healthy six-year old." That is roughly 50 cents a day. Even as a poor college student, could you afford 55 cents a day? In an essay, argue for a school-wide campaign to get students to donate to such a cause.
5. **Finding Reading Connections.** Compare Singer's persuasive strategies to Tom Haines's description in "Facing Famine" (Chapter 2). Which is more effective and why?
6. **Exploring Links Online.** Did you know that some colleges have food banks for students? Using online sources for examples and background, write an essay in which you argue for or against establishing one at your school.
7. **Writing the Research Paper.** When nations are ranked by the amount of money they give as a percentage of their gross national income, including both official development assistance and national charitable giving, the United States is 19th in the world. Is that too much or too little? In an essay arguing either side, take a stand on our nation's foreign aid policy.

For Further Study

Focusing on Grammar and Writing. Choose one or more of Singer's longer paragraphs and analyze how it is organized. Does it exhibit unity, coherence? How is that achieved?

Working Together. Working in small groups, use the information provided in "Statistics About Worldwide Need" to construct a print advertisement aimed at students.

Seeing Other Modes at Work. Singer also makes use of comparison and contrast, especially in the use of analogy.

PERSPECTIVE ON SINGER'S ARGUMENT

Andrew Kuper's "Facts, Theories, and Hard Choices: Reply to Peter Singer," originally appeared in *Ethics & International Affairs* in Spring 2002.

People starve, suffer, and die because of political and economic arrangements. To address the causes of such exclusion, we need empirically grounded theories that enable us to go behind appearances. Singer dispenses with this need, asserting simply that his "solution" to global poverty (widespread charity) is established by "the facts." He provides no way to determine which facts matter and how. That is, he gives us no theoretical tools for understanding the nature and causes of poverty, or for developing multiple methods to tackle it. Again, we should not be against charity in all instances. Rather, drawing on more reliable development theory allows us to recognize that charity is not a cure-all. Chronic reliance on this one strategy can harm the poor. We must not depend on mere (irregular) assistance, where the rich are exhorted to dispense aid beneficently; rather, we must carefully reform relations and systems of cooperation, such that they benefit the poor on an ongoing basis. Only a wider range of institutional reforms and political strategies, derived from this cooperative approach, can generate sustained inclusion in governance and the global economy.

STATISTICS ABOUT WORLDWIDE NEED AND HOW TO HELP

The Measles and Rubella Initiative (www.measlesrubellainitiative.org)

A partnership of national and international agencies that aims to ensure that "no child dies from measles or is born with congenital rubella syndrome."

Magnitude of the problem: Measles kills an estimated 139,300 each year—mostly children less than five years of age, roughly 380 deaths every day.

How to Help: For just $1, a child can be safely and effectively vaccinated against measles and rubella.

Malaria (www.nothingbutnets.net)

Magnitude of the problem: Malaria causes 200 million illnesses per year and kills 600,000 people, mostly children under the age of five. In Africa, it is a leading killer of children. Every second sees 10 new cases of malaria; every 60 seconds, a child in Africa dies from a malaria infection.

How to Help: For $10, you can send a long-lasting insecticide-treated bed net which can reduce the transmission of the disease by as much as 90%.

Food for the Poor (www.foodforthepoor.org)

For a slightly larger donation, consider what you can provide:

+ For just $14.60, you can feed a family of four for a month.

+ For just $24, you can give 100 lbs. of rice and beans.
+ For just $43.80, you can feed a hungry child for a whole year.

Using and Documenting Statistics and Facts

1. Write a persuasive paragraph using some of the information provided here or on the websites from which they were taken. Think of your paragraph as the copy that would be used on a print advertisement. Using the Web, locate appropriate images that might also be included in that advertisement.

2. Prepare a list of works cited for each of the websites above. Use the current date as the time when you accessed the online information.

ADDITIONAL WRITING SUGGESTIONS FOR ARGUMENT AND PERSUASION

The following list presents topics with suggestions about how they might be approached in an essay. Also listed are topics that could be expanded into an essay. Remember, argument does not embrace only extreme positions on an issue; often it involves acknowledging limits or facts and suggesting a compromise.

Possible Topics Expanded

1. Youth and alcohol
   a. The legal age for drinking ought to be lower in the United States as it is in many European countries.
   b. Given the problems with alcohol-related violence and crime, the legal drinking age ought to be strictly enforced in the United States/this state/this community/this campus.
   c. Companies should not be allowed to produce advertisements that portray drinking as "the thing" to do in social situations and that encourage the sale and use of alcoholic beverages among those who are underage.
2. Tobacco use
   a. Tobacco has clearly been linked to forms of cancer; therefore, the advertising and sale of tobacco products should be outlawed.
   b. Government has no right to infringe on an individual's personal choice to use tobacco.
3. Cell phone and texting
   a. It ought to be against the law that drivers talk on cell phones or text on cell phones while driving.
   b. Drivers should be able to use cell phones while driving, provided the phones are not handheld.
   c. Government has no right to infringe on an individual's personal choices about using cell phones.

4. Study abroad/internships/community service/service learning/ mission trips
   a. Before graduation, every student should be required to complete a service learning, study abroad, or volunteer experience.
   b. College is already expensive and requires too many courses.
5. High school or undergraduate foreign language requirements
   a. Our ability to interact in and to understand the world is greatly increased by exposure to other languages and cultures.
   b. Statement "a" is correct, but such courses should be electives, not requirements.
   c. Everybody ought to learn English.

Other Possible Topics That Could Be Expanded

6. Guaranteed student loan programs
7. Required math courses
8. Reinstituting the military draft
9. Debt-relief for foreign nations
10. Stem cell research, genetically modified crops
11. Going green
12. Birth control, abstinence
13. Fuel-efficient automobiles
14. Seat belts, motorcycle helmets
15. Public prayer
16. Spring break—volunteering or partying?
17. Marriage
18. Women serving in combat
19. Handgun or automatic weapon ownership
20. Mandatory physical education classes

10 | The Research Paper

LEARNING OBJECTIVES
In this chapter, you will learn how to
   1. Recognize the distinctive features of a research paper
   2. Distinguish among a subject, topic, and thesis
   3. Plan a search strategy for gathering information from sources
   4. Evaluate the information found in your sources
   5. Integrate sources into your paper
   6. Document your sources appropriately
   7. Revise your research paper to increase its accuracy and effectiveness

WRITING A RESEARCH PAPER
Getting Ready to Write
What is a research paper and why are you writing one?

Key Questions

How much of a research paper is direct quotation from sources?
How do you find a topic for a research paper?
How do subject, topic, and thesis differ?
Starting Your Research
How do you plan a search strategy for gathering information?
How do you locate books on your subject?
How do you find sources published in magazines and journals?
How do you locate online sources for your paper?
How do you evaluate your sources?
How do you interview people for a research paper?
Writing
How does researching help you write your paper?
How do you integrate sources into your paper?
How do you shorten a quotation using an ellipsis?
Why do you need to acknowledge and document your sources?
Why are sources cited differently in magazine and newspaper articles?
What documentation system do you use in your paper?
Can you find software programs to help with documentation?
How do you work quotations into your text?
What if quotations are too long to work into a sentence?
Revising
What should you check in your final review?
How do you prepare a "list of works cited" or "references" page?
Student Research Paper
   Kristen LaPorte, "Music as a Healing Power: A Look into the Effect of Music Therapy on Alzheimer's Patients"

Writing a Research Paper

GETTING READY TO WRITE

What Is a Research Paper and Why Are You Writing One?

A research paper involves gathering and using information from a variety of reliable sources, and includes formal documentation (such as parenthetical citations, endnotes, and a bibliography). Of all the types of papers you will write in school, the research paper will be the one you encounter most often. As a result, a research paper is required in most first-year writing courses because it gives you the opportunity to tackle a large problem, to learn how to use your library's collections and other online sources, to evaluate the quality of your sources, to learn how to integrate quotations into your text, and to practice using a formal system of documentation.

Although all writing uses sources (printed, online, memory, observations, interviews), not all writing meets the special demands of the research paper. A research paper not only documents its sources, but it also exhibits a particular approach to its subject. It is not just a collection of information about a subject like an encyclopedia article. Instead, a research paper poses a question or thesis about its subject and then sets out to answer that question or test the validity of that thesis.

How Much of a Research Paper Is Direct Quotation from Sources?

The research paper provides an important experience in learning how to integrate source material such as quotations and statistics into your own prose. The verb *integrate* is crucial. A research paper is not a collection of quotations stitched together with an occasional sentence of your own. A research paper is written in your own words. Quote your sources where necessary, but do not quote any more than necessary. The ideal research paper—in any college course—is probably 80 percent your own prose and no more than 20 percent direct quotation (and even that number is fairly high). Later in this chapter, you will find advice on how to reduce the amount of quoted material and how to know when to quote.

Because a research paper involves using sources, you must be careful not to plagiarize and you must quote accurately. Plagiarism and how to avoid it is explained in detail later in this chapter. Under no set of circumstances should you buy a paper or copy a paper from a friend or from the Internet. Plagiarism from the Web is increasingly easy to detect. In addition, every person has a distinctive writing style that is manifest in elements such as vocabulary choices and sentence structures. Someone else's prose does not sound like your prose. It is rather like lip-synching to a song sung by a professional artist—no one is going to believe it is you!

How Do You Find a Topic for a Research Paper?

A possible research paper topic can be found after every essay in this book. In addition, your instructor might assign a topic or suggest a particular approach. Since a research paper will require several weeks of work, you should choose something that appeals to you. Kristen LaPorte, whose research paper is included in this chapter, was enrolled in a course intended for music majors and everyone in the class was to chose a topic related to music. Kristen started with the idea of music therapy since she was thinking of that as a possible career choice. As she worked on the paper, she decided to focus on music therapy for people with Alzheimer's disease.

How Do Subject, Topic, and Thesis Differ?

Whether you select one of the research paper topics provided in this book or one suggested by your instructor, remember how *subject*, *topic*, and *thesis* differ. As you move from one to another, you narrow the scope of your paper. Kristen's original idea for a research paper was a subject—"music therapy," which was already much more focused than simply saying "music." As she thought about that subject, however, she narrowed its scope, which made her paper more focused and, therefore, easier to research and write. Her topic became "music therapy and the Alzheimer's patient." Her thesis, the final step, had to state a definite position on that topic: "Although other forms of therapy may be beneficial, music therapy proves to be one of the most effective treatment options for Alzheimer's patients, either individually or in a

 Student Writer: Selecting a Topic

It took me a little time to actually get to my final topic for my research paper. Since our class was a music-oriented English class [a section intended for freshman music majors], we all had to choose some topic in the field of music, but it was fairly open. Since I am going into music education, I naturally wanted to research and write about something in the area of how music can help people. Music therapy has also always been an interest of mine. Since my passion lies with elementary students, I originally thought of writing something about music and students with exceptional needs. Since other students in the class had the same idea, I decided to stick with that general subject but concentrate instead on how music is used with the elderly. Since that was still too broad, I eventually decided to look at music and the Alzheimer's patient.

group, to help in areas such as concentration, general attitude, and communication." Notice how in each step the statement gets more sharply defined:

Subject:	Music
Narrower subject:	Music therapy
Topic:	Music therapy and the Alzheimer's patient
Thesis:	"Although other forms of therapy may be beneficial, music therapy proves to be one of the most effective treatment options for Alzheimer's patients, either individually or in a group, to help in areas such as concentration, general attitude, and communication."

The key to planning, researching, and writing the research paper is to define progressively what it is that you are writing about. Think of the impossibility of trying to research the topic "music" or even "music therapy." You would have thousands of potential sources. Moreover, when you try to write about a *subject*, you are much more likely to fall into the trap of thinking about your paper as an informational, encyclopedia-like article (e.g., "here is a general overview of the types and methods of music therapy"). Remember, a research paper is not an informational summary.

STARTING YOUR RESEARCH

Research takes time, but the key to getting quality sources that are truly related to your topic—and getting them in the shortest amount of time—is to plan a search strategy. Your instructor will probably tell you that you need to have a variety of sources—books, articles from magazines and journals, information from websites or government documents, interviews with experts. No research paper should be based on one or two sources; no research paper should be based solely on Web resources. Either strategy poses problems: You will not get a range of information and opinions if you use only one or two sources. Websites can be full of erroneous information—you can post anything on the Web and make it look professional and trustworthy.

How Do You Plan a Search Strategy for Gathering Information?

Finding quality sources of information requires knowing how and where to look. For an academic research paper, you should always start not with the Web, but with your library's online catalog. At my university, for example, the online catalog initially displays two options:

1. *Search WorldCat.* Do not start here since it lists other libraries which own the material for which you are searching. Start with your own library.

2. *Search the Library's Catalog.* The screen offers four different ways to search

    a. the catalog itself (a listing of separately published items such as books, but not including articles in periodicals (search by keyword, author, title, and subject)

    b. databases that can be accessed (search by title, subject, or keyword)

    c. e-journals (electronic, online) held by the library (search by subject or title)

    d. research guides (search by subject)

The options might seem overwhelming, but it is not as complicated as it might seem. A search strategy involves four elements:

- a keyword or phrase
- a subject heading
- an author's name
- a title of the source

Searching by a Keyword or Phrase   Computerized databases, library catalogs, and Web search engines (like Google) can be searched by using a *keyword*, a significant word (almost always a noun) that is associated with what you are looking for. Keywords are convenient, but they have limitations. Often you are just guessing what that keyword might be. Computers will never prompt you to modify your search or suggest that you use another term. Also, keywords work only if the word or phrase appears in some part of the record.

Searching by Subject Headings   Subject headings use a controlled vocabulary, grouping all information about a particular subject under a single heading with cross-references from other related headings. Most libraries use the subject headings provided by the Library of Congress. Your school's online catalog will allow you to search by subject and, when you access an entry online, it will display the subject headings under which it is classified. The most effective search strategies use both keyword and subject-headings searches.

Searching by Author or Title   These are the easiest searches to perform, but they require some prior knowledge. You must have the author's name and/or the title of the work and both must be spelled correctly and in the right order; otherwise your search will come to a dead end.

How Do You Locate Books on Your Subject?

Every book or separately published item held by your school's library is listed by the author's name, the title of the item, and by a few of the most prominent subject headings. A keyword can be used as long as that word appears somewhere in the computer's record. Most online catalogs include the call number and even information about the availability of the item. Often you can search the library's online catalog from home or your dorm room.

When you start to search for books, remember these key points:

- Read the "help" menu to see how to use the catalog.
- Remember that your library's catalog lists only those items owned by that library. No library owns a copy of every book.
- Be aware that the catalog will not list articles contained within a book or a periodical.
- Consider how recent or technical your subject is. Certain subjects might not be treated in a book since they are too current or too specialized. That is why you cannot search just for books.
- Browse your library's shelves. Libraries organize their book collections by subject. Whenever you locate a helpful book, check the shelves immediately around it.

How Do You Find Sources Published in Magazines and Journals?

Colleges and universities do not use the term "magazine"; they refer to "periodicals" or "serials." Both terms indicate that the publication appears periodically or that it is an installment in a larger series. Most of the magazines that you might find in a store will not be found in your college's library. Most of the journals (periodicals or serials) found in your library cannot be bought in a store. They are too specialized; they appeal only to a limited audience; they contain research and are aimed at a scholarly audience.

Because journals are quite expensive and aimed at a specialized audience, most libraries have discontinued their subscriptions to print copies and instead are providing electronic access to journals. The switch has significant advantages. Many of the journal databases provide a full text of the article. Online databases have significantly increased access to periodical literature, but that does not necessarily mean that it is easy to find the information you need. For example, no single index covers all periodical literature.

When you are ready to start your research for sources in periodicals, go to your library's online catalog to see what databases are available. Typically you can access databases in a variety of ways. At my university, the options include the following:

- Broad subjects (e.g., Arts and Humanities)
- Specific subjects (e.g., African American Studies)
- Title
- Keyword

Your library might have a different arrangement and even a different selection of journals. Ask a reference librarian at your school for help if you have questions on how to access or search those databases.

How Do You Locate Online Sources for Your Paper?

The most recent guess is that the Web has one trillion Web pages. Not surprisingly, no *search engine* (a term applied to software programs that index information on the Web) can retrieve it all. In fact, search engines do not really search the entire Web each time that you type in a word or a phrase. Rather, the search engine searches within its own database which has been compiled by robot programs called "spiders" that crawl over the Web locating possible sites to include.

Choosing a Search Engine   You search the Web by typing a word or phrase into a search engine, probably Google. Immediately, a list of websites appears, but the list is not arranged by the quality of the information. With Google, for example, the listing appears in order of their popularity. Remember also that what you retrieve depends on what keyword or phrase you enter. Varying the keywords (e.g., using a synonym) will produce different results. Finally, what you find depends on the search engine you use. Studies have shown that more than 80 percent of the pages retrieved by one search engine are not retrieved by another.

The University of California, Berkeley, maintains a series of tutorials on "Finding Information on the Internet" which is regularly updated. One tutorial is "Recommended Search Engines" (www.lib.berkeley.edu under "find information" "websites"). Their tutorials are an excellent place to learn how searches work and how you can control and maximize your results from every search. You can learn how to use "operators" (words or symbols that signal the relationship between words in a search entry). Each search engine, for example, has a "help" feature which shows you how to use it more efficiently.

How Do You Evaluate Your Sources?

From Print Sources   At this point in your research, you have identified a number of sources to use in preparing your research paper. Your paper should be based on a variety of sources, not just one or two. A single source represents one point of view and contains a limited amount of information. Your instructor might specify both the number and the nature of the sources you are to use, but even if the choice is yours, select a varied group, not one.

Guidelines for evaluating sources from print and online databases of periodical literature include the following:

1. *Is the Source Objective?* You can assess objectivity in several ways. Does the language and even the title of the work seem sensational or biased? Is the work published by an organization that might have a special, and possibly biased, interest in the subject? Is the information it contains documented? Who published it?

2. *Is the Source Accurate?* Reputable journals make serious efforts to ensure that what they publish is accurate. Similarly, books published by university presses or large, well-known publishing houses are likely to be reliable, as are the journals they sponsor.

3. *Is the Source Current?* In general, the more current the source, the greater the likelihood that new discoveries will be included. In scientific fields or medicine, for example, this will make a great difference.

4. *Is the Author Someone to be Trusted?* What can you find out about the author's credentials? Is this person an expert?

From Websites   Locating information on the Web that looks promising and relevant is only part of the problem. Anyone can post anything (or nearly anything) on the Web. Just because it is there, just because it appears at the top of the sources your search engine lists, just because it looks professional and scholarly, that does not guarantee that you can trust the information it contains. An excellent guide to evaluating online sources is "Evaluating Web Pages: Techniques to Apply and Questions to Ask," prepared as part of the "Finding Information on the Internet" by the Library of University of California, Berkeley *(www.lib.berkeley.edu/teachinglib/guides/internet/evaluate.html)*.

 ## Caution: Using Wikipedia as a Source

Everyone at one time or another uses Wikipedia. The name is derived from a combination of two words: *wiki* (a type of collaborative website) and *encyclopedia*. Wikipedia is what is called an open-source information website, which means that anyone—including you or your teacher—can contribute an article or edit an existing one. The articles in Wikipedia must draw upon existing knowledge, that is, on material that has been published elsewhere. In that sense, nothing is "original"; all entries must be documented from other sources. This is why contributors do not need special qualifications. However, because articles do not initially undergo editorial checking and scrutiny, it is possible that the articles might contain inaccurate information. Articles in some fields, most of the sciences for example, are generally quite accurate, but that is not true for every field.

Wikipedia has the advantage of timeliness. On its website, Wikipedia notes that it is "continually updated, with the creation or updating of articles on topical events within seconds, minutes or hours, rather than months or years with printed encyclopedias." You can find information in Wikipedia that cannot be found in print volumes or online encyclopedias.

Most instructors, colleges, and universities will *not* accept information from Wikipedia as a source for a research paper because it is not regarded as a reliable scholarly resource.

How Do You Interview People for a Research Paper?

Depending on your topic, you may find that people—and not just books and articles—will be an important source of information. If you decide to interview someone in the course of your research, choose a person who has special credentials or knowledge about the subject.

Once you have drawn up a list of people to interview, plan your interviewing strategy. When you first contact someone to request an interview, always explain who you are, what you want to know, and how you will use the information. Whether you are doing an interview in person, on the telephone, or through e-mail, establish guidelines for the interview. Once you have agreed on a time for an in-person or telephone interview, be on time. If you are using e-mail for the interview, make sure that your source knows when you will need a reply.

No matter what the circumstances of the interview, always be prepared: do some fairly thorough research about the topic ahead of time. Do not impose on your source by stating, "I've just started to research this problem, and I would like you to tell me everything you know about it." Prepare a list of questions in advance, the more specific the better. However, do not be afraid to ask your source to elaborate on a response. Take notes, but expand those notes as soon as you leave the interview, while the conversation is fresh in your mind. If you plan to use any direct quotations, make sure that your source is willing to be quoted and that your wording of the quotation is accurate. If possible, check the quotations with your source one final time.

Quotations from interviews should be integrated into your text in the same way as quotations from printed texts. Make sure quotations are essential to your paper, keep them short, use ellipses to indicate omissions, and try to position them at the ends of your sentences. When you are quoting someone who is an expert or an authority, include a reference to her or his position within your text, setting off that description or job title with commas.

 ## Student Writer: Locating Sources

Finding sources was actually not that difficult a process at all. I found a few websites by using a search engine, but in the end most of my sources were books. Our library had many books that were incredibly useful for researching. Since I did not have time to read a number of books, I looked at their tables of contents and indexes for things that I thought sounded useful. Then I would skim the chapters as needed.

WRITING

How Does Researching Help You Write Your Paper?

You can, of course, start writing as soon as you have a topic, or preferably a thesis. But because of the length of the research paper and because the paper involves using sources and documenting them, do not expect to complete all of your research before you begin writing. As you gather information, your paper and your thesis might change. Despite your most diligent efforts to find a specific topic within a larger subject, you might begin your research strategy with a topic that is really just a subject—too large to research effectively and write about within the limits of a freshman English research paper. If you accumulate a mountain of published sources, you need to focus your topic and your thesis more precisely. The research stage actually helps you define your thesis.

How Do You Integrate Sources Into Your Paper?

Even though much of the information in a research paper—facts, quotations, statistics, and so forth—is taken from outside sources, a research paper is not a cut-and-paste collection of quotations with a few bridge sentences written by you. A research paper is written in your own words with quotations and documentation added whenever necessary. You can control your quotations by remembering several points:

- **Ask Yourself If a Quotation Is Really Necessary.** If something is common knowledge, you do not need to quote an authority for that information. Any information that is widely known or that can be found in general reference works does not need to be documented—provided that it appears in your own words.
- **Keep Your Quotations as Short as Possible.** Do not let your paper become large chunks of indented direct quotations.
- **Avoid Strings of Quotations.** Never pile up quotations one after one. Rather, interpret and control the material that you are using and provide transitions that tie the quotations into your text.
- **Learn to Paraphrase and Summarize Instead of Giving Direct Quotations.** What is important is the idea or the facts that you find in your sources, not the exact words. Paraphrasing means putting a quotation into your own words; summarizing means condensing a quotation into the fewest possible words.
- **Use Ellipses to Shorten Quotations.** An ellipsis consists of three spaced periods (not two, not four). It is used to indicate that a word, part of a sentence, a whole sentence, or a group of sentences has been omitted from the quotation.

How Do You Shorten a Quotation Using an Ellipsis?

An ellipsis is a series of three spaced periods (. . .) that is inserted into a quotation to show the omission of words or phrases or even whole sentences. An ellipsis helps to shorten a quotation, to omit what is unnecessary. Under no circumstances should an ellipsis be used to change or obscure the meaning of the original quotation.

If you omit a sentence or more from a quotation, then you add a fourth period to the three. If you remove either the opening or closing part of a quotation, you do not need ellipses in either place.

Original:	"My teacher observed that many writers in introductory writing courses find that writing becomes easier the more frequently it is done."
Removing words:	"Many writers . . . find that writing becomes easier the more . . . it is done."

Style guides for writers offer extensive advice on using ellipses when quoting sources.

Why Do You Need to Acknowledge and Document Your Sources?

Research papers require documentation. As a writer, you need to document and acknowledge all information that you have taken from sources. The documentation serves three purposes:

1. *Documentation Acknowledges Your Use of Someone Else's Work.* Whenever you take something from a published source—statistics, ideas, opinions, whether quoted or in your own words—you must indicate where it comes from, thereby acknowledging that it is not your original work. Otherwise, you will be guilty of academic dishonesty. Students who borrow material from sources without acknowledgment—that is, who plagiarize—are subject to some form of academic penalty. People in the real world who do so can and will be sued.

2. *Documentation Gives You Greater Credibility as a Writer.* Documentation lets your readers know that you did not create these statistics, facts, quotations to suit your paper or to strengthen your argument. Your readers can see and evaluate, if necessary, the sources that you used.

3. *Documentation Helps Your Readers Locate Other Sources of Information on the Topic.* Notes, lists of works cited, and bibliographies are vital to someone who is researching the same topic.

Why Are Sources Cited Differently in Magazine and Newspaper Articles?

Most readers of popular magazines and newspapers would not welcome parenthetical citations, footnotes or endnotes, or lists of works cited or consulted. Scholarly articles and books, however, always include documentation. Magazine and newspaper articles typically attribute information to a source within the text without providing an exact reference. For example, Pete du Pont quotes a passage from a law in his newspaper article, "Have a Heart—but Pay Me for It" (Chapter 9) by just identifying where it occurs and by placing the exact words within quotation marks: "That's because the National Organ Transplant Act (1984) prohibits 'any person to knowingly acquire, receive or otherwise transfer any human organ for valuable consideration for use in human transplantation.'" Readers can find a copy of the act by searching for it, for example, on the Web.

What Documentation System Do You Use in Your Paper?

Different disciplines use different documentation, or citation, systems. Later in your studies, you may be asked to use a system different from the one you learn in an introductory writing course. Nearly all English courses use the MLA model; other humanities and social science courses typically use the APA form. MLA stands for the Modern Language Association, an organization of teachers of modern foreign languages and of English. A full guide to that system can be found in either the *MLA Style Manual and Guide to Scholarly Publishing* (3rd edition, 2008) or the version intended for students, the *MLA Handbook for Writers of Research Papers* (7th edition, 2009). The APA is the American Psychological Association, and its style guide, *Publication Manual of the American Psychological Association* (6th edition, 2010) is widely used in the social sciences.

Documentation systems are standardized guidelines that have been agreed on by organizations and fields. There is nothing sacred or "right" about one versus another. Standardization provides a fixed format for giving bibliographical information. Even the marks of punctuation are specified. No one expects you to memorize a particular citation system.

Style guides are intended to serve as models. Look at each of your sources, noting its particular features. What type of source are you dealing with? How many authors or editors did it have? In what format was it published? Then look for a similar example in the style guide for the citation system you are using; use that sample as a model. Citation formats for the types of sources most commonly used in a first-year research paper in a writing course are given on the next few pages. The range of possible sources for any topic is large, so you might have a source that does not match any of these common examples. For a complete guide, consult the MLA or APA manuals. Both can be found in the reference area of your school library.

Can You Find Software Programs to Help with Documentation?

In recent years, a number of software programs, referred to as "individual bibliographical management products," have become available. They allow you to import data directly from an online database available through your school's library or to enter your own sources and convert the bibliographical citations into a number of different formats such as MLA, APA, Turabian, or Chicago. Programs such as RefWorks, EndNote, ProCite, and RefMan are popular and in widespread use. This type of program makes doing bibliographical citations simple and foolproof. Check with your library's reference section to see what is available. In all likelihood, there will be workshops or handouts to show you how to use these products.

How Do You Work Quotations Into Your Text?

Both the MLA and APA systems acknowledge sources with brief parenthetical citations in the text. These refer the reader to the "List of Works Cited" (the MLA title) or "References" (the APA title) at the end of the paper for the full bibliographic reference. For in-text references in the MLA system, the author's last name is given along with the number of the page on which the information appears. For in-text references in the APA system, the author's last name is given along with the year in which the source was published and—for direct quotations—the page number. Note in the following examples that the punctuation within the parentheses varies between the two systems.

Here is how a quotation from an article, "Immuno-Logistics," written by Gary Stix, that appeared in the June 1994 issue of *Scientific American* would be cited in the two systems:

MLA: The major vaccines—those for diphtheria, pertussis, tetanus, polio, measles, and tuberculosis—cost less to make than they do to distribute: "The United Nations Children's Fund, for example, spends a total of $1.50 on the vaccines. . . . A tenth of what a government then has to disburse for labor, transportation, training and refrigeration to get these vaccines to infants and young children" (Stix 102).

APA: The major vaccines—those for diphtheria, pertussis, tetanus, polio, measles, and tuberculosis—cost less to make than they do to distribute: "The United Nations Children's Fund, for example, spends a total of $1.50 on the vaccines. . . . A tenth of what a government then has to disburse for labor, transportation, training and refrigeration to get these vaccines to infants and young children" (Stix, 1994, p. 102).

Note that in both cases, the parenthetical citation comes before any final punctuation.

If you include the author's name in your sentence, you omit that part of the reference within the parentheses.

MLA: According to Gary Stix, the major vaccines—those for diphtheria, pertussis, tetanus, polio, measles, and tuberculosis—cost less to make than they do to distribute: "The United Nations Children's Fund, for example, spends a total of $1.50 on the vaccines. . . . A tenth of what a government then has to disburse for labor, transportation, training and refrigeration to get these vaccines to infants and young children" (102).

APA: According to Gary Stix (1994), the major vaccines—those for diphtheria, pertussis, tetanus, polio, measles, and tuberculosis—cost less to make than they do to distribute: "The United Nations Children's Fund, for example, spends a total of $1.50 on the vaccines. . . . A tenth of what a government then has to disburse for labor, transportation, training and refrigeration to get these vaccines to infants and young children" (p. 102).

What If Quotations Are Too Long to Work Into a Sentence?

A quotation of more than four lines (MLA) or more than forty words (APA) should be indented or set off from your text. In such cases, the parenthetical citation comes after the indented quotation. Here is how a quotation from "A Weight That Women Carry" by Sallie Tisdale, which appeared in the March 1993 issue of *Harper's* magazine, would be cited in the two systems:

MLA: Sallie Tisdale points out the links between weight "reduction" and the "smallness" that society presses upon women:

> Small is what feminism strives against, the smallness that women confront everywhere. All of women's spaces are smaller than those of men, often inadequate, without privacy. Furniture designers distinguish between a man's and a woman's chair, because women don't spread out like men. (A sprawling woman means only one thing.) Even our voices are kept down. (53)

APA: Sallie Tisdale (1993) points out the links between weight "reduction" and the "smallness" that society presses upon women:

> Small is what feminism strives against, the smallness that women confront everywhere. All of women's spaces are smaller than those of men, often inadequate, without privacy. Furniture designers distinguish between a man's and a woman's chair, because women don't spread out like men. (A sprawling woman means only one thing.) Even our voices are kept down. (p. 53)

Note in both cases that the parenthetical citation comes after the final period.

If you are quoting material that has been quoted by someone else, cite the secondary source from which you took the material. Do not cite the original since you did not consult it directly. In "Little Princesses and Fairy Tale Stereotypes" (Chapter 8), the author quotes a sentence from another book. Here is how that quotation would be cited:

MLA: Explaining the dominance of the "princess" stereotype in popular culture, Lyn Mikel Brown, in *Packaging Girlhood*, commented, "When one thing is so dominant then it is no longer a choice: it's a mandate, cannibalizing all other forms of play" (qtd. in "Little Princesses").

APA: Explaining the dominance of the "princess" stereotype in popular culture, Lyn Mikel Brown, in *Packaging Girlhood*, commented, "When one thing is so dominant then it is no longer a choice: it's a mandate, cannibalizing all other forms of play" (cited in "Little Princesses").

In both cases, readers can then find the full citation—in this instance an online essay—in the "Works Cited" or "References" page.

In certain situations, you may need to include additional or slightly different information in your parenthetical citation. For example, when two or more sources on your list of references are by the same author, your citation will need to make clear to which of these you are referring; in the MLA system you do this by including a brief version of the title along with the author and page number: (Tisdale, "Weight," 53). (Note that this is generally not a problem in the APA system because works by the same author will already be distinguished by date.) For works that do not indicate an author, mention the title fully in your text or include a brief version in the parenthetical citation.

Unless a quotation is only a few words long, try to place it at the end of a sentence. Avoid "sandwich" sentences in which a quotation comes between two parts of your own sentence. If you introduce a several-line quotation into the middle of a sentence, by the end of the sentence the reader will probably have forgotten how your sentence began.

When you place a quotation at the end of a sentence, use a colon or a comma to introduce it. The colon signals that the quotation supports, clarifies, or illustrates the point being made.

> In his classification of why people want children, Bernard Berelson in "The Value of Children" (Chapter 4) acknowledges that the last reason he includes is the first reason mentioned by people: It is "altruistic pleasure of having them, caring for them, watching them grow, shaping them, being with them, enjoying them."

Caution: Plagiarism, Academic Dishonesty, and the Misuse of Sources

The Writing Program Administrators (WPA) website offers the following definition of plagiarism: "In an instructional setting, plagiarism occurs when a writer deliberately uses someone else's language, ideas, or other original (not common-knowledge) material without acknowledging its source" (www.wpacouncil.org). Every college and university has a policy on plagiarism and academic dishonesty. If a student is found guilty, the school assesses some form of penalty, typically ranging from a failure on the paper to suspension from school.

Plagiarizing sources occurs on a variety of levels—all of which are serious. This section offers a quick overview with some examples. Most likely, your college will have guidelines on defining and avoiding plagiarism. Your instructor can explain the types of plagiarism and show you how to avoid each.

Several forms of plagiarism are obvious: submitting a paper obtained from a paper-writing service or from another student; using chunks of someone else's writing and simply inserting it without quotation marks and documentation into your paper. Material taken from the Web is easily identifiable when certain search techniques are applied. Remember, you have a distinctive writing style—you use a certain level of vocabulary and a certain type of sentence structure. You have a written "voice." After a short time, your instructor develops a sense of when the words on the page are really yours and when they are not. Your writing style is as distinctive as your speaking style.

Plagiarism is not limited to copying a whole paper or even a group of paragraphs. It is not defined by the quantity of material that is taken from a source without acknowledgment. Other forms of plagiarism (sometimes called "misuse of sources") include the following abuses or mistakes.

- **Misuse of source: using exact words from source without quotation marks**

- **Misuse of source: using someone else's ideas, words, and structure of sentences and paragraphs without using quotation marks and without acknowledgment of the source**

Adding some words or synonyms does not change the fact that the paragraph is structured in form and content around the source.

If the introductory statement is not an independent clause, always use a comma before the quotation. For example, in the following sentence, the introductory clause ("In writing about . . . observes") is not a complete sentence.

> In writing about the prevalence of caffeine in American society, Mark Penn in "Caffeine Crazies" (Chapter 7) observes, "Americans already sleep an average of 25 percent less per night than we did 100 years ago, and so to some degree we are trying to make up for it with beverages turbo-packed with caffeine."

If a complete sentence follows a colon, the first word after the colon may or may not be capitalized. The choice is yours, as long as you are consistent. However, if the colon introduces a quotation, the first word following that colon is capitalized.

REVISING

The process of revising a research paper is no different than revising a regular-length essay. Because the research paper is longer, more detailed, and written over an extended period of time, make sure you get feedback from readers. Often your instructor will ask you to submit a complete first draft before turning in a final copy. In some cases, you might be able to take your finished paper to a writing center or a writing tutor for additional help. Not everyone has problems with the same parts of a paper, but as you see in the comments from Kristen below, she had trouble with the beginning and ending.

What Should You Check in Your Final Review?

Before you hand in your research paper, check again each of the following items:

1. If your instructor specified a certain format (e.g., double-spaced pages, margins of a certain size, cover sheet laid out in a certain way), make sure you followed the directions.

2. Check each quotation in your text—do not skip proofreading them! Verify that you quoted your sources accurately.

 ## Student Writer: Revising

Writing a research paper can sometimes be a little overwhelming. Everyone has trouble with different sections. For me, it is introductions and conclusions. About 100 percent of the time, I do not write an introduction until the paper is completely finished. I have a topic and a thesis, of course, but it is hard for me to write an engaging introduction until the body of the paper is finished.

Quick Guide to MLA Documentation

With the publication of the 2008 edition of the *MLA Style Manual and Guide to Scholarly Publishing* (3rd edition) and the *MLA Handbook for Writers of Research Papers* (2009, 7th edition), the Modern Language Association reworked the format for documentation of sources. The new system reflects the changes in how researchers access information through libraries and computers. Increasingly, lists of works cited include Web documents and articles and even books accessed through electronic databases rather than print sources. An abbreviated guide to the order of components in a citation follows. For more information consult either of the MLA guides.

Article or Essay in a Print (as Opposed to an Online) Periodical

1. Author's or authors' name(s) followed by a period
2. Title of the article or essay in quotation marks followed by a period
3. Italicized title of periodical
4. Volume number or date of publication followed by a colon
5. Page numbers on which the article appears followed by a period
6. The word *Print* to indicate the form in which the article appeared

Examples

Milgrom, Mordecai. "Does Dark Matter Really Exist?" *Scientific American* August 2002: 48–52. Print.

Monasterky, Richard. "Searching for Extra Dimensions and the Ultimate Theory." *Chronicle of Higher Education* 18 July 2008: 45. Print.

Article or Essay Accessed in an Online Database

Order of information is identical to a print citation with the following additions:

1. Italicized title of the database
2. The word *Web* to indicate how the article was accessed
3. Date on which the material was accessed

Examples

Monasterky, Richard. "Searching for Extra Dimensions and the Ultimate Theory." *Chronicle of Higher Education* 18 July 2008: 45. *Expanded Academic ASAP*. Web. 16 Sept. 2010.

Lederman, Leon. "What We Will Find Inside the Atom." *Newsweek*. International edition. 15 Sept. 2008. *LexisNexis*. Web. 16 Sept. 2012.

Printed Book

1. Author's or editor's name followed by a period
2. Italicized title of the book followed by a period

3. Edition, if other than first, followed by a period
4. Place of publication, publisher, date of publication followed by a period
5. The word *Print* to indicate the form in which it was accessed

Example

Thomas Armstrong. *Multiple Intelligences in the Classroom*. 2nd ed. Alexandria VA: Association for Supervision and Curriculum Development, 2000. Print.

Web Document

1. Author's or editor's name followed by a period
2. Title of the document in quotation marks followed by a period
3. Italicized title of the website
4. The word *Web* to indicate the form in which it was accessed
5. Date on which the material was accessed

Examples

"Cosmos." *Encyclopedia Britannica Online*. Encyclopedia Britannica Online, 2013. Web. 16 Sept. 2013.

"Dark Matter." *Imagine the Universe*. NASA Goddard Flight Center, 22 Aug. 2008. Web. 16 Sept. 2013.

Other Types of Sources

MLA now adds a word at the end of a bibliographical citation to indicate exactly what medium the work was produced in—for example, Radio, Television, CD, DVD, Videocassette, Audiocassette, Film, Performance, Print, Photograph.

3. Make sure that you have not unintentionally misused a source (review that section in this chapter). Have you placed quotation marks around every group of words or every sentence taken word for word from a source?
4. Check to see if your parenthetical documentation is done correctly (review that section in this chapter).
5. Review your documentation. Do you have your List of Works Cited or References in proper format? Check each item, following either the MLA or APA system. Getting it right is part of the assignment.
6. Consider your title. Does it accurately reflect your essay? Every paper must have a real title—"Research Paper" is not an option.

How Do You Prepare a "List of Works Cited" or "References" Page?

At the end of your essay, on a separate sheet of paper, list all of the sources that you cited in your paper. In the MLA system, this page is titled List of Works Cited (with no quotation marks around it); in the APA system, it is titled References (also without quotation marks). This list should be alphabetized by the authors' last names so that readers can easily find full information about particular sources. If a source has not indicated an author, then alphabetize it by its title. Both systems provide essentially the same information, although arranged in a slightly different order.

- **For Articles:** the author's or authors' name(s), the title, the name of the journal, the volume number and/or the date of that issue, and the pages on which the article appeared
- **For Books:** the author's or authors' name(s), the title, the place of publication, the publisher's name, and the year of publication
- **For Electronic Sources:** the author's or authors' name(s), the title, date of publication, information on how the source can be accessed, and the date on which you accessed the material. Dates are important in citing electronic sources because the source may change its electronic address or even disappear.

Note in the following sample entries that in MLA style, the first line of each entry is flush with the left margin and subsequent lines are indented five spaces. If you are to use the APA format, ask your instructor which of APA's two recommended formats you should use: the first line flush left and subsequent lines indented five spaces (as shown here) or the first line indended five spaces and subsequent lines flush left.

Articles

An article in a journal that is continuously paginated (i.e., issues after the first in a year do not start at page 1)

MLA: Lenz, Nygel. 'Luxuries' in Prison: The Relationship Between Amenity Funding and Public Support." *Crime & Delinquency* 48 (2002): 499–525. Print.

APA: Lenz, N. (2002). "Luxuries" in prison: The relationship between amenity funding and public support. *Crime & Delinquency, 48,* 499–525.

Note: When each issue of a journal does begin with page 1, also indicate the issue number after the volume number. For MLA style, separate the two with a period: 9.2. For APA style, use parentheses: 9(2).

An article in a monthly magazine

MLA: Milgrom, Mordecai. "Does Dark Matter Really Exist?" *Scientific American* Aug. 2002: 42–52. Print.

APA: Milgrom, M. (2002, August). Does dark matter really exist? *Scientific American,* 42–52.

An article in a weekly or biweekly magazine

MLA: Gladwell, Malcolm. "The Moral-Hazard Myth." *New Yorker* 24 August 2005: 44–49. Print.

APA: Gladwell, M. (2006, Aug. 24). The Moral-Hazard Myth. *New Yorker*, 44–49.

An article in a daily newspaper

MLA: Lacey, Marc. "Engineering Food for Africans." *New York Times* 8 Sept. 2002, Sunday National Edition, sec. 1:8. Print.

APA: Lacey, M. (2002, September 8). Engineering food for Africans. *New York Times*, Sunday National Edition, sec. 1, p. 8.

An editorial in a newspaper

MLA: "Stem Cell End Run?" Editorial. *Washington Post* 24 Aug. 2005, sec. A14. Print.

APA: Stem cell end run? (2005, August 24). [Editorial]. *Washington Post*, sec. A, p. 14.

A review

MLA: Hitchens, Christopher. "The Misfortune of Poetry." Rev. of *Byron: Life and Legend, by Fiona MacCarthy. Atlantic Monthly* Oct. 2002: 149–56. Print.

APA: Hitchens, C. (2002, October). The misfortune of poetry. [Review of *Byron: Life and legend*, by Fiona MacCarthy]. *Atlantic Monthly*, 149–56.

Books

A book by a single author

MLA: Boyer, Paul. *By the Bomb's Early Light: American Thought and Culture at the Dawn of the Atomic Age*. New York: Random House, 1985. Print.

APA: Boyer, P. (1985). *By the bomb's early light: American thought and culture at the dawn of the atomic age*. New York: Random House.

An anthology

MLA: Ibieta, Gabriella, ed. *Latin American Writers: Thirty Stories*. New York: St. Martin's, 1993. Print.

APA: Ibieta, G. (Ed.). (1993). *Latin American writers: Thirty stories*. New York: St. Martin's Press.

A book by more than one author

MLA: Burns, Ailsa, and Cath Scott. *Mother-Headed Families and Why They Have Increased*. Hillsdale, NJ: Erlbaum, 1994. Print.

APA: Burns, A., & Scott, C. (1994). *Mother-headed families and why they have increased*. Hillsdale, NJ: Erlbaum.

A book with no author's name

MLA: *Native American Directory*. San Carlos, AZ: National Native American Co-operative. 1982. Print.

APA: *Native American Directory*. (1982). San Carlos. AZ: National Native American Co-operative.

An article or story in an edited anthology

MLA: Quartermaine, Peter. "Margaret Atwood's Surfacing: Strange Familiarity." *Margaret Atwood: Writing and Subjectivity*. Ed. Colin Nicholson. New York: St. Martin's, 1994. 119–32. Print.

APA: Quartermaine, P. (1994). Margaret Atwood's Surfacing: Strange familiarity. In C. Nicholson (Ed.). *Margaret Atwood: Writing and subjectivity* (pp. 119–132). New York: St. Martin's Press.

An article in a reference work

MLA: "Film Noir." *Oxford Companion to Film*. Ed. Liz-Anne Bawden. New York: Oxford UP, 1976. 249. Print.

APA: Film Noir. (1976). In L.-A. Bawden (Ed.), *Oxford companion to film* (p. 249). New York: Oxford University Press.

Other Sources

An interview

MLA: Quintana, Alvina. Personal interview. 13 June 2010.
Worthington, Joanne. Telephone interview. 12 Dec. 2009.

Note: APA style does not include personal interviews on the References list, but rather cites pertinent information parenthetically in the text.

A film

MLA: *Silkwood*. Writ. Nora Ephron and Alice Arden. Dir. Mike Nichols. With Meryl Streep. ABC, 1983. Film.

APA: Ephron, N. (Writer), & Nichols. M. (Director). (1983). *Silkwood* [Motion picture]. Hollywood: ABC.

More than one work by the same author

MLA: Didion, Joan. *Miami*. New York: Simon & Schuster, 1987. Print.
—— "Why I Write." *New York Times Book Review* 9 Dec. 1976: 22. Print.

APA: Didion, J. (1976, December 9). Why I write. *New York Times Book Review*, p. 22.
Didion, J. (1987). *Miami*. New York: Simon & Schuster.

Note: MLA style lists multiple works by the same author alphabetically by title. APA style lists such works chronologically beginning with the earliest.

Electronic Sources   Increasingly the sources that we use for writing research papers are electronic—full-text articles taken from electronic databases available through libraries, journals that exist only in electronic form, documents taken from websites, e-mail from people whom we have interviewed. Even books today are available—and sometimes only available— in an electronic format. The most recent edition of the *MLA Handboook for Writers of Research Papers* (7th edition, 2008) includes a section on citing electronic publications, as does the *Publication of the American Psychological*

Tips for Citing URLs and DOIs

A URL [Uniform Resource Locator] is defined as the global address of documents and other resources on the World Wide Web. The *MLA Style Manual* notes that the inclusion of URLs of Web sources in "Works Cited" lists has "proved to have limited value . . . for they often change, can be specific to a subscriber or a session of use, and can be so long and complex that typing them into a browser is cumbersome and prone to transcription errors." It continues, "Readers are now more likely to find resources on the Web by searching for titles and authors' names than by typing URLs. You should include a URL as supplementary information only when the reader probably cannot locate the sources without it."

A DOI refers to the Digital Object Identifier (DOI®) System that identifies "content objects in the digital environment." Their website explains, "DOI® names are assigned to any entity for use on digital networks. They are used to provide current information, including where they (or information about them) can be found on the Internet. Information about a digital object may change over time, including where to find it, but its DOI name will not change." If a document has a DOI, it will appear on the published document. The APA citation system cites DOIs, but will use URLs if no DOI has been assigned.

Association (6th edition, 2010). The most common types of electronic sources used in freshman English research papers are listed here. For a fuller guide, consult the *MLA Handbook*. If you want additional help, ask your instructor or the reference department in your library for assistance in locating a published style guide in your area of study.

An E-Mail Message

MLA   Miller, George. "On revising." Message to Eric Gray. 7 May 2012. E-mail.

APA   E-mail messages are not included in the list of references, though you parenthetically cite them in your text: (G. Miller, personal communication, May 7, 2012).

Full-Text Article from a Periodical Available Through a Library Database

MLA   Nadis, Steve. "Exploring the galaxy-black hole connection." *Astronomy* May 2010: 28. *General OneFile.* Web. 11 May 2010.

APA   Nadis, S. (2010, May). Exploring the galaxy-black hole connection. *Astronomy*, 28.

When material is taken from online library database, APA does not use database information.

Article from an Online-Only Journal

MLA   Finnerty, Páraic. "The Englishman in America." *Genders Online Journal* 51 (2010): n.pag. Web. 10 May 2010.

With a DOI number:

APA   Di Carlo, A (2009, January) Human and Economic Burden of Stroke. *Age and Ageing* 38(1), 4-5. doi: 10.1093/ageing/afn282

Information from a Website

MLA   *The Purdue Online Writing Lab.* Purdue U, 2008. Web. 10 May 2010.

APA   *The Basics of APA Style.* Retrieved from http://www.apastyle.org/learn/tutorials/basics-tutorial.aspx

Student Research Paper

The paper that follows was written to fulfill the research paper requirement using the MLA documentation style as required by the instructor. Be sure to consult your instructor to determine which documentation style you should use.

Kristen LaPorte's paper has been annotated to point out important conventions of research writing and documentation. Notice that the paper does not begin with a title page. Check with your instructor to see whether you need a title page or an outline.

Kristen LaPorte

Dr. Taylor

ENGL110, Section 43

15 May 2012

① LaPorte 1

① Page numbers in the upperright corner with author's last name

Music as a Healing Power: A Look
into the Effect of Music Therapy on
Alzheimer's Patients ②

② Tide centered and not in quotation marks or italicized

③ Text is double-spaced throughout

③ The major motion picture *The Notebook*, released in 2004, followed a love story between Noah and Allie Calhoun, a couple who met while they were teenagers and never truly found love anywhere else. Because of a tragic accident, Allie began to suffer from severe dementia to the point that when she looked at Noah, the love of her life, he was unrecognizable to her. However, even in her condition, she was able to sit down at a piano and play a piece by Chopin by memory that she learned as a teenager (*The Notebook*).④

④ 'Hook' introduction to catch the reader's attention

Even though a fictional movie serves as the inspiration for this example, it could realistically be possible. Music has an intangible power that continues to be increasingly explored, and it truly works miracles where some medical treatments have fallen short. As illustrated in *The Notebook*, Allie still has the ability to remember music even though she suffers from severe dementia. Alzheimer's disease is the most common form of dementia and has no cure. However, different therapies are offered to help memory restoration. Although other forms of therapy may be beneficial, music therapy proves to be one of the most effective treatment options for Alzheimer's patients, either individually or as a

LaPorte 2

⑤ Thesis
statement

group, to help in areas such as concentration, general attitude, and communication. ⑤

In order to see the impact of music on Alzheimer's patients, a general overview of the disease itself is necessary. Alzheimer's is the most common form of dementia, a disease that affects the brain. Symptoms of Alzheimer's can be as minor as losing your house keys or forgetting a hair appointment. However, more symptoms, such as disorientation, impaired speech, or even forgetting family members, begin to take over as the disease progresses. There are many hypothesized causes of Alzheimer's, and they all tend to point to brain cells. Whether it be the death of brain cells due to viral infection, collection of toxins in brain cells (which leads to damage), genetic factors, or a decline in the immune system due to age, damage to brain cells takes the lead for causing Alzheimer's (Check 40–47). ⑥

⑥ Parenthetical citation with author's last name and page numbers. No punctuation. Information taken from source, but not a direct quotation

As mentioned previously, no cure can completely eliminate Alzheimer's from the system; however, antidepressants or tranquilizers are usually given to help with the patient's state of mind. In addition to these treatment options, music therapy continues to grow in popularity today as an alternative treatment. The use of music therapy does not rid the brain of Alzheimer's, but, in conjunction with medical treatment, music's power produces positive steps towards a better means of living and dealing with the disease.

LaPorte 3

⑦ Notice proportion of author's own prose to quotations. Quotations kept to a minimum, no long indented quotations

⑦ Many definitions of "music therapy" exist in the professional world. In their book *Music Therapy in Principle and Practice*, Donald E. Michel and Joseph Pinson describes music therapy as "a relationship among . . . the individual, the therapist, and the music" (4). The word "relationship" plays a key role in this definition. An Alzheimer's patient may not be the easiest person to deal with, but the creation of a bond between patient and therapist needs to occur for progress to be achieved. Therefore, a music therapist must have patience and the willingness to spend time with an individual. In order to get Registered Music Therapist (RMT) certification, one must successfully complete four years at a school with an accredited music therapy program in addition to completing a six-month internship. Music therapists should also be knowledgeable about music in general if they wish to use music as a medical tool. Michel and Pinson summarizes these qualities quite well by saying, "The music therapist can design strategies that use the motivating power of the medium to encourage listening, performing and composing in a way that addresses individual needs" (19). Music therapists can use discretion to evaluate their environments, patients, and other similar factors to decide what activities to use in a therapy session. For example, different styles of music therapy can include exercises in singing, rhythm, movement, instrumentation, or a combination of all four. As Gary Ansdell states

LaPorte 4

in his book *Music for Life: Aspects of Creative Music Therapy with Adult Clients*, "music involves an irreducible alchemy between mind and body, self and other . . . and it is the music therapist's job and skill to help anyone to the point where they can 'become music'; where music can act within and between them" (13). ⑧

⑧ Author's name and title of book given in text, parenthetical citation needs only page number

The medical aspect of Alzheimer's and the world of music therapy fit together like pieces of a puzzle to create a working, intertwined relationship. To begin with, music therapy generally occurs in a scheduled session-type atmosphere instead of a casual meeting in the patient's bedroom or similar setting. There are many reasons why music therapists sometimes choose to conduct a one-on-one therapy session with an individual patient. Depending on the patient's stage in the disease and current mental capacity, among other factors, a group setting might be too overwhelming. Frustration and aggravation are common personality characteristics of Alzheimer's patients. It would be unwise to place a patient with these traits into a group setting because he or she could potentially setback the progress of the entire group. Also, Dr. Frans Schalkwijk points to "poor ego-function" (33): working in groups can either help or hinder a patient's ego. If successful, the patient can feel more confident about himself or herself. Conversely, if a patient is struggling with a certain task, such as playing the right rhythm with mallets, and sees other patients successfully completing the same task, that could be the source of possible regression.

LaPorte 5

One-on-one therapy has also proven enormously helpful with keeping attention. Alzheimer's patients often struggle with keeping focus on a task at hand and often wander with no purpose. It proves much harder for the patient to get distracted and lose concentration with just the patient and a therapist in the room. Gudrun Aldridge conducted a study with a 55-year-old woman who was having a hard time with everyday activities such as cooking on her own or even finding words to speak. She had some past musical interest and ability, which made her family consider music therapy as a option. She demonstrated the ability to produce simple rhythms using two sticks and a drum. Aldridge also used improvisation in the therapy. Because the patient had the responsibility of creating an improvised rhythm to go with a certain melody, her concentration increased (G. Aldridge 146).⑨ As Aldridge states in her study, "intentionality, attention to, concentration on and perseverance with the task in hand are important features of producing musical improvisations" (161). Her success with the rhythms caused the patient to experience a more uplifted and hopeful attitude (160–61).⑩ Aldridge also discussed a study conducted by Fitzgerald-Cloutier in 1993. The procedure consisted of several reading sessions where the therapist simply read to the patient. The patient sat still for twice the amount of time in the music therapy sessions than in the reading sessions (G. Aldridge 144). These results further prove the positive effect that music has on a patient's attention span.

⑨ Sources include two different people with last name Aldridge so first initial is given

⑩ First citation included a quotation, the second attributes information to source, but nothing is quoted

LaPorte 6

Although individualized music therapy involves only the therapist and the patient, the format actually helps the patients control their behaviors toward each other outside of the session. Because of a positive experience with music therapy, patients show increased sociability and apply what they just learned in the session. For example, Sambandham and Schirm referenced a study conducted by Pollack and Namazi that "showed that individualized music therapy resulted in increased social interaction both during and after music sessions for eight AD [Alzheimer's Disease]⑪ residents" (79). Another study conducted by J. R. Wolfe concluded that patients who underwent music therapy seemed to have better participation in activities as well as better attitudes in general in contrast to other patients who were not subjected to music therapy (Sambandham and Schrim 80). Based on these two examples, one can clearly see the effect that individualized attention achieves in patients. Alzheimer's patients are not a different species; they like to feel valued and cared for like any other human being, and individualized music therapy helps to achieve that goal.

⑪ Brackets indicate that the writer provided the explanation for AD

LaPorte 7

One-on-one therapy sessions are not the only environments where Alzheimer's patients show an increase in socialization. In fact, there are many arguments for implementing group therapy sessions instead of individual ones. David Aldridge draws a conclusion based on Clair and Bernstein's research by saying, "working in groups [helps] to promote communicating, watching others, singing, interacting with an instrument, and sitting" (195). Many patients only have interactions with the other residents during a once-a-week music therapy session, so this socialization time proves to be quite important. Music therapy truly serves as one of the only therapy options that promotes unity among the patients. Other types of therapy, such as reading and exercise, are strictly individual. By creating a group atmosphere, the patients can simply enjoy making or listening to music while temporarily building relationships with one another, even though they may not remember them in the future.

Similar to individualized therapy, group music therapy helps patients with focus and attention. Imagine the patience needed to get young children to sit still and focus in a small group, and then imagine what a difficult time a music therapist would have keeping a group of fading Alzheimer's patients on the same track. In reality, attentiveness in group therapy sessions with Alzheimer's patients truly surpasses any previous notions. When the patients know they must work together to complete a common goal, their concentration increases. Schalkwijk discusses a case study with Miranda, a patient who struggled to pay attention and not talk when it was not her turn. The conductors of the experiment decided to put her into a new group setting to see how she would interact and fit in with new people. The group did an activity where one person created a rhythm and then the rest of the group imitated it on their instruments. Miranda was absolutely overjoyed and very proud when the others repeated her original rhythm. The exercise turned into a popular activity where different patients would create unique melodies and the others would copy them. The exercise helped to maintain the patients' attention, while giving them a sense of accomplishment (Schwalkwijk 74–75).

Music therapy directly relates to communication and speech as well. Specific songs often are used to express exactly what someone is feeling because music evokes intense emotions. Alzheimer's patients are no exception to this phenomenon, and communication, or even a lack thereof, plays a role in music therapy. Gudrun Aldridge supports the use of music therapy in relation to language. She states, "While language deterioration is a feature of cognitive deficit, musical abilities appear to be preserved. This may be because the fundamentals of language are musical and prior to semantic and

LaPorte 9

lexical functions in language development"
(G. Aldridge 140). Aldridge brings up a very
important point. Infants often make incompre-
hensible musical noises before they can speak
their first words. Because of the nature of language development, music never leaves us. As a
result, even when the mind wanders in stages of
Alzheimer's, a musical foundation can always be
found and rediscovered.

As mentioned previously, there are many
treatment options available for Alzheimer's. No
single medicine can prevent memory loss from
occurring; however, certain drugs help control
certain symptoms. Antidepressants are commonly prescribed to assist with the patients' attitudes, especially if they are still aware of the
deterioration of their memory. Tranquilizers
such as Valium are sometimes prescribed as
well. However, with these medical approaches
come the normal physical side effects such as
dizziness, drowsiness, and even decreased motor
control (Check 64–65). Why then go through
these side effects, when none of these medicines
will improve the patient's condition? Although
an antidepressant might help with the attitude of
a patient, music therapy can produce the same
result without putting any added chemicals into
the body and results in nothing but positive
effects.

LaPorte 10

When I began writing this research paper, I intended to conduct an interview with a music therapist in the Newark area about working with elderly Alzheimer's patients. However, I called every nursing home and assisted living center in the area, and not one had a music therapist on staff. This astounding realization speaks about the growing nature of the field of music therapy. The profession has not become a standard treatment yet, though this research indicates that more and more facilities should consider incorporating music therapy into their programs. With Alzheimer's patients, music therapy can drastically improve concentration, attitude, and communication through individual or group sessions. Overall, music can help connect people through a common medium and also helps patients reconnect with themselves despite their state of memory.

William Check reports a number of eye-opening statistics in his informative book about Alzheimer's. He observes, "Health experts predict that if no advances in treatment or prevention of the disease are made, in the year 2040 . . . ⑫ half the American population will suffer from dementia before they die" (16).⑬ This figure is sobering. Music therapy may not be able to cure half of America in 2040, but it can make a difference. Music truly has an indescribable, intangible power to heal, and a patient suffering from Alzheimer's can benefit remarkably from music therapy treatment.

⑫ Ellipsis (three spaced periods) indicates words omitted to shorten the quotation

⑬ Vivid quotation provides effective closure for the essay

LaPorte 11

⑮ Sources are
alphabetized
by author's
last name or
by title if no
author

⑮

Works Cited⑭

⑭ 'List' is on
a separate page

Aldridge, David. *Music Therapy Research and Practice in Medicine: From Out of the Silence.* London: Jessica Kingsley Publishers, 1996. Print.

Aldridge, Gudrun. "Improvisation as an Assessment of Potential in Early Alzheimer's Disease." *Music Therapy in Dementia Care: More New Voices.* Ed. David Aldridge. London: Jessica Kingsley Publishers, 2000. 139–65. Print.

Ansdell, Gary. *Music for Life: Aspects of Creative Music Therapy with Adult Clients.* London: Jessica Kingsley Publishers, 1995. Print.

Check, William. *Alzheimer's Disease.* New York: Chelsea House, 1989. Print.

Michel, Donald E., and Joseph Pinson. *Music Therapy in Principle and Practice.* 2nd ed. Springfield: Charles C Thomas, 2012. Print.

The Notebook. Dir. Nick Cassavetes. Perf. Ryan Gosling, James Garner, Rachel McAdams, and Gena Rowlands. New Line Cinema, 2004. DVD.

Sambandham, Mary, and Victoria Schrim. "Music as a Nursing Intervention for Residents with Alzheimer's Disease in Long-Term Care." *Geriatric Nursing* 16.2 (1995): 79–83. *ScienceDirect.* Web. 20 April 2012.⑯

⑯ source
accessed
electronically
includes date
of access

Schalkwijk, F. W. *Music and People with Developmental Disabilities: Music Therapy, Remedial Music Making and Musical Activities.* Trans. Andrews James. London: Jessica Kingsley Publishers, 1994. Print.

Glossary and Ready Reference

This Glossary and Ready Reference has two purposes. First, it is a quick and simple guide to the terms used in discussions of writing. Second, it is a quick reference guide to the most common writing and grammar problems. For a fuller analysis of grammar and the mechanics of writing, refer to a grammar handbook.

Abstract words refer to ideas or generalities—words such as *truth*, *beauty*, and *justice*. The opposite of an abstract word is a concrete one. Sarah Lin in "Devotion" (Chapter 8) defines the abstract term *devotion* by describing specific actions that she wished she had been capable of performing.

Allusion is a reference to an actual or fictional person, object, or event. The assumption is that the reference will be understood or recognized by the reader. For that reason, allusions work best when they draw on a shared experience or heritage. Allusions to famous literary works or to historically prominent people or events are likely to have meaning for many readers for an extended period of time. If an allusion is no longer recognized by an audience, it loses its effectiveness in conjuring up a series of significant associations.

agr **Agreement** problems commonly come in three areas. Subjects and verbs must agree in number (both singular or both plural) and person (first, second, third).

> The paper are due. (paper is)
>
> The requirements on the syllabus is not clear. (requirements are)

Pronouns and their antecedents must agree in person, number, and gender.

> A student must preregister to ensure getting their courses. (his or her courses)

Verb tenses need to agree within a paper—that is, if you are writing in past tense (the action happened yesterday), you should not then switch to present tense (the action is happening).

Analogy is an extended comparison in which an unfamiliar or complex object or event is likened to a familiar or simple one in order to make the former more vivid and more easily understood. Inappropriate or superficially similar analogies should not be used, especially as evidence in an argument. See faulty analogy in the list of logical fallacies in Chapter 9.

Argumentation or persuasion seeks to move a reader, to gain support, to advocate a particular type of action. Traditionally, argumentation appeals to logic and reason, while persuasion appeals to emotion and sometimes prejudice. See the introduction to Chapter 9.

Cause-and-effect analyses explain why something happened or what the consequences are or will be from a particular occurrence. See the introduction to Chapter 7.

Classification is a form of division, but instead of starting with a single subject as a division does, classification starts with many items, then groups or sorts them into categories. See the introduction to Chapter 4.

cliché **Cliché** is an overused common expression. The term is derived from a French word for
d a stereotype printing block. Just as many identical copies can be made from such a block, so clichés are typically words and phrases used so frequently that they become stale and ineffective.

Everyone uses clichés in speech: "in less than no time" they "spring to mind," but "in the last analysis," a writer ought to "avoid them like the plague," even though they always seem "to hit the nail on the head."

coh   **Coherence** is achieved when all parts of a piece of writing work together as a harmonious whole. If a paper has a well-defined thesis that controls its structure, coherence will follow. In addition, relationships between sentences, paragraphs, and ideas can be made clearer for the reader by using pronoun references, parallel structures (see **Parallelism**), and transitional words and phrases (see **Transitions**).

coll   **Colloquial expressions** are informal words and phrases used in conversation but inappropriate
d   for more formal writing situations. Occasionally, professional writers use colloquial expressions to create intentional informality. David Bodanis in "What's in Your Toothpaste?" (Chapter 4) mixes colloquial words (*gob, stuff, goodies, glop*) with formal words (*abrading, gustatory, intrudant*).

Comparison involves finding similarities between two or more things, people, or ideas. See the introduction to Chapter 5.

Conclusions should always leave the reader feeling that a paper has come to a logical and inevitable end, that the communication is now complete. As a result, an essay that simply stops, weakly trails off, moves into a previously unexplored area, or raises new or distracting problems lacks that necessary sense of closure. Endings often cause problems because they are written last and hence are often rushed. With proper planning, you can always write an effective and appropriate ending. Keep the following points in mind:

1. An effective conclusion grows out of a paper—it must be logically related to what has been said. It might restate the thesis, summarize the exposition or argument, apply or reflect on the subject under discussion, tell a related story, call for a course of action, or state the significance of the subject.
2. The extent to which a conclusion can repeat or summarize is determined in large part by the length of the paper. A short paper should not have a conclusion that repeats the introduction in slightly varied words. A long essay, however, often needs a conclusion that conveniently summarizes the significant facts or points discussed in the paper.
3. The appropriateness of a particular type of ending is related to a paper's purpose. An argumentative or persuasive essay—one that asks the reader to do or believe something—can always conclude with a statement of the desired action—vote for, do this, do not support. A narrative essay can end at the climactic moment in the action. An expository essay in which points are arranged according to significance can end with the major point.
4. The introduction and conclusion can be used as a related pair to frame the body of an essay. Often in a conclusion you can return to or allude to an idea, an expression, or an illustration used at the beginning of the paper and so enclose the body.

Concrete words describe things that exist and can be experienced through the senses. Abstractions are rendered understandable and specific through concrete examples. See **Abstract**.

Connotation and denotation refer to two different types of definition of words. A dictionary definition is denotative—it offers a literal and explicit definition of a word. But words often have more than just literal meanings, for they can carry positive or negative associations or connotations. The denotative definition of wife is "a woman married to a man," but as Judy Brady shows in "I Want a Wife" (Chapter 8), the word *wife* carries a series of connotative associations as well.

Contrast involves finding differences between two or more things, people, or ideas. See the introduction to Chapter 5.

Deduction is the form of argument that starts with a general truth and then moves to a specific application of that truth. See the introduction to Chapter 9.

Definition involves placing a word first in a general class and then adding distinguishing features that set it apart from other members of that class: "A dalmatian is a breed of dog (general class) with a white, short-haired coat and dark spots (distinguishing features)." Most college writing assignments in definition require extended definitions in which a subject is analyzed with appropriate examples and details. See the introduction to Chapter 8.

Denotation. See **Connotation**.

Dependent clauses are also called subordinate clauses. As the words *dependent* and *subordinate* imply, they are not sentences and cannot stand alone. A clause is made dependent by a subordinating word that comes at the beginning of the clause, reducing it to something that modifies another word in the sentence. Common subordinating words are either conjunctions (such as *although, because, if, since, when, where*) or relative pronouns (such as *which, that, what, who*). Dependent clauses are set off from the rest of the sentence with a comma:

> Although you have a test on Friday, your paper is due on Friday.

> Your paper, which must be at least 10 pages in length, is due on Friday.

Description is the re-creation of sense impressions in words. See the introduction to Chapter 3.

Dialect. See **Diction**.

Diction is the choice of words used in speaking or writing. It is frequently divided into four   *d* levels: formal, informal, colloquial, and slang. Formal diction is found in traditional academic writing, such as books and scholarly articles; informal diction, generally characterized by words common in conversation contexts, by contractions, and by the use of the first person (I), is found in articles in popular magazines. Bernard R. Berelson's essay "The Value of Children" (Chapter 4) uses formal diction; Judy Brady's "I Want a Wife" (Chapter 8) is informal. See **Colloquial expressions** and **Slang**.

Two other commonly used labels are also applied to diction:

- **Nonstandard** words or expressions are not normally used by educated speakers. An example would be *ain't*.
- **Dialect** reflects regional or social differences with respect to word choice, grammatical usage, and pronunciation. Dialects are primarily spoken rather than written but are often reproduced or imitated in narratives. William Least Heat Moon in "Nameless, Tennessee" (Chapter 3) captures the dialect of his speakers.

Division breaks a subject into parts. It starts with a single subject and then subdivides that whole into smaller units. See the introduction to Chapter 4.

Documentation involves acknowledging the use of direct quotations and facts taken from   *doc* someone else's writing. If you do not document your sources, you are guilty of plagiarism (see Chapter 10: "The Research Paper"). Documentation involves enclosing direct quotations within quotation marks ("), providing a parenthetical citation in your text, and listing the source on a list of sources or references at the end of your paper. Detailed advice and helpful models can be found in Chapter 10.

Essay literally means "attempt," and in writing courses the word is used to refer to brief papers, generally five hundred to one thousand words long, on tightly delimited subjects. Essays can be formal and academic, like Bernard R. Berelson's "The Value of Children" (Chapter 4), or informal and humorous, like Judy Brady's "I Want a Wife" (Chapter 8).

Example is a specific instance used to illustrate a general idea or statement. Effective writing requires examples to make generalizations clear and vivid to a reader. See the introduction to Chapter 1.

Exposition comes from a Latin word meaning "to expound or explain." It is one of the four modes into which writing is subdivided, the other three being narration, description, and argumentation. Expository writing conveys information; its purpose is to inform its reader. This purpose is achieved through a variety of organizational patterns, including division and classification, comparison and contrast, process analysis, cause and effect, and definition.

Figures of speech are deliberate departures from the ordinary and literal meanings of words in order to provide fresh, insightful perspectives or emphasis. Figures of speech are most commonly used in descriptive passages and include the following:

- **Simile** is a comparison of two dissimilar things, introduced by the word *as* or *like*.
- **Metaphor** is an analogy that directly identifies one thing with another. After Scott Russell Sanders in "The Inheritance of Tools" (Chapter 3) accidentally strikes his thumb with a hammer, he describes the resulting scar using a metaphor: "A white scar in the shape of a crescent moon began to show above the cuticle, and month by month it rose across the pink sky of my thumbnail."
- **Personification** is an attribution of human qualities to an animal, idea, abstraction, or inanimate object. Gordon Grice in "Caught in the Widow's Web" ("How to Revise an Essay") refers to male and female spiders as "lovers."
- **Hyperbole** is a deliberate exaggeration, often done to provide emphasis or humor. In describing the ingredients that go into making toothpaste, David Bodanis in "What's in Your Toothpaste?" (Chapter 4) makes hyperbolic comparisons when he likens the ingredients to chalk, paint, seaweed, antifreeze, paraffin oil, detergent, and formaldehyde.
- **Understatement** is the opposite of hyperbole; it is a deliberate minimizing done to provide emphasis or humor. In William Least Heat Moon's "Nameless, Tennessee" (Chapter 3), Miss Ginny Watts explains how she asked her husband to call the doctor unless he wanted to be "shut of" [rid of] her. Her husband, Thurmond, humorously uses understatement in his reply: "I studied on it."
- **Rhetorical questions** are questions not meant to be answered but instead to provoke thought.
- **Paradox** is a seeming contradiction used to catch a reader's attention. An element of truth or rightness often lurks beneath the contradiction.

frag **Fragment** (sentence) is anything that is not a complete sentence but is punctuated as if it were. Fragments can be intentionally written—advertisements, for example, make extensive use of fragments ("The latest discovery! Totally redesigned!"). Fragments are common in written dialogue. In most college-writing situations, though, make sure that you write only complete sentences. Fragments can be either long or short—their length has nothing to do with whether they are fragments. Since every sentence must contain a subject and a verb, fragments are lacking one or the other, typically the verb. The presence of a word at the beginning of the fragment can subordinate a clause, changing what would have been a sentence into a fragment.

> Rain fell. (subject + verb) = sentence
>
> Despite the high winds and rains. (no verb) = fragment
>
> Although it was windy and rainy ("although" subordinates what follows) = fragment

Most fragments occur when a long subordinate clause comes at the end of a sentence and it is then separated and punctuated as if it were a sentence:

> Our class decided to walk to the library to see the video. Although it was very windy and raining heavily. ("although" clause is separated from the sentence to which it belongs).

Generalizations are assertions or conclusions based on some specific instances. The value of a generalization is determined by the quality and quantity of examples on which it is based.

Bob Greene in "Cut" (Chapter 1) formulates a generalization—being cut from an athletic team makes men superachievers later in life—on the basis of five examples. For such a generalization to have validity, however, a proper statistical sample would be essential.

Hyperbole. See **Figures of speech**.

Illustration is providing specific examples for general words or ideas. A writer illustrates by using examples.

Independent clauses are complete sentences. As the word independent suggests, they are capable of standing alone.

Induction is the form of argument that begins with specific evidence and then moves to a generalized conclusion that accounts for the evidence. See the introduction to Chapter 9.

Introductions need to do two essential things: first, catch or arouse a reader's interest, and second, state the thesis of the paper. In achieving both objectives, an introduction can occupy a single paragraph or several. The length of an introduction should always be proportional to the length of the essay—short papers should not have long introductions. Because an introduction lays out what is to follow, it is always easier to write after a draft of the body of the paper has been completed. When writing an introduction, keep the following strategies in mind:

1. Look for an interesting aspect of the subject that might arouse the reader's curiosity. It could be a quotation, an unusual statistic, a narrative, or a provocative question or statement. It should be something that will make the reader want to continue reading, and it should be appropriate to the subject at hand.

2. Provide a clear statement of purpose and thesis, explaining what you are writing about and why.

3. Remember that an introduction establishes a tone or point of view for what follows, so be consistent—an informal personal essay can have a casual, anecdotal beginning, but a serious academic essay needs a serious, formal introduction.

4. Suggest to the reader the structure of the essay that follows. Knowing what to expect makes it easier for the audience to read actively.

Irony occurs when a writer says one thing but means another.

Metaphor. See **Figures of speech**.

Misplaced and dangling modifiers occur when a modifying or limiting element in a sentence *dang* cannot be clearly connected with what it modifies. A misplaced modifier creates a sentence that *mod* is awkward and confusing for the reader:

> The instructor returned the papers to the students with grades. (Did only the students who had grades receive their papers?)
>
> The instructor returned the graded papers to the students.

A dangling modifier has no element to modify, so it "dangles" unattached to the sentence.

> Returning the papers, the students were relieved.
>
> After the instructor returned the papers, the students were relieved.

Narration involves telling a story, and all stories—whether they are personal-experience essays, imaginative fiction, or historical narratives—have the same essential ingredients: a series of events arranged in an order and told by a narrator for some particular purpose. See the introduction to Chapter 2.

Nonstandard diction. See **Diction**.

Objective writing takes an impersonal, factual approach to a particular subject. Bernard R. Berelson's "The Value of Children" (Chapter 4) is primarily objective in its approach. Writing frequently blends the objective and subjective together. See **Subjective**.

Paradox. See **Figures of speech**.

¶ **Paragraph** is both a noun and a verb. A paragraph (noun) is a block of text set off by white space and indented. To paragraph (verb) means to construct those blocks. The length of paragraphs varies considerably in printed texts. Newspaper articles, because they appear in narrow columns, often put each sentence in a separate paragraph. Articles in magazines or books generally have longer paragraphs. Paragraphing, then, does depend on the format of the printed page. Paragraphing can also achieve emphasis by setting something apart. In a composition class where papers are word-processed on full sheets of paper, you should avoid extremes—no one-page or two-page long paragraphs (allow your reader to rest!), no large clumps of tiny paragraphs (unless you are writing dialogue!).

Even though paragraphing can vary because of print format and emphasis, most paragraphs in college essays are constructed using a model such as this:

> Topic sentence (which states the controlling idea in what follows)
>
> Body sentences (which provide the details that support that idea)
>
> Concluding or transition sentence (which summarizes, extends, or provides a transition into the next paragraph)

Typical problems with paragraphs include these:

> Not enough paragraphs—not marking for the reader the structure of the paper, making it difficult to read
>
> Too many paragraphs—paragraphs not developed with enough details or skipping quickly from one idea to another, creating a choppy disconnected effect
>
> Paragraphs not logically organized—ideas out of sequence, lacking topic sentences

// **Parallelism** places words, phrases, clauses, sentences, or even paragraphs of equal importance in equivalent grammatical form. The similar forms make it easier for the reader to see the relationships that exist among the parts; they add force to the expression.

Parts of speech is the phrase that traditional grammar uses to refer to how a word is used in a sentence. It classifies words into eight categories: the verb, the noun, the pronoun, the adjective, the adverb, the preposition, the conjunction, and the interjection. It is often important to be able to recognize the first five.

- **Verbs** typically express an action or state, or signal a relationship between things. In English, they can change in form (inflected) primarily to signal tense (past, present, future), voice (active, passive), and to agree with their subject or object.
- **Nouns** are words that name a person, animal, place, thing, and abstract idea. In English, they are frequently preceded by an article (such as *a* or *the*), have plural and possessive endings (book, books, book's), and serve as either subjects or objects in a sentence (This *book* features a *lighthouse* on the *cover*).
- **Pronouns** are words that can replace a noun or another pronoun. The most common, traditional classification of pronouns includes personal (*I, you, she, it, we*); demonstrative [pointing out] (*this, these, that, those*); interrogative [asking a question] (*who, whom, which, what*). Because pronouns replace nouns, they must agree in number (a pronoun

replacing a singular noun must also be singular in form). Consult the separate entry under **Pronouns** in this Glossary that deals with pronoun agreement.

- **Adjectives** are words that function as modifiers of nouns (the *yellow* book). In English, they can have comparative and superlative endings or forms (*fair, fairer, fairest* or *good, better, best*).

- **Adverbs** are words that function as modifiers of verbs, adjectives, or other adverbs or adverbial phrases. In English, they often end in an *-ly* and indicate *how* or *when* or *where*, or *how much*.

Person is a grammatical term used to refer to a speaker, the individual being addressed, or an individual being referred to. English has three persons: first (*I* or *we*), second (*you*), and third (*he, she, it,* or *they*).

Personification. See **Figures of speech**.

Persuasion. See **Argumentation**.

Point of view is the perspective the writer adopts toward a subject. In narratives, point of view is either first person (I) or third person (he, she, it). First-person narration implies a subjective approach to a subject; third-person narration promotes an objective approach. Point of view can be limited (revealing only what the narrator knows) or omniscient (revealing what anyone else in the narrative thinks or feels). Sometimes the phrase "point of view" is used simply to describe the writer's attitude toward the subject.

Premise in logic is a proposition—a statement of a truth—that is used to support or help support a conclusion. For an illustration, see Chapter 9 ("How Do You Structure an Argument?").

Process analysis takes one of two forms: either a set of directions intended to allow a reader to duplicate a particular action, or a description intended to tell a reader how something happens. See the introduction to Chapter 6.

Pronouns are words used in place of nouns. For a full discussion of the eight types of pronouns, *prn* consult a grammar handbook. In writing, two types of problems are extremely common. First, always use *who* when you are referring to people—never *that* or *which*. Second, pronouns must agree with their antecedent (i.e., the word to which it refers) in person, number, and gender. Typical pronoun problems:

> A student <u>that</u> was late missed the assignment. (who)
>
> <u>A student</u> must hand in <u>their</u> paper on Friday. (student is singular; *their* is plural)

Proofreading is the systematic checking of a piece of writing for grammatical and mechanical errors. Proofreading is quite different from revision; see **Revision**.

Punctuation marks are a set of standardized marks used in writing to separate sentences or *pn* parts of sentences or to make the meaning of the sentence clear. Punctuation marks exist only in writing; they have no oral equivalent. Punctuation marks are used to signal the boundaries or parts of a sentence; they reveal the sentence's meaning. It is very difficult to read a passage in which the punctuation marks have been removed. The choice of when to use what mark is determined by how the sentence is structured. The most common problems with punctuation in writing come in a limited range of situations:

- **a.** **Periods (.)** come at the end of complete sentences. Before you use a period at the end of what you think is a sentence, make sure that it is a **sentence** and not a sentence **fragment**.

- **b.** **Colons (:)** are used in only two situations in writing: first, to introduce a quotation, a list, or a series (just as it is used in this sentence); second, to signal a link between two parts of a sentence. In this second instance, a colon works as an equals (=) sign, signaling that what comes after the colon is an example or restatement of what comes in the first half of the sentence.

> Jose had one goal this semester: to write an "A" paper.

c. **Semicolons (;)** are "half" colons and are used primarily in two writing constructions. First, they are used to link together two sentences either without a connecting word or with a certain group of connecting words:

> Your research paper is due on Friday; it cannot be late.
> Your research paper is due on Friday; moreover, it cannot be late.

Second, a semicolon is used to separate items (phrases, clauses) in a series that already has internal commas. The semicolon helps the reader to see what belongs with what.

> An effective research paper shows several characteristics: the use of accurate, appropriate, and varied source materials; careful *and* accurate documentation of those sources; and clear, effective prose.

d. **Commas (,)** have the widest range of uses of all of the punctuation marks. Commas are used to link, to separate, and to enclose. They link when they are used with a coordinating conjunction (such as *and, but, for*) to link two sentences together.

> Your research paper is due on Friday, and it cannot be late.

They separate items in a series (Bring a bluebook, a pencil, and a dictionary to class), or two or more adjectives that could be linked by *and* (Revising can be a slow, painful process), or introductory elements at the start of a sentence:

> If you are uncertain of the spelling of a word, always look it up.
> Finally, do not forget to bring your dictionaries to class.

They enclose elements that are interjected or inserted into a sentence—things like nonessential phrases and clauses (the meaning of the sentence is not changed if the interrupter is omitted):

> All students who miss three or more classes will fail the course. (The words "who miss three or more classes" cannot be omitted from the sentence without changing its meaning.)
> Mr. Rodriguez, the instructor of the course, has a very strict attendance policy. (The interrupter could be omitted without changing the meaning, and so it is set off with commas.)
> Your exam, unfortunately, falls just before spring break.

poss　e. **Apostrophes (')** are used in three situations in writing: first, to mark the omission of letters in a contraction (can't = cannot); second, to signal ownership or possession ("It was Tanya's paper"); and third, to mark plurals of letters and numbers (Tanya got all A's on her essays).

f. **Dashes (—)** are two unspaced hyphens with no spaces between the dash and the letter that precedes and follows it and no space between the two hyphens. Dashes are used either alone (to add something to the end of a sentence) or in pairs (to surround or enclose something that is interjected into a sentence).

> The paper is due on Friday—don't forget!
> The paper—and it must be typed—is due on Friday.

g. **Parentheses ( )** always occur in pairs. Like commas and dashes, they are used to insert something into a sentence. Typically, parentheses minimize the importance of the insertion, while dashes emphasize it.

> The paper (it must be at least 10 pages long) is due Friday.
>
> The paper—it must be at least 10 pages long—is due Friday.

h. **Quotation marks (")** are used to enclose dialogue—words that characters or people speak—and to enclose direct quotations taken from print sources.

Purpose involves intent, the reason why a writer writes. Three purposes are fundamental: to entertain, to inform, and to persuade. These are not necessarily separate or discrete; they can be combined. An effective piece of writing has a well-defined purpose.

Revision means "to see again." Revision involves the careful, active scrutiny of every aspect of a paper—subject, audience, thesis, paragraph structures, sentence constructions, and word choice. Revising is more complicated and more wide-ranging than proofreading; see **Proofreading**.

Rhetorical questions. See **Figures of speech**.

Run-on sentences are also called "fused" sentences and occur when two independent clauses *run-on* (sentences) are fused or run together because a mark of punctuation or a connecting word has *f sent* been omitted. The independent clauses in such a sentence (compound) must be separated.

> Your paper is due Friday it cannot be late (run-on sentence)
>
> Your paper is due Friday, and it cannot be late.
>
> Your paper is due Friday; it cannot be late.

Satire pokes fun at human behavior or institutions in an attempt to correct them. Judy Brady in "I Want a Wife" (Chapter 8) satirizes the stereotypical male demands on a wife, implying that marriage should be a more understanding partnership.

Sentence variety is achieved by mixing up structural sentence types (simple, compound, *sent* complex, compound–complex). No essay should contain only one sentence type. *vary*

Sentences are traditionally defined in English as groups of words that express a complete thought, beginning with a capital letter and ending with a final mark of punctuation such as a period, question mark, or exclamation mark. Grammatically, a sentence must contain a subject and a predicate (verb). Sentences are not defined by length; anything that is punctuated as if it were a sentence but does not express a complete thought and does not have both a subject and predicate is called a sentence **fragment**. Sentences can also be called **independent clauses** or main clauses. Sentences are classified in a variety of ways, but the traditional classification by structure is most helpful to the writer.

- **Simple** sentences contain one independent clause, that is, one subject and one predicate. A simple sentence is a stripped-down sentence that contains no other clauses (either independent or dependent). Typically, simple sentences are short and easy to read and understand. They are not necessarily only a few words in length since they can contain modifying words such as adjectives and adverbs. The danger of using too many simple sentences is that it makes your paper sound like something written for grade school students.

> Your paper is due on Friday. (complete thought, one subject, one predicate)
>
> Your research paper with photocopies of your sources is due on Friday. (complete thought, one subject, one predicate, modifying words and prepositional phrases)

- **Compound** sentences contain two independent clauses (sentences) linked by a coordinating word and a mark of punctuation (typically a comma or semicolon).

    Your paper is due on Friday, and it cannot be late.

    Your paper is due on Friday; it cannot be late.

- **Complex** sentences contain one independent clause and one or more dependent clauses (not sentences on their own).

    Although we also have a test that day, your paper is due on Friday.

    ("Although . . . day" is not a sentence; it is a dependent clause)

    Although we also have a test that day, your paper, which must be at least 10 pages in length, is due on Friday. ("which . . . length" is another dependent clause)

- **Compound-complex** sentences contain two independent clauses and at least one dependent clause

    Although we also have a test that day, your paper is due on Friday, and it cannot be late. (dependent, independent, independent)

Simile. See **Figures of speech**.

d **Slang** is common, casual, conversational language that is inappropriate in formal speaking or
ww writing. Slang often serves to define social groups by virtue of being a private, shared language not understood by outsiders. Slang changes constantly and is therefore always dated. For that reason alone, it is wise to avoid using slang in serious writing.

sp **Spelling** errors are common—every writer misspells words occasionally. Advice on being aware
ww of your tendency to misspell and on coping with the problem can be found in "How to Revise an Essay." Many misspelled words are simply typographical errors that can be caught by carefully proofreading your paper. Always allow time to do so; always use a dictionary if you are unsure of the spelling. Automatic spell-checkers on word-processing programs will eliminate many misspellings, but they will not signal when you have written the wrong word in the context. For example, be aware of the differences among these commonly misused words:

1. affect—verb, "to influence"
    effect—typically a noun meaning the "result"; as a verb, "to bring about"

2. than—signals comparison, as in "faster than"
    then—signals time sequence, as in "and then the race began"

3. its—the possessive form (think of *hers* and *his*, which do not have apostrophes)
    it's—the contraction for "it is"

4. there—a pronoun that "points out," as in "there are the books"
    their—a plural possessive pronoun signaling belonging to, as in "their apartment"
    they're—the contraction for "they are"

Frequently, words do not mean what we think they do. Do not use a word in a paper unless you are confident of its meaning. If you are unsure, always check a dictionary first.

Style is the arrangement of words that a writer uses to express meaning. The study of an author's style would include an examination of diction or word choice, figures of speech, sentence constructions, and paragraph divisions.

Subject is what a piece of writing is about. See also **Thesis**. Linda Lee's thesis in "The Case Against College" (Chapter 9) is "not everyone needs a higher education."

Subjective writing expresses an author's feelings or opinions about a particular subject. Editorials or columns in newspapers and personal essays tend to rely on subjective judgments. Writing frequently blends the subjective and the objective; see **Objective**.

Syllogism is a three-step deductive argument involving a major premise, a minor premise, and a conclusion. For an illustration, see Chapter 9.

Symbols are objects, pictures, words, sounds, or particular marks that represent something else by association, resemblance, or convention. For example, a red octagon can be a symbol for "Stop," or Uncle Sam (see the visual in Chapter 9) can be a symbol of the United States.

Thesis is a particular idea or assertion about a subject. Effective writing will always have an explicit or implicit statement of thesis; it is the central and controlling idea, the thread that holds the essay together. Frequently, a thesis is stated in a thesis or topic sentence. See **Subject**. A detailed explanation of a thesis and how to write one can be found in "How to Write an Essay."

Titles are essential to every paper, and "Essay 1" or "Paper 1" or "Cause and Effect Essay" do not qualify as titles. No company would call its product "Automobile" or "Breakfast Cereal." A title creates reader interest; it indicates what will be found in the essay. Consider some of the strategies that writers use for their essays in this *Reader:*

1. Place or personal names (typically in narrative or descriptive essays): "Nameless, Tennessee," "Po-Po"
2. The promise of practical or informational value: "What's in Your Toothpaste?" "How to Devise Passwords That Drive Hackers Away"
3. An indication of subject and approach (especially in argument essays): "The Case Against College"
4. A play on words relevant to the subject of the essay: "Virtual Love" (about Internet dating) and "Mother Tongue" (about how the writer communicates with her mother in English)
5. A provocative word or phrase used in the essay: "Salvation," "Games, Not Schools, Are Teaching Kids to Think" "The Inheritance of Tools," "I Want a Wife"

Writers often use a **colon** in a title, separating a title from what is called a subtitle. A colon (:) is like an equals (=) sign. It signals that what is on one side is roughly equivalent to what is on the other. Typically, the title (to the left of the colon) is a catchy or a general phrase; the subtitle (to the right of the colon) is a more specific statement of what is to be found in the essay; for example, "The Value of Children: A Taxonomical Essay," or "Revision and Life: 'Take It from the Top—Again'."

Tone refers to a writer's or speaker's attitude toward both subject and audience. Tone reflects human emotions and so can be characterized or described in a wide variety of ways, including serious, sincere, concerned, humorous, sympathetic, ironic, indignant, and sarcastic.

Topic sentence is a single sentence in a paragraph that contains a statement of subject or thesis. The topic sentence is to the paragraph what the thesis statement is to an essay—the thread that holds the whole together, a device to provide clarity and unity. Because paragraphs have various purposes, not every paragraph will have a topic sentence. The topic sentence is often the first or last sentence in the paragraph.

Transitions are links or connections made between sentences, paragraphs, or groups of paragraphs. By using transitions, a writer achieves coherence and unity. Transitional devices include the following:

1. Repeated words, phrases, or clauses
2. Transitional sentences or paragraphs that act as bridges from one section or idea to the next
3. Transition-making words and phrases

Transitional words and phrases can express relationships of various types:

- Addition: *again, next, furthermore, last*
- Time: *soon, after, then, later, meanwhile*
- Comparison: *but, still, nonetheless, on the other hand*
- Example: *for instance, for example*
- Conclusion: *in conclusion, finally, as a result*
- Concession: *granted, of course*

Typographical devices are used to indicate subdivisions, sections, or steps within an essay and to call the reader's attention to a particular section or even word. As the word *typographical* implies, these are devices that have to do with typesetting (or word processing) and include such things as **bold face,** *italics,* <u>underlining</u>, subheadings, numbers, letters, and bullets (•, +) used to mark off sections of a text, as well as extra white space to separate blocks of paragraphs or sentences. Newspapers, magazines, Web pages, and business documents all make extensive use of typographical devices.

Understatement. See **Figures of speech**.

Unity is a oneness in which all of the individual parts of a piece of writing work together to form a cohesive and complete whole. It is best achieved by having a clearly stated purpose and thesis against which every sentence and paragraph can be tested for relevance.

ww   **Wrong word** is simply a word that is not used appropriately. Typically, the writer has chosen a word that does not mean what the writer thinks it does. Sometimes it is used to refer to a word that is too formal or too learned for the context and audience. Other inappropriate words include **clichés**, **slang**, and **colloquial expressions**.

Credits

Photo Credits

Index